THE HOLLYWOOD REPORTER

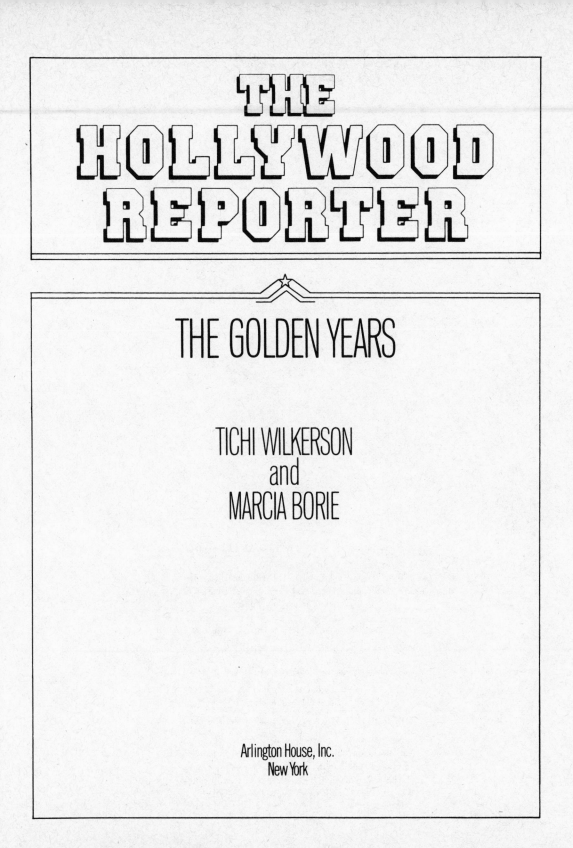

THE HOLLYWOOD REPORTER

THE GOLDEN YEARS

TICHI WILKERSON
and
MARCIA BORIE

Arlington House, Inc.
New York

For William R. "Billy" Wilkerson, who came to Hollywood in pursuit of a dream, and had the genius, courage and perseverance to make it a reality . . .

Library of Congress Cataloging-in-Publication Data

Wilkerson, Tichi.
The Hollywood reporter.

Originally published: New York: Coward-McCann, 1984.

Includes index.
1. Moving-picture actors and actresses—United States.
I. Borie, Marcia.   II. Hollywood reporter.   III. Title.
[PN1998.A2W627   1986]   791.43′028′0922   85-30657
ISBN: 0-517-60740-9

h g f e d c b a

Photographs for this book were coordinated by **MARVIN PAIGE'S** Motion Picture and Television Research Service, Hollywood, California. The majority originally appeared in the regular and special editions of *The Hollywood Reporter*, beginning back on September 3, 1930. The authors wish to acknowledge and thank the following corporations and individuals for their kind assistance in permitting us to use this material:

Allied Artists Corporation
American Broadcasting Company
The Bison Archives
The Caddo Company
Charles Chaplin Studios
Columbia Broadcasting System
Columbia Pictures Corporation
Walt Disney Productions
Fox Film Corporation
Samuel Goldwyn Productions
Las Vegas News Bureau
Metro-Goldwyn-Mayer Film Company
Monogram Pictures
National Broadcasting Company
Paramount Pictures Corporation

Republic Studios
RKO-Pathé Studios
RKO-Radio Pictures
Sands Hotel, Las Vegas
Screen Actors Guild
Selznick-International Pictures
Daniel Mayer Selznick
Mack Sennett Studios
Triangle Pictures
Bruce Torrence Historical Collection
20th Century–Fox Film Corporation
Universal City Studios, Inc.
United Artists Corporation
Warner Brothers–First National
Warner Brothers, Incorporated

Over the years, *The Hollywood Reporter* printed dozens of bylined pieces. The authors wish to acknowledge the contributions of the following celebrities who appear in this book:

June Allyson	Alice Faye	Fred MacMurray
Lauren Bacall	W. C. Fields	Hattie McDaniel
Lucille Ball	Judy Garland	Dean Martin
John Barrymore	Betty Grable	Victor Mature
Milton Berle	D. W. Griffith	Robert Mitchum
Humphrey Bogart	Jean Harlow	Jean Negulesco
George Burns	Helen Hayes	David Niven
Gary Cooper	Rita Hayworth	Gregory Peck
Joan Crawford	Buster Keaton	Mary Pickford
Bing Crosby	Gene Kelly	Ronald Reagan
George Cukor	Dorothy Lamour	Mickey Rooney
Linda Darnell	Mario Lanza	Barbara Stanwyck
Doris Day	Laurel and Hardy	Gene Tierney
Cecil B. DeMille	Jerry Lewis	John Wayne
Jimmy Durante	Carole Lombard	Jane Wyman
Doug Fairbanks, Jr.	Jeanette MacDonald	

The authors wish to acknowledge the following people for their generous assistance:

Fred E. Basten	The Gossards	Carlotta Monti
Carol Bruce	Wilson Heller	Carl Schaefer
George Cukor	Paul Kohner	Daniel Mayer Selznick
Samson DeBrier	Sue Carol Ladd	Rosalind Shaffer
Vic Enyart	Betty Lasky	Cynthia Wilkerson
Kayla Garen	Rouben Mamoulian	Willie Wilkerson, Jr.

A special thanks to Terry Roach, Linda Mehr, Carol Cullen and the rest of the staff of the Academy of Motion Picture Arts and Sciences . . . Mark Locher, public relations director of the Screen Actors Guild . . . Our wonderful editors at Coward, McCann: Chris Schillig, Lee Ann Chearneyi and Tom Miller . . . Arthur and Richard Pine, our hardworking literary agents . . . The secretarial assistance of Teri Diller, Lynn Helsel and Larry Merritt . . . And, last, but surely not least, an enormous debt is owed to many editors, reporters, reviewers and columnists of *The Hollywood Reporter*, especially Frank Pope, Edith Gwynn, Irving Hoffman, Mike Connolly, Don Carle Gillette, Radie Harris, Hank Grant and Arthur Knight.

CONTENTS

THE FIFTIES: HOLLYWOOD TRAUMA, BIG SCREEN VS. SMALL SCREEN 229

THE HOLLYWOOD REPORTER

PREFACE

1 n September 3, 1930, William R. "Billy" Wilkerson left his office at 1606 North Highland Avenue, across the street from Hollywood High School. He was carrying several neatly tied bundles of the debut issue of *The Hollywood Reporter*. As founder, publisher and editor-in-chief of the first daily show business trade paper ever to come off the press from the heart of filmland, he was proud of the accomplishment—and confident. After all, in his premiere issue, and the one which came out the following day, Billy had printed facsimiles of letters and telegrams from motion picture moguls, film stars and other industry leaders. They welcomed him to Hollywood, and wished him and his paper every success.

1 The offices of *The Hollywood Reporter* as they appear today. (Courtesy of Lida Hadas)   2 William R. Wilkerson, publisher and editor in chief of *The Hollywood Reporter* from September 3, 1930, to September 2, 1962.

Within ten days, having digested his editorial policy, all hell broke loose. The studio brass decided that the last thing they needed was an *independent* film paper, especially one that printed accurate news daily of what happened in Hollywood and throughout the entertainment industry.

Times were tough. The Depression was here. The movie business was going through a terrible crisis converting from silents to talkies. Before *The Hollywood Reporter*, studio heads controlled the flow of news. Words of puffery and optimism were sent to film distributors, movie house owners and newspaper editors throughout the country. Suddenly, there was someone named Wil-

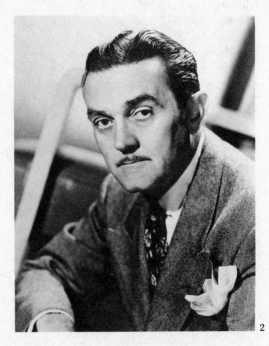

kerson actually telling it like it was, in cold hard print. Billy's reporters were barred from studio lots, not all at one time, but one that week, another the following. Phone calls from *The Reporter* soliciting news went unanswered. So staff members hopped fences, sneaked by dozing studio gatemen, made friends on the inside—and managed to get the news.

Then Winfield "Winnie" Sheehan, head of production at Fox, started a ritual. One of the mail room boys was instructed to gather up the entire morning's delivery of *The Hollywood Reporter* and pile them in a heap outside his office. Each day at high noon the papers were set on fire. Winnie liked to look out his window and see the wisps of smoke rising.

At the end of the second month, it was Wilkerson, not the industry, who was in trouble. Having run out of money, he informed his tiny staff that unless the revenue picked up, he would have to post a closing notice. All the while, he was determined to keep going. He confided in a friend, who loaned him some money. Then a couple of his salesmen brought in a few small ads. It wasn't much, but he decided to hang tough.

Meanwhile, the opposition was unifying. They boycotted *The Hollywood Reporter*. They literally told him to take his sheet and stuff it, reasoning that with combined studio pressure he couldn't last. Still, they had not yet figured Wilkerson out. Where was his money coming from? They were not taking out any ads, and yet he *looked* prosperous enough. Billy was the epitome of class. He dressed elegantly. He resembled a casting director's ideal of the suave, handsome riverboat gambler. His moustache was waxed just so. With his hand-tailored suits, he frequently wore gray spats, and always sported custom-made shoes, natty ties and fine linen handkerchiefs.

The Motion Picture Producers Association, with every studio head on its board—L. B. Mayer, Jack Warner, Sam Goldwyn, Winnie Sheehan, B. P. Schulberg, Harry Cohn—agreed to fight him. They were in the process of holding frequent meetings to discuss the current industry crisis. Hours of their time were spent talking about how to get rid of Billy Wilkerson.

After a few months, when they couldn't force him out, Billy received a handsome offer to *sell out*—plus the promise of an important studio job. Vic Enyart, one of *The Reporter*'s first advertising salesmen, remembers seeing a big check on Wilkerson's desk. "It had lots of zeroes. Billy just flicked it off onto the floor, and smiled. Later, he told me that he knew the battle had been won. By their show of such concern, the Association had convinced Billy of just how important his paper was. So, the harder they fought him, the more he resisted." The survival of *The Hollywood Reporter* can be attributed to Billy's keen perception of the industry plus his unique temperament and talent.

He was not a particularly pleasant man. He was tough. Resilient. Stubborn as they come. But honest. He could be ruthless, because he was fearless. He was totally loyal, but only to those whom he felt deserved that treatment. Starting with the first issue, Billy staked out a premiere position, on page one, from which he could give exposure to his own candid opinions. Under the title "Tradeviews," by W. R. Wilkerson, he gave the town a piece of his mind—literally.

No one in town was too big to be immune. In his editorials, Wilkerson told $500,000-a-year moguls day after day how to run their studios. The funny thing was, he knew exactly what he was talking about. Even his enemies secretly respected him. When they eventually became friends, his advice was much sought after.

In the beginning, though, Billy was one huge, belligerent burr rubbing up against the biggest backsides in the business. He loved the industry as much as the moguls did. He knew every nuance and phase of it as well as anyone in town. And he considered himself a crusader with a mission. He had to convince them that he, and the truth he printed, did *not* represent the enemy. It was the lack of good pictures—and the resulting sag in boxoffice grosses—that were their priority problems.

He was the same kind of man as they were. Determined. Shrewd. Ambitious. He respected the moguls for what they had accomplished. He knew how hard they had fought and scraped, worked and sweated, to turn the business from a nickel-and-dime, storefront operation into one of the top six industries in America. They should have understood that the louder they screamed and threatened, the more important it became for Billy Wilkerson to meet their challenge.

Billy Wilkerson had been a gambler all of his life. It was a trait he inherited. He was born in Nashville, Tennessee, on September 29, 1890, the only child of Mary and Richard Wilkerson. "Big Dick" was one of the last of the old-time courtly Southern gamblers, whose fortunes rose and fell with the turn of a card.

Billy was educated at Mount St. Mary's College, in Emmitsburg, Maryland, and Jefferson Medical School in Philadelphia. In the middle of his third year, he was forced to leave. His father had died—penniless. Billy's first job was managing a nickelodeon in Fort Lee, New Jersey. He ran the business for two years before it was sold at a nice profit. In the process, Wilkerson had been bitten by the movie bug. The world of film fascinated him. He was determined to learn about it—from every angle.

First, he managed the Jewel Exchange in New York, acting as middleman between producers and exhibitors. Next, he worked for a picture company which made one-reelers, became a film salesman, and went on to a position selling advertising for a New York trade paper, *Film Daily*. It was there he first realized the potential of such a paper. Wanting to understand the studio setup from the inside, he then became district manager for Universal Pictures in Kansas City. Subsequently, he returned to New York and managed several large theatres. Billy even tried to make a few film shorts and features on his own. But, as a producer, he was unsuccessful.

In 1929, he was briefly involved with a New York trade paper, but sold out for $20,000. Shortly before the Stock Market Crash, he ran into a Wall Street friend who gave him an inside tip. Wilkerson borrowed an extra $25,000 and put the whole bundle on his friend's hot stocks. Forty-five minutes later, the market went twenty-three skiddoo. Billy was penniless. Not so easy come. Very easy go!

A few months later he left his home, in Ferndale, New York, and drove west in a secondhand car, with a borrowed three hundred dollars in his wallet. In the summer of 1930 he formed the Wilkerson Daily Corporation together with Herbert Sonn, a New York financier. It was time to start his Hollywood trade paper.

He wangled an introduction to Frank Whitbeck, head of advertising and publicity for the West Coast chain of movie houses—soon to become the very extensive Fox West Coast Theatres. Wilkerson needed someone with the proper knowledge to lay out the dummy for his newspaper format and to create a logo which presented the name he was going to use—*The Hollywood Reporter*—in the most attractive way.

Whitbeck told Wilkerson he was crazy. This was no time to start such a venture. Business was bad. Besides, no one had ever published a trade paper from Hollywood before. But Billy was determined, so Whitbeck created the basic format of the paper, and John Wentworth designed the logo.

Nine months into his publishing venture, Billy was out at MGM conferring with Louis

B. Mayer about much needed advertising revenue. Mayer needed to be convinced of *The Reporter*'s nationwide impact. Together, they cooked up a scheme. Billy would write an editorial about MGM's biggest up-and-coming star, Clark Gable, and purposely sprinkle it with special details not included in any MGM publicity release. Wilkerson would then have his clipping service follow the column across country. Mayer gleefully agreed. It was a good way to get Billy off of his back about MGM advertising.

Wilkerson returned to the Metro lot sixty days later. Ushered into Mayer's presence, he silently opened a box and dumped close to 3,000 clippings on L.B.'s desk. Of course, Billy *had* loaded the editorial in his favor. The column was so forcefully written, stealing from it had proved irresistible.

Mayer was astounded but convinced. Wilkerson got his MGM advertising—a whole year's worth. As Leo the Lion roared, so the other jungle animals followed. The more the studios advertised, the more they saw its value. *The Hollywood Reporter* functioned, in many ways, as a middleman. Every tiny theatre owner and film distributor knew what was going on by reading *The Reporter*. To be totally accurate, some of the ads became vanity pages. But the majority both informed and served the industry in all the far-flung corners of the country and overseas.

By the time *The Hollywood Reporter*'s Fifth Anniversary had come and gone, Billy was a member of the establishment. With his paper doing just fine, he branched out. Over the next decade and a half, he opened numerous trend-setting restaurants and nightclubs. The Vendome, across the street from *The Reporter*, came first. Then, gifted with foresight and his gambler's instinct, Billy spotted a stretch of land on Sunset Boulevard, which connected Laurel Canyon on the east with Beverly Hills to the west. At that time it was an unincorporated area with very little development. Soon, largely owing to Wilkerson, it would become known worldwide as the glamorous Sunset Strip. There, Billy created the Cafe Trocadero, which rapidly became a famous celebrity mecca.

At the Troc every Sunday, Billy held Talent Night. He gave important exposure to up-and-coming young performers such as Judy Garland, Mary Martin, Jackie Gleason, Phil Silvers and Deanna Durbin, to name but a few. Several years later, he started Ciro's, another nightclub which became known on an international scale. Eventually, he added LaRue's, on the Sunset Strip, and L'Aiglon, in Beverly Hills, both exclusive restaurants that quickly became Hollywood "in" spots.

Every enterprise made money, but Wilkerson tossed back his profits—constantly redecorating, upgrading, importing new chefs and the finest of gourmet foodstuffs. He stayed with each venture until he got bored or the place began losing money. Then he closed one and started another.

In 1936, *The Hollywood Reporter* moved into its own three-story building at 6715 Sunset Boulevard. The printing was done in back; the editorial and business offices were upstairs. Downstairs, Billy created an exclusive men's barbershop and an elegant haberdashery. The building's sumptuous interior featured elegant woods, floor-to-ceiling mirrors and exquisite marble fireplaces. Within a short time, however, both enterprises were gone. The idea had been spectacular—it just hadn't worked. Harry Drucker, the head barber, whom Billy personally selected, went on to do rather well for himself, becoming the barber to the stars. To this day, he still cuts the hair of many famous people, including longtime patron President Ronald Reagan. The haberdasher, Jerry Rothschild, opened one of Beverly Hills's finest men's shops.

With Drucker and Rothschild gone, the paper spread out over the entire building.

Nineteen thirty-six interior of *The Hollywood Reporter*. A haberdashery and barbershop were located downstairs. Today, this room is filled with desks and busy journalists.

That elegant establishment, with its hand-finished wood paneling, its marble fireplaces, but sans mirrors, is still the corporate headquarters for *The Hollywood Reporter* and its various subsidiary companies.

Billy had an eye for talent. In 1936, he walked to the corner cafe for one of the twenty Cokes he drank each day. At the fountain, he spotted a cute kid, who had run across from Hollywood High to plunk down her nickel for a Coke. He saw something in the teenager. After the owner had reassured the girl that the gentleman staring at her was a respectable businessman, Billy walked over and asked if she had ever thought of going into pictures—and that was how it all *really* began for a kid the world would come to know as Lana Turner.

Another close friend of Billy's was Howard Hughes. Wilkerson and Hughes had Hollywood in common. Billy was among the few people whom Howard trusted. In his early days as a producer, Hughes was not adverse to publicity. But, unbeknownst to Billy, he had a paid informant on *The Re-*

porter staff, who was honor bound to warn him in advance about any mentions of him that were scheduled to be printed. Whenever he got wind of something, Hughes would request that the item be removed. *It never was*. And Billy, learning of Howard's inside tipster, bluntly told Hughes to save his money.

During the Forties and Fifties, Wilkerson and Hughes, each in his own way, fought against communism in the motion picture industry. In 1947, the House Un-American Activities Committee (HUAC) began conducting hearings into the alleged spread of communism within all areas of the film community. Wilkerson considered the possibility untenable. For nearly a decade, *The Hollywood Reporter* led the crusade, often to Billy's detriment. When this painful chapter in Hollywood's history ended, Wilkerson was credited with having helped stop the communist infiltration.

The Hughes-Wilkerson friendship was a lifelong one. Howard was a proven, if erratic, genius. But even before *he* fixed his gaze upon the Las Vegas desert, Wilkerson had discovered the nearly barren land and had made plans for some of it. He organized a syndicate to build the Flamingo Hotel. Subsequently, when the Wilkerson group ran out of money, the project was taken over by "other interests," led by Benjamin "Bugsy" Siegel. Still, Hollywood sat back and marveled at Billy's constantly innovative brain from which each new enterprise sprang forth—and was pursued to the hilt— or dumped.

Speaking of pursuits, even by Hollywood standards, Wilkerson was a great lover. He wooed, won, wed and was shed by five wives—all very beautiful women—several of whom were also very clever and talented. He was sixty years old, and had made a fortune, much of which he gambled away in high-stakes poker games with the studio bigwigs. It was at a party in the home of a card-playing crony, Joseph Schenck, one of the industry's mightiest moguls, that he spotted a gorgeous young lady. Although he had come with a beauty, Billy could not resist finding out the girl's name from Schenck. He walked over, introduced himself and asked for a date.

Tichi Noble, who had seen Billy arrive with a doll draped on his arm, promptly turned him down. Tichi, half American, half Mexican, a descendant of the Verdugos, pioneer settlers of California and Mexico, had come to Schenck's home through an introduction from relatives. Shortly after her conversation with Wilkerson, Schenck wandered over and asked if she would be interested in an acting career; he wanted to set up a screen test for her. Tichi's answer was plain and straightforward: "I don't want to be an actress. I've watched them work. It's a very difficult and demanding profession. I'd rather marry a rich man."

Joe looked at her and laughed. "I just steered a wealthy gentleman in your direction. But when he asked you out, you turned him down."

Tichi explained that she had seen him come in with another woman to whom he seemed quite close. Under the circumstances, she explained, she had felt obliged to say no.

"Well," Schenck replied, "you made a big mistake. Billy *always* has a beautiful girl draped on his arm . . . Doesn't mean a thing."

A few days later, Wilkerson phoned, turned on the charm, and his courtship of Tichi began in earnest. She still lived at home with her mother, who hardly spoke English. On their first date, Billy took her to LaRue's. She was very impressed with the elegant restaurant, even though she had no idea he owned it. Once they ordered, she tried to dazzle him with what she believed to be stimulating talk. After a decent interval, Billy looked at her and said, "Stop trying to make conversation."

He was curt. She was hurt—but hooked.

Tichi Noble as she looked when Billy first met her.

No one had ever spoken to her like that before.

On their next date, Billy sat in the living room, "talking" to Mrs. Noble as he waited impatiently for Tichi. While she took her time deciding what to wear, Wilkerson, whose only words of conversational Spanish were "adios" and "taco," grew increasingly more uncomfortable. Mrs. Noble was extremely gracious, but after thirty minutes, Billy got up, pointed to his watch, made sure she understood his anger and left.

When Tichi came downstairs and discovered she had been stood up—in front of her mother—she made up her mind. Billy Wilkerson was not like the young boys she was used to. Guys who spoiled her. Who were only too happy to sit and wait—for hours, if necessary—just for the pleasure of taking her out. Wilkerson was a *man*. A challenge. He was much older—but she was determined to marry him!

Within a few months, Tichi Noble became Mrs. William R. Wilkerson, and moved into his Bel Air mansion. It was a sweeping

French Colonial home Billy had built for his third wife. It came fully equipped, including two maids, a cook, a chauffeur, a butler and several gardeners. Shortly, however, the new bride received a shock. She discovered that her husband was spending and living on every penny he took in. Deliveries came to the house COD. Billy was actually in the red. His gambling debts had eaten up more than anyone knew. Boldly, she asked if she could handle the household finances. She wanted to help turn things around. To her relief, he agreed.

A year later, when their first child, William R. Wilkerson, Jr., was born, Billy, in ecstasy, quit gambling cold turkey. A couple of years later he became the father of Cynthia Diane. In his twilight years, he was a truly fulfilled man. He still ran the paper, kept up several restaurants and continued to go into and out of numerous enterprises. But his home life was unlike any he had known before. If one could use the word in his context, Billy Wilkerson finally had begun to mellow.

Every year the family traveled to Europe, Acapulco, Hawaii. When the children were in nursery school, Tichi became interested in the paper. She asked her husband if she could come to work with him. Billy set up another desk in his office. He showed her how the paper was put together, discussed business deals and treated her like a gifted protégée.

The marriage flourished for eleven years. During the last two, Billy suffered from emphysema, partially as the result of smoking three to four packs of cigarettes every twenty-four hours. One day before the thirty-second anniversary of his founding of *The Hollywood Reporter*, Billy had a heart attack and passed away.

Utilizing the professional training which Wilkerson had given them, his staff did *not* make his death *The Reporter*'s banner headline. But it *was* a page-one story. After all, he had been the most colorful figure that ever graced motion picture trade journalism.

After a suitable period of mourning, Tichi Wilkerson took up the reins of the business and became *The Hollywood Reporter*'s second publisher and editor-in-chief. She has continued to maintain and enlarge the scope of the paper's operations. Today, in addition to offices in New York, Washington, D.C., London and Australia, *The Reporter* maintains correspondents in twenty-two countries around the world.

Tichi, a civic and philanthropic leader in Southern California, is also among the nation's top printers through her Verdugo Press, which prints the daily paper and contracts outside accounts. The second generation of Wilkersons is very much a part of the dynasty Billy founded. Daughter Cynthia is managing editor of the daily paper and publisher of the international edition, which comes out every Tuesday. Willie Wilkerson, Jr., a musician and composer of classical and contemporary music, lived in London until recently, where his wife, Natalie, headed *The Reporter*'s bureau. They now reside in Beverly Hills, where he composes music for films, television and records.

Research for *The Hollywood Reporter—The Golden Years* was based on entertainment news stories, film reviews, gossip items and special features contained in more than 7,800 issues of *The Hollywood Reporter*, as published between September 3, 1930, and December 31, 1959. It was supplemented by investigative reporters' files and interviews, both with personalities who were part of Hollywood's beginnings, as well as with those who are involved in the contemporary cinema scene. There are also dozens of celebrity byline pieces written by the stars exclusively for *The Reporter*'s special editions, which began back in 1930.

MARCIA BORIE
Hollywood, California
1983

THE MOGULS

Wilson Mizner, renowned wit, top-notch reporter, world traveler and famous screenplay writer, once cracked: "Hollywood is like a play with a bad cast," which proved that even the most brilliant of people could make dumb remarks. To the contrary, the history of the motion picture industry, and of the moguls who helped to shape it, is the story of a marvelous, ever-changing cast of characters.

Originally, many of them earned their living as store clerks, factory workers, vaudevillians, bookkeepers, fur merchants, glove salesmen, amusement park employees and even sellers of junk. Some had their first experience in "the industry" when they bought or managed nickelodeons; others were fascinated patrons of these storefront theatres. All of them saw a future in *making* films. So they came to Hollywood and turned the thriving community into a stable "company town."

Collectively, these moguls, as they came to be called, comprised as extraordinary a mixture of talent and toughness, instinct and inspiration, ambition and arrogance, energy and ego, as had ever assembled in one place, for one purpose—to entertain—albeit the by-product was individual fame and fortune.

UNIVERSAL

Carl Laemmle was president of both Universal Pictures Corporation in New York and its West Coast Studios. Raised in Laupheim, Germany, he grew to his full height, five feet, two inches, when he was in his teens. All of his life he had to look up to others. But it was Laemmle who became "the giant."

In 1906, Laemmle opened his first storefront flicker parlor. He was immediately successful and added others to his chain. Three years later, he realized the necessity for more and better product and started an organization to produce films: the Independent Moving Pictures Company of America. People in the business called it IMP, for short. In 1912, together with a group of successful New York film executives, Laemmle formed the Universal Film Manufacturing Company. Three years later they opened new studios, in the San Fernando Valley, a few miles west of Hollywood. They were now officially Universal Pictures.

The industry owes a debt to Laemmle and Universal for their innovative contributions. Always the largest studio in area, the sprawling four hundred acres housed everything from the first electrically lighted soundstages, to the first woman producer, Lois Weber, to the first industry wunderkind, Irving Thalberg.

When Laemmle first spotted him, Thalberg was a secretary-clerk in Universal's

New York offices. He saw something special in the boy and made him his own private secretary. During a trip to the West Coast, Thalberg's brilliant suggestions convinced Laemmle to leave him behind as the studio's general manager. Irving's keen instinct for both a good story and outstanding talent proved invaluable. One of Thalberg's last selections, before he left the company for MGM, was to pick an extra, Lon Chaney, and star him in *The Hunchback of Notre Dame*—still regarded as a classic.

In 1930, Universal released *All Quiet on the Western Front,* another classic. It was produced by Carl Laemmle, Jr., who replaced Thalberg as general manager of the studio. Over the years, Junior Laemmle was not the only relative "Uncle Carl" employed. His son-in-law, M. Stanley Bergerman, was in charge of short subjects. While both Junior and Stanley proved extremely competent, Laemmle had a sentimental penchant for promising jobs to all of his other relatives, plus half of the population of his European hometown. Family by family, Laemmle's Laupheimers sailed to America and right onto the Universal lot. Eventually, this nepotism proved harmful. By 1935, he had a cash flow problem and decided to retire at age sixty-eight. He sold his holdings to a group headed by financier John Cheever Cowdin. Although he lived out the rest of his life away from the daily studio activity, Laemmle's contributions were inestimable.

PARAMOUNT

Adolph Zukor, born in 1873 in the Hungarian village of Ricse, was orphaned at age fifteen and sailed for America with the equivalent of forty dollars sewn into the lining of his vest by an older brother. His first job, as a New York upholsterer's apprentice, brought him two dollars a week.

In 1905, Zukor formed a partnership with William A. Brady to operate "Hale's Tours." They were a chain of imitation railroad carriages which jolted and creaked realistically while, on a screen at one end, scenic pictures gave "passengers" the illusion of a train ride. When the interest in this novelty waned and the supply of two-reel motion pictures became more plentiful, Zukor opened five-cent "store-shows." The first, the Comedy, was at 14th Street and Union Square, next to his original penny arcade, and featured motion picture reels as part of a vaudeville bill.

Zukor foresaw the great destiny of "flickers." As an exhibitor, he campaigned constantly for a better grade of pictures. He felt that longer narrative films would win public favor. But "The Trust," a powerful monopolistic group controlling film production and distribution, could see no reason to depart from the established success of two-reelers.

Unable to convince the big boys, Zukor became his own film producer. He haunted D. W. Griffith's sets, studied various picture companies at work, determined that he would present important actors and actresses in *full-length* screenplays. Long before his company was organized, he already had decided upon his motto: "Famous Players in Famous Plays."

At that time, he obtained the American rights to *Queen Elizabeth*, a French four-reel picture which starred "the Divine Sarah Bernhardt." The Broadway crowd thought him a hopeless optimist. People would not go for such highbrow stuff, they told him. But the public *did* enjoy it, and flocked to the boxoffice. *Queen Elizabeth* became the first really artistic, full-length screenplay shown in America. It paved the way for the abandonment of two-reelers and the adoption of feature-length subjects starring important performers.

In 1912, Adolph Zukor launched the Famous Players Film Company in association with Daniel Frohman, a leading Broadway producer. The first three pictures released by the new company were *The Prisoner of Zenda, The Count of Monte Cristo*, with James O'Neill, and *Tess of the D'Urbervilles*, with Minnie Maddern Fiske. These were filmed versions of Broadway plays which featured the original stars. He even wooed Ethel Barrymore from the theatre—temporarily. Zukor's success encouraged other new production companies to enter the field. His conviction that the public would respond to better pictures had been proven. The big push toward filmmaking, as we know it, had begun.

At the same time, Jesse L. Lasky, Sam Goldwyn and Cecil B. DeMille were combining their talents to organize the Jesse L. Lasky Feature Play Company. They raised $26,000 and filmed *The Squaw Man*, which had been a stage success with Dustin Farnum, as their company's first feature-length production. It was also the first five-reel feature ever made in Hollywood. It was 1913, when they rented half-a-barn in a pastoral suburb of Los Angeles called Hollywood.

Very few people ever said a bad word about Jesse L. Lasky, which made his mogulhood unique. He was one of the motion picture industry's most beloved pioneers, starmakers and innovators. Lasky's company later became the nucleus of Paramount's first studio, located at Sunset and Vine.

Meanwhile, Zukor had signed some of the greatest names of the theatre in addition to James O'Neill (playwright Eugene's father), Lillian Langtry, John Barrymore, Fanny Ward and Geraldine Farrar. In 1913, he brought a young Canadian girl, Gladys Smith, already renamed Mary Pickford, to the screen. She was the first film discovery to receive billing and became Zukor's first great star.

In 1914, William Wadsworth Hodkinson left General Film Company, the major trust of the day, to form the Paramount Picture Corporation. He also took over distribution of Zukor's films and the product of Lasky's Feature Play Company, plus several others. In 1916, The Famous Players Film Company and Lasky's Feature Play Company combined to become Famous Players–Lasky, with Zukor as president. Then twelve other production companies joined the merger. Zukor controlled his pictures from the moment the raw film went into the camera until they had reached the theatre. By combining production and distribution, he established a precedent for the entire industry.

The company's films were produced on both coasts. In New York, there was a studio on West 56th Street. In Hollywood, they rapidly expanded the Vine Street studio, which had sprung up around the original Lasky barn. Their gigantic Astoria, Long Island, studio opened in 1921. By 1926, Paramount Pictures Corporation had consolidated its operations when they took over Famous Players–Lasky and added to the already existing facilities on Melrose and Marathon avenues, where they remain to this day.

Lasky became head of production for that studio. Basically, blessed with an artist's talent—he was originally a musician—Jesse did not have the cutthroat temperament necessary for true and lasting mogulhood. But he did have an eye for talent, and was credited with discovering the movie potential of such greats as Gloria Swanson, Pola Negri, Maurice Chevalier, Gary Cooper and the Marx Brothers.

In the early Thirties, Lasky was forced out of Paramount, a studio he had helped to build—and his once enormous fortune seesawed from millions to zero—several times. But more of Jesse's personal saga later.

1 Carl Laemmle, Senior and Junior.
Laemmle was founder and president of Universal; his son was vice president.
2 Early portrait of Sam Goldwyn.
3 The Warner Brothers. Left to right: Harry, Jack, Sam and Albert.   4 Jesse and Bess Lasky, 1929. Bessie was loved by Goldwyn until Lasky swept her off her feet. So she fixed Sam up with her sister-in-law, Blanche Lasky, whom Goldwyn married and subsequently divorced. (Courtesy of Marc Wanamaker, Bison Archives)

picture, which became a boxoffice sensation. The brothers grossed nearly a million dollars and were a company to be reckoned with. So they established permanent headquarters in Hollywood and signed up a series of stars, including the "wonder dog" Rin Tin Tin, and John Barrymore, and also enlisted the services of director Ernst Lubitsch.

In 1925, Major Nathan Levinson, a former Signal Corps officer who had joined the company as a technical expert, brought the first word of a process that eventually revolutionized the industry—and established Warners as one of the great pioneers in entertainment. In Western Electric's New York laboratories, Levinson had witnessed a short motion picture "that could talk." He asked Sam Warner to investigate the process. Sam took one look and immediately decided that the innovative development offered a great opportunity for exploitation. He probed the possibilities of adapting the process for full-length films. This necessitated refining the synchronization of camera and sound recording devices in order to quiet the noise of the cameras and klieg lights, and perfec ng a studio stage technique fe naking pictures in an entirely new way.

In 1926, Warners produced *Don Juan*, which starred John Barrymore and featured a fully synchronized musical score by the New York Philharmonic Orchestra. Then came *The Jazz Singer*, the first motion picture with speech. The brothers made the picture, bit by bit, in a technique that was absolutely new to the world. In August of 1927, it was completed. The print and sound tracks were shipped to New York. Sam Warner planned to join brother Harry for the metropolitan opening. The weeks of worry and work, however, had taken their toll. Sam Warner contracted a cold which developed into a fatal case of pneumonia. Ironically, the one brother most responsible for trying the new process passed away on the eve of its biggest test. Clearly, their company's fate rested on the public reception of *The Jazz Singer*. Because of Sam's death, opening night, October 6, 1927, was both a memorable and a sad occasion.

An eager, fashionable crowd poured into the Warner Theatre for the premiere. When they *saw* and *heard* Al Jolson sing "Mammy," they applauded. Then they rose in stunned delight. It wasn't just the songs that brought them to their feet, it was *one spoken line*, which had crept in by accident. On the studio lot, Jolson had stepped up to the microphone to sing "Blue Skies." To help create the proper mood, he had leaned toward the microphone and said, "Come on, Ma, listen to this."

Those six words, brought into the picture by chance, *and left in*, electrified the crowd and assured the enormous success of the picture. New York audiences jammed the theatre. Eventually, *The Jazz Singer* swept the nation. In 1928, buoyed by their triumph, Warners purchased the First National Studios in Burbank and immediately began to expand.

COLUMBIA

By 1930, Harry Cohn was ensconced in Hollywood as vice president and general manager of Columbia Pictures Corporation. Back East, Joseph Brandt was president, while Harry's brother Jack functioned as secretary-treasurer. Ten years earlier, the Cohn boys had worked for the old Universal Company. Once they learned enough about the film business, they pooled their entire resources, two hundred and fifty dollars, and wangled a contract to release some two-reel comedies on their own.

Native New Yorkers, they knew nothing about Hollywood and had never actually produced films. So they hired a West Coast producer to make a series of shorts at a budget of $10,000 each. The first four that came through were terrible. Then they discovered that their "Hollywood connection" had spent only $2,000 per film and had pocketed the rest. They canceled the contract and "Hot Headed Harry," as Cohn would come to be known, traveled to California to produce shorts himself.

The Cohn-made two-reelers were an instant success and developed into a series called "The Hall Room Boys" comedies. Next, they made a series of one-reelers, "Screen Snapshots," which were a kind of filmed fan magazine. By the end of their first year, the Cohns had added a partner, Joseph Brandt. They called their new firm the CBC Film Sales Corporation. As soon as their feature film venture was a success,

they renamed the corporation. People in the trade had referred to CBC as "corned beef and cabbage." The Cohns needed a name with *dignity*, so they chose Columbia Pictures Corporation.

In 1932, Joe Brandt retired. Harry Cohn became Columbia's president, and Jack moved up to assume the vice presidential role. Between the brothers there was a constant East–West Coast feud. Jack felt vastly overshadowed by his volatile brother. He seemed hurt that *his* role in the company appeared to be so secondary. Over the years, publicity releases appeared in the nation's entertainment columns—all singing Jack Cohn's praises for *his* contributions to Columbia. Each time, Harry hit the ceiling— since the releases rarely mentioned *him*. The brothers continued their love-hate relationship for much of their lives.

DISNEY

Walt Disney arrived in Hollywood from Kansas City, in 1923, with one suit of clothes, a sweater, some drawing materials and forty dollars. For several months, he tried to sell a fairytale cartoon he had made back home. Nobody wanted it, and he sent it back East to some prospective buyers.

In anticipation of a sale, his brother Roy, who had faith in Walt's talent, came up with a couple of hundred dollars. Their Uncle Robert lent them another five hundred. The eastern buyers liked Walt's cartoon, gave them an order for a series and finally they were in business.

The Disneys rigged up their garage with an old camera and stands made out of packing boxes. Walt taught Roy how to work the camera and then started drawing day and night. With the help of two girls, hired for $15 a week each, they made their first cartoon. Walt later married one of his helpers—Lillian Bounds.

By 1925, they had moved into a regular

store, and Roy looked for land to build their own studio. He found a few acres out in Glendale, where they constructed a small green and white studio, with one big room for the artists. Walt and Roy each had his own cubbyhole. There were a couple of offices for miscellaneous help. At that time, Disney's main character was Oswald Rabbit.

In 1928, Walt needed financing to improve his pictures. He went to New York and asked the head of his distributing firm for an increased budget. The money was *not* forthcoming. Walt headed back to Hollywood with a studio but no pictures to make. Then Disney created a new character and became an independent producer. Dogs, cats and rabbits had all been used. So Walt, remembering the mice he used to tame back in Kansas City, drew a mouse and named it Mortimer. Mrs. Disney thought that sounded too stuffy. She suggested the name Mickey.

Walt turned out the first Mickey Mouse film, *Plane Crazy*, in a couple of weeks. But 1928 was the era of *The Jazz Singer*. Nobody was interested in a *voiceless* and rather unglamorous little mouse. Disney had already started work on a second silent Mickey Mouse cartoon, but put that aside. He realized that synchronized cartoons were not only possible but inevitable. He went on to his third cartoon, *Steamboat Willie*, which featured both Mickey and Minnie Mouse in sound. Since Walt and Roy could not afford to hire voices, Walt spoke for Mickey, and one of the studio girls, who did inking and painting, was drafted to be Minnie's voice. Audiences loved *Steamboat Willie*. Disney had arrived!

In 1933, Walt signed up four new stars— three little pigs—and a duck named Donald. Disney's staff numbered one hundred and fifty, and he bought more land next door. His cartoons were done in Technicolor; Mickey's gray pants became red. By 1936, Disney had three hundred employees, and his biggest desire was to make a full-length picture. Three years later, *Snow White* made its debut. It was an instant success around the world. Mickey Mouse had started the dynasty. *Snow White* enhanced it. Disney Studios moved to a sprawling complex in Burbank, and Walt eventually became the recipient of more Academy Awards than anyone else in Hollywood history.

RKO, FOX, UNITED ARTISTS, CADDO COMPANY

To round out the studio setup at the beginning of the Thirties, William Le Baron was vice president in charge of production at RKO Radio Pictures, with Pandro Berman as his assistant. Simultaneously, Charles R. Rogers headed production at RKO-Pathé, which was housed in separate studio quarters.

At Fox Studios, Winfield "Winnie" Sheehan was head honcho in charge of West Coast production. William Fox, who had founded the company, was already out, but continually suing to get back in. Harley L. Clarke, president of Fox, headquartered in New York.

United Artists, formed in 1919 by Mary Pickford, Doug Fairbanks, Sr., Charles Chaplin and D. W. Griffith, was the first organization to give artists creative control over production and distribution. By 1930, Pickford's own company was headquartered on the lot, as was that of independent producer Sam Goldwyn, who had become an owner-member of U.A.

Howard Hughes, one of the "second wave," who was neither poor, nor poorly

educated, but heir to the Hughes Tool dynasty, was president of the Caddo Company, named for the Louisiana parish where his daddy had first struck it big in oil. As a further example of the unique Hollywood infrastructure, Hughes was also a director of the Hughes–Franklin Theatres, with Joseph Schenck as his vice president. Meanwhile, Schenck, president of United Artists, was the brother of Nicholas Schenck, who was head of both Loew's Incorporated and MGM. And Noah Dietrich, treasurer of Hughes' Caddo, and secretary-treasurer of the Hughes–Franklin Theatres, was also an officer in the Hughes Tool Company.

Recently, Betty Lasky, former motion picture magazine writer and editor and author of *RKO: The Biggest Little Major Studio of Them All*, reminisced about her family and what it was like to grow up as the daughter of one of the most important pioneer moguls in the history of Hollywood.

When her father was production head of Paramount, the Laskys spent their winters in New York. They lived on an entire floor at 910 Fifth Avenue, directly across from Central Park. The home was furnished in European antiques. Tapestries hung on the walls. For Betty, as a child, "it was like living in a museum . . . a very depressing place.

I had a governess who shared my life. I rarely saw my parents. Occasionally, I glimpsed Dad at night, while he was having a massage. I played tag, and went in and out of his room before he left for the evening. My mother went to Europe every winter, where she bought our clothes. She dressed me in silks and laces, and I never looked like the average child. I was driven to school in a Rolls-Royce. It was agony getting out of the car. I felt the other kids were staring at me. I used to walk through Central Park with my governess. Once, Gloria Vanderbilt was there. We were photographed together: two "poor little rich girls." I have two brothers. Jesse Jr., is considerably older than I. As a child, I hardly knew he existed. He was grown up and out of the house. My other brother, William, was closer to my age, but he was always at school.

Every summer, we lived in California, when Dad came out to oversee the studio. We had a fifty-room beach house at 609 Ocean Front Avenue. It was an Early Spanish-style hacienda, with a patio in the center, and loads of guest rooms, which were always full of people. I'm not sure Dad knew half of their names. You could see the ocean from our solarium . . .

My parents were extraordinary, and constantly active. Dad had his studio business. Mother had her painting, her friends and her lovers. She was a very beautiful woman. Samuel Goldwyn had been in love with her when they were young. She was the Elizabeth Taylor of her day. But she met Dad and was swept off her feet. She came from an Orthodox Jewish family, but was convent educated. My grandfather sent her there to protect her. She was also trained at the Boston Conservatory, as a pianist . . . She had the spiritual soul of the true artist. Then she married into a show business family. It was difficult for her, until Dad did well and she could live her own lifestyle . . . She was elegant and always discreet.

During the summer, whenever there was a party, I was packed off with my governess to the Miramar Hotel, in Santa Monica, for the night. Even though the children's wing was in the rear, I was sent away so I wouldn't be disturbed, and so I wouldn't see anything. Consequently, I never viewed "wicked Hollywood." Although I do have one memory of opening my mother's bathroom door and seeing a nude man with a beautiful body. It was John Burton, the famous glassmaker from Santa Barbara. I later learned that he had been my mother's lover in the late Twenties. . . .

When my parents had beach parties, the preparation started a week in advance. Frequently the Albertina Rasch Ballet would perform. Our servants hung up a paper moon and installed a dancefloor over the large salt water pool. Pits were dug in the sand, and the food was cooked luau-style . . .

Others may have envied me, but I was a lonely child. When she was home, my mother was always in her studio painting. Then she would take off for Europe. She had a great love affair with Jascha Heifetz, in the late Twenties, when he was the toast of Paris. Her best friend was one of Heifetz's wives, actress Florence Vidor. Florence never knew; she was very straitlaced.

In essence, my parents had come to an accommodation. He did what he wanted to do. She did what she wanted to do. Yet they maintained the air of respectability in a marriage which lasted until the day he died . . . Their feeling was that he had a very important position, and that divorce was a bad thing. Besides, the press covered for them, and protected them, as they did all of Hollywood's important people.

Down at the beach, my mother also had an affair with Rex Ingram, Rudolph Valentino's director. Then there was John Monk Saunders, the man who wrote *Wings*. And Antonio Moreno, a very dashing actor. I'm sure Dad had his favorites, too. But I never knew who they were. We never found out.

In 1932, Dad was booted out of Paramount by that terrible man, Emanuel Cohen. He was just plain dethroned. He lost a fortune, and went through bankruptcy. But it wasn't reflected in our lifestyle. *We* still lived like Kings. Before Dad was kicked out, we rented the gorgeous King Vidor mansion on top of a mountain. When the ouster came, we moved to a house on North Roxbury Drive, in the *flat* part of Beverly Hills. We still lived on a street of mansions, but they were much smaller. After Dad left Paramount, in the fall of 1932, Sidney Kent, who had become head of Fox, made a place for him, and he became an independent producer.

My father was a wonderful man. Everybody loved him—except, I guess, Emanuel Cohen! But Dad was the only "mogul" whom everyone had a kind word for. He didn't really belong in this business. He was an artist, a musician. He couldn't be tough. During the course of his life, he made and lost three fortunes. With Dad, it was easy come, easy go. He never planned much for the future, unlike Mary Pickford, or C. B. DeMille. They were afraid of losing their money, so they made smart investments. Dad was never interested in money, although he liked what it could buy.

My father stayed at Fox, where he had his own independent production unit, until they merged and became 20th Century–Fox. Then he went into partnership with Mary Pickford, and released his films through her company, United Artists. Next, he was briefly at RKO. Then he moved to Warner Brothers where he produced all of those famous biographical films. But my father had a lot of trouble with Jack Warner, who was a vulgar man with no vision. I saw some of the inter-office memos he and Dad exchanged. They were full of crudity and lack of respect.

During that period my family lost our place at the beach because of debt. It was Harry Warner, a very good man, who helped my father out. He loaned him money and arranged to take over the house . . . But whatever my father's financial condition, he always kept his mother and us in style . . .

After my mother died, I discovered that the great love of her life had been Edward G. Robinson. That was in the Thirties, when he was an enormous star. Audiences may have thought of him as the tough guy, with the cigar and the rat-ta-tat delivery. But off screen, he was charming and worldly; gentle and kind. He was also very good-looking in a charismatic way . . . At one point, I think Robinson and my mother might have wanted to marry. But I guess neither of them thought it was proper. So they just enjoyed one another. Eddie's keen appreciation of art—he was one of the town's most prolific collectors—was enhanced after he and mother became close. My mother was a great artist. Her paintings were on exhibition in all of the fine galleries across the country. She did a series of California Missions that became classics. Her still-lifes were very much coveted by art lovers all over the country. All of her canvases were signed Bessie Mona Lasky.

Eventually, my dad had a mistress that we all knew about. Her name was Jean Kohler. She looked like Loretta Young, and she *was* younger than I. They wanted to marry. Mother considered divorcing Dad. She even packed up and started out for Reno. Then she changed her mind and came home. It was the smartest thing she ever did. She and Dad decided to live out their lives together.

My father died broke. It was a result

of a tax case over Dad's film *Sergeant York*, which starred Gary Cooper, and made millions. Ten years after the picture was finished, the Internal Revenue Service swooped down on Dad and took away everything he had. They would have thrown my mother out of her house, but the other moguls passed the hat, and loaned us enough money so that my mother could remain in the house until the day she died . . . It was all repaid, eventually.

Jesse L. Lasky, whose name is synonymous with early Hollywood, and whose famous Lasky barn would, in the 1980s, become the focal point for the establishment of the Hollywood Museum, died happy, but broke . . . The one man who was "too sweet to be a real mogul."

His daughter's recollections were told in candor, and with love. They offered an accurate picture of what life was like—at the very top of the Hollywood heap.

THE THIRTIES

HOLLYWOOD IN TRANSITION

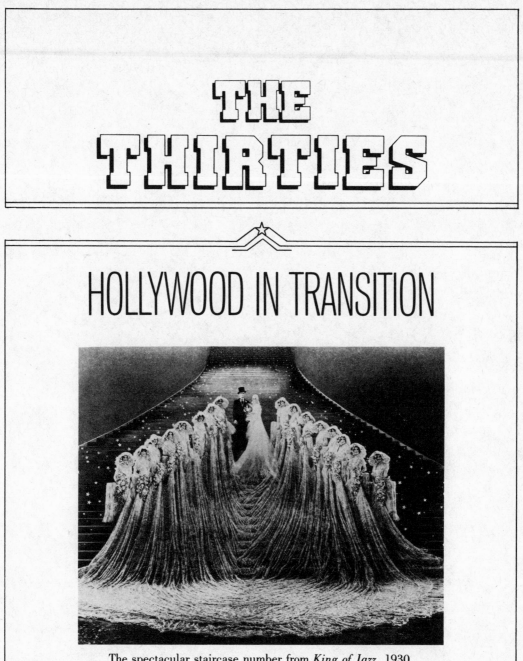

The spectacular staircase number from *King of Jazz*, 1930.

HOLLYWOOD: A TOWN IN TRANSITION

Hollywood, in the generic sense, has always been an industry in crisis. The movie business has ebbed and flowed from one transition to another, frequently in a state of panic, constantly looking over its collective shoulder to see how close "the enemy" was. In 1920, they were frightened by the potential impact of radio. A few years later, the first talkies were a cause for great alarm. Then came the Crash of 1929, the Bank Holiday of '33 and the European War in 1939. The bombs which devastated Pearl Harbor in 1941 simultaneously exploded over Hollywood with terrific force.

In between national or international crises, even card games such as bridge, gin rummy and canasta caused tidal waves of terror to rush through Tinseltown. Mah-Jongg, miniature golf, charades, horse and dog racing—any form of gambling—was considered as dangerous to Hollywood as an outbreak of the Black Plague. Fads, which kept audiences away from the boxoffice, were looked upon as a personal affront to the industry's survival.

But Hollywood, uniquely adorned with surface trappings of glamour, fantastic faces, frantic goings-on and the seductive allure of its own product, was able to mask its insecurities under a luscious layer of pancake makeup and a fantasyland atmosphere. The public never saw the acne scars of celluloid puberty. They never read about the town's continuous troubles. That would have spoiled the illusion.

In the early 1930s, Hollywood was a town full of secondhand roses and two-time tulips. To hide their fading profits, movie studios premiered their films with an extra-special flair. Invariably, they opened pictures at the plushest theatre palaces, such as Grauman's Chinese, the Egyptian, or the Carthay Circle.

Those evenings always began the same way. Incandescent lights, which radiated high-intensity beams visible for ten miles, crisscrossed evening skies. Makeshift barriers, set up out front, restrained the eager fans who had gathered to glimpse their favorite stars. Celebrities arrived in shiny limousines or snazzy roadsters. They alighted from their cars and glided across dazzling red carpets. Men were dressed in elegantly hand-tailored tuxedos. The ladies wore flowing chiffon, clinging satin or shimmering sequined gowns. After obligatory smiles and waves to the crowds, the stars entered ornate lobbies full of baskets and bouquets of exquisite flowers.

Following the ceremonious presentation of pastel posies to the picture's stars, studio heads spoke words of optimism and joy into standing microphones. Claques of sycophants beamed and applauded on cue. As the lobby lights dimmed and the movie began, all of the "show plants" were trundled back into trucks and redelivered to obliging florists. They were put back on ice—then resold to unsuspecting suckers—before even so much as a single petal had fallen from one fragrant rose.

Hollywood was a mass tableau of secondhand flowers. When clutched to mostly tiny, but heaving, bosoms, they made perfect free publicity pictures for the morning newspapers. It was pure sham. All show and no tell. The profusion of posies, rented by the hour or the event, were as necessary to the atmosphere as dress extras in a crowd scene.

Flowers were also used to impress the fans. Whether natives of Hollywood or tourists from Iowa, giant klieg lights always attracted them. Fans showed up, rain or shine, as mesmerized by the radiant glow as moths flocking to a bonfire. At every premiere, it was the same. Thousands of them—all, please God, prospective customers—breathing the fragrant aroma, jaws ajar, as they lived out their own secret fantasies in the reflected floral rainbow of Hollywood's most superficial splendor.

Lobby posters, an art unto themselves, were elegantly sketched, colorful depictions of stars. The come-on, written alongside the illustrations, was usually pure hyperbole. Universal Studios, for instance, purchased a book called *Mississippi* and turned it into a film with a catchy title. The poster was extremely effective. The stars stood shoulder to shoulder, their eyes full of love and determination. The copy beside them read:

A surging storm of romance and passion . . .
They called them white trash . . .
Born in poverty, they found riches in love . . .
Reared in rags . . . Love warmed them . . .
Just two kids seeking happiness where all was bitterness . . .

LEW AYRES and ANITA LOUISE
in
"HEAVEN ON EARTH"

Hopefully, the poster was enticing enough to make people—with holes in their soles—rush out to see the film. After all, if Lew and Anita could rise from the trash heap, why not them?

In September 1930, when *The Hollywood Reporter* started publishing, the movie industry was going through the final pains of the conversion to talkies. Ninety-five percent of Hollywood's films were being made with sound. Five percent—resisters to the end—produced only silents. Throughout America, 13,700 theatres already had installed sound equipment. Eight thousand movie houses still showed silents only. But the demand for sound equipment was so great that there were 234 different types of talkie systems on the market, many of them designed for use with a disk. These required that the sound and the film, two separate operations, be perfectly matched, exactly in sync, or else dramas suddenly sounded like comedies.

Conditions across the country were equally as confused—and growing worse. In the White House, Herbert Hoover seemed unable to handle the economic crisis brought on by the Stock Market Crash of 1929. Meanwhile, Franklin Delano Roosevelt, who had been renominated for governor of New York, was rumored to be waiting in the wings for "honorable Herb" to pack his presidential bags and vacate 1600 Pennsylvania Avenue.

The Roaring Twenties had given way to the Threadbare Thirties. Every section of the country was affected. In the industrial East, factories began to shut down. Large areas of the usually fertile Midwest became dust bowls because of an unprecedented dry spell. Poor cotton crops and overplanted land were weakening the South, which was still staggering from the residual scars of its own Great War. The embryonic Far West suffered from both industrial and agricultural failures. Everywhere, Americans were hurting.

In those bad times, people desperately needed periodic relief. They sought escape in picture houses, where reality was suspended and problems disappeared. Films were celluloid placebos—quickie panaceas guaranteed to last at least until the curtain came down.

To the moviegoing public, screen stars seemed to be God's *real* Chosen People. They were prettier, wittier, luckier, pluckier. They did things on camera—and off—that ordinary folks could only dream about. They even lived on their own Mount Olympus—Hollywood.

Everybody "knew" about Hollywood. It was that lush sin city, way out West, where stars bought all the luxurious possessions they craved and indulged in every human excess that pleased them. Tinsel township was inhabited by exotic actresses with bee-stung lips, long legs and firm breasts. And their co-stars, handsome broad-shouldered actors with pomade on their hair and the sexual scent of musk on their bodies. It was a magic place, where the famous were continually showered with all of life's bonbons as a reward for supplying beautiful pacifiers people could count on in hard times. There was only one problem: *Hollywood was in trouble, too.*

It was a town in transition. A community in crisis. Suddenly, the pot at the end of the rainbow was full of red ink instead of profits. In just two years, talking pictures had reached their peak and were headed for a nosedive. From 1928 until 1930, movies advertised as "100 percent talk" were assured boxoffice success. Industry leaders, who expected the cycle to continue indefinitely, hired novelists and playwrights at huge salaries to turn out screenplays full of dialogue. Then they imported stage actors to star in their films, some from New York, others from abroad.

But the movie industry had taken its public too much for granted. People suddenly began cooling on talkies. They grew tired of static films with actors they had never heard of before—stage folk who spoke with high falutin' accents. They wanted to see movies like the silents. Films that featured lots of adventure and action, starring their old favorites. If not, they would stay at home, turn on their radios, close their eyes and do a lot of imagining and fantasizing—for *free.*

Moguls with migraines worried about studio conditions plus competition from radio and ordered retrenchment and reorganization. Sound had come in too fast. All the quick coin they made turned out to be "curiosity money." They had been so anxious to rush into production, they hadn't stopped to analyze their precise situation:

Silent movies featured faces without voices . . .

Radio offered voices without faces . . .

Talkies were a *combination* of the first two . . .

But they had misused their new miracle. In their haste, they had forgotten the most basic principle. The true uniqueness of motion pictures was wrapped up in movement. Their industry had achieved greatness through pictures with MOTION . . . ACTION . . . REACTION.

Temporarily, the town turned into a tomb. In 1930, there was less production activity than at any time since the inception of talkies. Fox chopped three hundred from its payroll. Warners–First National, winding up production on a few odds and ends, prepared for a possible closing. Universal, which had been busy a few weeks before, stood idle. Paramount employees, playing guessing games, asked, "Who's who today, and do I still fit in?"

Sam Goldwyn was making *Raffles* at United Artists. He had two more scheduled to go, but they now were doubtful. Both Metropolitan and Tec Art Studios were shuttered. Columbia, stuck in the middle of shooting a talkie, discovered to its horror how much extra the use of sound hiked the cost of picturemaking. The company had sent a cast of five on location, twenty-six miles across the bay, to Catalina Island. Along with them went a crew of *ninety-eight,* mostly sound men or people connected with recording effects. In the silent days the same picture would have required a crew of only twenty and could have finished shooting within a few hours. This short sequence took two and a half days to set up before they even tested their sound equipment for maximum effectiveness.

Meanwhile, theatre owners across the country, desperate for business, gave away "better dishes," and featured "bank night." Most days, the cash prizes and crockery were barely covered by the money in their tills. One enterprising manager at the State Theatre in Cleveland thought he had the problem solved. He placed ads in local papers inviting his patrons to stay after the movies and dance. By the weekend, the word had spread. One thousand people swung and swayed in his immense lobby, with music provided by the theatre band. But even that novelty wore off. Throughout the movie industry the only word heard from the exhibitors in 1930 was one pathetic plea: "Help!"

Cecil B. DeMille
"THE SQUAW MAN"

Early in December 1930, Cecil B. DeMille was ready to start shooting a new version of The Squaw Man. *But he paused long enough to write this piece for* The Hollywood Reporter, *examining the progress the industry made since he first arrived in town.*

It was just seventeen years ago, December 13, 1913, to be exact that I began the making of the first silent *Squaw Man* in an old barn, formerly used by the Stern Brothers, at the corner of Selma and Vine Streets. The story has been told many times of how Jesse Lasky and I had to put our feet on our desks when the man who owned the barn, and used the other half, decided to wash his carriages!

It is not my intention, however, to plunge into historical reminiscence. I am concerned rather with the tremendous change which has taken place in the motion picture art since that time, in all of its branches.

When Mr. Lasky and I told friends in New York we were going to "take a flyer" in pictures, we were deluged with solemn warnings.

"Why," said one man, "what is the use of trying to make better pictures when the theatres are so small, dirty and ill-ventilated that decent people won't go in them?"

And in just seventeen years we have come from those tiny little storerooms, seating around two hundred people, to "Cathedrals of the motion picture," seating upwards of 6,000 persons, costing millions of dollars to construct, and containing every possible adjunct of comfort and beauty.

There is one thing I think we can be very thankful for, and that is the delay which occurred before talking pictures came in . . . I am a very definite advocate of talkies. I think

Lasky Studios, the historic barn where C. B. DeMille, Sam Goldwyn, and Lasky made the first feature, *The Squaw Man.* Photo taken in 1982 by Lida Hadas.

they have advanced the artistic possibilities of the screen art tremendously, and that we have not even made a start into their potentialities.

But I am glad they came no earlier, for the time which elapsed before their arrival made it possible for us to develop the splendid heights, the separate and distinct art of voiceless pantomime.

Had talkies been in existence at the very start of the film industry, I doubt if it would have achieved some of the heights it has touched. For when silent pictures first came out they went into direct competition with a very active stage. There were stock companies in every city, and traveling troupes galore. Without dialogue, picture directors and stars of those early days had to make their pictures good enough to survive this intense competition. Out of this necessity grew many of the devices used so advantageously in the building of our greatest silent pictures: i.e. the close-up, the fade-out, the dissolve, the cut-back, etc.

As to my new *Squaw Man,* it will be a very different picture than the first. It will talk, where the first was silent. It will have the advantage of the improvements in artificial lighting effects, where the original had only sunlight. It will be photographed on film many times more sensitive than the crude stock we bought in 1913. It will have entirely different people. The star of 1913, Dustin Farnum, is dead. The leading lady, Winifred Kingston, is no longer on the screen. Theodore Roberts is dead.

But the new *Squaw Man* will have the advantage of all the new things that we had to go without in 1913. It will be aided by the enormous amount of technical knowledge we have gathered to ourselves in the years between.

In closing, let me say a word about "depressions." From *Squaw Man* to *Squaw Man* I have seen about four of the gloomy periods we are now undergoing. Out of them all I have gained just one central thought and that is "depressions" are bad on bad pictures; but they never really affect good entertainment. In bad times people seek relaxation more energetically than in days of prosperity, but they shop more for their shows. You can't satisfy them with bunk. You must deliver the goods in entertainment, and if you do, good pictures have always broken records in even the worst of "panics."

THOSE FABULOUS THIRTIES FAVORITES

As the Thirties began, the personalities whose names meant the most on marquees were a pretty mixed bag. There was a collection of silent-film stars, unable to make it in talkies, who were destined to be rapidly replaced. In a second group were those silent stars, able to successfully bridge the gap, who continued to reign, many until the end of the decade and beyond. Third, a whole new batch of marvelous faces, figures and physiques—mainly untrained as film actors. A few had stage experience. The rest had nothing but looks as their passport to fame.

Thirties heroes and heroines came in all shapes and sizes. There were dazzling blue-eyed blondes, and shy, retiring ashen-haired beauties. Vivacious brunettes, with dancing velvet brown eyes, or green-blue orbs that twinkled and misted-up on cue. Some were piquant redheads with hazel eyes, or auburn-haired pixies with freckles marching across their faces. The men were mostly broad-shouldered Adonises with muscled forearms and trim moustaches, or outdoor-action types with slim hips that held holsters. A few were aesthetic-looking, pale, almost frail men. Several were the menacing types who knocked women around onscreen and looked like coiled cobras ever ready to spring into action. There were even a few definitely gorgeous males—those love gods whose faces and forms spelled perfection—and ruin to any woman who crossed their path. Of course, there were the unusual favorites, like Wallace Beery and Marie Dressler, homely almost to the point of being beyond redemption—were it not for their fantastic charms. And lastly, there were those funny-faced, wide-eyed comics, whose slapstick antics evoked audience laughter.

Douglas Fairbanks, Sr., and Mary Pickford reigned as King and Queen. Even the street they lived on was symbolically named. Pickfair, their twelve-acre spread, was perched on Summit Drive. They literally lived at the top, the peak, the pinnacle of Beverly Hills. From their sumptuous gardens, they could look down on their domain, suitably situated below them. Their rise to fame had been spectacular—and enduring. Doug enjoyed a screen career which had never been paralleled. Though many imitators tried to emulate him in his dashing roles, there was one Fairbanks. Wherever motion pictures were shown, his name was synonymous with colorful romance and fast action.

He was born Douglas Elton Ulman, in Denver, Colorado, on May 23, 1883, and took the name of Fairbanks when, at seventeen, he entered a Shakespearean repertory company in New York. His first big success was in George M. Cohan's play *Hawthorne of the U.S.A.* In 1914, he entered motion pictures and worked for D. W. Griffith at the then tremendous salary of $2,000 per week. After his first film, *The Lamb*, was a smash hit, his salary was doubled and he was established as a screen favorite. He made twelve pictures for Griffith and twelve for the old Famous Players Company before he became an independent producer.

In such pictures as *The Three Musketeers*, *Robin Hood*, *The Thief of Bagdad*, *The Mark of Zorro* and *The Black Pirate*, Doug's career rose to new heights. With Griffith, Mary Pickford and Charlie Chaplin, Fairbanks formed the original United Artists company in 1919. Under this banner, he would ap-

April 17, 1919. With the signing of incorporation papers, United Artists Studios becomes a reality. Seated: Charles Chaplin. Standing: D. W. Griffith, Mary Pickford, Douglas Fairbanks, Sr.; behind them, their attorneys, Albert Banzhaf, Dennis O'Brien.

pear in such successes as *The Iron Mask*, *Taming of the Shrew*, *Reaching for the Moon* and *Around the World in 80 Days*.

Mary Pickford was born Gladys Marie Smith in Toronto, Canada. She made her stage debut at age five playing Little Ted, a boy, in *Silver King* for the Valentine Stock Company of Toronto. She first appeared on Broadway as a child in *The Warrens of Virginia*, written by William DeMille, whose brother, Cecil, was one of the cast.

When she was thirteen, she took the professional name of Mary Pickford, and two years later made her film debut for the Biograph Company. Her rise was swift and sensational. The public adopted her and she became "America's Sweetheart," starring in such silents as *Tess of the Storm Country*, *Daddy Long Legs*, *Pollyanna*, *Rebecca of Sunnybrook Farm*, *Poor Little Rich Girl* and *Little Lord Fauntleroy*. Her talkies would include *Coquette*, for which she won the Oscar, *Taming of the Shrew* (with Fairbanks) and *Kiki*.

In 1916, she formed the Mary Pickford Film Company and was earning $4,000 a week, the highest-salaried star in Hollywood. In 1919, along with Doug, Griffith and Chaplin, she formed United Artists and became an independent producer.

Doug and Mary had been together for ten years, and Pickfair was Doug's wedding gift to her. It was a lavish, miniature estate tastefully crammed full of rare, priceless antiques. Delicate porcelains and jades from the Far East. A solid gold-rimmed dinner service, originally presented by Napoleon to his Josephine, was now Mary's, a present from *her* Emperor. Even the simplest pieces of furniture were finely crafted. The walls were covered with tapestries, paintings by the Masters, interspersed with oils of Mary and Doug in their respective roles as the *Poor Little Rich Girl* and *Zorro*.

The Fairbanks' surroundings suited their status as internationally beloved stars. The upkeep of Pickfair cost Doug nearly $200,000 a year. Servants' salaries amounted to $30,000 annually. In addition, Doug and Mary had a Santa Monica beach home and their 3,000-acre Zorro Ranch, in San Diego, California.

All of their estates, but especially Pickfair, became the mecca for the crowned heads of Europe. Instructions on how and when to bow were sent out to guests in advance of each royal event. Their Beverly Hills home also had a projection room where they screened the latest films following their elaborate dinners. Costume balls were another Fairbanks specialty. Ironically, stars required to wear costumes by day adored dressing in similar regalia by night. For weeks preceding one of Mary and Doug's fancy-dress soirées, local wigmakers were besieged. Seamstresses were worked to the bone. Some celebrities borrowed finery and fake hair from their studios, but the truly chic had gowns and hairpieces fashioned to order for each occasion.

During the summer months, Mary and Doug utilized their spacious, manicured grounds for parties featuring delicious buffets served by the pool. Guests who tired of swimming the breaststroke could relax and float around in one of the canoes, gliding back and forth on crystal-clear water. The whole setting was a perfect movie stars' Heaven.

The only well-known performers *not* welcomed on Summit Drive were Doug Fairbanks, Jr., and Joan Crawford. They had been married for six months and were readily accepted as the anointed Crown Prince and Princess of Hollywood's younger set. But they had not been invited to Pickfair since their elopement to New York in June of 1929.

However, their wedding *had* been witnessed by Doug's mother, Anna Beth Sully Fairbanks Whiting. She and her second husband, Broadway performer Jack Whiting, had given the couple a day to remember for always. Doug was especially happy for his mother's support. While Joan was equally grateful to her new mother-in-law, as well as to her handsome stepfather-in-law—who was only nine years older than Doug, Jr. Obviously, "Beth" Sully was an independent, down-to-earth, progressive woman. She had defied convention and gossip to marry a much younger man. She understood her son's love for Joan and wholeheartedly approved.

Doug, twenty at the time of the nuptials, and Joan, closer to twenty-five (but with an official studio biography which made her only one or two months older than her husband), appeared not to be worried about the "royal snub." They moved into their own "little castle" at 426 North Bristol Avenue in Brentwood. The home, owned by Joan, had been purchased with the first big money she'd earned. If the King and Queen could give *their* residence a name, so could the Prince and Princess. Since they called each other Jodie and Dodie, they dubbed their Spanish-style palazzo El JoDo.

Newlyweds Joan Crawford and Doug Fairbanks, Jr., seated before the fireplace in their home, nicknamed El JoDo.

Joan wore domesticity like a snug leather glove. She was determined to show her in-laws that she could be a fantastic wife. When she wasn't busy at the studio, she stayed home and planned Dodie's breakfast menus—"he never eats the same thing two mornings in a row"—sewed gingham curtains and hooked rugs to fit their Early American decor. She had read in a movie magazine that her mother-in-law, "America's Sweetheart," fashioned Doug, Sr.'s, old handkerchiefs into dainty maids' aprons. Well, she could sew, too, and hook as well. Albeit she'd heard rumors that the Senior Fairbanks thought she had been hooking things other than rugs for quite some time.

On the surface, Joan appeared happy as a clam. She *had* snatched handsome Doug out from under the wings of various younger debutantes. Inwardly, however, she was furious at the lack of familial acceptance. All of her life she had dreamed of being a great lady. Well, she was on her way. No one, nothing, could stop her now.

Then, six months later, there was a thaw in the relationship between the Senior and Junior Fairbanks. Mary phoned Joan to say that she and Doug, Sr., wanted to give young Doug (whom they called "Jayar"—for junior), a surprise twenty-first-birthday party at Pickfair, on December 9th. Joan was thrilled, and volunteered to help with the guest list.

The evening of the party, Jodie and Dodie arrived early. She, demurely dressed. He, beaming with happiness. It was a lovely evening. Joan came through with flying colors, cloaking her nervousness in the exuberance of the occasion. She was genuinely pleased that both Dougs were reunited and that Mary was pleasant to her. The ice was broken and invitations to Pickfair came more often. Joan was in Seventh Heaven.

Doug's father found Crawford to be beautiful, talented and very eager to please. Mary remained a little more reserved in her feelings for her stepdaughter-in-law. And, in truth, both Dougs would not become close for several more years.

Doug and Mary represented, in essence, the history of the motion picture business. Also during the start of the Thirties, Paramount's top stars were Clara Bow and Maurice Chevalier. Gary Cooper, William Powell, Claudette Colbert and new foreign import Marlene Dietrich were stars on the rise.

By the time Americans were headed for the Great Depression, Clara Bow, the teenage fan magazine contest winner from Brooklyn, had grown into Hollywood's number one flaming redhead. As the personification of the Twenties flapper, the "It Girl," she had made millions for Paramount. But by 1930, Clara was up to her beauty mark in booze bills, gambling debts and discarded lovers. Many of Clara's men friends kissed and told. They included the whole University of Southern California football team—first string! Another "friend's" wife sued and was awarded $30,000 for Clara's "misplaced passion."

MGM's boxoffice leaders were Greta Garbo, Joan Crawford, and the screen team of Wallace Beery and Marie Dressler. Norma Shearer was coming up fast. Roman Novarro, John Gilbert, William Haines and Lawrence Tibbett were on top but headed downward. They would eventually be replaced as the public's favorites by Clark Gable, Spencer Tracy and Jean Harlow, all of whom were then working at other studios.

In the early fall of 1930, Ella Rice, Howard Hughes' ex-wife, took her two-million-dollar divorce settlement and returned to Houston, Texas, where she became the belle of the ball. Meanwhile, twenty-four-year-old Howard had plucked lovely nineteen-year-old Jean Harlow, real name Harlean Carpenter, from the extra ranks. He started her on the road to stardom in his four-million-dollar production of *Hell's Angels*. After his press agent, Linc Quarberg, dubbed Jean the "Platinum Blonde," the nationwide hype swung into full gear.

At home, beautiful Mama Jean, who always called her beloved daughter "Baby," was pleased that her only child's first marriage—an elopement at sixteen with Charles McGrew, III, Chicago socialite— had finally ended in divorce and a nice settlement. Now Mama's second husband, Marino Bello, a charismatic roué with steel-gray hair, an Italian accent and a mascara-thin moustache, attempted to manage Baby's career himself. Mama stayed in the background, but cleverly pulled the strings. In her youth, she wanted to become an actress, but hadn't been allowed the freedom to try. Now she did everything she could to see that Baby had the fabulous career she was denied.

Garbo, at twenty-four, was already a legend shrouded in a smorgasbord of mystique. Early on in her career, Greta had innocently and honestly responded to a re-porter's question by stating that she and her mentor, Mauritz Stiller—"the man responsible for everything good that has happened to me in my life"—were sharing living quarters. After *that* was hushed up, she became semi-nonquotable. Eventually, Garbo turned into "The Totally Silent Swede." There were no more interviews granted—ever. The MGM brass, pleased that shy Greta *preferred* to remain mute off-screen, did nothing to encourage press relations. Consequently, GG had more stories written about her, based on *non*interviews, than all of MGM's cooperative stars put together.

Warner Brothers' biggest draw was John Barrymore, while Winnie Lightner, soon to be retired, headed the actress list. On the way up were two married couples, Bebe Daniels and Ben Lyon, and Frank Fay and Barbara Stanwyck. James Cagney and Edward G. Robinson were on the brink of enormous stardom. On the First National side of the lot, Richard Barthelmess and Dorothy Mackaill were tops, but soon gave way to the fast-rising popularity of Loretta Young and Doug Fairbanks, Jr.

Universal Studios, most important personalities were John Boles and Lupe Velez. Zany Lupe, always relegated to "B" films and destined to drop in fan popularity, remained a colorful Hollywood character. Velez, the Mexican spitfire, and Gary Cooper, the Montana shy guy, were unofficially playing house. They lived together, and split expenses, at Lupe's home, on North Rodeo Drive, in Beverly Hills. A handsome if incongruous couple, they enjoyed cavorting happily with his and her cars, his and her dogs and his and her birds. She had dozens of canaries. He had a couple of eagles.

Cooper's very proper parents, who lived in the neighborhood, thoroughly disapproved of the whole affair. They had seen Gary through his romance with Clara Bow, and sighed with relief when *that* ended. Now Judge and Mrs. Cooper were somewhat shocked that their soft-spoken, well-brought-up son, who had been educated in England, seemed to have fallen for another wild, extrovertish woman. Judge Cooper, in an effort to soften the blow, explained to his wife that, on occasion, even the finest bulls on their Montana ranch strayed into pastures full of less-than-well-brought-up young heifers. Mrs. Cooper did not appreciate the analogy.

Young Lew Ayres was definitely Universal's star-on-the rise. On the RKO–Radio lot, the comedy teams of Wheeler and Woolsey, and Amos 'n' Andy, rated supreme. While over at RKO's other lot, Pathé, the incongruous duo of cowboy star William Boyd and sophisticated Constance Bennett led the list. Columbia's top stars, Jack Holt and Evelyn Brent, were soon replaced by western hero Buck Jones and Barbara Stanwyck, who made pictures for them as well as for Warners.

In September of 1930, blond, blue-eyed Wilma Wyatt took out a license to marry a young band singer, Harry Lillis Crosby. She was a contract player at Fox, renamed Dixie Lee; he was a member of the Gus Arnheim orchestra, nicknamed Bing. On the 29th of the month, they exchanged wedding vows at the Church of the Blessed Sacrament on Sunset Boulevard. Only a handful of spectators were present.

The twosome announced the postponement of their honeymoon "because Dixie had film engagements pending, and Bing did not want to break up the personnel of the band." The *real* reason the couple did not leave town was purely monetary. They were both short of cash and could not even afford a nice place in which to live. They moved into the Los Feliz home of Dixie's best chum, actress Sue Carol. Eventually, they earned enough to rent the house next door.

Adorable, stuttering Marion Davies, née Douras, a delightful, big-hearted blonde from a very good family—"Da–da–day's a–a–ju–jud–judge"—was firmly ensconced as William Randolph Hearst's number one hostess. She was also the star of Hearst's Cosmopolitan Productions, headquartered at MGM.

In the fall of 1930, Marion moved into a palatial home built on her own Santa Monica beachfront complex. The place had fifty-five bathrooms and a platoon of servants who could scrub. There, she was surrounded by her close-knit family. Mama, Papa and siblings all lived within sight of the "big house." When Marion wasn't filming or tossing elaborate sit-down dinners and costume balls, she and her lover, whom she affectionately called "Droopy Drawers," frequently traveled to Hearst's castle, San Simeon. They invariably invited carloads of guests—who arrived with pyramid mounds of luggage—suitable for any sudden event or whim.

The really big news at the start of the Thirties was the fantastically fertile crop of young players destined to become widely known: John Wayne, Humphrey Bogart, Bette Davis, Irene Dunne, Joel McCrea, Ray Milland, Joan Blondell, the aforementioned Clark Gable, and a girl from the extra ranks moving up fast, Carole Lombard.

The tango was all the rage. Movie moguls played backgammon for $500 a game, and held all-night poker sessions at which thousands of dollars changed hands. Tea dances were terribly chic. Weekend beach homes were in vogue. Actresses wore designer pajamas of satin or crepe for evenings on the town. While the prostitutes and ponies of Agua Caliente, just 110 miles south of the border, down Mexico way, were good for laying, or betting on, in that order.

Even closer to home, Hollywood big shots could risk their large weekly salaries on either of two gambling barges, the *Mont-falcone* and the *Johanna Smith,* anchored between Seal Beach and Long Beach, beyond the three-mile limit. In mid-September, 1930, the *Montfalcone* caught fire and sank. The five hundred high rollers onboard were rescued by the crew of the *Johanna Smith.* Although they were given the option of going ashore to recover from the trauma, everyone remained and continued to gamble. The barge's bagmen were delighted to discover that celebrities could be such good sports—especially those that were slightly singed.

The Eighteenth Amendment, which ushered in Prohibition, had been the law for a decade. But everyone who could afford it had his or her own bootlegger. The booze they supplied was rarely watered down too much. For those who took their drinking seriously, however, a new status symbol came into vogue. "Arrangements" could be made to have a case or two of the "real stuff" picked up several times a month from boats which plied the harbor. A few of the more brazen rumrunners actually made onshore deliveries, especially to celebrities who lived in the beach areas.

Unemployed movie executives, performers and behind-the-scenes creative talent were forced to settle for gin of the bathtub variety. Unfortunately, in 1930, they were in the majority. Only ten percent of Hollywood's film players earned $5,000 a year or more—before agent's commission. Half of the actors made $1,999 a year or less. Day players received $15 per, but were glad to perform for whatever they could get. Only *thirty* of Central Casting's 17,000 extras worked more than three days during the entire year.

Times were so tough, local hotels claimed a 180 percent increase in rubber checks. Some establishments made out-of-work actors put on shows once a week in lieu of room rent. Many performers, down on their luck, earned eating money by selling perfume, novelties and greeting cards door-to-door.

Hollywood, a super microcosm of the rest of the country, was basically a two-class town. There were those who earned big bucks, and all the rest, who scrounged in order to exist. Priorities were turned upside down and inside out. Marion Davies and Al Jolson were among the celebrities who periodically took over Hollywood cafeterias and helped feed the unemployed. Simultaneously, famous screen sirens and wives of wealthy film executives dined on beef Wellington and cherries jubilee.

Al Capone, the highly publicized gangster creep, was offered $200,000 to play himself onscreen, while nonworking actors peddled oranges at two for a penny. Bread cost three cents a loaf, and bringing home the bacon meant an expenditure of eighteen cents a pound. But unemployed movie workers did their own share of fantasizing. They nicknamed Hollywood and Cahuenga, a few blocks east of Vine Street, the "Million Dollar Dream Corner." There, they took turns sitting on the fireplug, sharing their fancy daydreams. The plug, incidentally, was stamped by its maker, the L.A. Casting Company!

Despite the fabulous Thirties faces, the period from September of 1930 to September of 1931 turned out to be the most chaotic in the entire history of the film business. It was the first year in two decades that industry leaders had been caught flat-footed. The first period in which the business stood still, despite the fact that everyone was groping to find the right road.

Problems hit from all directions. In big cities, such as Philadelphia, ladies from various women's clubs organized to march against smut onscreen. They felt that many of the pictures were too "dirty," and also complained about theatres using too much sex in movie advertising. Meanwhile, smalltown theatre managers screamed at Hollywood to put more hoke back into pictures. They claimed that the sophisticated cycle brought on by talkies had laid a big fat egg with their public. It was wonderful that stars now talked. But when audiences complained that they couldn't understand half of what they heard, movie exhibitors demanded a change.

Simultaneously, European theatre managers also vigorously requested the return of silent films. They wrote letters to Hollywood declaring that American talkies were dying overseas. Their audiences were clamoring for the return of familiar faces in silent action swashbucklers and adventure dramas.

So, as the Thirties began, the industry found itself in a frustrating, no-win situation. They had no one to blame but themselves—Hollywood was a study in confusion. In October 1930, for instance, the studios said they were overloaded with film properties. The combined amount put out for screenplays totaled seventeen million dollars. Two months later, those same studios reported story shortages and pleaded for new material. During that period, the average film cost $300,000 to make while the typical theatre admission was twenty-three cents.

But all was not completely black. Some pictures did well in select locations. Howard Hughes' *Hell's Angels* was big in New York. Amos 'n' Andy's *Check and Double Check* cleaned up on both coasts for RKO. MGM saw profits from *Min and Bill* with Wallace Beery and Marie Dressler. Eddie Cantor's *Whoopee* and Barbara Stanwyck's *Illicit* at least broke even. Action westerns, which starred favorites such as Hoot Gibson, Ken Maynard, Buck Jones and William Boyd, continued to be popular.

Across America, the favorite song was "On the Sunny Side of the Street." It was soon replaced by anxious choruses of "Brother, Can You Spare a Dime" . . . And, in Hollywood, even those Fabulous Thirties Faces were not enough to keep Tinseltown from nearly drowning in a sea of confusion, lost profits and self-doubt.

On New Year's Day, 1931, a man in a rumpled suit walked along Hollywood Boulevard, wearing a sandwich board. On both front and back, six printed words told the whole story: DEPRESSION IS OVER. PANIC IS HERE. It was the most concise summary of what the next few years held in store for America as a nation, and motion pictures as an industry.

In addition to radio, Hollywood's latest "enemy" was a new outdoor sport called midget golf, Tom Thumb golf and eventually miniature golf. Under any name, the country had gone cuckoo over the idea. While rich folks played eighteen holes on grassy, sloping country club knolls, anybody with a quarter could go to his neighborhood "course" and play the game just like the swells. The moguls reached for their ulcer pills. They could hear the clink of the coins as people paid to putt instead of picture-go.

Howard Hughes' *Hell's Angels* premiere at Grauman's Chinese Theatre—complete with airplanes strung high above Hollywood Boulevard, 1930.

When things were blackest, studio hype was the wackiest. The Hollywood community awoke one morning to find billboards all over town with the cryptic words "OO-MOO-LOO" plastered in giant letters. The next day, the same signs appeared on hundreds of buses and streetcars. Eventually, the first line was joined by a second, third and fourth. Before "the mystery"was solved, the city had gone "OO-MOO-LOO" crazy.

OO-MOO-LOO
(MEANS "I LOVE YOU")
THAT'S WHY WE SAY . . . LOO-MOO
"TRADER HORN"

The advertising campaign was a $22,000 expenditure by MGM in advance of the release of their adventure film *Trader Horn.* Everybody loved it. Excitement over *any* studio's film was welcomed. The picture, a financial hit, was directed by W. S. Van Dyke, and starred Harry Carey, Edwina Booth, Duncan Renaldo, and a native actor—Mutia Omoola.

The only one who *didn't* profit was neophyte leading lady Edwina Booth. Duncan Renaldo's wife sued for divorce claiming that Booth, the only female on the remote African jungle location, had "alienated his affections from her." Edwina, a lovely blonde, who had actually spent half of the time fighting off rare tropical insects, and the other half trying to play scenes with wild animals, was shocked. She was also a newlywed. Her jungle evenings had been spent alone, under thick mosquito netting, pining away for her spouse. When the divorce suit was filed, she rolled her eyes heavenward. If this was what movie making was all about, she wanted none of it!

By the late spring of 1932, business in New York's biggest movie houses was the worst ever recorded. Theatres were playing to fewer admissions than at any time in their existence. The slump spread clear across the country. Within a six-month period, the only films that made any money at all were Garbo's *Mata Hari,* the Barrymore brothers in *Arsene Lupin,* Universal's thriller *Murders in the Rue Morgue,* with Bela Lugosi, and MGM's *Grand Hotel,* starring Garbo, John and Lionel Barrymore, Wallace Beery and Joan Crawford. It had just been released and all indications were very favorable.

Crawford, now one of MGM's reigning queens, had reached the point in her career where she could specifically request certain leading men. After Joan spotted Robert Young walking across the MGM lot, she asked Louis B. Mayer to cast him in her next film. L.B. was pleased to oblige.

On the home front, however, Joan had reached a new plateau. There were rumbles that her idyllic marriage to Doug, Jr., was on shaky grounds. Crawford would not even dignify the rumors. Meanwhile, she and her husband had passed the nickname stage. Although their house was still named "El JoDo," she now called him Douglas. He called her Joan. In more intimate moments, though, he referred to her as "Billie"—from the first professional name she had used when working in clubs and dance reviews, Billie Cassin. (Her *real* name was Lucille LeSueur.)

In August of 1932, Joan and Doug went on a six-week European holiday. Upon their return, she was terribly excited about the forthcoming premiere of her latest film, *Rain.* At that time, while they appeared to be as close as ever, persistent rumors still swirled around them.

Seven months later, all hell broke loose. Doug was accused by Jorgen Dietz, a chemical engineer, of false imprisonment, for which Dietz asked $20,000 compensation. More urgent was Dietz's allegation that Doug had alienated his wife's affections from him, for which he sought $50,000 in damages. The lawsuit made front-page headlines. Fairbanks was alleged to have had a romance with Mrs. Solveig Dietz, an actress, also known as Lulu Talma. He was further accused of having Mr. Dietz detained in the district attorney's office for two hours, and in a room at the Biltmore Hotel for more than four hours. The whole situation was bizarre, complicated and very messy.

Follow-up stories stated that Fairbanks was going to charge Dietz with extortion—a criminal offense. Meanwhile, Lulu had fled Hollywood and returned to her native Denmark. Then Dietz suddenly eloped with another woman after having shed Lulu in a quickie divorce. Only in Hollywood could such stuff have been the excuse for reams of copy.

The suit against Fairbanks had been filed on March 10, 1933. The following day, Joan announced their separation. Her public statement raised quite a few eyebrows: "I want it definitely understood that I do not contemplate any divorce action . . . and that the Dietz suit has nothing to do with our separation . . . I intend to do everything I can to help Mr. Fairbanks if the suit comes to a hearing. I know Doug is innocent, the victim of a plot. I'm sure he is innocent of the charges . . . We had been discussing separation for more than a year. The timing of my announcement has nothing whatsoever to do with this case, which I have known about for some time . . ."

Despite Crawford's words, the town took sides—mostly against her. Insiders recalled that, back in May of 1928, during the period when Joan and Doug were engaged, the shoe had been on the other foot. Two irate wives had accused Joan of having "relationships" with their husbands. One of the spouses, actor Edgar A. Neely, was alleged to have admitted that he and Joan had engaged in an "affair" while they were on location for a film at West Point. The other accused husband, musician-composer Sam Messenheimer, denied everything, stating that he had spent time at Joan's house only because he was giving her music lessons. Yet he admitted that Joan had not paid for his guidance, but did not deny that she had sent him a gift with a card that read: "To Sam, with love from Joan."

During the embarrassing front-page stories of Crawford's supposed indiscretions, she and Doug had laughed off the whole thing. Since neither case ever was heard in court, both episodes had blown over. Still, the town remembered how loyal Doug had been to Joan, and questioned the wisdom of her separation announcement. There was no question, however, that during the few years of their marriage, Crawford's screen fame—and salary—had far exceeded Doug's. Although he was doing very well at Warner Brothers at the time of their parting.

So, the love story of the Crown Prince and Princess was over and done with. Doug took his clothes, typewriter, books and a few odds and ends, and moved out. Joan, after a discreet length of time, removed the "El JoDo" nameplate from their home's front door. Meanwhile, there were whispers that both Ricardo Cortez and Joan's latest leading man, Franchot Tone, appearing with her in *Today We Live*, were vying for her affection. Joan refused to dignify the whispers, summing them up in one word—"ridiculous!"

Once Doug, Jr., was "unencumbered," he grew very close to his father. They traveled to England together. Simultaneously, there were rumors that the senior Fairbanks seemed to be spending quite a bit of time away from his Mary. He had been in London in February and had returned in May. Now it was June and he was back there again.

The combination of both dashing Dougs turned daily gossip-news items into glowing reports of their closeness, their popularity and their hobnobbing with all of England's top society. Doug, Jr., was personally escorted around town by the Earl of Warwick. Then the Fairbanks held a joint press reception and great Broadway and London stage star Gertrude Lawrence joined them.

Doug, Jr., was presented to HRH Princess Mary at a charity bazaar. A photo of them together, which showed Doug in the midst of purchasing some silk handkerchiefs from the Princess, made page one. The posh people who hosted parties for them, and were in turn entertained by them, read like a Who's Who of British aristocracy. The Fairbanks gave a tea for the Dowager Duchess of Sutherland and Lady Millicent Dawes, and the next day lunched with Lord Warwick, Lord Beaverbrook and Lord Castlerose. They houseguested for the weekend at Sandringham, one of the royal estates, with Edward, Prince of Wales, and Prince George. They spent two days at the castle of the Duchess of Sutherland. It was seemingly an unending mutual love affair between the Dougs and the Brits.

What started as a delightful holiday ended on a terribly sad note. First, young Doug contracted pneumonia. He wound up in a New York hospital, where his mother and stepfather helped nurse him back to health. Then, a few months later, in January of 1934, Mary Pickford received a call from Doug, Sr. He wanted to tell her—before she read it in the papers—that he had been named co-respondent in the divorce action brought by Lord Ashley against his wife, Lady Sylvia. Mary, who had suspected that there was "someone else," handled the situation with quiet dignity.

It was almost impossible to believe that their storybook romance had come to an end. But Hollywood's Reigning Monarchs did give up the joint throne which they had shared for more than thirteen years. Mary and Doug would continue to love each other, in a special way, for the rest of their lives. But now it was time for both of them to move on. To start all over again.

Although no one mentioned it—at least not in print—Pickford and Crawford had a great deal in common. They were both self-made women from poor backgrounds. They both had an inner core of residual toughness on which they were able to draw when problems arose. Very soon, Joan would join Mary in that rarefied atmosphere reserved for screen giants. And, for the rest of their days, each would remain Queen of her domain, no matter which man shared her bed and board.

CENSORSHIP
RAISE THE BLOUSES . . . AND LOWER THE SHADES!

On November 10, 1930, six hundred Hollywoodites attended the Third Annual Academy Awards dinner at the Ambassador Hotel's Cocoanut Grove. One interesting novelty was a talking picture speech by Thomas A. Edison, who had recently been named an honorary member of the Academy.

In the midst of the gala banquet, Will Hays, Hollywood's czar of the blue pencil, alienated the guests with a long-winded keynote speech, delivered as though it were a sermon preached from on high. He especially aroused his audience with some very negative closing remarks:

" . . . the motion picture industry has

created more wealth in less time than was ever amassed within the same period by any pioneer intelligence. But it has thrown more gold in the junk pile than it has put in its treasury and these millions in that junk pile keep increasing every year, because the industry's constructive discontent with its own standards, its own achievements, and its own successes has always been greater than its self-satisfaction."

What Will Hays said certainly had a ring of truth, but industry leaders didn't want any lectures from their censorship head. They were already disenchanted with the man whom they had appointed eight years before to lead them out of a severe crisis. Hays had come onto the scene as a direct result of the public's outrage over various 1920's scandals which involved well-known Hollywood personalities.

In 1920, Olive Thomas, Ziegfeld Follies beauty and screen actress, whose final films were *The Flapper* and *Footlights and Shadows*, took poison and died a painful death in a Paris hospital. Although the family said it was an accident, she had already been tainted by previous rumors of her penchant for taking drugs. Because she was married to Jack Pickford, America's Sweetheart's brother, her death was the occasion for large, cruel and shocking headlines.

Next came the rape trials of the world's beloved screen comic Roscoe "Fatty" Arbuckle. Although Arbuckle was tried three times—and stood acquitted—lurid details of his "San Francisco sex and booze orgy" were front-page fodder for months.

While Fatty awaited his second trial, William Desmond Taylor, one of Hollywood's foremost directors, was murdered. This still unsolved case indirectly involved two silent screen stars, in addition to a collection of shady and "unusual" characters known on the Tinseltown scene.

Then, in 1923, handsome screen idol Wallace Reid, the heroic star of dozens of silent films, died during a desperate attempt to cure himself of drug addiction. Gruesome tales of his struggles while confined in a padded cell filled the nation's tabloids.

Because the public was so outraged, and blamed the industry for lowering the nation's moral standards, Hollywood needed someone from the outside to clean up their image. If not, both the federal and state governments threatened to impose their own censorship laws upon the movie industry. Will Hays was the man they turned to. A lawyer from a prominent Indiana family, his interest in politics had gained him a nationwide reputation. In 1918, he served as chairman of the Republican National Committee. After Warren G. Harding was elected President of the United States, Hays was named postmaster general—the usual prestigious plum handed out for services rendered.

When Hollywood beckoned, Hays jumped at the chance and resigned his cabinet post. In 1922, he became president of the Motion Picture Producers and Distributors of America, Incorporated (MPPDA), and was immediately anointed filmdom's personal Julius Caesar, Emperor and Guardian of the nation's morals, Protector and Defender of America's right to be free from cinema sex and offscreen evildoing.

Hays was the perfect front man. He belonged to the right social clubs and fraternal organizations, was an elder of the Presbyterian Church and had instant access to top political and industry leaders. For his $100,000-a-year salary, he was supposed to get the government off the industry's back. Hollywood was running scared. Already three dozen states were considering the adoption of some form of censorship. Congress had passed a law making booze illegal—and the states ratified it. Might not the screen's exposure of *boobs* and bawdy behavior be outlawed next?

In a town noted for its glamour, Will Hays, whose face was more rodentlike than anyone should have been "blessed" with, nevertheless exuded self-confidence. Although the Harding administration would go down in history as America's most corrupt to that date, and Hays himself would later be somewhat tarnished, he proceeded full speed ahead. He gave studio heads strict orders. Each mogul was to personally lecture his stars on how to be circumspect in their private lives.

Celebrities were to be strongly advised to "at least pull down their shades, close their drapes and lock their doors if they planned to play around." Public scandals were to be avoided at all costs! Producers were instructed to tone down their film titles. Blatant double entendres were to be removed. Scanty costumes were to be sparsely, if ever, used. Studios were to submit film scripts and/or synopses of all stories in advance. Hays and his staff would then advise them as to which lines of dialogue had to be snipped, which scenes needed deleting altogether.

The moguls were not at all amused. Harry Cohn stood up at a private industry meeting and suggested they tell "Washington Will" to "go _____ himself!"

Then, in 1930, an official Motion Picture Code, written by publisher Martin Quigley and a Jesuit priest, the Reverend Daniel Lord, was adopted by the industry. Hays was its administrator. It was a paternalistic credo created for a Puritan moralistic society. America's citizens, considered a nation of innocents, were assumed to need protection from all the naughty things sophisticated society folk, the gangster element and members of the film colony indulged in—hopefully behind closed doors or drawn drapes.

The industry had created a Frankenstein. But Will was *their* "monster." Every studio had a representative on Hays' board and they were expected to accept his dictates as well as those provided for in the Code. Still, the problems continued. In-

dependents, producers who did not belong to the MPPDA, felt no obligation to live up to the rules—while producers who did belong wasted a lot of time and energy trying to avoid certain provisions.

Harry Cohn continued to be Hays' most vocal opponent. But an MPPDA spokesman commented, "Mr. Cohn joined with his eyes wide open. He *has* to abide by our rules and doctrines." Joseph Brandt, the president of Columbia, put an end to the feud. He commented tersely: "Harry just doesn't understand, that's all. He'll learn after a while!"

The Code, which hung over Hollywood like a heavy black drape for nearly three decades, did not appear too unreasonable. In general, it decreed that no picture was to be produced which would lower the standards of those seeing it. Therefore, the sympathy of the audience was never to be thrown to the side of evil wrongdoers.

The technique of committing murder was never to be presented in a way which would inspire imitation, nor were really brutal murders ever to be shown in explicit detail. Major crimes, such as theft, robbery, blowing up trains, safecracking or arson, were never to be presented in explicit detail.

The use of guns was "restricted to essentials." Smuggling details or illegal drug traffic were not to be shown. "The use of liquor in American life, when not required by the plot, or for some proper characterization," was forbidden.

Provision number two of the Code, which concerned sex, was most explicit. The sanctity of marriage and the home was always to be upheld. Adultery was never to be explicitly treated or presented attractively. Lustful kissing wasn't allowed—in fact, "scenes of passion" were to be included only when "essential to the plot." Seduction or rape, never to be more than suggested. Filmmakers could not even show scenes of childbirth.

The use of vulgarity in dealing with "disgusting, unpleasant, though not necessarily evil, subjects" was to be employed with all standards of "good taste and a regard for the sensitivities of the audience." Obscene words or gestures, included in jokes or songs—"even when it was likely to be understood by only *part* of the audience"— were forbidden.

Profanity of any type, especially taking the name of the Deity in vain, was not permissible. The use of Hell, sonofabitch, damn and even Gawd were not allowed. And salacious, indecent or obscene titles were never to be used in films.

Nudity in any form, even in silhouette, was not permitted. Undressing was to be avoided unless essential to the plot. Indecent exposure or undue exposure were forbidden. And dancing scenes that hinted at or suggested sexual actions or indecent passions were to be eliminated.

Religion was never to be ridiculed. Using the Flag in a disrespectful manner or casting aspersions on American history or institutions, or on prominent U.S. citizens, was forbidden.

The treatment of any scene that took place in a bedroom was to be strictly governed by good taste and delicacy.

Two years later, the Hays office was as active as ever. Their latest targets for 1932 were fan magazines that ran celebrity photos that Hays considered shocking. They placed a ban on all leg art, forbade "crotch" shots and insisted that stars be photographed *from the waist up* unless they wore long gowns.

Hollywood not only had the Hays office to contend with, but state censorship review boards also made producers' lives anything but pleasant. In Albany, New York, the State Education Department, after having viewed a film called *The Mystery of Life*, went into shock. They declared that the love lives of snails, spiders and one-celled animals were their own private business. All

such "mating scenes" were ordered deleted. However, Mother Nature was given a break. Scenes with naked young children were permitted to remain in the film.

By the summer of 1934, the moguls were frantic. It was unusually warm all over the country. Boxoffice receipts were down. To make matters even steamier, the censorship issue came to the forefront again. In Cleveland, at the Presbyterian General Assembly, the Reverend D. C. Buchanan, a missionary to Japan, leveled an attack against Hollywood. "I am ashamed of the films being shown in Korea and Japan," he said. "People in these lands seeing these pictures get the idea that every American woman is impure, and that every American man carries a gun . . ."

It was but the opening salvo of a renewed battle against motion pictures. Various other religious groups simultaneously declared war against "movie smut." All of the studios felt the sting of rebuke. Throughout the country, a Decency Movement was mounted, aimed not only at "dirty movies," but at salacious newspaper and magazine stories.

The most forceful attack came from the Catholic clergy. They were incensed by Hollywood's continuing "bad effect on the morals of its nationwide parishioners." The Legion of Decency was formed. Protestant and Jewish clergy concurred, although they still rarely condemned films outright from their pulpits. But what really hit Hollywood hard was the statement of a very important New York priest, the Reverend J. A. McCaffrey. He enunciated what seemed to be uppermost on the minds of the Catholic clergy: "The film situation will be cleaned up as soon as Will Hays is thrown out . . . Under Hays leadership, the motion picture industry has fallen so low that it seems high time he resign."

This personal attack, coming from outside the industry, shook Hays and galvanized him into action. He held a six-hour meeting at his office with all the studio heads.

When the cigarette butts and used coffee cups had been swept away, what emerged was a revolutionary idea. A *Purity Seal* had been voted upon and adopted unanimously.

The word went out. As of July 15, 1934, the seal, which would be shown onscreen directly after the main title, signified that the film upheld high moral standards and that all efforts had been made to comply with the Code. Once a picture had been denied a seal, there would be no further appeal. The picture would have to be altered before it could be shown.

Joseph Breen, whom Hays had appointed to enforce the laws, was given the power to withhold the Purity Seal from any film considered to be in violation of the Code. The movie industry in turn agreed not to distribute or to exhibit pictures that did not have the Seal. Finally, a method had been found which made the Production Code truly enforceable.

HOLLYWOOD POTPOURRI
1930

In September, Hollywood was shocked to hear that HOWARD HUGHES and theatre owner SID GRAUMAN had had a big fight in New York. Hughes was mad because Grauman had preceded him into town and grabbed all of the publicity for himself regarding Grauman's showing of Hughes' *Hell's Angels* . . . CAROL [sic] LOMBARD, formerly with MACK SENNETT and Pathé, was signed to a long-term contract by Paramount . . . MAURICE CHEVALIER's newest film, *Playboy of Paris,* was a big hit in its New York opening . . . JACKIE COOGAN hosted a kiddie matinee to honor the opening of the new Fox Wilshire Theatre in Beverly Hills . . . RICHARD BARTHELMESS opened a mini golf course on Vine Street . . . Local bootleggers met to discuss a merger "for the common good of the booze business" . . . AMOS 'N' ANDY turned down an offer of $10,000 apiece to do advertising for Lucky Strike cigarettes.

MARLENE DIETRICH was given a new contract by Paramount based on her work opposite GARY COOPER in *Morocco* . . . AL JOLSON opened at the Capitol Theatre in New York for the record salary of $20,000 a week, making him the country's highest-paid stage performer . . . JOAN BENNETT called off her engagement to JOHNNY CONSIDINE after he broke a date and she subsequently found out he'd been with another gal . . . LON CHANEY's will was probated. He left $550,000, making him one of the few silent stars who obviously had saved his money.

In October, CECILE B. DEMILLE was taken to Cedars of Lebanon Hospital after breaking a bone in his foot when he stepped off his yacht . . . HOWARD HUGHES said his next picture would be *Queer People*. He'd just purchased the book—an exposé on Hollywood . . . MGM contract player ROBERT MONTGOMERY and his wife welcomed a baby girl. They named her ELIZABETH.

GLORIA SWANSON's five-year marriage to the MARQUIS DE LA FALAISE DE LA COUDRAYE, was definitely on the rocks. "Hank" had been playing around and Gloria sued on the grounds of desertion. They were married in Paris in January 1925 and separated in September 1929 . . . Paramount dropped JEANETTE MACDONALD's contract . . . JEAN HARLOW went to New York to make two personal appearances daily for a week at the Gaiety with *Hell's Angels* . . . MADAME TUSSAUD's famous wax museum in London immortalized MICKEY and MINNIE MOUSE. They were to be placed alongside the wax statues of British royalty and famous celebrity figures . . . WILL ROGERS' new Fox contract paid him $300,000 a picture plus $10,000 a week extra if any of his films shot for more than ten weeks . . . And DOUG FAIRBANKS, SR., was drawing $8,000-a-day salary on *Reaching the Moon,* enhancing his bank account to the tune of $288,000 for the thirty-six days he filmed.

In November, TALLULAH BANKHEAD, for several years one of the favorite actresses in England, made her Hollywood film debut in Paramount's *Her Past* . . . Fox Studios was responsible for the two outstanding movie premieres of the month—both complete with "show plants" in the lobbies. The festive opening of *The Big Trail*, at Grauman's Chinese Theatre, was almost as spectacular as the film. JOHN WAYNE was excellent in his movie debut in a starring role. After the picture, EDMUND LOWE introduced the cast—Wayne shook visibly as he acknowledged the crowd's applause.

An even bigger world premiere was held for *Just Imagine,* a startlingly creative and innovative film set fifty years into the future—in 1980—when science had completely altered 1930 standards. For the opening, at the Carthay Circle Theatre, Fox had a futuristic rocket ship in the lobby. Searchlights filled the nighttime sky. As the ultimate gimmick—also a tie-in with the plot—they had a sixty-foot-high air balloon tethered at the corner of Wilshire Boulevard and San Vicente, at the edge of Beverly Hills. Inside the balloon's gondola, a traffic policeman whirled right and left and directed the thousands of cars which streamed below. It was sensational.

At the London opening in December of *Hell's Angels,* EDWARD, PRINCE OF WALES, headed a large royal contingent. His presence hyped the box-office appeal, and the film had the highest take of any American picture shown in England to date . . . MARLENE DIETRICH planned to sail to Germany and spend the Christmas holidays with her husband and daughter . . . JOAN CRAWFORD, whose latest film, *Within the Law,* was doing good business, was cast as the star of *Torch Song* . . . MAUREEN O'SULLIVAN received a fan letter from a nineteen-year-old Brooklyn boy. He told her he started to walk to California to see her, but had only reached as far as Denver when he was stopped by deep snow.

However, he had made plans to start walking to Hollywood again come spring.

In mid-December, the Los Angeles Police Department insisted that Hollywood's most prominent stars be escorted by armed guards when they went out. Reports were that some Chicago gangsters, bent on blackmail, had hit town. A few of the bigger names rode around in their cars not only with guards, but with sawed-off shotguns on the floor, ready for action.

Mrs. B. P. SCHULBERG held a charity tea in the Fiesta Room of the Ambassador Hotel. NORMA SHEARER, FAY WRAY, LILYAN TASHMAN and HEDDA HOPPER modeled furs and gowns . . . GARBO quarreled with director CLARENCE BROWN and wanted KING VIDOR to direct her next film . . . BETTE DAVIS, who recently signed a long-term contract with Universal, arrived in Hollywood from New York . . .

DOUGLAS FAIRBANKS left for the Orient by ship to film background shots for his next adventure-travelogue feature . . . Meanwhile, DOUG, JR., and his wife, JOAN CRAWFORD, spent Christmas in New York . . . JOHN BARRYMORE was confined to his bed with jungle fever that he had contracted during a recent cruise to Central America . . . MGM's *Dance, Fools, Dance,* JOAN CRAWFORD's newest film, was headed for a big boxoffice success. Newcomer CLARK GABLE, who played a racketeer, won excellent reviews . . . WILL ROGERS entertained the entire University of Alabama football team at Fox. His fee: two tickets to the Rose Bowl for New Year's Day.

1931

In mid-January, the *New York Daily Mirror* began a serialized story, "Why I Remain a Dope Fiend," written personally by once-great film star ALMA RUBENS. The series was still running when Alma died, at age thirty-four, in Los Angeles . . .

While Hollywood was recovering from the depressing news of Alma's death, another event occurred which had all of the moguls weeping into their collective crying towels. CHARLES CHAPLIN's latest picture, *City Lights,* a *silent* film, was rated a sensation. Not only had the "little giant" made an entertaining *talkless* picture, but he had thumbed his nose at the talkies by parodying them in the opening reel. And leave it to Charlie to make headlines. His personal premiere guests were the distin-

guished Professor and Mrs. ALBERT EINSTEIN, both of whom raved about Chaplin's production. MARION DAVIES arrived dressed in a black gown over which she wore a magnificent fox-trimmed green velvet wrap. In contrast, DOLORES COSTELLO BARRYMORE wore all white, while GLORIA SWANSON drew cheers for her sparkling gown of silver sequins. The biggest hit of the evening was blond CONSTANCE BENNETT, all dolled up in a pastel gown she had made in Paris. Connie's limo stalled in traffic and she was so perturbed she behaved "out of character" and tried to push it herself before her chauffeur came to her aid—much to the fans' delight.

In February, JOHN WAYNE's newest film, *Girls*

Demand Excitement, turned out to be a dud. Fox moguls were in a quandary. They thought they had a big star in Wayne, now they planned to drop him . . . And Paramount may do the same with CLARA BOW because of all the adverse publicity she had been garnering . . . JOAN BENNETT sued her ex-husband, JOHN FOX, a Seattle stockbroker, for child support . . . HAROLD and MILDRED LLOYD celebrated their eighth wedding anniversary with a dinner party at their hilltop mansion . . . And CHARLIE CHAPLIN turned down an offer of $680,000 to do twenty-six shows of fifteen minutes duration each. It was the highest radio offer ever made to a star.

March was a better month for the movie industry. MONOGRAM PICTURES, a new film company, announced that it would build a Hollywood studio to cost half a million dollars . . . And RKO's profits were up 102 percent over the previous year . . . DOUG FAIRBANKS, JR.'s, birthday gift to JOAN was a colonial-style portable dressingroom on wheels which Joanie could move back and forth at whim. The little white house had green shutters and came complete with a couch, a fully equipped dressingtable, an ironing board (Doug knew how particular his wife was about having all of her clothes absolutely wrinkle-free), a bridge table, plus all of the electrical conveniences that would have made any housewife jealous.

April brought sad news. Notre Dame's famed football coach, KNUTE ROCKNE, was killed en route to discuss the filming of some football shorts with Universal Studios. His plane crashed over Kansas, killing the two pilots and five other passengers. Rockne was slated to supervise the series, which was to be filmed at South Bend on the Notre Dame campus . . . A few days later, the only son of HARRY M. WARNER, twenty-two-year-old LEWIS, died from double pneumonia and blood poisoning following a tooth extraction.

But before April ended, MARION DAVIES had managed to put some gaiety back into the celebrity set. She tossed a gala bon voyage party for NORMA SHEARER and IRVING THALBERG, who were sailing to Europe for a three-month holiday. By the time the guests assembled at Marion's beach house, every fantastic detail had been planned down to the last string of brilliantly colored lights that hung suspended over the gardens, terraces, pool area and down onto the beach.

The theme of the evening was a "Night in Heidelberg." All of the men dressed in gorgeous gold-braided jackets, and jaunty caps were perched delicately on each head. The women came in everything from beer garden waitress costumes to heavily beaded gowns. The festivities, melodically orchestrated by German bands playing "oom-pah-pahs" in nearly every room, were nothing short of sensational.

Everyone from the MGM lot except Leo the Lion was there. Dinner preceded the dancing, drinking and madcap merrymaking. Processions of famous faces, beer steins in hand, were seen wandering off down the beach, then snaking back in chains and waves of frantic movement. It was a nonstop event that left Irving and Norma exhausted and ready for shipboard. Once again, Marion had proved to be a Hollywood hostess par excellence.

By summer things were looking up. Hollywood had a new young star, JACKIE COOPER. His huge success in *Skippy* had turned him into a nationwide sensation . . . JAMES CAGNEY scored in *Public Enemy,* and RICARDO CORTEZ and BEBE DANIELS had a hit in *The Maltese Falcon.* Cortez made a terrific Sam Spade . . . Meanwhile, over at FOX, SPENCER TRACY, who had formerly been associated with gangster films, scored big in a comedy, *Riding for a Fall* . . . But JOHN WAYNE, who had been dropped by Fox and picked up on a five-year contract by Harry Cohn's Columbia, was in trouble. His latest film, *Range Feud,* co-starring BUCK JONES received tepid reviews. The critics' consensus on Wayne: "Just adequate," was translated into "not so hot!"

Although it wasn't announced until early November, GLORIA SWANSON secretly married MICHAEL FARMER on August 16, at the New York home of DUDLEY FIELD MALONE. The wedding had taken place two days after Swanson and Farmer returned from Europe aboard the S.S. *Aquitania.* Since Gloria's divorce from "her Marquis" did not become final until November 9, the situation presented possible legal complications.

Gloria's lawyer said he did not anticipate any problems because the couple had not lived together as man and wife in California. But a California Superior Court judge was unable to remain silent and stated that Swanson's lawyer was incorrect: "Bigamy consists in contracting marriage while already in a married state, and if a person with only an interlocutory decree of divorce is not married, no one is."

Gloria, who didn't seem worried about "her crime," confided to friends that her real reason for marrying so quickly was that she wanted to have another child of her own as soon as possible. Swanson's love of children had manifested itself a few years earlier when she adopted a youngster as a companion for her daughter. According to rumors, the stork was already on its way to the Farmer family.

At the beginning of September, after less than one year of togetherness, DIXIE LEE decided to end her marriage to BING. She filed for divorce, alleging mental cruelty. Crosby, disheartened by the turn of affairs, managed to crack, "I hope people won't think that means I whacked her over the head with a golf club!" But DIXIE cooled down and the CROSBYS reconciled. Friends said he had taken to heart the title song of his newly released Mack Sennett short, *I Surrender Dear*.

In November, the MARX BROTHERS—and assorted wives and children—moved into separate bungalows at the Garden of Allah on Sunset Boulevard. The chic place was turned upside down. Groucho, Harpo and Zeppo had a thing for badminton. They set up a net between two Marx bungalows and played day and night when they weren't working. Shuttlecocks flew into open windows. Kids screamed. Finally some of the more intellectual tenants rebelled. The badminton net came down. The Garden of Allahites reported that Groucho took up a more sedate pastime—wenching.

HOWARD HUGHES and H. B. FRANKLIN won December's "no taste" award. Billboards had gone up all over Hollywood plugging their latest 300-seat theatre: TWENTY-SIX MEN DIED TO OPEN THE NEW HUGHES—FRANKLIN THEATRE, and heralding the first picture to be shown, *The Viking*. Truth in advertising did *not* always make for good copy. Twenty-six men *had* been lost when the ship, used in the picture, exploded and sank during filming. When it was pointed out to Hughes that the billboards were turning people off, they were hastily removed.

Just before Christmas, MGM's *Mata Hari*, another stunning GARBO starrer, won unqualified raves from reviewers . . . WINSTON CHURCHILL, in New York, gave local celebrities something to gossip about. When Winnie visited a swank Park Avenue speakeasy, the band struck up "God Save the King" in his honor. Visibly moved by the gesture, Churchill stood and the crowd joined him in toasting his sovereign. The amusing commotion started after fellow patrons wondered if Churchill realized he was breaking the law by even being in the booze club in the first place!

As the year ended, young BETTE DAVIS left Universal Studios to free lance . . . Performers LOLA LANE and LEW (*All Quiet on the Western Front*) AYRES eloped . . . The brother and sister dancing team of FRED and ADELE ASTAIRE signed to star in two Broadway Brevity shorts for Warners.

Christmas of 1931 was the gloomiest Hollywood had ever experienced. The studios tried to cheer up their remaining employees by hanging ornaments, tinsel and mistletoe. One studio "comic" said it would have been more appropriate if they had tacked up black crepe instead! . . . And, on the last day of the year, TYRONE POWER, SR., died of a heart attack. The famous Shakespearean actor had been working in films for some years. His last completed picture had been *The Big Trail*.

1932

In January, Hollywoodites were whispering about volatile LUPE VELEZ's new love interest. They had met shortly before the gala Mayfair Club New Year's Eve Ball. One look, so the story went, and Lupe had fallen hard. So, the luscious Mexican Spitfire had remained all alone during the early part of the evening, brooding. Then, just before midnight, *he* arrived. Big, blond, handsome RANDOLPH SCOTT, under contract to Paramount—and a definite "comer." As though someone had suddenly flipped a switch, Lupe lit up like a proverbial Christmas tree. She melted into Randy's arms and, as far as the town knew, they were still arm in arm—somewhere—all alone, together.

LIL TASHMAN and her husband, EDMUND LOWE, gave a snazzy tea dance at their home. The hostess, and one of Hollywood's top fashion plates, had received her guests all dressed up in the latest rage, silk pajamas. Lil's were sensuous red. Among the invitees were the SAM GOLDWYNS, GLORIA SWANSON, the B. P. SCHULBERGS, and that oh-so-loving couple, BILLIE DOVE

1 A very young Bette Davis and an equally young Howard Hughes in the days when the tycoon socialized.   2 Left to Right: Jesse L. Lasky, Mary Pickford, Maurice Chevalier, at a film industry dinner.   3 Left to Right: Robert Montgomery, Joan Crawford, Doug Fairbanks, Jr., and Heather Thatcher leaving the Cocoanut Grove, May 1932.
4 Portrait of the "Mexican spitfire," Lupe Velez.   5 Claudette Colbert helps to tack up her personalized Christmas wreath on Hollywood Boulevard, 1932. During this era, each lamppost along the boulevard contained the photograph of a different star. (Courtesy Bruce Torrence Historical Collection)

and HOWARD HUGHES. Billie wore white silk pajamas, a gardenia in her hair. Devoted Howard stuck to her like glue.

In February, everyone in Tinseltown was moaning about the economy. An atmosphere of doom and gloom was everywhere. In fact, the entire entertainment industry was in crisis. Even the MARX BROTHERS, always a sure-fire hit onstage, had flopped on Broadway. After playing to half-empty houses for a week, the boys fled back to Hollywood.

By March, MGM's *Grand Hotel,* with its all-star cast, had received smash reviews. There was a tingle of optimism until the horror of the CHARLES LINDBERGH baby kidnapping hit the headlines. Moguls and famous stars hired round-the-clock bodyguards and imported ferocious dogs for sentry duty.

In April, with the world "on hold," GARBO was up to her old tricks again. She told L. B. MAYER and IRVING THALBERG she was thinking of quitting movies . . . MARLENE DIETRICH, not to be out-done, "acted up," and Paramount suspended her. BEBE DANIELS sued Warners for $100,000 for not offering her suitable scripts . . . And JAMES CAGNEY walked off the Warners lot in a salary dispute . . . To make April a complete downer, SAM GOLDWYN and GLORIA SWANSON got into such a furious battle, she threatened to leave Goldwyn and United Artists and move over to Radio Pictures.

In May, JOAN CRAWFORD and the cast of *Rain* shipped themselves over to Catalina on location. The little island, off the coast of Southern California, was chosen as the nearest thing to the authentic South Pacific locale of the story of Sadie Thompson.

When summer came, Hollywood was treated to a refreshing actor when Britisher CHARLES LAUGHTON arrived in town. He asked Paramount *not* to spend any money publicizing him. "Let the public discover me for themselves," Charles said modestly—or confidently! . . . JOHN BARRYMORE and DOLORES COSTELLO BARRYMORE had a son . . . And a huge calamity occurred when the First National Bank of Beverly Hills collapsed. WALLACE BEERY stood to lose $80,000; ROBERT MONTGOMERY'S savings account had $40,000; some said GARBO would be strapped for funds, too, but her assets wound up being secure. JOHN GILBERT, however, who had established a $300,000 trust account with the bank, hired a lawyer to untie his loot. It was panic time again among the very rich!

Over at Universal, TOM MIX's latest flick, *My Pal,* featured a young MICKEY ROONEY. It was rumored that ROONEY would be the town's next top juvenile star.

In July, there was a massive slashing of studio salaries across the board ten to thirty percent. Tinseltown was hearing its own death rattle . . . GARBO calmly sailed off for Sweden, assuring the MGM bosses that she might not quit movies after all. One positive indication of that fact—Greta had leased her new home for only three months . . . Happily, CLARK GABLE and NORMA SHEARER turned out to be a winning combination. Their *Strange Interlude* won rave reviews and seemed headed for a heavy box-office return.

In August, there was a mass migration out to Malibu Beach where CLARA BOW and LUPE VELEZ alternated in playing hostess and trying to outdo each other. Lupe tossed a huge barbecue for seventy-five merrymakers. It went on for two days, nonstop . . . The overflow crowd headed for Clara's soirée, which included free-flowing booze, fried chicken picnic lunches, and twenty-four-hour gambling at poker tables and roulette wheels. One of the town's biggest VIPs tossed away three weeks' salary in less than an hour.

By September, the "in" crowd was flocking to a newly discovered hangout at B.B.B.'s Cellar. Inside, it was tiny, dark, noisy, featured a postage-stamp sized dance floor, but had the wildest entertainment in town—ten gorgeous female impersonators. All of the patrons were given little wooden hammers. Whenever a new guest arrived, it was the signal for the revelers to pound their tables with the tiny mallets. Among the surprise patrons who came back frequently were ETHEL BARRYMORE, TALLULAH BANKHEAD, BILLY HAINES and JEAN HARLOW. Even HOWARD HUGHES dropped in two nights in a row . . . Over on Sunset Boulevard, another quaint new spot with an equally "wicked" show was The La Boheme Cafe. Owner KARYL NORMAN delighted his patrons by dressing up in yards and yards of lace and feathers whenever he performed his incredible female impersonations. The hit number in his repertoire was an impersonation of JOAN CRAWFORD doing a scene as Sadie Thompson. It brought down the house nightly.

In November, celebrities flocked to the Palm Springs opening of a new hotel, the El Mirador. Everyone who was anyone showed up for the two-day celebration, which included a fashion show, a champion swim meet, and dancing under the stars until dawn. The SAM GOLDWYNS, NORMA and IRVING THALBERG, CLARK

GABLE and the handsome twosome LOMBARD and POWELL helped to launch the spot.

It was another gloomy Hollywood Christmas. Most studios didn't even bother hanging up the mistletoe and ivy. The only bright face in town belonged to MAURICE CHEVALIER, who arrived from Paris. Paramount, in an effort to chase away the gloom, tossed a delightful party in his honor attended by all of their current contract players.

HOLLYWOOD HAUNTS AND HABITS

Hollywood, the most libeled city since Rome was at its height, is perhaps the best known and most widely publicized town in the United States. It ranks with Washington, D.C., as one of the two celebrated capitals of America. Though it was incorporated as a city in 1903, Hollywood never had its own officially elected mayor, city hall, airport or divorce court. It was merely a designated suburb, annexed to Los Angeles in 1910. Its prominence was based on the growth of the movie companies that located there. The early studios were for the most part wooden structures or converted dwellings—such as D. W. Griffith's place. Jesse Lasky's studio was half a barn with one outside stage. Universal owned a ramshackle, tumbledown studio at Sunset and Gower. The Fox Company had no Western home. Marshes and grazing land for cattle flourished in Culver City, where MGM eventually was built.

Soon, though, Hollywood would become synonymous around the world with sin, sycophants and single-minded moguls. The community would be transformed from a lovely, pastoral setting into a thriving, bustling town full of painted ladies and hard-drinking men.

By the time *The Hollywood Reporter* published its very first edition, Hollywood socially resembled a small, tight, upper-class community. There were definite cliques. Certain "in" spots. Select restaurants. Special nightclubs. Specific sporting events. Above all, there was the Mayfair Club, a strictly for-members-only organization. Everyone in Hollywood wanted to be invited to join. Membership was restricted to three hundred—and there was always a waiting list. No one new could be admitted until an old member had died, or withdrawn. Being a Mayfairite was one of the ultimate status symbols reserved for film stars, moguls, writers, directors and producers, plus a few tycoons whose relationship to the industry was purely monetary.

The idea for Hollywood's Mayfair came about as the direct result of the Sixty Club, a prominent celebrity group in the early Twenties. But the Sixty allowed *anyone* who could afford the price of admission to join their festivities. In 1926, a few members of the film colony started a group strictly for the movie set. The chief organizers were Irving Thalberg, Conrad Nagel, Sid Grauman, United Artists producer Mike Levee, prominent motion picture attorney Edwin Loeb, and mogul Joseph Schenck. The Club was set up as a nonprofit organization with an initiation fee of one hundred dollars and annual dues of twenty-five dollars a person. Profits were turned over to the Motion Picture Actors' Fund.

Mayfairites gave themselves fantastic parties in the grand ballroom of the then very elegant Biltmore Hotel in downtown Los Angeles. They were held on the last

Saturday of every month except during the summer. Every dinner dance had a special theme. Sometimes it was a costume ball, or perhaps a party at which guests could wear only certain colors. Each of the nine evenings was arranged by a different committee—colleagues of one film studio would plan January's program, for instance, while the polo club members took February. But whatever the costume or the show, every event featured special European party favors. And each successive committee spent extra time, energy and money in an effort to outdo the previous month's soirée.

During the regular season, celebrities paid twenty dollars a couple for an elegant dinner, dancing, show and favors. At each table, cigarettes and mineral water came with the price of admission. The effervescent water provided a good mixer for booze, which everyone brought in hip flasks or chic hollow-tipped canes. In the early Thirties, the Biltmore, along with every other nightspot in the United States, "observed" the Prohibition laws.

On New Year's Eve, the ante for the gala Mayfair Ball was raised to fifteen dollars a person. The price included all of the regular goodies plus horns to blow at midnight and simulated snowballs made of cotton, which guests tossed at each other on the stroke of twelve. Orchids and gardenias, sold by circulating flower girls, were extra.

There were a few unique features of the Club. A nonmember could attend as a guest only once every three months. Exceptions were made for fiancées and/or any member brave enough to bring his or her current live-in playmate, even if there was no engagement ring in evidence and an official announcement had not been forthcoming. If two married celebrities divorced, each could retain membership and come alone—or bring a new spouse whenever he or she took the plunge again.

So it was that on the fourth Saturday of every month—except in the summer—the creme of Hollywood could be found dining together, vying on the dance floor for prizes, showing off new furs, jewels, lovers, or legal mates—and also rubbing shoulders with last season's husband and/or wife. It was all very civilized. Except for the occasional spurned spouse, seen to head discreetly for the ladies' room, handkerchief in hand, bravely holding in the tears as she caught a glimpse of her *former* hubby dancing cheek to cheek with his *current* wife.

Hollywood in the Thirties was a clannish town. Stars—on similar salary levels—tended not only to work together, play together and vacation togther, they even ordered their groceries from the same places and bought their cars, furniture, clothes and accessories from select merchants. The moment one femme fatale found a fabulous hairdresser or masseuse, the name was passed on to others in "the set." Weaver-Jackson's was one of the five top favorites for hair styles. Almost everyone purchased household furnishings from Barker Brothers in Hollywood. Jewels from Stromberg's were considered top drawer. For groceries, it was Young's—either their Hollywood store or the Beverly Hills branch. I. Magnin's and Bess Schlank sold the majority of fine clothes to actresses when they did not have the time or the desire for custom-made apparel.

Stars had their pipe tobacco blended and their cigarettes imported by Max Lickter, while the House of Flowers supplied the majority of posies for the town's well-heeled set. At one time, they had a standing order from Howard Hughes for a selection of orchids, gardenias and pale pastel roses—packed loosely in a golden box—to be delivered four times a week to his best gal, Billie Dove.

For a shop to be a supplier to the celebrities was the equivalent of those London merchants whose signs hung over British firms, reading: BY APPOINTMENT TO HIS MAJESTY KING GEORGE, ROYAL PURVEYORS

OF JAMS AND JELLIES . . . It meant that you had been singled out, selling goods fit for a king—or, in this case, one of Hollywood's own royalty.

In 1929, Hollywoodites discovered a nearby Riviera only twenty miles from their front doors. Malibu Beach suddenly became the favorite local playground for stars, studio heads, producers, directors, writers, their coterie of friends, servants and the usual hangers-on.

At first, modest beach shacks were hastily constructed. Some contained as few as four rooms, but still necessitated a minimum of two servants. Built one on top of the other, with only a few feet separating the kitchen of one residence from the bedroom of the next, the Malibu set *had* to be a close-knit group. Everyone knew each other's secrets, was privy to his or her neighbors' daily squabbles, and sometimes even shared vicariously in each other's lovemaking.

The whole setup was unique. Within the area called "The Colony," famous people, no matter how much or how little they spent on their homes, could *not* own the land. All of it belonged to May Rindge, known as the "Queen of Malibu." May, the widow of Frederick Rindge, one of the founders of the Southern California Edison Power Company, and Union Oil—among other holdings—owned 24,000 acres extending from the mountains to the sea, from Ventura to Santa Monica. She began leasing beachfront property at a dollar a foot per month. When the stars came, she raised the price to two-and-a-half per. Most celebrities leased a thirty-foot frontage.

Two of John Gilbert's ex-wives were householders. Barbara Stanwyck and Frank Fay weekended there. Dolores Del Rio, Ronald Colman, Clara Bow, Louise Fazenda and her husband, Hal Wallis, Warner Baxter and even the district attorney of Los Angeles, Buron Fitts, were Malibu weekend and summer residents. One of Gloria Swanson's early ex-husbands had a beach home close to Gloria's, which wasn't too embarrassing. What really hurt was that Gloria's *third ex*, the Marquis, was frequently seen lounging in the home of Constance Bennett, who was rumored about to become the new Marquise. Gloria had gladly given up her title in order to marry husband number four, Michael Farmer. But she *hated* the thought of Connie inheriting all of that prestige.

Perhaps the most exotic Malibu "shack" in the early Thirties belonged to lovely Lilyan Tashman and her handsome actor hubby, Edmund Lowe. The whole place, down to the last beach chair, was decorated by Billy Haines in various shades of red or white. Guests dressed in red and white, and even the napkins and toilet tissue were color-coordinated.

Despite the makeups, breakups, illicit scandals and just plain juicy gossip, Malibu continues to be one of the stars' favorite playgrounds. Over the decades, more and more celebrities have become year-round occupants. In the late Thirties, May Rindge finally allowed residents to purchase the property—at a very handsome price. Those who knew Malibu in "the old days" claim it was more fun, much freer. In the early Thirties, bootleg brew was consumed by the gallon. Private homes were the settings for round-the-clock gambling, complete with blackjack, dice and the whirring spin of the roulette wheels. As far as sex play among the sanddunes, with the surf pounding in the background, it was, as Clara Bow told a friend, ". . . a real perfect place for hey-hey. The guys wear bathing trunks, so you don't have to waste time unzipping flys."

Unfortunately, along with the relaxation it offered, Malibu has always been one potentially gigantic tinderbox or flood area. Within two years of its prominence, fire gutted dozens of houses. It spread from one rooftop to the next within a matter of minutes. So Malibu residents quickly became resigned to periodic rebuilding. Although it was hard to watch one's second home go up in flames or down in the high tide, piece by piece, Malibuites felt it was worth it for the glory of living there the rest of the year. As soon as the ashes cooled, or the rains and tides subsided, the construction crews were back again. After all, the homes were insured. And besides, where else could the famous make such elegant whoopee away from the glare of their fans—and only twenty miles from their own in-town front doors?

Life was not all fun and games. Studio heads, tired of dope scandals and stars who drank so excessively that they needed frequent drying out cures, sought to insure that personalities took better care of themselves. They inserted thirty-day illness clauses in film contracts. Players "sick" for more than a month were threatened with replacement and their contracts were subject to cancellation.

In between pictures, while the majority of stars played hard but sanely and traveled to exotic places to unwind, some stayed home and abused their beautiful bodies with hard liquor and other stimulants, downers, or euphoria drugs. Then, as soon as the next shooting date was announced, it became more and more difficult to go back on their health and fitness regimens.

Wiser celebrities, like Joan Crawford and Robert Taylor, who had worked hard to reach stardom, employed enormous self-discipline in order to keep themselves in shape. Friends said Joan had not eaten a square meal in years. She constantly dieted to keep the weight off. As for Bob, he was very active physically, enjoyed a social cocktail or two, and usually managed at least eight hours sleep a night. Garbo, always nutrition conscious, went on periodic fasts and then stayed on a vegetarian diet. Lila Lee went in and out of an Arizona sanitorium in a futile effort to control her fluctuating weight.

Unfortunately, she lost her desperate battle.

Most celebrities had doctors, chiropractors and masseurs on call. Some worked out with exercise coaches. Others took up tennis and golf or installed swimming pools— no longer just for their aesthetic beauty but for daily laps back and forth either before or after work.

Health spas, hot mineral springs, gyms, dude ranches and physical culture institutes sprang up within a hundred-mile radius. Weekends were spent relaxing in Palm Springs or Lake Arrowhead. Horseback riding and dancing lessons became regular routines for keeping in shape.

Some celebrities were constantly in an ambivalent state. They worked so hard to afford the best of food and drink, yet most often were compelled to dine on lettuce leaves, cottage cheese and carrot juice in order to keep in shape. Material possessions became substitute rewards. While stars could not sink newly capped teeth into corn on the cob oozing with butter, or candied nougats, they *could* live in style in Beverly Hills or Bel Air and drive very snazzy roadsters or wear a new sapphire bracelet— all of which helped to ease their hunger for excessive calories, sweets, booze and dope. There were a number of stars who were warmed by sable coats covering anorexic bodies.

Hollywood offered them the golden pot at the end of the rainbow, but was their prison as well. *Everything* was available for the taking. Too often the risk had far greater consequences than the rewards of self-control. Often, those who could not cope—and there were quite a few—found their film parts getting smaller, heard their phones ringing less and watched their fan mail dwindle. Still, there were always the chosen few, like Alma Rubens and Clara Bow, who *had* everything, *did* everything, and inadvertently *destroyed* everyone who tried to help them, and still survived—until their excesses finally did them in—or, for as long as they brought enough money into the box-office for their bosses to protect them, pamper them and pardon them for their harmful, self-destructive habits.

Several years before Las Vegas became the frequent watering hole of celebrities, Reno, Nevada, billed as "the Biggest Little City in the World," had already begun to attract the film crowd. There were two main reasons: gambling and quickie divorces. Unlike California's one-year waiting period between court appearance and the final divorce decree, people could be spliced after six weeks.

Reno was a wide-open town with gambling joints on every block, saloons hidden in the back behind respectable storefronts, and the Washoe County Court House, where judges granted divorces at the rate of ten an hour. Famous faces checked in at one of the swank hotels, like the Riverside, the El Cortez, The Overland, or The Golden, and settled down for six weeks' residence. For those who preferred a more sedate, less public existence, there were several fancy dude ranches where stars could relax, ride, read and sleep away the obligatory residence requirements, or else just lose their money at the tables.

In the early Thirties, Reno was a twenty-four-hour train trip, a five-hour flight, or a fifteen-hour drive from the heart of Hollywood. Then a celebrity group headed by Jeanette MacDonald, Ann Harding and Reginald Denny formed a partnership and started the Los Angeles to Reno Air Service, offering three faster and more convenient flights daily.

Among the famous who shed husbands and/or wives in Reno, perhaps the most celebrated and shocking was Mary Pickford. She took up residence way back in 1920, on a guest ranch, divorced actor Owen Moore, and shortly thereafter became Mrs. Douglas Fairbanks, Sr.

By the time Jack Dempsey, the heavyweight champion of the world, arrived and settled in to get his divorce from Estelle Taylor, Reno splits had become more commonplace. Dempsey liked the town so much, he stayed for a while and managed the local racetrack.

Even more important than cities in other states, Southern California itself offered literally everything anyone could desire. There were mountains, deserts, ski trails, fishing holes, beaches, sequestered hideaways, garish nightspots, quiet cafes, intimate hotels, theatres and museums. In essence, Hollywood was indeed the land of caviar and crepes: the Promised Land. And it flourished, and changed, and grew—and the movie industry grew with it.

LOVE STORIES

As the first year of the new decade ended, Radio Pictures previewed *Cimarron*. The entire industry took heart. It was a landmark epic in breadth and scope, albeit perhaps the last of the one-million-dollar talkies until the economy came around. The film, directed brilliantly by Wesley Ruggles, was an intense saga of Americana, wrapped up with the development and growth of a new town and the people who built it. Richard Dix, in the most demanding role of his career, triumphed. Screen newcomer Irene Dunne was not only beautiful, but her performance was topnotch.

The picture did very well. As more and more people saw their own lives diminished by the country's worsening conditions, they felt that watching a new town being built was the kind of inspiring movie they needed. The American public was always receptive to any entertainment or news which truly brightened their lives. So 1931 was a wonderful year for Hollywood love stories.

In mid-May, Carole Lombard, twenty-two, wearing a huge emerald-cut diamond engagement ring, confirmed that she and William Powell, thirty-eight, would be married as soon as both of them could get time away from their respective studios. Their romance had begun on the set of *Ladies Man*, in which Powell starred. Onscreen, she had played one of the ladies who fell in love with him—but lost. Offcamera, the combination clicked!

On June 20, Carole and Bill showed up at the local marriage license bureau, but still would not give reporters a firm wedding date. Frankly, both newsmen and friends of the twosome were surprised by the suddenness of their action—primarily because Bill was considered a difficult catch.

Powell, born in Pittsburgh, Pennsylvania, on July 29, 1892, was one of Hollywood's suavest leading men. He could kiss a girl, kill a guy or toss off a humorous line with just a tiny lift of the eyebrow and evoke gales of laughter in the audience.

Bill had studied at the American Academy of Dramatic Arts in New York before enjoying a successful stage career. In 1922, he came to Hollywood, under contract to Sam Goldwyn, to appear with John Barrymore in *Sherlock Holmes*. He went on to make numerous silent films, including *The Great Gatsby*. Then he created a whole new image for himself as Philo Vance in *The Canary Murder Case*. Of all the roles Powell

had done, or would do, his portrayal of Nick Charles opposite Myrna Loy in "The Thin Man" series would win him everlasting screen fame.

As far as his personal life was concerned, however, Powell had been married in April of 1915, but he and his wife, Jule, had separated in June of 1925. For many years, they lived apart, with Bill in Hollywood, while Jule and their son, William David, five and a half, resided back East. But after one look at Lombard—or so the story went—Mrs. Powell number one suddenly appeared in court and was granted a divorce on the grounds of mental cruelty. She alleged that Powell insulted her, told her she had the mentality of a twelve-year-old child, and that being married to her hurt his career. She also said that he refused to take her out socially. In their out-of-court property settlement, it was agreed that Jule would keep custody of their son until he reached his sixth birthday. From then on, the boy would divide his time equally between parents.

At this point in time, America's highest-paid comedienne, the nutsy, zany, marvelous "broad" that Lombard would be-

Carole Lombard and William Powell in *My Man Godfrey*, one of several pictures they made together. They were briefly married to each other.

come, had not yet emerged as part of her public persona. Bill Powell was the big star of the combination. Carole was still a young leading lady on the rise.

She was born Jane Alice Peters in Fort Wayne, Indiana, on October 6, 1908. When she was six, her family came to Hollywood for a visit and liked what they saw. There was Mama Peters and two older brothers. When she was twelve, little Jane was spotted by director Allan Dwan as she played with some friends on the street in front of her house. She appeared to him to be the perfect tomboy type and he cast her in *A Perfect Crime*, in the spring of 1921. Then she returned to her classes at Fairfax High School in Los Angeles.

Upon graduation in 1924, she actively went after a career. Winnie Sheehan signed her to a stock Fox contract at fifty dollars a week. By then she was calling herself Carol Peters. But the studio requested a new name with more zip. So Carol added an "e" and chose for a last name that of family friends. Once she had a high-tone moniker, Fox put her in a Buck Jones western!

By the time she was seventeen, Carole had played the lead opposite Edmund Lowe in *Marriage in Transit*. But she was considered an acting lightweight. So, much of her time was spent posing for cheesecake photos. While Carole was still in her teens, she was in a bad automobile accident coming home from a dance at the Cocoanut Grove in a date's fancy Bugatti. The crash shattered the windshield, and flying pieces of glass embedded themselves in her cheek. After a touch-and-go period and plastic surgery, Carole looked as good as new.

Through a school chum, Sally Eilers, Lombard heard that Mack Sennett needed another girl for his bathing beauty group. She went over to Sennett's, made a few shorts, and then the next few years were spent doing other less-than sensational silents. In 1929, she made her first talkie,

High Voltage, for Pathé. Then she was dropped. Rumors circulated that Constance Bennett, the queen of that lot, had ordered her dismissed because they resembled each other too closely.

Carole worked at several other studios before winding up at Paramount. She made *Safety in Numbers*, with Buddy Rogers, the first of more than twenty pictures she did there under a seven-year contract. Then, early in 1931, Lombard acted in two films with William Powell, *Man of the World* and *Ladies Man*. It was the latter film which brought them together—in what they believed would be a permanent arrangement.

Carole Lombard and William Powell were married on June 26, 1931. She wore a simple blue chiffon dress decorated with an enormous corsage of yellow orchids, selected to match the yellow-gold of her hair. They changed the hour of the actual nuptials three times in order to shake off the press. No one except members of both families attended. But a group of champagne-logged friends did escort them down to the dock where they boarded a Matson liner and sailed off on an Hawaiian honeymoon.

For a couple of years, the Powell-Lombard match was considered idyllic by friends and fans alike. In 1933, as if to prove the point of their happiness, Carole and Bill celebrated their second wedding anniversary with a lavish party. Nine days later, Carole left for Reno, established six weeks' residence there and secured a divorce. The news came as a shock to the public. Even more nonplussed were their close friends, who were still wiping the anniversary cake frosting from their lips. There was never a public statement issued about the whys and wherefores of their parting. The plain fact was that they were just incompatible as husband and wife. They adored each other. They just couldn't live together.

The Lupe Velez–Gary Cooper idyll was over by 1931. He had taken his cars, his books and his birds and moved back to his parents' home. When reporters inquired, Miss Velez said it was she who had called the whole thing off. Insiders maintained that the elder Coopers had finally prevailed upon their son "to come to his senses." Lupe countered by displaying telegrams and letters signed by Gary, which all asked for one more chance. Cooper, the only party at interest who hadn't made a statement, was then back East shooting a picture.

The following year, he took off for Europe. He needed time to relax. He had gone from picture to picture and from romance to romance. He told friends he felt entitled to some fun. When Gary arrived in Rome, he called the Countess di Frasso. He had brought a letter of introduction to the wealthy socialite from a mutual acquaintance. The Countess, delighted to hear from Cooper, invited him to dine at her palatial home, the Villa Madama. In his honor, she invited the creme of Italian society to join them.

From the first time they met, the twosome formed a close bond. Dorothy was an attractive, fascinating, worldly woman, older than Gary and beloved by the international set. The former Dorothy Taylor, of New York City, she was the heiress to a multimillion-dollar fortune created by her father, an industrialist and real estate tycoon.

When Gary came into her life, she was romantically uninvolved. Her second marriage, to the Count di Frasso, had gone sour. However, she was not yet legally divorced. Whatever her status, Dorothy and Coop became inseparable. Through her, Gary had immediate entrée to anybody and everybody of importance on the Continent. Through him, the Countess met all of the visiting Hollywood celebrities. She was pleased as punch to have such a handsome and devoted escort. And Gary, who had become accustomed to the trappings of stardom, was still mighty impressed by her social sphere. Together, they had everything.

Dorothy, who adored showering Gary with gifts, saw one area of his life in which she could be of immediate help. She introduced him to the finest tailors in Rome and personally selected a whole new wardrobe for him—from topcoats to undergarments. Then the pair went traveling. To London. Paris. Madrid. When they had "done" the Continent, Gary and Dotty headed to Africa on safari. He was an avid hunter; she was a willing pupil. When he finally returned to Hollywood, with the usual collection of animal skins and stuffed exotic beast heads to be mounted, he seemed more relaxed and at ease than ever before.

Shortly thereafter, the Countess, who had residences all over the world, checked into the Beverly Hills Hotel while she hunted for a local palazzo to buy. Gary and Dorothy continued to be "a couple" until the late summer of 1933. For all of those months, in between filming, he devoted his time to introducing Dorothy to all of Hollywood society. If there was anything Tinseltown folks loved, it was a title, particularly when its owner also came equipped with an apparently limitless bankroll. Besides, she was a marvelously generous hostess. Not only was the Countess welcomed into Hollywood's top echelon—they practically made her its ruling Queen.

Howard Hughes' fast-paced film *Front Page* did extremely well at the boxoffice in 1931. Meanwhile, having finished the picture, Howard personally concentrated on handling the contract of beautiful Billie Dove. He not only gifted her with diamonds, he hired five writers to doctor up her latest script. There were even reports in certain columns that HH had given "his Dove" a fantastically expensive full-length chinchilla coat. But Billie denied that. She said that she not only didn't have one, she'd never even *seen* one!

Wilson Heller, one of Hollywood's pioneer publicists, meaning he had been on the job before 1923, was Howard Hughes' first press agent. Recently, he talked about Hollywood in the early days and discussed his famous former boss.

In the Twenties, and for most of the Thirties, this town was a much more exciting place than it later became. Things were wilder and freer. The performers were mostly uneducated notoriety seekers. The town was wide open and the police didn't watch things so closely.

Among my women clients—and I mostly handled women—it was well-known around the business that only a few of them never laid a guy to get where they were: among them Bebe Daniels, Lois Wilson and Patsy Ruth Miller. They would go to parties now and then, but they wouldn't screw. They weren't on the make. Most of the others got their jobs by laying somebody. Among the early stars, I think every damn one of them laid some guy to get ahead, or further ahead after they got started . . .

Anyway, I handled publicity for General Service Studios, over on Las Palmas and Santa Monica Boulevard, in exchange for free office space. One of the tenants was a kid named Howard Hughes. He was only around twenty then. He just busted in there one day and rented the fanciest office on the lot. Word got around that he was worth millions. He took a liking to me and I was hired on a free-lance basis. I had fifteen other clients at the time, really big silent stars like Anita Stewart, Clara Bow, Blanche Sweet, Agnes Ayres, Richard Dix, Harold Lloyd and those three other ladies I mentioned before.

Howard found out I had been a flier in World War I. He was nuts about aviation. About every two or three months, he'd buy a plane, and whenever he got a new baby, he would insist I go up with him. We became pretty good pals. For about a year, he didn't really do anything but play around. I think he had invested some money in a couple of pictures, but he had a lot of time on his hands.

He had some wealthy dame from Chicago, who was living up in Montecito, right outside of Santa Barbara. Every time he got a new plane, we would fly up there. He would zoom down over her house, trying to attract her attention. A few times, he came damn near to hitting her chimney. He could scare you to death. Howard was a very good pilot, but he was a daredevil. He wanted to loop the loops, do stalls and everything. He was a brave man. I never knew a braver person than Hughes, and I'd flown in combat with the best.

Really, he was amazing. He could do so many things at the same time. But whatever else he did, he was always on the make for women. From what I heard, he was the world's worst guy in the hay. Two of his girlfriends told me he wasn't worth a damn as a lover. He was just no good in the sack. They said he just wanted to look and fondle.

Anyway, after a while, Howard began to think in earnest about becoming a movie producer. He really seemed to want to tackle it. Then he got all wound up with *Hell's Angels*. Suddenly, he was doing everything. Writing. Directing. Checking out all of the aerial shots. It was then that he asked me to go to work for him, full time. But I didn't want to. I had all of my other clients. Besides, I still wasn't sure about Howard's future.

At times, it seemed so nebulous. Even when he was hip-deep in production, I was never sure he wasn't going to run off after some dame. It's funny, I used to feel sorry for Howard. When it came to dames, I mean. Those women didn't give a damn about him personally. They all wanted a free ride . . . All the glamour and notoriety that came just from being with him. I guess, from a woman's point of view, he wasn't really terribly interesting. I know for a fact that, after he went with Billie Dove for a while, she got sick of him. But he had given her a lot of money. He was always lavish with his dough.

I recommended that he hire Linc Quarburg as his publicist. Linc was a fraternity brother of mine from Wisconsin. He stayed with Hughes for a couple of years. Howard fired him, though. He didn't like Linc's politics. But it was Quarburg that did all of the early Harlow publicity. He was the one who coined the phrase "Platinum Blonde."

Howard and I always stayed in touch. When he wanted some special glamour shots of Jean to promote *Hell's Angels*, he asked my advice. I put him in contact with a guy who was very well known in those days for shooting women's tits. He was a homosexual, and always photographed dames wearing very little. Hell, he was safe around the girls. Anyway, he took a few shots of Harlow. Howard was crazy about them. Those early tit pictures were delivered to papers across the whole country. Those photos made Jean famous before anyone had even seen her onscreen . . .

By the end of June 1932, Hollywood received bad news. Attendance at motion picture houses was down forty percent from the peak it had achieved in 1928. But the Depression was only partly responsible for the boxoffice plunge. The novelty of talkies had definitely worn off. Quality, not quantity, became every studio's goal. And to add to their woes, many producers continued to feud with Will Hays. The latest was Howard Hughes. He had become disgusted when his film *Scarface*, after undergoing extensive reshooting—at Hays' insistence—still failed to win approval. He decided to release the original uncut version. *The Hollywood Reporter* publicly backed him, calling the film a masterpiece of acting, directing, and producing, and congratulating Hughes for making a picture that candidly exposed the mobs and detailed gangland operations. Censor Hays was not at all pleased.

Howard was having trouble on another front as well. Ever since Jean Harlow had appeared in *Hell's Angels*, stardom had been indelibly stamped on her. When Hughes could not readily find a follow-up film for her, he loaned her out to Columbia for *Platinum Blonde*. That sent her stock soaring. When Harlow began to make constant salary demands, Hughes considered her ungrateful. He sold her contract to MGM for a reported $60,000.

Even before Jean stepped onto the Metro-Goldwyn-Mayer lot in 1932, her closest friend was powerful film executive Paul Bern, Irving Thalberg's righthand man. Bern, liked by everyone—studio heads and stars alike—fell in love with Jean. They began dating steadily. Paul was no Don Juan; on the contrary, he was a short, slight, plain-looking man with a pencil-slim moustache. But he had a reputation for great kindness. He was known as the father confessor to the stars. Anyone with a problem sought him out. Once they met, Harlow had immediately gravitated toward him, too.

Jean clung to Bern. He was the one man who did not want to exploit her obvious sexual charms. For all of their months of togetherness, Bern was content just to remain her friend. Outwardly affectionate, he never treated Harlow as less than a lady and constantly put her on a pedestal. In the course of time, their closeness ripened into more. Undoubtedly Jean felt that she loved Paul, as he loved her. They were married. She was twenty-one. He was forty-two.

The wedding took place on July 2, 1932, at her mother's home, with just a few close friends present. The following day, as the new mistress of Paul's cozy house in Benedict Canyon—he deeded it to her for a wedding gift—Jean and Paul entertained everyone who was anyone in Hollywood's celebrity and executive set.

The marriage seemed happy. But the Berns were not seen around town too much

Jean Harlow and her second husband, Paul Bern, on their wedding day. Bern committed suicide only weeks after this portrait was taken.

socially. Their excuse: that both were working very hard. Jean went from picture to picture, and Paul was wrapped up in MGM's business affairs. At the few parties they did attend, other guests subsequently remembered that Paul was overly possessive of his wife. And that she held on to him, listening to his every word, obediently following his lead.

On Labor Day, two months and eight days after their wedding, the nude body of Paul Bern was found on the floor of their bedroom. Apparently, he had committed suicide by shooting himself in the head. He had left behind a final cryptic note, subsequently spread over the nation's front pages:

Dearest Dear—Unfortunately this is the only way to make good the frightful wrong I have done to you and to wipe out my abject humiliation. I love you.

PAUL

You understand that last night was only a comedy—

Harlow had been at her mother's home at the time of Bern's death. The shock, publicity, headlines and clamor were hard on her, but Jean never publicly broke down. She never discussed Paul's note. She never expressed anything but disbelief that Paul could have taken his own life. She never admitted anything except that she had loved him very much.

Two days after Bern's suicide, the body of Dorothy Millette, who turned out to have been Bern's common-law wife, was fished out of the Sacramento River. Quietly, Jean paid for her burial.

At the outset, many Hollywoodites condemned Harlow. They blamed her for "Saint Paul's" suicide. However, after the autopsy report revealed—although in couched terms—that Bern was *physically incapable* of consummating their marriage, sympathy turned back to Jean. Surely, people reasoned, she must have known of Paul's condition prior to the nuptials. The fact that she had married him anyway, realizing that she could never be a wife to him in the normal sense, turned her into a martyr.

Still, there were unanswered questions. Many remain a riddle to this day. At the time, though, Harlow won great admiration when she insisted on returning immediately to work on *Red Dust*. Her co-star, Clark Gable, said in amazement, "That little lady has more guts than any *man* in Hollywood!"

A few days into the filming, she collapsed. But Jean was back on set early the following morning. *Red Dust*, one of her biggest hits, was completed on schedule. Every day that passed brought more and more revelations. For one, Harlow had *not* married Bern for his money. When his will, in which he left her everything, was probated, it turned out that Paul was in debt. The house he had given her as a wedding present was mortgaged to the hilt. After his bills were paid, nothing was left. His years of generosity had left Bern a man with no assets.

After Paul's death, Harlow continued to go from picture to picture. Meanwhile, there were dozens of magazine stories all conjecturing on her romantic future. Had she been too hurt by her marital experiences to risk giving her heart again? "Yes," said several well-known psychologists. "Nonsense," Harlow commented. "Of course, I'll marry again—if and when I fall in love."

"Being both a divorcée and a widow at age twenty-one is too much trauma for any sensitive person," said a third group of insiders, who claimed to know Harlow well. "Jean will obviously date again—but she won't take the plunge for many years."

The psychologists and the insiders were wrong. On September 18, 1933, a year and two weeks after Paul Bern's funeral, Jean Harlow and ace Hollywood cinematographer Hal Rosson boarded a charter aircraft. They flew off to Arizona, where they were joined as man and wife, at dawn, by Yuma's "Marrying Judge," E. A. Freeman. The couple had just completed filming *Bombshell*, with Harlow starring and Rosson behind the camera.

Hal had known Jean since her early days at MGM. They had, in fact, been introduced by Paul Bern, when Hal made camera tests of Jean for *Red-Headed Woman*. He was also a golfing buddy of her stepfather, Marino Bello. At the time of the marriage, Jean had turned twenty-two. Rosson was twice her age, plus.

Before they motored off to spend a brief honeymoon sequestered at a nearby mountain resort, Jean spoke with reporters: "I believe I know what I want. And I want Hal. He is, I think, the finest, kindest, most sincere and most honorable man I have ever known."

Harlow admitted that she had fallen in love with Rosson during the filming of *Red Dust*, just after the tragic suicide of Paul Bern. "During that picture," Jean said, "of all the eyes that were on me, I seemed to feel that Hal's were the kindliest . . . I sensed that he was in love with me. We saw a great deal of each other while we were shooting that picture, and during later productions. Then, all of a sudden, I knew the overwhelming truth. I was in love with him . . . and that this time it was forever!"

Jean Harlow was Mrs. Hal Rosson for five months and twenty-three days. On March 11, 1934, she filed for divorce.

While Christmas of 1933 was definitely a downer for the film industry, some stars did fairly well. Under their respective Christmas trees, Sylvia Sidney found a diamond bracelet from film executive B. P. Schulberg. Darryl gave Virginia Zanuck a diamond bracelet. Dolores Del Rio received a ruby and diamond clip from art director Cedric Gibbons. Lupe Velez was given two Mexican hairless puppies and a diamond and ruby wristwatch by her "Tarzan" fiancé Johnny Weissmuller. Virginia Bruce Gilbert gave her husband, John, a motion picture camera. Jean Harlow received a small sailboat for their pool from Hal Rosson. And Carole Lombard was given the key to a shiny new Ford, the gift from her ex-husband and best buddy.

The biggest New Year's Eve party of the season was given by Lombard. The evening's entertainment was topped off by a "tipsy quartette" which actually consisted of Bill Powell and one other guy—who thought there were four of them.

Over the years, Carole and Bill remained close. It was, in truth, one of Hollywood's rare friendly splits.

Bill went on to find love with Jean Harlow. Lombard, of course, had Gable. Eventually, he took a third wife, Diana Lewis. Their marriage continues to this day. William Powell, who enjoyed a long and enormously successful career, once said about his wealth, all earned in Hollywood, "Money is the aphrodisiac which fate brings you to cloak the pain of living."

Jean Harlow
"EXTRA GIRL GETS HER FIRST CLOSE-UP"

By September of 1935, it was a foregone conclusion that Bill Powell and Jean Harlow would become man and wife. Neither was anxious to rush into anything. They were content just to be together. Once or twice they ducked out on Hollywood and traveled up north to be the guest of W. R. Hearst and Marion Davies at San Simeon.

Bill told a friend that on one such occasion he and Jean borrowed a car and drove into the nearby village, where they visited the local movie house. When they were recognized they held an impromptu personal appearance. Both he and Jean, as well as the surprised moviegoers, got a big kick out of the whole afternoon.

It was while Jean was away with Powell for a few quiet days that she fulfilled her promise to Billy Wilkerson and wrote this story for a September 1935 anniversary issue of The Hollywood Reporter. *Billy was one of the few in town, incidentally, who realized that Jean was a serious writer. When he asked her to do a piece for him, he wasn't surprised when she turned in this fabulous semiautobiographical vignette.*

Suppose—oh, just suppose, it doesn't cost anything—suppose she could get a close-up today!

The thought warmed her. She had summoned it into mental existence hundreds of times, just for the sake of that warming tingle which came in its wake. After all, it wasn't IMPOSSIBLE! It DOES happen to extra girls—well, not regularly but frequently enough to justify the perennial visualization of its glorious possibility.

She thought about herself, very carefully. She surveyed her whole person, in critical analysis as if she were someone else, just as she had meticulously studied herself that morning in the bleary mirror of her bathroom door—a smooth white body, unflawed, taut with youth, curved with promise, clean with hope.

She found nothing much to criticize—except that she did not have artificial eyelashes.

She tried to compensate herself with the assurance that at least her eyebrows conformed to Hollywood convention. Of course it HAD been something of an effort to shave the brows cleanly off this morning, and to pencil the thin, highly-arched arcs of unreality in place of the silky ash-blonde hairs. She had postponed this for almost a year. It did not, however, give the complete effect. She must have the artificial lashes. Her own lashes, upper and lower, were adequate—even abundant—but they were REAL hence marked her as one of the rank and file.

She had stopped wearing stockings six months ago. Stockings cost too much, but more

Harlow studying her script in her MGM dressingroom.

important was the reason that bare legs may not be classified so readily as stockinged ones and she was conscious that the curves of her calves were vaguely irregular.

Her mouth was her strong point. Mouth—which means, on only visual contact—lips. She had made her lips important by long hours of study in the mirror. The carmine lipstick now outlined the upper lip in a sweeping single curve so brutally false as to provoke a second and interested glance; it was a cheap lipstick; she had found it in a boulevard drugstore; but it made provoking the wet smear of lambent color.

For seven weeks she had planned to buy the artificial eyelashes. It was not a tragic necessity for food and shelter which weekly devoured the eyelash appropriation. It was the thousand and one other little things even more important to an extra girl.

Shoes. Assistant Directors always look at your feet first.

Hair. No matter how simple a coiffure you evolve, the beauty shop cannot be dodged forever.

Makeup. You'll never get a close-up unless your makeup is satin-smooth with the very best grease and powder and shadings.

Telephone calls. Not only the daily routine to Central Casting, but the three or four calls every day to Marcella, or Red, or Tommy, the several various persons in different studios who had manifested a degree of friendliness sufficient to warrant a call reminding them of your existence.

Hats. You can't fake hats the way you can fake clothes. Hats CHANGE—irrevocably.

Transportation. The cruelest burden of all the burdens. First National, way over in the valley. Metro, far out in Culver City. Fox, in Westwood. Funny the way Easterners came out here and expected to find all the studios cuddled up in one handy group in the heart of Hollywood. Hollywood? Hollywood isn't a city. Hollywood isn't even a district. Hollywood is the name of an idea, and its ramifications stretch expensively far and wide for the extra girl. Her nose wrinkled delicately with the shadow of an impish grin—maybe she'd waive her spirit of independence long enough to accept that "hundred and a quarter" from Daddy and buy a second-hand Ford— maybe she wouldn't either.

Even without the artificial eyelashes she knew she looked "hot" today. There were only, she counted, twenty girls on the set. She knew very well that at least twelve of them had been selected from the Assistant Director's list. The other eight had come direct from Central Casting.

That's funny too, and she remembered what that nice woman at Central Casting had told her. How the real problem was not only finding work for extras but finding the right extras for the work. How few REALLY lovely well-dressed girls had she said were available?

She relaxed with satisfaction. Yes, she was undoubtedly the best-looking, best dressed, best made-up extra on the set. And that without counting her hair. Her hair would get her a break some day, she felt sure. Its pale ashen loveliness was natural. She liked to announce the fact somewhat arrogantly to the bleached sisters.

As a matter of fact, it was not her hair which attracted the Assistant Director. His roving eye flickered about and settled on her because she was the one girl in the lot he had not classified. He had actually nothing on her. He'd heard rumors, but rumors are nothing in Hollywood. His wife—who secretly "worked extra" under an assumed name—had sniffed quite vigorously one night at that "blonde dame" with her twenty-two-dollar Fifth Avenue shoes. Still, he could comfort himself on his selection of her with the reassurance that she was really the most striking girl of all the twenty.

"You," he said to her curtly, "be ready for a close-up at three o'clock."

She looked at him dully, not quite segregating his actuality from the endlessly dreamed visions of this moment. Then she knew that it was reality, because his eyes lingered on her for a second. His gaze was not lascivious nor acquisitive. It was kindly and gracious.

In a sudden warm flash of understanding she realized that Assistant Directors are human, probably dine on meat and vegetables rather than fire and brimstone, and even possibly might have been born through the ordinary human processes of life.

The Director was rehearsing a dialogue two-shot. From experience she knew the leading man would not acquire the proper emphasis for at least another hour. She walked proudly off the set with the sure knowledge that she was entitled to some preparation time. She was going to have a close-up.

The kindly hairdresser responded nobly. The ash-blonde hair was done and re-done and done again. The makeup was removed and put on anew with loving care and trembling hands.

If she only had those artificial eyelashes! Why hadn't she yielded to temptation this morning—why hadn't she turned her steps into that drugstore?

Now there is a God, even in Hollywood.

It was certainly one of His minions, this slim southern girl "in stock," who overheard the lament and proffered—a pair of artificial eyelashes for the great event.

"Hop to it, kid," were her words. "Your first close-up may get you plenty. You're telling me! And what's a buck to me? I'm in stock! Of course nobody but His Nibs . . . and the Cashier, and Allah il Allah to him . . . knows I'm in stock, but I've been collecting that little check every Wednesday for five months. Here—good luck—"

They were ready and waiting when she came back on the set. It was more important than an outsider would think. They would make several takes of that close-up, and the producer himself—to say nothing of his staff and secretaries and the Director and maybe even the Head Man who sat in his "mahogany hell" of an office—would be interested in that day's rushes and thus forced to look full into this lovely face of hers for several minutes.

With an approving nod the Assistant Director took her firmly by the arm and led her to a spot about which dazzling lights were concentrated. Her heart was bursting within her.

"Sit there on the arm of the couch." The Director himself was speaking. "Pull up your skirts, WAY up—above your knees!"

Then she understood. They were going to take a close-up of her LEGS.

Carole Lombard
"EVERY ACTOR SHOULD TAKE AT LEAST ONE WEEK'S WHIRL AT PUBLICITY"

Carole Lombard was not only a Hollywood beauty and a notorious zany, but she was also a very perceptive and clever woman. After she had achieved stardom, she spent a week working for David O. Selznick—not as an actress but as a publicist. She recorded her experiences in an exclusive article for The Hollywood Reporter, *run on October 24, 1938, and directed at her colleagues.*

Publicity is one of the most important—if not the most important topic—under discussion in Hollywood today. The motion picture capital has come to a long overdue realization that its publicity, foremost among its contacts with the rest of the world, has the power to make Hollywood the most beloved place on earth or the most hated. That, of course, goes for all the personalities in Hollywood.

A lot of us have wondered what makes a publicity office tick and what goes on behind the scenes where the big sales ideas are born and developed. I've had many contacts with film press agents while working in pictures but only when I spent a week as a working publicist at Selznick-International was I able to see the wheels go 'round.

It was a six-day, full-time job. I worked every minute of it. Fun? Never had a better time in my life. There's more romance in the everyday work of a publicity office than in the work of any other single department on a movie lot. And you can take that straight—without a chaser.

Carole Lombard.

The fun, of course, is merely incidental. Any star knows, or should know, the importance of publicity. This is not exactly a recital of what I learned in a week at Selznick-International's praisery, for you cannot learn much about publicity in that time. It has always been a prideful point with me that I have taken a personal and necessary interest in publicity, and believe I have come to know as much about it as any other person who has not made that branch of journalism a life career.

It is in the publicity offices of Hollywood's motion picture studios that careers have been made—and cracked. Here, every day of the week, are men and women who have in their hands millions of dollars' worth of careers. Theirs is the work of creating interest in players and pictures, jumping the value of an actor with every well-timed line of news or chatter. And at the same moment theirs is the power to blot a career with an ill-chosen idea that can ruin years of effort. Is it any wonder that stars must make it their business to know publicity from the ground up?

The business of putting all other interests aside for a week and doing publicity work myself, with my own hands, so to speak, was a new experience for me. Now that it's over, I can say with complete conviction that all film players should try it. The idea that publicity consists simply of writing pieces for the papers has gone to the same limbo where silent pictures now roost.

In the first place, publicity is not a pursuit dedicated to the grabbing of all the free space the traffic will bear. Publicity, I learned, is journalism, plus salesmanship, plus diplomacy, plus showmanship. In the second place, the space itself does not mean a thing. In the third place, it is far better to never get one's name in the paper than to have whole columns which say the wrong thing.

The entire workings of a well-ordered publicity department will teach one that every effort, even down to the smallest, is or should be directed along pre-conceived lines, with all of these dove-tailing into a definite sales campaign.

What features of a picture are to be sold heaviest? What angle will best convince the public the picture must be seen? How are the personalities in the cast to be handled? What is the best way to present them to the public, considering the type of roles they are playing?

These are but a few of the basic questions you will hear around the office . . .

A common charge leveled against press agentry in general is that it lives on a diet of hokum. That may be true in too many quarters today, but it doesn't hold among those who have kept pace with the technical improvements in other branches of the film industry. Hokum, one may learn in a publicity office, is as outmoded as the spinning wheel. Not only outmoded, but also outworn, ineffective and downright dangerous.

Your modern press agent believes that hokum is the resort of publicity men too lazy to dig for something truthful, which nine times out of ten makes a better story anyway. Remember, too, that the unseen welcome mat before the editor's door is not nailed down, and may be hauled in on short notice. There's a string attached to it for the man that tries to "put one across" the second time.

That leads us to another subject, which can be called . . . the "developing of news." One of the quickest-learned (and most deflating) truths around the publicity office is that city editors do not swoon at the sound of the names that glitter in lights. Names that come popping at city editors every week cease to be news in themselves, unless there is news attached to them. That is why "developing of news" is important.

In using this procedure, your publicist goes out and makes news happen. He gets his idea first, then executes it. When completed, the idea makes a story. It's all true enough, in the final analysis, because it *did* happen . . . and it has to possess the kind of newsworthy merit that practically cries out for printing.

We hatched a couple of such ideas . . . during my hectic week. One was for a round-the-world telephone poll of notables, getting their views on who should play Scarlett O'Hara in *Gone With the Wind*. The Duke of Windsor and George Bernard Shaw were a couple of the names on our list. Another was in connection with *Titanic,* and included the dropping of a wreath by the first Pan-American trans-Atlantic Clipper plane over the spot where the *Titanic* sank, the flowers bearing the legend "To those who showed the way to safety on the high seas."

The true test of publicity is not how much is said, but what is said, whether in a newspaper, a magazine, over the air or by word of mouth. President Roosevelt performed one of the best press agent services in months when, during the Birthday Ball in Washington, he called Janet Gaynor "cute as a button." Just four words there, but how well he described our good friend, and how the newspapers and magazines snapped it up.

In my opinion, the time is coming when the field of publicity will have reached such heights that it well may be the toughest branch in the business to break into. I wonder how many people in Hollywood realize there are more than 400 correspondents of one kind and another in town, every one feeding the world Hollywood news. Each individual style, a special preference in news, a different audience for his material. A press agent has to satisfy these markets and write for them.

Every star in Hollywood ought to take the time to work a week in a publicity department. They would find six full days of surprises and, I might mention, hard work.

Besides, they would hear from the press itself what it wants and why, without any triple-play relays in between.

Try it yourself some time.

AUTHORS' NOTE: ONE PUBLICITY SCHEME CAROLE HERSELF DREAMED UP NEVER CAME OFF. AS A GAG, SHE WANTED TO HIRE A PLANE TO FLY LOW OVER CLARK GABLE'S SET AT MGM AND DROP LEAFLETS WHICH READ "REMEMBER PARNELL"—ONE OF CLARK'S RARE BOX-OFFICE BOMBS. AT THE LAST MOMENT, THE PILOT CONSIDERED THE STUNT TOO MUCH OF A HAZARD. QUITE A GAL, THAT LOMBARD!

GRETA AND MARLENE

There was a glimmer of new hope for boxoffice gains in late summer 1931 with the first reviews of MGM's *Susan Lenox: Her Fall and Rise.* The studio's decision to co-star Greta Garbo and Clark Gable turned out to be exciting and potentially profitable. While the story itself was criticized as "warmed-over Garbo," the stars' love scenes compensated. Gable had gone "tender" in this picture, but it proved to be as provocative as his former "tough guy" image. As for Greta, she was her usual gorgeous self. When the public got a gander at the film, Gable's lover image garnered him a whole new collection of weak-kneed female *fans.*

By the end of August, there was also at least one weak-kneed *actress.* Two suits against Marlene Dietrich—one for alienation of affection, the other for libel—had been filed by the *former* wife of Josef von Sternberg. At the same time, the director's ex had hauled him into court for being late with alimony payments.

Ever since Marlene made her American debut in *Morocco,* opposite Gary Cooper, the public had eagerly lapped up any stories it could find that revealed the private life of the fantastic frau with the flawless skin, blue-green eyes and come-hither accent.

Marlene was born on December 27, 1904, as baby Mary Magdalene von Losch, in Weimar, Duchy of Saxe-Weimar, where her father, an army officer, was stationed. He was killed on the Russian front when she was eleven. After World War I, she entered Max Reinhardt's drama school in Berlin and changed her name to Marlene Dietrich. To supplement her income, she worked as an extra and bit player for Berlin's biggest film corporation, UFA.

While at UFA, she met Rudolf Sieber, an assistant director. Sieber, an attractive single man, spotted Marlene in a crowd scene and liked what he saw. So he handed her a lorgnette and focused the camera in her direction. When the reel was run, Marlene's glasses had picked up and reflected a beam of light—calling further attention to her. From this break came a bigger extra part. Sieber continued to help promote her career, and they were married only a few months later.

Dietrich worked onstage in Vienna for six months, playing in *The Great Baritone*. After a brief retirement in 1925, while she awaited the birth of her child Maria Sieber, Marlene landed a few lead roles in films, which she alternated with her stage work. She was appearing at the Berliner Theatre when famous Viennese director Josef von Sternberg spotted her. He had been working in America but had returned to Germany to fulfill a film commitment at UFA. The leading role called for a lady with great legs. Marlene fit the bill. So it was that the twosome made *The Blue Angel*.

When *Angel* was finished, von Sternberg returned to Hollywood and told everyone about "his Dietrich." His enthusiasm prompted Paramount into offering her a contract and the lead in *Morocco*. While she was making the film, a high-powered publicity campaign was started.

Since MGM had been so successful with Garbo, their Swedish import, Paramount decided to exploit its German leading lady in the same exotic manner. Before either press or public had seen one frame of film on her, huge billboards with Marlene's face—and particularly her legs—had been plastered all over the key cities in America. When *Morocco* won good reviews, Marlene was on her way. After *The Blue Angel* was shown in the United States in 1931, her stardom was assured.

There was one problem, however, that continued to plague her for quite some time. Many reviews of *Morocco*, including *The Hollywood Reporter*'s, had tossed brickbats Dietrich's way. Critics claimed that she was nothing more than an imitation Garbo. While Billy Wilkerson had rapidly changed his opinion and *The Reporter* hailed Dietrich as a potentially enormous star, other papers

Mae West and "The Blue Angel," Marlene Dietrich.

kept picking at her for years. The Garbo comparison, while personally *odious* to Marlene, was not at all helped by her own behavior.

As "strange and peculiar" as Garbo's offscreen antics sometimes were, Dietrich matched her stride for stride. First, she took to wearing men's clothing. Then she started hanging around with certain types who were not calculated to emphasize her femininity. Contrary to Garbo's total silence about such matters, Dietrich *always* had a ready defense. After all, *she* was a wife and had become a mother at age twenty-one. Before long, her baby girl was coming to join her in America. So, Dietrich loudly proclaimed, she was one hundred percent female, even if she *did* enjoy dressing in male trousers and shirts and carrying a mannish walking stick.

And yet, it was true: Dietrich and Garbo had so much about them that was alike. Garbo had been born Greta Louisa Gustafsson on September 18, 1906, and the family lived in an apartment building at 32

Blekingegaten Street on Stockholm's south side. The youngest of three children, she was fourteen when her father died. She left school and went to work in order to contribute to the family finances. Her first job was lathering men's faces in a friend's barbershop. She graduated from that to selling ladies hats in Bergstrom's Department Store. In 1921, she was given an opportunity to model hats for the store's spring catalogue—that was the unusual springboard which started her on the road to an acting career.

From the time she was a small child, Greta had been fascinated by actors. She spent hours standing outside the Southside Theatre near her home just to catch a glimpse of the performers coming and going. Her hat modeling led to a tiny part in an advertising film made about Bergstrom's Store. Her first footage showed Greta looking purposefully comical in an outsized riding habit. This led to other industrial films. In 1922, Greta had the opportunity to get a small part in a Mack Sennett-type bathing suit comedy, *Peter the Tramp*, for director Erik Petschler. She decided to take it and gave up the security of her clerk's position.

Next she auditioned for entrance to Stockholm's Dramatic School. She was accepted and worked hard during the seasons of 1922–23 and 1923–24. By February of 1924, she already called herself Greta Gustafsson Garbo, and had been seen by famous director Mauritz Stiller. He cast her in his film *Gösta Berling*.

The rest, as they say, was history. Another film with Stiller . . . MGM's offer for Stiller to direct in America . . . His refusal unless they also signed Garbo . . . The twosome's arrival in 1925. Once in Hollywood, Stiller had been unable, or unwilling, to catch on to the American system. His first efforts at directing Garbo, in *The Torrent*, were disastrous. Still, Greta clung to him. Hung on to his every word. But "the master" had been humiliated—and sailed back to Sweden. Garbo wanted to give up her chance at stardom and return with him, but Stiller insisted she stay. He literally ordered her to remain in America. And so she went on to fame and fortune, while Stiller, a broken man, died on November 18, 1928, shortly after his return home.

When she learned of his passing, Greta was in the midst of shooting *Wild Orchids*. She walked off the set and remained at home for three days, alone, brooding. Then she returned to MGM, and only once afterward did she even mention his name publicly. She insisted that "He was the man responsible for everything good in my life." Mauritz Stiller's photograph was the only one Greta ever displayed in her own home, along with a small snapshot of her family. She had been named his sole heir—but what Stiller gave Garbo could never be measured by material possessions.

With Marlene's extraordinary success came a public awareness of her apparent symbiotic relationship with von Sternberg. Dietrich acted; von Sternberg pulled the strings. Unlike Garbo, who had desperately wanted her mentor, Mauritz Stiller, to be by her side forever, but had lost him, Dietrich still had von Sternberg close to her. And while Stiller had failed to understand American film techniques, Josef von Sternberg's work in Hollywood was considered brilliant.

After several more pictures together (*Dishonored* and *Shanghai Express*), von Sternberg had Paramount's front office negotiate new contracts for himself and his star pupil. Professor Henry Higgins never did more for his "fair lady" than Josef did for "Legs" Dietrich. She received $125,000 a film, while he was paid a handsome sum for directing Marlene, plus a pecentage of the *gross* of each production. The new contracts turned Josef and Marlene into Paramount's "royal couple." In each of their subsequent pictures, the twosome would have complete control over the screenplay, the writers, the cutters who edited their films and even their technical crews. There were other unusual contractual provisions, including their control over all publicity releases and photographs of Marlene. Even Greta never had such an all-encompassing deal.

But once Mrs. Riza von Sternberg had filed her suits in New York, the newspapers were free to print all of the juicy details. The legal brief against Marlene claimed that she had "acted like a wife" to von Sternberg and even charged clohing to his account. It was also alleged that von Sternberg had furnished Marlene's apartment. For this, Riza wanted $500,000 damages. The director's ex-spouse also claimed that Marlene had libeled her in a magazine interview given prior to the von Sternberg divorce, in which she said that the director was planning to leave Riza because she was an undutiful spouse who neglected her marital obligations. Marlene was also alleged to have accused Riza of taking an active part in fomenting a move to have Dietrich's pictures boycotted in America. For this charge, Mrs. von Sternberg wanted $100,000 in damages.

Marlene did not appear in court the day von Sternberg admitted having withheld some $10,000 in alimony from Riza. He did it, he said, because Riza had agreed not to harass him; and he considered her suits against Dietrich as harassment also directed at him. He stated, however, that the alimony had subsequently been paid.

After much teutonic name calling on both sides, the lawsuit was put to rest. If there was an out-of-court settlement, it was never made public. The only further news of the whole affair involved a mutually loving exchange of letters. Marlene wrote to Riza saying the whole incident had been a misunderstanding. In her letter, Dietrich enclosed an apology from the magazine editor for misquoting her.

In Riza's reply, she graciously accepted the explanation and sought to put an end "once and for always [to the] unfortunate publicity to which both of us have been subjected."

The matter no longer made the nation's front pages. But while it had raged on, the public eagerly digested every word.

As the summer of 1933 was about to go into the record books, Laurence Olivier, imported from England to co-star with Greta Garbo in *Queen Christina*, was hastily removed from the cast. Olivier, judged too young to play opposite Garbo, was replaced at the last moment by John Gilbert. Still, he was very much in demand as a leading man. MGM offered to sign him for seven years. Unfortunately, Olivier's stage commitments at that time prevented it.

Meanwhile, Garbo seemed delighted about something for the first time in years. She was so pleased that she uttered her first official press sentences in years: "Nothing could make me happier than again to play in the same picture with Mr. Gilbert. Our association has been a most pleasant one, and it will be most gratifying to resume our careers together." Gilbert was similarly gratified.

Even the nation's theatre exhibitors applauded. They felt that Garbo and Gilbert together again was money in the bank. During the making of *Queen Christina*, Garbo and her director, Rouben Mamoulian, forged a close personal bond. They began being seen together socially, always at out-of-the-way spots. They even traveled together, but always incognito. They continued to be an "item" for the next couple of years. To this day, they remain close friends.

One typical Garbo-Mamoulian social outing took place in September of 1933. A dude ranch near Victorville, California, received a mysterious call asking whether a reservation could be made for the weekend—one which assured that the guest would

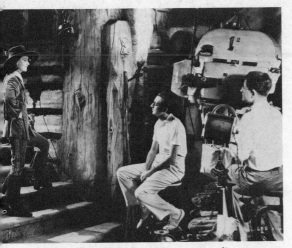

On the left, Garbo; in the center, director Rouben Mamoulian. The film: MGM's *Queen Christina*.

have the utmost privacy and seclusion. The manager said it would be arranged, in spite of the fact that the place obviously accommodated other visitors.

Two days later Greta Garbo arrived with her chauffeur, her maid and Mamoulian. Whereupon the party (with the exception of the chauffeur) secluded themselves. Each time Garbo wanted to take a stroll, her maid walked out first. She tried to run interference, and even asked the manager to have the other patrons get out of the way so that Miss Garbo might stroll "unspied upon."

After a number of such requests, guests being asked to empty the porch, the hallways and the immediate grounds, the manager had had it. He told the maid, "If you people wish to conduct yourselves as any other paying guests, you may remain. But if you insist that we put blindfolds on everyone each time Miss Garbo wants to take a walk, or a ride, you had better go someplace else."

Garbo and Mamoulian had arrived on a Saturday. They departed on Sunday.

As far as Garbo's alleged romance with John Gilbert, there has always been a difference of opinion around Hollywood as to how serious their love affair had been. Close friends of Gilbert's have said that he was madly in love with her, that he even had an entire wing built onto his home for her during a period when he had hoped to make her his wife. Those same friends also admit that when John showed Greta the new rooms, she was indifferent. Nonetheless, she did feel a sincere affection for him . . .

When *Queen Christina* was released, in December of 1933, it was an artistic triumph for Garbo and Gilbert. And the critics said it was the best directorial work Rouben Mamoulian had ever turned out. The illusion of Garbo was again a work of art.

Recently Mamoulian talked about Garbo and the qualities that made her so special.

What made Greta unique? First, it was her look. She had the ideal photogenic face. Before we started shooting *Christina*, I made some tests so that I would know how to light her properly. I had her cameraman, Billy Daniels, try using a few different lights. When we looked at the finished film, I thought, "Am I crazy, or is it possible that whatever we use she looks beautiful?" I challenged Daniels: "Let's see if we can ruin her." So he took a light and put it *below* her face, in the harshest kind of grotesque angle. She still looked magnificent. It was a God-given gift Greta had, as opposed to, say, Dietrich. Marlene looked beautiful on film, but it sometimes took two hours to light her.

Second, Garbo was thoroughly intuitive. Her subconscious had sensitivities to moods, to subtleties of emotion and feeling that cannot be reasonably explained. With Garbo, there was no point in being logical. Instead, I used metaphors. For instance, once I said: "Greta, you know the way a flower opens to the light? That's the way your face will look when you see John . . ."

From those few words, she knew instinctively what I meant—and gave it to me. It was one subconscious talking to

another. Third, Garbo had grace of movement, which can make or break a performer. She moved beautifully. But, in her case, there was an added element which was something of a mystery. It was her capacity for stirring up the spectator's imagination. With certain actors, they call it charisma . . . charm.

Some people can walk into a room, you look at them, and there is nothing there. Someone else walks in, and you can't take your eyes off of her, or him. There's something there! With Garbo, there was *always more in the spectator's eye and mind than there was onscreen.* That's a talent. An unconscious gift . . .

Yes, it's true, Greta and I saw each other for a couple of years. You know, she was very childlike in a way. On the other hand, she had a kind of basic subconscious wisdom. Those two things were quite contradictory, and the combination was very charming and attractive. But Garbo, the *person*, and Garbo, the *actress*, were two different things . . .

As far as her no-interview policy, most actors are more social. It is part of their business to communicate. But I think, in Garbo's case, the original, illusive Greta was somewhat premeditated. Her early interviews were difficult, and not too productive. So, the studio got smart. They decided it was *best* to keep her away from reporters—to let her remain a mystery. Actually, I don't think a Garbo interview would have been of much interest. That was where the difficulty came in—the magic of the onscreen Garbo, as contrasted with the real Garbo just answering mundane questions.

Obviously, from the first, the whole ploy had to appeal to something within Greta. Finally, it became part of her. Her *modus operandi.* The more she shied away, the more publicity she got. Her aloof style made her more famous and written about than if she had talked. A mystery woman stops being one if she speaks. At least, with Garbo, the illusion would have been gone. Without answers, one's imagination takes flight. Greta was just not very social around strangers. At a dinner party, with a few friends, she could be charming, lively, and was capable of enjoying herself.

Yet, on balance, she was not a very happy person. That's the last thing you could say about Garbo, that she was happy. But then, most performers are not happy. It's a tough job—being a star. You reach a pinnacle. There's only one way to go—down. It's inevitable. Stars look at themselves. They see that their beauty is gone. Their youth is past. It's a tough experience, and much harder on actresses. Beauty has so much to do with their fame.

In that respect Garbo was and is lucky. The public thinks of her in only one way: beautiful, young, charming, unblemished. She contributed a legend to the screen. It still remains.

Jimmy Durante
"NO MORE WOMEN!"

On September 18, 1933, The Hollywood Reporter *ran this piece written by Jimmy Durante in his own inimitable style.*

Garbo sent for Gilbert!
Well, that lets me out—I'm a complete nonentity or its equal in Swedish! After all the publicity I've gotten Greta. Posed for pictures waiting with bouquets outside her dressing room. Even if the publicity department did buy the flowers, I had my heart in them, just the same.

So Garbo sent for Gilbert. And after five years!
To the victor belongs the spoils . . .
All I can say is—you're a better man than I am, John Gilbert. But my nose is still longer than yours!
Am I off women?
Ha! Get 'em out of my path! From now on,

it's Durante, the hermit of Ocean Park—Durante, the laugh-clown-laugh guy who won't wear his heart on anybody's sleeve.

No more women!

Durante's through. From now on I'm a woman hater—no matter how mortifying!

The other day I'm walking down the main drag of the MGM studio and I finds myself an island floating in a sea of femininity—you know, women. Chorus girls, in shorts and bathing suits and some had on even less as far as I could see . . . and I couldn't help but seeing!

What do I do?

Here I am. Women to the right of me. Women to the left of me. It's positively mortifying—me, whose giving Garbo the air. The situation is acuter and acuter. One of the blonders giving me the eye is acuter and acuter too. I act quick.

"Girls," I shout. "There's no use following me. I'm completely out of circulation. To be more subtle—SCRAM!"

The blonde hauled off and socked me in the jaw. A beefy brunette tore off my coat. Another gave me the high heels. The rest AD LIBBED.

When Peggy, the nurse, brought me to, I blinked the only eye I could blink and looked up in astonishment.

"What happened?" I says, naturally being curious minded.

Peggy sponges arnica into my wounds and starts to embroider an ear into place.

"Don't talk to me, you wolf in Brooks clothing," she says. "Insulting those little ladies just because you think you're a big shot and can get away with it—I've a good mind to wallop you in the other eye!"

Well, that's how it is. A guy just can't convince he's on the level. They won't believe he don't want nothing to do with them.

Like when I'm walking down the boulevard the other afternoon with my family tagging

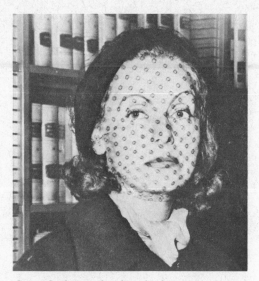

Greta Garbo on the day she became a United States citizen.

along—you know, taking the kids out to see the funny sights on the beach—as if they don't see enough at home. Anyway, there I am walking down the boardwalk with the kids trailing along.

Suddenly up comes a policeman.

"You're under arrest!" he says, grabbing me by the coat collar like a Baxter street suit salesman.

I'm aghast. I'm nonplussed. In fact, I'm mad.

"See here," I says. "You're making a frightful mistake, my good fellow. I'm a citizen and a taxpayer. I'm peaceful and law-abiding. How can you place me under arrest when I haven't done anything?"

The cop yanked me around.

"You musta done something," he growled, "to have the crowd following you!"

So here I am again. Disconsolate. Or maybe it's only chagrin.

Maybe I oughter go back after Greta.

HOLLYWOOD POTPOURRI
1933

After a brief flurry of holiday business, the movie industry was back in a slump. The big New York theatres reduced their admission prices while some houses just closed their doors altogether . . . It was announced that in 1932 motion pictures had lost *one hundred million dollars*, which certainly gave

all of Hollywood pause for thought.

For the next few months, with rare exception, people stayed away from picture shows in droves. MAE WEST and CARY GRANT scored in *She Done Him Wrong*, despite a huge protest from some of the women's groups that "the film was steeped in sin and sex." In fact, during this period, S and S seemed to be the *only* commodity that *was* selling.

The very next boxoffice hit was *Gold Diggers of 1933,* a big splashy musical with scantily clad dancing girls for enticement . . . Then along came GABLE and HARLOW in *Hold Your Man,* which featured JEAN in a sufficient number of clinging satin gowns to raise the temperatures of the male audience . . .

BILLY WILKERSON opened a mini-restaurant, The Vendome, on Sunset Boulevard across from *The Reporter.* Soon, the stars were dining out again, and Billy had most of their business. But it took the chic and wealthy COUNTESS DOROTHY DI FRASSO to actually christen the place. On the first Saturday in June, she took over the entire restaurant and tossed an Old English Costume Ball. The Countess led the way by changing her costume several times until she had worked up to an ensemble that included a stylish wig and an expensive set of false teeth. Director EDMUND GOULDING put his hair up and appeared garbed as an English nursemaid. LILYAN TASHMAN arrived as Gainsborough's "Duchess of Devonshire," while gorgeous JOAN BENNETT appeared as "the fair maid Elaine." BILLY HAINES wore an Eton schoolboy's uniform. GEORGE CUKOR appeared in monk's robes as a friar. The SAM GOLDWYNS, DAVID O. SELZNICKS and CLARK GABLES were also suitably costumed; Gable looked especially fetching in a Tower of London guardsman's regalia—albeit reluctantly! From that evening forward, The Vendome was the place to be seen.

In June, child star JACKIE COOGAN turned eighteen, while another "juvenile," JACKIE COOPER, had an appendectomy . . . OLIVER "BABE" HARDY sued for divorce, charging mental cruelty and intoxication. The Hardys had been married since 1921 . . . On June 29, ROSCOE "FATTY" ARBUCKLE died of a heart attack in New York. He had recently finished a comedy short, *In the Dough.* It had been one of only six small films that he had been allowed to make after seven years of not working following his rape trials. Film mogul JOSEPH SCHENCK wrote a glowing tribute to Arbuckle, which appeared in *The Reporter:* "His was the tragedy of a man born to make the world laugh, and to receive only suffering as his reward. And yet, to the end, he held no malice . . . He felt that he had done no wrong, the courts of justice confirmed him in his belief and yet—Destiny had turned its back on him. That is how he felt, that no one personally was against him, but merely fate."

GARBO rented a home on San Vicente in Los Angeles but was having trouble hiring servants to staff the place. There were rumors that she required a butler-chauffeur who was "neither too formal, nor too cold; well-educated, polite and, above all, discreet!" . . . And, before summer grew too old, the JOHN GILBERTS anxiously awaited the arrival of a mate for their pet Guatemalan squirrel, who was definitely "ready for love-making."

The DARRYL ZANUCKS tossed a beefsteak on their outdoor patio with DFZ personally grilling all of the filet mignons to perfection. Among the guests were HELEN HAYES, JIMMY CAGNEY, the COUNTESS DI FRASSO with GARY COOPER and JOE SCHENCK . . . There was trouble reported in the GEORGE BRENT—RUTH CHATTERTON marriage . . . In mid-July, IRVING and NORMA SHEARER THALBERG sailed into New York harbor and practically the entire staff of MGM was at the dock to greet them. Irving looked fit and rested—his weight was up to 129 pounds, four more than usual.

The romance between CONSTANCE BENNETT and GILBERT ROLAND was definitely out in the open. They were happily dining in public and unchaperoned . . . TALLULAH BANKHEAD made a killing on the stock market, but wouldn't say where she got her inside tips . . . HARPO MARX had all of his hair shaved off so water wouldn't drip down his face when he worked under his tousled wig . . . GABLE had his tonsils removed and the nurses were doing nipups fighting to attend everybody's all-time favorite leading man . . . And GRETA GARBO spent the weekend on JOE SCHENCK's yacht, *The Invader,* along with WALTER WANGER, who borrowed the craft in order to hold a private story conference with GG about her next film, *Queen Christina.*

There were several very loud summertime fights around Tinseltown. CHARLES CHAPLIN and PAULETTE GODDARD'S was so serious, insiders said their romance was off. Paulette left for London by way of Chicago. She stopped off in the Windy City hoping to receive a message from Charlie asking her to turn around and come home. After all, she had dyed her hair brunette to please him. What greater sacrifice could a leading lady make?? . . . And the heat was still rising after the donnybrook between AL JOLSON and WALTER WINCHELL, who got into a terrific fight at Hollywood Legion Stadium, where both had gone to see the weekly bouts. But Joley wound up poking Walter in the snout even before the main event got under way. The whole thing started after someone told

Jolson that Winchell had sold a script, "Broadway Through a Keyhole," which purported to be "the real inside story of the Jolson-Keeler marriage." Winchell, who had been punched by surprise, was furious because he'd had no opportunity to land a right cross of his own. Besides, he vehemently denied that his story had anything to do with Jolson's intimate life. Round one was over. Round two still to come . . .

By August, the MIRIAM HOPKINS—KING VIDOR romance was on ice. Hopkins' intimates said she liked going places, while Vidor preferred staying home and holding on tightly to his purse strings . . . CLARK GABLE was rushed back to the hospital, this time to have his appendix removed. He was very sick for a few days. The same nurses were still fighting over who brought him pills and put the ice pack on his sore spot . . . The JOHN GILBERTS had a baby daughter . . . TALLULAH BANKHEAD had lunch at the Assistance League. Some say it had a strange effect on her—on the drive home she stopped and bought a monkey . . . Speaking of the animal kingdom, JEAN HARLOW was spotted lunching in her MGM dressingroom alone—except for two English sheepdogs . . . And the JOHN BARRYMORES and their entire retinue returned from Juneau, Alaska, having caught enough fish to start their own hatchery.

September was a quiet month—LUPE VELEZ bought herself only one diamond bracelet . . . And the rumors were roaming around Hollywood that CHAPLIN and GODDARD were secretly man and wife, in contrast to equally strong whispers that they would never wed.

In October, Hollywood took a hiatus on the social front. There was not even one drunken Halloween party to report on. But by November, the partying was back to a frenzied peak.

1 Left to Right: George Raft, Fredric March, Adolphe Menjou, Groucho Marx, James Cagney; seated: Warner Oland. This photo was taken at a Screen Actors Guild meeting held in Hollywood, October 9, 1933. The Guild, headed by Eddie Cantor (not shown here), assembled to protest unfair competition and the reduction in wages, both hot issues among actors during that period.   2 An MGM gala premiere night. Left to Right: Irving Thalberg; his wife, Norma Shearer; and Louis B. Mayer.   3 Interior of Wilkerson's world-famous Cafe Trocadero, where Hollywood's elite gathered.

On November 7, beginning at 10 P.M. and continuing until dawn, there was a *new* New Year's Eve celebration held at The Vendome. PROHIBITION had officially come to an end, and one hundred couples were invited to join the pilgrimage "to the resurrection of John Barleycorn." GROUCHO MARX, JIMMY DURANTE, TED HEALY and CHARLES BUTTERWORTH presided over the formal ceremonies. All of Sunset Boulevard was one massive party that evening, as was every main street across America. Conditions in the country, and specifically in the film industry, were still bad and growing worse. But at least now all of the folks who cared to could drown their sorrows—legally.

CLARK GABLE was in a bad way when he discovered that some cad had run over his pet chow dog. He felt so awful that he and a few cronies took off for a weekend in San Francisco . . . The HARRY COHNS gave a dinner party at The Vendome along with co-host MADAME FRANCES, the friendliest owner of the poshest brothel in Los Angeles. Among their guests were JOAN CRAWFORD and FRANCHOT TONE, the BRUCE CABOTS and SOPHIE TUCKER, who sang for her supper and didn't quit until the wee hours.

France's top plastic surgeon, DR. SERGE VORONOFF, just finished a film short of one of his operations. Called *The Cry of Youth*, it had provoked a lot of interest among the celebrity set . . . In mid-November, a flu epidemic sent half of the film performers under the covers . . . Those who were well enough continued to pack the latest "in" spot, the Colony Club, where behind-the-door gambling was extremely popular. CONSTANCE BENNETT made a killing at the roulette wheel, while CLARA BOW, with her bright red hair, all dressed up in green and wearing orange gloves, did fairly well for herself at the blackjack table. When someone joked that she had better be careful

or she'd lose the diamond buckles on her shoes, Clara just grinned: "Honey, these days I'm wearin' rhinestones, particularly to places where there's gamblin'!"

By the time Thanksgiving was over, Hollywood was in a state of shock. The weekly boxoffice grosses for the entire film industry had hit rock bottom. During the week of November 27, it was announced that losses for the previous two and a half months had amounted to ten million dollars. Hollywood cooks and maids were saving the family turkey carcasses to make soup . . . Despite the bad news, there were *still* some who could afford to toss lavish parties. JOAN BENNETT'S cronies gave her a lovely baby shower. She received lots of lovely loot, including golden baby spoons and lacey coverlets from IRENE SELZNICK, EDIE GOETZ, BESSIE LOVE and the rest of the gals.

In mid-December, KATE HEPBURN opened in Washington, D.C., in *The Lake*. It was one of the gala social events of the winter season. The audience was full of congressmen, senators, and foreign diplomats . . . MAE WEST'S unsolicited check to the Motion Picture Relief Fund in the amount of one thousand dollars came just in the nick of time to give a brighter holiday to many unfortunate Hollywood families . . . On the 15th, GARY COOPER married socialite-actress SANDRA SHAW, real name, VERONICA "ROCKY" BALFE, in his suite at the Waldorf-Astoria. Afterward, they boarded a train headed for a honeymoon in Arizona . . . One of the most popular, inexpensive gifts around Hollywood that Christmas was a metal flower dish that resembled pewter but was pliable enough to look lovely when filled with gardenias. The attractive object, which sold for $7.50, was one of the favorite gifts celebrities gave to their household staff and studio crew.

1934

As the year began, FRANKLIN ROOSEVELT was firmly ensconced in the White House. He received an air mail copy of *The Hollywood Reporter* each morning. FDR kept in touch with all of filmland's big events, despite his main preoccupation. The state of the economy, while improved, was still far from anything to cheer about . . . But, in Hollywood, HOWARD HUGHES was cheering. He had finally won his two-year battle with Illinois censors. *Scarface* was shown in Chicago for the first time. However, no one recorded the mob's review of the film.

Los Angeles police drew extra duty at the Marcal Theatre. Armed with rolls of adhesive tape, officers carefully cut strips and stuck them over the exposed breasts of the poster cuties who advertised BRYAN FOY'S nudest picture to date, *Elysia* . . . On the 10th of February, CARY GRANT married VIRGINIA CHERRILL, CHARLIE CHAPLIN'S *City Lights* leading lady. Shortly before the nuptials in London, the bride came down with a sore throat and the groom had a tooth pulled. It was a painful portent of things to come. The beautiful blue-eyed blonde, and

the charming Cary, who had been marvelous unmarried lovers, turned out to be incompatible spouses. Eleven months later, the Grant-Cherrill merger was only a memory . . . Also having marital troubles was comedian STAN LAUREL. Because of alimony problems, he said that he was leaving America to live abroad. It signaled the end of the LAUREL–HARDY combo, at least for a while.

In March, after she had won an Oscar for *Mornig Glory*, KATE HEPBURN asked RKO for a salary raise. She was earning $1,000 a week and wanted at least double that amount. To bolster her point, Hepburn cited some current weekly salaries she'd read about in local papers: GARBO—$9,000; CONNIE BENNETT—$7,000; NORMA SHEARER—$6,000 per, and JOAN CRAWFORD—$4,000. She had made her point! . . . Meanwhile, young leading man RAY MILLAND, who had just been signed by Paramount, read the same article and was overjoyed. Despite the Depression, Hollywood wages certainly beat the money he had earned acting in England.

April brought SHIRLEY TEMPLE and her remarkable performance in *Little Miss Marker* to an adoring public. It was a smash hit, although certain women's clubs objected to the amazing four-year old's rendition of a torch song in the film. They said it made her seem too precocious . . . Springtime found CHARLES CHAPLIN extremely happy. Although he would not publicly admit it, he was in love again with beautiful green-eyed PAULETTE GODDARD, and his immediate film plans involved her. They were working on *Street Waif* and then were expected to do *The Women of Paris*. Afterward, while Paulette rested, Charlie was expected to star in a film on his own, *Napoleon Bonaparate*. Insiders said it was the perfect Chaplin role—Charlie acted like an emperor anyway.

In London, MAE WEST'S *I'm No Angel*, did fabulous business the second time around. The British had taken Mae to their collective bosom. Obviously, her comic turn of phrase and her outright audacity struck a responsive

1 Maurice Chevalier, Mae West, and Cary Grant pose for photographers.   2 Left to right: Franklin Ardell, Norma Shearer, Paulette Goddard, and Charlie Chaplin cruise on the yacht *Invader*, owned by film mogul Joe Schenck, 1934. (UPI)   3 Wedding portrait of Ginger Rogers and Lew Ayres, November 14, 1934.

chord in the English psyche . . . STAN LAUREL had not gone to Europe after all. Instead, he only complicated his alimony troubles when he eloped to Mexico with RUTH ROGERS. Since his divorce was not final for five more months, living with Ruth was legal in every state—but California. BABE HARDY, back in Hollywood, seemed confused.

In May, there was a marvelously exciting polo match between the actors and producers at the Uplifters Club for the benefit of the Marion Davies Clinic. When all of the horses and men had "done their thing," it was the actors' group which romped home triumphant. Led by WILL ROGERS, the team consisted of LESLIE HOWARD, JOHNNY MACK BROWN, SPENCER TRACY and JIMMY GLEASON. The defeated producers were: JACK WARNER, WALT DISNEY, LUCIEN HUBBARD and FRANK BORZAGE. The event, witnessed by a star-studded crowd, ended when the winners received trophies—elegant cocktail shakers—personally presented by CAROLE LOMBARD . . . And HEDDA HOPPER, who gave up acting to become an agent, turned to writing gossip for various fan magazines.

June was the month when religious groups, women's clubs, and the movie audiences in general gave Hollywood moguls a collective case of the heaves. It seemed as if everyone was marching against smut and sex on screen—and the industry was told to clean up its act. So, they adopted the Purity Seal the following month.

On July 28, MARIE DRESSLER lost her fight against cancer. She died in Santa Barbara; funeral services were held at the Wee Kirk o' the Heather, in Forest Lawn, Los Angeles . . . JEAN HARLOW and WILLIAM POWELL shared a table at WILKERSON'S Vendome. Since an appearance at Billy's restaurant was tantamount to sending everyone a Western Union telegram, the twosome's togetherness was duly noted . . . In Martha's Vineyard, Harlow's ex-boss, HOWARD HUGHES, spent a night in jail. He was arrested for speeding and driving without either a license or registration.

As summer warmed up, Fox had some heated discussions with representatives for their new "Little Queen," SHIRLEY TEMPLE. Papa Temple asked for $2,500 per week. Before her triumph in *Little Miss Marker*, Shirley had earned only $150. Fox offered five hundred, but Temple, a banker, stood pat. Shirley was upped to $1,000 a week—with the promise of future bonuses . . . BILLY WILKERSON opened a rather fabulous new club on the Sunset Strip, com-

plete with French decor, striped awnings and the West Coast's first oyster bar. He called it CAFE TROCADERO, and it rapidly became a new celebrity "in" spot.

On September 2, 1934, a tragic accident took the life of popular stage, screen and radio singer, twenty-six-year-old RUSS COLUMBO. He had been cleaning one of the guns he used for hunting when it went off and fatally wounded him. Russ and CAROLE LOMBARD had been seriously dating for some months. The suddenness of his passing stunned Carole and all of his friends and fans. Funeral services were held at Hollywood's Church of the Blessed Sacrament, with BING CROSBY, GILBERT ROLAND and ZEPPO MARX among the pallbearers.

WALTER WANGER signed a young Broadway actor, HENRY FONDA, to a long-term contract. The same week, FONDA and his closest pal, JIMMY STEWART, toasted Hank's forthcoming Hollywood trek as well as Stewart's rave reviews for his performance on Broadway as JUDITH ANDERSON's son in *Divided by Three* . . .

On November 14, LEW AYRES, whose marriage to LOLA LANE had fallen apart, went to the altar again, this time with dancing-acting star GINGER ROGERS. It had been a somewhat long and frustrating courtship. Ginger's pal, SUE CAROL, admitted that Rogers was so head-over-heels in love with Ayres in the early days of their courtship that she had stretched out on the floor of Sue's car while Miss Carol drove back and forth in front of Lew's house just to make sure he wasn't seeing another girl while dating Ginger! Roger's persistence had paid off. What Lola (Lane) didn't want, Ginger happily got! The nuptials took place at the romantic Little Church of the Flowers.

In December, WILLIAM POWELL moved into a huge new mansion, which his friends nicknamed the Palace of Versailles, and gave a gala housewarming. Since the place was totally bare—except for the rugs and a few chairs—the biggest "happening" of the night occurred when JEAN HARLOW helped Bill light his new marble fireplace. Despite the warmth of the fiery glow, Powell subsequently got cold feet, sold the palazzo and moved into a smaller home . . . By midmonth, Hollywood held its collective breath. Indications were that the worst of the boxoffice slump was over. Holiday business was the best it had been in years. As one positive reaction, MGM rewarded its employees with a Christmas bonus: salaries were brought back up to pre-1932 levels.

Stan Laurel and Oliver Hardy
"YOU, TOO, CAN BE A COMEDIAN!"

These two internationally beloved comedians wrote this amusing piece for The Hollywood Reporter *in September of 1935.*

This is not a gag. Others have given advice to the lovelorn, secrets of worldly success to diploma holders; straight-from-the-shoulder talks on every subject from raising the baby to running the country. It's high time that someone from the ranks of the screen's so-called funsters steps forward and "teaches the young how to shoot," or at least how to throw custard pies, so to speak, and that's what we propose to do here and now! Yes, you, too, can be a comedian—and without correspondence, at that. All it takes is what you've got, plus a little common sense, if you know what we mean.

If there is a dearth of film funsters today it's your fault. However, it is not too late for you to get into this easy-money class. There is no obligation nor nothing to buy. Not even a coupon to sign! This is to be our contribution to posterity or what is left of it. Now then, let's get down to business.

So you want to be a comedian? Before embarking on this line of endeavor, one should first check their qualifications against the following questionnaire which has been standardized by the Association of Alleged Funny Fellows of Filmland, of which organization the writers of this article are associate members without portfolio:

1. Do your relatives and friends laugh at your jokes? (Answer Yes or No or Both.)
2. Are you a student of Madison's Budget or The World's Greatest Collection of Jokes, or are you just naturally funny?
3. Do you own baggy trousers, a derby or straw hat, oversize shoes and unusual cravats?
4. Can you exist without food for days at a time? Why?
5. Name the two funniest comedians in pictures today. (Remember who it is who is helping you get into the movies!)
6. Does your wife understand you now? If so, why do you want to get funny?
7. Are you good at cracking (1.) parlor jokes; (2.) practical jokes; (3.) bedtime stories; (4.) your knuckles?
8. Are you the life of the party, and will they laugh when you sit down to eat?

Having answered the above questions satisfactorily there remains but little for you to do before securing a job, and this should be comparatively easy if you study your approach.

Some advocate the Friend or Relative Studio Executive entree to accomplish this end, while there are others who hold out for the Give-Until-It-Hurts system. Then again there are plenty of protagonists of the Rest-On-Your-Own-Merit plan who are willing to do or die along these lines.

Regardless of what system you employ in making your studio contact, it is necessary that you be able to talk fluently on the subjects of golf, bridge, night spots and Shakespeare in order to lead up to the business of securing employment as a funnyman. And speaking of bridge, not a few aspiring comics have made the grade by filling in as a fourth at this game. One highly important qualification for screen jester fame is one's ability to meet newspaper and magazine writers as man to man without flinching. Here, we give you a few tried and true remarks to toss off for the benefit of the third degree-ers of the fourth estate during the course of such a grilling:

(1.) I am looking forward to the day when I can do Hamlet.
(2.) There is no secret of my success. I guess I was just born funny.
(3.) No, custard pie isn't my favorite dessert.
(4.) Chaplin and W. C. Fields are all right in their way.
(5.) One has to have suffered to be a comedian.

Now then, we almost overlooked a very essential bit of advice that you will need if you hope to climb the ladder to success as a screen funster. Hire yourself a high-powered press agent at once to exploit your personality, your social activities and the fact that you are good to your mother. This breaks the ice and assists in securing an entree for you in the offices of the moguls of moviedumb. Be sure and carry your press clipping book with you at all times so that you can meet any emergency. Also, it may be necessary to refer to this volume from time to time so that you consistently live up to the things your press agent says about you. But always call him "my publicity counsel" when addressing a supervisor or producer.

If you have carefully read and digested all of the above you are just about ready to crack down on the studios. But before doing so, hire an old Model T break-away Ford so that you can drive up in front of a producer's sanctum and do your stuff in front of his office window prior to making personal contact. This is sure-fire and some of the boys have been invited into his presence before they had a chance to send in their cards after executing a few comical didoes as outlined. And this brings us to the subject of your professional cards. And this, too, is highly important, so important, in fact, that we are giving you here a sample of the style of card that is being used this season by we boys of the profession. Of course, the name is fictitious:

I. M. NUTZ
Professional Comic
(Own My Own Wardrobe)
Expert at Pratt Falling—108's, High Gruesomes and Double Takems.
Nifty Dresser On and Off
Facial Contortionist
and Can Double Brass.
(Address and Telephone Number here)

This is a proven ticket of admission to the most impregnable offices. It is yours for the taking and with it go our blessing and best wishes.

Oh, yes, there is one other thing we almost forgot. Be sure and arm yourself with a bunch of letters of recommendation from your Sunday School teacher, the village elocutionist, your favorite bartender and such other influential citizens as you can think of, before bearding a potential employer in his den. Most producers can read and have a lot of time on their hands and love to peruse such testimonials.

HOLLYWOOD POTPOURRI

1935

MAE WEST hit Paramount where it lived—in the checkbook. Her manager flew to New York to arrange a new deal. Mae's contract paid her $10,000 a week when she worked, with a minimum guarantee of seven weeks per picture. The new demand was for a percentage of her gross boxoffice receipts. Although she had almost singlehandedly helped Paramount out of a deep financial crisis when her first two films made the studio a fortune, Mae's timing was off. Paramount Studios was in deep trouble. Eastern banking houses were about to take over if reorganization plans, currently under way, did not meet with their satisfaction. So for the moment it was a standoff.

During January, GRETA GARBO'S "best pal," writer MERCEDES DE ACOSTA, wrote what she thought was a marvelous role for GG. Greta had encouraged her to do the script, and Mercedes had worked long and hard over the material, which she declared was "sheer poetry." But at the last minute GG turned cool toward the idea, Mercedes was offended, and a long and loud behind-closed-doors discussion went on—for days. When they had fin-

ished talking, Mercedes tossed the screenplay into the nearest wastebasket and went off to New York in a huff. But the whole matter was subsequently "forgotten," and de Acosta returned to Greta's side and resumed her role as Garbo's chief business spokesman with MGM.

Despite the continuing competition from radio and the latest industry financial crisis, the usual social activities went on among the very solvent. Friends who visited the DARRYL ZANUCK home had themselves a ball inspecting the children's playhouse which Darryl and Virginia had given their kids for Christmas. It had three rooms and included a fully equipped kitchen with running water, electricity and a working refrigerator and stove. There were quite a few unemployed actors who would have loved such accommodations—permanently.

JOAN CRAWFORD and FRANCHOT TONE tossed a smashing soirée at their Brentwood mansion to bid a temporary farewell to both HELEN HAYES, who was returning to Broadway, and the FRED ASTAIRES, who were going to Europe. The dinner party, which began with dollops of caviar and wound up with flaming crepe suzettes, was superb. Joan's best china and crystal gleamed at the elegant dining room table, and the guests could barely waddle into Crawford's playroom for the after-dinner charades which followed. PHYLLIS ASTAIRE won the prize for the best charade, and Fred honored his hostess by leading the guests in a community songfest.

The Trocadero, nicknamed the "meeting place of the stars," rated itself an unqualified success. GRETA GARBO showed up there the last Sunday in January. During the evening, a gentleman entered and spotted a lady who looked like his friend LILI DAMITA from the back. He thought it was Lili because of the unique hairdo. So he snuck up, touched her on the shoulders and simultaneously yelled "Hello, Toots!" The head attached to the shoulders swiveled. The guy looked into the face of the Gorgeous Swede and literally collapsed on the floor. Greta smiled and continued eating her steamed vegetables.

In February, the SAM GOLDWYNS opened their new home and gave an elegant tea party in honor of the COLE PORTERS. Among the guests were the FRED ASTAIRES, the IRVING BERLINS, MARY PICKFORD and CONNIE BENNETT with GILBERT ROLAND. The same crowd was also at a party the Berlins gave the next night for the Porters and MOSS HART. In the wee hours of the morning, the guests of honor, who hadn't been to bed, departed on an around-the-world cruise . . . Meanwhile, JOHN BARRYMORE was already in Europe where he had his famous face lifted by one of the Continent's best plastic surgeons. Before he left, buddy W. C. FIELDS pleaded with Barrymore to be sure he was sober when the doctor worked on his face. Even Barrymore thought that was funny . . . And the advertisement for the latest feature at Grauman's Chinese Theatre raised some eyebrows: "Three Gay Stars! CRAWFORD, GABLE, and MONTGOMERY in MGM's *Forsaking All Others*."

By March, local bars were featuring a new drink guaranteed to make even movie moguls forget their dwindling profits. The concoction: fifty percent peach brandy, fifty percent sweet whipping cream, plus lots of finely chopped ice. The trick was to have the bartender shake vigorously while he counted to fifteen—fast. Hollywoodites, who made batches of the brew at home, were advised to have all of the ingredients ready to go. The problem was that the exotic beverage had to be downed immediately. If not, it tasted like wallpa-

per . . . Another "new brew" was MAX FACTOR's introduction of a startling new liquid foundation makeup, "Satin Smooth," which had all of Hollywood agog. It was a panchromatic foundation guaranteed to cover every blemish.

April was a bad month for Fox Studio. They unceremoniously dropped SPENCER TRACY in the belief he would never win public acceptance as a big movie star. A few hours later, Tracy signed with MGM. The rest would become box-office history . . . New young leading man DAVID NIVEN, whose only acting experience had been limited to the screen test that won him a contract with SAM GOLDWYN, went to work at the Pasadena Playhouse in order to gain some experience . . . There was a serious and tragic accident in May which sent JACKIE COOGAN to the Physicians and Surgeons' hospital. His father and three others, including the Coogans' ranch foreman, died in the crash.

By summertime, business was looking up. *David Copperfield* and *Anna Karenina*, with GARBO, were among the big boxoffice winners . . . But, playing a losing game, mogul HARRY COHN moved out of the family home and went to stay with his attorney. There were rumors of a pretty young actress, JOAN PERRY, in his future . . . CLARK GABLE broke records in a speedboat race to Catalina . . . Garbo signed a new MGM contract and began her eleventh year at the studio . . . W. C. FIELDS was ill and confined to his bed at home in Encino. His medics would not permit visitors, and he could not return to work for two months . . . Young BETTY GRABLE was borrowed for a Paramount picture, *Collegiate*. She had an extra glow when she reported for work. Friends said it was because Grable was in love with a guy named CHARLIE MACE, a member of TED FIO RITO's band.

By September the overwhelming success of the FRED ASTAIRE—GINGER ROGERS musicals, and the fans' acceptance of ELEANOR POWELL in *Broadway Melody* had every studio sending talent scouts across country to look for new musical talent . . . GEORGE RAFT led a caravan of Hollywood stars back East for the MAX BAER—JOE LOUIS fight. The group, which included EDWARD G. ROBINSON, RICARDO CORTEZ, BERT WHEELER, the RICHARD BARTHELMESSES and WALLACE BEERY, all stayed at the Waldorf, and after the fight, they made merry at the Stork Club and Leon and Eddie's.

Over in Berlin, CHARLES CHAPLIN's productions were the latest to be banned by the Nazis. All of them. The reason given for the ban:

"Chaplin is not 'pure Aryan.'" ... Back in Hollywood, all pool owners with children were warned to put up fences or guard rails around their pools following the near-fatal accident which happened to FREDRIC MARCH'S daughter, PENELOPE. She rode her tricycle into the deep end of the swimming pool. Fortunately, Freddie saw the accident and rescued his young child in time.

Even Hollywood's uppercrust set was stunned by the opulence of COUNTESS DI FRASSO'S beautifully redecorated Beverly Hills mansion, especially after the lavish dinner party she tossed for one hundred celebrants, who wined and dined, played backgammon and bridge, and then danced until dawn. Among the guests were the SAM GOLDWYNS, the CLARK GABLES, GEORGE CUKOR, MARY PICKFORD, the RICARDO CORTEZES—but Dorothy's "best pal," GARY COOPER, *didn't* show up! In New York, wealthy industrialist WALTER CHRYSLER gave a cocktail soirée in honor of newlyweds JOAN CRAWFORD and FRANCHOT TONE.

The following evening, socialite JOCK WHITNEY tossed a dinner pary for the popular pair.

In November SHIRLEY TEMPLE, under yet a new "arrangement" with 20th Century–Fox, was raised to $4,000 a week, for fifty-two weeks a year. The six-year-old thus became the highest-paid child in the world. Under a special bonus clause, Shirley also received an extra $20,000 per picture, plus a weekly "tip" of another $1,000 for endorsing certain commercial products, namely a doll, a hat, a dress and a breakfast food. One hundred dollars a week was paid to Shirley's mother for driving her daughter to and from the studio. Shirley had become the biggest little gold mine in Tinseltown history.

As Hollywood celebrated the Christmas season, over in Germany ADOLF HITLER confiscated all movie theatres owned by people of Jewish origin. His stated objective was to remove all the Jews from any connection with the German film industry.

1936

January began with a big bang. Paramount decided they had had all of MAE WEST'S temperament they could take. The studio planned not to pick up their option on her services—and let Mae sashay her hips straight off their lot. Madame West, never one to let any grass grow under her tiny feet, was unofficially dickering with other studios. Everyone who knew her claimed that when Mae dickered, she always came out on top.

The winter season saw a pickup in movie business with *Anything Goes,* the smash BING CROSBY–ETHEL MERMAN starrer. Then VICTOR McLAGLEN hit big in *The Informer,* ROGERS and ASTAIRE clicked in *Follow the Fleet,* and the WALTER WANGER–Paramount production of *Trail of the Lonesome Pine* became the first outdoor Technicolor thriller to find audiences lined up at the boxoffice.

On the 3rd of April, KATHARINE HEPBURN returned to the United States, aboard the S.S. *Paris,* the same ship that had just transported her abroad. After four days in France, Kate suddenly had decided to come home. Hepburn said her quickie holiday had been " . . . a salute to impulse. I don't know from one moment to the next what I'm going to do. My plans are usually pretty much uncertain. I'm going to rest for a while, and then do another film."

Three weeks later, a woman registered at the Hotel Itza, in Yucatan, Mexico, as Mrs. Ludlow Smith. A petition for divorce had been filed on her behalf by a local attorney, Francisco Arcovedo Guillermo. When reporters got wind of the fact that "Mrs. Smith" was KATE HEPBURN, they pleaded for a press conference. Kate would not discuss her private life. Her petition alleged that she and Smith had been married on December 12, 1928, in West Hartford, Connecticut. The thirty-two-year-old Smith, contacted in New York, also declined comment. He was from a socially prominent Philadelphia family, and had married Kate four years before Broadway took notice of her in *The Warrior's Husband.* Not only was divorce granted, but the usual three-hundred-day legal waiting period before remarriage was waived at the request of both parties. There were rumors that Kate was paving the way for a marriage to LELAND HAYWARD. At the time, Hayward, although separated from his wife, was still technically married. The twosome *was* subsequently seen out on the town, both in Hollywood and New York. But if there ever was anything serious between them, it eventually became just a close friendship.

In mid-April, TYRONE POWER, JR., appearing on Broadway in *St. Joan,* was signed by DARRYL

1

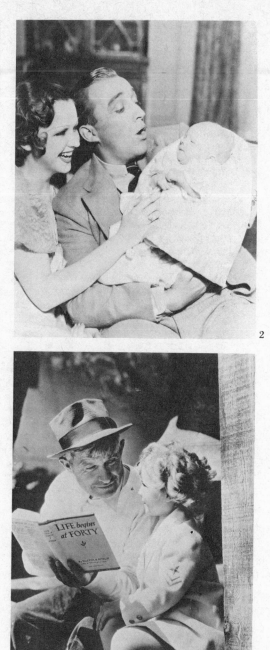

2

3

4

1 Mae West attends an industry dinner—and as usual is surrounded by men. Seated to Mae's left, Gary Cooper. Standing behind Cooper, W. C. Fields.   2 Bing and Dixie Lee Crosby with their first baby son, Gary. Bing was starring at the time in Paramount's *We're Not Dressing*, 1934.   3 Sonja Henie, the great Norwegian ice skating champion, Olympic gold medal winner, and 20th Century–Fox star.   4 America's most beloved humorist, Will Rogers, with Shirley Temple on the 20th Century–Fox lot.

ZANUCK to an exclusive 20th Century—Fox contract. Ty finished playing the juvenile lead opposite KATHARINE CORNELL, and flew to Hollywood on the first available plane.

On the very same April day, SONJA HENIE, European champion figure skater, signed an MGM contract. Eventually she wound up working at Fox with Ty, and they became "a close romantic duo," courtesy of the 20th publicity department.

In May, the high price celebrities paid for stardom was evident when the studio advised the TEMPLE family that SHIRLEY "looked chunky" and the child was put on a diet until she shed her excess poundage . . . In June, the success of the famous Canadian DIONNE QUINTUPLETS in their film *The Country Doctor* had Universal praying for another miracle. Mama Dionne was pregnant again.

At the beginning of July, Censor Czar WILL HAYS insisted that a movie chimpanzee's bare spots around its fanny be covered with MAX FACTOR's pants-of-hair. The ape was appearing in *Girl of the Jungle*.

Two screen newcomers made an impact with the public. MARTHA RAYE debuted in BING CROSBY's *Rhythm on the Range,* while French import SIMONE SIMON did well in 20th's *Girls' Dormitory.*

On August 15, 1935, in the dense fog of an early Alaskan evening, WILL ROGERS, America's homespun king of humorists, met instant death in the fiery crash of a plane piloted by WILEY POST, famous globe-circling air ace. The pair, on a leisurely flight around the world, found their final destination on the banks of a shallow stream near Point Barrow, an Arctic frontier town.

Rogers, the most beloved performer of his time, was honored by every studio, by every star, by every mogul, all of whom mourned the tragic passing of an American institution. Ten thousand mourners filled the Hollywood Bowl to honor him.

Rogers' last two films, *Steamboat 'Round the Bend* and *In Old Kentucky,* were released on schedule, just the way the number one boxoffice star of the 20th Century—Fox lot would have wanted it . . .

As summer ended, the film's top boxoffice favorites were: ROGERS—ASTAIRE, SHIRLEY TEMPLE, CLARK GABLE, NORMA SHEARER, CLAUDETTE COLBERT, ROBERT TAYLOR, JAMES CAGNEY, JOAN CRAWFORD, DICK POWELL and MYRNA LOY . . . But movie theatre exhibitors were screaming again. Now that business looked a little better, they com-

plained that some of the biggest studio stars were appearing on radio and hurting their profits . . . And Columbia decided to cancel MARY ASTOR's contract. They utilized the "morals clause" because of all the negative publicity that had surfaced during her divorce petition, which concerned the candid revelations of her extracurricular activities with playwright GEORGE S. KAUFMAN.

In September, GEORGE GERSHWIN gave a party for MOSS HART in honor of the playwright's new teeth . . . GRACIE ALLEN was taking driving lessons and GEORGE BURNS warned his friends to stay off the streets in Beverly Hills for the duration . . . FRANCES FARMER and her husband, LEIF ERICKSON, went on a camping trip. Leif drove their motorcycle while Frances rode in a tiny sidecar, holding onto their suitcase . . . The relationship between LAUREL and HARDY was sorely strained because Stan refused to sign a new long-term contract with HAL ROACH.

October was a big month for CBS. They announced the immediate construction of a million-dollar radio studio on the corner of Sunset and Gower . . . Little JUDY GARLAND, who made her picture debut in her first major role in *Pigskin Parade,* was being touted as the town's next new star . . . EDDIE CANTOR, who had made several very strong anti-Nazi speeches, was forced to hire special bodyguards after receiving numerous death threats . . . JOHN WAYNE, hoping to help his career, co-authored an original screenplay called *Alcazar.*

JOE DIMAGGIO, the outfielder for the New York Yankees, signed with an agent for both stage and movie representation. The handsome baseball star could have a big future in the business . . . MRS. JAMES CAGNEY was lucky she had any future at all after being trapped in her automobile following a three-car collision. Fortunately, she walked away with only minor injuries. Her grateful husband celebrated both his wife's miraculous escape and the $4,000 he earned doing a Lux Radio Theatre broadcast . . . A few days before Christmas, *Intermezzo,* a Swedish film, introduced American audiences to the beauty and charms of young INGRID BERGMAN.

The year ended on an optimistic note with a dazzling holiday party given by JOAN CRAWFORD and FRANCHOT TONE. Joan, one of Hollywood's truly great hostesses, invited one hundred celebrants to a deluxe open house. She and Franchot had wrapped presents under their huge tree for every guest. Tone, with lots of padding, played Santa Claus, while Joan, gorgeous in a long red velvet gown, served hot mulled wine and gaily decorated Christmas cookies for dessert. But her mother, MRS. LeSueur, had made huge batches of pickles and relish to surround the delicious baked hams and turkeys she'd turned out. Among the delighted guests were the JACK BENNYS, BOB YOUNGS, ROBERT MONTGOMERYS, the FRED ASTAIRES, assorted visiting Tone relatives, and even studio head LOUIS B. MAYER dropped in. It was a delightfully elegant way to say so long to 1936.

Douglas Fairbanks, Jr.
"JUST A MATTER OF ACCENT"

Fairbanks, Jr., loved England, and made many films over there. In October of 1936, he wrote a piece for The Hollywood Reporter *explaining the difference between shooting a film in London as opposed to working on a Hollywood soundstage.*

People are always asking what I think about British studios as compared to American, if ever they have nothing better to do. I invariably give the same answer. There is *no* difference, or in any case very little. The equipment is naturally the same. People over here in England use mostly American cameras and American lamps, just as you will see on any set in Hollywood. Cameras are handled in precisely the same way, clapperboards in England vary not one jot from clapperboards in America, tracking trucks look like tracking trucks, laboratories still scratch negatives, and so on. The only difference which exists is in sound—*not* the track—but the human voice.

I defy anyone on an English set to say whether he is in London or California until people begin to talk. Then only is it banged home to you in which country you are.

The English accent always surprises me every time I hear it on the lot or in one of the soundstages out here at our studios. It seems somehow so out of place. You see a camera being dollied along and suddenly a voice yells: "Oy, 'oo the 'ell put this track together?," or again, a hand on one of the two-b'-fours will shout down to the floor "juicers" in a rich fruity Cockney: "Gor' blimey, mate, it ain't 'arf 'ot hup 'ere!" All of which makes an old Hollywoodian smile.

I remember the first time I worked in a British studio. There was a Cockney "juicer" (or "Sparks" as they call them over here), and he used to look up at the rows of arcs and spots, and shout "Syve 'em!" At first I couldn't think what he meant. The new settlers from L.A. are often mystified. Sometimes they give up in desperation the possibility of ever learning the mother tongue. Then comes the dawn and "Syve 'em" becomes "Save 'em." And so it goes on like that famous brook and Columbus.

Of course a great amount of American accent is now heard in British studios. I am not referring to the young army of stars, both male and female, from Hollywood, who have invaded our own studios (Worton Hall) and those at Denham, Elstree, Shepherd's Bush, Teddington or any of the other big British production studios which are centered all around the outskirts of London. I am speaking now of the technicians of the business—of the directors; people like Thornton Freeland, who made *The Amateur Gentleman* and *Accused* for our company, Criterion; Tay Garnett, who is going to make our next picture, and many other famous directors who have come over here to work with a British crew around them. Of American cameramen there is also a plentitude, while several of the best publicity directors have worked on newspapers in the United States or in American studios, and have absorbed a sufficiency of the American mode of expression to become more or less bi-accented.

I don't want to talk unnecessarily about our own pictures, but naturally the material nearest to hand is the easiest to write about. Let's take our last picture, *Accused*. This was heralded by the trade papers over here as "A British picture." Fine. Now let's take a look at the studio lineup. Nobody could accuse Thornton Freeland of an English accent, nor Dolores Del Rio, who played the female star role, either. Our cameraman was Victor Armenise, an Italian. My partner, Marcel Hellman, is Roumanian, so if you add to this a hearty leavening of unaspirated Cockney, throw in a little German from the point of view of young Conrad von Molo, our head cutter, you will get some idea of the babble of tongues which reverberates across the set when the cameras are not turning. In other words, my answer to the question as to what difference there is between a British and an American studio, boils down simply to one of the spoken language. We have as many accents here as we have in Hollywood—from the supervisors on up to the extras. British visitors to picture studios over here are getting used to seeing American stars on the set, and it is no longer any surprise for them to see people like Marlene Dietrich, or Constance Bennett, or Miriam Hopkins, or Wallace Beery and practically any famous Hollywood star you like to mention, basking in the glow of a London fog.

Personally I am all for this sort of thing. You know the old internationalist. Art for art's sake, and all that sort of thing. However the importation of Hollywood customs and efficiency is becoming a curse. Tea-time (which is the excuse for saying "No" to tea and having a drink instead) is going out, and pictures are attempting to finish on schedule. I'm afraid it's going to be successful. The only remnant that will soon be left for all early colonizers and half-time exiters will be the tang of ale-laden Cockney floating through the rafters of an air-conditioned stage.

LEGENDS AND LOVERS

O n the ninth of January, 1936, John Gilbert, thirty-nine, died of a heart attack. His career, which began in 1915 with *The Mother Instinct*, had spanned nineteen years.

Gilbert, one of the most popular of the early romantic stars, reached his peak in 1925. It was then he had played the lead in *The Big Parade*, the most successful silent film ever made. But he soared to even greater heights two years later when he starred opposite Greta Garbo in *Flesh and the Devil*.

He was born John Pringle, in Logan, Utah, in July 1897. During his career, he was married four times, to Olive Burwell, Leatrice Joy, Ina Claire and Virginia Bruce. When talkies came into vogue, Gilbert had problems. He spoke with a slightly high-pitched voice. It did not match his devilishly handsome macho exterior. Because of this, Gilbert's early talkies nearly sent him into oblivion. But John was a man full of pride. Unable to accept such a fate, he studied with vocal coaches until he reached the point where he had control over his voice pitch. Still, the illusion was gone. While he never again reached the magnitude of fame he had known for ten years, his 1933 starring role opposite Garbo, in *Queen Christina*, did a lot to revive a career which was on the skids.

Gilbert, who made his last film, *The Captain Hates the Sea*, in 1934, left his entire estate to Virginia Bruce. It was valued at $363,494, close to two hundred thousand dollars of it in cash.

Exit one formerly great leading man, enter a new swashbuckling hero. Originally, Warners had wanted Robert Donat for the lead in *Captain Blood*. But a bad bout with asthma eliminated him. After testing quite a few well-known actors, newcomer Errol Flynn got the part. It would make him famous. Flynn was originally signed by Warner Brothers in London. With his tall, slim, elegant grace, his devastatingly handsome exterior and his mellifluous, exotic British voice, Errol was perfect. With just one picture under his belt, he grabbed as much attention—particularly from female ticket buyers—as any of the top stars in the industry ever had—or would. Because of his last name, and the fact that his face had the map of Eire bred into it, the studio's first official biography marked down his birthplace as Ireland. After the release of *Captain Blood*, Flynn received smash notices. His real native land was heard from.

He had been born in Hobart, Tasmania—an island off the southern tip of Australia—on June 20, 1909. The islanders, who hadn't produced many potential screen idols, wanted recognition. His father, a professor, and his mother, an elegant English lady, had settled there some years before their son was born. The elder Flynns, who traveled to Hollywood frequently, remained close to Errol. But once he had reached adulthood, no one really had much control or influence over him.

Flynn was just too handsome, too charming, for his own good. Every female with whom he came in contact turned weak at the knees. And those who didn't weaken at first were conquered by Flynn, ultimately.

Soon after *Captain Blood* was completed, Warners sent him to New York. Errol was put up at a swank hotel and scheduled for the usual four-to-five-day whirlwind round of press interviews and photographs. The very first afternoon, the telephone rang. Flynn answered it, fixed a pained expression on his face and said, "I'll be right there."

He turned to the studio publicist assigned to travel with him and said, "Frightfully sorry, old boy, but I've just had an emergency call. I have to go off now, but I'll be right back."

Flynn was gone for three days. The publicist was in a panic. The studio was in an uproar. What cruel and evil fate had befallen their newest star? He had simply vanished from the face of the earth. Discreet inquiries were made to the police. The whole thing had to be kept under wraps—at least for the moment.

Seventy-two hours later, Flynn showed up. He walked back into his suite, a broad smile on his kisser, picked up his press schedule and said calmly, "I'm ready now, sport."

The publicist, who would gladly have hauled off and hit him, exclaimed, *"Where have you been, you sonofabitch?"* Flynn just grinned. He couldn't understand all the concern. Of course he hadn't disappeared. He had been right here in the hotel all the time—a couple of flights up. He was only enjoying the delights of a few luscious lovelies, along with a fellow actor who was generous enough to share the wealth.

Back at the studio, all was forgiven. It was only the first example of the notorious Flynn exploits. What came later would make his three-day "dame detour" seem slight indeed.

Much of the credit for Flynn's *Captain Blood* success lay with director Michael Curtiz. The "mad Hungarian" had managed to communicate with the "wild Tasmanian." During the early days of production, Flynn had been nervous and somewhat stilted. But Curtiz had worked with the young man night and day, attempting to bring out the spark he saw in Flynn. Other directors might have taken such pains. But it is doubtful that anyone could have succeeded as well as Mike did.

With all that Errol owed to Mike Curtiz, a practical joke that Flynn played on his favorite director a few years later remains one of Hollywood's funniest legends. During the filming of *Elizabeth and Essex*, rumors were that one of the stand-ins was a young lady who could be had.

While they were shooting, practically every man on set capable of breathing had enjoyed a matinee quickie with the girl in question. Then, according to former Warner publicist Carl Schaefer, near the end of filming, Flynn and the cast noticed that the stand-in and director Curtiz had gone

Olivia de Havilland, Errol Flynn and Ann Sheridan during the filming of Warners' *Dodge City*.

off to lunch together. When Mike returned, alone, Errol and the crew were standing around waiting to begin shooting.

"Out of the clear blue," Schaefer recalled recently, "Flynn, who could put on the most innocent expression, said to Curtiz, 'Mike, a terrible thing happened to Ken, the electrician, while you were out.'

" 'Oh, that's awful,' Curtiz replied. 'Did he slip and fall off the catwalk?'

" 'No,' Flynn answered, looking solemn. 'He became very ill. We called the doctor. He said Ken had this unusual strange disease—kind of a V.D. It can hit a man without a moment's warning . . .

" 'Well, it serves him right,' Curtiz answered unsympathetically. 'Who was the damn fool playing around with?'

" 'I'm afraid it was one of the girls in our *own* family . . . one of the stand-ins.' Flynn dropped the name of the lady casually.

"Curtiz turned white as a ghost and ran off the set, headed for the Warners' First Aid station. Shooting was held up for hours. Poor Mike never did find out that it was only one of Flynn's practical jokes.

"No matter what Errol did," Schaefer concluded, "regardless of all the shenanigans he pulled, everybody on the lot loved him."

The 1936 press preview of MGM's *Romeo and Juliet* drew as many celebrities as normally would have attended the world premiere. Six officers, four plainclothesmen, plus an equal number of highway patrol officers were needed to restrain the crowds that had gathered as soon as word of the "sneak" circulated. The police formed a human chain to hold back the fans as the film's star, Norma Shearer, and its producer, Irving Thalberg, arrived. When the as-yet unmarried duo of Gable and Lombard appeared, it was hysteria time. Among the other stars who attended were John Barrymore, Jeanette MacDonald, Nelson Eddy, Freddie Bartholomew and Rosalind Russell.

The film, directed by George Cukor, was considered so special that *The Hollywood Reporter* invited several distinguished "critics" to contribute their comments.

Anita Loos, the author of *Gentlemen Prefer Blondes* and other such witty, brilliant literary efforts, put everything into its proper perspective:

I have just come from the press preview of Irving Thalberg's production of *Romeo and Juliet*. It was an electric occasion, sparkling with a thousand high points of achievement—from the brilliant and heart-touching Juliet of Norma Shearer, through a list of performances, many inspired—all excellent—on down to the subtlest detail of a magnificent production.

I think the modern American girl has many things to learn from the Juliet of Norma Shearer, and I advise her to go about learning them right away, for believe it or not, within a space of twenty minutes, Juliet grabs off the best man in Verona, and does it at a time when he is singeing his fingers carrying a torch for another girl.

I have always been led to believe that girls should keep men guessing, and that no girl should ask a man his intentions regarding matrimony. These two rules Miss Shearer breaks the very first night she meets her man, which causes one to stop and another to ponder. Maybe the rules are no good, and then again maybe the Shearer technique of breaking them is what does the trick.

Girls, see Norma Shearer as Juliet, and good luck to you.

Five weeks after its West Coast preview, *Romeo and Juliet* opened at the Astor Theater in New York. The crowds were as jubilant and unrestrained as the celebrities in attendance. Cole Porter, upon leaving the theatre, said that it was "The finest production of Shakespeare's works ever conceived."

But it remained for the staid *New York Times* to give the picture its ultimate tribute: ". . . It is a dignified, sensitive and entirely admirable Shakespearean—*not Hollywoodian*—production."

Many years later, George Cukor, who directed the film, reminisced about it.

Studios, in the "old days," were so very well organized. They had the best cameramen, the top lighting experts, the finest technicians in every field, and they knew how to use them. It was just a very pleasant experience. Some of the producers were absolutely brilliant. Creative. Helpful. Men like Thalberg and David Selznick . . .

Thalberg was creative in that he brought something of himself to every production. There was a give and take. There were long discussions in his office which preceded the production. Then, of course, we were in daily contact . . . I guess it was also always a special situation when a film was being made starring his wife.

Irving was so kind and polite. He had a lot of class. Of course, he was very interested in that particular production, and especially generous in the input he gave me. As for Norma, she had great respect for Irving. She did the best she could. She worked very hard . . . But I don't think Irving could be dispassionate about Norma's films. He wanted her to play Juliet because he thought it was the ideal role for a woman. Of course, in the play, Juliet was a very young girl. Norma was *not* a girl, anymore. But Irving saw her in the role. Consequently, we had many pre-production discussions about how to transpose this play, as a motion picture with words, onto the screen.

Irving was interested in every detail, down to the sets, the costumes which, in this particular film, I thought were absolutely beautiful . . . You know, Hollywood and New York appreciated the picture, but overall I don't think it received the critical reviews it deserved. Most critics weren't accustomed to tackling a work of this kind.

Leslie Howard, in particular, came in for some negative comments. Well,

Irving Thalberg and Norma Shearer at the Pasadena train station on their arrival from New York.

perhaps he wasn't the picture image of Romeo. Although he played the part beautifully, and to me, he was very moving.

I'm often asked if L. B. Mayer was as intimately involved with the productions as Thalberg. The answer is no, at least not in my case. Mayer didn't like me. He thought I was a wisecracker. But since I was such a close friend of his son-in-law, David Selznick, he left me alone. Yet he was never particularly nice to me. I don't think he quite trusted me . . . But Irving—he was a prince of a man.

In August of 1936, there was some cause for optimism. Nationwide, theatre boxoffice receipts had skyrocketed more than twenty-five percent over the previous year. The following month it was announced that forty musical films would be made in the coming year. The whole Hollywood production situation had definitely taken a turn for the better. There was only one jarring note. Irving Thalberg was ill at home. On Monday morning, September 14, *The Hollywood Reporter* noted that he was recuperating at his beach house. But while industryites were digesting breakfast and reading their trade paper, a bulletin came over the radio: "Irving Thalberg is dead at thirty-seven."

Within minutes the whole town was plunged into gloom. Work at every studio stopped as people gathered to share their grief. The shock was greater than anything that had ever happened in the film industry.

It had not been until the previous evening that anyone in the Hollywood set realized Irving was in such critical condition. He had been in an oxygen tent for two days. But that was construed only as a precautionary measure brought on by the cold from which he suffered. Not even his closest friends or studio colleagues knew of the imminent danger.

Early on Monday, September 14th, a few hours after Thalberg went into a coma, stu-

dio associates and close friends began to assemble at Louis B. Mayer's beach home. They wanted to be closer to Irving. Meanwhile, Mayer had gone to the Thalbergs', where Irving died at 10:16 A.M. When Mayer brought the news back to the group at his home, there was utter disbelief and dejection.

Funeral services were held on September 16th. MGM was completely closed down. For five minutes, during the services, all other film studios observed silence . . .

Situation Wanted: SECRETARY-STENOGRAPHER. SPANISH. ENGLISH. HIGH SCHOOL EDUCATION. INEXPERIENCED. $15.

This advertisement, which appeared in the classified section of *The New York Journal of Commerce* in November 1917, was the first step Irving Thalberg had taken in a business career which saw him rise to the top in the motion picture industry.

He was born May 30, 1899, in an old-fashioned brownstone house at 19 Woodbine Street, Brooklyn, the son of Mr. and Mrs. William Thalberg. His father was a lace importer. Thalberg graduated from grammar school, but illness halted his high school studies. Once he was well again, he preferred working part-time in his grandfather's department store. During that period he studied shorthand and Spanish, which had enabled him to advertise proficiency in both. Thalberg was hired by Universal in 1917. He soon became private secretary to "Uncle" Carl. On Laemmle's next trip to the West Coast, Irving had gone along. The rest of his story is part of show business history.

Of all the stars he nurtured, Thalberg's most important personal discovery was Norma Shearer. He had spotted her in a small picture he saw in a neighborhood theatre while he was attending a preview. He immediately signed her to a contract. She joined the MGM stock company and eventually rose to stardom. They were married in 1928. In 1930, Irving, Jr., was born. Little Katharine came into the Thalberg family in 1935. Irving and Norma were considered one of filmdom's happiest couples. They lived in a modest French-Norman home at the edge of the ocean in Santa Monica. *Romeo and Juliet*, with Norma starring, had been his last personal production. But even after his death other pictures Thalberg had planned and worked on were in preparation: *The Good Earth, Maytime, Camille* and the Marx Brothers' *A Day at the Races*.

In the will drawn up fifteen months before his death, Thalberg left his wife their residence and all of his personal effects. Norma was also co-trustee of the bulk of an estate estimated at more than $5,000,000. Sums were set aside for his parents, sister and other relatives. There were also three trusts of $1,500,000 each. Not bad for a still-young man who had begun his career as a fifteen-dollar-a-week clerk.

The last words Irving Thalberg spoke before dying were, "Don't let the children forget me . . ." His son was going on six. His baby daughter was one year old. The name of Thalberg has lived on, and will continue to live as long as the art of motion pictures remains.

With Irving Thalberg's instinct for talent, he would have loved to see the name Lana Turner on an MGM contract list. But she was not discovered until a month after his death. Lana, herself, told the story best:

I wasn't even sixteen yet. It all happened so suddenly. I was having a Coke at this place right across from Hollywood High School, when I noticed a gentleman on the other side of this U-shaped fountain.

I could tell he was looking at me. I remember, my eyes blurred. I went on sipping my Coke. Then I saw him call over the owner of the cafe. The two of them talked for a while. A few moments later, the owner, who knew all of the kids from Hollywood High, came over to

Billy Wilkerson's "discovery," Lana Turner, on the left in a scene from her first film, Mervyn LeRoy's *They Knew What They Wanted.* Look familiar?

me. He said, "Judy, that gentleman is Billy Wilkerson. He'd like to meet you."

"Why?" I asked him.

"He just wants to talk with you for a few minutes. He's the man who owns *The Hollywood Reporter*, down the street." I said if he thought it was okay, then sure. But I asked him to stay close!

Billy Wilkerson walked over to me, presented his business card. "How do you do?" he said. "What's your name?" I blushed. "Judy Turner."

Then Billy articulated those few magical words that have become so cliché over the years: "How would you like to be in pictures?" I looked at him, and replied, in a very sophisticated manner, "I'll have to ask my mother!"

Over the years, those words have been attributed to others. The magazines have had me being discovered on a stool at Schwab's Drugstore, or by God knows how many other people. But I owe it all to Billy. He introduced me to an agent, who brought me to Mervyn LeRoy. It's so odd, the way things happen—being at the right place, at the right time, I mean. Meeting Billy Wilkerson that day changed my life. He's always had a deep place in my heart . . .

Fred MacMurray
"I Play a Saxophone: Is Civilization Doomed?"

Fred MacMurray, one of the most versatile actors ever to appear on Hollywood screens, wrote this lovely tongue-in-cheek piece for the October 14, 1937, special issue of The Hollywood Reporter.

Back in Beaver Dam (that's in Wisconsin, in case you didn't know, and the place I come from) the folks begin laying in a supply of coal along about this time of year, and start getting the storm windows out of the basement.

Here in Hollywood we burn gas, and the native sons never heard of storm windows. But signs of winter's approach are no less apparent. They consist of a lot of guys like me, who can just barely spell, huffing and puffing in a great literary effort for *The Hollywood Reporter* Annual.

When I first learned I was to have this opportunity to take pen in hand and pour out my very all for the enlightenment of the readers of this great family Journal, I called around at the Paramount publicity department and got hold of some back issues of previous Annuals. I thought I'd read up and see just what the boys and girls wrote about, and thereby gain some inspiration for my own literary offering.

The principal thing I discovered is that it's surprising how much dust can gather on a printed page in the space of a few seasons—especially a printed page which is adorned with burning messages to mankind, penned by guys like me in the heat of creative fervor.

However, the fact that *The Reporter* does give space to such burning messages to mankind is heartening, because it just happens that I have a load which I've wanted to get off my chest for a long time. And I guess it will be perfectly fitting for me to do so, since I noted several essays on such subjects as Soviet Russia, The Cinema as an Art, and Is Civilization Doomed?

If it's acceptable for the authors of such pieces to work up steam over their pet ideas, I guess it's okay for me to give vent to something that's pretty close to my heart.

It's a subject I didn't find discussed in any back numbers of *The Reporter,* and I think it's time for somebody to do something about it.

I'm referring to the persistent campaign of ridicule, vilification and slander which for years had been directed against as fine a body of men as you'll find anywhere in America or any other country.

I mean saxophone players.

As I said, this is a subject very close to my vest. I used to be a saxophone player myself—yes. I not only used to be a saxophone player, but I *am* a saxophone player to this day. If you don't believe it, ask the neighbors.

And furthermore, I speak of my Art with my head held high. And why shouldn't I? Stokowski isn't ashamed of being a musician, is he?

I have played the saxophone ever since I was a kid (nobody ever had a better pal than that old tin gourd of mine), and I deeply resent the things which people say about it and its cousins.

A good case in point is a conversation I overhead during the production of *True Confession*. Claude Binyon—you know, the roundish sort of guy who wrote the screenplay—was telling Carole Lombard, John Barrymore and Wesley Ruggles about a law he is proposing which would require all musical instrument manufacturers to whittle saxophone mouthpieces from poison oak!

Of course, Binyon is notorious around Hollywood for his loose talk and his utter lack of appreciation for the finer things of life, and I know I shouldn't have let what he said bother me in the least.

But I just couldn't help it. That night I dreamed I was playing my sax in a command performance before the King and Queen of Denmark and discovered, too late, that Binyon had put a poison oak mouthpiece on it and had stuffed a suit of his red flannel underwear down the bell.

I awoke in a cold sweat just as dawn was breaking over the Hollywood hills, shaken and unnerved by this monstrous thing which Binyon had implanted in my subconscious. But as my self-control returned, a great resolve grew and flowered in my breast. I made up my mind that some day, some way I'd do something to help end these attacks upon the finest, most beautiful musical instrument ever created.

So really I suppose I should thank Claude Binyon. Unknowingly, in his crude way, he started something in my life which is rather fine. Without the motivation he provided, it is possible this article would never have been written.

It is my hope that this tribute to the saxophone and the men who play it will serve as the beginning of a great wave of public indignation that will force Binyon and others like him to shut their big mouths about a fine and noble instrument.

Can you imagine what a Salvation Army Band would sound like without its saxophones?

Can you imagine the dull dreariness of a college dormitory without the sweet sounds of a dozen or so scholars learning to play the instrument? It would be unthinkable!

And if these thoughts aren't enough to arouse you to action, consider the fact that if Binyon and his ilk have their way they'll drive forever from this earth the instrument which makes the finest hanging flower pot you ever saw.

Arise, citizens, arise!

HOLLYWOOD POTPOURRI
1937

Universal Studios started the year on a very positive note. Without waiting for WILL HAYS to give them orders, they voluntarily changed the word "goose," in the script of *Class Prophecy,* to geese. The altered line read: "So, he gave her a geese."

On January 7th, seven hundred people from all over the world gathered at Paramount Studios to honor ADOLPH ZUKOR on his sixty-fourth birthday, and his twenty-fifth year in the picture industry. After dinner, another thousand guests arrived to toast the film prince. One hour of the event was broadcast over NBC. The show, emceed by JACK BENNY, featured WALLACE BEERY, CECIL B. DEMILLE, DOROTHY LAMOUR, CAROLE LOMBARD, MARTHA RAYE, BING CROSBY, plus a comedy sketch, done by W. C. FIELDS, from a remote pickup in his sanitorium room, where he was convalescing.

The guests "crossed studio lines." Every studio was represented, from MGM's LOUIS B. MAYER and CLARK GABLE, to former Paramount vice president JESSE L. LASKY. The guest of honor was given a massive autograph album which contained handwritten tributes from many of the world's notables. Speaking quietly and humbly, Zukor thanked them for "the outstanding gift of his career."

Between the beginning of February and mid-March, almost all of the nation's theatres had done away with "bank night." They showed their confidence in the quality of films being produced as being enough incentive to lure patrons to the boxoffice. Blockbuster hits like FRANK CAPRA's *Lost Horizon,* for Columbia, and MGM's *Maytime,* with JEANETTE MACDONALD, NEL-

SON EDDY and JOHN BARRYMORE, started bringing the public back into theatres.

DAVID O. SELZNICK began negotiations with MGM to borrow CLARK GABLE for the role of Rhett Butler in *Gone With the Wind.* Metro seemed willing if they were given the right to release the film. Since everyone, from the author, MARGARET MITCHELL, to tens of thousands of readers, felt Gable *was* Butler, it seemed likely the two factions would consummate their deal.

Spring brought word that DON AMECHE would host NBC's new Chase and Sanborn radio show with regular guests, ventriloquist EDGAR BERGEN and his dummy, CHARLIE MCCARTHY. With Ameche gone, his former sponsors, Campana, set out to rebuild their "First Nighter" program. They hired TYRONE POWER to star opposite their regular female lead, BARBARA LUDDY.

May was "make-a-buck" time for the latest commercial venture. An advertisement in *The Hollywood Reporter* offered to sell recordings of KING GEORGE of England's coronation speech for $1.85. For fifty cents extra, they tossed in EDWARD VIII's farewell speech—the one in which he had given up his throne for "the woman I love" . . . Two days later, headlines hailed the fact that television had "turned the corner in England." The entire coronation pageant had been viewed on a thousand tiny screens throughout the south of England, scooping the inadequate newsreels that arrived in theatres twelve hours later. The television reception had been perfect, thus confirming the U.S. Government's opinion that competition from both European and British television would outstrip America's product if the television industry did not get on the ball and secure co-operation among TV companies.

Back home, EDDIE CANTOR signed an unprecedented six-year radio contract with Texaco. NBC announced it would broadcast the JAMES J. BRADDOCK—JOE LOUIS fight from Comiskey Park, in Chicago, on June 12. Between the immediacy of radio and the apparent progress of British television, Tinseltown once again felt the hot breath of competition on its collective neck . . . At the end of the month, a film short, *How to Undress in Front of Your Husband,* starred ELAINE BARRIE BARRYMORE and provoked a lot of comment. It was the first time the illustrious Barrymore name had ever headlined a striptease act. The film offered a lot of suspense, particularly when Elaine could not undo the last button on her black panties. Unfortunately, the preview audience not only laughed with Elaine, they laughed *at* her as she peeled off her gown. Her slip came next, revealing a pretty pair of panties and brassiere. As the pants started downward, Miss Barrie covered up with a nightgown. Three-hundred-pound TRIXIE FRIGANZA, who also stripped, revealed more skin than Elaine. But she was not supposed to have a figure. Elaine's performance was wooden. While she was not called upon to talk, she *did* smile once, when the brassiere came off. Barrie, who had been married to JOHN for six months, filed for divorce on April 24, 1937. Perhaps the strip show was a form of "sweet revenge!"

That was *not* the only act of revenge being contemplated. Magazine photographers stuck together and planned to play up the MARY PICKFORD—BUDDY ROGERS wedding above the JEANETTE MACDONALD—GENE RAYMOND nuptials in their forthcoming issues because they felt that they had been mistreated at the MacDonald-Raymond affair . . . MARY PICKFORD blushed beet red at her wedding reception when CHARLIE CHAPLIN kissed her for the first time in 20 years . . .

July turned out to be so hot in Hollywood that all social events were curtailed as VIPs took off in yachts, sat in their pools, or sailed to Alaska to escape the unusual humidity.

By August, things were back to normal. On the 19th, *The Hollywood Reporter* noted the very successful screen debut of RONALD REAGAN, in *Love in the Air,* a Warner Brothers "B" picture, with a "B" cast and low-budget production values, but surprisingly rated "A" for its entertainment values. Reagan played a young announcer who became "Uncle Andy"

of the bedtime story hour and via his radio show promoted athletic bouts and other recreational events for poor kids. When one of his young fans called upon him for help to find a missing brother, Andy became involved in solving the mystery of a murderous gang. Reagan, who had been discovered announcing in a Des Moines, Iowa, radio station, proved to be completely at home in his role. *The Reporter* rated him "a natural talent who had given one of the best first picture performances ever seen in Hollywood."

September brought progress for another outstanding discovery, when JOE PASTERNAK'S Universal film *100 Men and a Girl* was released; DEANNA DURBIN was described as "a teenage SHIRLEY TEMPLE, physically, and a JEANETTE MACDONALD, vocally"—which made her close to being rated as the eighth wonder of the world as far as Hollywood was concerned . . . On the radio front, NBC, not to be outdone by CBS, announced they would build new radio studios on two full city blocks at the corner of Sunset and Vine. The building would also house structural plans for future *television* operations. The movie moguls read the announcement and panic set in again!

While Hollywoodites finished the last of their leftover Thanksgiving turkey, Universal Studios fired virtually all of its New York executive staff. In an almost total purge, the company's president, R. H. COCHRANE was removed and replaced by RKO's head honcho, NATE BLUMBERG . . . Speaking of eating, Hollywood summoned young ORSON WELLES in December, but admonished him *not* to partake of any holiday goodies heavier than goose or turkey *feathers*. The brilliant performer, who scored big in a New York production of *Julius Caesar,* had numerous film offers. But all included the same message: lose a few pounds. Ironically, Welles was *heard* weekly over the radio starring as "The Shadow."

As the year ended, half of Hollywood jammed into the Trocadero to attend the first gala of the winter season, the Bal Cap d'Antibes. It was a costume ball in which guests were advised to dress in beach clothes or sportswear, any garment reminiscent of togs worn on the sun-drenched Riviera. The evening was a spectacular success. The cafe re-created the Côte d'Azur down to the smallest detail. BILLY WILKERSON brought in everything French except the Mediterranean Sea. Hosting the biggest party was CARY GRANT, along with his "steady,"

PHYLLIS BROOKS. Phyllis, whom everyone called "Brooksie," was obviously head over heels in love with Cary. They had been steady-dating since July of 1937, and friends said it was only a matter of time before they merged.

Also in Cary's party was LANA TURNER, who wore an orange sweater and blue shorts; MARLENE DIETRICH, draped in mannish-tailored slacks, came with director EDMOND GOULDING. JACK OAKIE led a group "Big Apple" dance with Lana as his partner. CLAIRE TREVOR and agent VIC ORSATTI sat under the Troc's canopy and sipped long, tall, cool drinks, pretending to get a suntan. KAY FRANCIS and BILLIE DOVE and dates, and ANNE SHIRLEY with JOHN PAYNE, were just a few of the guests whom Cary paid for . . . And the Troc was also jammed for New Year's Eve. NELSON EDDY gave the patrons a surprise treat when he headed for the stage and sang almost the entire score from *Rosalie* . . . The crowd seemed to flow up and down Sunset Boulevard as revelers also stopped by the Clover Club for drinks and a few turns at the roulette wheel.

Other Tinseltown celebrants hit the track at Santa Anita and lost some of their hard-earned loot on the ponies . . . And dozens of VIPs segued to the desert, but went into mourning when they discovered that their favorite gambling establishments, The Dunes and the 159 Club, had been closed down by the local police. However, for those who only wanted sun and fun, it was heaven at CHARLIE FARRELL'S Racquet Club. The most attractive sight there was MARLENE DIETRICH, who wore sandals, with her *heels* painted red, as she sat and watched CHARLES BOYER play tennis. At one point, fearing that Charlie was exhausting himself, Marlene walked out to center court and carried him champagne.

"Adios" 1937!

1 Warner Brothers' star Errol Flynn and first wife Lili Damita, seated on the staircase of their Beverly Hills home.   2 Charles Boyer and Marlene Dietrich on the set of Selznick-International's *The Garden of Allah*, 1937.   3 Clark Gable and Jean Harlow with director Jack Conway, relaxing on the set of MGM's *Saratoga*. A few days after this photo was taken, in July 1937, Jean Harlow was dead.   4 Walt Disney and Shirley Temple at the 1938 Academy Awards.

Warners' about-to-be stars HUMPHREY BOGART and ANN SHERIDAN replaced BARTON MacLANE and GLENDA FARRELL in the "Torchy" series, and played the lead roles in *Torchy Goes to Panama* . . . KATE HEPBURN turned red as a winter watermelon when a gateman at 20th failed to recognize her. She had gone to that studio to do some action shots on Fox's jungle set for *Bringing Up Baby*. When she told the guard, "I'm Katharine Hepburn," he looked her straight in the eye and replied, "Oh, yeah. Well, I'm Abe Lincoln." Hepburn pressed down on her horn and drove right up under DARRYL ZANUCK's window, and kept honking until a few executives leaned out their windows. Then Kate yelled out that she wanted in, and Zanuck's personal assistant escorted her onto the lot . . . On a less noisy note, SAM and FRANCES GOLDWYN sailed off to find tranquillity during their month's holiday in Hawaii.

In February, the Troc held a rhumba contest. The winners were four semi-odd couples: JOE SCHENCK and VIRGINIA ZANUCK; DOUG FAIRBANKS, SR. and his SYLVIA; RUDY VALLEE and DOROTHY LAMOUR, and the biggest hip-shaker in the group, gorgeous MARLENE DIETRICH with DOUG, JR. . . . Meanwhile, over in Germany, yet another awful decree was handed down—music by Jewish composers such as GEORGE GERSHWIN and IRVING BERLIN could still be played as long as the tunes were identified as having been written by pure Aryans . . . There were rumors that HOWARD HUGHES was about to re-enter the movie business by purchasing a large hunk of Universal.

MARY ASTOR and MANUEL DEL CAMPO celebrated their first "Sweet Valentine's Day" wedding anniversary in Palm Springs . . . Juvenile star FREDDIE BARTHOLOMEW was ordered by the court to pay his parents and sister twenty percent of his earnings. Freddie still lived with his AUNT CISSY, who raised him, and the kid still claimed she was "the only mother he had ever known" . . .

March brought Hollywood the most torrential rainstorms in decades. Many areas of the city were flooded. For the first time in history, the Oscar show was postponed for a week. Many stars, caught at their studios, spent several nights sleeping in their dressing rooms. RALPH BELLAMY, whose San Fernando house was literally swept away, rescued his five dogs and three suits and took refuge in the home of producer HARRY LACHMAN . . . Good-hearted CAROLE LOMBARD donated the five-hundred-dollar fee she collected for a radio show to help the flood victims.

On March 13, HITLER invaded Austria. World conditions were deplorable and getting worse . . . On March 23, JOAN CRAWFORD celebrated her birthday at the Trocadero during a surprise dinner party arranged for her by FRANCHOT TONE. Other guests included BARBARA STANWYCK and ROBERT TAYLOR, the RAY MILLANDS, the IRVING BERLINS and CESAR ROMERO . . .

In April, GRACIE ALLEN took up painting. She called her latest canvas "Dog Standing on a Corner Watching Two Men Fight" . . . DAVID O. SELZNICK gave his wife, Irene, a birthday party, and invited MADELEINE CARROLL, GEORGE CUKOR, socialite-film investor JOCK WHITNEY and Irene's sister and brother-in-law, EDIE and BILL GOETZ . . . Two weeks after her festive birthday party, Crawford left for New York with hubby FRANCHOT TONE, quieting rumors that their marriage was over, and that Joan was filing for divorce . . . Her next film, incidentally, was called *Fidelity*, from a script by F. SCOTT FITZGERALD . . . The Swedish royal family felt obliged to write a letter to MGM deploring all of the international publicity given the supposed GARBO—LEOPOLD STOKOWSKI romance during Greta's recent trip abroad. They claimed it reflected poorly on the Swedish image. Greta, back in Hollywood, fumed over the stories, said: "I will never leave Hollywood again as long as I remain in the arts; it is the only place in the world where I can be left alone!"

JACKIE COOGAN filed a lawsuit against his mother and stepfather, Mr. and Mrs. ARTHUR BERNSTEIN, demanding that they turn over four million dollars in property plus other assets he earned as a juvenile star. The angry stepfather told reporters, "The law is on *our* side. He'll not get a penny from us. My lawyers told me that every dollar a kid earns before he turns twenty-one belongs to his parents" . . . Meanwhile, another underage performer, seventeen-year-old LANA TURNER, beat out two hundred other girls for the role of one of MICKEY ROONEY's sweeties in *Love Finds Andy Hardy*.

In May, back in New York, GLORIA SWANSON was having a ball "being domestic." Gloria did her own shopping, and the Fifth and Park Avenue merchants loved her, although they said she was "a little screwy." When she wanted Ritz Crackers, she asked for a box of the Ritz

Brothers, and when a grocer asked if she wanted any chicory blended with her coffee, Swanson smiled and started singing, "Chickory, dickory, dock!"

JOHN WAYNE signed a contract with Republic and will make eight of the "Three Mesquiters" series films during the next year. He left Universal and started at Republic on the following day . . . CAROLE LOMBARD was having a house built for her mother, and was personally overseeing its construction . . . Hollywoodites had a new place to lose their money. They took a water taxi three miles out and boarded the ship *Rex*, which was anchored off Santa Monica just beyond the legal limit . . . Insiders said that while MARLENE DIETRICH loved being escorted by DOUG, JR., he was carrying a mile-high torch for LORETTA YOUNG.

BETTY GRABLE moved in with her family while hubby JACKIE COOGAN made some personal appearances in an effort to earn money . . . At the end of May, JUDY GARLAND was injured in an auto crash while riding in a studio car on the way home from MGM. She was rushed to Cedars of Lebanon Hospital and X rays disclosed she had three broken ribs, a punctured lung and a sprained back. But doctors said she would have to miss only three weeks of filming on *Love Finds Andy Hardy*.

FRANCES LANGFORD admitted that she and JON HALL had slipped over the border and were married in Prescott, Arizona, on June 4 . . . Totally unrelated to the last item, LOUIS B. MAYER bought a huge ranch which he will use as a breeding farm—for his thoroughbred horses . . . At NORMA SHEARER's small dinner party for HELEN HAYES there were several new surprise couples: MERLE OBERON and GEORGE BRENT; MARY PICKFORD with MGM executive EDDIE MANNIX; SONJA HENIE with CESAR ROMERO, and JOAN BENNETT with WALTER WANGER . . . And a beautiful Creole Madame opened a swank "establishment" right in the heart of Beverly Hills. Most of her clientele was from the "Who's Who" of filmdom. Patrons who had charge accounts were personally reminded by one of Madame's boys—every Monday morning.

The start of the Hollywood racing season attracted OLIVIA DE HAVILLAND, MICHAEL CURTIZ, MARY LIVINGSTONE, who left JACK BENNY at home, and came with GEORGE and GRACIE, AL JOLSON, JACK OAKIE and GEORGE BRENT . . . Membership invitations went out for the new Rhumba Club to be held every Tuesday at the La Conga Club. CARY GRANT and PHYLLIS BROOKS were the first couple to accept . . . RONALD REAGAN was spot-ted with SUSAN HAYWARD. Pals said it was just for publicity purposes . . . Silent star CARMEL MYERS and her agent husband, RALPH BLUM, who owned GLORIA SWANSON's former mansion opposite the Beverly Hills Hotel, had an interesting party the other evening . . . The highlight was a psychic/fortune teller Carmel hired to amuse the guests. Instead, the lady "really told off quite a few celebrities" who sought readings. Glimpsed in the crowd: the new twosome of ANNABELLA and TYRONE POWER; the JACK BENNYS, BURNS and ALLEN and SIMONE SIMON—all alone.

By July, their mutual pals were bemoaning the breakup of the CRAWFORD-TONE marriage . . . DICK POWELL and JOAN BLONDELL had a baby girl whom they named ELLEN . . . NELSON EDDY and JEANETTE MACDONALD had such a feud on the *Sweethearts* set that it cost director W. S. VAN DYKE five precious days of his shooting schedule . . . RONALD REAGAN got a break with a featured part in *Brother Rat* . . . FRANCES FARMER and LEIF ERICKSON dined at the Hollywood Brown Derby and looked like they just jumped off their motorcycle . . . ERROL FLYNN and LILI DAMITA had a shooting match over corned beef and cabbage at the House of Murphy. This marriage looks to be headed for the divorce courts.

SHIRLEY TEMPLE, who visited FDR at Hyde Park, had simultaneous covers released on *Time*, *Life* and *Saturday Evening Post*, plus about a dozen fan magazines . . . *Marie Antoinette* was a smash hit at its Carthay Circle premiere. Afterward, LOUIS B. MAYER gave a party at the Trocadero (no longer owned by BILLY WILKERSON). Among his guests were: GABLE and LOMBARD; TAYLOR and STANWYCK; star of the flick, NORMA SHEARER; TYRONE POWER and ANNABELLA, the grown-up-looking couple of FREDDIE BARTHOLOMEW and JUDY GARLAND, the ROBERT MONTGOMERYS and JEANETTE MACDONALD and GENE RAYMOND.

In August, *Alexander's Ragtime Band* had the greatest audience mob ever to storm the Roxy boxoffice in New York . . . It broke a nine-year attendance record . . . In Paris, ANNABELLA'S marriage to French actor JEAN MURAT fizzled . . . Sad to report that director FRANK CAPRA'S three-year-old son died at the Children's Hospital while under ether for a tonsillectomy . . . W. C. FIELDS had to turn down a $50,000 offer to appear in *The Wizard of Oz* because he was still tied up on *You Can't Cheat an Honest Man* . . . And GEORGE BRENT qualified for his private pilot's license . . .

As September started, ANN SHERIDAN, in New

York, filed for divorce against actor EDDIE NOR-RIS . . . SHIRLEY TEMPLE made her Technicolor debut in *The Little Princess,* adding one million dollars to the budget . . . ALEXANDER KORDA flew in from London under an assumed name just to visit MERLE OBERON . . . Broadway stage actor JOHN GARFIELD, winning critical acclaim in *Four Daughters,* is headed for top stardom . . . RHEA GABLE told reporters she was tired of denying stories that she won't give CLARK a divorce. She says the reason she hasn't divorced him is because he hadn't asked her to, and didn't want one . . . Meanwhile, LILI DAMITA sailed for Europe, but there was still no news on whether or not she and ERROL FLYNN would split.

In October, shortly after Lili sailed, Errol took seriously ill with influenza. He'd just finished *Dawn Patrol.* Doctors were monitoring him closely, watching for a possible recurrence of jungle malaria . . . Gable returned from a Canadian hunting trip to help CAROLE LOMBARD celebrate her birthday on October 6th . . . A move was afoot to establish a pension plan for old actors based on an idea proposed by JEAN HERSHOLT to the Motion Picture Relief Fund

Committee . . . The JACK WARNERS, in London, traveled in very social circles. They were wined and dined by Ambassador and Mrs. JOSEPH P. KENNEDY on their trip to open a new Warners Theatre in the heart of London.

In November, GRETA GARBO wound up hiding out in Santa Barbara on a ranch owned by LEOPOLD STOKOWSKI, whom she swore she'd never see again—because she considered him a big publicity hound . . . By the time Thanksgiving was over, JAMES ROOSEVELT was in Hollywood, where he accepted a position with the Samuel Goldwyn Company. Roosevelt will start to work after he spends Christmas at the White House with his family . . . And, as the year ended, the new 1939 edition of the British "Who's Who" was published. Among the actors listed were CHARLES CHAPLIN (described as married twice, now single), CLARK GABLE and ROBERT TAYLOR (who made it for the first time, but failed to list their ages), LILY PONS, PAUL MUNI, EDDIE CANTOR and LIONEL BARRYMORE, who were not shy about their birthdates. Cantor was noted as being forty-six, while Barrymore admitted to sixty-one.

Betty Grable

"FROM THE CRADLE TO THE GRABLE"

Betty Grable was not only talented, and pretty, she also had a very good sense of humor, often self-deprecating, but always charmingly effective. In October of 1937, she wrote a vignette for The Hollywood Reporter. *It was autobiographical, and typical of Betty's down-to-earth attitude about her early struggles to win fame. Five years after she wrote this piece, she was known around the world, and on her way to becoming one of the all-time boxoffice favorites.*

Hundreds of years ago someone advised my great grandfather to come out west and grow up with the country, and so the screen has Betty Grable.

Isn't that just too ducky for the fans?

It took granddaddy eight weeks to cross the plains—and baby Betty eight years to see her name above the title of a movie.

Fine thing.

But the movies are like that. I've been in their hair out here since I can remember—since I was in pigtails and swiped my big sister's dresses and switches and paraded up and down in front of the house in the wild hope that a producer would get run over by a garbage wagon and I could rescue him and tap him for a job just before he died.

Just the other day I had a fan letter which said, "Gee, but time flies. I've been watching your work on the screen since I was eight. Can't we get together?"

I'd have felt ancient if I didn't know that I was only twelve when he was eight.

They took my nursing bottle away from me and ushered me into Producer Goldwyn's sanctum and he dandled me on his knee and I was the first Goldwyn girl, then and there. I was just turning thirteen.

I guess I was fourteen or so when I began singing with Ted Fio Rito's orchestra, just killing time between spankings, so to speak. And I have never played a child part in my life.

But what were we talking about? Oh, yes. They previewed *This Way Please,* just the other night, and for the first time since I came to Hollywood I saw my name up there above the title.

Was I thrilled? It was the thrill of a lifetime for me. Pardon the plug, but my heart's in my work, and I've just finished *Thrill of a Lifetime*. That makes it two plugs.

They're funny that way, in Hollywood. A prophet is not only without honor—he's lucky to be alive.

Maybe they were waiting for me to grow up.

For eight years I've heard: "Here's that Grable kid—hello, kid." And: "Nice little part, let's give it to Grable. Nice kid, that Grable. Pretty, too. Sure, she'll do that fine." And: "You wanna dame to lay your cornerstone? Sure, we got one. Pretty, too. Blond. Yeah. Name's Betty Grable. Sure, she'll come." And: "Radio singer? Sure we got one. Ever hear of Betty Grable? You HAVE? How come? Well, anyway, we'll have her over there at nine sharp."

And so on. But never: "Hey, why not put Grable in that big one . . . give her the lead, too. The dame's got something!"

That is, not until a few weeks ago, when they called me in at Paramount and yelled, "Hey, where you been?"

I'd been right there under their noses for a couple of months, only they'd been going along, saying, "Here comes Betty, let's buy her a Coke or something. Nice kid, that Grable."

They'd have been lonesome if they hadn't seen me underfoot half the time. I've had my arms squeezed so many times a day while big shots grinned and said, "Hello, Betty, how's-a-kid?" that I'm black and blue.

All of a sudden somebody said, "Look! Whadda I see? She can dance! Heard her sing? Hey, look—the figger she's got!" And they called me in and said, "Shake hands with a new star Betty—we mean, Miss Grable. Shake with yourself—you're it!"

So they put me in *Thrill of a Lifetime* and some people and some lingerie sales managers, and some toothpaste men all crowded around me and took my picture with their products, and somebody else said, "Oh, we have a spot on the radio for her," and they began blowing up my photographs from 8 x 10 to 30 x 67, or something, and this meant that I was to be a star, and I got a headache and had to go to bed. Eight years is a long time.

How does it feel to be a star?

Wait until I get through with *College Swing*, the big one I've been cast for, and the big one after that, and then another one, and wait until I can feel sure of walking out on a set without hearing someone yell, "Here comes Grable, nice kid, she'll stand on her head and wiggle her ears. Oh, boy, how she can wiggle her ears!"

Wait until I can pick and choose the cornerstones I have to lay, and until they say, "You wanna dame to meet the train when Whoozis gets in? You want Grable? Sorry, you can't have Betty—she's taking a nap and we can't disturb her, ever, when she takes a nap."

Now that it's happened, I feel as though I could out-nap old Rip himself.

LOVES WON AND LOST

In April of 1934, Joan Crawford, only weeks away from receiving her final divorce decree from Doug, Jr., spoke with reporters. She emphatically stated that she had no intention of remarrying. She had learned her lesson. "An actress should not marry, I'm convinced of that. It is better to say no, and cause a small hurt now, than to say yes and cause a great hurt later on."

Despite the sincere ring of Joan's words, rumors had circulated for months in *The Reporter*'s newsroom that she would marry Franchot Tone. He had even admitted proposing. And there *were* changes being made over on Bristol Avenue. Crawford's entire Brentwood home was undergoing a face-lift. Almost all traces of the original Spanish structure were gone, including the symbolic red tile roof. Workmen had added a swimming pool, a theatre, an office-studio and a bathhouse. "All of the reconstruction," Joan said, "is for the purpose of enabling me to assume a new life, one in which mental activities will be of paramount importance."

Her at-home theatre featured a small stage, which she planned to use for putting on private productions. One of Joan's closest friends, Francis Lederer, was scheduled to dedicate the theatre by putting on a playlet. Crawford, Lederer, and a few close friends had been getting together on Saturday evenings for discussions, often lasting into the wee hours. Joan said her new life-style had replaced the active social life she led as Mrs. Fairbanks.

"I had had too much of it," she commented. "But that was in the past. And, I have no regrets, nor am I heartbroken at my breakup with Doug . . ." Then she agreed to discuss some gossip items which had been cropping up in London papers.

"Yes, I do think Douglas will marry Gertrude Lawrence . . . and I am hoping for his happiness . . . I say this in all honesty. After all, *I* took the step toward divorcing Doug. That never would have happened if I had loved him to the extent that I could not bear to be separated from him . . . That I have ever really been in love, I doubt. Hollywood itself stands in the way of any great, true love. If a woman, an actress, is in a position where she can give up her career, marry, and give her husband children, she can be happy here. But the career must become incidental. If two people are in the profession, they should both leave it if they want to marry, and then they could, perhaps, be happy."

Crawford also admitted that she was no diplomat when it came to concealing her moods: "That's too difficult in married life, especially if one's husband is in the same profession as oneself, and that profession is acting. I don't think it is fair to the man . . . I just don't want to go through life causing unhappiness, great unhappiness, where a little unhappiness, of perhaps a very transitory character, might be substituted instead."

Joan seemed to be shutting the door on any future marriages, at least as long as she was a Hollywood star. But, when it came to both prognostications and self-predictions, Crawford struck out. Young Doug never did marry Gertrude Lawrence. As for Joan, well, it was only a matter of time before she said her "I do's" again.

Meanwhile, Franchot Tone's stock was rising at MGM. He had been cast opposite Jean Harlow in *100 Percent Pure,* and the studio was very high on him. An offbeat type physically, he seemed extremely versatile, able to turn on the comedy charm or give a fine dramatic performance at will. A New York stage performer who had originally turned actor as a lark, Tone was one of those natural talents that Hollywood latched on to.

On October 11, 1935, Joan Crawford, giving her age as twenty-six, and Franchot Tone, thirty, were secretly united by Mayor Herbert W. Jenkins, of Englewood Cliffs, New Jersey. The ceremony was witnessed by Nicholas Schenck, who had made all the arrangements, and Leo Friedman, both executives of the Loew's-MGM Corporation.

Joan wore a blue suit and carried a bridal bouquet. Tone was dressed in a gray pin-striped suit, sans flowers. For the happy occasion, Franchot had gifted Joan with a seven-karat emerald-cut diamond ring set in a platinum band. Her wedding ring was platinum set with diamonds. Joan gave Tone a thick platinum wedding band for the double-ring ceremony. The newlyweds honeymooned in a lavish suite at the Waldorf-Astoria Hotel on Park Avenue. The couple stayed in New York just long enough to do several radio interviews in which they extolled the virtues of marriage. Then they flew back to Hollywood.

Joan and Franchot moved into her refurbished home, which one Hollywood wag suggested should be called "JoFran" or "ElTono." But for this marriage, Crawford

Joan Crawford and husband number two, Franchot Tone, at home with the family dachshunds.

did not feel it necessary to give her house a name. For the second time, Joan had married a man from a wealthy family background. Tone's grandfather, on his mother's side, was a New York state senator. His father, Frank Tone, was an important industrialist—the president of one of America's largest firms manufacturing abrasives. Franchot, a graduate of Cornell University, was definitely Ivy League through and through. Once again Crawford had married up.

For the first couple of years, Joan and Franchot seemed the ideal couple. Both worked steadily, with Crawford's career once again outshining that of her husband. But Tone was very secure in his talent and did not seem disturbed by his wife's more flashy and glamorous roles. To the contrary, it was Joan who learned from him. Under Tone's guidance and tutelage, her metamorphosis became complete. The girl, whose early education was garnered mostly in chorus dressingrooms, became extremely well versed on literature (begun when she first married Doug, Jr.), read all of the classics, and was very involved in social problems and work with the poor. She was, in fact, the classic young society patron of the arts and good works.

In March of 1938, Crawford celebrated her birthday with an elegant bash at the Trocadero. Franchot had made all of the arrangements. Joining them were the Robert Taylors, Ray Millands, Irving Berlins and Cesar Romero, all of whom helped Joan blow out her candles.

In May, Crawford was one of those performers named in an advertisement taken out by the Independent Theatre Owners of America and addressed to all Hollywood producers. It chided studio heads for paying large salaries to performers such as Crawford, Mae West, Greta Garbo and Kate Hepburn, "whose dramatic ability is unquestioned, but whose boxoffice draw is nil."

Stung by this public rebuke, Joan only intensified her career plans. She refused to allow the label "boxoffice poison" to be attached to *her* name. MGM came through, signing Joan to a new contract calling for her to star in fifteen films. There would be three Crawford pictures a year, at $100,000 per, with the total contract amounting to $1,500,000 for five years—one of the biggest deals ever made by any studio.

However much that new contract meant to Joan, she was about to break an even more sacred agreement. On July 19, 1938, it was confirmed that she and Franchot Tone had separated and that he had already moved out of their Brentwood home. For the moment, Joan said, she was not filing for divorce. In four months, Tone's movie contract was expiring. He was expected to return to the New York stage, after which Joan undoubtedly planned to seek a divorce. She filed in February. But then went East, dined with Tone and was photographed in his arms on the dance floor.

In April of 1939, at around the same time that Joan's first Hollywood husband, Doug Fairbanks, Jr., took a second bride, society beauty Mary Lee Epling Hartford (shades of déjà vu—columnists referred to them as the *new* Doug-Mary combo). Joan was in court divorcing Franchot Tone.

She finally arrived costumed as an "orchid lady." She wore a crepe dress, wool tailored coat, a big, floppy-brimmed straw hat (she admitted to reporters that she had been up until three that morning steaming the brim over a tea kettle so it would fall just right!), accessorized by suede pumps, bag and gloves, all in harmonizing orchid tones ranging from lavender to deep purple. Beautifully color-coordinated, she was stunned when the judge publicly berated her. Why, he wanted to know, after she had filed mental cruelty charges against Mr. Tone, had she gone dancing with him in public? Joan batted her cobalt-blue eyes and answered demurely. She said that she and Tone were in the same profession. They might even be making future films together. Therefore, wasn't it more civilized to remain on cordial terms?

She then proceeded to explain that living with Franchot had become oppressive. He had been sullen and resentful. He had absented himself from their home for weeks at a time. Holding her agent's hand as she spoke, Joan nervously continued. "Then he came right out and told me that our marriage had been a mistake . . ."

Joan's statement was corroborated by her former sister-in-law, Kasha LeSueur. The judge granted the divorce. Tearfully, Joan stood. Her wide-brimmed orchid hat flopped perfectly—covering the top half of her face. Slowly, she walked out of the courtroom. The only sound heard was the staccato noise of her high, slim, purple suede heels clicking away on the tile floor.

Across the continent, Kate Hepburn, rehearsing *The Philadelphia Story*, in 1939, made another kind of noise. A local paper had criticized her for being so outspoken in her dislike for Hollywood. Hepburn *had* to reply:

The publicity people out there hate me. I never cooperated with them. If that's done me in, so be it. But, I suffered the most idiotic interviews out there. They kept asking me stupid personal questions and I answered them stupidly, thinking they'd understand: "Was I married? Who was my husband? Did I have any children?" And I replied, "Sure I'm married. I've had four husbands and I have seven children—all colored." And they printed that!

RKO gave me a six-year contract. It was too long, so I bought my freedom. I made a lot of money, but Hollywood always pays people nine million times more than they are worth. I was overpaid. I was never a big boxoffice draw. The films they do are too pleasant . . . too amiable. There's no excitement. Censorship has become a terrible cross. There are all manner of thrills in daily life: sitdown strikes and trouble everywhere. But they never use that for story material. If you eliminate sex and politics, what's left? Besides, their film budgets make no sense. I don't think a comedy picture should cost more than a few hundred thousand dollars. They spend too much out there—on everything.

"Out there," Hollywood studio heads were finally giving in to the screams of their exhibitors. MGM had decided to cancel its radio shows. Darryl Zanuck ordered Tyrone Power to quit appearing on the programs. He claimed that Ty was being overexposed. So Power stopped broadcasting. Zanuck's move and Louis B. Mayer's decision led the way. For a time there would be less and less studio cooperation with "the enemy."

Ty not only lost his radio show, things at home were not running all that smoothly for him either. He had fallen in love with his *Suez* co-star, Annabella. By prearrangement, Tyrone had gone off on a South American "holiday" in November of 1938. There, under romantic Rio skies, he and his French lady had spent several glorious weeks together. Then, Louella Parsons broke the news in her column. Ty, of course, denied everything. He said he and Annabella "were just friends."

Ty's mother was upset. She had been fond of "little Sonja," whom Ty dated. Annabella was a different story. She had been married twice, had a child and was a divorcée. The Powers were Catholic. The studio was equally concerned. Power was their number one romantic idol. For publicity purposes, they had "arranged" the Power-Henie duo, yet they were *not* keen on Ty's being *really* involved with anyone "as womanly" as Annabella. But Power had fallen hard and was determined to have his way.

After many weeks of fast talking, he "secured permission from *both* his mother and his studio." On April 23, 1939, Ty, twenty-four, and Annabella, twenty-five, were married in a small ceremony at Annabella's rented home. Don Ameche was best man. Mrs. Charles Boyer was matron of honor. There were no reporters or photographers allowed at the ceremony. When it was over, Annabella's secretary announced, "Well, it's done."

Tyrone Power and Annabella during the filming of *Suez*. They were married shortly after this film.

Photographers were allowed to take pictures of the glowing bridal couple. Reporters asked the few obligatory questions. Standing together, Ty, so darkly handsome, Annabella, lovely in her Nile-blue afternoon dress, announced that within a short time they would be off on a European honeymoon.

While his flying buddy, Tyrone Power, had taken himself a bride, Howard Hughes had been down in Bermuda on yet another of his intricate business deals. But Hughes, who managed to discuss oil, airplanes and movie deals simultaneously, always had his in-built antennae at the ready; on a moonlit evening, he spotted Brenda Frazier across a ballroom floor and wangled an introduction. She was the nation's number one glamour girl–debutante, having been so chosen in 1938. Only eighteen, she lived on an allowance of $52,000 a year and was the most photographed socialite in America.

Brenda was petite and had hazel eyes, black wavy hair and ruby red lips. Hughes liked what he saw—tremendously. But she was not the usual run-of-the-mill beauty. The heiress to a sizable grain fortune, she needed a special kind of wooing, or so Howard thought. Still, when he held her in his arms for the first time, he offered to make her a star.

Brenda dismissed that offer. But they began dating, and eventually were engaged. The "romance" was typically short-lived; the engagement broken. Howard went back to his airplanes, oil and movies. Brenda dated the world's most eligible men: a Vanderbilt; an Astor; Franklin Roosevelt, Jr.; and John F. Kennedy, before settling down with socialite-playboy John "Shipwreck" Kelly.

On June 7, 1937, at 11:37 A.M., the glamour over Hollywood was switched off. The first bulletin came over the radio: "JEAN HARLOW IS DEAD . . ."

While many of the nation's theatre marquees headlined her name in lights, co-starring with Robert Taylor in *Personal Property*, the twenty-six-year-old platinum blonde died in Hollywood's Good Samaritan Hospital after lapsing into a coma that had lasted for two hours.

She began her career in films as an extra, known by her legal name, Harlean Carpenter McGrew. She had died a full-fledged international star, beloved by tens of millions as the glorious "Platinum Blonde."

Ten days before that final morning, Jean had been on the set of her latest film, *Saratoga*, in which she starred opposite Gable. She had not felt well and had been forced to leave the set. Doctors subsequently would describe what killed her as uremia, a poisoning of the bloodstream.

Her resistance had been low. Earlier that year she had gone to Washington, D.C., to celebrate President Roosevelt's birthday. On the way home, she'd suffered a severe cold. A few months later, a badly impacted wisdom tooth had been pulled. All of these ailments had contributed to her weakened physical condition.

At her bedside when she died were her mother, Mrs. Jean Bello, her latest flame, William Powell, and her former stepfather and manager, Marino Bello. While in the hospital, she appeared to be improving, then went into respiratory failure. The heroic efforts of a special fire department oxygen inhalator squad had been unable to rouse her.

In only a comparatively few years, Harlow's name had become world famous. Everything she did was accompanied by headlines. Less publicized was her warm off-camera personality, highlighted by her delightful self-deprecating humor. Hers was pure, original wit, somehow tinged with a modicum of sarcasm. "All they see when they look at me is my breasts," she'd complained. "I have a brain, too." Then, she followed with that trace of a smile, and added, "But they can't see THAT part of me as easily!"

Outside the Wee Kirk o' the Heather Chapel, at Forest Lawn, William Powell stumbled. His face was milk white. Tears streamed down from beneath his dark glasses. Slowly, he reached for Mrs. Bello's arm. Together, they entered the flower-banked chapel. A broad-brimmed black hat and dark glasses cloaked her emotions. The chapel was filled with famous faces—all the greats were there.

Gable sat, weeping. The usually unemotional Robert Montgomery wiped tears from his eyes, Spencer Tracy, Ronald Colman, Myrna Loy and Norma Shearer hid emotions behind dark glasses. L. B. Mayer openly wept. Howard Hughes was there, pale and motionless. Everywhere you looked, there were stunned, still disbelieving mourners. Somehow, it was incomprehensible that a twenty-six-year-old woman, in the peak season of her life, was gone.

Outside the cemetery gates, thousands of fans stood quietly. Everywhere, there were summer flowers, and sprays, and wreaths and bouquets.

Joan Crawford and Carole Lombard walked solemnly out of the chapel together. Kay Francis stood comforting Barbara Brown, Jean's stand-in, so hysterical she'd had to leave in the middle of the services. Bill Powell, Hal Rosson and screenwriter Carey Wilson left, with Jean's mother, headed for her home in Beverly Hills. Marino Bello and Dr. Carpenter, Jean's natural father, followed, separately. They were joined by many of Jean's friends, who had come to be all together one more time—in Jean's memory.

On the MGM lot, Harlow's dressingroom was locked. It would be left that way, for the time being, in tribute to Jean.

Five weeks after Harlow's death, *Saratoga* was sneak previewed in Glendale. The audience reception was unmistakably enthusiastic. They were somewhat surprised, but never shocked by the fact that the story was a riotous comedy. Each time Jean's name appeared on the screen, and upon the occasion of her first appearance, the house rocked with applause.

Jean's performance was by all odds her finest. At no sacrifice to her vivid personality, she appeared a more authoritative actress. Gable had returned to the roughhewn role that brought him his first popularity and carried it off beautifully. Lionel Barrymore, Walter Pidgeon and Una Merkel scored solidly. The whole picture, under the direction of Jack Conway, was received extremely well.

Louis B. Mayer, satisfied with the *Saratoga* preview, left town in the company of Joe Schenck. He was drained by the emotional loss of one of his greatest stars—and closest friends.

For weeks after Harlow's death, a car was seen every day parked across the street from her home. Inside, a man sat, alone, his eyes covered by dark glasses. Usually he stayed for half an hour or so, sitting motionless, his head bowed. When he was finally able to "let go," William Powell released his sorrow—and went on about the business of living and loving again.

FAST FRIENDS
FIELDS AND BARRYMORE

If all the multitalented human beings that have been famous on the Hollywood scene, no individual was more talented—or more eccentric—than a bulbous-nosed, fey creature the world knew as W. C. Fields.

He was born on February 20, 1879, in Philadelphia, and named William Claude Dukenfield. During his colorful lifetime he performed in circuses and vaudeville, onstage and in films. He was also a prolific writer, and, some say, "a certified genius."

No one knew him better than the exotically beautiful Carlotta Monti. She was his mistress for fourteen years, and shared every phase of his life. Recently, she reminisced about him. She talked free-style, saying whatever popped into her head. Throughout the discussion, she referred to W.C. most often as either "Woody" or "the old man." He, in turn, had called her "Chinaman" because of her penchant for dressing in exotic Chinese silk pajamas.

I don't live today like I did when I was

with the old man. But I have no regrets. Tomorrow is here now. Yesterday is gone. Woody and I were very devoted. When he was sick—which was a lot of the time—I would never leave his side. He was a hard man to live with. But he was never drunk. I wouldn't have stayed if he had acted the way they said he did. I can't stand drunks. At home, he was never a showoff. He rarely told jokes, except sometimes, at dinner, if someone asked him to. Most of the time, he was very quiet. He never behaved like an actor away from the studio.

I never slept one whole night in the same bed with him, not that we didn't have an affair. But he couldn't sleep for more than two or two and a half hours at a time. So he was up and down, and I was up and down. I had another bed set up alongside of his, in addition to having my own separate bedroom. When he got up at night, I'd make him a snack, and we'd stay up and talk.

Woody could be very temperamental . . . especially when he

was writing. When I first met him, he had a secretary. One day, he started swearing in front of us, using bad cuss words. So I told him, "If you want to keep seeing me, you have to treat me like a lady." Then his secretary said, "Mr. Fields, I was just about to say the same thing to you."

He never swore again. At least, not in my presence.

Monti, who began working in pictures in 1926, gave up her career when Fields objected.

I exchanged movie work for being with him. I knew his reputation. Before me, he had lived with eight other women. They all left him—fast. But I really cared for him, so I stayed.

He was very down to earth, and had a lot of good qualities. But he never gave me any money, and I never thought about the future. From the very first, when I went to stay with him, almost everybody accepted me. I think because we were honest and open. A lot of people lived together in those days—but on the Q.T. But everyone knew about W. C. Fields and me.

At the beginning, one of Woody's friends, director Greg La Cava, gave me a rough time. He was mean when he drank, and he drank quite a bit. One night, we were having dinner at the house. Woody never liked to have too many people at one time. There was Fields and me, Gene Fowler, Mack Sennett and Greg. Suddenly, out of the blue, La Cava put his hands on my throat and began choking me. Then he shouted, "You better be good to him, or I'll kill you!"

I walked out into the other room and started to cry. I'd never been treated like that before. Fields came out to find me. Then he ran back into the dining room and yelled at La Cava, "You sonofabitch, you get out of here, and don't you ever come back. You can't treat my Chinaman like that!" He didn't

see Greg for a year, not until we left Encino and moved to De Mille Drive.

People have asked me if it was very difficult—being Fields' mistress. Well, honestly, it wasn't, because I cared for him. Besides, I was very young, and he wasn't really old. He even used to play tennis. He didn't annoy me. We would take long walks. I had deep feelings for him. But still, there were some things I couldn't do. Not even for Woody. He wanted me to go to the studio with him every day. If he could, Fields would have kept me like a bird in a gilded cage.

But other women had it rough, too. Sometimes I used to feel sorry for Elaine Barrie, when she was married to John Barrymore. When Woody and I lived at 655 Funchal Road, overlooking Beverly Hills and the ocean, Barrymore lived nearby. Whenever John got drunk, he was mean. Once, we all went out to a big affair. Barrymore had been drinking, and he hadn't bathed. No one wanted to sit next to him, so I did. That night, just before the lights went down at this industry dinner, with everybody important there, Mae West came in. I'll never forget it. She made a grand entrance, trailing her white fox. She got mean in the end, too . . .

Woody usually hated drunks, but he cared for Barrymore, so he tolerated him. John usually came to our house when no other guests were there. I also didn't like Mack Sennett. He used to chew tobacco, and it dribbled down his chin.

W.C. didn't really like to go out. He was a homebody. But, one day, we went to the races with Bing Crosby, down to Agua Caliente, Mexico. Bing gave Woody a pair of binoculars. They cost $750. When Fields died, I was broke, so I pawned them for fifty dollars.

When Fields died, on Christmas Day, 1946, he left a fortune. Carlotta knows for sure that there were at least forty-eight different bank books, large deposits all over the country. As for her "rewards," well, in

Carlotta Monti, W. C. Fields' mistress, as she looked when he first met her.

those days before "palimony," she was *not* protected. Amazingly, she holds no bitterness. From the day Fields died, Monti has worked hard for a living. For a while she received checks in the amount of fifty dollars a week from his estate, but these stopped coming years ago.

But the fortunes of many Hollywood stars—even those who made millions—were often dissipated. One of W.C.'s closest friends, another artist in the "genius" category, was John Barrymore. Because of his erratic life-style, his numerous wives, and various other problems, "the Great Profile" was down and out years before his life ended in May of 1942.

Nearly four years before his death, in September of 1938, *The Hollywood Reporter* ran a startling advertisement. Although it personally affected only *one* performer, it deeply touched each of his colleagues. The ad copy described the Barrymore home in exquisite detail:

THE ESTATE OF
JOHN BARRYMORE
For Sale at a Sacrifice

In a romantic, wood setting . . . on the crest of a hill . . . twelve hundred feet above sea level . . . with a magnificent view of Beverly Hills, Bel Air, Westwood Hills and the blue Pacific at Santa Monica . . . the estate, comprising seven-and-a-half acres developed at a cost of $448,000 . . . presents an extraordinary opportunity for seclusion and better living in the exclusive community of distinguished families.

There are 2 master houses containing 22 spacious rooms . . . including 8 bedroom suites and 5 bathrooms . . . There is a separate 6-room house for servants; 2 roomy garages; 2 garden houses and dog kennels.

There is a typical old tavern room containing a bar transplanted from the Alaska goldmining country . . . A trophy room with Mr. Barrymore's collection of rare birds, animals and fish adjoins a projection room.

The chandelier in the music room comes from the palace of the Archduke of Austria, and originally cost $8,500. All buildings are modern Spanish and include Mr. Barrymore's private collection of antique doors.

The spacious grounds include a large kidney-shaped swimming pool encircled by a water spray that is rainbow-hued when it is lighted. A large bathhouse contains dressing rooms, lavatory and complete filtering system for the pool.

In the center of an illuminated Japanese fish-pond is a $14,000 sun and moon dial from Cambridge, England . . . There is also a massive bird aviary, roofed with glass, which may be converted into a ballroom or indoor pool.

Mr. Barrymore spent $110,000 for landscaping, which includes everything growable in California. There is also a wine-cellar, film vault, play garden, wading pool and bowling green adequate for tennis.

Barrymore intimates knew with what love and care John had acquired and collected all of the possessions which had become part of his life-style. Upon reading the advertisement, they realized he had come to some desperate moment in his life. The entire estate, which had set him back close to a million dollars, was on the open market for *ninety thousand dollars*—less broker's fee!

Hollywoodites who did not know Barrymore might have shrugged off the pathetic tenor of the whole situation with a funny crack or a cruel aside. But, down deep, every high-living celebrity realized that he or she *could* wind up the same way: selling costly possessions because the fates had turned on them . . . because the magic was gone.

W. C. Fields
"NOW I'M A GENTLEMAN FARMER"

In 1934, W. C. Fields had been cast in the role of Micawber in David Copperfield. *The film's director, George Cukor, said: "Fields had never really played a character role before—but he was born for this part.*
"He was charming to work with. He added so much dimension to the role. Even his ad libs were brilliantly in character. There was a scene where he was sitting at a desk writing. He asked me if he could have a cup of tea placed next to him. Then he proceeded to write furiously—and he dipped his pen into the teacup instead of the inkwell. It was perfect!"
It was during Fields' David Copperfield *filming that he wrote this vignette for* The Hollywood Reporter. *It ran in December 1934.*

I think "Squire W. C. Fields" looks good on calling cards. And that, in short, or shorts as the case may be, is why I became a gentleman farmer.

I have a little 7½ acre ranch in Encino, not far from the studio and there I commune with nature. I have trees. Such lovely, gorgeous trees of all kinds. And vegetables. And a tennis court. And a goldfish pond. It is all so pastoral.

You should see me behind my patient, plodding mules as I harry the fields. I think harry is the word. The only trouble comes when the mules go on one side of a tree and I steer the plow on the other. But these are only minor matters.

I love nature. Beauteous, bounteous, beneficent nature. I love the sun and the moon (particularly the moon) and the stars. I love the soft winds, and the gentle dripping rain. So darn much rain dripped over that dirt road up to my house that I was marooned for two days. But I still love nature.

It thrills me deeply to see the little stalks of corn, the tiny something-or-others of wheat pushing their way up through the ground into the sunlight. I enjoy my trees and my vegetables and my flowers. I even like the animals. I have one potato patch that I planted just to keep a little family of potato bugs fed during the winter.

There, in my little home, I am away from the hustle and the bustle of this work-a-day world. There is peace, and quiet, and solitude in the country. Nothing but the mooing of cows, the neighing of the horses, the grunting of the pigs, the crowing of the roosters, the cackling of the hens, the chirping of the crickets, the baaing of the goats, the buzzing of the bees, the howling of the coyotes, the infernal twittering of the dratted birds, and the chunk of a lot of one-lunged pumping motors to keep a feller awake. As I say, it's all so calm and serene and peaceful and quiet.

In my own quiet way I am attempting a few experiments in vegetation. I am attempting to do a few things that the late Luther Burbank left undone.

Portrait of four Barrymores. Standing, John; seated, brother and sister Lionel and Ethel, with John's newest baby.

For one thing I am watering my orange trees with gin instead of water. Then all I have to do is to squeeze the juice into a glass.

I am also perfecting a type of asparagus that will be a boon to humanity. I am crossing the asparagus with raisins. The iron in the raisins will cause the asparagus to assume an erect position and it will then be a joy, rather than a feat fit for a contortionist, to eat.

When I am through with these little things, I plan to develop a watermelon with the seeds in the center like a cantalope and also an ear of corn with handles.

Being busy in a picture, I haven't much time to devote to these scientific achievements, however, but just give Fields a chance. What he starts, he finishes. As I can easily prove with the aid of a number of empty bottles.

In the spring a young man's fancy may lightly turn to any number of things. The Fields fancy turns to productivity. He leaps into the fields, spade and fork in hand, and turns over the soil. He digs little holes, and in them places seed of various flora. He waters them tenderly, and watches them blossom. Usually they turn out to be weeds, but that is nothing. They are the results of his tender, lavish care. He has a paternal instinct toward each little stalk, each tiny bud. In him glows the pride of parenthood. And ah, my friends, it is a lovely feeling.

The life of a gentleman farmer is indeed a delightful one. He rises at 9 A.M. By that time the hired hands have fed the chickens, milked the cows, cut the wood, and accomplished other odd jobs hither and thither about the premises.

He is served a breakfast of eggs from his own hens, bacon from his own pigs, bread from his own wheat fields, and honey from his own bees. Later he drives to the nearest golf course and spends the day wandering around the links.

He returns home for dinner—all of his own produce—and then drifts out to visit friends for the evening, returning home late, and sleeping the sleep that comes from honest toil.

At the end of the year he totals up his assets, and his outgoing bills, and finds himself considerably in arrears. He sells the farm, pays these off, and goes back to work again. But he has had a lovely time.

John Barrymore
"MEMORIES"

John Barrymore, in his prime, was one of the greatest actors ever to appear on a stage or before a camera. Even half sober, he was more articulate, more urbane and twice as witty as the majority of his peers. In 1937, when Billy Wilkerson asked if he would like to write a piece for The Hollywood Reporter, *Barrymore was delighted to comply. He had spent one of his earlier years as a professional artist-journalist, and had never lost the literary touch.*

According to an old song, memory is the only friend that grief can call its own. That's nice and sentimental, but memory is a great deal more than that. I wouldn't take anything for mine. It furnishes a companionship as fresh as the day it first existed.

In my memories, I can always find myself in a circle of wonderful people. I can relive experiences that are both amusing and interesting—sometimes a bit nonsensical—and always be in good company.

I can remember Edward Sheldon, the playwright, for instance. He was a marvelous wit. In fact, it was his wit that led me to do Richard the Third.

We were going through the New York zoo and happened on an insect room. In a glass cage was a big red tarantula with a bald spot on its back—quite the ugliest thing I had ever seen.

"It looks," I remarked, "like Richard the Third."

"Why don't you play him?" demanded Sheldon.

We laughed, but it germinated the idea.

I can always get a laugh out of my memories. One of the funniest is of a monkey.

While I was playing Hamlet in London, I fell heir to an old English valet who had, at one time, been a servant for Beerbohm Tree. I resolved to take him back to the United States with me.

One night I came home from the theatre and found a big cardboard box awaiting me in my hotel room. Presently, the box began to jump about. At first I thought I was seeing things.

Then I realized it was no hallucination and upon opening the box discovered a small monkey, a playful little thing and very affectionate.

I christened her Claire. The English valet and Claire formed a deep attachment for each other, so when I left for America I took both of them along. We all wound up in Hollywood.

There are memories of fellows like Walter Deffenbaugh, the brilliant newspaperman and actor. We used to fool around New York together and, finally, when Lionel and I went on the road, we persuaded Frank to come along and try his hand at acting.

Frank was a big asset to us. He had a gold tooth and when we went broke we used to pawn it.

Frank was fired when we got to Minneapolis, but he got a job as dramatic critic. Every day he took delight in panning our show. He paid particular attention to Lionel. We had a great laugh over it when we met nightly to dine with him.

Frank got along all right until one day when he roasted Minneapolis. They fired him for that.

I knew all the newspaper crowd in the old days. I had decided to become a newspaper artist. I didn't want to act. Finally I got a job with the *New York Journal*. Arthur Brisbane was my boss. He tolerated me for more than a year. Then he called me into his office and gave me my walking papers.

I recall that he told me I came from a family of actors and I should go on the stage, pointing out that I couldn't possibly be the failure there that I was in the newspaper office.

So I went back to acting, but not until I nearly starved to death. I lived on free lunches while I was making a desperate effort to sell some of my sketches. During a period of six months I sold one sketch—for $10.

My travels took me to San Francisco where I did a lot of chumming with Ashton Stevens, one of the most brilliant dramatic critics of all time.

I remember that one night, after the show, I got into a place where a group of thugs eyed me furtively. I was wearing the dress suit I wore in the play and the atmosphere was tense until Stevens showed up.

Later I found out that the thugs had me all divided up. They had planned to take me into the alley and grab watch, studs, cuff links and the other embellishments. "Ash," as a newspaperman, knew them all and his appearance saved my jewelry and possibly my life.

Then there's the old fellow I know up in Alaska, a hunter and trapper whom I visit whenever I get up that way. For a living he raises foxes and does quite well at it.

Once, about nine years ago, he visited Los Angeles. He and his wife hired a wing at the Ambassador Hotel, but when they went out they were afraid to cross the street on account of the automobile traffic. So they packed up and went back home! I never blamed them.

These people are all real to me. So, for instance, is John Sargent, the artist, one of my best friends. I was always a worshipper of his art and even more so of the man himself. I wanted him to do a portrait of me, but, somehow, we never got around to it.

Meanwhile, he had vowed never to paint another picture, but imagine my surprise one day when I called on him in Boston, to be presented with a picture he had painted of me from memory.

My father, Maurice Barrymore, is one of my real memories. I felt a terrible sense of loss when he died, but even in such blows there is consolation, for in the example of those we love and admire, and the memory of them, is an incentive to carry on that spurs one along the roadway of life.

I remember his performances, as I watched them from the wings and recall that we children, Ethel, Lionel and myself, used to talk about being stage actors when we grew up.

We put on a play in an old barn. It was *Camille,* with Lionel the elder lover, Ethel as Camille and myself as Armand. It was quite the most original script ever written because we made it more original than the authors. Youngsters of 8, 10 and 12 do these things.

I remember Tully Marshall when he was in my father's company, and Joe Grismer. Likewise, Modjeska, who was Lionel's godmother. Down the years I have played with many brilliant actors and there is still a freshness to the performances of those of the past in my memory.

I recall my first motion picture engagement and my best part in the old days of silent films. It was *Dr. Jekyll and Mr. Hyde,* produced at Paramount 17 years ago.

Now I'm back at the studio where I started, having played recently in two *Bulldog Drummond* pictures, in *Night Club Scandal* and in *True Confession*—quite apropos, don't you think in view of what I've written?

The talkies have given me a brilliant set of new memories—almost too fresh to be called memories, but which, in the future, will mean a great deal to me.

HOLLYWOOD POTPOURRI
1939

WAYNE MORRIS was the first groom of the New Year. He married socialite BUBBLES SCHINASI on January 7, in a private room at the Victor Hugo Restaurant. Wayne and Bubbles honeymooned on a cruise to New York via the Panama Canal. Then they visited her mother, who lived in a forty-eight-room "shack" on Riverside Drive. At least the handsome Warners star won't run out of cigarette money anymore . . . ANNABELLA, back in America, houseguested with TYRONE POWER'S mother. Ty lived with Mom, too, which made the arrangement very cosy . . . CLAUDETTE COLBERT'S maid was the most popular female on the Paramount lot—the lady happened to be an expert horse handicapper—and picked winners when she wasn't busy picking up after Claudette. And LESLIE HOWARD introduced VIVIEN LEIGH and LAURENCE OLIVIER to the American game of football. When the fans spotted Leslie, they rushed past Larry and Vivien to get to Howard, who was very embarrassed that his British colleagues went unrecognized in the Los Angeles Coliseum.

In February, SONJA HENIE, who originally dated TY POWER under instructions from the 20th publicity department, really fell for the guy. Now that he and ANNABELLA were "for real," SONJA'S determined to make him jealous. She's bringing back a wealthy Russian suitor she met on a recent trip to South America . . . LANA TURNER and GREG BAUTZER went to the La Conga on February 7th, and stayed until after midnight, so they could celebrate Lana's eighteenth birthday together . . . CLARK GABLE gave CAROLE LOMBARD a mule for her birthday and then put the poor critter to work on his farm . . . JUDY GARLAND and her family moved into a beautiful new Bel Air home . . . And zany LUPE VELEZ said she had a wealthy suitor in New York, and as soon as she finished her current film she was headed for Nevada to divorce JOHNNY WEISSMULLER, and then to New York to meet her new beau.

On February 18, Pasadena Junior College student WILLIAM BEEDLE signed a stock contract with Paramount. His name was changed to WILLIAM HOLDEN, and he debuted in a small part in JACKIE COOPER'S film *What a Life* . . . ANNABELLA told a reporter she would rather have TY POWER than willpower . . . HUMPHREY BOGART developed such a female fan following, Warners allowed him to exchange his six-guns for more romantic roles . . .

In March, JACKIE COOGAN had really hard luck. His latest personal appearance tour was canceled, and BETTY GRABLE told him she wanted a divorce . . . The young British royal princesses, ELIZABETH and MARGARET ROSE, "confessed" that their own personal favorite movie star was GENE AUTRY. So Republic Studios sent prints of Gene's latest flicks to be screened for them at Balmoral Castle in Scotland . . . A Hollywood bartender came up with a mild drink for celebrity entertainers who needed the boost from a drink before performing but couldn't afford to get tipsy. Called the "Tornado," it was actually a mild mixture of: one jigger of sherry; one teaspoon of grenadine; $\frac{1}{2}$ fresh lime; plenty of ice, put into a tall highball glass with club soda.

SAM GOLDWYN signed DANA ANDREWS, a handsome gas station attendant, to a contract the second week in March. Dana debuted with JOEL McCREA in *Black Gold* . . . Complications developed in the TY POWER—ANNABELLA merger. Unless they can get a papal dispensation, the wedding may not take place. Ty's Catholic; Annabella was widowed once and divorced once . . . And on March 29th, GABLE and LOMBARD *did* marry in a ceremony performed in the Kingman, Arizona, hometown of Gable's best pal, ANDY DEVINE. There was an open house at Carole's on the 30th for all of the reporters. The groom reported to work early the next morning on *Gone With the Wind*.

In April, LANA TURNER had hysterics. She and GREG BAUTZER had made a pact. If one grew tired of the other, he/or she would send the other "partner" one dozen red roses, no card attached. So Greg left town and Lana received her dozen roses and went into a nonstop crying jag. When Greg returned and called, Lana was shocked. But the mistake was cleared up. Greg had instructed the florist to send *white* roses— and there had been a mixup . . . A new professional baseball team was organized called the Hollywood Stars. The players were financed by a combine headed by CECIL B. DeMILLE, GARY COOPER, BARBARA STANWYCK, BOB TAYLOR and HARRY WARNER. The "Stars" will play at Gilmore Stadium, located close-in at Beverly Boulevard and Fairfax Avenue . . .

In mid-April STANWYCK and TAYLOR had another new "business deal." They got together with the architect who will build their honeymoon cottage . . . BETTY GRABLE and JACKIE COOGAN reconciled. They'll head for a second honeymoon in Hawaii after they finish co-starring in *Million Dollar Legs* for Paramount . . . LOMBARD moved her three dogs out to GABLE'S ranch. She moved into the newly redecorated place in mid-April . . . The SPENCER TRACYS headed for New York on their way to a European vacation they had planned for twenty-two years . . . And newcomer LINDA DARNELL debuted in 20th's *Hotel for Women*, a film ELSA MAXWELL helped write.

In May, CHARLES CHAPLIN, not noted for readily parting with his cash, gave PAULETTE GODDARD a $75,000 necklace of emeralds and

1 Lana Turner in a scene from *Dancing Co-Ed*. On the bandstand, Artie Shaw, her first husband.   2 Sylvia Hawkes Ashley Fairbanks, Louella O. Parsons, and Douglas Fairbanks, Sr., attend a Hollywood premiere, June 1939.   3 Newlyweds Robert Taylor and Barbara Stanwyck.

diamonds that was the talk of the town . . . JIMMY CAGNEY's crazy about boats—but hates the sea. So, when he invites cronies aboard his yacht, they have a ball but never leave the dock . . . Yet another Hollywood High School student received a movie. Eighteen-year-old NANETTE FABERE [sic] got a Warners contract and was cast in a small role in *Elizabeth and Essex* . . . At the end of May, RONALD REAGAN went back home to Des Moines to do the radio commentary at the annual Tin Can Derby . . . And DAVID O. SELZNICK will never play golf with PAULETTE GODDARD again. She beat him out of $1600.

In June, Hollywoodites, who were always looking for a new drink, discovered a great brew to cure insomnia: a jigger of Jamaican rum in a cup of hot chocolate—guaranteed to put you to sleep pronto . . . JOHN WAYNE had his Republic contract rewritten. He's committed to five pictures a year—but permitted to do any outside picture he can fit into his schedule! . . . Director ERNST LUBITSCH and his *Ninotchka* star got along so well, he began calling her "Greta." No director had ever called her anything but "Miss Garbo" since she made her second Hollywood film . . . And LESLIE HOWARD described his *Intermezzo* co-star, INGRID BERGMAN, as looking like a "sexy virgin."

In July, young PHYLLIS ISLEY, who was given the lead in *Raiders of the Wasteland*, was identified as the daughter of theatre owner PHIL ISLEY, who owns twenty-three movie houses in Oklahoma, Missouri and Kansas. Miss Isley will get her name changed—to JENNIFER JONES . . . ERROL FLYNN left for New York on his way to a six weeks' tour of South America . . . And Warners' big publicity hype for their "Oomph Girl," ANN SHERIDAN, has paid off. Her face and figure have been on over six hundred European magazine covers in the past nine months . . . MARLENE DIETRICH arrived in Paris to make a French film. On Bastille Day, she sang before a huge crowd at the Place de l'Opéra and was a smash.

By August, SUSAN HAYWARD was hit with a $100,000 lawsuit by her former model agent; he claimed she owed him ten percent of the million-dollar contract she just signed . . . CAROLE LOMBARD's emergency appendectomy held up shooting on RKO's *Vigil in the Night* for six weeks . . . Hungarian director MICHAEL CURTIZ had his crew in hysterics when he asked his prop man for a mohair-covered throne chair, and specified, "Be sure it's from a genuine moe." In midmonth, MGM screened *The Wiz-ard of Oz* at the studio, and it was a smash hit. JUDY GARLAND and MICKEY ROONEY made personal appearances with the picture in Washington, and 6,000 fans lined up to see them . . . BRIAN AHERNE and JOAN FONTAINE became man and wife on August 20 . . . And Warners, in an effort to separate the identities of their two young contract players, JANE WYMAN and JANE BRYAN, have changed Wyman's first name to Janet.

In September, sixteen-year-old KATHERINE [sic] GRAYSON, from St. Louis, who arrived in Hollywood only a few weeks ago to prepare for an opera career, was signed by MGM, and will be featured on EDDIE CANTOR's radio show . . . TY POWER put ANNABELLA on a plane for Europe. She was frantic about her family's safety in France and will try to bring them back to America . . . RONNIE REAGAN, in town with LOUELLA PARSONS and her group of young stars, was bedded with an infected jaw. Young tourmate JANE WYMAN (yes, she pleaded with Warners to let her keep the name Jane) had been providing Ronnie with tender love and care during his illness . . . And CHARLES BOYER was called up to serve with the Free French Army. He had volunteered the moment war was declared.

When October came, HEDY LAMARR, who earned $750 a week at MGM, insisted on a raise, to $5,000 per. Leo the Lion had an attack of asthma just thinking about Hedy's request! . . . HOWARD HUGHES "discovered" OLIVIA DE HAVILLAND—and gave her the usual rush . . . JIMMY STEWART and MARLENE DIETRICH were all over town together . . . JIMMY's pals say "it's nothing but pure fun."

In November, DANA ANDREWS married MARY TODD . . . REAGAN and WYMAN closer than ever, still on LOUELLA's junket, but due home soon . . . AL JOLSON rather bitterly told friends he was "through with women," and from now on would concentrate on his racing stable—period! GENE MARKEY tossed a posh birthday party at the Beverly Wilshire for HEDY LAMARR . . . HOWARD HUGHES and DE HAVILLAND a thing of the past. His newest flame is gorgeous brunette actress PATRICIA DANE . . .

When Christmas arrived, GABLE gifted LOMBARD with a $5,000 ruby and diamond clip . . . TY gave ANNABELLA a lovely fur coat . . . JACK and MARY BENNY exchanged his and hers convertibles . . . And HOWARD HUGHES sent showers of flowers to at least half a dozen Hollywood beauties—he was "between girls" and wanted to hedge his bet.

THREE VOICES ON "THE GOOD OLD DAYS"

Milton Berle
"THEM WERE *NOT* THE GOOD OLD DAYS"

One of the most versatile performers in show business, Milton Berle began working when he was a child. In October of 1939, he wrote for The Reporter *this candid piece about his early life as an actor.*

Invariably, when I meet old friends and acquaintances—people who were brought up with me in New York's Harlem when it was a fashionable neighborhood, or people who worked with me in vaudeville or pictures—the conversation usually gets around to "Say, do you remember when—?" I've stood on a corner or sat in a restaurant for hours on end talking about the "good old days"—the time when the kids on 118th Street in Harlem (I was one of them) got 15 cents and three thick sandwiches so that we could go on a hike, only to discover that we had to walk three miles at the end of the day because the fare was 20 cents altogether (the good old days!) or the time the other boys in my gang denounced me with the terrible epithet, "hey actor," because my mother made me wear Buster Brown collars and sissy socks in keeping with my job as a child player at the old Biograph studios (the good old days!) or the time—but I could go on indefinitely.

Them were *not* the good old days. Though it may sound brutal and caustic, the "good old days" exist only in the memories of those who have nothing to look forward to, like people who have retired and whose main pastime is indulging in retrospection, or in the minds of the young and defeated whose solace is the "good old days" when they had what they now miss.

I don't miss the early days. Why should I miss hardship and semi-poverty? When I was five years old, I did imitations and everybody thought I was "cute" except my mother, who whaled the daylights out of me when I cut up her cheap, sleazy imitation fur coat, her only protection against a tough winter, to make "Charlie Chaplin mustaches." At the age of six, I became an "actor" after my mother read somewhere that the Biograph Studios were going to make *Little Lord Fauntleroy*. One of my most searing memories is the day my mother dressed me in an eton jacket (where she borrowed the money to buy it even she doesn't remember), little socks and other sissy garments.

Then she combed out and "finger waved" my long yellow curls (yeh, long yellow curls and maybe you want to make something out of it?) took me by the hand, wiped my nose and two hours later I was a "child extra" at Biograph. Those were the good old days, all right, when unless I had my mother with me, the members of my former "gang" would bombard me with "hey actor!" and slightly aged tomatoes or a small rock.

I toured in vaudeville for years after being in pictures long enough to become pale and emaciated from standing under hot lights and getting very little sleep between going to school and working in the films. I worked with Flora Finch, John Bunny, Pearl White, Mabel Normand, Jack Holt, and many others of the early film era. Not that I am sorry for the tough life I led at the ages of six, seven, eight and upwards, because my earnings filled that coal scuttle and the bread basket for a family that included my mother, an ailing father, three older brothers and a younger sister. But you wouldn't call them the good old days. At least I wouldn't, and I lived them.

Getting back to vaudeville, they didn't have air-conditioned trains in the "good old days." Sleepers cost a lot of money so we slept in a day coach, covered by a blanket of cinders in the summer and a covering of frost in the winter. Mom and I couldn't afford the better hotels and in some of the towns we played the best hotel would be a rat-trap that made our home in Harlem—railroad flat that it was—seem like a palace by comparison. The food wasn't any better—but, as my friends say, them were the good old days!

Sure, that's all over with now. I've recently finished a long engagement at the International Casino on Broadway, and I'm currently rehearsing for a new George Abbott play and for a new radio program that Quaker Oats brings to the air over NBC (advt.). Mom, my steady guide and inspiration, has enough fur coats to start a retail establishment (although I can't figure out what she could possibly want with a mink bathing suit) and I feel fine.

There have even been nibbles from the movie firms in the last few months. I'm 31 years old. I've been in show business for 25 of them. There have been moments of joy, of sorrow and days when I drew consolation prizes after shooting for the big blue ribbon for a long time.

So I never want to look back, unless it is to remind myself of a mistake I made that I don't want to make again. I haven't cut off the old acquaintances and friends. They are the part of the "good old days" that I want to remember, because they too have learned to be of the present and of the future. Sure, we reminisce about the "good old days," but with a shudder and an avowal that we wouldn't want to live those days over again for all the tea in China. Them were NOT the good old days!

Buster Keaton
"I'M THE ORIGINAL 'I WAS THERE' GUY"

On October 28, 1939, Buster Keaton, one of Hollywood's first authentic superstars (way before the word was even coined), wrote this amusing vignette for The Hollywood Reporter. *Because Buster had been around for so long, people always asked him about "the old days."*

They tell me I'm a movie veteran. Just because I've been around this town called Hollywood since 1917, they think I was the first on the scene during every important step the industry ever made. A guy starts telling a Hollywood story that he heard another fellow say he heard and when the story is ended, he turns to me and says: "Isn't that the way it happened, Buster?"

The story he told may have been news to me but I've become "tell-shocked" enough to answer automatically: "Exactly! Exactly!"

When I went to work for 20th Century–Fox in *Hollywood Cavalcade,* everyone on the set wanted my version of how it all happened. You'd think from their questions that I furnished the scratch pads while Thomas Edison sketched plans for his first motion picture in 1888; that I got sunburned on the roof of the San Fernando Building at 6th and Main Streets while Col. Bill Selig's company filmed the first movie in Los Angeles back in '08; that I held Mack Sennett's seat for him in 1935 when he went backstage of the old Empress Theatre in Los Angeles to pick up Charlie Chaplin for a role in a one-reeler called *Kid's Auto Races.*

You'd think I was the guy who held up that stage actor, Hobart Bosworth, when he almost fainted at an offer from Selig to appear in pictures. He recovered quickly enough, however, when mention was made that there would be $125 added to the Bosworth bank account for two days' work. That wasn't tin in those days—it ain't tin today, either—and Hobart went into a picture called *The Power of the Sultan.* They filmed it in back of a Chinese laundry in Los Angeles, and a sheet was borrowed for Bosworth's robe while a bath towel served as his turban. Folks think I held the tickee while the company used the washee.

Bosworth fell hook, line and sinker for the business and started to write, direct and act in his own shows. Bosworth says he bought quite a few stories from a certain Gladys Smith, who later became known—but well!—as America's sweetheart, Mary Pickford. One guy recently asked me why *I* changed her name!

That barn on the Paramount lot where today shapely young lassies and muscle-conscious lads do their exercises is the same building where Cecil B. DeMille directed *The Squaw Man* in 1913 with Dustin Farnum. As the story goes, DeMille and Farnum left New York, prepared to shoot the picture in Flagstaff, Arizona. But when they arrived there, they found that Flagstaff resembled a dance-hall in a Blue Law state at 9 o'clock Sunday evening. So they choo-chooed to Hollywood and rented the barn for seventy-five iron men a week. You can take it for granted that I was the guy who rode with Casey, the engineer, on the same train, greeted Flagstaff with a loud raspberry, came to Hollywood and slept in the barn's hayloft and then got up and tried to chisel the owner of the barn down to one seventy-five.

Mack Sennett, when he was writing for

D. W. Griffith, used to turn in comedies using policemen as victims. Griffith didn't encourage him too much, but he wrote them anyway. Those scripts were a standing studio joke but Sennett had the last laugh when the Keystone Cops [sic] began to tear around. I'm the guy who laughed the loudest, then whispered to Mack: "Save 'em for yourself."

In 1909, the industry disapproved of the use by newspaper comic strips of the term "movie." People began repeating the word so much that the Essanay Company, with a keen eye for publicity, offered a handsome award of $25 for a new tag for the motion picture. Edgar Strakosch, a musician and exhibitor in Sacramento, whom many insist was my second cousin, submitted the word "photoplay." He won the contest, impressing everyone but the comic artist who still liked "movie."

In 1921, a night spot was opened in Los Angeles and soon became the place to see and be seen. Opened by the Ambassador Hotel and christened the Cocoanut Grove, the cafe became the mecca for stars and movie executives as well as tourists looking for stars and executives. As the story goes, many stars were discovered by producers while dancing there. Among them, I hear, were Joan Crawford, Carole Lombard, Loretta Young and Ricardo Cortez. If you can keep a secret, it was Keaton, himself, who waltzed with Crawford,

pinned an orchid on Lombard, sang off-key choruses with Young while the band played, then gave up his table so Cortez could be lamped by a producer.

But that isn't all. I'll have you know—rather, my friends will have you know—that I was washing elephants at the Miller Bros. 101 Circus Ranch in Santa Monica when Thomas Ince signed them for pictures.

I was sneezing under a pepper tree near the junction of Hollywood and Sunset boulevards when Griffith talked over production problems on the lawn outside the studio. He didn't like the way pictures were titled so he hired a young girl who had sent him several stories from San Diego to do the job. Her name was Anita Loos, and my pals blushingly admit I was the guy who pedaled a bicycle to San Diego and rode her back to Hollywood on the handlebars. And that ain't all. She wrote *Gentlemen Prefer Blondes* because she didn't like to see me running around with a certain brunette!

Yessiree! The movie business is a three billion dollar industry. More than two hundred million people see a movie during a week. And thirty years ago I was getting sunburned on a roof at 6th and Main, telling people this business would grow into a three billion dollar industry.

I'm the original "I Was There" guy.

D. W. Griffith
"THE GREATEST PERSONS ARE THE SIMPLEST"

Objective Hollywood authorities knew that D. W. Griffith contributed more innovative techniques to the art and skill of film direction than anyone else in the history of the industry. But by 1939 he seemed to be "the forgotten man." Friends said he was both pleased and grateful when Billy Wilkerson asked him to contribute a piece for The Hollywood Reporter's *ninth anniversary issue.*

Reminiscing at length is a sure-fire way of clearing out a room, leaving the narrator delivering solitary and magnificent monologues. I have been asked to reminisce at length.

Perhaps one way of skirting the pitfall of being a bore under these circumstances is to avoid dwelling upon one's own accomplishments, minor or otherwise. That shouldn't be difficult.

Anything I might have done during my long association with the film industry isn't impor-

tant enough for recapitulation. No one man is important enough, nor what he does worthy of long and continual comment.

The brightest, most significant memories I have carried with me are concerned with personalities. The good people I have met, the fine folks with whom I have worked. They alone matter.

As a rule, you'll find in our business that the greatest persons are the simplest in heart.

The real people of the world, regardless of station, are the best fellows. The would-bes in all walks of life are afraid of having their dignity injured. The real ones aren't worried about that.

As a director I have never had any great difficulties with human beings in so-called high or low walks of life. None were hard to get along with—when they had brains.

Lionel Barrymore, Lillian Gish, Mary Pickford and Dick Barthelmess among others, were not only easy to get along with, but fun to work with. I can't imagine any happiness that could compare with that of having a good story and these geniuses to work with in translating that story to the screen.

The loudest and longest laughs I have ever had, in my screen experience, came when I directed W. C. Fields in *Sally of the Sawdust,* way back.

It seems a far cry from the days when Mary Pickford was trying to get a $25-a-week guarantee. We broke an ironclad rule of the industry in giving it to her. I remember that one day Mary got a little indignant. The Irish in her cropped up and she declared:

"Mark my words—some day I'll be making $100 a week!"

Four years later, she was earning $10,000 per week.

A certain actor came to the old Biograph Studio in New York one day and insisted he would make a good film policeman, for five bucks a day. He was told he wasn't big enough, that men of six feet and more were wanted for policeman parts. The actor put up a good argument, to the effect that one comparatively small man in uniform would make his fellow-cops all the more impressive. We hired him.

The combination prop-boy, errand-boy and jack-of-all-trades at the studio asked the actor his name.

"Barrymore," the man replied, "Lionel. Not the handsome Barrymore."

One time, way back, I was invited to the home of a friend, Elmer Clifton, for a spaghetti dinner. I told Clifton I did not care much for spaghetti. He told me I would get spaghetti the like of which I had never tasted before. He said a cook, not a professional, but an Italian, who loved to prepare the dish for his friends, was the chef for the evening, and that the cook would himself bring the food from the kitchen to the dining table. The cook came in with the spaghetti. Clifton said to me:

"Meet Mr. Valentino—Rudolph Valentino!"

I took one look at Valentino's profile and he was put on the extra list the next day. We made him reduce 20 pounds. He played extra bits, then heavies. As soon as we got him to stop gesticulating—washing the air—he quickly developed the style which afterwards made him the most popular leading man the screen has ever known.

In the making of *Way Down East,* we used a lot of extras in various scenes, and as usual the extras were hard to handle. When we wanted to get action, we would shout to one young girl who had more sense than the rest of us combined to "get in there and give us action." Perhaps you know her name—it is Norma Shearer.

Perhaps the most memorable period in my film work was during the World War [I], when I was making pictures in England. The folks with whom I came in contact then, from members of nobility down, form a dearly remembered gallery.

Dowager Queen Alexandria of England, widow of King Edward VII, was one of the most gracious ladies I have ever known. She actually appeared for a bit in *Hearts of the World.* That was in 1917. She was extraordinarily anxious to please. It was literally impossible to outdo her in courtesy and consideration.

When I was over there, and men were needed for active war duty, some ladies of the greatest families in England were scrubbing a studio floor one day and helping adjust props for a set in a picture. Lady Mary Montague, wife of the Viceroy of India, made a complaint. It was that she wasn't given enough work to do—not enough scrubbing.

In all fields, the worthwhile people are the simplest and least affected. I have met three presidents of our United States. I found them entirely free from arrogant egotism, remarkably easy to know and get along with.

I am back now, after a period of semi-retirement, engaged again in active motion picture work. It came about through what was intended to be purely a social visit with my old friend, Hal Roach.

Roach asked me to look over story material and go to work on any story that impressed me. One did, very much—a story having to do with the dawn of culture among prehistoric men.

Now I am busy preparing to produce this picture, entitled *1,000,000 B.C.*

So many people ask me if I am going to "work" again. My answer is—"I hope not." Just give me a good story and some good actors to translate that story to the screen.

"Say, that's not work! It's a picnic!"

GOD SAVE "THE KING"

In the late fall of 1938, "Topic A" in Hollywood still revolved around whom David O. Selznick would select to play Scarlett O'Hara. The nationwide search for an "unknown" had been unsuccessful, except for the numerous "casting couch" experiences shared by DOS and his various talent scouts.

All of the actresses in Tinseltown wanted the part. Tall. Short. Blond. Brunette. Young. Middle-aged. Bette Davis, Joan Bennett, Kate Hepburn, Paulette Goddard, Loretta Young and Tallulah Bankhead would have killed for the chance to star opposite Gable. George Cukor had been selected to direct the film.

It was rumored that the role was offered to Norma Shearer. Cries of "foul" . . . "unfair" . . . "unbelievable" were heard throughout the hills of Hollywood. "Now that Thalberg was dead, did she *still* have to get all the good parts? God, wasn't starring in *Marie Antoinette* enough for her?" other leading ladies bleated in agony. But in truth, Norma did want to be Scarlett more than she had ever wanted any role. More, even, than Juliet. *That* had been dear Irving's idea. So she had been working—hard. She read *Gone With the Wind*. Reread it, and studied the script with more care and attention than she had ever employed on any of her vehicles. But thousands of letters came to her attention. Letters from ticket buyers whose opinions she valued. Ninety-nine percent of them wrote the same thing: "Norma, please, *don't play Scarlett!*"

So, even though production was scheduled to start between November 15 and January 1, 1939, there was still *no* Scarlett.

By the second week in December, one of the key scenes, the burning of Atlanta, had been started in order to do away with the destroyed sets and begin construction on the exterior of Tara. During this period, Selznick's brother, Myron, came to the set bringing Vivien Leigh and Laurence Olivier with him. Myron had told David he thought Vivien was perfect for the part. Now he was presenting "his evidence" in person. David took one look and agreed that, at least physically, she was indeed like Scarlett. So Leigh became the unofficial dark-horse candidate. Throughout the next few weeks, the tests continued. Jean Arthur, Paulette Goddard, Joan Bennett and Vivien made the finals.

January of 1939 arrived. It marked the beginning of the last year of the "Threadbare Thirties." Somehow the country, the industry, the world, had managed to survive—so far. And in Hollywood, there was special excitement in the air. Over at Selznick's, hundreds of technicians: costume sewers, Civil War buffs, explosives experts, animal trainers and actors' agents were buzzing about. It was the year of "GWTW"—and everyone wanted in!

By the 13th, the greatest talent hunt in cinema history was over. Scarlett, at last, had been decided upon. The winner was twenty-five-year-old Vivien Leigh, the green-eyed, brunette British actress, then still married to a London attorney-barrister, Herbert Leigh Holman, and the mother of five-year-old Suzanne. Vivien, of course, was jubilant.

But so was her costar-to-be, Clark Gable. He and Carole Lombard had finally set their wedding date. They were married on March 30, and soon moved into Gable's Encino ranch house, where they settled down to enjoy the same closeness which they had

Seated left to right: David O. Selznick, Vivien Leigh; standing behind them Leslie Howard and Olivia de Havilland discussing the script for *Gone With the Wind*. (Courtesy Selznick Properties, Ltd.)

shared for the previous couple of years.

The second week in December 1939, Lombard fussed over the packing of Clark's suitcases. The phone never stopped ringing. There were deliveries all through the day. Last-minute schedule changes arrived. Reporters wanted Gable quotes on all of the fanfare surrounding him. Selznick's publicity people were in and out. Executives from MGM, the studio distributing *Gone With the Wind*, came to discuss strategy and to put Gable at ease. He disliked all of the premiere hoopla to which he would be subjected. He was shy about being plunked down in the middle of the huge Atlanta crowds. Reluctantly, he had agreed to go along with some of the fanfare for the sake of the picture—but he didn't have to like it!

Actually, Clark was somewhat numb at this point. So much time, energy and effort had gone into this whole production. Now the picture was in the can. There were no more lines to learn. No more horses to ride through battle-scarred towns. No more cos-

tumes to fit, and change, and fit again. No more hours of nighttime shooting. So all of this fuss seemed somehow anticlimactic.

Gable supposed he *should* be grateful. Just nine years earlier, he had been out on some dreary location, playing a less-than-secondary role in a turkey called *The Painted Desert*. No one knew his name—or cared. He wasn't even considered a leading-man type in those days. His own agent said that his ears stuck out and his teeth needed fixing. Now he was in the eye of a hurricane, the lead in the biggest epic film ever made. And people kept calling him "The King." The number one male star in the world!

Personally, Gable felt a little odd about that title. After all, Doug Fairbanks had worn the crown for years. And Fairbanks, Sr., was his idol. *His* "King." The one actor he had looked up to as an example of the best in screen excitement.

On December 12th, twenty-four hours before Gable and Lombard were due at the airport, they heard the news—Douglas Fairbanks, Sr., had died suddenly of a heart attack. He was fifty-six years old and had been ill for only a few hours when he passed away. In England, word of his death overshadowed war bulletins.

His wife since 1936, the former Lady Sylvia Ashley, happened to be in their London home at the time. Plunged into deep shock, she left the arrangements to others and prepared to fly to California for the funeral. In Hollywood, *Gone With the Wind* excitement played second fiddle to the headlined words: DOUGLAS FAIRBANKS, SR., DEAD.

Mary Pickford, who had been Mrs. Buddy Rogers since June of 1937, was in Chicago when she received a phone call from her niece. Stunned by the news of her former husband's passing, she secluded herself in her room and canceled a scheduled press conference. Hours later, when pressed for a statement, Mary said: "Douglas' sudden going is a great shock and a deep sorrow to his family and friends, but I'm sure it will prove a consolation to us all to recall the joy and the glorious spirit of adventure that he gave to the world. He has passed from our mortal life as quickly and as spontaneously as he did everything, but it is impossible to believe that the vibrant and gay spirit could ever perish."

While stars gathered for the Fairbanks funeral, it was like Mardi Gras time in Atlanta. The governor had declared a state holiday. The town was overflowing with celebrities from social, political and theatrical circles. The sirens of motorcycle escorts made a continuous, spine-tingling wail. Never in the history of shows, circuses, carnivals or fairs had there been such a fuss. Election days and New Year's Eves paled into insignificance before the "GWTW" excitement.

The parade traveled from the airport through Atlanta and down famed Peachtree Street. Instead of bands marching in the parade, both musicians and choirs were spotted in special locations en route. The fifty flower-bedecked automobiles which carried Gable, Vivien Leigh, Olivia de Havilland, Ona Munson, Evelyn Keyes, Ann Rutherford, Laura Hope Crewes and other cast members, literally rode through a sea of music and confetti. The population of Atlanta was close to 300,000. But at least a million and a half people lined the streets.

The car caravan wound up at the Georgian Terrace Hotel. There was a big civic reception for the stars, who were introduced by Mayor Hartsfield. After gifts were presented, the Confederate flag was raised— *Gone With the Wind* was officially launched— and would eventually be seen all around the world.

In Hollywood, Fairbanks was being buried. The small church was filled to capacity, the extra crowd sat on the grass outside the Forest Lawn Chapel. Several thousand

fans stood silently in a roped-off area. The service was conducted by the Reverend Neal Dodd. Pallbearers were Charles Chaplin, Joseph M. Schenck, Sid Grauman, Clarence Ericksen, Chuck Lewis and Tom Geraghty.

Back in Atlanta, the Junior League gave a *Gone With the Wind* Ball in a huge auditorium. Eight thousand guests were inside, eighty thousand on the outside. Kay Kyser and his band played. Vivien Leigh was Queen of the Ball. Clark Gable was King. Always before, he had felt skittish about that title. Now that Fairbanks was gone, and perhaps by "Divine Right," the throne was legitimately his.

Atlanta adored the film. Authoress Margaret Mitchell was thrilled by the faithful re-creation of her words onto the screen. Selznick had an unqualified sensation on his hands. The three years of work and aggravation . . . the long talent search for Scarlett . . . the thousands of ups and downs, had all been worth it. Vivien Leigh and Clark Gable, Leslie Howard and Olivia de Havilland, Hattie McDaniel and all the rest of the cast were truly magnificent.

On December 18, "GWTW" took New York by storm. The press devoted front-page space plus reams of inside copy to extoll its virtues. Short of a proclamation of martial law, Manhattan saw itself under as complete a siege of armed forces as it had ever experienced. A special detail of three hundred policemen and thirty-eight sergeants had surrounded the Astor and the Capitol theatres for the public's protection during the first twin premiere since Howard Hughes' *Hell's Angels* back in 1930.

In the Capitol lobby, television cameras brought the crowds—and interviews with celebrities—into the homes of thousands of viewers in the metropolitan area. Klieg lights in front of the theatre turned the sky so fiery one might have thought Atlanta was burning

The culmination of Gable's official succession as "the King." Clark puts his handprints and footprints in the forecourt of Grauman's Chinese Theatre. Looking on (left to right): Sid Grauman, director W. S. Van Dyke, and Gable's secretary, Jean Klossner. (Courtesy Bruce Torrence Historical Collection)

all over again. There was an evacuation—a social one—of the entire East Side to Broadway. The mood was so Southern you could almost smell the blossoms and taste the grits. New Yorkers took "GWTW" into their hearts. The "eastern sophisticates" laughed and cried, and stood and cheered. It was the greatest spectacle the town had ever witnessed.

On December 27, the most brilliant premiere in the history of Hollywood ushered in the West Coast opening. There had never been such a star-studded audience, nor so large a crowd of spectators. Huge batteries of arc lights, dozens of spotlights of all sizes, and clusters of incandescents turned night into daytime. Celebrities left their limousines and walked up the esplanade under this massed flood of lights, through a runway banked with sprays of brilliant poinsettias, offset by blue and silver eucalyptus leaves. The lobby was full of baskets of Christmas flowers—not "show plants" but floral tributes specially *purchased* for the occasion.

The enthusiasm of the fans reached two peaks. First, when Vivien Leigh arrived with Laurence Olivier. Second, when Gable and Lombard arrived. Inside, the picture had already started. The esplanade was empty. There were tremendous screams which signaled the coming of the Gables. One collective ear-piercing cheer was sustained and continued until after Clark and Carole had disappeared through the lobby doors.

Gone With the Wind was a fitting end to the Threadbare Thirties. Hollywood was no longer a town in transition from silents to talkies. The decade had been the worst that the motion picture industry had ever experienced. But it ended with the greatest talking Technicolor motion picture that had ever been conceived and brought to fruition on screen.

THE FORTIES

HOLLYWOOD "BATTLEGROUND," THE WAR YEARS

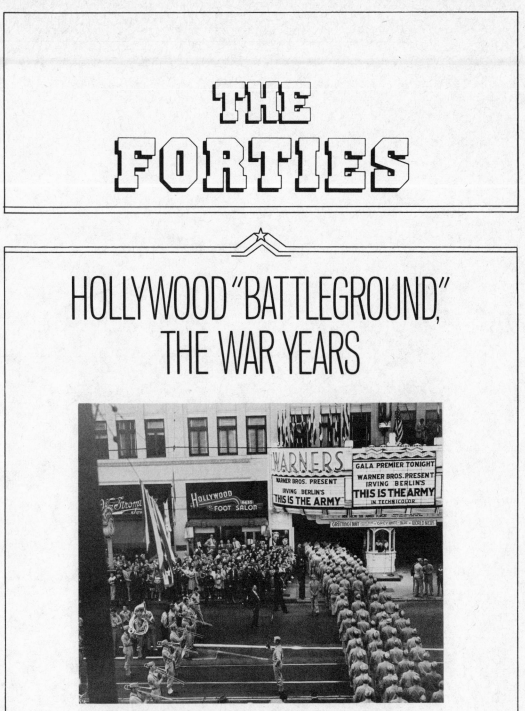

The wartime premiere of Irving Berlin's *This Is the Army*, at Warner Brothers' Theatre on Hollywood Boulevard.

HOLLYWOOD ON THE BRINK

For one brief shining moment, the scent of magnolia blossoms was in the air. Hostesses tossed "Gone With the Wind" parties. The ladies wore hoop-skirted gowns and the men ruffled dress shirts and Rhett Butler outfits. The taste of mint juleps was tangy and effervescent. Selznick's 1939 blockbuster had gone national—and business was sensational. But that wonderful euphoric period was all over before Hollywood could take one deep easy breath. The first six months of the "Frantic Forties" had come and gone. It was panic time again.

The motion picture industry, dependent on foreign revenue for much of its profits, felt the economic effects of the war in Europe before the rest of the country. Hitler had overrun Poland, Norway, Denmark, Holland, Belgium and triumphed over the fall of France. Britain alone remained to be conquered. Meanwhile, Japan had invaded China.

As of January 1, 1940, there were 67,129 motion picture theatres throughout the world. The United States had 17,003. When World War II started, the possibility of a Nazi invasion threatened Europe's 36,000 movie houses. While in the Far East, which had nearly seven thousand theatres, the situation was also unstable and growing worse. Hollywood braced itself as it tallied the weekly receipts. Within a few months, they had their answer—forty percent of its income was in jeopardy, much of it had already been lost.

In the United States, isolationist groups were determined America should remain neutral. The Hollywood community was divided about taking part in actual combat. But within each studio the battle for financial survival had already begun. All of the major lots announced curtailed production. Yearly output was reduced from sixty films each to a low of forty pictures or less. To add to the bad news from Europe, America's own boxoffice grosses were at their lowest in ten years.

Nationwide, radio was at its peak. People became so deeply interested in war news that they spent their spare time *listening* to developments from abroad—and stayed away from picture houses in droves. Adding insult to injury, studio workers brought their radios onto movie lots. The continual broadcasting of events was slowing down production. Moguls held meetings to decide whether they should ban all radios from the premises.

Meanwhile, Congressman Martin Dies launched a cruel attack on the picture business and the people in it. He authored a national magazine article accusing Hollywood of being a hotbed of communists intent on provoking America into the war through its propaganda films.

Nineteen forty was a national election year. FDR ran for an unprecedented third term. The Republicans searched high and low for a candidate who could defeat him. They chose a fine man, Wendell Willkie, who lost.

All British actors of draft age working in American pictures or stage plays were summoned home on the first available transport. The situation was grave. The British had suffered a stunning defeat at Dunkirk. At a mass meeting of Hollywood's British set, all of the men reaffirmed their willingness to serve in any capacity. Herbert Marshall, Alan Mowbray, Ronald Colman, Sir Cedric Hardwicke, Nigel Bruce, Brian Aherne, Charles Laughton, Laurence Olivier, Cary Grant, Errol Flynn, Basil Rathbone and Ray Milland had all volunteered at the very outbreak of the war.

A committee under Dame May Whitty and Boris Karloff handled the evacuation of sixty British children. Cary Grant donated nearly his entire salary from MGM's *Philadelphia Story* to underwrite their expenses . . . the rest went to the Red Cross. Douglas Fairbanks, Jr., acted as the children's American-born sponsor. Charles Laughton gave his radio earnings to both war relief and the Red Cross. Ronald Colman donated a sizable sum for ambulances. And a special filmed appeal made by Anna Neagle had already raised $100,000 for the Red Cross.

Meanwhile, Hollywood's celebrity set celebrated January 1940 in a frenzied social whirl. William Powell eloped with young actress Diana Lewis after a twenty-one-day courtship—catching the town flat-footed. It was rumored that the week prior to his elopement, Bill had proposed to three *different* ladies—and it was the *last* one who said "Yes." (This match, however, would become one of the town's most enduring mergers.)

Marlene Dietrich was accused of robbing the cradle when she continued to date twenty-six-year-old Orson Welles. And Joan Bennett eloped to Arizona with producer Walter Wanger. By the time the Wangers had returned from their Phoenix nuptials—literally in a matter of hours—Marlene had dropped Orson and was seen dining out in Beverly Hills with old flame Howard Hughes. Insiders said that all Howard wanted from Marlene this time was a picture commitment.

Greta Garbo and her girlfriend, screenwriter Mercedes de Acosta, went out on the town with nutritionist Gayelord Hauser and his friend, Frey Brown. Norma Shearer went skiing at Sun Valley, Idaho, and made several telephone calls a day to her beau, George Raft, who was stuck in Hollywood, filming.

On January 26, Ronnie Reagan climbed out of his flu bed, secured a license to marry Jane Wyman, then went back under the covers until time for the ceremony. The wedding, attended by a small group of relatives and friends, took place at the Wee Kirk o' the Heather Church in Glendale. The couple was married by the Reverend Cleveland Kleihauer. Jane's sister, Elsie Wyatt, was matron of honor, while William Scott, a college chum of Reagan's, was best man. The couple honeymooned in Palm Springs.

The handwritten will of Douglas Fairbanks, Sr., was filed for probate. His widow, Sylvia, received one million dollars. Doug, Jr., got six hundred thousand. Some relatives were left the remainder of the cash assets. All other property was divided equally between Sylvia and Doug, Jr.—much of it stock in United Artists Corporation.

Sylvia Hawkes Ashley Fairbanks was now a very wealthy woman, having taken possession of, among other things, the lovely Fairbanks beach home. She preferred living in England, though, or in New York. Over the next few years, she would be only an occasional visitor to Hollywood.

Joan Crawford's divorce from Franchot Tone became final, and she informed a reporter that she had gone through the trials and tribulations of marriage for the last time. There would be no more Crawford husbands. The whole ordeal was just too painful. It was not that she was renouncing men—or giving up sexual relationships. "Sex," she confided to a close friend, "was part of what kept her young." She needed the close companionship that a man could provide. As for exchanging wedding rings and what went with it, that was behind her.

Before the town could rest up from all of those coming and goings and splicings and splitting of millions, young and naive Lana Turner up and eloped with sophisticated Artie Shaw. Everybody wondered whether to throw rice or send sympathy cards.

Week after week the news from Europe grew more unbelievably tragic, and Hollywood was facing its own greatest crisis to date. The foreign markets were dead or dying. The Federal Government, in an antitrust suit, was attempting to split the studios from their theatres. The unions were talking strike. The independent producers were siding with the government against the major studios. Nazi sympathizers were raving and ranting against Hollywood films that they considered anti-German. American motion pictures were banned in all countries under German occupation. Most studios were forced to close down their overseas offices. And from Washington, D.C., Congressman Dies continued his attacks on Hollywood's "commies." Feelings in the industry ran very high about how best to counter the awful charges.

In the spring of 1941, Orson Welles had his own troubles. *Citizen Kane*, which he produced, directed and co-starred in, had been extensively press previewed, yet no theatrical release date had been announced. There were rumors that RKO would never let the picture be shown nationwide. The alleged "unspoken reason" boiled down to three words: *William Randolph Hearst.*

Unlike Welles' brilliant science-fiction radio show, "The War of the Worlds," adapted from the H. G. Wells tale by Howard Koch, *Citizen Kane* was *not* a mythical story about Martians. The word was that Welles had, indeed, written a thinly disguised version of the powerful Hearst's *real*
life—something which Orson never admitted and in fact vehemently denied.

Orson threatened to sue on the grounds of "interference with freedom of the moving picture industry as the foremost medium of artistic expression in the country." RKO backed down. *Citizen Kane* was released and won many prizes and awards. At Oscar time, however, although the film was nominated in nine categories, it picked up only one award—for best original screenplay. Still, Welles was vindicated. He became known around town as Hollywood's "boy genius."

By the time Orson's "crisis" was over, Hollywood itself was once again a study in organized confusion. No one was quite certain where world events were leading America—and what specific role Hollywood would play. Meanwhile, there was more potential trouble at the boxoffice. Having conquered miniature golf, dog races, bowling and night baseball, the industry faced a new enemy— *gin rummy!*

Incredible as it seemed, the latest box-office analysis disclosed that three out of every ten regular moviegoers were staying home, going to other people's homes or to clubs to play cards. The number of "addicts" grew every day. It seemed the old ten-card rummy—first played in 1907— had come back with a vengeance. Everyone was playing. Already many neighborhood picture houses had started running gin rummy tournaments before and after every matinee. But the bigger theatre owners frowned on this practice—it might encourage *more* people to become addicted to the game.

Bette Davis, two-time Academy Award winner, was elected president of the Academy of Motion Picture Arts and Sciences, the first woman to win the post. She succeeded Walter Wanger, who now became first vice president. Almost immediately there were rumors of trouble. Bette, working in a film, and not feeling too well, suddenly discovered that the Academy office held much more responsibility than she had anticipated. Within weeks, she resigned. Wanger was back in as president.

On December 7, the Japanese attacked Pearl Harbor, Hawaii, as well as the Philippine Islands. It was no longer just a European conflict. Ninety million people listened on their radios as President Roosevelt spoke to the nation about "this day that will live in infamy"—and declared war on Japan.

Unless you were a resident of Hollywood during World War II, it would be impossible to fully convey the frantic sense of urgency that hit every corner of the community on December 7, 1941. For all intents and purposes, Hollywood became an instant armed camp—"a battleground." Immediately, there were rumors that California was extremely vulnerable to possible Japanese attack. Every area of life was suddenly conditioned by a war going on many thousands of miles away. It might as well have been raging on the corner of Hollywood and Vine for all the activities that it curtailed or accelerated.

On that fateful Sunday evening, a benefit for a Catholic Charity had been scheduled for Ciro's night club. Despite the situation, it went on. In the middle of the evening, a young army lieutenant came into the cafe and asked for a microphone. People stopped dancing; those at the tables rose to immediate attention as the officer asked all servicemen to report immediately to their respective posts. He continued, "And as far as you—the civilian population—are concerned, you are aware that we are in a state of extreme emergency. But there is nothing to be alarmed about. Keep your high morale. This is something *we* did not want. *They* started it. Please be assured that *we* know how to finish it! All we ask is—keep your thumbs up!"

It was like a surrealistic dream, or a Hollywood movie. But there were no weird flashes of color, no hidden violins to play background music. Only silence. For a community that dealt in make-believe, the reality of war seemed doubly frightening.

All over town, moguls met in emergency sessions to discuss the possibility of moving production facilities out of Hollywood. Simultaneously, studio managers set plans for the defense of property from sabotage and enemy activity. Overnight, security was beefed up on every lot, and all studio personnel ordered to identify themselves upon entering. Japanese employees were suspended, all visitors barred—except press with very good credentials—and private planes were grounded. Studio machine guns and other weapons were confiscated by the army. Studio trucks and vehicles were put on standby to be requisitioned by the military. Portions of soundstages were converted into air raid shelters. Hollywood was "at war."

The Women's Emergency Corps of Beverly Hills found itself overrun with volunteers. Glamour girls, in sables and limousines, came in to offer their services. The first of Hollywood's big names to register were Rosalind Russell and Linda Darnell. Meetings were scheduled for Tuesday evenings on the 20th lot. The first night the ladies were taught how to march—for two hours—with Roz and Linda setting the pace.

The following day Darnell—obviously not too tired from drilling—left with Carole Landis and Sam Levene for St. Louis to attend a "Victory Rally." Twelve thousand tickets had been sold. Melvyn Douglas and Helen Gahagan joined them, as did Universal's Carol Bruce, who headed for St. Louis from New York. Humphrey Bogart and Phil Silvers were also en route by train.

While local doctors were swamped with requests for nerve tablets, neighborhood food markets were standing room only. Hollywoodites made a run on canned vegetables and fruits—afraid that fresh produce might have been poisoned by the predominantly Japanese people who raised a large percentage of California's vegetables and citrus crops.

Hollywood's citizens were furious about Japan's unprovoked attack. The small isolationist block in the community was in an uproar. Former pacifists readied their affairs for early enlistment. Those over draft age volunteered for Home Defense duty. Most of the active Reservists eagerly stepped back into uniform. Many not called in the draft prepared to enlist. The country was facing its most serious crisis. Everybody in Hollywood wanted to do something—to contribute in some way.

The Clark Gable household was experiencing a small crisis of its own. For over a year, ever since they had returned from the Atlanta premiere of "GWTW," Carole had talked to Clark about retiring. She had been in the business long enough. Wouldn't it be wonderful if, after she finished her latest film, *To Be or Not to Be*, she could just stay on their Encino ranch and be "Ma" Gable— *literally?* She wanted desperately to have Clark's child. There had been some concern by her personal physician that, at best, it would be difficult for Lombard to bear children. But maybe if she stopped the rat race and just sat nice and easy by the fireplace—maybe she could get pregnant.

Gable was delighted. He *wanted* children of his own. He had been a devoted stepfather to his second wife's two kids. But it wasn't exactly the same as having his own child. On the other hand, he realized that Carole, Hollywood's highest-paid light comedienne, was at the peak of her career. She would be giving up so much—inwardly, that appealed to his male ego— Carole *wanted* to toss it all aside to have *his* baby.

As she wrestled with her decision, while busily shooting *To Be*, with her co-star Jack Benny and director Ernst Lubitsch, the war news grew grimmer. In between long days of filming, she and Clark attended benefits for British War Relief, Greek War Relief, the Red Cross, and also helped organize the Hollywood Victory Committee.

One day, Carole was inadvertently provoked into making a public statement. She overheard some studio people griping about how much tax they paid. Suddenly Lombard couldn't restrain herself: "This is the best damned country in the world. I'm grateful I earn enough to pay a lot of taxes. I'm going to keep making as many pictures as I can so I'll be able to pay *more* taxes. The government *needs* this money. Don't you know the whole world is in trouble!"

In her exuberance, Carole had not realized that she had been overheard by a reporter. Her statement made the front pages: LOMBARD HAPPY TO PAY TAXES—FEELS IT'S HER OBLIGATION.

She had gone and shot off her big mouth again. But she *meant* every word of it. Besides, she told Gable, there was no reason why she couldn't continue working—and still get pregnant. *Then* she would retire from the screen.

On Christmas Eve, there was a "wrap party" for *To Be or Not to Be* over at 20th. The film was finished, and everyone felt they had a big hit on their hands. Stage center, Jack Benny was his usual humorous self, while Carole, looking gorgeous, talked a mile a minute, terribly witty and full of fun, as Clark stood by her side. The group broke up just as Christmas Day was dawning. Presents were exchanged between cast and crew. There were lots of "I'll be seeing you's" as the company parted for the final time.

During Christmas week of 1941, the celebrity community was galvanized into action. The people would need movies more than ever—and there was money to be raised for any number of causes. Hollywood stars would have to travel the country in between pictures, selling War Bonds . . . keeping up the country's morale.

Unification of Hollywood's all-out talent effort for United States victory in the war crystallized on January 12, 1942. Lowell Mellett, the government's liaison for films, was notified by the Hollywood Victory Committee for Stage, Screen and Radio that it had completed its plans for coordinating all contributions of free entertainment to patriotic and humanitarian campaigns. The committee's work as a talent-request clearing house was launched on January 15. Carole Lombard was scheduled to appear in her home state at a huge Indiana War Rally in Indianapolis. Her mother, Elizabeth Peters, and her press agent, Otto Winkler, went with her.

Carole left the Gable's Encino ranch with mixed feelings. She and Clark quarreled over the holidays. He had given her a beautiful pair of diamond earrings as a makeup gift. She had not taken them off since. It was difficult for her to leave home at that moment. Still, she would be gone only a few days. And, after all, she was only leaving Clark for a good cause.

Carole was a smash hit in Indianapolis. Her speech was marvelously received—and many thousands of dollars in war bonds were sold. Afterward, she, her mother and Winkler stopped off in Fort Wayne, the town where Carole was born. There, she addressed another rally. Just before she boarded the plane, Carole said: ". . . we are fighting a war to win a peace. We know what it will cost, but the peace will be priceless."

Carole and her party had been scheduled to return home by train; all commercial aircraft were commandeered for service personnel on a priority basis. But she was so eager to get home that she wangled three seats at the last minute on a flight otherwise occupied by military men.

Over a rugged mountain range thirty-five miles southwest of Las Vegas, Nevada, the TWA Skyclub smashed headlong into a perpendicular cliff known as Double Up Peak. The furious impact—against a wall of solid rock—telescoped the tail section into the nose of the plane, which fell forty-five feet in a heap of twisted debris. There was wreckage strewn everywhere on the snowy slopes.

Six bodies, all of them members of the Army Ferry Command, were thrown clear of the wreckage. The rest of the passengers and crew were killed instantly.

Gable, grief-stricken, traveled to Las Vegas and kept a lonely vigil until "the remains" of his wife, mother-in-law and Otto Winkler were brought down from the mountain.

The tragedy had many ramifications. Clark, who was four days into filming *Somewhere I'll Find You*, with Lana Turner, went into seclusion. The MGM production was shuttered. Sneak previews for *To Be or Not to Be* were postponed. Jack Benny, Carole's final co-star, chose not to appear on his weekly NBC comedy program for one of the few times in his long career. An all-musical show was presented. It ended with Dennis Day and a chorus singing "America the Beautiful."

Everywhere, moviegoers mourned the thirty-three-year-old star and the irony of her death while "in the service of her country." It seemed so incomprehensible, so unfair, that this beautiful, fun-loving, wisecracking creature should have died on a bleak, remote mountain peak on that January 16th day.

On January 21, there were private funeral services for Carole and her mother at the Church of the Recessional in Forest Lawn. Their bodies lay in dark-gray steel coffins banked with blankets of gardenias and huge sprays of orchids. After a simple ceremony, they were placed in crypts in the mausoleum known as the Sanctuary of Trust, nearby those of Marie Dressler, Jean Harlow, Will Rogers and Irving Thalberg.

Later in the day, a funeral service was conducted for Otto Winkler, with his eulogy given by Walter Pidgeon.

When all of the plane's wreckage and debris had been cleared, Gable received one diamond earring which had been undetected in earlier searches.

Crisis situations kept coming in continuous waves. Hollywood prepared itself to face facts: forty to fifty percent of its top male stars would be in the service before the year ended. To meet the loss of star names, studios concentrated on story values, on accomplished directors and on Technicolor whenever possible. As never before Hollywood was a *story*, rather than a star, market.

Among those already in active service or slated to go by July were: 20th's Richard Greene, in service in England; Tyrone Power, about to enter the Marine Corps; Victor Mature and Robert Sterling, leaving, for branches to be determined. From Warners, Ronald Reagan was already in the Army, as were Jeffrey Lynn and Herbert Anderson. George Brent was scheduled to go into the Navy.

Dan Dailey, at Universal, planned to join the Army, and would be in the air service. Among some of the free-lance players already in the war were David Niven, in England; Gene Raymond, Burgess Meredith, Laurence Olivier, and Buddy Rogers. At RKO, William Holden was scheduled to join up as soon as he finished his present commitment. Robert Montgomery was in the Navy, Jimmy Stewart was in the Army air force.

Somewhere I'll Find You was completed. Clark Gable went back to his Encino ranch on a full-time basis. There were no early-morning calls. No lines to be learned. No all-day shooting schedules. The inactivity got to him. But more than that—he couldn't bear rattling around the house without Carole. He wanted to get into the fight. In any branch. He didn't care.

At the end of May 1942, Gable wrote to the President. He offered his services wherever he could best be used. But Roosevelt replied: "Stay where you are. Continue doing work you are doing as we feel that's the best service you can offer."

On June 18, Clark went to Washington. He was determined to enter the armed forces—through enlistment or otherwise. But he was collared by Lieutenant General "Hap" Arnold, head of America's air force. They were in conference for three hours, and it was subsequently understood that Clark Gable would be heading up a morale division of the air corps. A commission was said to be following within days.

Gable had been preceded to Washington by the president of Loew's, Inc., Nicholas Schenck, two MGM vice presidents, Eddie J. Mannix and J. Robert Riben, as well as Howard Strickling, the studio's head of publicity. But whatever might have been arranged between studio brass and government people, Gable decided to have none of it. He wanted to enlist.

Clark would not see any newspapermen. He asked a close friend to beg newshounds to forget about him as a picture star and to consider him as just a candidate for any branch of the service for which he could be slotted. Through his friend, Gable said: "Picture acting is one thing and the war effort is still another. Everyone has been trying to sell me the idea that my proper place is before the cameras. But I can't agree with them, although they may be right. I have no interest in acting as long as this big war is going on. I hope some branch will take me, and I am not looking for a commission."

Word of Gable's possible entrance into the service worried Hollywood studio heads.

If Gable went, there was sure to be an even larger exodus of other big-name stars—men, not in the draft, who reasoned that they *should* be in, too, rather than feeling that people were pointing a finger at them.

Seven months after Carole Lombard's death, Clark's restless and lonely vigil ended. On August 12, 1942, Gable raised his right hand and repeated the oath of enlistment. At the end of the ceremony, making him a private in the U.S. Army, Clark left for Miami, Florida, for three months of basic training. Along with him was Andrew J. McIntyre, a studio cameraman and close friend, who had enlisted at the same time.

Soon after Gable left for camp, Gene Autry enlisted in the Army air service and completely devastated Republic Studios. He was their top star, and had been scheduled to make eight films in a row. Now they were canceled. Next, two of 20th's biggest names, Tyrone Power and Henry Fonda, enlisted.

Ty, whose application for a chief specialist rating in the Navy was rejected, joined the Marine Corps as a private, and went in immediately after the filming of *Crash Dive* was completed. Fonda enrolled as an apprentice seaman third class, the Navy's lowest rating. Fonda had enlisted at the Navy recruiting center in the Los Angeles Hall of Justice without informing his studio in advance. He was sworn in immediately and left five days later for boot camp at San Diego, slated for the Navy's gunnery school. Hank, who had recently finished *The Ox-Bow Incident*, was offered a chief specialist's rating. He turned it down—he wanted to be a gunner.

The mass exodus was on. Hollywood, desperate to turn out pictures as fast as possible—in order to satisfy a nation at war—was in the process of losing half its most famous faces.

1 Lieutenant (j.g.) U.S. Naval Air Force and Mrs. Robert Taylor (Barbara Stanwyck).
2 Lieutenant and Mrs. Ronald Reagan (Jane Wyman) at the Ice Capades, 1942.
3 Tyrone Power as he enters the Marine Corp.

HOLLYWOOD ON THE HALF-SHELL

The Hollywood community was very insular. Throughout the Forties and Fifties, a clannish atmosphere pervaded celebrities' off-set lives. Stars formed cliques —and stayed within them. Close friends went to parties and premieres together and did benefit shows as a group. If they were under contract to the same studio—and they tended to be—they traveled on personal appearances and junkets with each other. A feeling of camaraderie existed then which seemed to evaporate at the end of the Fifties.

During the Forties, only a handful of hotel ballrooms, nightclubs and restaurants were "in" spots. Hollywood's social life revolved mainly around at-home parties or soirées at one of "their" places, where the VIPs were left alone among their peers—free to let their hair down and be themselves.

For many stars, "being oneself" was synonymous with "being on." Not that JACK BENNY was a stand-up comedian offstage, or that GEORGE BURNS and GRACIE ALLEN went around doing routines. But for star cliques, relaxation frequently meant playing charades, sitting at the piano and singing tunes, screening each others' films, or doing things which, most often, were industry-related.

He-men like GABLE went off hunting. TY POWER took to the skies in his own plane. GARBO mainly hung out by herself or with women pals such as MERCEDES DE ACOSTA and SALKA VIERTEL and her family. JOAN CRAWFORD traveled between Hollywood and New York a great deal. GARY COOPER and his group enjoyed skiing trips to Sun Valley, Idaho. Within the cliques, there were the gamblers who played cards for high stakes. Even some of the ladies adored cards. BETTY GRABLE was one of the shrewdest lowball poker players in Hollywood. Other celebrities enjoyed the racetrack. BING CROSBY and PAT O'BRIEN'S set religiously followed "the nags" at Santa Anita and Del Mar. Many sports nuts, like GEORGE RAFT and his cronies, went to Hollywood Legion Stadium on Friday nights to watch the fights, and to the Los Angeles Coliseum on Saturdays and Sundays to see football games.

There were also favorite "near town" resorts: Palm Springs, Lake Arrowhead, Santa Barbara, Carmel, Tijuana, or Baja California. Hollywood also had quite a large seagoing contingent. The yachting crowd included LOUIS B. MAYER, CECIL B. DEMILLE, HUMPHREY BOGART and ERROL FLYNN.

There were some outstanding party-givers in Tinseltown. Even a casual invitation to JOAN CRAWFORD'S always meant a swank evening. SONJA HENIE'S affairs were guaranteed to be a mix of the social register and celebrity sets. ERROL FLYNN was a noted party-tosser, the SAM GOLDWYNS always entertained in style. And a DAVID O. SELZNICK "do" was bound to be a superspecial event.

No one gave bigger, better, or more exclusive shindigs than ELSA MAXWELL, who was usually *paid* for her efforts, and always came through. Personally, Elsa resembled an unmade bed: short, square and rumpled. But by the time the Forties rolled around, Maxwell was the number-one continental soirée-tosser. She hosted parties around the world for royalty, society and the celebrity set.

Elsa was especially good at bringing impoverished but authentic noblemen together with rich American debutantes. In the late Forties, she was responsible for such "fabulous matches" as that of RITA HAYWORTH and PRINCE ALY KHAN. Maxwell's only visible source of income was the money earned from newspaper and magazine articles on the comings and goings of high society.

Even the mighty DUCHESS OF WINDSOR trembled when Maxwell barked orders. Their famous feud, over some trivial party guest list, had their whole set taking sides. Elsa claimed the most supporters. Eventually, the duchess apologized!

Aside from the rare, purely social event, most of the Forties decade was devoted to war work. There was hardly a private party that was not simultaneously a benefit for a worthy cause. Stars spent weekends and time in between films on bond-selling tours or on visits to camps and/or hospitals. Almost every top celebrity made at least one junket overseas. Some had their bags perpetually packed. Their arms resembled pincushions from the numerous shots they needed to keep from getting strange "native" diseases.

In January, BRENDA MARSHALL'S divorce from RICHARD GAINES was in the works, and she and young WILLIAM HOLDEN began dating for more serious reasons. His family, out in Pasadena, were none too thrilled by this latest development . . . DOUG FAIRBANKS, JR., bought ELISSA LANDI'S Pacific Palisades home for $30,000 and spent an extra $20,000 to redecorate. The exquisite place originally cost Landi $110,000 . . . Speaking of money, CLARK GABLE had his MGM salary raised from $4,000 to $7,500 per week, and his new seven-year contract provided that "the King" be given twelve weeks off every year to go hunting . . . The first MRS. ORSON WELLES won her freedom after a six weeks' stay in Reno, Nevada . . . And GARBO'S family was in town, so she took them to the posh Perino's for dinner four nights in a row.

In February, ERROL FLYNN and LILI DAMITA split . . . MRS. GEORGE RAFT'S tough alimony demands kept NORMA SHEARER and GEORGE from making their relationship more permanent . . . AL JOLSON took RUBY KEELER to see *Meet the People*, then on to Ciro's where, just like in the movies, everything grew quiet as EMIL COLEMAN and his orchestra played "April Showers" in Joley's honor . . . The HENRY FONDAS had a son they named PETER . . . And RAYMOND BURR, nightclubbing with ONA MUNSON, was identified as a young San Franciscan anxious to break into the movies . . .

In March, GINGER ROGERS openly admitted that if her divorce were final, she and HOWARD HUGHES would be married. HH gave Ginger an emerald as big as Madison Square Garden. Insiders said it was an engagement ring . . . GABLE and LOMBARD packed their bags for a trip to Wyoming to go bear hunting . . . DAVID O. SELZNICK wired MARGARET MITCHELL that he was sending her his "GWTW" Oscar. "Without your great book there would have been no award and I shall take the liberty of forwarding to you the reward for the production of 'GWTW.' " Miss Mitchell declined and wired back: "You are amazingly generous in offering to send me the trophy but I cannot think of accepting it. The award was not for novel writing but for moviemaking, so the trophy's proper place is with you."

DR. LASZLO, the Viennese skin specialist, revealed one of GARBO'S beauty secrets. He had taught her how to mix a raw egg with either hamburger or milk and apply it to her face.

GG then allowed it to dry and removed it with lukewarm water. Laszlo swore that was what made Greta's skin glow so.

As April arrived, JANE WYMAN and RONALD REAGAN made their first film together since their marriage, *An Angel From Texas*. They played a husband and wife who constantly nagged each other . . . CHARLES CHAPLIN'S yacht, *Panacea*, on which he, PAULETTE GODDARD and Charlie's two sons went cruising, was purchased as a gift for Goddard. Friends said she was tired of receiving jewels and was happy to accept the boat instead . . . And, as the month ended, talk from back East was that HOWARD HUGHES and GINGER were no longer lovebirds. His newest: KATE HEPBURN.

In May, mutual friends predicted that OLIVIA DE HAVILLAND and JAMES STEWART would elope any day . . . Ditto for LORETTA YOUNG and TOM LEWIS . . . NORMA SHEARER got tired of waiting for GEORGE RAFT, so he switched to ANN SHERIDAN . . . The VIVIEN LEIGH—LAURENCE OLIVIER stage production of *Romeo and Juliet* received very bad reviews in New York.

June was the month in which FRANCES FARMER, who used to be Hollywood's "problem child," returned to work at Warner Brothers, and was very cooperative . . . With the war raging in Europe, there were estimates that about seventy-five percent of the German domestic servants working in the homes of Hollywood's biggest stars or as studio helpers were Nazi sympathizers. HARRY WARNER held a mass meeting to urge industryites to report any suspicious activities . . . HOWARD HUGHES donated $25,000 to the Red Cross Emergency Fund . . . And doting hubby CLARK GABLE went on location with CAROLE LOMBARD when she started *They Knew What They Wanted* in Napa Valley, California.

In July, LAURENCE OLIVIER tried to go to Canada to enlist, but they told him to stay in America and act . . . Every theatre in France was closed as a gesture of mourning for the country's defeat by Hitler's forces . . . The war news was heating up as each day passed. IDA LUPINO and LOUIS HAYWARD gave a farewell party for handsome 20th star RICHARD GREENE who left to join the British Army . . . On the last day of the month, LORETTA YOUNG became MRS. TOM LEWIS.

In August, LANA TURNER, who left ARTIE SHAW, returned after a couple of weeks of "recuperation" in Hawaii . . . ORSON WELLES tossed a press party to launch his production of *Citizen Kane*. . . . All American films had been banned in countries occupied by Hitler . . . LUCILLE BALL and DESI ARNAZ began dating . . . JUDY GARLAND and DAVID ROSE were "acting serious" . . . MARY LIVINGSTONE became pregnant, and JACK BENNY was as nervous as a Mother Hen. Unfortunately, Mary suffered a miscarriage a few weeks later . . . And, on the 30th of August, VIVIEN LEIGH became MRS. LAURENCE OLIVIER. They were married at the San Ysidro ranch of RONALD COLMAN, with KATE HEPBURN and GARSON KANIN as witnesses.

At the start of September, CARY GRANT and BARBARA HUTTON's dates became more public . . . A new redhead in town, SUSAN HAYWARD, was causing heads to turn.

A tribute from PRESIDENT ROOSEVELT to the late KNUTE ROCKNE highlighted the premiere-eve banquet for Warner's *Knute Rockne—All American,* held at the University of Notre Dame on October 3, 1940. FDR's message was contained in a touching letter written to Mrs. Rockne and read by FRANKLIN D. ROOSEVELT, JR., one of the more than forty national celebrities who occupied the speaker's dais. Two thousand people gathered to see and meet PAT and ELOISE O'BRIEN, RONALD REAGAN, JANE WYMAN, RUDY VALLEE, ROSEMARY LANE, ANITA LOUISE, CHARLES RUGGLES and IRENE RICH. The REVEREND HUGH O'DONNELL, president of Notre Dame, opened the program. Then BOB HOPE, emcee for all of the premiere events, presented PAT O'BRIEN, the film's "Rockne" and KATE SMITH, who sang "God Bless America."

More than 100,000 people from other towns and cities jammed into South Bend, Indiana,

to see the Hollywood stars and celebrate "Knute Rockne Week." Warners premiered the film, *Knute Rockne—All American,* in four local theatres, and the stars appeared prior to the start of each showing. Then, the exhausted but exhilarated bunch hopped aboard the Super Chief and trained back to Hollywood.

In November, LUPE VELEZ announced she would marry "BIG BOY" WILLIAMS. She didn't . . . RITA HAYWORTH and her husband, EDWARD JUDSON, bought a home in Westwood . . . FRANCHOT TONE and CAROLE LANDIS started dating . . . Eleven-year-old RODDY McDOWALL, a refugee from England, was tested by 20th for *How Green Was My Valley.*

GEORGE BRENT and ANN SHERIDAN spent the holidays on his yacht with a gang of party-goers . . . The gin rummy fad took Hollywood by storm. PAULETTE GODDARD began December by moving out of CHAPLIN's house. Insiders said she had started divorce proceedings . . . DEANNA DURBIN's parents tossed her a big engagement party. She will become MRS. VAUGHN PAUL . . . FREDDIE BRISSON introduced ROSALIND RUSSELL to his parents . . . GARBO left to spend Christmas in New York. Dr. GAYELORD HAUSER joined her and then hit the lecture circuit . . . BARBARA HUTTON was very concerned about her divorce from Danish COUNT REVENTLOW coming through now that Hitler had occupied Norway; she feared the rest of Scandinavia was sure to fall . . . LANA TURNER tossed a big Christmas bash for her latest love, TONY MARTIN . . .

On New Year's Eve, GENE TIERNEY dated OLEG CASSINI for the first time as they joined the merrymakers at BILLY WILKERSON's Ciro's.

1941

BETTE DAVIS married ARTHUR FARNSWORTH at the Arizona ranch of JANE BRYAN and JUSTIN DART . . . On January 18, BARBARA HUTTON gave an elegant supper for one hundred guests in honor of CARY GRANT's birthday . . . JANE RUSSELL was being given a huge publicity build-up and was hailed as the "hottest discovery" since HEDY LAMARR.

Though they denied it, the word went out that GARBO and GAYELORD HAUSER had definitely planned to be married late last December aboard the very social WENNER-GREN yacht while they visited Nassau. Everything was fixed so that the DUKE and DUCHESS OF WINDSOR would be

aboard for the event. But the whole thing was postponed when the Nassau trip fell through . . .

LUCY and DESI ARNAZ spent the last week in January honeymooning in Miami Beach while Desi appeared at the Rhumba Casino . . .

As of February, it was reported that GODDARD and CHAPLIN were back together, staying at MYRON SELZNICK's beach house . . . NANCY KELLY eloped with EDMUND O'BRIEN on February 19th . . . ERROL FLYNN went back to LILI DAMITA and told pals he had bought a ranch in Hawaii where he and Lili would vacation after their child was born . . . The set of *A Woman's Face* was closed because JOAN CRAWFORD brought her adopted daughter, CHRISTINA, to work with her. No photos were allowed as the adoption would not be final for some months.

In March, HOWARD HUGHES discovered HEDY LAMARR and began showering her with gifts . . . BARBARA HUTTON'S divorce came through, and she and CARY GRANT were closer to marriage than ever . . . Lovely STEFFI DUNA became Mrs. DENNIS O'KEEFE . . . And JIMMY STEWART packed one set of underwear, two pairs of socks and left to report for duty.

CHARLIE EINFELD, vice president for publicity and advertising at Warner Brothers, tossed a two-day "party of the Pacific," for the premiere of the *Sea Wolf*. It was a knockout from the ship's tug start to roaring airplane finish. Everyone had a wonderful time on the S.S. *America,* the latest word in modern ships. EDWARD G. ROBINSON'S identification badge read "SHIRLEY TEMPLE." When Eddie posed for the still cameramen with PRISCILLA LANE, Einfeld said, "You sure look like a 'Sea Wolf' now."

"Yeh," cracked Eddie, "but what's the good of it—my '*She*-wolf' is aboard." He wasn't kidding.

The dance after the premiere was terrific. Robinson led the orchestra. JOHN GARFIELD played the drums, and the regular passengers had a whale of a time mixing with the Hollywood gang. By midnight of the first evening, JOHNNY MEYER, HOWARD HUGHES' "buddy," had already promised screen tests to seventeen girls— but the gals were too smart for Johnny. They all asked for straight seven-year contracts— or no dice. The boys tagged handsome JOHNNY GARFIELD "The JEAN GABIN of the Bronx." MARIA MONTEZ made as many entrances and exits aboard ship as she usually did at Ciro's. When RONNIE REAGAN introduced the stars after the screening, he said, "Two weeks ago we wouldn't have had to come to sea for this premiere. We could have had a boat fixed right on Hollywood and Vine." (Unusual rains had flooded all of the town's famous streets a couple of weeks previous to the party.)

1 "Pa" and "Ma" Gable at their Encino Ranch, 1940. Come and get it! Carole was under contract to RKO Radio Pictures at this time.　　2 Judy Garland on the bandstand, pal Mickey Rooney seated at the drums, and standing between them, choreographer-director Busby Berkeley.　　3 Lana Turner shares lunch with two GIs on the lot at MGM.

In May, SHIRLEY TEMPLE signed a new studio contract which permitted her to do at least eight radio shows a year, provided they did not interfere with her film schedule. Shirley decided to appear on several LUX RADIO THEATRE programs.

In June, RON and JANE REAGAN dated the stork again . . . FRANCES FARMER tested for *The Yearling,* but Wyman got the part . . . DAVID NIVEN wrote to pals that he had been promoted to major. Niven, who was serving with the British Army, had already seen quite a bit of action . . . LILI DAMITA FLYNN brought ERROL's new baby son, SEAN, home from the hospital . . . GENE TIERNEY and her family were still feuding over her quickie elopement with OLEG CASSINI . . . ALEXANDER KORDA wanted to marry MERLE OBERON, but his wife was making their divorce settlement difficult . . . And the government asked HOWARD HUGHES to concentrate on making aircraft at his Los Angeles and Houston plants. HH had no plans to make any more films for the duration.

By mid-July, with the intercession of columnist COBINA WRIGHT, GENE TIERNEY's parents seemed reconciled to their daughter's marriage. OLEG, who came from a formerly prominent, titled European family, was considered one of America's finest dress designers. But, frankly, father Tierney had hoped for more from their gorgeous offspring.

When August arrived, reporters tried to track down rumors of a Mexican elopement by CARY GRANT and BARBARA HUTTON. They discovered the twosome together in a posh suite at Mexico's swank Hotel Reforma. They were properly "chaperoned" by a whole slew of pals. While the twosome remained unmarried, Hollywood had already nicknamed them "Cash and Cary." Meanwhile, lovely blond actress PHYLLIS BROOKS was still trying to get over Cary's loss. She and Grant had gone steady for years before Hutton entered the picture.

In September, LANA TURNER and TONY MARTIN broke up, and she began dating GEORGE MONTGOMERY . . . MARLENE DIETRICH had her legs insured by Lloyds of London for one million dollars . . . And BING CROSBY passed ENRICO CARUSO's phenomenal records sales figure, and admitted to earning $125,000 per year just in royalties.

In October, BUDDY ROGERS and MARY PICKFORD entertained LORD and LADY LOUIS MOUNTBATTEN of Great Britain at Pickfair. It was also the occasion for bidding farewell to DOUG, JR., who was about to leave for Naval duty . . . And the GARY COOPERS and ROBERT TAYLORS took off for a holiday in Sun Valley, Idaho . . . Just to be sure everything was legal, MAE WEST sought "an official divorce" from her husband, FRANK WALLACE. The couple had been split for years.

By November, FRANCHOT TONE and his new wife, JEAN WALLACE, were on their honeymoon at Tone's home in Niagara Falls, New York . . . And JUDY GARLAND and musician-composer DAVE ROSE celebrated their marriage with a trip to New York.

In December, OLEG CASSINI signed a contract with 20th. His first assignment was to design clothes for RITA HAYWORTH. Meanwhile, his wife's parents were suing Gene "for loss of income" due to her marital status . . . And director ERNST LUBITSCH's butler was picked up by the FBI and named as a relative of one of the top-ranking Nazis in Europe. He was the "paymaster" for the U.S. Nazi sympathizers. Lubitsch was shocked.

The Japanese bombed Pearl Harbor and the Philippines: AMERICA WAS AT WAR!

On a happier note, AVA GARDNER and MICKEY ROONEY went house-hunting . . . And CLARK GABLE and CAROLE LOMBARD headed up a committee to help coordinate bond sales and camp shows.

1942

With the United States directly involved in the war, almost all social events were curtailed. Only those appearances that aided morale were considered of top priority. CAROLE LOMBARD, the first major star to go on a war bond sales tour, in January of 1942, was killed on the 16th in an air crash.

One of the few annual events that Hollywood stars still attended was President Roosevelt's Birthday Ball—with proceeds from their appearances going to charity. CAROL BRUCE, barely out of her teens, and the rage of Broadway for her performance in *Louisiana Purchase,* had just been signed by Universal Studios and was thrilled to be included in the February 1942 event. CAROL, who also had been AL JOLSON's featured vocalist on his weekly radio show, was dating FDR's son, FRANKLIN, JR. When she received an invitation to the White House, she was doubly excited—and nervous. She was going to meet her beau's parents.

"It was really something," Carol reminisced recently.

First came the preparation. Universal had

a spectacular long white organza ball gown made for me, complete with ostrich feathers and hand-sewn pale pink, blue and violet beads on the bodice. During my fittings, someone from the publicity department primed me on a whole series of "dos" and "don'ts."

My most important assignment was to make sure that, when I arrived at Uline Arena [the big outdoor stadium] for the cutting of the president's cake, I was standing *alongside* the cake. That was the one shot the newsreels always picked up. They stressed how important it was to the studio, and to me, their "new star" [who had only done one film to date].

Among our group were Rosalind Russell, Joan Crawford, Pat O'Brien, Betty Grable, Jimmy Stewart, Doug Fairbanks, Jr., Robert Montgomery, Wayne Morris, and Ava Gardner and Mickey Rooney, who were still honeymooners. Even the train trip was fantastic. I marveled at being included in such a star-studded contingent.

When we arrived in Washington, D.C., the first big event was a private luncheon for all of us at the White House. Mrs. Roosevelt greeted us. She was so warm and radiant, with sparkling blue eyes, and much prettier than she photographed. Suddenly, the doors swung open. President Roosevelt was wheeled in. He was the most imposing figure I had ever seen. His cigarette in its holder jutted out of his mouth, and his smile was worth a million dollars. A chill ran up my spine.

During lunch, he chatted informally, and addressed us all by our first names. When it was over, the President left ahead of us. Then we took a tour of the White House. The first room I entered was a bathroom. I later reported to my parents that the White House towels were plain white—nice and fluffy—but not any different from those that *we* had at home!

Everything became a fantastic blur. We made four or five quick stops to meet the fans, and were mobbed. Then we arrived at the huge Uline Arena. Suddenly, Universal's instructions ran through my head: "Whatever you do be sure you're next to the cake." I looked down and saw Mrs. Roosevelt standing by an enormous frosted goodie—the size of a whole table.

They started a fanfare of music. I latched on to Betty Grable's arm. After all, she *was* the biggest star of the moment—the G.I.s' favorite pin-up girl. Mickey Rooney took Betty's left arm. The three of us started walking toward the cake. Suddenly, there was Mrs. Roosevelt, knife in her hand, just ready to cut.

Quickly, I stepped to her side and put my hand on top of hers. And together, Eleanor Roosevelt and *I* cut the President's first slice.

The Movietone Newsreel cameras started whirring. When the film appeared in theatres all over the country the following weekend, there we were—just Mrs. Roosevelt—and me—Betty and Mickey weren't in the shot! Universal was thrilled at all of the publicity. In my short, but rather delightful career, the President's Birthday Ball was one high spot I could never forget.

Sixty-year-old John Barrymore died on May 29, 1942, of complications from a chronic kidney and liver ailment. His funeral, at Calvary Cemetery, had been attended by a top celebrity crowd, including Gable, who made his first public appearance since the death of Carole Lombard.

According to Carl Schaefer, former head of Warner Brothers' International Publicity Department, a junket the studio threw in Mexico, mid-1942, was really a lulu. "Warners decided to make a contribution to Inter-American affairs, and offered a special showing of *Yankee Doodle Dandy*—which was cleaning up millions in the United States—and considered a perfect film for the occasion. The society leaders of the Mexican Red Cross were very excited. They booked the ornate, sedate Palacio de las Bellas Artes—which had never screened a movie before . . ."

Schaefer gathered a group of Warners stars, which included Errol Flynn, Ann Sheridan, Dennis Morgan and Faye Emerson, and invited a huge press contingent. Nelson Rockefeller, an expert on Latin-American affairs, flew up from New York to join them.

The gang stayed at the Hotel Reforma. As with most junkets, there were a few minor problems.

Because Errol Flynn was having "girl trouble" at the time [Schaefer said], it was decided not to tell him about a big luncheon being tossed at the American Embassy. There was some concern that his presence "might offend" Mrs. Messersmith, the Ambassador's wife. So I took the other stars, and we piled into limousines and headed for the Embassy. When we walked in, Flynn was already there. He had a drink in one hand, and was chatting away, charming the pants off the Ambassador's wife. No one could figure out how he had heard about the soirée. But Errol and party-time sort of went together.

Meanwhile, Ann Sheridan, in between beaus, was having a fling with OSCAR BROOKS, the unmarried and very attractive head of Warner Brothers in Mexico. Ann really cared for Brooks, and the feeling was reciprocated. The evening of the premiere neither Ann nor Brooks was in the lobby at the appointed time. So I phoned upstairs and, from the conversation, realized that the twosome was engrossed in something more intimate than a showing of *El Canto de la Victoria* [the Mexican title for *Yankee Doodle Dandy*]. I told Brooks the limos were leaving in fifteen minutes, and that he and Sheridan had better be ready.

In twelve minutes flat, gorgeous Annie, Warners' hard drinking, fun-loving star, was downstairs—pretty as a picture. Right behind her was Oscar Brooks. The film was a big hit. The Mexican Red Cross collected a lot of money. The Ambassador's wife couldn't stop raving about Errol Flynn's charms. And Ann and Oscar cemented the bond between them. In fact, everyone was thrilled except Jack Warner—when he received the bills.

On August 19, 1942, all of the gala floodlit premieres were banned until the war was over. The night before Hollywood "grew dim," SAMUEL GOLDWYN's *Pride of the Yankees* had the honor of closing the series of brightly lit premieres that had begun back in 1923 with *The Covered Wagon*. Proceeds went to the Naval Aid Auxiliary.

Thousands of fans stood outside the Pantages Theatre, on Hollywood and Vine, and watched as stars and high-ranking Naval, Army and Marine officers entered. The San Diego Naval Station band played both outside and inside the theatre to entertain the crowd before the picture started. Among the celebrities who attended were: MICKEY ROONEY and AVA GARDNER, RITA HAYWORTH and VICTOR MATURE in his Coast Guard uniform, LT. RONALD REAGAN and JANE WYMAN, JEAN-PIERRE AUMONT and HEDY LAMARR, WYNN ROCCAMORA and DOROTHY LAMOUR, IRENE DUNNE and DR. FRANCIS GRIFFIN, Mr. and Mrs. BOB HOPE, Mr. and Mrs. SAMUEL GOLDWYN, JACK BENNY and MARY LIVINGSTONE, GINGER ROGERS and the CHARLES BOYERS.

When the picture ended, most of the crowd gathered at the nearby Brown Derby for a late supper.

The first junket contingent of Hollywood stars left by train on August 27, 1942, for Washington, D.C., to be part of the September billion-dollar War Bond Drive. Each carried a suitcase full of prized personal mementos to be auctioned off as a special hype for the War Bond sales. Other celebrities headed for various parts of the country. By Labor Day, JOHN PAYNE and JOAN LESLIE were in Tacoma; RONALD REAGAN and LYNN BARI sold Bonds in and around Colorado Springs; JAMES CAGNEY was auctioning his memorabilia in Madison, Wisconsin; GREER GARSON visited Roanoke and Lynchburg, Virginia; IRENE DUNNE was in New York City; CHARLES LAUGHTON spouted Shakespeare and sold bonds in Waterbury, Hartford and New Britain, Connecticut. Meanwhile, BETTE DAVIS was busy "hustling" bonds in Kansas City, Oklahoma City and throughout the Midwest.

Simultaneously, a two-hour national radio salute to the industry-led billion-dollar drive was broadcast from Hollywood and New York. RED SKELTON, BOB BURNS, AMOS and ANDY, EDWARD G. ROBINSON, NELSON EDDY, FANNY BRICE and HANLEY STAFFORD headlined from Hollywood. ORSON WELLES and DINAH SHORE topped the New York portion of the program.

At the end of August, NORMA SHEARER married MARTY ARROUGE, businessman–ski instructor . . . And, when September started, TYRONE POWER enlisted in the Marine Corps and HENRY FONDA signed on as an able-bodied seaman with the Navy . . . As the month ended, AVA G. divorced MICKEY ROONEY.

In the fall, *The Reporter*'s BILLY WILKERSON added to his string of impressive cafes and clubs by opening an exclusive restaurant in Beverly Hills called L'Aiglon. Debut night was a smashing success. SONJA HENIE came with GREG BAUTZER—who would soon begin a torrid romance with JOAN CRAWFORD. HEDY LAMARR showed up with MARK STEVENS. The VAN JOHNSONS, JOAN BENNETT and WALTER WANGER, TONY MARTIN and JOSEPH SCHENCK were others spotted among the well-wishers. The place had been suitably "christened" by some of Hollywood's biggest names.

In October, the Hollywood Canteen officially opened at Sunset Boulevard and Cahuenga . . . Down in Miami, CLARK GABLE, in training, was given guard duty—eight thousand local women found out and marched with him. Gable was reassigned to stand guard from 1 A.M. to 3 A.M., which did nothing to discourage the ladies—and upset the whole camp. Private Gable was relieved of guard duty.

In November, the evidence of how much MICKEY ROONEY *really* loved Ava was revealed. He gave her an alimony settlement of $75,000—quite a sum for less than a year of wedded "bliss" . . . And HEDY LAMARR had second thoughts about breaking her engagement to GEORGE MONTGOMERY. Unfortunately, it was too late. She had already given the ring back... Hollywood lost cowboy star BUCK JONES, who died a hero's death in Boston's Cocoanut Grove, trying to rescue patrons during a nightclub fire.

By December, MARY PICKFORD was holding down the fort at Pickfair alone. BUDDY ROGERS had left home to fly for the Navy... SPENCER TRACY was in Washington, D.C., being briefed prior to a junket to Casablanca to entertain the troops... BETTE DAVIS, president of the Hollywood Canteen, had arranged for all postcards sent from there by G.I.s to go out postage-free... And ANN SHERIDAN and ERROL FLYNN, both between marriages, discovered each other. When Errol left for Mexico to divorce LILI DAMITA, Ann decided she might get her divorce there, too.

LANA TURNER'S on-and-off marriage to STEVE CRANE had complications. She was pregnant... In mid-December, GLENN FORD was sworn in as a Marine... CLARK GABLE came home on a brief leave for a few days of rest at his ranch. But without Carole there, he spent only a few hours with the family pets, saw some chums, and then bunked elsewhere... And GENE TIERNEY spent the holidays visiting with OLEG at Fort Riley, Kansas.

George Cukor
"THE 'NEW' KATHARINE HEPBURN"

No director in Hollywood knew more about Kate Hepburn than George Cukor. They were professional associates and friends, and Kate even became a Cukor tenant. Both of them shared a candor, a tell-it-like-it-is approach to life. For the December 31, 1940, issue of The Hollywood Reporter, *Cukor wrote this piece which exemplified his Hepburn expertise and their relationship.*

It is only fair to admit my perplexity in the first sentence. During several years of a most pleasant friendship and professional association, I have come to feel that I know something about Miss Katharine Hepburn. Apparently I have been laboring under a delusion. It seems from what I read that I am one of the few who has not yet discovered the "New Katharine Hepburn."

My perplexity was predicated on the disbelief that any major transformation in Miss Hepburn could possibly have come without my detecting at least a few symptons. But on carefully analyzing this alleged change in personality, it less puzzled me than amused me. Seriously, the most interesting observation to be made about Miss Hepburn is that fundamentally she has never changed at all, either as the actress with a rare and gifted talent I directed in *A Bill of Divorcement* in 1932, or as a person whose charm and strength is her uncompromising individuality. It goes without saying that she has improved as an actress and that she is a more delightful and intelligent person than she was eight years ago.

In 1932, Miss Hepburn, being very young, lacked experience and therefore technique.

Katharine Hepburn.

In *The Philadelphia Story,* both on the stage and screen, she had fully developed and perfected her technique. This was only the complete realization of the ability she always possessed.

What I have to say about Miss Hepburn should not be interpreted as the usual banalities, which have been written in a bogus way so many times in the past. I have no pedestal for Miss Hepburn. She can be wrong. She can be difficult. We have had our arguments. But Miss Hepburn can most sincerely be judged by the almost tearful affection with which the crew regarded her at the completion of *The Philadelphia Story.*

Too, my impressions, formed long ago, were amply verified by the scores of newspapermen who talked with her while she was in Hollywood. They went away to write enthusiastically about a normal, highly intelligent and extremely honest, pleasant and likeable young woman.

Since these qualities seemed to be at odds with those of a girl whose superficially undeserved reputation had recorded her as being temperamental, rude and unreasonable, and a proper target for similar scabrous adjectives, it was accepted that she must have reformed. But the truth of it is that, from the beginning, Miss Hepburn chose a direct line, and stuck to it.

If Miss Hepburn were not the challenging personality she is, she would still be somebody, but certainly not Katharine Hepburn. In 1932, she was shocking Hollywood by wearing slacks, which she considers the most comfortable garment ever invented, then inelegantly referred to as "men's pants"; driving a station wagon, classified at the time as a "truck" for want of a better descriptive word, and by sitting on curbstones, because studios do not provide benches for stars whose feet hurt. These activities today would hardly cause the lifting of an eyebrow, being considered quite normal. This is merely offered in evidence that Hollywood has at last gained some of the naturalness which Miss Hepburn always has had.

I will never forget the day Miss Hepburn came into the studio to make a test for *A Bill of Divorcement.* She impressed me with her freshness, spirit and also because she was one of the oddest looking girls I had ever seen. She had run a sliver into her eye, which was bloodshot, and was wearing an arty, strange and eccentric dress by Elizabeth Hawes. Afterwards, she admitted that the dress was supposed to make us all "take notice." She was self-possessed, a bit patronizing, and a little silly, giggling like a college girl one moment, and being superior the next.

When she was shown her costumes for the picture, Miss Hepburn expressed decidedly emphatic opinions about them, mostly negative. To this outburst, I recall remarking, "just from the way you look, I can hardly take your judgment seriously." Our friendship started on this frank and open basis, and has remained so. But in the several pictures in which I have directed her, she never at any time has been unreasonable. She has good ideas, for which she will fight at the drop of a hat, at the same time admitting being in the wrong if such happened to be the case.

As for the often made charge that she is rude, that is not true. Her manner is direct and definite. She will stand on her own ground against anyone. But neither I, nor anyone else, has ever seen Miss Hepburn be rude to anybody not in a position to answer her back on even terms.

We have gotten along in complete harmony, I believe, because she thinks she handles me more than I handle her, putting up with more vagaries and nonsense from me than I do from her. Whatever the basis on which we work together, it always has been solid and satisfactory to a high degree.

When I went East to see her on the stage in *The Philadelphia Story,* Miss Hepburn was very tired after more than a year-and-a-half in the play. She acts on the stage with a picture technique, rather than just giving a performance. By this, I mean that she tries to feel every performance, going at top speed, with no letdown. This is good on the screen, with short scenes and a chance to relax in between, but on the stage it is devitalizing.

The night I saw her, she gave a bad performance. When I told her this backstage, Miss Hepburn replied that she would have considered me dishonest if I had not said so. Having a friend in the audience bothers her. All she can see is his head looming out above the others. The next night, more at ease, she was excellent.

When Miss Hepburn came to Metro-Goldwyn-Mayer for the picture, she knew the play backwards and forwards. So we made slight changes in dialogue and situation to give them a new freshness, vitality and spontaneity for Miss Hepburn . . .

It was a pleasure to see her back in Hollywood, because the screen and the stage both need her great talent. And nothing can break her spirit, since Miss Hepburn, who has never changed in those things that count in the years I have known her, is not likely to change in the future.

Humphrey Bogart
"CENSORSHIP"

On October 31, 1941, Humphrey Bogart wrote this very thoughtful vignette for The Hollywood Reporter. *He tackled a very important subject, one with which he was personally quite conversant. While some of his views about the possible effects of the relationship between violent crime films and the actual copycat commission of same have changed over the years, much of what he wrote still remains valid.*

The blanket of censorship covers practically every country in the world these days, except our own. And, judging from the editorials, whenever the threat of censorship rears its head in this country, most of us seem agreed it is the Number One enemy of a free democracy.

This is where my pet peeve comes in. While people are always quick to take up the cudgels against censorship of the press, or radio, any crackpot can advocate new forms of censorship for the movies, and not a voice is lifted in protest. There's something illogical about this indifference to censorship of the movies. After all, it's just as much a medium of public expression as are the radio and newspapers.

My own type of film has shown me how wrong and unfair advocates of censorship can be. For several years now, various groups have urged the banning of crime pictures on the ground that they influence youths to turn to crime. When Jimmy Walker was minority leader of the New York Legislature, there was a censorship fight on the floor of the House. A powerful group of pious bluenoses wanted to bar from circulation good books that dared to mention certain well-known facts of life. The bluenoses said the books were indecent, bawdy, lascivious and would lead their young and innocent daughters astray. Jimmy stood the debate as long as he could, then he said, "I have been around a good deal, but I have never heard of a woman's being seduced by a book." That killed the censorship bill.

I have never heard of any youngster going wrong, turning to crime, because of the movies. It simply isn't possible. Our relation to crime is, in a sense, the same as the prison warden's. We don't create it. We deal with it after it has happened, and we always make the criminal look bad.

Humphrey Bogart with Ingrid Bergman in Warners' classic film *Casablanca*, 1943.

When I went to college, I studied under a professor of geology who wanted to make us understand how the different peoples of the world got the way they are, their racial tendencies and characteristics, dark-skinned Africans and fair-haired Swedes. He cited geography and climate and food and opportunities, and he summed it all up with the phrase: "We are what we are largely because we are where we are."

The proof of that argument can be found in the Uniform Crime Reports and the Department of Justice. The spot maps of cities show it. Not so long ago, I examined some maps showing juvenile delinquency, diphtheria, tuberculosis and murder quotients in a number of cities from New Orleans to Los Angeles. The maps all looked alike. Disease, crime and delinquency were invariably grouped in the same parts of the cities—in the slum districts. That is the cause of crime, not the motion picture.

About ten years ago, I was a guest at a little dinner party in Hollywood, and my hostess' son, a boy of about nine, sat across the table from me. He was an obnoxious little brat. His manners were very bad. He was hard-boiled, truculent and talked out of the side of his mouth. His mother finally whispered to me, "Don't pay any attention to him now, but he is your greatest admirer. He thinks you are wonderful, sees all your pictures, and he's acting for you."

That didn't make me happy. I made friends with the boy and took him over to the studio one day. We rode along in silence for a little while, and then he said, "Say, Bogie, are you bad in this new picture?" I had a good part in the film, so I replied, "Why, no, as a matter of fact, I think I'm pretty good."

"Aw, nuts," said the kid. "Don'tcha smack anybody down?"

He felt better when I admitted I did put a couple of guys on the spot, and his next suggestion was that we ought to stick up the First National Bank, and when he grew tired of that we talked about baseball. The boy turned out all right, in spite of me and my bad acting. He came from the right kind of home, had the right kind of parents, and he attended the right kind of school. His environment was right, and no amount of motion pictures could have made a criminal of that boy. He could take the Cagneys and the Rafts and Bogie, or leave them alone . . .

Movies don't cause crime any more than prison wardens cause crime. It has been charged against the motion picture industry that we take a sympathetic attitude toward gangsters, thugs, racketeers and criminals. I deny that. After the things that have happened to me and my fellow screen heavies, I don't see how they can say that. So many criminals get killed in *The Maltese Falcon* that there's a special announcement at the end of the film saying, "If any persons are alive in this picture, it is purely coincidental."

There are groups that would like us to show the criminal always outmatched, poorly armed, and all policemen a good six inches taller, armed with tear gas and tommy guns, while the poor, dear, miserable rat of a gangster has to fight it out alone with only one measly little pistol. The object would be to de-glamorize the gangster.

That's all right, but it seems to me they are asking us to go about it in the wrong way. It seems to me that disarming the gangster tends to add glamour rather than to remove it and, in some instances, even makes him seem gallant. What these critics forget is that the sympathies of the crowd are always with the underdog.

It is better, I think, to de-glamorize His Excellency the Rat as we do it at Warners, by showing him well-armed, with an up-to-date arsenal, with smokescreens for his automobile, expensive short-wave radios and other good equipment for the art of murder and arson. When we show a criminal on the screen like that, there is no doubt in the mind of the weakest low-grade moron who the hero is. The hero is unquestionably your friend and mine, the cop.

I have dealt with only one phase of the attempt to impose censorship on the movies. It is the phase with which I am most familiar. But there are men who advocate even more dangerous types of film censorship, and if America is to continue to have freedom of the press and radio, as well as every other type of freedom, these insidious enemies of freedom must be emphatically discouraged. Because once the movies are gagged, these men will move on to the other mediums of public expression. We have seen it happen in other countries, and it can happen here.

HOLLYWOOD'S WARTIME STARS

There was a song which became popular during the war—"They're Either Too Young or Too Old."

Part of that line happily expressed one reason for Hollywood's hold on some of its top male stars. John Wayne, Jimmy Cagney,

Spencer Tracy, Edward G. Robinson and Humphrey Bogart were examples of the "too old" set. That group, joined by those who were young enough, but medically or otherwise deferred, formed the civilian cadre from which most of the early Forties films were cast.

By the time America entered the war, Bogart had just reached top stardom at Warner Brothers. He was Mr. Versatility, plus. He could be tough. Tender. Cruel. Crude. At times, he could even be romantic and cute. Although no one ever dared accuse him of the latter attribute—not to his face.

He was born Humphrey DeForest Bogart, in New York City, as legend has it, on Christmas Day, 1900. His father was a family physician. His mother was a well-known illustrator who painted under the name of Maude Humphrey. She even used Bogie as a child model for a series of magazine covers she did for *Delineator* magazine. With his good upper-middle-class background, he was sent to—and tossed out of—several very good prep schools. He had developed a high spirit and an independent nature which were not geared to the conformity required of him.

When World War I broke out, he joined up as a common seaman and served aboard several transport ships, including *The Leviathan* and *The Santa Olivia*. He also spent a good deal of time in the brig. By the time he was discharged, he had decided to become an actor, and headed for Broadway. In his first role of any substance, critic Alexander Woollcott roasted him. But Bogie was determined to succeed.

He made two abortive attempts in Hollywood. Both times he just didn't seem to fit in. Then he was cast as the cruel gangster, Duke Mantee, in the stage version of *The Petrified Forest*. He was a big hit. When he heard that Warners was going to make the film version, he decided to give himself another chance. But the studio had Edward G. Robinson in mind for that role. In desperation, he called Leslie Howard in Scotland. Howard had already committed himself to the picture. He asked Leslie to intercede. Howard made the call and said he wanted Bogart. The studio was reluctant. Robinson fumed and fussed. But Bogie got the part.

In 1936, the release of the film launched Bogart's screen career. There was only one problem. Warners had a whole stable of "tough guys"—Robinson, Cagney, Paul Muni. So Bogart had to be content to take their "leftovers." Finally, in 1941, he was given the lead in *High Sierra*, a role originally intended for Paul Muni. It was the turning point in Bogart's career. It made him a star.

While he was a success as an actor, Humphrey was less than a perfect mate. By the early Forties, he was one-half of a Hollywood duo quaintly known as the "battling Bogarts." His sparring partner was stage and screen actress Mayo Methot, his third wife.

The first woman who shared Bogie's nest was stage and radio star Helen Mencken. She divorced him in 1927. The second Mrs. Bogart was actress Mary Phillips. They were married on April 3, 1928, in Hartford, Connecticut, stayed together nine years, and separated in January of 1937. Finally convinced that her man had no intention of coming home, Mary went into court.

"My husband was always pining for his single blessedness," she told the judge. "In the presence of friends, he told me he wanted a divorce . . . that he didn't love me anymore. He said I was depriving him of his freedom. Then he began staying out until all hours of the night . . ."

The judge granted the divorce. Exactly one year later, Bogie was "back in harness" again, married to Mayo. In Hollywood, the Bogarts were regarded as generous hosts who frequently gave parties that involved a lot of imbibing. Bogart, the tough guy on screen, was an intelligent, cultivated man. He just had trouble holding his booze. Mayo matched him shot glass for shot glass. Frequently, they were seen around town, usually arguing, sometimes coming to blows.

At the end of October 1944, they were apart. By the beginning of November, they were back together. On December 3, the marriage appeared to have ended. Mayo hired famous attorney Jerry Giesler. When questioned by reporters, she shrugged her shoulders. "What can I do? He says he's not coming home. But it is *his* home and I want him in it. Our marriage has weathered a lot of storms in the last six years . . . I don't want a big settlement. I want him. It's become a habit to love Bogie and it's hard to break that habit."

Bogart told *his* side to another reporter. "While it's hard to break up a marriage of six years, we have had so many fights, I believe it's the right thing to do. I told Mayo I am not coming home. She can have anything she wants if she'll just let me go. And I believe she is too sensible to want to hold me after six years of the continual battling we've been having."

But three days after Christmas, Bogie was back home. Mayo was ecstatic. "We're going to make it this time. I'm very happy. The holidays brought us together. This was the first time we were ever separated at Christmas. But he did give me a diamond and ruby ring . . . and he came to visit me on Christmas Day." Mayo, who had taken off weight because of her love for Bogie, anticipated that this would be the happiest of New Year's for them. It was during this period that Bogart had completed work on *To Have and Have Not*. Shooting had already begun on a follow-up film. In both screen epics his co-star was tall, slim, sultry fashion model Lauren Bacall, age twenty. Rumor had it they had fallen in love.

By January of 1945, Bogie was ensconced in Suite 901 of the Gotham Hotel in New York City; his marriage to Mayo was officially ended. Bogart publicly stated his plans for a divorce. In the next breath,

Mr. and Mrs. Humphrey Bogart at sea.

he quietly added that he and "Baby" were engaged.

"I know that I open my big fat yap too much. Maybe my announcement is a little premature. But, what the hell, I could never keep a secret. I live in a goldfish bowl anyway . . . I have for ten years. Have you ever tried to keep a secret in a goldfish bowl?"

So much for Mayo's dreams of "their happiest New Year's." Lauren and her mother checked into Suite 801 at the Gotham Hotel. Bacall had come to New York to do publicity for their film. From the moment she registered, the sidewalk in front of the hotel became a way station for groupies. The kids vociferously debated. Some said Bogart was too old for Bacall, others thought the love match idyllic.

Bogie, meanwhile, was so euphoric that he continued to "open his yap." Talking to a group of reporters, he admitted that he and Betty were going to be married. When? Well, that was up in the air. "It all depends on where Mayo obtains her divorce. We've agreed on the settlement. We're already through with the preliminary stages . . .

"Mayo is a fine girl. We just couldn't make a go of it. Hell, it was just a clash of personalities. Frankly, I'm not the easiest guy in the world to live with. But I can't say that I think our constant battling is an extra added attraction to any marriage. I don't want to end my life punch-drunk and walking on my heels . . . My engagement to Betty had nothing to do with the divorce. That was arranged a long time ago. She's a swell kid. I've made it kind of tough for her, shooting off my big face the way I have."

When questioned about the potential success of a fourth marriage, Bogart was very positive: "I'm not disillusioned, either about marriage or women. Hell, they're both a wonderful institution. You need a woman around the house to make a home of it."

By the middle of March, the Bogarts had reached a settlement. Mayo was already on her way to Las Vegas for a six-week quickie. Bogie had been very generous, endowing her with much of his worldly goods. By April of 1945, everyone who could read knew that it was only a matter of time before Lauren Bacall became the fourth Mrs. Bogart.

Suddenly, William Perske, Bacall's "long lost daddy," emerged to make a statement: "In my opinion, Lauren is far too young to marry a man more than twice her age. But she's a girl with a mind of her own. The chances are good that she will marry Bogart. If the wedding happens, it sure won't be with my approval." Perske said that his daughter's studio had insisted he "keep his trap closed." Then he added, "But I just felt like opening it!"

On May 21, 1945, in Mansfield, Ohio, in the spacious hallway of novelist Louis Bromfield's home, Malabar Farm, Lauren Bacall, 20, and Humphrey Bogart, 45, were married by Municipal Judge Herbert S. Schletter. The ceremony lasted three minutes. Hope Bromfield, the eighteen-year-old daughter of the novelist, played the "Wedding March" on the piano. George Hawkins, manager of Malabar Farm, gave the bride away.

The Bromfield family and a few friends witnessed the nuptials. Lauren wore a light pink, two-piece dress with brown accessories. Her only jewels were the ring given by Bogart and a bracelet on each wrist. She carried a bridal bouquet of two orchids. Bogie was in a gray suit, maroon tie, with a white carnation in his lapel. After the ceremony, he swept Lauren into his arms and brushed his lips across her cheek. This time, he was convinced, he had a lasting marriage.

Bogart's popularity was even greater after his fourth "merger." With Betty Bacall by his side, Bogie had taken on a new luster—now he was not only one of the biggest wartime stars, but a national sex symbol.

At the other end of the spectrum, a new star loomed on the horizon. He wasn't "too old," just 4-F, deferred because of a punctured eardrum. His name was Frank Sinatra, a skinny, dark-haired kid with a voice straight from heaven.

Suddenly, from out of nowhere, he had become the answer to every maiden's prayer. He burst onto the national scene in 1943, when the men were away at war and their women were lonely.

Frank had been an obscure band singer with both Harry James and Tommy Dorsey. Then, in 1943, he was signed for a two-week engagement at the Paramount Theatre in New York. From the moment he hugged the stage microphone, crooning words of romance . . . love . . . hope . . . and a brighter tomorrow, his audience, ninety percent female, went into fits of ecstasy. The engagement was extended for six more weeks. Sinatra shattered a fifteen-year attendance record.

His next stop was a step up. Frank appeared at the Waldorf-Astoria and sang his heart out for an entirely different crowd, the Sutton Place, Southampton and Westchester champagne and caviar set. Again, he scored—big.

Matrons with blue-tinted hair joined the bobbysox brigade. Frank was definitely the man of the moment!

Francis Albert Sinatra was born on Monroe Street, in Hoboken, New Jersey, on December 12, 1917. From the moment of his birth, he was the pride and joy of his parents, Dolly and Marty, and a delight to the rest of his huge Italian family.

Music was part of his heritage. Even as a high school kid, he sang with local bands. His only other love was journalism—he was a hotshot on the school newspaper.

The "big time" for undiscovered talent in those days was an appearance on "Major Bowes' Amateur Hour." As a teenager, Frank managed to wangle a spot on the show. He won first prize—singing a kid's romantic rendition of "Night and Day." From there, Frank worked small local radio stations, then landed in a tiny New Jersey nightclub. Big-time bandleader Harry James dropped in one evening, liked what he heard and signed Frank on as his vocalist.

From the James organization, Sinatra went with Tommy Dorsey. When he sang with the mellow Pied Pipers, Frank had the kids standing by the bandstand—holding each other and just listening. They believed he was fashioning his lyrics just for *them*.

While he was with Dorsey, Sinatra and the group recorded "I'll Never Smile Again," "Night and Day" and "This Love of Mine," all top sellers. Frank even made his film debut in 1942 in a picture called *Ship Ahoy*. Sinatra sang a few songs with the band, but didn't speak a word of dialogue. He went unnoticed.

After his recordings with Dorsey hit big, Frank moved on. He worked for CBS, and eventually wound up as one of the soloists on the "Hit Parade" radio show.

In 1943, RKO signed Sinatra to make his *acting* debut in *Higher and Higher*, co-starring Michèle Morgan and Jack Haley. Once he had a picture contract, the publicity really snowballed. Frank and his wife, the former Nancy Barbato, together with their baby girl, Nancy Sandra, moved West. They settled in a modest home in Toluca Lake, where Nancy, Sr., did all of her own housework while adjusting to her new Hollywood life-style.

Frank's second film was *Step Lively* with Gloria DeHaven. In between shooting, he returned to New York briefly and caused a riot. Thirty thousand youthful fanatics, Sinatra devotees, put on a demonstration in Times Square. It was so chaotic that hundreds of police reserves were called out to try to prevent the mob from self-destruction.

The phenomenon was so unusual that Professor Henry E. Garrett, a psychologist from Columbia University, was called to explain it. In scholarly fashion, the doctor

Pamela Britton and Frank Sinatra in MGM's *Anchors Aweigh*.

labeled the whole scene a case of "mass hysteria" complicated by the war. "You see," he continued, "this little fella represents some kind of an idealized hero, much like the story of Prince Charming . . ." Then, off the record, he added that, frankly, he had heard better singers!

Frank was everybody's brother . . . sweetheart . . . lover. He wasn't handsome in the matinee-idol sense. He lacked an impressive physique; in fact he was almost frail. But it was this very vulnerability that evoked a maternal response in every female over the age of eleven.

There were rumors that his rise had originally been a publicity gimmick—started by a claque of girls who had been hired to cheer and swoon. Even if it were true, the sight of thirty thousand weak-kneed women and girls in Times Square waving his photos and screaming his name was *genuine*. Sinatra had arrived—for real.

On January 11, 1944, the Sinatras welcomed a son, Frank, Jr. While her husband was busy with films, recordings, radio shows and personal appearances, Nancy Barbato Sinatra was preoccupied moving the entire household into a new home. It was a long way from Hoboken—but the family now resided in a Beverly Hills mansion. There were nannies and nurses. Maids and gardeners. Secretaries and managers. And Nancy stopped doing her own dishes.

In 1945, Sinatra co-starred with Gene Kelly in MGM's Technicolor musical *Anchors Aweigh*. It was such a smash hit that fans went back week after week to see it again and again. By the end of the year, it was nominated for an Academy Award as one of the five best films. Frank Sinatra had become one of the biggest wartime stars in the world.

Between the polish of Bogart and the personality of Sinatra, there was another whole batch of leading men who kept Hollywood busy during the early 1940s. In addition to making as many films as they could, stars like Gary Cooper, Cary Grant, Bing Crosby, Fred Astaire, Fred MacMurray, Ralph Bellamy, Brian Donlevy, Ray Milland and Dane Clark joined the aforementioned Eddie Robinson, Spencer Tracy, James Cagney and Paul Muni in dedicating their spare time to visiting camps, doing USO-HVC shows and going on exhausting fund-raising drives in order to help the war effort.

John Garfield was among the most active leading men. He and Bette Davis had been the driving forces behind the establishment of the Hollywood Canteen. The twosome had begged, borrowed, wheedled, pleaded and coerced anyone in town who could help make their dream a reality. Studio moguls, union leaders, wealthy society people—and their own peers—were all buttonholed to contribute.

The first fund-raiser for the Canteen was held on August 29, 1942—a premiere of *Talk of the Town*, followed by a supper party. The film was donated. The theatre was given free. Ciro's opened its doors especially for the occasion. Thousands of dollars were raised. The "reality" was coming closer.

Five weeks later, on October 3, the Hollywood Canteen officially opened. Davis and Garfield stood watching as the first G.I.s rushed through the door. Outside there was almost a carnival-like atmosphere. The bleachers were full of fans. Several bands played. There was so much noise and gaiety that the whole area off Sunset Boulevard and Cahuenga echoed and re-echoed with the solid sound of success.

Ten thousand dollars' worth of admission tickets had been sold. On this one night it cost everyone—not in uniform—to enter. For the privilege of broadcasting the event, several thousand more was collected. Dr. Jules Stein, president of the Music Corporation of America, and the Canteen's "business advisor," personally greeted all of those "anonymous" donors from whom

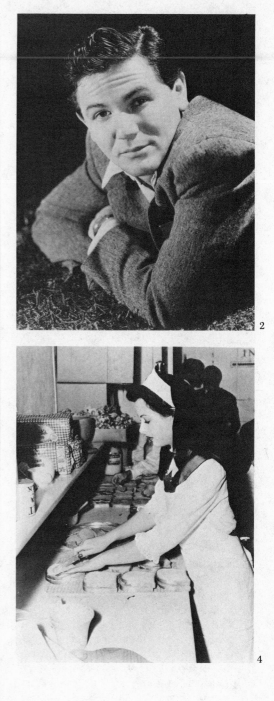

1 The world-famous Hollywood Canteen with GIs lined up to get in. For four years, this was the home away from home for thousands of service personnel.   2 One of Warner Brothers' "tough guys," John Garfield. He was co-founder, with Bette Davis, of the Hollywood Canteen.   3 Bette Davis, president of the Hollywood Canteen, and friends.   4 Hedy Lamarr prepares sandwiches for the Canteen. One of the most generous celebrity volunteers, she appeared there every Friday night for several years.

he and his wife had collected large sums. With "Mr. MCA" behind it, the Canteen had been on solid financial ground from the beginning. Still, from inception to reality, it had been miraculous.

At the end of the first six months, the Canteen staff estimated that 600,000 servicemen had consumed 24,000 loaves of bread, 300,000 half-pints of milk, 2400 pounds of butter, 15,000 pounds of milk, 180,000 gallons of orange juice, 450,000 packs of cigarettes and more than 900,000 sandwiches. They had danced with every glamorous star from June Allyson to Vera Zorina, and had been entertained by the greats of the show business world.

Seven nights a week, the Canteen required a minimum of three hundred volunteer workers. Stars not only performed and fraternized, they also helped sweep up and serve food. But most rewarding of all was the word-of-mouth reputation that the Canteen received all over the world. Every G.I. who spent a few hours inside told some of his buddies. Eventually, guys on Saipan, and in the deserts of North Africa, and all the tiny atolls in between, knew about the Hollywood Canteen. By the time the war was over, millions of them had been there.

One of the most gratifying experiences of John Garfield's connection with the Canteen came in the form of a letter handed to him in February of 1943. For stars like himself—who weren't in actual combat—it meant everything. The message, in part, read:

Dear Movie Star:
You've got it rough. To a few this may sound crazy, but I wouldn't change places with you even if I could act. You beat yourself all the time because you're not carrying a gun. You think we scorn you. You imagine everyone is pointing a finger at you saying: "What's the matter with him? Is he afraid? Doesn't he want to defend the country that's been so good to him?"

Let me tell you, Mister, you're all wet . . . I have seen six months action in the South Pacific War Zone. I know what it is to be cut off from everything . . . to sit on my bunk with my head in my hands . . . to walk a post in some lonely nowhere . . . to wait and wait for God only knows what. Those hours can stretch into centuries—and would, if it weren't for a movie now and then. Movies that stop us from thinking of ourselves and our surroundings. Movies that remind us there are such things as pretty girls, gay music, and a civilization worth living for . . .

Sure, we'd like to have you with us. But we're selfish, we want movies more. We'd rather you keep on making entertainment for us. As a man in uniform you might stop a bullet or, if you're lucky, you might eliminate a dozen of the enemy. But as an actor you'll help us hand out a thousand wallops.

Beat yourself if you must, but, for our sake, please don't stop making movies.

Private Briddell
U.S. Marines

Hollywood's new crop of young actors appreciated the Marine's letter as much as Garfield. Van Johnson, Peter Lawford, Robert Walker, Montgomery Clift and a whole host of others performed *their* duty, and kept the home fires churning, turning out entertaining pictures that reached our service personnel around the globe.

Alan Ladd, also one of the new wartime stars, had a taste of both worlds—civilian and military. All of his life he had worked hard, paid his dues, but had never been lucky. Then, he caught the golden ring on the carousel of stardom. It was in December 1941, when *This Gun for Hire* opened to smash reviews at Paramount's theatre on Broadway. For the first time in his life, Ladd traveled to New York City, deluxe. He stayed in a fancy hotel and gazed up at his name on a billboard so big he couldn't believe it.

Alan Ladd was born in Hot Springs, Arkansas. When he was three, his father died. His mother, a young English beauty named Ina Rawley, married again—unhappily. All Ladd remembered was that his first stepfather's name was Tom—and that the man had been cruel to him.

His second stepfather, Mr. Beavers, was a kind, hardworking person. But the family was very poor. While still a young boy, Alan and his family moved to Southern California, eventually settling down in the North Hollywood area. Beavers, a house painter and carpenter, found enough lumber to put together a makeshift garage—their home for quite some time.

It was a far cry from a lean-to in North Hollywood to a billboard on Broadway. But after years of struggling, and a first marriage, at a young age, he met Sue Carol, a former screen star, beautiful and brilliant. She was then an actors' agent—and the first person "with connections"—who believed he could become a star. After a couple of years of small roles, and a juicier cameo part now and then, he was cast as Raven in *This Gun for Hire*.

Ladd had faster impact on the American moviegoing public than any other leading man of his day. Without the benefit of television, his name and face were known across the country in a matter of weeks. For the first time in his life, he had the beginnings of security within his grasp.

He and Sue were married early in 1942, and he started his second film under his Paramount contract. But there was a gnawing feeling inside his gut. The war was on and he wasn't in it. As a high school kid, he had been a championship swimmer and diver. Years of constant double somersaults off the high boards had caused a chronic stomach injury. It was this ailment which made his first attempt to enlist futile.

Still, as it got closer to Christmas of 1942,

Mr. and Mrs. Alan Ladd (Sue Carol). The Ladds dedicated every free moment to visiting Army camps and hospitals.

Ladd found himself unable to look any man in uniform straight in the eyes. So he tried to enlist again, and was accepted. By this time he had finished a third starring film, *China*. Alan went off to basic training and was stationed in Walla Walla, Washington. Stardom was still so new, he was awed to learn that his fan mail continued to pour in at a rate of over 15,000 letters a month. From the first, he and Sue were determined to answer every one of them. While he was away, Paramount paid for a secretary to help. Several times during his Army stint, the old stomach injury plagued him. Finally, after eleven months, he wound up in a military hospital—and was given a medical discharge. By this time, Sue had presented him with a baby, Alana. He already had a son, Alan, Jr., and Sue had an older daughter, Carol Lee, each from a former marriage.

Ladd came home from the wars to a full household, and immediately went back to work. But, having been in the service, and having been hospitalized, he knew what overwhelming feelings of loneliness the men in uniform experienced. He and Sue decided to dedicate every free moment to visiting Army camps and hospitals. They kept up the pace all throughout the war.

One day in 1945, while the Ladds were walking through a military hospital, stopping to speak to each patient, they spotted a handsome young man lying in bed, stripped to the waist. One of his legs was in a steel brace. He told them he had been shot down over Bougainville. He was so outstanding-looking that Alan asked if he had ever thought of being in the movies. The G.I., whose name was Johnny Veitch, said he hadn't.

Then Ladd offered to help him get into pictures if he came to Hollywood. Veitch expressed his gratitude, but said he had other plans. When he was well, he was going back to Buffalo, to enter a General Motors executive training program. The Ladds wished him luck—and gave him their home phone number just in case. One year later he called long distance. "Do you remember me?" he asked. Although Sue and Alan had spoken to thousands of wounded G.I.s, they did indeed remember the handsome kid from New York.

"I'd like to come to California," he continued. "How's the situation out there?"

"As good as anywhere," Ladd assured him. "C'mon ahead, we'll do everything we can to help you."

From the moment Veitch arrived, the Ladds befriended him, welcomed him into their home. He became like a big brother to their children. Carol Lee was then fourteen; Alan, Jr., nine; Alana, five; and David, a toddler. Frequently, when they went out to dinner, Johnny babysat. Often, he remained overnight.

Meanwhile, he had been introduced to some studio people. He found work as an actor, but once he was more familiar with the business, he preferred the other side of the camera. He began scouting locations for producers and directors. Veitch was a fast learner, and the Ladds were understandably proud of him. Eventually, he became a location manager—and kept on moving—upward.

To give this particular Hollywood wartime "Cinderella" story more impact, it should be noted that Carol Lee Ladd grew up and became Mrs. John Veitch. John, meanwhile, had progressed so far that eventually he became president of a major studio, in charge of *all* production for Columbia Pictures Corporation. His advancement took many years of hard work. But it never would have happened at all if Alan and Sue Ladd had not offered a wounded G.I. their friendship—and meant it.

HOLLYWOOD ON THE HALF-SHELL
1943

January began with the shortest interview on record. A female reporter asked GEORGE SANDERS what he would do if he had only twenty-four hours to live. He told her—in one word . . . It must have been love: DINAH SHORE gave GEORGE MONTGOMERY singing lessons—daily . . . FRANCES FARMER, in the process of making a picture for the King Brothers, "acted up," and was replaced by MARY BRIAN . . . On the 20th, ALAN LADD went into the Army . . . PAULETTE GODDARD was rumored to be on her way to Reno to get a *second* divorce from CHARLIE CHAPLIN—just in case her Mexican splicing was declared invalid.

By February, ANN SHERIDAN was denying that she would marry ERROL FLYNN, or even that she cared for him. But she had done the same thing before wedding GEORGE BRENT, so no one believed her. Flynn, meanwhile, was busy defending himself on a morals charge in court . . . And a young actor named GREGORY PECK was signed by RKO after having been spotted in two outstanding Broadway stage performances.

On February 23, the Legion of Decency condemned HOWARD HUGHES' *The Outlaw* because they claimed it "glorified crime and immoral actions" . . . INGRID BERGMAN and her husband, Dr. PETER LINDSTROM, took out their first citizenship papers . . . Actor DON BARRY kept busy rounding up signatures petitioning the Academy because RONALD REAGAN's name was not placed in nomination as Best Actor for *King's Row*.

In March, DOROTHY LAMOUR told friends that she had accepted the proposal of Captain WILLIAM ROSS HOWARD . . . RITA HAYWORTH was dating ORSON WELLES . . . And MGM was having fits because MICKEY ROONEY had been classified 1-A . . . At Pueblo Air Force Base, where CLARK GABLE was taking additional training, there was a sign posted at the gate which read: "The Officers and Lieut. Gable will appreciate it if the public will not interfere with his heavy training program and will treat him as just another member of the armed forces. He will not be available for any appearances and cannot be reached by phone."

The wives of the actors making *Sahara,* on location in the desert city of Brawley, California, formed a "Sewing Circle and Gin Rummy" club. They voted for MRS. HUMPHREY BOGART as their president—which meant that MAYO was responsible for bringing the gin.

By April, many of Hollywood's top stars took every opportunity to be with their husbands or beaus. LANA TURNER visited STEVE CRANE at his Army post, and they were remarried . . . While GINGER ROGERS was honeymooning near San Diego, California, and living in a three-dollar-a-day motel room waiting to be with her Marine groom, JACK BRIGGS, whenever he could get off duty . . . When news hit Hollywood that a certain big studio executive was being drafted, a Tinseltown wag cracked, "What did they do, reclassify him one-ape??"

A few weeks before BETTY GRABLE and GEORGE RAFT broke off their relationship, he had gifted her with a $4,000 sable jacket. But then Betty started seeing HARRY JAMES, and Raft was very upset—not about the jacket—but about losing Betty.

By the middle of May, HOWARD HUGHES was wooing AVA GARDNER, but she was resisting his honeyed cards, flowers, and other tokens of affection . . . Down in Palm Springs, the Army took over several posh hotels and converted them into military hospitals . . . LINDA DARNELL and cameraman PEV MARLEY cut their honeymoon short. He reported back to the Signal Corps, and Linda, staying nearby, busied herself entertaining the troops . . . CHARLIE CHAPLIN was dating playwright EUGENE O'NEILL's seventeen-year-old daughter, OONA . . . ANN SOTHERN married ROBERT STERLING . . . And HEDY LAMARR and JOHN LODER took out a marriage license, became man and wife, and honeymooned in a borrowed cabin at Big Bear Lake.

On the 2nd of June, aesthetic actor LESLIE HOWARD was killed overseas in a plane crash . . . ROBERT PRESTON, BRUCE CABOT, GILBERT ROLAND and JOSH LOGAN all graduated as lieutenants from the Air Force Intelligence School in Harrisburg, Pennsylvania, and headed overseas . . . It was revealed that FRANK SINATRA now earned several thousand dollars per week, but had to still give twenty percent to TOMMY DORSEY, plus another piece to his agent. Frank was trying desperately to get out from under the obligations. Meanwhile, NANCY was pregnant with child #2 . . . And GENE TIERNEY wrote to a few Hollywood friends from the little Kansas house she was living in near OLEG CASSINI's Army post. She said she was very content— and very much in love.

By the end of June, CHAPLIN and young OONA O'NEILL were honeymooning, and her family was fuming . . . LANA TURNER was expecting her baby in three weeks . . . Rumors were that RITA HAYWORTH and ORSON WELLES were headed for Vegas . . . But OLIVIA DE HAVILLAND needed to exercise patience, because JOHN HUSTON's wife had changed her mind about divorcing him . . .

In July, JOAN CRAWFORD surprised everyone when she left MGM, after being there almost two decades, and signed an exclusive contract with Warners. It turned out that LOUIS B. MAYER had been very understanding after Joan told him: "I felt like I was yesterday's newspaper because I'd been at Metro so long. I need a new start somewhere else . . ." So L.B. excused her from fulfilling the last sixteen months of her contract, and Joan exited . . . Meanwhile, KATE HEPBURN signed a new MGM contract and went to work in *Without Love* . . . VAN JOHNSON, after recuperating from an accident for three months, reported back to work on *A Guy Named Joe.*

VERONICA LAKE's premature baby son, WILLIAM ANTHONY DETLIE, was still in the hospital fighting for his life . . . And HANK FONDA wrote pals that he had been assigned sea duty aboard a destroyer . . . Meanwhile, in boot camp, trainee TYRONE POWER made the mistake of calling his rifle "my gun." His punishment: he had to write one thousand times "My gun is a rifle!" He was also assigned extra guard duty . . . In Texas, RED SKELTON made eighteen camp show dates, and played before 230,000 G.I.s . . . SUZANNE BURCE, a fourteen-year-old singer, was spotted on the "Hollywood Showcase" program and signed by MGM. They renamed her JANE POWELL . . . And CARY and BABS HUTTON celebrated their first anniversary.

By August, both JAMES STEWART and RONALD REAGAN had been promoted to captain . . . VERONICA LAKE was still in shock over the death of her baby son . . . MARIA MONTEZ had become Mrs. JEAN-PIERRE AUMONT . . . GENE TIERNEY and OLEG CASSINI were expecting a child . . . Pals said HOWARD HUGHES and AVA GARDNER were secretly engaged . . . The JUDY GARLAND—DAVID ROSE marriage had collapsed . . . JACK BENNY was in Cairo entertaining the troops . . . And rumors were that MCA's JULES STEIN paid TOMMY DORSEY $60,000 to free SINATRA from any further contractual obligations.

In September, the ORSON WELLES—RITA HAYWORTH marriage was confirmed, leaving VICTOR MATURE heartbroken . . . It was announced that BETTE DAVIS would star in a movie called *Hollywood Canteen,* for Warners, and that the studio would share their profits with both the local Canteen and New York's Stage Door Center . . . MARIA MONTEZ tossed a going-away party for hubby JEAN-PIERRE AUMONT, who left Hollywood to join the Free French Army . . . CRAWFORD officially checked into the Warners lot . . . And GINGER's husband, JACK BRIGGS, left for an overseas assignment with the Marines.

In October, TURHAN BEY was loaned by Universal to MGM to play an Oriental opposite KATE HEPBURN in *Dragon Seed* . . . Juke box record spins jumped from a nickle to a dime . . . ROBERT ALDA's eight-year-old son, ALAN, a victim of infantile paralysis, left the hospital to recuperate at home . . . ALAN LADD was so ill he may receive a medical discharge from the Army . . . The Hollywood Canteen celebrated its first birthday. More than a million service personnel have been entertained there.

In November, DANNY KAYE was rejected by the Army and headed overseas to entertain the troops . . . CLARK GABLE returned to Hollywood after one year's absence. He wore cap-

tain's bars, flyer's "wings" and two campaign ribbons. Gable was headquartered at the Roach Studio, with the First Motion Picture Division, until he finished editing 50,000 feet of combat film shot over Europe . . . GARBO was rumored to have made a deal for a film at RKO. It never came off . . . And LANA TURNER was back in the MGM portrait gallery for the first time since the birth of her baby, CHERYL CRANE.

At seven o'clock, on Christmas Eve, 1943, EDDIE CANTOR, dressed as Santa Claus, arrived at the Hollywood Canteen and started to dispense gift duffel bags to the first group of ten thousand G.I.s who attended between that evening and Christmas Day. The entertainment was extra special. Several orchestras played until midnight, and BING CROSBY, RED SKELTON, VIRGINIA O'BRIEN, AMOS 'N' ANDY, JESS BARKER and EDGAR BERGEN performed.

On Christmas Day, BURNS and ALLEN, DINAH SHORE, JOSÉ ITURBI, LENA HORNE, DENNIS DAY, JOHNNY JOHNSTON and NAN WYNN contributed their talents. Besides those who entertained onstage, the back-of-the-Snack-Bar was run by BETTE DAVIS, JOHN GARFIELD, SPENCER TRACY, RICHARD WHORF, FRANCHOT TONE, RONALD COLMAN and his wife, BENITA HUME, CHARLES COBURN, BILL BENDIX, PAULETTE GODDARD, JINX FALKENBERG, GALE SONDERGAARD, ALEXIS SMITH and OLIVIA DE HAVILLAND. They served a festive holiday dinner with all of the trimmings.

In addition to the celebrities, a large number of the Volunteer Workers, composed of

Out on the town. Left to right: Rocky (Mrs. Gary) Cooper, Jack Benny, "Coop," Joan Crawford, and Phil Terry.

members of forty-two unions and guilds affiliated with the motion picture industry, served in various capacities. Christmas carols were led by groups of the stars, and it was both a joyous and tearful occasion. Holidays were superspecial events at the Canteen. Christmas of 1943 was typical of the manner in which the Hollywood set gave their all "for the cause." The Canteen doors swung open at two o'clock and did not close until midnight. KAY KYSER'S orchestra played from 9 o'clock until the last G.I. left.

As the year ended, INGRID BERGMAN gave up the holidays with her husband and daughter to spend five weeks entertaining troops in Alaska . . . JOAN CRAWFORD, in a melancholy mood, told *The Hollywood Reporter:* "Love is a fire. But whether it is going to warm your hearth, or burn down your house, you can never tell!"

1944

In January, DEANNA DURBIN admitted that as soon as her divorce from VAUGHN PAUL was final, she would marry film producer FELIX JACKSON . . . BETTY GRABLE and HARRY JAMES told friends they expected a baby come spring . . . EDDIE CANTOR became the world's number one war bond salesman. As the result of a twenty-four-hour continuous radio broadcast, he sold close to twenty-eight million dollars' worth of bonds.

The industry saluted ANNE LEHR in February for the contribution of her Hollywood Guild, in operation for twenty months. She gave free beds and meals to some 5,000 G.I.s each week . . . DONALD O'CONNOR, due to leave for the Army, just signed a new contract with Universal. The studio continued to pay him $200 a week while he was in the Army . . . Lt. DAN DAILEY was at Fort Riley, Kansas . . . JOHN PAYNE pulled the garbage detail at Buckley Field in Texas . . . And Captain CLARK GABLE, on leave, spent his evenings with Yeoman STEWART PETERS, LOMBARD's brother.

February was the month CHARLIE CHAPLIN was indicted on a morals charge brought by JOAN BARRY . . . JOAN BLONDELL and DICK POWELL went into court in a custody battle over their kids . . . And JUDY GARLAND was frantically trying to divorce DAVID ROSE.

In March, BETTY GRABLE brought her new baby daughter, named VICTORIA, home from the hospital . . . And still LORETTA YOUNG was "expecting" . . . ROBERT TAYLOR signed a fabulous contract with MGM, guaranteed to run for seventeen years . . . VIVIEN LEIGH, who could have picked any American film in which to star, decided it was her duty to remain in England for the duration . . . HOWARD HAWKS announced that he had signed his protégée, LAUREN "BETTY" BACALL, to star opposite BOGART in *To Have and Have Not.*

In April, BILLY WILKERSON opened his swank LA RUE Restaurant on the Sunset Strip. It rap-

Spencer Tracy attends a dinner with Father Flanagan of Boys Town.

idly became one of Hollywood's "in" spots . . . SYLVIA ASHLEY FAIRBANKS showed up in Hollywood with another titled spouse, LORD STANLEY . . . And CAROLE LANDIS denied rumors she was divorcing her husband, Captain TOM WALLACE, but she did.

By May, GARBO told friends she might consider making an appearance at The Hollywood Canteen. But she never did show up . . . SINATRA went on loanout to MGM for *Anchors Aweigh* and also signed a two-picture pact with that studio . . . JOAN CRAWFORD and PHILLIP TERRY worked at the Hollywood Canteen every Monday night . . . And producer JOE PASTERNAK gave a smash party for CLARK GABLE, before "the King" left for overseas again. At Joe's soirée, JOSÉ ITURBI played the piano, GENE KELLY danced, JIMMY DURANTE had the guests in hysterics with his comic antics, and GABLE just relaxed and enjoyed the evening with his date, gorgeous KAY WILLIAMS.

In June, the largest number of Technicolor films ever scheduled was announced. Color was to be used not only in feature films and cartoons, but also for government training pictures. G.I.s would soon be able to learn how to shoot a rifle or avoid social diseases—all in living color . . . At the end of the month, any thoughts of Gable marrying Kay Williams were put on the back burner. Her most recent groom, South American millionaire MACOCO, planned to block her divorce attempts.

By July, SUSAN HAYWARD was engaged to JESS BARKER . . . VERONICA LAKE, not yet unhitched from husband JOHN DETLIE, announced she would marry director ANDRÉ "BUNDY" DE TOTH . . . And SINATRA made another contribution to the war effort when he starred in a radio show, "Something for the Girls," a Navy-oriented show geared to recruiting more WAVES.

ERROL FLYNN hosted a marvelous soirée when his pal BRUCE CABOT came home from the service in July of 1944. Tables were set up around Flynn's pool, and the tented terrace made the dinner picturesque as well as delicious. There was outdoor dancing, plus a floorshow put on by swimming and diving stars, who performed somewhere between the suckling pig and the ice cream. Errol's drinking buddy, artist JOHN DECKER, came up with a very constructive idea. He suggested that next time, instead of filling the pool with water for swimming, Errol should load it with champagne and let the guests jump in.

Among those glimpsed poolside: MARY (PICKFORD) and BUDDY ROGERS; the PAUL LUKASES (he raved about what a wonderful down-to-earth girl INGRID BERGMAN proved to be on their recent bond-selling tour), PAULETTE GODDARD and BURGESS MEREDITH, KAY FRANCIS, DAVID SELZNICK, the REGGIE GARDINERS, the JACK WARNERS, the DARRYL ZANUCKS, party-giver extraordinaire ELSA MAXWELL, Sir CHARLES and Lady MENDL and Errol's beautiful NORA EDDINGTON.

August was a lackluster month, but by September, gossip was popping all over Hollywood. CARY GRANT and BARBARA HUTTON were about to divorce . . . LUCILLE BALL went to Las Vegas, Nevada, to shed DESI ARNAZ . . . VIRGINIA GILMORE married a "foreign-born" actor with a name no one seemed to be able to remember, YUL BRYNNER . . . TALLULAH BANKHEAD, who claimed not to be athletic, was spotted playing tennis with both KATE HEPBURN and GRETA GARBO, while top pro BILL TILDEN coached her from the sidelines.

BANKHEAD hosted a small dinner party. She was annoyed when one of her guests, CLIFTON WEBB, told her he had brought along an unexpected date, "a Japanese trapeze artist." Talu was furious, but went out into her foyer to greet the lady—who turned out to be GARBO, on a rare evening out.

By mid-September, SPENCER TRACY had arrived in Honolulu to entertain the troops . . . L. B. MAYER was recuperating from a horseback riding accident . . . FRANK SINATRA's father, MARTY, had been promoted to chief of the Fire Department of Hoboken, New Jersey . . . And Warners signed a nineteen-year-old former coed from Southern Methodist University, DOROTHY MALONE, of Texas . . .

STEVE CRANE told *The Reporter* that he and divorced wife LANA TURNER were dancing together (in true Hollywood tradition) when he noticed she was wearing a diamond and ruby ring he had given her at the time of their parting. Lana had promised never to wear it, but to put away for their baby, CHERYL, because it was a Crane family heirloom. When he called her on it, Lana took off the ring and told Steve to keep it until the evening was over, and then she would take it home. TURHAN BEY (Lana's date) evidently saw or heard only part of this conversation; he misconstrued the whole thing and began deriding Steve for "taking back a gift, etc." Steve took the insults up to a point, and then he and Turhan "went outside." Lana was left alone, strictly in the middle—one of the reasons she had been so cozy with Steve was to make Turhan jealous after *he* had cozied up to several other ladies. In the end Crane and Bey left right after the fight. No one remembers how Lana got home—or with whom.

In October, the national elections heated up, with Hollywoodites taking sides for and against FDR . . . "Cash and Cary" reconciled . . . JENNIFER JONES decided to go ahead with her plans to divorce actor ROBERT WALKER . . . LUCILLE BALL was dating PETER LAWFORD, while DESI ARNAZ still carried a torch for Lucy . . . And, on October 30, CLARK GABLE made his first appearance as a civilian on the "Cavalcade of America" radio broadcast.

In November, GEORGE MURPHY was elected president of the Screen Actors Guild . . . JOHN

PAYNE was about to divorce ANNE SHIRLEY . . . And a national magazine (*Look*) named Hollywood's four most beautiful faces: HEDY LAMARR, INGRID BERGMAN, GENE TIERNEY and LINDA DARNELL.

As December arrived, JOHN WAYNE said he would marry Mexican actress ESPERANZA BAUR. She was under contract to Republic Studios, but her "film career" had been very quiet . . . Lt. HENRY FONDA was stationed on Wake Island . . . GLORIA VANDERBILT and PAT DI CICCO announced they were suing HEDDA HOPPER for one million dollars because she said on her radio show that they were about to be divorced . . . And young LAUREN BACALL was spotted dancing cheek to cheek with a very happy looking HUMPHREY BOGART.

New Year's Eve rang out 1944, featuring some spectacular at-home parties. Definitely *the* party of the evening—and the one used as a yardstick by which to measure other "great parties" in the future—was given by the JACK BENNYS. The coveted invitation was for a dinner-through-breakfast affair. Jack and Mary had a huge tent put up in their backyard. It was garlanded with flowers and large enough to accommodate the more than one hundred guests. They had a dance floor big enough to really move on, a full orchestra and a flock of round tables, each of which seated six or more.

It was a formal affair. All of the guests came in their finest gowns, jewels and tuxedos. Jack

scored a personal triumph in this area. He pleaded with CROSBY to please wear a tie—a black tie. Bing, noted for his casual garb, showed up not only with a black tie, but in an evening suit set off by jeweled studs and cuff links. Crosby must have hated himself by morning when "the news" of his sartorial splendor spread across Hollywood. It broke a long-standing Crosby precedent for being himself at all times down to his argyle socks and fancy sports duds.

Poor Crosby! By the end of the evening, someone had misplaced his car. While he was waiting for it, he sang for two sailors who stood in front of the Benny mansion to spot some of their favorites. They weren't disappointed. Among the Bennys' guests were MERLE OBERON and ALEX KORDA, GENE TIERNEY with OLEG CASSINI, JOAN CRAWFORD, wearing a stunning sequined evening suit, seated with JUDY GARLAND (in a white filmy IRENE gown) and VINCENTE MINNELLI. The SAM GOLDWYNS, GINGER ROGERS, the ROBERT TAYLORS and the DAVID SELZNICKS shared a table. CLAUDETTE COLBERT was glimpsed chatting with her favorite co-star, CLARK GABLE. VAN JOHNSON, the RAY MILLANDS, and DOROTHY LAMOUR, who looked stunning in a bare-topped black velvet gown, sat together. NORMA SHEARER, JOAN BENNETT and WALTER WANGER, TY POWER, and MARGARET SULLAVAN were there. Maggie looked wonderful—while ERROL FLYNN just looked. And that was only a partial list.

Gene Tierney
"FACT AND FICTION"

Gene had trouble with the press from the very beginning of her career. On December 31, 1945, The Hollywood Reporter ran this piece she wrote in an attempt to set the record straight.

I've always felt so much fiction has been written about Hollywood actors and actresses that it might be fun to write the facts. So I am taking this opportunity to refute some of the fanciful fiction printed about me.

Here are some of the squibs—some amusing to me, some annoying—I'd like to debunk.

Fiction: There's a choice tidbit gone the printed rounds of the country that I have "a mad room." It sounds like a good idea—only it happens to be one of those dream-ups not even the studio publicity department would inflict on me. Of course, I can imagine an Ivan-

the-Terrible needing a mad room, but me, I'm just an ordinary gal who gets angry once in a while. My mads take on a peculiar, but far from violent flavor.

Fact: When I get a mad-on, I don't throw things; I don't cry; I don't shout, much—though any of those symptoms would probably be the fastest way out of a mad-jag. I do talk a blue streak about whatever has annoyed me, until I have exhausted myself. Then I generally laugh helplessly and I am over it. But I don't need or have a special room to explode in!

Fiction: Speaking of rooms, one columnist

Actress Gene Tierney as she appeared in 20th Century–Fox's *Laura*.

dreamed up a sumptuously extravagant establishment which sounded like a 40-room mansion before he got through with where and how I supposedly lived.

Fact: I live in a beautifully-old remodeled, New England type house which contains exactly six rooms, two master bedrooms, a combination living and dining room, a den, a maid's room and a kitchen. There is also a tiny three-room guest house on my two acres, boasting one bedroom, one living room and one kitchen.

Fiction: Another imaginative writer quoted me as boasting a full size menagerie including a pet snake.

Fact: There was a time when I had three cats and a dog. I now have one dog, Butch. I have never owned the snake he credited me with. I have an utter horror of reptiles. At one time I did have a baby hawk I found injured in the desert. I nursed it back to health and then turned it loose.

Fiction: Someone else said that a still picture I once made as a Powers model was bad because I was given the wrong make-up, inferring I had complained about the inefficiency of whoever made me up.

Fact: The truth of the matter is I have never used make-up, other than lipstick, in real life or for any still picture either in private or professional life. I rarely used make-up for the screen except in such an instance as *Heaven Can Wait*, where I aged 30 years. Even when I played such roles as the Chinese girl in *China Girl*, the Polynesian girl in *Son of Fury*, the Eurasian in *Shanghai Gesture*, the Arabian in *Sundown* I never, as was reported, resorted to eye make-up or taping to get the Oriental effect. I used no make-up, except lipstick, for the role of the Sicilian in *A Bell for Adano*, nor for *Leave Her to Heaven*. Luckily, because of my mixed ancestry—I'm Irish and English on my father's side; French, Spanish and Swedish on my mother's side—I can look like any nationality.

Fiction: And speaking of heritage, I am getting some highly indignant fan letters from Port Arthur, Texas, since someone reported that town was named for my husband's grandfather, Count Arthur Cassini. Another writer inferred, and bald statements have been made to the same effect, that my husband's title is a myth.

Fact: The truth is that my husband, Lieutenant Oleg Cassini, happily discarded the title of "Count" in favor of becoming an American citizen. As for the title's authenticity, and the Port Arthur named for his grandfather—anyone can go to the neighborhood library and find considerable authentic information on both in history books on Russia, China and the United States. They also can look up the Congressional Records during Theodore Roosevelt's presidential administration and find considerable data on Count Arthur Cassini, who was the last Imperial Russian Ambassador to the United States—from 1896 to 1905. Further, they can read the "memoirs" by John Hay, who was U.S. Minister of Foreign Affairs during the same administration, for information about Count Arthur Cassini. Before his American post, Count Cassini made history as the Russian Minister to China. He effected such fine conditions for China following the Japanese-Chinese War in 1895, during what is historically known as "The Cassini Conference," that the Chinese government deeded to Russia a port in the province of Kwang-Tung, naming it Port Arthur in Count Cassini's honor.

Fiction: I didn't mind it before, when I was too young, that everyone seemed to add a year to my age, BUT:

Fact: I must be getting to the sensitive stage. I was born in Brooklyn November 19, 1920. I think the papers listed my birth the next day, and the fact that I resided at 119 Brooklyn Ave.

Fiction: I didn't know whether to be amused or furious when I read that I'm a night club habitué. If I'm not mistaken, I was called "A Pub Crawler." Really it sounds horribly unsanitary, and veddy blasé and sophisticated or just plain moronic. I was fascinated by this strange species I was supposed to be, but it sounds like much too harrowing a life to live up to.

Fact: I'm a frightful stay-at-home who rarely even drinks a glass of wine. I prefer home parties, but I do love to dance to a good orchestra as much as any other girl my age, so I occasionally go to a night club.

DUTIES AND DESTINIES

Living under wartime blackout conditions cast a gloomy shadow across a town accustomed to bright lights. But production on every lot was at the fullest capacity possible—and not even one new card game, or dog race, now interfered with previous moviegoing habits. People were seeing films in record numbers. The lost foreign grosses were nearly all compensated for by the increase in domestic boxoffice receipts. Everyone—including Rosie the Riveter, from the nearest defense plant—needed to see a movie at least once a week in order to relieve the tensions of wartime.

Walt Disney stopped his feature-film-making. He had chosen to use the facilities of his studio for working on government films. *Bambi* turned out to be his last commercial effort for the duration. Also, the Army had shifted its center for the production of training pictures from Fort Monmouth, New Jersey, and Astoria, Long Island, to Hollywood. Major Frank Capra had flown in, conferred with Colonel Darryl F. Zanuck, and then had taken over the responsibility for overseeing the government-issued product.

On July 21, 1942, Joan Crawford, who vowed never to remarry, reported for work on the MGM set of *Reunion*. There was an extra glow on her face, and a new ring on her finger. Dramatically, she announced her

Joan and husband number three, Phil Terry.

marriage, earlier that day, to Phillip Terry. With that mischievous Crawford grin on her crimson lips, she confessed that keeping the whole thing quiet had been quite easy. She and Phil had obtained their wedding license three weeks before, in Ventura County, using their real names—Lucille Tone and Frederick Kormann.

Joan's studio clique gathered around to hear all of the details. The ceremony had taken place at the Hidden Valley ranch house of attorney Neil McCarthy. Justice of the Peace David Flynn performed the rites. Many of the Metro people knew of Terry, a tall, dark-haired, handsome leading-man type, whose recent films had been Paramount's *Wake Island* and *The Parson of Panamint*.

Joan seemed ecstatically happy, especially after her bridegroom joined her on set. Life was wonderful, she said. This was "Mr. Right." The two of them were going to live happily ever after in the newly redecorated Brentwood home—which had had more "face-lifts" than an aging starlet.

Although she didn't say it, Joan, who had a penchant for all things monogrammed, felt doubly lucky. She could still use the same towels, napkins and hankies that she had had embroidered when she was Mrs. Franchot Tone.

At the beginning of the marriage, the couple had seemed devoted. When he was not working, he visited her at the studio every day. Joan would greet Phil very warmly, as would Pupchen, the family dachshund, whom she took to the studio with her every morning.

But the week before Christmas of 1945, on December 17, to be exact, Joan publicly announced that she and Phil were separated. He had moved out the night before. With her shoulders squared and her chin held high, Crawford announced that, thank God, she still had her children, her career and her Brentwood home.

The Terrys' separation came close on the heels of Joan's magnificent performance in *Mildred Pierce*. It was intimated that Crawford's success had been too big a cross for her third husband to bear.

In securing her divorce, Joan testified that on many occasions Phil had criticized movie roles she picked—even when they turned out to be big successes. Also, that when she came home after a hard day at the studio, and wanted to relax, he had insisted on discussing parts and stories. Her secretary, Theodora Larson, testified that

Joan had lost twenty pounds as a result of Terry's criticism.

Crawford also stated that her husband had been jealous of her. He wanted to keep her all for himself and, for the first year and a half of their marriage, they rarely went out.

Divorce granted. Exit Phil Terry. All of her monogrammed linen was now truly obsolete. Joan said she would never marry again (particularly a man whose last name began with a "T"—some Hollywood wags commented).

In September of 1942, Colonel Darryl F. Zanuck took a leave of absence from 20th Century–Fox. He resigned as vice president and director of the corporation in order to devote his full time to military duties.

In October of 1943, Clark Gable, then a captain and fresh from the European air front, held a press briefing at the Pentagon. Women outside oohed and aahed as he made his way into a conference room. He had come to report on his latest project: doubling in a Flying Fortress, both as a director-photographer and a gunner. Gable had just returned from missions over Antwerp, Paris and several cities in the vicinity of the Ruhr Valley.

During his first six months overseas, Clark had directed a crew of six, supervising the shooting of a color film record of all of the activities of every bomber group in England. Following the conference, he left for Hollywood to supervise the cutting and editing of the more than fifty thousand feet of footage which would be turned into a concise, instructive training film. He worked very hard on the project, supervised by Colonel Darryl Zanuck.

Zanuck's war effort was, for the most part, skillfully executed. He accomplished a lot by trying to ride herd on his men just as he had done as production head of 20th. Distinguished director Rouben Mamoulian

Captain Clark Gable visits with Louis B.
Mayer at MGM during a brief wartime leave,
1943.

talked about such accomplishments, and
reminisced, years later, about that brand
of ego and special talent inherent in Hollywood moguls of Zanuck's stature.

"They were real showmen—gamblers.
Even though they were uneducated, with
no cultural background, they all had this
gut level feeling. There was one common
denominator that united them. They were
all cut from the same mold when it came
to being very potent. All throughout history,
power, and the *feeling* of power, was of
primary importance when it came to creating something, implementing something.
Sure, it was corrupting, or it could be. But
all of the moguls, along with their use of
power, had a very pragmatic way of achieving things. That was the essence of their
success. When you stripped through all of
their rhetoric, they had power, and used it
pragmatically."

Prior to Zanuck's return as head of production at 20th, William Goetz, his wartime
replacement, resigned to form International
Pictures, along with Leo Spitz. Eventually,

this company merged with Universal Studios, which resulted in the creation of Universal-International.

Speaking of "creations," the word around
town was that Garbo was anxious to begin
"creating" again. She had not been seen
onscreen since *Two-Faced Woman* turned
out to be such a boxoffice failure. Now that
her MGM contract had expired, for the first
time since coming to Hollywood, in the
Twenties, GG was at loose ends.

Initially, she used her free time to
rest . . . to meditate . . . to travel . . . to
walk along the beach with her close chum,
Mercedes de Acosta. They had become
friendly during the late Thirties when de
Acosta wrote screenplays for MGM.

Mercedes, a very skilled author, would
one day detail her years as Garbo's best
friend in a candid autobiography, *Here Lies
the Heart*. She would discuss their closeness. How hard it was for Greta to form
intimate friendships. How very much their
relationship meant to her. She would also
"confess" that her public revelations about
Garbo's life-style were something Greta
would probably abhor. But that, all things
considered, she had been obliged to write
about it. After all, the book was *her* life
story. Garbo very definitely had been part
of *her* life.

They met through Salka Viertel, the wife
of the well-known director Berthold Viertel.
Between them, there had been an immediate bonding. Greta, who had never married, was virtually alone. She rarely took
to people, but she had responded instan-
taneously to something within de Acosta.
Mercedes, with an unhappy marriage behind her, was also by herself, and equally
as responsive. For Garbo, it was a real
blessing. She had only an infinitesimal circle of close friends—so small, they could
all have fitted comfortably into a medium-
sized bathroom.

On first acquaintance, Greta spontaneously picked a flower and gave it to

Mercedes. It was the beginning of many of nature's joys they would exchange. Sometimes they just sat quietly, staring into space. Other times Garbo fixed them simple meals, which they shared in the solemnity of Greta's moonlit bedroom. ("It was a simple and rather empty room. It had a bed, a desk, a dressing table and a few uncomfortable straight-backed chairs, all in heavy oak.")

At the beginning of their friendship, Greta opened up. She talked freely of her childhood . . . of her dreams . . . of her love for a sister, Alva, who was dead. Then, self-consciously, she had stopped, saying shyly, "I have never spoken like this before."

Sometimes the ladies took long drives together, with Greta's chauffeur, James, at the wheel. The closer they became, the more Garbo depended upon de Acosta's advice. After a while, Mercedes was officially known at MGM as the person who handled "the Swede's" business affairs.

The poetic word-portrait that de Acosta painted of her friend revealed Garbo to be very sensitive, painfully shy, capable of rare moments of happiness, mixed mainly with somber, gloomy moods. The woman, whose onscreen face, form and acting ability had enchanted tens of millions, did not enjoy doing films. Each one seemed to sap every ounce of her strength. Yet each was made with painstaking discipline, attention and care. Somehow, it was as if Garbo lived only onscreen. She glowed in the camera's magical glory because it reflected her image as perfection. But she grew pale and wan offstage, merely a beautiful shadow of her celluloid self. She was, literally, two separate people. Her public reputation was so dazzling that her private persona suffered by comparison. But when she shared the beauty of this rare friendship, and was unafraid of being compared with "the other Greta," Garbo learned to relax, to feel free—and safe.

Once, the twosome traveled together across the desert to Nevada. There, they stopped on top of a mountain from which they could see Silver Lake in the distance. Greta, excited, stretched out her hand and pointed. "There is our lake and there, that island in the center, is our island!"

The remote cabin belonged to Wallace Beery. He had loaned it to Garbo. She, in turn, had taken Mercedes there to share it. For six weeks, the two stayed alone, together, and rejoiced in their peaceful surroundings. Greta was so happy at this taste of freedom that one morning she threw off her clothes. " 'We must be baptized at once.' Then she dived into the chilly waters, swimming with long, powerful strokes . . ."

During this period, Mercedes saw another side of Greta—a luminous, humorous, almost child-like, devilish side—so seldom glimpsed by others. Magically, they stayed the entire six weeks without glimpsing another soul, and returned refreshed and revitalized.

But that closeness had come—and gone. By the mid-Forties, Garbo seemed restless and ready to go back to work. Amazingly, not one of the major studios offered her a contract. However, she did constantly receive scripts from various independent producers. These she gave to Rouben Mamoulian or George Cukor and asked them for an appraisal. Ultimately, she rejected them all.

As the years slipped away, it became very evident that if Garbo did not return to the screen soon, the chances were she would be too frightened to return at all. Then, in 1947, after George Schlee became her close companion, he tried to find scripts for her. Schlee, the husband of dress designer Valentina, was on more or less a temporary "loan" from his wife. He brought some fun into Greta's life—but no film prospects she considered worthwhile.

In 1948, Garbo took matters into her own hands. In mid-August, it was announced that she had actually *signed* a contract. She had entered into a percentage deal to do a picture for producers Walter Wanger and Eugene Frenke. A new company had been formed to make the film, Walter Wanger International. The deal had been set personally by Greta herself. She had gone to the home of Wanger and his wife, Joan Bennett, and there everything was consummated.

Within a few months, Garbo, optimistic and happier than she had been in years, sailed for Europe to begin preparations for her comeback in *The Duchess of Langeais*. Greta's good humor was short-lived. Upon her arrival, there was no one from the company to meet her. Startled, she went to her hotel, alone. For a star of Garbo's magnitude to have had no "greeting committee," no studio representative to carry her bags, smooth the way, was unthinkably rude—and very ego-deflating.

Soon, she discovered the problem. Wanger's company was having money troubles. They were $500,000 short of production costs and were having no luck getting finances. James Mason, who was to have co-starred with Garbo, had been expected to put up $100,000. But at the last minute Mason backed out. Then Howard Hughes had been contacted. There were times when even Hughes turned down a deal—this was one of them.

Next, a wealthy Italian magazine publisher, Angelo Rizzoli, was involved. He agreed to put up the money, until he heard Greta's terms.

Garbo, by this time highly insulted, had laid down some preconditions. She was to be paid $175,000 in cash *before* shooting began. Second, she would film only in Italy and Paris. Third, she would NOT remain in Italy more than thirty days. Now the Italian millionaire was insulted, and *he* backed out. Through his writers, word was spread that he had lost interest because Garbo was no longer glamorous and beautiful. She had

lost her charm and sex appeal, which was why she had been seen of late hiding her face and figure behind a droopy hat and a large coat.

Greta's Swedish friends, who had just seen her, were furious. Garbo was more beautiful than ever, they said. Her only problem was a touch of rheumatism. It was because of this condition that she had imposed a time frame on filming. She wanted to be finished and out before the weather turned bad.

One insult followed another. Finally, Garbo packed her bags and returned to America. Those few who knew her well said she had been hurt beyond redemption. Obviously, they were right. She never even got close to making another picture deal. Her career was over. The Garbo of the Thirties legend would remain intact.

On May 15, 1944, Captain Clark Gable walked into the Pentagon. He emerged four hours later as a major. His gold leaves had been personally pinned on his uniform by General Hap Arnold, head of the Army Air Force. After Clark wound up his business, he left immediately by train for Hollywood.

While he was still there, on June 6, the Allies launched D-Day, invading the Normandy coast. The war in Europe would go on for nine more months—but it *was* winding down.

On June 11, it was announced that "the King" would soon resume his $5,000-dollar-a-week acting career at MGM. His commanding officer, Colonel Roy M. Jones, stated that Gable would be placed on the Army's inactive list as soon as he completed editing the film photographed under his supervision.

Gable's enlistment had started the mass exodus of leading men. Now that he had come home, the studio heads breathed easier. It was only a matter of time before the rest of the screen heroes came marching back onto their respective lots.

MAMOULIAN ON ZANUCK

*When Colonel Zanuck resumed his "throne" at 20th Century–Fox, he
once again exemplified the type of supreme "mogulhood" that director
Rouben Mamoulian saw as both effective and terrifying. In an
interview, Mamoulian told* The Hollywood Reporter . . .

In my opinion, Darryl Zanuck was the best symbol of studio power. His whole manner, and the aura which surrounded him, was one of power. At Fox, he had this enormous office, and what I called his "Greek Chorus," which always surrounded him. There were these fifteen men who went everywhere with him, including his barber. They were always there saying "Yes" to everything. Zanuck was definitely the most tyrannical of all the moguls I worked with. I watched him talk to men earning $5,000 a week and saw them turn green with fear. The higher their salary, the more they had to lose and the more they groveled. Because in the late Thirties and early Forties, it was really true that if you lost a job at one studio, you might never get another one in town. The word went out, and you wouldn't be hired anywhere else. People said I was courageous in my personal dealings. It was not really courage so much as it was part of my character, based on my luck. If things didn't work out for me in Hollywood, I could always go back to New York, to the Broadway stage. [Among other landmark shows, Mamoulian directed *Oklahoma!* and *Lost in the Stars*.]

At the beginning of the Forties, my agent at that time, Charlie Feldman, told me I'd never work at 20th. Zanuck was an absolute dictator there, and he didn't like me—also, he had never met me! But over the months,

we saw each other socially at various parties and, suddenly, Zanuck asked me to direct *The Mark of Zorro* with Tyrone Power.

I was surprised and pleased. I had seen the silent Doug Fairbanks, Sr., version, and loved it. But when I read his script, I thought it was awful. Feldman said I should forget the deal. Zanuck had spent two years, with numerous writers, working on the project— and *he* liked it. I told Charlie to set up an appointment anyway. I wanted to meet "the tiger of Fox" in his den.

I entered this enormous office. We exchanged hellos. I told Mr. Zanuck that I was very interested in making the film, but that I did not care for the script. He banged down hard on his large desk with a polo mallet. The conversation was about to end. Then I added, "Would you be interested in hearing my reasons?" He agreed to listen.

I went over the script, scene by scene. To give the devil his due, he paid attention. Then he asked, "How long would it take you to get rewrites?"

"Six weeks."

"All right, Mamoulian, it's a deal."

As I was about to leave, I added one final note. "I've heard that when a director does a picture for 20th, *you* cut it. Well, on this film, *I* must have the first cut and my own preview . . ."

"Forget it," he yelled. "Look, Mamoulian, *I* even cut *John Ford's films*." [He had evoked the name of 20th's top director.]

"But you can't cut a picture I've made until you've seen how I intend to use it," I said. "Anyway, it was nice meeting you, Mr. Zanuck."

I was halfway out the door, when he shouted, "How long would it take you to cut the picture?"

I told him I needed a week.

"All right, I'll go to Palm Springs—then people can't say that Zanuck was on the lot, but Mamoulian was cutting his own film!" He needed an out in order not to establish any precedent.

I made the film . . . took seven days to cut it . . . and we previewed it in a 20th projection room. Zanuck was there, surrounded by his Greek Chorus. Their reaction was terrific, until the head man ordered me back in the projection room at eight the next evening. "We're going to run the film again—by the time we finish, it will be a great picture."

I showed up and sat through a harrowing experience. Zanuck had his film cutter alongside him. Every few seconds, he would punch the man in the ribs. Obediently, the cutter wrote down the key words of that scene, so that he could go back and find the places Zanuck wanted to change. I cringed, and thought to myself that 20th's boss obviously had a nervous tic. He couldn't possibly have wanted *that* many changes.

When it was finished, he explained his deletions. Every time he mentioned a changed scene, his chorus said in unison, "Oh, that's great, D.F.; that's wonderful, Mr. Zanuck . . ."

Actually, he had decided to cut every lyrical, poetical scene and leave in only the action. "What do you think, Mamoulian?"

I stood up and said, "Darryl, you have just ruined a very good picture. Please, take my name off of it—and forget about me ever doing another film on this lot."

The chorus trembled. Zanuck's face was beet red. It was four o'clock in the morning, and he kept yelling at me. Then he said, "You had *your* cut and preview, I want mine."

I couldn't argue with *that* logic. He took *his* version of *The Mark of Zorro* out to a theatre in suburban Riverside and ran it before a packed house. The film laid an egg. The audience hated it. Afterward, Zanuck and his group walked out with me. He put his arm around my shoulder and said, "You see, Rouben, you and I *together* are the best cutting team in Hollywood. Now, put every scene back in—and ship it."

"HOLLYWOOD BATTLEFIELD"
(WORD FROM THE FRONT)
1944–1945

Most of the time, parents, wives, sweethearts and relatives of American G.I.s overseas waited weeks—sometimes months—between letters from their loved ones. The Hollywood stars who visited with their men were the one tangible link that helped them to fight their own "enemies"—loneliness and concern.

Returning stars always gave instant press

conferences—which were wonderfully informative and encouraging—for the home folks' consumption. The majority of them also brought back letters to mail and made personal phone calls to servicemen's families.

Jack Benny, for instance, took small notebooks wherever he traveled. Dozens of these were filled with names, phone numbers and personal comments. The moment he returned from the front, Jack personally sat at his telephone for hours each day, calling families—reading from his notes: "I saw that red-headed kid of yours in New Guinea," he'd say. "He wants you to know he's growing a moustache . . ."

Just these few words from a star who had seen "that red-headed kid" meant everything to anxious parents.

Many Hollywood celebrities never received due recognition for the countless private kindnesses they did for their fans, especially during the war years.

"The Army is now doing a great job of getting the picture industry's gift of new movies to troops in the forward areas of war," John Wayne told a press conference, talking about his three-month (January through March 1944) Hollywood Victory Committee–USO Camp Shows tour of Pacific bases and battle lines from Brisbane, Australia, to the front lines of New Britain.

"War is not only fighting," Wayne said, "it is work and sweat. And the Army has realized that the boys must have entertainment and relaxation from the monotony of hard work, in order to keep morale high. The boys want to laugh; they do not mind walking through mud and sitting in the rain to see a show. The important thing is that there *is* a show for them to see, and this is being taken care of now. Up on the forward lines on New Guinea I found movies that were just being released when I left Hollywood. The ability to bring 'home' to the

men is the chief value of Hollywood players going overseas.

"I was worried about not being able to do anything on the stage," Wayne explained, "but I did not realize how much just a familiar face means to them. I just made a few cracks about the tropics not being what I had dreamed about, and pulled a couple of gags about the Battle of Brisbane, and they howled. One thing they have not lost is their sense of humor."

Wayne played five daylight shows with a G.I. band on New Britain, where American forces had recently established beachheads to open the fight for Rabaul.

"Overseas is where I belong," Wayne concluded. "I have some picture commitments that I have to fill, but aside from that, I have told the Hollywood Victory Committee that as long as I can contribute something to the war by visiting our troops, that I shall do."

Repeating the word that motion pictures rank with food and mail from home as vital elements of morale in combat areas, Humphrey Bogart, seaman 2/c as well as a Warner Brothers star, returned to Hollywood, on April 14, 1944, with his then wife, Mayo Methot (he would marry Bacall in 1945), from a 35,000-mile, three-month entertainment tour of Italy and North Africa.

Bogie reported that in his visits (within three or four miles of the fighting front in Italy), he found soldiers viewing the free 16mm movies donated to the Army by the film industry and declared that everywhere commanding officers stressed the vital function of screen entertainment. His most recent film, *Sahara*, released in America while Bogart was overseas, was playing the Italian circuit while he was there. The Bogarts, with emcee Don Cumming and accordionist Ralph Hark, spent seven weeks in Italy, most of the time directly behind the front line.

"We wanted to stay in Italy as long as possible," Bogart said, "because there seemed to be such a terrific need for entertainment there. Usually we were playing to boys who had just left active combat for three or four days' rest, and we would spend the entire leave period with one division. We always played at least two shows a day, not counting the time spent visiting hospitals. We gave shows on board platforms laid between two trucks, or in the remnants of buildings. Sometimes we played in theatres, and that was worse than being outdoors. There was always a wall missing or part of the roof gone, and never any heat.

"You don't appreciate the difference between America and Europe until you have been over there and watched a crowd of people when an airplane goes overhead. When we were playing to five thousand men, we'd see five thousand heads go up at the first sound of a plane. Fortunately, we never found out what happens when the plane is not friendly. Many times we arrived at a town which had been bombed the day before, and left the day before it was bombed again. But we were never actually under fire."

The Bogart troupe used Naples as headquarters through most of their Italian tour, spending an average of two days a week in the city, five days at the front. Playing seven days a week, they gave approximately 150 shows in all. In Africa, they played from Algiers to Casablanca, which Bogie reported was somewhat different from the locale of his film of the same name.

"Munitions and movies are just about equally vital to American fighting men in the Far East," reported Paulette Goddard, who flew back to Hollywood on May 11, 1944, after a tour of more than 38,000 miles

through the China-Burma-India theatre of war.

Paulette, Keenan Wynn, William Gargan and accordionist Andy Arcari comprised the first Hollywood Victory Committee—USO—Camp Shows troupe to visit these Asiatic battle areas and bases, and Goddard was the first white woman seen in some of the advanced areas.

"In China," she said, "where every ounce of material, fuel and food must be carried over the Himalayan peaks by plane, some of the precious space and poundage is devoted to new movies which are our industry's gift to U.S. forces in the war zones. More and more projection equipment is being flown in and distributed to isolated units of the air and ground forces.

"No matter how many of the new pictures reach the men," she observed, "there never are quite enough. You can hardly imagine how hungry they are for entertainment. The army has stepped up the film service marvelously. We realized, too, how our own appearances there were appreciated, because we found that our party and luggage represented a thousand pounds of cargo.

"The tour was perfectly managed. We were flown from Miami to China without stopping to give shows, and then worked our way back. That put the most strenuous part of the trip at the beginning, before we were tired out."

Even so, Paulette, the Paramount star, was grounded for a three-day rest because of the exertion and tension of the tour in China, sometimes with flights of 400 miles between shows.

"The real glamour girls of this war," the actress said, "are the flight nurses who come in on the ambulance planes, take their wounded aboard, and care for them on the way back to the bases. They're all former airline hostesses, and very trim and pretty.

"Since I was the first woman to really tour the region, General Stilwell—who called me 'Girlie'—used me as a sort of guinea pig to decide whether others could take it.

"We played 130 shows, including every American base and every hospital in China, Burma and India. Seeing and knowing those men was a tremendous emotional experience for me," she said. "They're homesick, of course, but they're also grimly determined to stay at their jobs and fight their way to Tokyo. Meanwhile, they're grateful for the pictures that give them visual reminders of their homes."

On June 21, Marlene Dietrich sat on a table at USO Camp Shows headquarters in New York and told a group of Manhattan reporters what it felt like to be home from the wars. For ten weeks she had been entertaining troops in Italy and Africa, on a tour arranged by the Hollywood Victory Committee. Hers was the first show to play on the Anzio beachhead. Also in the troupe were Danny Thomas (little known at that time), actor-singer Wilton Frome, comedian Lin Mayberry, and Jack Snyder, accordionist-pianist.

Miss Dietrich's biggest thrill was announcing to an audience of G.I.s that D-Day had begun. "It was in Italy," Marlene said. "I was getting ready for a show when an officer told me that the Normandy coast had been invaded. I was still in my traveling uniform, but I dashed out on the stage and made the announcement. There was a vast audience out in the open. It was their first news of the invasion . . . They went wild—but not over me!

"Another thrill was riding in a jeep into Rome on the second day after its fall to the allies."

"Were you ever under fire?" a reporter asked.

She smiled. "I know it would be a better story to say yes, but it wouldn't be true. The Army took good care not to let us get into danger."

"Did you meet any Generals when you got to Rome?"

"No," said Miss Dietrich, again with candor and poise. "They were too busy."

Answering an inquiry as to whether, because she had been born on German soil, the Nazis might not have relished picking her up as a prisoner, she countered, "But they didn't, did they?"

In one spot, to prove to her G.I. audience that she really was "Miss Legs" and "Goldilocks" who had been publicized all over the world, she lifted her skirt and let her hair fall around her shoulders. For stage appearances and hospital visits, she wore beaded formals.

"I may have seemed slightly incongruous walking into hospital wards in long shimmering gowns . . . but the look in the men's eyes when they saw me made up for the inconvenience of trying to pretend I was just strolling on to a Hollywood movie set."

On September 4, 1944, refreshed after a two-day sleeping session, Bob Hope, who just completed an eight-week, thirty-thousand-mile air trip to the South Pacific, was raring to get going again. The comedian, together with his all-star troupe consisting of Jerry Colonna, Frances Langford, Patty Thomas, Tony Romano and Barney Dean, played 150 shows in the very heart of the Japanese-infested area.

"It was plenty rugged," Bob admitted, "but it was worth it. I guess we played to about a million G.I.s out there in the Pacific and they sure were a great audience and plenty appreciative. Look what they gave me," he said, gesturing to reporters in his home. His bedroom was practically a trophy-room, littered with captured enemy loot.

"The Japanese have got to lose this war," he grinned. "I have most of their equipment right here!"

His pet gift was an ivory carved cane, given to him by a tribal chief somewhere

Carpenter, Barbara Ruick; third row: Arthur
Loew, Jr., Carolina Cotton, Robert Tucker;
top row: Lionel Ascher, Elsie Gould.
2 Mickey Rooney entertains the troops.
3 Bob Hope, voted America's Number One
Entertainer with the troops.   4 An assort-
ment of stars about to board the train for a
Hollywood Victory Caravan War Bond Tour—
Left to right: Frances Langford, Joan Bennett,
Claudette Colbert, Frank McHugh, Eleanor
Powell, Groucho Marx, Joan Blondell, and
Risë Stevens.

1 Eleven Hollywood performers who gave up
Christmas vacation to entertain G.I.s from
Iceland to North Africa. Left to right, first
row: Keenan Wynn, Audrey Totter, Walter
Pidgeon; second row: Betsy Butler, Carleton

in New Guinea after he had put on a special show for some natives. Hope explained they didn't understand a word he was saying, but they had laughed along with the G.I. audience.

His biggest show was at Pearl Harbor, where more than fifty thousand men were assembled. At some other bases, they played before a mere handful. This South Pacific tour completed Bob Hope's fourth overseas trip. He had played to six million men in Europe, Africa, Alaska, the Aleutians and the Caribbean.

Because he had done the greatest job of entertainment for servicemen both here and overseas, Hope was named the number one "Soldier in Greasepaint."

"An overseas tour raises the entertainers' morale as well as that of the troops," Jack Benny said.

He had just returned from nine weeks playing to G.I. audiences in the Pacific theatre of war. Carole Landis, harmonica virtuoso Larry Adler, Martha Tilton and June Bruner were the other members of the "Benny Gang."

They had traveled approximately thirty thousand miles in the Marshalls, Gilberts, Solomons, New Hebrides, New Caledonia, New Guinea, Australia and Hawaii, presenting over 140 shows to a total of some 600,000 men, usually in what Adler described as "horizontal rain." In all that time, only two shows were given indoors—aside from their hospital tours—where each member took a ward so as many as possible could see the visitors in action.

This was the second overseas trip together for Benny and Adler, who had previously visited the European theatre and North Africa, also toured by Carole Landis the previous year. "The boys in the Pacific are more in need of live entertainment since civilization there is where they make it," Jack said.

Setting aside his own personal discomforts, Jack raved about his female companions. "The girls were terrific, unbelievable. Carole and Martha and June always looked so glamorous, so very special. It took effort. For the shows, Carole Landis and the girls dressed to the hilt in evening gowns, although the rain came down in sheets almost constantly. They never covered themselves with coats—after all, the boys wanted reminders of the girls back home. Larry and I made it a point to wear civilian clothes and bright ties which inevitably elicited rousing cheers from our khaki-clad audience.

"It was such a joy to see the morale those guys have—especially under such lousy conditions—and I'm not talking about enemy fire. Some of those islands were so remote the men could go nuts under the strain and isolation—but, thank God, they've kept their sense of humor intact."

Advance notice of the quintet's arrival at a base precipitated the posting of signs and gags about Fred Allen, Benny's Maxwell, or other jokes used on the comedian's radio program. Warner Brothers' *George Washington Slept Here* came in for a few plugs, and signs read, JACK BENNY SLEPT HERE.

"You'd be surprised at the set-ups they had for us. Almost every camp had an impromptu stage and their p.a. systems were good," Jack commented. In order of "morale builders," Benny listed mail from home first, movies second, the Armed Forces Radio Service programs third, and then live entertainment.

"One of the greatest thrills afforded the G.I.s by visiting shows is that they also provided something to write home about— I mean what else can a guy say to his mother—'It's raining . . . All we see are coconuts or Japanese firing at us.'!"

Reporting that the French foxhole circuit was beginning to look like Hollywood, Dinah

Shore returned to the United States on September 20, 1944, after an eight-week tour of France and England.

"We met up with Bing Crosby and gave a show with him for an engineer's unit at Châlons-sur-Marne," Dinah said. "We also played another show with Fred Astaire at the Palace of Versailles.

"Our chief trouble in France was keeping up with the Army," Shore reported. "At one point, our troupe played to an Army unit two miles behind the lines. The next day we played to other members of the same unit at a more advanced point—but by then the front was twenty-five miles away. At one place, we were billeted in a house which had been the quarters of a German officer. He had departed so hurriedly that he had left all of his shaving stuff in his room."

Dinah's troupe spent seven weeks in France, one in England, and put on 130 shows. Most of the "theatres" were pastures close to the front. "We lived G.I. lives, sleeping on the ground," she continued, "eating K-rations, traveling by jeep, command car, weapon carriers, trucks, planes and even a horse and wagon. But it was so inspiring—*for us*. When the guys knew we were coming, they took time and made special preparations. At one stop, the engineers had changed signs. They named a bridge over the river Seine for me . . . and those Army nurses were really something. We arrived at another remote area and they had painted a special sign: DINAH'S PLACE—right alongside my foxhole!"

Spencer Tracy had been skeptical—like John Wayne—about what he could do to entertain the troops. Before he left for a two-week USO Camp Show tour of Hawaii, he had expressed some doubts.

"Hell, I don't sing or dance—and I'm not another pretty face—are you sure they'll want to see this Irish kisser of mine?"

On his return, in late September of 1944,

Tracy sat for a press conference along with an Army spokesman. He was red-faced and embarrassed as the officer told the press just how *effective* he had been.

"Tracy was terrific," the captain said. "He visited thirteen Army and Navy hospitals in thirteen days. It wasn't an easy task, but he was a real trouper. He made informal, friendly visits in the wards, walking in unannounced and just introducing himself. He talked to each patient, signed thousands of short-snorters, photographs and scraps of paper, and brought back hundreds of messages to deliver to relatives and sweethearts."

Tracy started each day at five o'clock in the morning and stayed in the hospitals until nightfall—with an hour out for a swim and lunch. On nine of the thirteen evenings, he showed up unexpectedly at G.I. theatres where his newest film was playing. He made a brief stage appearance in the middle of each show, talked to the guys and then just left unobtrusively.

Listening to himself being praised, Tracy just sat—speechless. At least, now the press corps had their answer as to exactly what a great dramatic actor did on a USO tour.

In somewhat of a switch, David Niven, who was serving with the British forces, wrote a letter to a friend who worked on *The Hollywood Reporter*. When excerpts were printed the first week in December 1944, Niven's Hollywood friends were shocked at its somber tone—something they had never associated David with before.

I have no further news since my last long dreary epistle. In the meanwhile, I have made a definite decision as far as what happens after the war. Once this thing is over and I have been demobilized, I hope I shall never have to mention this again.

I have slugged along for five years with millions of my countrymen and I am

just as happy as they are that the end is in sight. During these five years I have seen too much misery, horror and suffering, twice in France at the beginning of the war, and again in '44, and in my own country during the whole time, ever to want to brag about being even a small part of it all.

And more important, with the one blessed exception of my elder brother, who is still with the Eighth Army in Italy (and has been all the way from El Alamein), all my closest friends and most of my male relatives have been killed in this war.

So witness this, if I ever get back to Hollywood you will never hear me giving interviews along the lines of the "returning warrior," and above all, you will never hear me get into arguments as to who or what won the war and when. As far as I am concerned, it will have been five of the best years of my life not, pray God, wasted. Though that we shall see later when the politicians get on with their job of winning the peace.

I am proud to have been fit enough in body and mind to have had those years to give for our cause. It must be awful for young and healthy men to have stayed away from all this. They will have lost something, however thick skinned they may be. They may have made themselves famous and wealthy during the last few years, but their insides will still be rotten at the end of it. We pity them. I met one the other day. He took out his American citizenship papers in 1942 to avoid the war over here. He was in the uniform of one of Uncle Sam's G.I.'s. I laughed a lot.

This all looks rather bitter on reading it, but don't worry, it won't be mentioned by me again. I just want to forget it all—except the funny bits which were legion and which I shall never forget. See you soon, I hope . . .

And, finally, here are excerpts from a letter Phil Silvers wrote from overseas—not about himself—but mainly about Frank Sinatra.

Have been a lot of places. There is still a strict army censorship so can't tell too much of where we've been but we're doing a helluva job—and what an experience . . . The men like our unit because we've concentrated on the best way to get to them by first making the show as good as we can—and next, to fraternize. We eat with the soldiers, talk to them about home, movie stars, etc. . . . About Sinatra. Believe me, I've been out with just about all of them, but he is the biggest sensation the USO ever had. He's the most cooperative, regular kid you've ever seen. Every camp we've been to—he was greeted by derisive screams from the men because of his swooning publicity. But when we leave, they love him to a man and are for him a million percent. This is gratifying, for the show was planned with that in mind. I use him as a stooge, slap him around for most of the show—and then, when he sings, the guys are really ready for him . . .

Judy Garland
"BACK TO FOUR-A-DAY"

In October of 1942, Judy Garland, one of the most tireless of stars, wrote this piece for The Hollywood Reporter *about her experiences while entertaining troops here in the States.*

A new cradle for talent has been found! For years the producers and directors of stage and screen bemoaned the loss of small-time vaudeville and burlesque houses, for they were a treasure trove of talent. From there sprang the great personalities of today's world of entertainment. With the passing of vaudeville, there arose the problem of finding the stars of tomorrow. The answer is to be found in the hundreds of units touring the country's army camps.

This was revealed to me when I made my trip east and visited seven camps in seven different states. At each camp I joined a troupe currently playing there. In every show were young boys and girls gaining experience not to be found anywhere since the era of one-night stands and two-a-day vaude perform-ances. Youngsters starting in show business knew there must be a starting place. Stars aren't made overnight. But where? Now they know. While gaining this invaluable experi-ence they enjoy the thrill of bringing enter-tainment to the boys in our armed forces.

Embryo performers are not the only ones who gain this two-fold benefit. There are also to be found the men and women who were one-time stars in vaudeville. Forced to turn to other forms of livelihood when vaudeville rang down the curtain they, too, are back in har-ness.

Touring the camps was reminiscent of my old vaudeville days. Making overnight jumps on milk trains, and playing four-a-day instead of the usual two. It was really like "old home week." Many of the performers were people who had played on the same bills with my sisters and me. It was wonderful to see these people, headliners twenty-five years ago, re-turn to "bring down the house" in army camps all over the country. One of these troupers told me he never hoped to experience a more thrill-ing moment than the day he opened at the Palace Theatre eighteen years ago. But he did, when with the very same act, he received an even greater ovation at Fort Knox, in Louis-ville, Kentucky.

Willie Shore, the "Abba-Dabba" man, who was my favorite comedian when I was a little girl, played with us at one camp. He did an act with a seltzer water bottle and I would sit out front with the soldiers and watch him. He never failed to squirt the water so that it would land on me. This often resulted in my ap-pearing on the stage in a slightly wet and bedraggled condition, but it was wonderful. These people were all my own friends and it was grand to see them back in front of an audience where they belong.

Another thing I discovered—it's easy to en-tertain soldiers. You don't always have to sing and dance. All you have to do is talk. Just pull up a chair, sit down, and be prepared to an-swer a barrage of questions. Besides, there are always plenty of others on the bill who can do the singing and dancing. All the boys want to hear about Hollywood and the motion picture stars. But though they asked me ques-tions, it didn't compare with the quiz I put them through. I had to know about each one, where he came from and what he did.

The first time I sang for the soldiers I was scared to death. My knees shook and my voice trembled with a severe case of stage fright. It seems silly now, as I look back on it. Every performer dreams of stopping a show, but be-lieve me, no show was ever stopped with the thunderous applause and appreciative re-sponse that greets an entertainer playing to a group of soldiers.

We did four shows a day. One at the re-ception center where the newly inducted boys gather, one in the hospital and two in the camp auditorium. At each show I sang two set songs, and then did request numbers. It seems the boys favor the old songs. In my case the two outstanding requests were for "Over the Rain-bow," and "Dear Mr. Gable." The first time they asked for the "Gable" song I was stumped. It had been a long time since I had sung it, but after ad-libbing the lyrics a few times, the original ones came back to me. All shows were staged at night, and my days were spent touring the camp. There wasn't a spot I missed seeing, from the kitchen to the rifle range.

Meal times were fun. The only bad part was that the food was so good I gained eight pounds. We ate in the mess hall with all the boys and a steady diet of steak and potatoes, fried chicken and pie wrought havoc on the brand new figure I had worked so hard to acquire. Now I understand why the boys come home on furlough looking so strong and healthy. That army food puts the pounds on.

There's one thing about the army. It has a swell sense of humor. When I started out I couldn't tell the difference between a private and a general. I was introduced to a colonel one night and to the great amusement of all the boys I acknowledged the introduction with a "I'm very happy to meet you, Corporal!" They howled and when I arrived home they sent me a huge chart showing all the insignias and what each one stood for. Just to keep me straight, they wrote. They laughed with me—not at me, for which I'll be eternally grateful.

Another thing that touched me deeply was the interest of both the boys and the other performers in me. If it hadn't been for the soldiers at Camp Robinson and the other actors in the troupe I would never have had the thrill of a wedding cake.

The day we played there was my wedding anniversary. My husband David Rose, who accompanied me on the trip, and I were talking about it. The boys overheard, and that night we were given a surprise party. Highlight of the evening was a huge wedding cake topped with a miniature bride and groom. A wedding cake was the one thing I felt cheated of when we were married. Now, I had it, thanks to a swell bunch of people.

I could go on forever telling the many wonderful things I've experienced on camp tours. The immense thrill and gratification of doing what little I could to entertain came first, but then there was the meeting of old friends, the knowledge that so many young people were getting their start, the friendships made with the boys and the knowledge that we can never do enough for the soldiers who have left their homes and families to fight our battles. If, in any way, I brought happiness to them it can never equal the joy made possible for me.

WARTIME BLUES

It was President Franklin D. Roosevelt's fate to die in office before World War II came to its final conclusion. He passed away on April 12, 1945.

Because FDR meant so much to the film industry, almost every one of America's 16,000 theatres stayed closed until six o'clock on the Saturday following the tragic loss. Many of the bigger houses remained shuttered for one complete day. All studio home offices in New York were closed. Every legitimate theatre canceled its matinee performance. All entertainment industry social events were postponed for one week. And the motion picture theatre owners of New York City pulled their newspaper advertisements and substituted FDR tributes and death notices.

Hollywood had been somewhat preoccupied with death, and other depressing news, for nearly a year. In March of 1944, Myron Selznick, only forty-five, and one of Hollywood's most important agents, died suddenly of abdominal hemorrhages. His brother, David, and other family members, were distraught. Dozens of both Hollywood and England's most important stars-directors-producers and writer clients, along with the rest of the industry, mourned the tragic

loss. It was decided to keep the business going. For years after he passed away, the Myron Selznick Agency continued to flourish.

In October of 1944, Wendell Willkie, 1940 presidential candidate, industry friend, legal counselor, and chairman of the board of 20th Century–Fox for two and a half years, died suddenly.

Then, on December 14, 1944, thirty-four-year-old Lupe Velez, the "Mexican Spitfire," took her own life. It was ironic that her suicide should come right before the year-end holidays. Everyone always said that the adorable, fiery Lupe looked like a Christmas tree when she was dressed up. It was true. She loved *real*, sparkling jewelry. In fact, over the years, she had bought herself drawersful of diamond, sapphire, ruby and emerald rings, necklaces, bracelets, earrings and brooches. Frequently, she was seen on-the-town all loaded down with gems. "I can't live without them," she said. "They make me feel alive."

Lupe took poison rather than give birth to a child who had no legal father. She had been dating handsome Austrian actor Harald Ramond. According to Lupe, when Harald learned of "her condition," his passion suddenly chilled. He finally agreed to marry her—providing that she first sign a paper which acknowledged that he was doing so only to give the child a name. That way, of course, Ramond would have had no financial responsibility for the baby. (Following Lupe's death, Harald admitted asking Velez to sign such a paper, but said that he had done so only after they'd quarreled, and that he really hadn't meant it.)

Lupe was devastated. Despite her freewheeling personality, down deep, the sanctity of marriage—and particularly motherhood—meant a great deal to her. She could not face the birth—but was too deeply Catholic to seek an abortion.

Instead, she decorated her bedroom with candles and statues of saints and madonnas. Then she dressed in long filmy blue pajamas, wrote two suicide notes—one which accused Ramond of "faking" his love for her and their unborn child—and swallowed pills.

Several months later, it was discovered that Lupe's estate had dwindled to very little by the time of her death. A public auction conducted on the premises of her Beverly Hills home revealed that even with the jewelry—once thought to have been so valuable—her legacy amounted to a comparative pittance. Still, Lupe was somewhat vindicated, if not in life, then in death. After a vigorous fight, she was allowed to be buried in consecrated ground. Dressed in her favorite full-length ermine cape, her body was lowered into the hallowed soil of her native country—glamorous to the end.

David Niven came back from the war in May of 1946 with his young English bride and their two small babies. Since everyone wanted to meet "Primmie," the Ty Powers gave a party in the Nivens' honor. It was an informal, fun evening. After dinner, the gang assembled in the Powers' living room. Someone suggested a game of hide and seek—and, believe it or not, all of the sophisticated crowd joined in.

As everyone split up, looking for their own secret niche, David went in one direction, Primmie in the other. Unfamiliar with Ty's home, she opened a door to what she believed was a closet and plunged twenty feet straight down. She landed on the cellar floor and sustained a fatal concussion.

For David, who had spent five years "in the trenches," it was almost too much to bear. He was inconsolable and retreated into a shell of loneliness. His Hollywood friends all rallied to his side. Numerous film offers awaited him. Most important was his awareness that his two babies needed him now more than ever. So Niven picked up the pieces of his life and went on.

Jane Wyman
"FOR BETTER UNDERSTANDING"

In October of 1948, Jane Wyman delivered this moving vignette to The Hollywood Reporter *concerning her experiences while making* Johnny Belinda.

I've got a story to tell—

Of *Johnny Belinda,* the picture in which I have nothing to say. It's the first time on the screen an actress neither speaks nor hears.

If by it, the problems of the deaf are more compassionately understood by those who have the blessing of hearing then I think all of us on the production will have accomplished our purpose. I'm speaking here of Director Jean Negulesco; Jerry Wald; who produced the film for Warner Brothers; the cast—such able artists as Lew Ayres, Agnes Moorehead, Charles Bickford, Jan Sterling and Stephen McNally who appear in types of roles they never before attempted; and the crew, to the last cooperative man. *Johnny Belinda* represents ensemble effort. Let me say that we were inspired to our very best efforts by the sensitivity of the theme and by the message of tolerance it might help to spread.

Johnny Belinda, from the successful Broadway stage play by Elmer Harris, is the story of a waif, an uncultured little animal, denied speech and hearing from birth, dwelling among the simple fishing and farming people of Prince Edward Island, Nova Scotia. A sympathetic young doctor from "the outside world" penetrates the girl's world of silence by teaching her sign language and lip reading by which she can attempt to communicate her thoughts to those around her who previously had been denied, or failed to attempt, any contact whatsoever due to her affliction.

It's an utterly absorbing characterization, an emotional challenge to any actress, particularly to this one who prefers character roles any day to leading women. I wholeheartedly accepted the challenge. *Johnny Belinda* provided what looked to be a neverending succession of blocks to overcome before I could even begin an actual interpretation of the role in front of the camera.

To begin with, *Johnny Belinda* came to me out of the blue. I had completed *The Yearling* and was on tenterhooks awaiting public opinion on Ma Baxter, a job of acting that I knew to be completely out of the Wyman sphere as Jane Wyman had come to be known on the screen in light comedy and musicals.

Jerry Wald telephoned in the midst of my anxiety to say that he had caught a rough cut of the picture, admired it, and wanted to suggest a property for my next vehicle. He spoke of *Belinda*. Here was another opportunity for characterization! I read it, loved it and, with Jerry rushed to Jack Warner and begged him to buy it for me. Jack shared mine and Jerry's enthusiasm. He realized that here was something entirely different, the like of which had never been seen before in motion pictures.

When Jack gave the "go ahead" signal, I plunged into the task of creating Belinda. Illness prevented me from starting the picture on the original date planned. So it happened that I had the script a full year. It was a year of study and six months of actual, intensive preparation. I read the script night and day and memorized everybody's lines.

There's a lucky angel perched on my shoulder, I'm sure. Elizabeth Gesner, who has devoted years of energy and her brilliant talents to teaching and working with the deaf, was assigned as technical advisor. May I add here and now that I would never in this world have been able to play the part without her instruction and guidance. She taught me sign language and lip reading.

Mrs. Gesner also found a young Mexican girl, who had been born deaf, to serve as my model for emotion. The girl came to my home and to the studio, and we made innumerable tests of her in 16 and 35 mm. for me to study. I spent hours with the youngster—a cheerful, delightful little thing despite her handicap—watching her every move and reaction.

What I fought most to get in my characterization was what I call the "something quality" that I saw in her eyes. How may I describe that expression? An "anticipation light" possibly. Anyhow, it was the look of one who wanted eagerly to enter in, to share. With all deaf people, you'll observe this expression—inquiring, interested, alive—as they watch you, to understand by lip reading or by your actions and expressions what you want to impart to them.

Weeks of tests followed. Desperation gripped me whenever I viewed these tests. Something was missing, something intangible. Then, one day, I realized what was wrong. I could hear. Small wonder I was missing out on that vital key to a realistic portrayal of a deaf girl.

So I had plastic, wax and cotton ear stops made for my ears to block out all sound and conversation. I wore these throughout shooting to give me the necessary quality of indecision, of faltering. Negulesco and I were put to evolving a sign language of our own so he could direct me when I had my ears plugged. The cast and crew, as well, developed their own set of signals in order to speak to me.

I completely altered the timing of my acting to where I was always one beat late; never re-acting squarely on the line or cue. And having, for the sake of my career, been trained to walk gracefully, with correct posture and to display clothes to the best of my ability, I had to overcome the problem of Wyman entering into Belinda's physical appearance. Wyman had to be ruled out.

So, whenever I walked in the scene, I began with my left foot instead of my right and used my left hand to get over the feeling of unsureness. In other words, it was a reversal of Jane Wyman who had worked all these years to make herself into a positive personality.

Regarding wardrobe, experience has taught me an important fact—that materials mean more than anything in correctly and dramatically achieving the effect you want. Milo Anderson's clothes are wonderfully pathetic for Belinda, I believe. But it cost us weeks of testing. To achieve the dinginess we wanted, the clothes were soaked for weeks in lysol and thoroughly beaten by rocks and brushes.

Another important factor in the characterization of Belinda was her hair-do. I studied hair styles, thumbing magazines showing photographs of the rustic Nova Scotians which we were portraying. An example of what we saw in these photographs was blended with a homely coiffure (if you can call it that!) to result in what we thought Belinda would wear. It looks like the style of the 1900's, as if I were typical of the kids of that time who looked as though they had a bowl set on their heads and then had their hair cut. I had my hair cut that way.

Here I want to repeat that *Johnny Belinda* represents ensemble effort. No matter how many screen veterans were there among us, we decided on a policy of mass approval—that is for the actors. It put us on our mettle.

We all sincerely hope that *Johnny Belinda* proves that we knew what we were doing. But the final verdict rests with the public.

HOLLYWOOD ON THE HALF-SHELL
1945

By January, JUDY GARLAND and VINCENTE MINNELLI firmed up their wedding plans . . . LAUREN BACALL headed to New York for a personal appearance, proudly wearing a yellow sapphire ring set in gold BOGIE had given her. Rumors were that HUMPHREY and MAYO METHOT had already agreed on a property settlement. The third Mrs. Bogart was on her way out . . . PAT DI CICCO and GLORIA VANDERBILT *did* separate—but both claimed they still loved each other.

In February, EDGAR BERGEN married beautiful cover girl—model FRANCES WESTERMAN . . . BETTY GRABLE anticipated the birth of her second child . . . LAUREN BACALL complained to Warner Brothers because they were only paying her $200 a week.

By March, SUSAN HAYWARD and JESS BARKER announced they were expecting twins . . . KAY WILLIAMS reconciled with MACOCO. The South-of-the-Border millionaire had purchased Kay's mother a home in the East, and gifted beautiful blond Kay with a fortune in jewels.

In April, insiders said VIRGINIA GREY was the girl "most likely" to become the next MRS. CLARK GABLE . . . And famous war correspondent ERNIE PYLE was killed in an accident . . . HEDY LAMARR made the announcement in May. She and JOHN LODER were expecting . . . BARBARA HUTTON gave a smashing dinner party and handsome PHILIP REED helped her receive guests . . . SONJA HENIE not only sent $45000 to aid the Norwegian Relief Society, she headed overseas to entertain the troops.

May was a marvelous month. On the 8th, the war was over in Europe, and the country celebrated VE-Day. Thirteen days later, CLARK GABLE started shooting his first postwar film, *Adventure*. It co-starred GREER GARSON, and was directed by his "GWTW" mentor, VICTOR FLEMING. It was not a terribly exciting vehicle, but Gable's mere presence onscreen—after a three-and-a-half-year absence—brought out legions of fans.

There was a lot of excitement in Hollywood on the first Saturday in June. Many stars and an enormous crowd flocked to the Los Angeles Coliseum to honor Generals GEORGE S. PATTON and JAMES H. DOOLITTLE. "God of Battles," a poem written by General Patton, was read by BETTE DAVIS. EDWARD G. ROBINSON narrated a tribute to Patton. General Doolittle, of the Air Force, received an equal fanfare. A trio of operatic voices—LAURITZ MELCHIOR, EZIO PINZA and JEANETTE MacDONALD—had opened the program with "The Star-Spangled Banner." JIMMY DURANTE, CARMEN MIRANDA and her troupe, GINNY SIMMS and DANNY THOMAS entertained. JACK BENNY was the master of ceremonies, Director MERVYN LEROY produced the gala welcome in collaboration with the Army. The show followed a downtown parade and late-afternoon reception for the returned heroes.

On June 18, JUDY GARLAND married VINCENTE MINNELLI. LOUIS B. MAYER gave the bride away . . . On the same day, DONNA REED married agent-producer TONY OWEN. Both couples left on their honeymoons by train, and even had adjoining compartments.

In July, LANA TURNER spent a cozy weekend with TURHAN BEY, on leave from the Army Training Camp at Fort Roberts . . . JOAN CRAWFORD, looking like a star from head to toe, in a slinky black dress, draped by a white fox stole, celebrated her third anniversary at the Mocambo with hubby PHILLIP TERRY. And LUCY and DESI ARNAZ reconciled. Lucille, glowing with hap-

1 A shot from Gable's first MGM film after his release from the Army, *Adventure*, co-starring Greer Garson. The advertising slogan for the picture read: "Gable's back and Garson's Got Him." 2 Judy Garland and Vincente Minnelli celebrate her 23rd birthday on the set of *The Harvey Girls*. 3 Errol Flynn and second wife, Nora Eddington, in the spring of 1945, during one of their troubled marital periods. (UPI) 4 Charles Boyer, Merle Oberon, Pat Paterson (Mrs. Boyer), and David Niven stop for the camera. 5 Two great Hollywood filmmakers: David O. Selznick and Alfred Hitchcock. (Courtesy Selznick Properties, Ltd.)

piness, said she and her Cuban hubby would adopt a baby (they didn't).

On August 6, the first atomic bomb was dropped on Hiroshima . . . PAULETTE GODDARD, decked out in "CHAPLIN diamonds," showed off her new husband, BURGESS MEREDITH . . . BOB MITCHUM, an Army private, was on a brief leave to make a personal appearance with his first important film, *The Story of G.I. Joe.* Mitchum had an RKO contract waiting for him as soon as he was discharged . . . PHYLLIS BROOKS, who doused the torch she was carrying for CARY GRANT and married Eastern socialite Lieut. TORBERT McDONALD, was living in Lexington, Virginia, and expecting a child . . . And Lieut. HENRY FONDA passed through Hollywood on his way to begin a Washington, D.C., assignment . . . GARY COOPER was taking instructions in the Catholic faith, which pleased his wife, "ROCKY," enormously . . . And IRENE and DAVID O. SELZNICK confirmed rumors that their marriage had ended.

If the costs of the elegant new gowns the ladies wore to Sonja Henie's stupendous party on Saturday night, September 8, 1945, had been totaled, the Treasury Department could have relaxed. CLAUDETTE COLBERT, JOAN CRAWFORD, MARY LIVINGSTONE BENNY and the hostess all looked gorgeous. But it was LANA TURNER who took first prize. She wore a tight-fitting white beaded gown, topped by her blond-white hair and set off by a white fox coat. Somebody said she looked like LADY GODIVA on a white horse in a snowstorm! Lana was escorted by "her fiancé of the moment," TURHAN BEY. There were exactly 212 people at the dinner-dance and not one crasher—which was news. Among others under the huge tent were the DARRYL ZANUCKS, JOAN BENNETT and WALTER WANGER, CARY GRANT with his current heartbeat, BETTY HENSEL, BOB and MARY CUMMINGS, the FRANK SINATRAS, BILL and DIANA POWELL, JACK WARNER, JR., MERVYN LEROY, the VAN HEFLINS, the KEENAN WYNNS, the CHARLES BOYERS, the JULES STEINS and ROBERT WALKER.

Glamour photographer PAUL HESSE raved about JOAN FONTAINE's dress as she walked in, and remarked "You must have bought it in New York."

"Yes," Joan replied, "and thank heavens—I won't be seeing myself in duplicate all evening."

Five minutes later, they bumped into Mrs. RONALD COLMAN, and BENITA was wearing the same gown. When Joan looked as though she were about to cry, Hesse cracked, "If it will make you feel any better, JACK BENNY and I are wearing the same suits."

The party went on until the wee hours without Sonja splitting a seam or dropping a diamond as she flitted from table to table, always the perfect hostess. But the *best* scene of the evening was watching CLARK GABLE and his date, model ANITA ("The Face") COLBY, seated at a table seriously engrossed in trying to pat their tummies with one hand and rub their heads with the other. Gable's secret was out—Rhett Butler was *not* terribly well coordinated.

On September 2, it was all over. The war with Japan had ended. VJ-Day arrived—and the nation was in a euphoric mood. Hollywood, in its usual glamour tradition, pulled out all the stops. Crowds gathered. Families and strangers, stars and "civilians," embraced in an outpouring of unity. The boxoffice was in great shape throughout the United States. With the end of the war and theatres all over the world once more eager for their films, Hollywood studio heads should have been very optimistic about the future. Unfortunately, they were *not*. In an industry where "crisis" situations cropped up with the regularity of the common cold, moguls were once more looking over their shoulders. This time, however, their chronic paranoia was somewhat justified.

Television—which would have been available sooner had World War II not interfered—was about to rear its "ugly head." Predictions were that by the end of the decade there would be five million homes equipped with TV receivers—not to mention thousands of bars and diners. With yet another "new enemy" threatening, this one potentially more virulent than radio, the moguls reached for their headache powders in larger and larger doses.

Also in September, KAY WILLIAMS' recent marriage to sugar tycoon ADOLPH SPRECKELS was already shaky . . . SYLVIA FAIRBANKS and her LORD STANLEY were rumored to be drifting apart . . . And the wedding event of the season was that of grown-up SHIRLEY TEMPLE to handsome JOHN AGAR, scion of a very wealthy family. The only hitch came when they went to check into the bridal suite of the exclusive Town House only to discover that another bridal couple had been given their room by mistake.

In November, Hollywood newcomer ELLA RAINES turned TURHAN BEY's turban. He split from TURNER to Raines, and Lana was fuming . . . TYRONE POWER and ANNABELLA took off on a two-week vacation motoring through America. When they returned, Ty was mustered out of the Marines.

As another Christmas rolled around, ERROL FLYNN sold off part of his handsome Mulholland Drive estate . . . HOWARD HUGHES was counting the profits derived from his fifty-one-percent ownership in TWA . . . MRS. MIKE TODD asked for a quarter of a million in alimony to free MIKE so that he could marry JOAN BLONDELL . . . And LANA TURNER and GREG BAUTZER, handsome motion picture attorney, celebrated their first New Year's Eve of togetherness.

Lauren Bacall
"BABY CHOOSES TO BE ADULT"

Lauren Bacall, who went from model to film star in one rapid leap, contributed to a 1948 special issue of The Hollywood Reporter.

A smart motion picture wife is not her husband's best friend and severest critic. This tired old cliché may be applicable to wives who are content to stay home and play house and put all their "yesses" and "noes" in the right places. But with the pair of career people that are in our house, I've taken quite another approach to the matter.

I've decided that in the film business a really smart wife is her husband's most disinterested observer.

Something more than three years ago, I became Mrs. Humphrey Bogart and a motion picture wife at the same time. And from then on, I plotted a campaign of professional casualness and one of marital enthusiasm as far as Bogie was concerned.

What I mean is that I never interfere with my husband's screen life. We work together as members of the same craft, not as man and wife. I respect his opinions, of course, and sometimes he respects mine, I hope, but we never offer them except on request.

That's what I mean by being a disinterested observer.

I try to view Bogie's career with about the same attitude that I do—well, say Van Johnson's or Gary Cooper's. Actually, to be sure, H. Bogart's career is the second most important thing in the world to me (our marriage is the first) but I try not to look at it from a personal viewpoint.

When Bogie and I went back to Ohio to be married in May, 1945, the Hollywood gloom set shook their collective heads and moaned, "It won't last." We knew better. What the catastrophe-anticipators didn't consider was that the Bogarts were in love and were going to

Lauren Bacall.

try to act like sensible adults. Which I think we have.

It's ridiculous for anybody to say that there is a specific formula for a successful marriage that will apply to everybody—and certainly not to everybody in Hollywood.

I know people in the profession who operate much differently but probably just as successfully in their professional and marital relations as Bogie and I. One Hollywood wife, for example, wouldn't think of letting her husband go before the cameras without first reading his lines with him. She practically directs him.

And still another film wife won't go on a set where her husband is working, nor will she see any of his films. She wants to think of him as just her husband who reports to duty every day (and comes home with a nice fat paycheck), and what he does at the office is none of her concern. That's carrying indifference too far.

Of course, by appearing together in the same pictures as we frequently do, Bogie and I have one distinct advantage. During the making of *Key Largo*, for example, we both worked at the same time, rested at the same time, and played at the same time. It was never a matter of one of us coming home tired to find the other well rested and charged with a lets-go-somewhere attitude. Or vice versa.

We usually got up at the same time and drove to work together, and quit at the same time and drove home together. This, of course, is an ideal arrangement, and one that not very many Hollywood couples can work out. And, believe me, you have to be mighty compatible to live and work together as closely as my husband and I do.

It's not always easy for a film wife—or a film husband, for that matter—to take a completely objective view of her (or his) spouse's career. It's much easier to let your personal feelings take over, and I frequently have to restrain myself to keep from trying to advise Bogie one way or another. The results in our relationship have been well worth the effort of restraint.

Humphrey has always been one to point out that the private lives of the motion picture people are no more bogged in sin and distress than the lives of people anywhere else. And I think the same thing applies to the marital happiness of Hollywood couples—they don't get any more divorces or marry any more frequently than the couples in Sioux City or New Haven. The publicity spotlight is just hotter in Hollywood.

The burden of being looked at through the big end of a telescope is something that members of the acting business in Hollywood must expect to bear, and most of them bear it with good grace in the knowledge that it's part of the business.

All of these things don't help to make marriage in Hollywood comfortable and effortless, but it's amazing how many people come through

Alice Faye.

it glowingly, year after year. The Robert Montgomerys, for instance, and the James Cagneys and the Robert Taylors and the Jack Bennys and the George Murphys, etc.

It's screen couples like these who are constant examples to the rest of the world that Hollywood people, too, can live normal decent lives. Although the Bogarts have been married only something more than three years, I hope that seventeen years from now, they will join the list of Hollywood's 20-year couples.

Because I think Bogie is an easy, able performer, he has been immeasurably helpful to me in my acting. It isn't what he has ever told me to do, because he isn't a dramatic coach. But acting with him and catching his spirit and pace have given me great confidence.

Our life is really pretty exciting—at least to us—and playing the dual role of Bogie's off-screen missus and his on-screen leading lady gives me a lot of pleasure.

When we are on the boat or at home, I'm strictly Mrs. Bogart, and not the Lauren Bacall of the studio. It pleases me to notice that when most people telephone me at home, they ask for Mrs. Bogart. These same people, calling at the studio, ask for Miss Bacall.

It shows that I've managed to keep my two lives separate—even if I do live them with the same man.

Alice Faye
"FANS—LONG MAY THEY WAVE"

Alice Faye, one of the screen's most charming leading ladies, was always an audience favorite. On November 2, 1943, she wrote this article for The Hollywood Reporter *in which she discussed how much the public support meant to her.*

It seems to me that in all that's said and written about Hollywood from day to day, there's usually an oversight. Too little is said about the movie fans. They're being neglected and they're entitled to better treatment on several counts, the most obvious being the boxoffice count. So, now that I have the opportunity, I propose to do my level best to correct this condition.

I owe a good deal to my fans and so, I'm sure, does every other star in Hollywood. In fact, it's doubtful whether anyone can rise to top billing in this bewildering business without a devoted fan following. They form, in a sense, the foundation on which Hollywood success is built.

The picture in which you appear may be good or it may, unfortunately, be bad. But your true fan doesn't stop to weigh the pros and cons of the particular picture. If you're in it, he'll see it. And that, definitely, is something, because I recall a couple of pictures in which I appeared which must have taxed these devoted people no end. I know I couldn't sit through them.

Individually, and in the mass, the dyed-in-the-wool fan is interesting, intelligent and helpful.

Something like 30,000 of them have been writing me every year for the last three years. They have taught me a lot not only about the particular business I'm in, but tastes, customs, prejudices, sectional differences and attitudes, and all manner of other things. It's been like a post-graduate course in Americanism, one that's given me a far better insight into the people of this great land than I could possibly have obtain otherwise.

Contrary to general belief, there is surprisingly little "gush" in this mail. On the whole, the fans are full of suggestions, kindly advice, curiosity and their own hopes and aspirations.

Some of the advice and suggestions I have received through the mail, I might add, has been really helpful. For instance, I'll never forget one of my first fan letters. It reached me at what we call a "crucial" period. It was almost eight years ago. I had been in Holly-wood a relatively short while and had made one picture, *George White's Scandals*.

Thereafter I sat back to rest. I was a starry-eyed stranger in a strange town. I felt lonely and I was homesick for New York. I wanted to devote some time to getting acclimated.

But the studio had other ideas. They decided to make me over to fit the Hollywood conception of what a Hollywood celebrity should be. They sent coaches and tutors over to instruct me in elocution, singing, deportment, selection of a wardrobe and even carriage.

As far as I was concerned, the limit of endurance was reached when they called me over to an empty soundstage where a feminine coach put three books on my head and instructed me to walk up and down without dislodging them. That was to teach me proper carriage.

I guess the Irish in me boiled over. Anyway, I let the books fall and kept on walking. In fact, I walked out on all the coaches at the same time. Naturally, the studio frowned on my conduct. A player may be right on occasion, but usually the men who have devoted their lives to this business know quite well what they're up to.

At any rate, the report went out that I was proving difficult to handle. It was then that I received the fan letter from a mother of nine in Brooklyn, who had taken a long-distance interest in my career. She told me to stick to my guns.

"You'll never be anything," she wrote, "unless you can be yourself."

That letter helped enormously to cheer and encourage me and I have tried to follow her advice ever since.

There's an ebb and flow in the mail a star receives. You receive more of it in the winter months than in the summer, and more in February than in any other month, particularly if you have just made a good picture.

There is one qualification to this, however. A good picture will bring forth a veritable avalanche of fan mail, and a bad one will cut it down almost to a dribble. Which leads me to believe that the true fan would rather praise than condemn.

Yet, the loyalty of a real fan will surmount a poor picture. For instance, some years ago a young woman who's been writing to me for years asked me about a picture which I had recently completed. Candor compelled me to answer that it would be just as well if she passed it by.

Several weeks later, I received another letter from her. Enclosed was a statement from eighteen theatre managers in and around St. Louis attesting to the fact that she had seen this particular picture at their houses. In other words, she had been through the ordeal eighteen times. She came out here a couple of years ago, and I did my best to make amends.

At times, of course, fan attention may become a little embarrassing. Yet, it is usually so well meant that you can't become offended. We've all been mobbed at times, but I, for one, hope that it will continue to happen to me. I've always regarded these things as an exuberant display of affection, and so the experience has been rather more exhilarating than terrifying.

Then, of course, there are the kindly fans who like to pay their respects in gifts. Not so long ago, I received two prize pigs from a fan in Sacramento, California. The pigs posed me a pretty problem. In the first place, there is a law against keeping porkers within the corporate limits of Encino, where I live, and, in the second place, I know nothing about the care, feeding, and habits of such animals.

Now I'm paying a farmer in the San Fernando Valley to board and feed them, while trying to decide what to do with them. I might be able to induce the fan who sent them to take them back.

Another time, I received two hundred golden trout in a tank from an admirer who raises them for commercial purposes in Colorado. They were a welcome gift, of course. Everyone working with me had trout for dinner for several days.

In addition, there are innumerable smaller tokens of affection sent by fans. They range from cakes and hams, usually from the South, to jewelry and pictures.

Some of the fan mail goes romantic. Before I was married to Phil Harris, there was hardly a week went by that I didn't receive some sort of marriage proposal through the mail.

A wealthy Argentine cattle man offered me a 500,000-acre ranch and 10,000 head of cattle as a wedding present.

A Swiss offered me jewels and a castle. A member of the Royal Canadian Mounted Police wrote me a touching note in which he said he had nothing to offer me but his love and an opportunity to share his loneliness in Canada.

I wrote a nice note to the Mounted Policeman.

But, all in all, I prize my fans. They're thoughtful! They're considerate, and they're understanding. They mean more to this business than any star. May they increase and multiply.

THE TERRIFIC TRIO: RITA . . . AVA . . . BETTY

Some of them were touched with magic. The great ones. They were blessed with an extra dimension: an overabundance of charismatic onscreen charm that immediately set them apart. It was an instantaneous connection between star and public. A love affair carried on right in front of everybody else.

Many of them had great talent. Others were possessed of a rare personality. Some were so beguiling, it didn't matter whether they had talent or not. But all of those "special stars" had one thing in common—a silent siren-song. They had the ability to make you care.

Among the great female stars of the Forties were three dazzling sex symbols—a blonde, a brunette and a redhead. One of them, Rita Hayworth, was "created." Her hair was colored. Her hairline lowered. Her lips rounded. Her eyebrows tweezed. Her cheekbones sunken. But when the creation was finished, it was a masterpiece.

Ava Gardner was a natural. Straight off the farm, she was the personification of beauty. But she lacked confidence, poise. After the studio—and several husbands—worked their magic, a whole new magnificent creature emerged . . . and thrived.

Betty Grable, the third great Forties star, was nearly "authentic," except for her chestnut-brown hair, which she turned almost straw-blond and kept that way. Betty's beauty was harder to type; in fact, she wasn't a classic "looker" at all. There were actresses in Hollywood who could sing more sweetly, dance better and emote with more proficiency—yet Grable topped them all. She had a natural warmth, a down-to-earth, gutsy quality, and a sincerity that glowed through even the thickest studio makeup.

It was Betty's charm, plus those incredible legs, that made her the All-American Girl. She eventually would become the most famous "Pin-Up Girl" of the Forties and, for quite a few years, the highest-paid actress in Hollywood.

Grable's stardom, however, was achieved through very hard work and sheer courage. In fact, she almost gave up. A few years before her famous pinup photo hung in tens of thousands of barracks from Little Rock to London, she nearly quit the business—because she thought it had quit on her.

When Rita—née Margarita Cansino—was seventeen, and under a stock contract at Fox, businessman Edward Judson asked her out on a date. He saw her dance in a film, and was struck by her beauty. Eventually they got together. Judson, many years older, looked on Rita as a child who needed to be molded. She, in her first dating relationship, fell for his kindhearted ways.

In 1938, they were married. From the outset, Judson took complete control of both Rita's domestic and professional life. He told her she was incapable of making decisions—he would do all of the thinking for her. Rita's "job" was to make herself as beautiful as possible. And she was to learn how to *act* with the same perfection that she had acquired as a dancer. It was a tall order. But Judson commanded, and Rita bowed to his every whim and wish. Outwardly, she radiated sex appeal and a talent she never knew she had. Rapidly, she was given more and more important parts. But she retreated further into a shell of shyness and inner self-doubt.

For six years, Judson pulled the strings. One day the puppet revolted. Rita Hayworth had become a star, a somebody. She was able to stand on her own. Judson refused to let go.

On May 23, 1943, Hayworth filed for divorce. Judson countersued. He had "created her," he said. He had "made her a star"; he felt that he deserved some compensation. The whole situation became very messy. Finally, Judson demanded $30,000. With the studio's help, the case was settled out of court. Rita was free—but not for long.

Handsome hulk Victor Mature, who won screen fame wearing a loincloth in *One Million B.C.*, was Rita's co-star in *My Gal Sal*. The twosome fell in love and became engaged. For months, they were seen everywhere together, always the most devoted of couples. Then, Vic had to go into the service. After all, there *was* a war on and it took precedence—even over Rita.

Mature entered the Coast Guard. Rita swore "she would wait." But, while Vic found himself shipped out to the icy Atlantic, an "authentic genius," Orson Welles, entered Hayworth's life—and her heart shifted directions.

On September 7, 1943, Rita became Mrs. Orson Welles. On her wedding day, along with the wires of congratulation, Rita received "another message." It was a long-distance call from a Coast Guard ship, somewhere in the North Atlantic. Vic had secured permission from his executive officer to phone her. They talked briefly. Rita began to weep, while Chief Boatswain's Mate Mature began to curse. His anger spilled out, directed not only at his "ex-love," but also at the helplessness he felt over circumstances that had placed him in the middle of an ocean, unable to stay "in the competition." Between curses, he apologized to the censor monitoring the call. The understanding individual exclaimed with relish, "That's all right, Mature—go right ahead!"

At the beginning, Rita's life with Welles was wonderful, especially after the birth of their daughter, Rebecca, in 1944. But when the first excitement was past, it became apparent that Orson was hell to live with. He refused to keep regular hours. He was always discussing business—even from their bed—on a seemingly twenty-four-hour-a-day schedule.

Still, Orson opened Rita up to a new world of art, theatre, books and current events. They traveled in very intellectual circles. Rita credited "her formal education" to Welles. But living with him, which even at first had been difficult, finally became unbearable.

Meanwhile, she was working steadily. After *Gilda*, with Glenn Ford—which the critics hated and the fans loved—Rita made a film directed by Welles, *Lady from Shanghai*. It was during this picture, shot at the end of 1946, that the Hayworth-Welles marriage fell apart.

One reporter who visited the *Shanghai* set commented: "You should have seen the 'act' put on by Orson in the middle of directing a scene. People got hysterical (though not out loud, of course), watching Welles, standing in the middle of a courtroom set, giving out orders in all directions—while *shaving*. Not only that, but a barber was trying to cut his hair at the same time.

"Of course, with Welles leaping forward, or sideways, every few seconds, the poor barber was snipping at thin air (maybe thin hair, too), most of the time."

A few days later, Walter Winchell attributed the breakup of their marriage to the fact that one morning "Welles stepped out of the shower—and Rita forgot to applaud!"

After four years of marriage, in March of 1947, they separated. Rita filed for divorce that fall. She made a couple of other films, *Affair in Trinidad* and *Miss Sadie Thompson*, and then traveled to Europe for the first time.

She was absolutely captivated by the foreign scene. So, in 1948, Rita went back to Europe, this time with her secretary, Shisia Haran, who had worked for Orson before he and Rita were married. When the Welles were divorced, Rita "got custody" of Miss Haran. She became Hayworth's constant companion and eventually a buffer between Rita and the press.

While they were in France, the two of them drove down to the Riviera. Rita was an honored guest at a party given by international hostess Elsa Maxwell. Elsa saw to it that Rita was seated next to the handsome and dynamic Prince Aly Khan. From that moment on, Rita's life was never the same.

The Prince and the film star left the party together and took a long drive in the moonlight. They were still together when the sun came up. An instant twosome, they traveled to Spain and went on to tour Europe. Finally, with film commitments awaiting her, Rita had to return home. When reporters asked her about the status of the relationship, Rita smiled, and said, "We are good friends, nothing more."

Two weeks later, however, Aly turned up in Hollywood. Soon, they began traveling together again. They flew to Mexico, then to Havana, Cuba, then back to America where they toured New Orleans. When it was time for Aly to leave for Europe, Rita was unwilling to be separated from him.

They booked passage on the steamship *Britannic*. Aly had cabin 51A, Rita, cabin 53A. When the ship docked at the seaport of Cobh, in Ireland, Aly took Rita to stay at his Irish castle. And all hell broke loose.

It was "a question of morality." Prince Aly Khan was a very much married man. His wife was the former Joan Yarde-Buller Guinness. When they originally met, Joan was already married. Her husband was an heir to the Guinness Brewery fortune. But she and Aly fell in love and in 1935 Guinness divorced her. He named Aly as co-respondent and also won custody of the couple's four-year-old son, Patrick. Subsequently, Aly and Joan had married, and she gave birth to Khan's two sons, Karim and Amyn. But now the tables were turned. Joan was the "lady in waiting," while her husband went gallivanting across oceans and continents with Rita Hayworth.

Aly Khan was a fascinating and powerful man. There was no doubt about the fact that the Prince was possessed of the manly qualities, and the worldly goods, guaranteed to turn the head of any woman—even a famous screen star. He had domiciles all over Europe. There were residences in London and Paris . . . three estates in Ireland . . . a house in Switzerland . . . and homes in Syria, Bombay and Calcutta. Aly was a famous horse breeder. He owned stud farms in Ireland and India. Khan, a magnetic personality, was half Persian and half Italian. He had been educated in England, spent his boyhood on the Riviera and, after he was mustered out of the British Army, had purchased the Château d'Horizon, on the French Riviera.

1 Orson Welles and Rita Hayworth on their wedding day, September 7, 1943. (Wide World Photo)　　2 Rita Hayworth with her two children. On her lap, Princess Yasmin Khan (Prince Aly Khan's daughter); seated next to them, Rebecca Welles (Orson's child).　　3 Prince Aly Khan and Rita.

For Margarita Carmen Cansino, from Brooklyn, New York, all of this was pretty exciting. After Ed Judson, and even the great Orson Welles, Prince Aly appeared to be a fabled knight straight out of some heroic novel.

Still, once the twosome had driven off to his castle, "reality" set in. The outspoken, frequently brazen British tabloid press had a field day. One of the papers, *The People*, headlined: THIS AFFAIR IS AN INSULT TO ALL DECENT WOMEN.

The article said, "This is the last time that this newspaper will report in its columns details of the squalid love affair of the film star Rita Hayworth and Aly Khan. We have taken this decision on the grounds of public decency, because we believe that the extravagant expeditions of this colored [sic] Indian Prince and his 'friend' has become an insult to decent-minded women the world over . . ."

The London *Sunday Pictorial* headline read: A VERY SORDID BUSINESS, and stated that: "The current behavior of Miss Rita Hayworth and millionaire Prince Aly Khan, if described in a film script, would never get by the censors, either here or in America . . ."

Despite the negative publicity, Rita kept her mouth shut and continued her romance with Aly. There was no question about the fact that she was very deeply hurt. Meanwhile, Columbia was furious, and Rita's career was in jeopardy. Even her fitness as the mother of Orson Welles' daughter was held up to ridicule. Still, she and Aly continued their romance, mainly in Switzerland. They were waiting for permission from Aly's father to marry as soon as Aly received his divorce from Joan.

The old Aga Khan—the annual recipient of his weight in gold—was quite a hefty ruler, whom his people considered a God-on-Earth. Before Aly could make a move, the Aga had to give his blessings to the "new attachment." Finally, the Aga gave Aly permission to bring Rita to meet him and his wife, the Begum. Hayworth was nervous, but came through with flying colors. She was absolutely charming, and managed to win the Aga's approval.

On January 18, 1948, Prince Aly Khan was permitted to make his first public statement, issued from Château d'Horizon:

I have hitherto refrained from making any comment upon the uninformed and often scurrilous reports which have recently appeared in some sections of the press in connection with my domestic affairs.

I should now like it to be made known that, by mutual consent, my wife and I have lived apart for over three years; that appropriate proceedings have been in progress for nearly a year; and that immediately after these terminate, steps will be taken to remedy a position which appears to have provided material for the press comment complained of.

I am going to marry Miss Hayworth as soon as I am free to do so.

In these circumstances, I hope that my private affairs will be treated with the consideration which is usually extended to the private affairs of individuals in general.

Rita gave out her own comments: "I am fully conversant with the statement which Prince Aly Khan has issued today to the press and am in full agreement with what he says and have only been waiting for him to be free to marry him."

Afterward, the Prince answered a few of the reporters' questions. "Yes, my father has consented to the marriage." . . . And, "No, it will not be necessary for Rita to embrace the Moslem faith."

Hayworth and her Prince were married in Vallouris, France, on May 27, 1949. On December 28 of the same year, Rita gave birth to a five-and-one-half-pound baby girl, at the Mont Choisi Clinic, in Lausanne, Switzerland. The child was named Yasmin. Rita and Aly, who were staying in a suite at the Palace Hotel, had driven to the hospital a few hours before the birth. Rita's time had come on so suddenly that she tossed a fur coat over her pajamas, and Aly had helped her to his car.

There were no complications, although at one point there had been the possibility of a cesarean. But the doctor, Rudolphe Rochat, who had ushered quite a few royal babies into the world, decided to proceed with natural delivery. It was announced that Princess Yasmin would be raised as a Moslem.

In Hollywood, Harry Cohn looked on the whole situation as a mixed blessing. All of the publicity that Rita had garnered for Columbia Studios was priceless. But then, she had let it be known that she did not intend to fulfill her full contractual commitment with Cohn, under the original Beckworth Productions agreement made with Columbia two years before. It was a deal for fourteen films in seven years—with Columbia owning fifty percent of Beckworth—while Rita and her representative, Johnny Hyde, of the William Morris Agency, owned the other half.

Cohn, who did not get to be a mogul by playing dumb, decided to bide his time. He announced that Rita—"Princess Rita" as some movie marquees were billing her—would remain on suspension and would not receive her $5,000-a-week salary.

Then, news was released from one of the "Khan palaces." Rita would not return to Hollywood until late 1950, at the earliest, and she would make only one film a year. She also sent word that she was no longer a William Morris client. Mr. Jules Stein, of MCA, had taken over her professional life.

Cohn, never noted for his subtlety, was reported to have said: "Wait . . . She'll be back . . . And I lay you five to one, after a year she'll be grateful to *play* the Palace—not *live* in one!"

Ava Gardner, tall, slim, green-eyed and gorgeous, with a prominent dimple in her chin and an even more pronounced Southern accent, showed up one day at MGM. Born on a farm just outside of Smithfield, North Carolina, she had been signed by a Metro talent scout after he saw her picture in a shop window on New York's Fifth Avenue. It had been taken by her sister Bea's husband, Larry Tarr, a professional photographer.

Ava, fresh out of high school and a postgraduate course in stenography, had gone East to visit Bea and Larry before seeking employment as a secretary. She had absolutely no yen to act. But, in true Cinderella fashion, she suddenly wound up in Hollywood. There she was, a stock contract in her handbag, walking across the MGM lot—the magical home of legendary stars.

On her first day at the studio, she was spotted by one of MGM's most spectacular "legends," Mickey Rooney. He was then among the nation's boxoffice favorites, especially because of his popular "Andy Hardy" series. It was mid-1941. Mickey took one look and asked her out. They began dating steadily. After a few months, as Ava said, "We just knew that one day we would marry."

She was still in her teens, a raw talent being groomed by a major studio. Mickey, on the other hand, had been performing since the age of two. During working hours, vocal coaches trained Ava to lose her Southern drawl. At night, Mickey brought her flowers and candy, and bolstered her confidence. It was pretty heady stuff for a teenage kid with no real ambition.

Oddly enough, it was Ava's very lack of a frenzied drive to succeed that originally attracted Mickey. He had dated dozens of girls who were consumed with their careers. Ava, on top of being gorgeous, and sweet, couldn't have cared less about filmmaking.

The week before Christmas of 1941 the twosome went house-hunting. Mickey's

The young Ava Gardner.

mother, who found Ava to be a charming girl, was very supportive of her son's choice. Yet she told friends she was sure their marriage would not last three weeks. Mickey, by nature, was a born performer, "always on." Everyone else in his life had to be content to remain part of his audience. There was nothing any girl could do to compete with the talent and drive oozing from every one of his pores.

Mother was right. Ava and Mickey were married at the beginning of 1942. By June, Ava had gone home "for a visit." She and Mickey were separated. Before the year was out, they had been divorced. As Ava told reporters: "It was pretty hard keeping up with Mickey. I was born and raised in a Southern tempo background. Mickey just had too much speed for me. If he wasn't busy at the studio, he was always taken up with something else: his writing; his music; his golf. The breakup was not really his fault. He can't help the way he was constructed. Unfortunately, I didn't find out until too late that I was not the right girl for him. We were just incompatible."

It was now 1943. The twenty-year-old divorcée began to take her career a little more seriously. MGM, realizing her potential, was delighted. They stepped up her grooming process. She was given lessons of every kind . . . taught how to dress . . . to make up . . . to use the best of her tremendous natural assets. Meanwhile, the studio put her in a few films, in small roles, just to get her over that "camera-shy" period.

In April of 1944, Ava was at work in a Dr. Kildare film, *Three Men in White*. Sister Bea, newly divorced, moved to Hollywood. The gals shared a small, two bedroom bungalow in Bel Air. By this time, Ava had become the favorite "target" of every unattached actor and tycoon in Hollywood. Her kind of beauty was rare, and hard to resist. But while she played the field, Ava *did* concentrate on her career.

Happily, she told reporters: "It will be a long time before I marry again. I'm really in earnest about acting."

On October 17, 1945, Ava Gardner became the fourth Mrs. Artie Shaw. It was as though MGM were running a "training stable" for potential Shaw wives. He had already scooped up Lana Turner and made her one of his brides. Now, Louis B. Mayer held his head between his hands in anguish. Shaw had made off with yet another Metro girl.

Ava, one of L.B.'s brightest potential young stars, was playing house again. This time she had married a handsome "ladykiller." Shaw was an intellectual—a brilliant musician—but definitely erratic husband material.

Ava should have realized the storm warnings when Artie took a suitcase of books along on their honeymoon. She should have grown wary when he spent hours every day trying to correct her educational "shortcomings." But she was in love, so she crammed in literature, took a crash course in culture, and found the going very oppressive.

Marriage number two lasted for only ten months. In August of 1946, Ava, at twenty-three, filed suit in Superior Court against thirty-seven-year-old Artie Shaw. In part, her complaint stated that: ". . . Since the marriage, the defendant had treated the plaintiff in a cruel manner, causing . . . grievous mental suffering."

On the 24th of October, 1946, Ava, barely able to hold back the tears, testified that one month after their wedding, Shaw had become "utterly and completely selfish. He disregarded even my smallest wish. He persisted in humiliating me every chance he got. If I remained silent when we were with friends, he said, 'Why don't you talk? Have you nothing to contribute to the conversation?'

"When I *did* try to say something, he would look at me and shout, 'Shut up!' "

By the summer of 1947, Ava was considered a major star-on-the-rise. After making a successful personal appearance tour, she was greeted by reporters eager for a statement on her current romantic status.

"I'm just so happy to be home," she said, "I could kiss the nearest palm tree!"

"Why not kiss a man?" one reporter jested.

"Because," Ava laughed, "he might kiss back." As an afterthought, Ava told the reporters that she would like to make a statement. "Temporarily, I'm through with love. Mind you, I did say *'temporarily.'* You see, for me, marriage is a full-time job . . . and I just don't have the time and energy now to devote to building both a home and a career. That's why I don't want to become romantically involved at this time."

Ava was making her biggest picture to date, *The Hucksters*, opposite Clark Gable. In November 1947, her divorce became final. Once more, she was legally free. Artie Shaw, meanwhile, had not waited for legalities. He eloped to Mexico with another brunette beauty—albeit *not* one belonging to MGM.

The fifth Mrs. Shaw, Kathleen Winsor, had been the rage of the nation ever since she had written the most shockingly sexual romantic novel of the decade, *Forever Amber*.

When the news of Shaw's latest marriage broke, one Hollywood wag commented: "At last, Artie's found the perfect woman—she can not only *read* a book, she *wrote* one!"

Elizabeth Ruth Grable was born in St. Louis, Missouri, on December 18, 1916. When she was a child, the family vacationed in Los Angeles, took a liking to it, and were determined one day to move back. They did. And, by that time, Betty was a twelve-year-old who sang, danced and had no desire for anything except a theatrical career. Her formal education had ended the year before, at the Mary's Institute, a St. Louis girls' school. Now, her mother enrolled her in the Hollywood Professional School, and she started dancing instruction, first with Albertina Rasch, later with Ernest Belcher.

The following year, Betty lied about her age and found employment in bit parts at Fox Studios. After a brief stint there, they dropped her, and she was hired as a dancer in Eddie Cantor's *Whoopee*, for Sam Goldwyn. By 1931, she was doing a stage play, *Tattle Tales*, with Frank Fay.

Grable's early career was a checkered affair. She would get a break—think she was on her way—only to find herself back on the outside again. She sang with Ted Fio Rito's band, then was put under contract at RKO in 1932. There, she had her first "substantial" role, in a Wheeler and Woolsey comedy, *Hold 'Em Jailed*. A series of low-grade "B" pictures followed, and RKO let her go.

Betty went to San Francisco and sang with Jay Whitten's orchestra. Once again, an RKO talent scout signed her. Grable almost got "the break," when she was cast in a marvelous Fred Astaire–Ginger Rogers film, *The Gay Divorcee*, and featured in a specialty production number, "K-nock K-nees," with Edward Everett Horton. She received good notices, but then was given a few more films in which only her legs were prominently displayed. RKO dumped her again.

Grable hit the road in the mid-Thirties. She toured the country in a variety show which starred Jackie Coogan, the famous child star, now fully grown. They fell in love, and were married in 1937, but separated two years later. Betty got her interlocutory decree in October of 1939. By November 10 of 1940, it was final. At the time of their marriage, Jackie, who had earned millions, was penniless. The first year of their life together, Grable's earnings supported the couple, while Jackie sued his mother and stepfather to recover part of his fortune. He lost the suit, but helped to establish the "Coogan Law," protecting other child stars. Through all of this messy business, Grable was there to lend her moral and financial support. The marriage ended without bitterness. Betty just felt she had been "too young." They parted as friendly as a couple can after divorce has entered the picture.

Betty, by this time, had been under contract to Paramount. But that studio let her go, too. It was a key period in her life. The year 1939 had come to an end, and Grable made a decision. She faced reality, and thought of completely quitting show business. After Paramount dropped her, no other studio seemed inclined to pick her up. Although she was only twenty-three, Betty figured she had been around too long. She had been in and out of films for ten years. Then Buddy De Sylva offered her a featured spot in his Broadway musical *Du Barry Was a Lady*. She accepted. But this was to be her *last* attempt. She decided that if she didn't click in the show, she would give up trying to make it as an actress.

Meanwhile, Darryl Zanuck picked up a newspaper, saw a picture of Betty, took one look and called his casting director, Lew Schreiber. He wanted a rundown on Grable. Schreiber told him that Paramount had just let her go. Zanuck said two words: "Find her."

Everyone was under the impression that 20th signed her on the strength of her success in *Du Barry*. Actually, Zanuck had her name on a contract even before she left for Broadway. That was all right with Zanuck. Wisely, he realized that success onstage would give her added value as a motion picture property. He had a strong hunch she would be a hit. He was right.

Grable took New York by storm. She became the girl of the hour. By June of 1940, she was back in Hollywood, and justified Zanuck's belief in her by doing the lead in *Down Argentine Way*. She replaced Alice Faye, who had taken ill. At that time, Faye was 20th's top star, and Betty's selection to step into her role was the entrée to stardom.

Betty, a totally candid lady, admitted that even though she had been under contract to various studios, including the old Fox Company, Zanuck had been the first important executive who ever talked to her.

She dated Vic Mature for a while, but her most serious romance involved George Raft. They had originally met when she was a kid in the chorus of Frank Fay's *Tattle Tales* revue. She hadn't seen him again until she was married to Jackie Coogan, and under contract at Paramount. George, a better friend of Coogan's than of hers, helped Jackie select gifts for Betty. After their divorce, Raft asked her out.

From the moment they began dating, Betty fell madly in love. She had three-dimensional pictures of George plastered all over the walls of her home. The photos were virtually the only things which weren't put there by her interior decorator. But Betty unfortunately fell into the same trap as other women with whom Raft had been involved—there seemed little chance of marriage. Raft was unable to obtain a divorce from his estranged wife, Grace. They had been married in 1923, and, for a while, the marriage worked. But when love disappeared, and Raft wanted out, Grace refused to give him a divorce. Then, when Raft and Norma Shearer fell in love, Grace's settlement demands became impossible. She wanted everything—which would have stripped Raft of his savings and future earnings. So, for all of these years, he had gone with other women—never free to marry.

By this time, Grable's star was rising. She was going from one film to another at 20th, and the public loved her. Meanwhile, Grable adored Raft. She considered him the perfect companion. They had a marvelous time together. They danced, they dined, they took in the weekly prizefights at Hollywood Legion Stadium, and they had a running gin rummy game—with Raft the big winner.

In 1941, Betty and George made a serious attempt to secure his freedom. There was a meeting set up with Grace in the hopes that Betty could implore her to give George the divorce. Grace retained her stiff terms. Betty, who was earning good money, didn't care that George would lose everything. But Raft could not, and would not, give in to the untenable terms.

In April of 1943, Grable, the most popular actress on the 20th lot and the favorite star of G.I.s around the world, confessed to a reporter that she would have married George Raft a week after she met him because she was so desperately in love with him. But now, after two and a half years, she had concluded that there was no future in romance with a married man. She was making *Sweet Rosie O'Grady*, with Robert Young, and talked about the fact that she had just made up her mind her relationship with George was over. So she called him and said "goodbye."

Another man walked into Betty's life. His name was Harry James, and he was one of

1 George Raft and girlfriend Betty Grable. She's being kissed by director Gregory Ratoff. The man on the far right is unidentifiable.   2 Betty Grable and husband Harry James at the Ice Follies. (And look who's in front of them—Jane Wyman!)

America's most popular bandleaders and a genius when it came to playing the trumpet. They originally met in Chicago, in 1941, when Betty did two weeks of personal appearances, and James and his orchestra played at a hotel. Grable admired the James group because she had followed bands all of her life. "But, when we met, all we said was 'Hello. How do you do.'

"When I returned to Hollywood, I told

everyone that I had heard a wonderful band in Chicago. I talked Harry up. The next time I saw him was in 1942, when Harry was cast in my picture *Springtime in the Rockies*. Again, all we said was, 'How do you do.'

"I was still going with George Raft at the time. But Harry and I really got to know each other well early in 1943, at the Hollywood Canteen. It was what you would also call a Canteen romance. He went there every day to play for the boys. I went there on Mondays to dance with them. We had six dates before he went back to New York. In the nine weeks that we were separated, I had a telephone call, a letter, or telegram every day. It was what you might also call a long distance romance!"

For the second time, Betty had fallen in love with a married man. But in this case, things were different. Harry and his wife, Lois, had been separated for a long time. The first Mrs. James obligingly went off to Juarez, Mexico, at the end of June 1943, and divorced Harry, leaving him free to marry Betty.

At 4:05 A.M., on July 5, 1943, Betty Grable became Mrs. Harry James, in a room at the Last Frontier Hotel, in Las Vegas. Betty, dressed in an ice-blue, tight-fitting dress, "bought at the nearest store," was visibly nervous, and trembled as she murmured her "I do's." James wore a somewhat harassed air and picked at his blue pin-striped suit. Their license listed Betty as twenty-six, and Harry Haag James, of Beaumont, Texas, as twenty-seven. It took only five minutes for the minister, Dr. C. H. Sloan, to complete the ceremony, which was witnessed by actress Betty Furness; Manny Sacks, an executive for a recording company and a friend of James'; and Mrs. Edith Wasserman, MCA executive Lew's wife, a mutual friend.

After a hasty wedding breakfast, Mr. and Mrs. Harry James left for Hollywood, where Betty was due to start work later that day.

At the time of her marriage, Betty Grable, who had once wanted to give up show business out of discouragement, was the highest-paid actress in the United States, and on the top of the boxoffice list. Her films, such as *Tin Pan Alley*, *Moon Over Miami*, *A Yank in the RAF* and *Footlight Serenade*, all done in glamorous Technicolor, showed off Betty's "pastel charms" magnificently. They had made her the biggest female star in Darryl Zanuck's "glamour stable."

When Grable first married, the 20th moguls were concerned about her status as the "Number One Pin-up Girl." They need not have lost any sleep. The G.I.s' reaction could best be summed up by a letter Betty showed a reporter, during a lunch break, a few months after she had put on her wedding ring. It was addressed to Harry and read in part: "We ought to be mad at you for marrying the sweetheart of our camp, but it couldn't happen to a nicer guy . . . good luck!"

Betty explained that she and James both had the same public. The young guys, away from home, overseas, or in stateside camps, who went for both of them. "A lot of them have written asking for our wedding photo," Betty grinned. End of problem.

Stardom and total financial security hadn't changed her. She remained unpretentious, handled her own business affairs, still loved the prizefights, ponies and weekly card games. But, even more, her happy marriage put Grable in a motherly mood.

In March of 1944, Betty gave birth to a seven-pound, twelve-ounce baby, after a cesarean section. She was named Victoria, after the character Betty played in *Springtime in the Rockies*, the first film she had done with Harry. Then, after another succession of hit films, such as *Pinup Girl*, *Four Jills in a Jeep*, *Billy Rose's Diamond Horseshoe* and *The Dolly Sisters*, all of which brought many millions to the boxoffice, Grable was ready for the next "personal production."

In December 1946, Betty went into retirement to await the birth of her second child. It was a happy pregnancy. The "Queen of Technicolor" remained easygoing, seldom worried, rarely took a drink, but chewed gum constantly. She was still getting more fan mail than any other star at 20th Century–Fox. The marriage was wonderful. "The sweetest thing that ever happened to me," she said, "was Harry James. I'm a nicer person since I married him. He's a real gentleman!"

The only least bit pretentious thing about the James family in those days was the racing stable which they had acquired. But then, as the highest-paid woman in the United States, she was "entitled" to snuggle up to a few of her own ponies.

During the last week in spring, 1947, Jessica James arrived. She did not make her formal debut until ten weeks after her birth. Then, on July 28th, with a bow stuck in a tuft of hair, she was presented to the press—and weighed in at eleven pounds, three ounces.

Betty and Harry and their two daughters spent the rest of the Forties as contented as a family could be. Grable made a few more Technicolor musical hits, such as *That Lady in Ermine, When My Baby Smiles at Me* and *The Beautiful Blonde From Bashful Bend*. As the decade ended, she remained one of the most fortunate "hunches" Darryl Zanuck ever had.

Rita Hayworth
"NOTHING BUT FUN, ALL DAY LONG"

Rita Hayworth's tongue-in-cheek piece "Nothing But Fun, All Day Long" detailed the frantic work schedule of a screen glamour girl. It appeared in The Hollywood Reporter *on October 8, 1940.*

To paraphrase a well-known columnist [Sidney Skolsky], don't get me wrong, I love motion pictures.

It's so much fun to get up at 5 o'clock in the morning, to take a brisk shower and a brisker rubdown, to gulp a hastily prepared breakfast of fruit juice and coffee and to dash off to the studio while other people are still asleep.

It's delightful to wonder what director Charles Vidor will think about those circles under your eyes, results of studying your script the night before, or what new causticity Director Ben Hecht will spring during the day.

It's heaven to dart from soundstage to portrait gallery where a feverish photographer is waiting to make leg art, fashion pictures and portraits, to change into myriad costumes, to have such things done to one's hair that you begin to feel like a chameleon, or whatever it is that reacts to light and color suggestion.

It's nice to know that when the day's shooting is completed, you can rush to makeup, have that heavy layer of cosmetics removed, slip into an evening gown, grab a sandwich and hurry off to the benefit where people will be so-o-o-o disappointed if you fail to appear.

It's lovely to dye your hair for this part, redye it for the next, to wear dresses that you would get arrested if you thought for a minute of appearing in them in public, to take dramatic lessons by the hour and flirt with tongue-twisting sentences that would be fine tests for a drunken driver.

It's glorious to know that you are only as good as your last picture, that your future, your career and your happiness depend upon an ability to act when you would sooner die, to smile when you're fretting about headlines and to weep when you feel like laughing.

It's wonderful to get a fresh batch of fan mail, to discover that a lot of people think you're terrible, that another school is carping about your publicity, that still more people believe they should be handling your business affairs.

There's nothing like the glow that comes with "blowing" a line, the dismay that follows an awkward gesture, the impatience of skilled workmen with a girl who is trying to get along.

When the thermometer is flirting with 90, it's grand to step in front of lights that might well be used in scouting hostile air maneuvers, to wonder how long that makeup's going to last, to be gay when it would be much more fun to faint.

Then there are the interviews, with sharp, intelligent young men flinging questions that leave no secrets, delving into your life, finding out more about yourself than you knew yourself. Your head whirls and it's like being on a merry-go-round, only you are clinging to the sides of the chair and wondering just how much will appear in the paper, and if so, about the public reaction.

You finish a picture, but can't rest. What if there are no more pictures, or if you're given a part that isn't suited to your personality? You hear about a part you would give ten years of your life to play and you learn that some of the biggest names in the business are being discussed for the role.

Then there are the previews, when you see yourself in the witness box as *The Lady in Question* and wonder why you didn't think about your hands when that particular sequence was being filmed. You see every imperfection and every flaw in your characterization and you smile brightly so that people sitting near you won't know the disquiet and the fear that is gnawing at your vitals.

And the reviews, those beautifully written words that dissect a picture, that make or break an actress. They're such fun to read, with your heart in your throat and a great fear to go on to the next line.

There is the necessity of being a great guy all the time, of being nice to people you never knew before and probably will never see again, of talking gaily about people and places that are only dim meanings in your mind, of dressing always and keeping fit when you would sooner be alone on a desert island.

But, like the lad who did so much griping that one of his colleagues reminded him sarcastically that he had asked for the job, I do love motion pictures and everything about them. Perhaps I've been caught in the maelstrom that's Hollywood, but I don't believe I would trade places with anyone else in the world. Certainly, it's hard work, but there are a lot of other things I can think of I would not rather be doing.

HOLLYWOOD ON THE HALF-SHELL
1946

In January, the JOHN GARFIELDS welcomed a baby . . . and SONJA HENIE and DAN TOPPING split.

In mid-February, HOWARD HUGHES scooped up a bunch of pals and flew them to New York on what was referred to as a "platinum junket." The whole event became the talk of both coasts. Some of the executives who were supposed to be aboard the Constellation with Hughes at the controls failed to show up. But in Hughes' gang were BILL and DIANA POWELL, PAULETTE GODDARD and BURGESS MEREDITH, CARY GRANT and BETTY HENSEL, and one passenger who was kidnapped. CONNIE MOORE, without a hat, toothbrush or coat, had gone to the airport to see JOHNNY MASCHIO off. She was supposed to report to Republic Studios the following morning at eight o'clock, but Howard refused to let her off the plane. He said he would explain everything to her boss, then he locked the doors—and they were airborne.

Everyone who made the trip was given a three-room suite at the Sherry Netherland, plus a car and chauffeur, individually assigned at Howard's expense. Guests' rooms were filled with flowers and fruit. No one was even permitted to tip. The trip was satin smooth—until the last ten minutes—when the big Constellation descended from 20,000 feet through foul weather. But Howard's hospitality was exceeded only by his skill at the controls. He set the plane down in a sixty-two-mile wind for a perfect bumpless landing.

Hughes never left the cockpit during the trip, but invited his guests, one at a time, to sit beside him. An hour before they landed, Howard said to Diana Powell: "Please ask someone to bring me a drink." Diana did a double-take, knowing that Hughes never drank. But he repeated the order. Others, hearing him, thought, "Ohh brother—here we go—he's cracked under the strain!"

Diana went back and told restaurateur DAVE CHASEN (who had provided the champagne supper en route) that Hughes wanted some booze. Dave brought out the pièce de résistance—an eighty-five-year-old bottle of vodka he had been saving. It was delivered to Howard on a tray bearing a crystal glass. Chasen was the only one who was delighted that his host was about to have a nip. Then, to Chasen's horror, Howard took out a big rag, poured the entire contents of the precious bottle over it and wiped the frost from the plane's windshield.

By early April, both JOAN CRAWFORD and RITA HAYWORTH were having marital problems. PHIL TERRY had already moved out of 426 North Bristol, bag and baggage. He had signed a prenuptial agreement waiving any rights to Crawford's money. So the Terrys parted as "amicably" as any two former lovers could—once the affection between them had died . . . But Rita's problems were a bit more complicated. Just as life with ORSON WELLES had been difficult, so, too, parting from him turned into a rather gigantic task.

Meanwhile, BING CROSBY and PAT O'BRIEN sold their interest in the Del Mar Race Track for a handsome profit . . . And VAN JOHNSON was still recuperating from his accident at the home of best friends KEENAN and EVIE WYNN. *That* eventually turned out to be a big mistake for all concerned.

The best party of the 1946 spring season was hosted by four of the town's most handsome and eligible bachelors: CARY GRANT, JIMMY STEWART, EDDIE DUCHIN and JOHNNY MCCLAIN. For weeks before the big evening, they held nightly meetings and planned everything down to the tiniest detail.

They invited three hundred guests and took over the old Clover Club on the Sunset Strip for the occasion. Cary thought the place—which had been shuttered for months—needed some redecorating. By the night of the event, it resembled a tiny palace—complete with tons of gardenias strung up all over the room. MIKE ROMANOFF catered the food. The orchestra was just right. Everything was perfection.

Cary, Jimmy, Eddie and Johnny stood at the door and personally greeted every one of their hundreds of friends. Among the most elegantly dressed were: FRANCES (MRS. HENRY) FONDA, in a gown cut down to *there;* PAULETTE GODDARD, who wore emeralds to match her eyes; JOAN CRAWFORD (complete with her blinding set of star sapphires and diamonds) and RITA HAYWORTH, in a strapless gown that defied gravity.

Spotted in the crowd was the beautiful LADY JERSEY (VIRGINIA CHERRILL), Cary's ex-wife. Rumors circulated that the twosome would get together again now that the "Lady's" current husband was about to be her former spouse. But Virginia quashed the talk. She said she was just visiting Hollywood and had no intention of resuming her picture work, or her romantic attachment to Cary. But she admitted that no matter what—she would *always* love him! As for Cary, he was with pretty blonde BETTY HENSEL (someone remarked that she and Virginia Cherrill looked enough alike to be sisters).

VAN JOHNSON left at midnight with tennis on his mind. But his date, SONJA HENIE, stayed on until way past dawn. IDA LUPINO and BING CROSBY did a marathon rhumba, and "The Groaner" (having a wonderful time) "closed the show" with a song—at 7:30 A.M.—by which time great gobs of guests left for home in the broad sunshine.

At the beginning of May, JOAN FONTAINE became MRS. WILLIAM DOZIER. They were married in Mexico City . . . And BARBARA HUTTON was in love again and romancing international playboy and tennis star BARON VON CRAMM . . . One of the allegations in RITA HAYWORTH's divorce suit against the great ORSON stated that her husband stayed away from their home night after night, just like a common tomcat!

CONSTANCE BENNETT was a June bride when she married Colonel JOHN COULTER. MRS. DARRYL ZANUCK was her matron of honor . . . LAUREN and HUMPHREY BOGART confirmed those stork rumors, as did the ALAN LADDS, who were expecting their second child . . . And OLIVIA DE HAVILLAND began instruction in the Catholic faith in preparation for her marriage to Major JOE MCKEON. But the wedding never took place.

On July 8, 1946, while flying his new XF-11 experimental reconnaissance plane over Beverly Hills, HOWARD HUGHES crashed and the plane burst into flames.

Fortunately, a passerby was able to pull Hughes from the wreckage. He was rushed to Good Samaritan Hospital in critical condition. But four days later, "Lucky" Howard was taking nourishment and dictating letters to his secretary.

While he was still hospitalized, he received word from Washington, D.C., that he had been awarded the Congressional Medal of Honor for his "achievements in advancing the science of aviation, thus bringing credit to his country."

In order that his temporary confinement would not be a total loss, Hughes invented a special bed in which to recuperate at home. The "Hughes Special" had thirty-four separate motors which could do everything from raising and lowering sections to performing fascinating personal accommodations!

ADOLPH and KAY WILLIAMS SPRECKELS gave one of the best parties of the summer of 1946 as attested to by exactly 320 guests who sat down to dine at the lavish outdoor ball that obviously cost a lot of sugar. Since Kay's husband was one of the heirs to the Spreckels Sugar fortune, money was no problem. But many wealthy Hollywood people did *not* have the finesse or know-how to pull off such a soirée.

Everything was exquisitely planned. There was the obligatory overhanging canvas tent (no sides, just a tent top), which was strung over all of the tables. Kay had the largest dance floor this side of the Cocoanut Grove Ballroom set up, and PHIL OHMAN and his orchestra played at dinnertime and were still making music at 5 A.M. The Spreckels even went to the trouble of having the ropes, which harnessed the tent top, strung with garlands of colorful flowers and anchored to the ground by bowls of blossoms.

Among the best dressed was JOAN CRAWFORD. She looked smashing in Wedgwood blue. Crawford arrived with FREDDIE DE CORDOVA, but grabbed GEORGE BURNS and spent half of the dinner hour swinging and swaying with him. LOUIS B. MAYER brought LORENA DANKER (soon to become the second Mrs. M.), and JENNIFER JONES appeared with DAVID O. SELZNICK. Spotted at various tables were the GARY COOPERS, the TY POWERS, GEORGE CUKOR, ESTHER and BEN GAGE and the JOE PASTERNAKS. MARY BENNY, SONJA HENIE, GRACIE ALLEN and ROZ RUSSELL, their heads together, gabbed away most of the evening, while their husbands and/or escorts danced with others. It was a lavish opulent fun party. The guests didn't leave until dawn.

In August, DAVID SELZNICK tossed a spectacular shindig honoring newlyweds EVELYN KEYES and JOHN HUSTON. He invited one hundred and fifty of his "most intimate friends" and dined them outdoors in a setting so effective in lighting, decor and comfort, it was no wonder a lot of them stayed until the sun came up over the mountains—and the band was still playing. At one point in the evening, JIMMY STEWART sat at the piano singing some amusing deadpan songs, with patter provided by HENRY FONDA; in another room, WALTER HUSTON, father of the groom, favored a group with his famous rendition of "September Song." By midnight, a fortune-teller, whom David hired to amuse his guests, collapsed in a heap. Trying to tell famous and beautiful people how *much more* famous and beautiful they would become had taken its toll.

NORMA SHEARER shook everything she had in the right direction and won the jitterbug contest with MARTY ARROUGE. IDA LUPINO won the rhumba contest partnered with RORY CALHOUN. Among others dining and dancing were JOAN CRAWFORD and GREG BAUTZER, the LOUIS JOURDANS, CARY GRANT (still with BETTY HENSEL), LANA TURNER with BOB HUTTON (TURHAN BEY, her ex-fiancé, was nowhere in sight). Also glimpsed were MARIA MONTEZ and JEAN-PIERRE AUMONT, JENNIFER JONES, the host's date, JOAN FONTAINE and BILL DOZIER, and MARLENE DIETRICH and ORSON WELLES—together again! When GEORGE JESSEL proposed the toast to the bride and groom, he ended with, ". . . and I only hope they'll be as happy as I might have been on several occasions."

The REX HARRISONS were the last to take the Tanner bus, which Selznick had so thoughtfully provided, down the hill—parking facilities on the edge of his own cliff being what they were. David was such a great host, many of his guests were still raving about the party long after the newlywed Hustons had had their first serious quarrel.

TYRONE POWER was a big enough star to go on a "private junket" in late August. He piloted his own plane, *Saludos Amigos,* on a goodwill tour of Latin America. Ty explained to local newsmen that when he was a Marine, fighting on Saipan, Okinawa and Kyushu, he had promised himself that "if I ever get out of this I want to travel through Latin America again." His wish came true.

Power and his companion, CESAR ROMERO, were luncheon guests of MADAME EVITA PERON, the First Lady of Argentina, in Buenos Aires. Several days before they had houseguested at the Carrasco showplace residence of ALBERT DODEROS, Argentine shipping and aviation magnate. After dining with Evita, they took off for Rio where they visited President DUTRA. Ty and Cesar also dined with the leaders of Guatemala, El Salvador, Panama, Peru, Argentina and Uruguay.

Mobs greeted them at every airport, and became enthusiastically unruly at Guatemala and Uruguay. The Carrasco landing was followed by a mad autograph session. Women

1

2

3

4

5

6

1 Rita Hayworth at age sixteen, still known as Rita Cansino and signed to a contract by Fox.   2 Gossip-talk between three of MGM's biggest stars: Lana Turner, Esther Williams, and June Allyson.   3 Lana Turner, and the man she claimed was the love of her life, Tyrone Power.   4 Here's the "most beautiful couple": Linda Christian and Ty.   5 Wedding portrait of Hedy Lamarr and John Loder, 1943.   6 Liza Minnelli visits her mother on the MGM lot.

magazine writers found Ty even more irresistible this trip than on his last visit. Their favorable comment meant a lot, especially in Buenos Aires, where the attitude of reporters was considered a barometer of the popularity of Hollywood stars.

In early September, ORSON WELLES returned from Mexico, and he and RITA HAYWORTH reconciled. Lovely FELICIA PABLOS, who just married CORNELIUS VANDERBILT, was the same lady who had been in Hollywood previously under the name PHYLLIS PABLOS. At one point she had almost married composer JIMMY MCHUGH. The new Mrs. Vanderbilt had a young and handsome son who would soon become known in Hollywood as movie star JOHN GAVIN . . . ORSON and RITA split again. She went on to date TONY MARTIN while Welles "returned" to DOLORES DEL RIO.

In October the news that FRANK and NANCY SINATRA had separated hit Hollywood like an exploding bombshell . . . And EVIE WYNN took off for Las Vegas to divorce KEENAN so she could marry their "best pal," VAN JOHNSON. Understanding Keenan even drove his about-to-be-ex wife to the airport. Evie landed in Nevada, had second thoughts, and flew home to Wynn and their two sons.

In November, Hollywood's handsomest couple, LANA TURNER and TYRONE POWER, were glimpsed dining together in a dark romantic corner of a Sunset Strip restaurant . . . ARTIE SHAW was in Las Vegas dating authoress KATHLEEN WINSOR, while AVA GARDNER, Shaw's fifth wife, was furious. MERLE OBERON became MRS. LUCIEN BALLARD . . . And 20th re-signed OLEG CASSINI to design gowns for GENE TIERNEY no matter how long their marriage lasted.

At the end of November, KATHLEEN WINSOR became the sixth Mrs. ARTIE SHAW in Mexico . . . EVIE WYNN and VAN JOHNSON resumed their romance, even though rumors were that Mrs. Wynn and Keenan expected another baby . . . And ANNABELLA reluctantly agreed to divorce TYRONE POWER.

In December, NORA EDDINGTON FLYNN was staying at the Palm Springs Racquet Club and expecting *her* baby momentarily. ERROL, nowhere in sight, was expected to arrive home in time for the blessed event . . . JAMES MASON, seen around Hollywood with a very large entourage, could afford the hangers-on. His wife, PAMELA, was independently *very* wealthy . . . DINAH SHORE and GEORGE MONTGOMERY sent their agent a thank-you gift on their first wedding anniversary. He had originally introduced them at the Hollywood Canteen.

On Christmas Day, W. C. FIELDS died in his bed at Las Encinas Sanitorium. He had been in residence there for a year. Although his 1946 obituary listed a son, and a brother and sister as his next of kin, it was his mistress, CARLOTTA MONTI, who was by his side when he died. W. C. had left instructions in his will ordering his cremation. Instead, he lay for two years in an unmarked grave while various relatives fought over the body—and searched for his missing bank books.

As a pre-Christmas fling, JANE WYMAN and RONNIE REAGAN gave a party at Ciro's for twenty-eight guests, including the GREGORY PECKS, GEORGE and GRACIE, and the JACK BENNYS . . . ROBERT TAYLOR gave BARBARA STANWYCK a fabulous set of earrings, bracelet and choker of rubies and diamonds . . . SUE LADD gifted ALAN with a convertible Buick . . . But the Christmas gag of the season was pulled by young MAUREEN REAGAN, who announced: "Mummy gave Daddy a wonderful big bottle of perfume . . . It's called Four Roses!"

1947

In January, LANA TURNER flew to Mexico just to spend one day with TY POWER . . . GINGER ROGERS and JACK BRIGGS celebrated their fourth wedding anniversary . . . LINDA CHRISTIAN and TURHAN BEY began dating . . . And grown-up juvenile star BONITA GRANVILLE married wealthy Texan JACK WRATHER at the posh Bel Air Hotel.

Between February and March, the marriage of GREER GARSON and RICHARD NEY was over with . . . RITA and ORSON had split for good . . . JOAN CRAWFORD denied she would marry GREG BAUTZER . . . And AVA GARDNER sued MICKEY ROONEY on an old, unsolved income tax matter.

In April, JOAN CRAWFORD gave GREG BAUTZER a

smashing birthday party . . . LANA and TY went to Easter Mass celebration together . . . ORSON and RITA, still shooting on *Lady From Shanghai*, were having terrible tension problems on the set. It was pretty tough for RITA to be directed by her soon-to-be-ex . . . JEAN WALLACE retained a Las Vegas attorney and planned to divorce FRANCHOT TONE . . . LOUIS B. MAYER was granted a divorce from his first wife . . . And insiders, who predicted that VAN JOHNSON would lose his gigantic film following if he married EVIE WYNN, were surprised and happy for Van, who signed a new two-million-dollar contract ten days after the ex-Mrs. Keenan Wynn became his bride!

In the spring of 1947, people were fighting over Frank Sinatra. He was caught in the middle between two cigarette sponsors, both of whom wished to air his radio show. In the end, Lucky Strike's came out on top and Old Gold retreated.

By May, LANA was keeping her fingers crossed that ANNABELLA would hurry up and become the *former* Mrs. TYRONE POWER so that she and her "cherished Ty" could marry . . . Also in the marrying mood, STERLING HAYDEN wed BETTY DE NOON . . . But CARY GRANT and BETTY HENSEL ended their long courtship, and Betty was known to be very despondent . . . HEDY LAMARR divorced JOHN LODER . . . And BETTY GRABLE and HARRY JAMES had a second daughter they named JESSICA.

At the start of summer, JANE WYMAN signed a new multimillion-dollar Warners contract . . . Fourteen-month-old LIZA MINNELLI made her film debut with Mama JUDY GARLAND in *The Pirate* . . . LAURENCE OLIVIER was knighted . . . ANNABELLA still debated on whether to stay in Paris and make a film or fly to Reno, Nevada, and divorce TY. POWER was hoping his wife would be kind enough to give him the Nevada quickie . . .

After a few brief months, ARTIE SHAW's sixth marriage—to author KATHLEEN WINSOR—went sour . . . MIKE TODD and JOAN BLONDELL broke up . . . The HEDY LAMARR—JOHN LODER divorce turned messy when she asked him to pay her room and board for the months that they lived together when he didn't work! . . . And on the 27th of June, Hollywood learned that JANE WYMAN had given birth to a premature baby. The infant subsequently died. Meanwhile, RONNIE was hospitalized with pneumonia.

As July hit Hollywood, there was yet another breakup as ANN RUTHERFORD and department store heir DAVID MAY separated . . . JUDY GARLAND, who had been consulting a psychiatrist for many months, had a nervous collapse. Friends said her marriage to MINNELLI was on the verge of collapsing as well . . . And TY POWER and LANA TURNER were back dining together in dimly lit cafes . . .

August and September were quiet in Tinseltown. The biggest news was that JANE WITHERS and rich Texan BILL MOSS were married in a huge church wedding with twelve hundred guests, followed by an elaborate reception for the same number . . . And, at the beginning of October, VICTOR MATURE, who had bided his time, was back dating his former sweetheart RITA HAYWORTH.

Even baby showers in Hollywood were spectacular. At the end of October, one such event turned out to be so special, it was a long time before any other "daytime—ladies only" affair topped it. Mr. and Mrs. ART STEBBINS (he was DINAH's manager) tossed MRS. SHORE—MONTGOMERY a baby shower. The food- and flower-laden living room looked like the infant department at Saks Fifth Avenue. What loot! Dinah, positively glowing, said she would not eat again until December 16th—the date she expected her first offspring to sing its first notes.

In the center of the dining table was a huge bowl filled with blooms—and a little bouquet of baby roses for every guest. The hosts gave Dinah her baby carriage. ANNE BAXTER HODIAK brought a gorgeous bassinette. BETTY HUTTON showed up with a flower-filled perambulator; OLIVIA DE HAVILLAND came with a pink satin carriage set; MRS. ALAN LADD provided the baby's christening dress. The EDGAR BERGENS sent a wardrobe stand with every outfit an infant could possibly wear hanging from it. MRS. FRED MACMURRAY, GRACIE ALLEN, TERESA WRIGHT and MRS. LOU COSTELLO were among those who admired everything from silver picture frames to monogrammed bibs. JOAN DAVIS took one look at the enormous pile of gifts and sniffed, "Hmpf! *Some* shower! Nobody gave the baby a swimming pool!"

Dinah's husband, GEORGE MONTGOMERY, came later, in a truck, to cart all the presents home.

By November, CLARK GABLE and SYLVIA ASHLEY FAIRBANKS STANLEY had "discovered each other." The twosome became regular diners at BILLY WILKERSON's chic L'Aiglon Restaurant in Beverly Hills . . . JANE WYMAN and RONNIE REAGAN, both sufficiently recovered from the emotional shock of losing their baby, appeared together on the Lux Radio Theatre in *Nobody Lives Forever* and won the highest rating of the season . . . And around town everyone who could afford them was ordering the latest fad product with which to gift their favorite sweetie—full-size juke boxes—perfect for celebrity rumpus rooms.

In December, although ANNABELLA had decided to give TY POWER the rapid divorce he wanted, something had gone wrong with the TURNER-TY "idyll." Quietly, Lana took off alone for New York to make some radio appearances . . . Famed director ERNST LUBITSCH passed away at age fifty-five. He had just signed a fifteen-year contract with 20th and was in the midst of shooting a film, prophetically titled

This Is the Moment . . . And three days after Lana left town, Tyrone Power was spotted with a beautiful young woman dining at L'Aiglon. *The Hollywood Reporter* noted the date, but misspelled the lady's name as "LINDA CHRISTIANS." Soon enough, everyone would *know* who Linda was—and how to spell her name properly.

The brief marriage of heiress DORIS DUKE and the Dominican Republic's playboy-diplomat PORFIRIO RUBIROSA was over before it began . . . And GREER GARSON received a marvelous Christmas gift from MGM—a new seven-year contract which guaranteed her $30,000 a year for life, whether she remained at Metro or not.

Joan Crawford
"THE STAGE IS NOT ALL THE WORLD"

Billy Wilkerson asked Joan to write this vignette for the September 29, 1947, issue of The Hollywood Reporter. *Joan happily complied in her own inimitable style.*

I've been reading in the newspapers and magazines about how noble it is of Joan Crawford to adopt four children.

That is not only embarrassing, but it isn't true. The situation is exactly in reverse. The children are doing the noble things for me—and not I for them.

Regardless of what the legal papers say, the children adopted me. Day after day, in a hundred little ways—the things they say, the smiles they give me, the love they offer me—they have brought me a happiness I have never known before. They've kept me abreast of life, given me new ideas and new hopes.

As soon as I wake up, Christina, who's eight, and Christopher, who's four, start off my day by jumping into bed and wanting to play. I wrestle with them for a half-hour—and sometimes I really take a pummeling—before I send them scooting off to wash up for breakfast. I get more fun and exercise out of those early morning tussles than I would at golf or riding—and when a scene comes along, such as I had in *Daisy Kenyon,* helping Henry Fonda carry a load of lumber, I've got the muscle for it!

Usually they show up at breakfast well washed and neatly dressed but if they don't, back they go. They've taught me the value of molding firmness with love. They get spanked

Joan surrounded by her four adopted children. Left to right: Christina, Cynthia, Cathy, and Christopher.

the same as any youngsters when they're naughty, which isn't very often, and I don't delegate the spanking to others. I administer them myself—and then feel badly the rest of the day until I see them and they kiss me and make up, and everything's fine once again with the world.

They've shown me the beauty of unselfishness. When the babies came—Cynthia and Cathy, who are four and five months, Christina and Christopher had to give up their quarters. They did so without a word and moved into my bedroom to await the time when we can build an addition to the house. They thought it was grand fun.

They've taught me new games and sports. Somehow I never had gotten around to learning to swim. Now the three of us take lessons once a week. They're both good little waterdogs and I run a poor third.

They've rediscovered the comic pages for me. What happens to "Little Orphan Annie" is important in our household and it's a sad day when "Little Beaver" runs afoul of trouble. We yip and yell with high humor over what happens to all of them. Sunday mornings we're up earlier than usual—sometimes it seems to me like the middle of the night—to get the Sunday comic pages.

They've brought back for me the joys of little homey pleasures, such as picnics. Often Sundays we pack a picnic basket and drive to a secluded wooded spot we found a long time ago, and we share our hardboiled eggs and sandwiches with the ants and see how many birds we can identify. We return home dog-tired and hot but with the comfortable outdoor feeling that only a picnic can bring.

Evenings are now something grand to anticipate—even though Two-Gun Christopher and The Outlaw may be shooting up the place. No, it isn't quiet at the Crawford house. Recently when a friend called to spend a "nice, quiet evening," she told me on leaving, "Joan, it was sweet of you to ask me over but the next time I want peace and rest I'll go down to the Union Depot." But there's relaxation in the noise for me. Before the youngsters adopted me, it was entirely too quiet in the house nights and I would rattle around in the place like a ghost.

My own problems don't worry me so much anymore because I've got theirs to think about and somehow, theirs often seem much more important.

Christina goes to public school and Christopher will in another two years. I want them, and the babies, to grow up normally and in the same way as other youngsters, studying the same things, taking part in the same sports and good times. They already have their home studies, their own little responsibilities around the house, and they have their dog, Pupschen, a little dachshund which Otto Preminger gave them. Right now they are having a wonderful time helping the nurse with the babies.

Because I'm afraid they might get false ideas about glamour, I seldom permit them to come to the movie sets. During the filming of *Daisy Kenyon* at 20th Century—Fox, I did make an exception. When Christina finished school, she decided she wanted to go to summer camp. She had only a few days in between and I let her come on the set so that we could be together more.

Because my pictures lately have dealt with adult problems, I haven't permitted Christina or Christopher to see them. Christina amused me the other day when she came to me and said, "Mother, I don't even know what Mildred Pierce did." She still doesn't.

But getting back to the love they have brought me, I had a note from her at camp. It said: "Mummie dearest—I got the candy. It was beautiful. I love you."

It's little things like that which bring me more joy than all the praise from a role well done. Their love constantly reminds me that if "all the world's a stage," the stage is not all the world.

THE REAGAN AFFAIR

On August 15, 1946, Ronald Reagan was nominated to serve as third vice president of the Screen Actors Guild under the incoming president Robert Montgomery, who was succeeding George Murphy. Two weeks earlier, Reagan had become involved in an exchange of correspondence with *The Hollywood Re-*

porter's publisher Billy Wilkerson.

On August 8, Wilkerson wrote a front-page editorial criticizing the American Veterans Committee for intruding in what Billy considered strictly an "industry matter." The situation concerned the rehiring of some MGM publicists who had been in the armed forces. They returned expecting not only to get their positions back but also what would have been their normal promotions and salary increases had they not been in the service.

Billy's accusations against the AVC triggered a letter from Reagan which *The Reporter* printed. Reagan's letter, in turn, provoked a response from an anonymous "wounded Marine." As a result, all hell broke loose.

In part, Wilkerson's editorial said:

Official portrait of Ronald Reagan as president of the Screen Actors Guild. (Courtesy SAG)

We in the industry can settle all our fights, can handle all our negotiations. We not only do not need but will *not* countenance "outsiders" jumping into these fights and negotiations. The American Veterans Committee, which we construe as one of the "fronters" [a commonly used euphemism for communist infiltrated organizations] injected itself into the discussions between MGM and the Screen Publicists Guild about the six publicists who were notified by MGM that their services were no longer needed . . .

MGM's point was that the publicists should be left in the classification they had when they left for the wars, giving MGM time on their return to enable the publicity heads at the studio to determine which of them would be qualified for advancement . . . The Guild thought otherwise and demanded that the years spent in the armed forces should be added to their studio years, thereby shoving them ahead, when in fact they had done no studio work to fit them into the more advanced positions.

MGM and SPG are in positions to straighten out this argument, but the American Veterans Committee, in the

hope of gathering publicity and influence for its work, jumped on the band-wagon . . .

Reagan's reply ran on August 13th under the heading "Open Forum."

Dear Bill:
I have read your editorial in the August 8th Reporter, and sincerely believe that you have been badly informed on several points concerning the American Veterans Committee. First of all let me say that in writing this letter, I am writing as a member of A.V.C. and am in no way speaking officially for the organization.

Number one, you referred to our outfit as "fronters." The inference of course being "red front." That seems a little strange when a few months ago the members of any veterans group were the "heroes" who were defending our country. But rather than hide behind this, I would like to call to your attention the fact that at the recent A.V.C. National Convention in Des Moines, Iowa, a tentative pink infiltration was met and dealt with in true democratic fashion, with the result that everyone was

convinced that the vast majority of A.V.C. members were interested only in perpetuating our forms of democracy. Of course, to deny that there are some "commies" aboard, would be ridiculous as those guys inkle in just about every place.

My second "beef" has to do with your statement that we were outsiders butting into a strictly picture business fight, namely, discharge of the several veteran publicists at MGM. I don't feel free to use other people's names without their permission, but if you will check you will find that the local A.V.C. roster lists an overwhelming majority of the motion picture veterans as members, including many of the big names among producers, directors, actors and writers. That, I think, takes care of the charge that we are outsiders. However, even if we were not members of this business, can you really find anything wrong with a veterans' organization investigating to determine whether an injustice has been done to fellow veterans?

Actually I can't think of any veterans group better qualified to seek justice because no organization has taken such a definite stand in opposition to veterans seeking special privileges. One line from our statement of principles best explains this: "We are citizens first and veterans afterwards."

Without going into the merits of the MGM case I would like to remind you of one thing about veterans' seniority: There is a difference between veterans' special privileges and the right of a veteran not to be penalized for having spent four years away from his career soldiering while those at home in his absence forged ahead. For example, does it seem fair to you that a man who attained the rank of major on the staff of a combat infantry outfit should come back and become a second assistant director to assistants who were behind him prior to the war, and only got ahead of him because he was somewhere on the Western front?

Well, Billy, this is about all I have to say, although I would be happy to sit down and talk this over with you any time. I know that you have the best interests of our industry at heart and I hope I have convinced you that we do, too. Again, may I say, I am speaking as an individual and not officially for the A.V.C. whose record I am sure can speak for itself.

Sincerely,
RONALD REAGAN

In response to Reagan, the following letter ran under the same Open Forum heading the next week.

Gentlemen:

The Open Forum letter from Ronald Reagan made me shed a tear from one eye, because the other is on a landing beach in the South Pacific. I shed this tear because I remember during the war how Reagan, as a Cutting Room Commando at Fort Roach, so bravely fought the war from the polished night club floors of Hollywood, while some of us wallowed in the blood and guts of a dark South Sea Islands front.

On the battlefield a job had to be done and it was done by American lads, like myself, when the chips were down. To come back to a daily life with "brave soldiers" like Reagan spouting off is just a little bit, let's say, nauseating. I went to a couple of the meetings of AVC and if that isn't loaded with Molotov vermin then Joe Stalin is getting ready to become a minister.

General Bradley is doing a great job for the veterans. It doesn't take an organization to get over a plan for rehabilitation! The American people are well aware of the fact that the boys who fought the battle on the battle lines are going to get a real voice in their future. It is the group of Parlor Pinks, it is the well-tailored stay-at-home-boys who fought the war in the night clubs and behind the gates of a well-protected studio, it is the group who trounced the

Japs, on film, while their wives earned hard cash and while they hit the silk sack far, far away from the dull thud of mortar shells—and who now bow toward Moscow, when Stalin speaks, who lead groups like AVC and other pink outfits— that disgust wounded front line fighters.

I'm not bitter. I wouldn't take a million for the experience overseas. A shell didn't hunt out a captain, major or GI during the war. Everyone's number was up. There were no special privileges under fire, and it makes a fighting man mad to read the drivel of a stay-at-home special privileged character because he "happened" to be a name—and being a name was chosen to protect the dance floors of Hollywood from a last-stand Jap invasion.

Time heals all wounds. Time also reveals some of the cover-ups which took place during the war. Washington is getting a load of that now. When the Hollywood history is written, Ty Power, Wayne Morris, John Howard and a host of others who served well overseas will come in for just glory. A page should be devoted to the "Hero Group of Sunset Strip" who should pray to their God that they did not have to go over to drop blood and limbs *but* who now blab for "rights" which every well-deserving veteran is getting—as fast as things can be done.

Sincerely,
A Wounded Marine

On August 21, in the *Reporter*'s main gossip column, the following item appeared:

Personal to Ronald Reagan: It would have done your heart good to know (as we discovered yesterday) how many friends you have in Hollywood—and whose fury at the injustice done you in the letter carried in these pages under Open Forum, kept our phone ringing incessantly. We already knew, as they did, what a fine job you did during the war; that without your glasses you're

"blind as a bat"; how you tried for overseas duty time and again; how you (as Reserve Officer) were one of the first to report for duty and put on "limited service" immediately thereafter. The very, very "courageous" man who signed himself merely "a wounded Marine" must be blind, not only in one eye, but both—and deaf as well. Otherwise he would know (despite the bitterness he denies) that there were lots of "desk-commandos" in lots of places, *but* plenty of guys who were held here despite their sincere efforts to get overseas. Perhaps, Ronnie, he was using his indictment of you as a means of cracking at the AVC which you defend. Well, there are plenty of "wounded Marines" and others who have lost more than one eye in that outfit. And any *informed* person knows that the organization started "cleaning its own house" of crimson elements months ago—and is still sweeping. The Luce publications for instance, which don't even have pink cheeks, were noticeably cool on AVC until recently. But three weeks ago, *Life Magazine* gave it a "clean bill of health" in a signed story; and two weeks ago in its own editorial gave it a plug ending with, "The American Veterans Committee has the right slogan: Citizens first, veterans second." This is the attitude all vets must adopt if they are to avoid damaging from within what they fought so hard to preserve from without.

Then, on August 22, an advertisement appeared which read:

A Letter to the Hollywood Reporter
Someone who signed himself "A Wounded Marine" recently wrote a letter which *The Hollywood Reporter* deemed sufficiently important to print in its Open Forum column.
Those of us who fought in the Marines, or side by side with them, know that most "Gyrenes" worthy of that service would have guts enough to use

their names in connection with their opinions.

The person or persons who actually wrote this letter chose to attack Ronald Reagan for presuming to talk for the GI when he served all of the war here in the States.

As several who have served in various theatres of the war overseas, we will not even attempt to answer and thereby dignify the scurrilous remarks of your correspondent. Even a below-average reporter could have ascertained the facts that Reagan enlisted in the cavalry of the United States Army as early as 1934 and immediately requested a transfer from reserve to active duty at the start of the war. His request for overseas duty was turned down on the score of eyesight so poor that it is a wonder he was able to persuade any Army medico to pass him for any kind of duty.

We who were in the service didn't pick our details. We were assigned to them. Those of us who served in the various war theatres were there for the same military reasons which prompted the assignment of many Hollywood people to at-home posts. We were all placed where the higher echelons wanted us.

The attack on Ronald Reagan is an attack on all in our community who served during the war in work for which their valuable motion picture training best fitted them, work which had to be done at home.

Those who are inimical to our industry for reasons of their own are spreading exactly the type of propaganda to which you have opened your columns. It is shocking to find those who profess to be a friend and spokesman for this industry supporting the dissemination of such unmitigated tripe minimizing the magnificent accomplishments of Hollywood in the war effort . . . both in and out of the armed forces.

Unlike the letter in *The Hollywood Reporter*, this one appears signed with our names.

Eddie Albert
Doug Fairbanks, Jr.
Melvyn Douglas
William Holden
John Howard
Jeffrey Lynn
Gene Markey
Wayne Morris
Audie Murphy

(The men whose names appear above fought in virtually every theatre of World War II. They hold many decorations among them. Audie Murphy is America's most decorated soldier, veteran of eight campaigns, winner of the Congressional Medal of Honor and sixteen other decorations.)

As usual, when Billy Wilkerson was wrong about something, he allowed his paper to give free rein to all of those who disagreed with him. In the end, Wilkerson realizing the error of his original editorial, personally apologized both to Reagan and to the American Veterans Committee. Always a crusader for the conservative point of view, Billy and Reagan remained lifelong friends.

As for the MGM publicists for whom Ronnie had gone out on a limb, precipitating the whole "Reagan Affair," once the smoke cleared and a suitable amount of time had passed, several left Metro to seek their fortunes elsewhere, while the rest received the promotions and salary increases they'd sought. But the whole incident was illustrative of the beginning of Reagan's deep public commitment to causes he considered worth championing, as well as to his ability to clearly articulate a point of view in which he believed.

Another note of historical significance was to be found in Reagan's rapid rise to a key position of leadership in the Screen Actors Guild—his springboard to immortality. Seven months after his August 15, 1946, election as third vice president of SAG, Robert Montgomery, the president, resigned. He was going into film production and felt there might be a conflict of interest. So, in March 1947, Reagan ran for Montgomery's office, and won. That November, he was re-elected president and served six successive one-year terms as Hollywood's extremely visible and highly articulate spokesman for the actors' most powerful organization.

In the October 26, 1948, issue of *The Hollywood Reporter*, there was an ironic item which read: "The Man in the White House [Harry S Truman] would certainly like to get his name on a ballot like the one Ronald Reagan, as incumbent, has on the Screen Actors Guild ticket. SAGers have only one choice for president, one for vice-prexy and one for second veepee only . . .''

THE STARS SPEAK OUT

The year-end special anniversary issues of *The Hollywood Reporter* were always a great therapeutic outlet for celebrities who wrote byline pieces about what was happening in their lives at that moment. Some chose to offer Billy Wilkerson vignettes that revolved around their current films or their career lives in general. Others adored reminiscing about where they had been—and the miracle of how far they had come.

It is interesting to note how many very good performers also had a facility for writing, for expressing themselves with style and a certain flair. They seemed to get a genuine kick out of reversing the tables, so to speak. Availing themselves of the opportunity to see their names in print attached to something *they* had written—rather than something *written about them*.

The following group of pieces, all contributed to *The Reporter* in the Forties, is illustrative of the quality of literary talent the stars possessed.

Humphrey Bogart
"LOCATIONING IN MEXICO"

Bogie employed his famous offscreen wit and wisdom in a September 1947 vignette he wrote for The Hollywood Reporter.

Somehow, I don't get this routine. I mean a guy calls me up and says he wants a piece for the paper.

What am I supposed to do? Be Humphrey Bogart, the way my mother reared me, or be the Humphrey Bogart like they see on the screen.

I consult my crystal ball, and get a wrong number. I consult my wife, Lauren, and—well, she's a pretty good number, but I get a wrong answer.

I even consult my publicity department—and they tell me *I'm* the wrong number. So I've got to do this thing myself, and I'll be just as surprised as you are what comes out at the end of 1000 words. If I've got that many.

So let's do it this way. John Huston calls us together one day and tells us what the caper is. We're flying down to Mexico for a picture called *The Treasure of the Sierra Madre*. That's a plug, brother, and the last one. From now on we're on our own.

It's one helluva story by a guy—or is it a gal?—named B. Traven. Nobody knows who B. Traven is, but Warner Bros. didn't have too much trouble in sending him (or her?) the check for the rights to the story. [*Author's Note:* At the time this piece was written, and for many years afterward, the actual identity of writer B. Traven *was* a mystery at *his* request.]

Anyway, the picture is about three guys who are on the bum and who go into the mountains of Mexico in search of gold. Sounds like Roy Rogers and Trigger could do it with no trouble at all, doesn't it? Well, they could—but to get serious for a minute, I'm glad they picked Bogie for the piece. And Walter Huston and Tim Holt.

I'm not sentimental about this motion picture business. It's a living and a good one. But every so often you get your teeth—courtesy Dr. Cowan—into a part and this was it.

So to get back to that caper John Huston was telling us about. He wanted us to go into Mexico. Down into those sultry mountains for eight weeks. Heat and mountain climbing and snakes and all that. It sounded rugged, but he sold us on the deal.

And I'm glad we went. As long as the guy says I can write anything I want, I'm going to tell you something about Mexico. It's a great country. Not only those spots like Mexico City, Acapulco, Cuernavaca or Taxco. Those are wonderful places, but they are tourist spots.

We went high into the mountains more than 100 miles north of Districto Federal. We met the people at home—their own homes. And you'll never meet better people.

You've heard of beavers? They're drones compared to the way these Mexican boys work. We had a few of our own technicians down there, but they were backed up by experts from the motion picture industry in Mexico. Those boys know their business—and what they didn't know they wanted to learn. And they learned fast.

And another thing. Come six o'clock or whatever quitting time "Simon Legree" Huston decided on, they didn't head for the nearest pub and a glass of cerveza. They'd whip out those guitars and mandolins and give us one of the nicest concerts you'd ever want to hear.

We taught them a few things about making motion pictures—they taught us how to live. I even tried a few bars on the guitar myself.

And I find I'm much handier with a tommy-gun.

They've got a great spirit down there. They know that their educational system isn't all that it should be, just for instance. And they're working towards one like we have in this country. But meanwhile, until the school construction program can catch up, everyone who can read or write is teaching somebody who can't. And I mean *everyone.* They're progressive. They're ambitious. They're proud of their country—their nationality—and they are determined to make the world proud of them.

And they'll do it, too.

But to get back to this *Treasure* . . . It was the damndest location I ever was on. And I've been on some pips. We had nice quarters—sure. But that John Huston didn't make any shots around that beautiful little resort village where we stayed. No. He had to go up into the hills. Hills? I mean *mountains!* High ones and rugged. We'd go as far as we could in a cab, and then walk. Walk for miles until Huston said, "This is it."

We'd stumble over rocks and stones and cactus and sagebrush. We'd dodge snakes and scorpions and things that must have been Gila monsters. The guy was a bundle of energy and I was a bundle of old, tired, left-over atoms.

And who do you think was the guy who made with the laughs and quips and told us "youngsters" to "chin up, stout fellah"?

Walter Huston, of course!

Maybe John was just trying to show up his dad by making us go on all those rough trips. If he was—he missed! Walter took the heat, the climbs, the rocks and the snakes like they were something you found on Stage 14 at Warner Brothers.

Well, anyway. We went to Mexico. And we made *Treasure*—I mean we made a picture. We liked the country and the people. And after it was over do you know what happened?

Walter went up to his ranch to round up a lot of dogies.

Tim went back to his studio to make some westerns.

Bogart collapsed.

He's planning on a vacation. In Mexico.

Jeanette MacDonald
"HALF THE WORLD IN HALF A DECADE"

In September of 1947, Jeanette MacDonald, one of Hollywood's greatest stars, wrote this article for The Hollywood Reporter. *It gave some insight into Jeanette's "other life"—as a singing star on tour.*

You can study your geography from the fifth grade on, making careful note of the location of the headwaters of the Missouri River and the principal exports of South Dakota and still know very little about your country. That's what I found when I took a sabbatical leave from pictures five years ago and set out upon my concert tours. It was no definite thought of studying my country. My uppermost thought was to sing well enough in concert to bring home some good reviews as a lyric soprano rather than as an actress.

Now that I am back on the screen, I find that, rather unwittingly, I have absorbed a great deal about the western hemisphere and the British Isles, through my concert tours as well as camp shows and hospital appearances, which I still continue. I have found, too, that there is no such thing as an American type. True, certain locales produce certain colloquialisms, but I have seen gabby Yankees and taciturn Texans, gay Scotchmen and dour Irish. No blood strain has a corner on any attribute, be it good or bad.

I have thought, since my tours, that we in Hollywood run a great danger of becoming too insular. I know I was near it when I left. Hollywood is such a tight unit in the American scene that a Hollywoodite's map of the world is apt to show one large eastern seaboard area labeled "New York," and one west coast section labeled "Hollywood." There are a few pin dots scattered over the map reading, "Sun Valley," "Palm Springs," "Miami Beach," "Bermuda." The space between is arid waste. There are no dots reading "Cincinnati," "Sioux City," "Augusta," "Spokane."

During my tours, I found they were not only dots but thriving cities with people buying life insurance and washing machines, with money earned from the growing of wheat and the manufacture of egg beaters.

I was scheduled for a concert in Robin Hood Dell in Philadelphia and I reached the city at noon the day before the concert. I went to my hotel and directly to the Dell to rehearse with my accompanist. We worked on the entire program and the next morning we were back again, doing the same thing. We took time out for lunch and I decided to rehearse one more song and then go back to the hotel for some rest. I walked on the stage facing the rows of empty seats and I noticed a half dozen nuns sitting quietly way at the back.

A man who had been working on the lights came up to me and said, "Miss MacDonald, those nuns have come in on the bus from their convent thirty miles out to hear you rehearse. They are not allowed to attend public gatherings at night." I was anxious for my rest so I sang the one song we were still smoothing out and turned to walk off the stage. There was a timid spatter of applause from the back of the house. I signaled to my accompanist to play another song. We ran through the entire program before we were through, playing to our six-woman audience.

When we were through they walked to the edge of the stage and one of them said, "Miss MacDonald, we want to thank you so much for singing for us. I have heard you sing before but never your concert numbers. You see, before I entered the order, I was in the chorus at MGM when you made *Naughty Marietta*." They turned and left and I went back to my hotel determined that never again would I try to categorize people. They have a way of slipping out of the tidy cubby-holes your mind builds for them.

When I sang at the Zoological Gardens in Cincinnati, the management had not anticipated as many ticket buyers as appeared. It was during the war and the lumber shortage was acute and they had built as many temporary seats as possible. Then they began to sell standing room. When I got to my dressing room, there wasn't a scrap of furniture in it. The built-in dressing table and mirror were still in place and there were some hangers on a pole, but there was nothing to sit on. I called the stage manager and he said, "My God, I *told* them to take every chair in the place and they did! They've sold your chair for someone to sit on out front!"

I began to put on my make-up leaning down in front of the mirror when a tap came on the dressing-room door. I opened it. There stood a little man straight from a print of the Paris Boulevardiers. He wore striped trousers, spats and a cutaway and carried a derby. Without a word, he whipped out a hunting seat at me, the kind preferred by the 'orsy set, with the small platform on top of a cane thing. Then he covered the top with a linen handkerchief, handed it to me and still without a word, frisked out. At great risk to my sacroiliac, I balanced on the thing while I finished my make-up. This fey creature appeared in Cincinnati—not Vienna, Prague or Paris.

When I was in Scotland, I was scheduled for a concert in Edinburgh and, during an interview, I mentioned that I was disappointed in being unable to take back any tweed yardage with me. It was forbidden by the government because I had no ration points. The thoughtless remark appeared in print and the next day, a man came to my hotel with two suit lengths of luscious tweed in a wonderful smoky gray and an earth brown. The girls in the woolen mill had read the interview and had pooled their clothes coupons to secure the wool for me.

These are three things, small things, yes, which happened during those memorable five years I was away from the picture business. Not one moment would I erase. Waiting on cold train platforms at midnight—muddy coffee served as an entire breakfast—getting to towns before my trunks and having to buy some weird dress covered with pompom things from the local Bon Mode shop—all of them are precious memories. But mostly, it was wonderful to meet people. I kept remembering that old lyric from the revue,

"Climb down from your steeple,
Meet the common man;
You'll find him wonderful;
He's not the kind that the papers extoll—
But he's a power in the Gallup poll."

The five years have taken me from the Pacific coast to the highlands of Scotland, and I loved all of it. When I went back to MGM to make *The Birds and the Bees,* I stepped back into the studio world with a long backward look over my shoulder. I love making pictures but I'll never again think the world is bordered by Washington Boulevard and the MGM back lot.

Gene Kelly
"DANCING MEMORY"

Fame did not come easily to Gene Kelly. In September of 1947, he wrote this vignette for The Hollywood Reporter. It was a perfect example of a genuine talent "paying his dues."

Every actor has his own fond memories about his first professional engagement. Some are good, some are bad. As for me, I'd rather forget the whole thing. Trouble is, it's the kind of memory that sticks. It happened in Chicago in 1932.

I had just arrived from Pittsburgh, where I had been operating a dancing school. Believing I needed some additional experience, I decided to close the school for a few months and see what I could learn in Chicago. I hit town jobless.

The Windy City was really living up to its reputation. A stinging gale whipped across town that March afternoon and the thin overcoat I was wearing flapped around my legs. Bucking the raw wind, I went to the office of a booking agent I knew.

"How about it, Mac?" I said. "Have you got anything for a needy hoofer?"

"When do you need it?" he asked, watching me pull a couple of cold hands out of my overcoat pockets.

"Three guesses."

"Gene," he said, "I've got just the right spot for you. Best of all, you can start tonight. It's in a night club on the outskirts of town and you play three shows. Pay isn't much, but it'll help get you started."

"How much is the pay?" I asked.

"Well," he fumbled, "as I say, it isn't much. But it will help you get started. And it's only three quick shows. Five dollars."

I gulped a couple of times.

"You want it?" he asked.

"I'll take it."

The one truthful thing Mac told me about that job was its location. It certainly was on the outskirts of town. The trip took an hour and two trolleys.

I knocked on the door of the club at 8:30. The manager greeted me frostily and told me, in a few well chosen words, about my routine.

"Dance a little, sing a little," he said. "Then break the monotony with some patter. Make it last about 25 minutes."

I had 15 minutes to get my act in shape. I think of that snappy time limit every once in a while when I'm working in a musical film. Let's see, we spent more than five months on *The Pirate*. I do five dance numbers in the picture, so that's about a month to a dance, if you want to figure it that way.

Well, that night I put on my little act for three shows, at 9, 12 and 2. At 2:45 A.M., I dragged myself to the manager's office.

"May I have my five bucks and leave now?" I asked.

"Not until after the fourth show, buddy," he answered.

"What do you mean, fourth show? I was told there are only three."

"There are four shows. Four shows!"

"For five bucks?"

"For five bucks."

So I stayed for the fourth show, which went on at 4 in the morning.

When I finally got out of the joint it was raining and I had to wait an hour for the trolley. I got back to town at 7. My feet ached, my eyes were raw, and I was famished. I bought breakfast and shuffled across the street to a hotel. After some sleep and a shower I felt better. I decided to go back to Mac's. Perhaps he'd have something less exhausting.

"Well, Gene," he smiled, "how was it?"

"Lousy," I told him.

"I guess it was," he admitted, "but maybe I can find you a better spot for tonight. By the way, haven't you forgotten something?"

I looked at him in surprise. "No, what?"

"My commission, old man. You know as well as I do—ten percent."

I left four-bits on Mac's desk and jingled the few coins left in my pocket. I had to smile. Discounting carfare and commission, I had played four long shows for $1.02½ each!

Any wonder I'd rather just forget the whole incident?

I'd rather dwell, in recollection, on the past five years, right here in Hollywood. They've been very exciting and interesting.

The transition from stage techniques I'd used in *Pal Joey* to dancing before a camera has been accomplished, I believe. Closeups don't scare me anymore. I have, I hope, become a screen actor, in the interim between *For Me and My Gal* and my current picture, *The Pirate*, both for Metro-Goldwyn-Mayer, where I'm under contract.

But I remember how awed I felt when I got my first closeup. The stage can't give you anything like it. A closeup can even be made to show what you're thinking! Nothing in the whole field of drama offers greater psychological possibilities, or offers the actor a greater chance to show himself as he really is in his role.

Then, too, I have outgrown the first impatience I used to feel during filming. Shoot a few minutes, then hold everything! It seemed to me like an awful lot of starting, commencing, beginning, getting ready, to get something done—like, say, to create a fleeting impression that would be on the screen only twenty seconds!

Like every newcomer, I wondered if possibly I might not create a sensation by pointing out new ways to save time.

Well, I'm over that, because, many pictures since, I have come to understand that this is an industry that strives for perfection. Being the "worrying type," I had to figure it out for myself.

And the conclusion goes something like this: Millions and millions of persons see a motion picture.

Suppose only forty millions—a really small total—say, see a given motion picture; for example, the picture with our 20 second fleeting shot that took four hours to make. Forty million people times twenty seconds each of their time, equals more than twenty-five *years* of audience time! So what're four hours to give them the fleeting scene that may remain one of the unforgettable memories of the film.

No, I don't believe there are many shortcuts when you play to the millions and millions!

Incidentally, this little bit of arithmetic I've given you, shows, from a new angle, I believe, just how tremendously important our world motion picture audience is.

For one hundred million people—or whatever the figure is—I think I'm a little low—you'd better try to be right!

That's why, in my opinion, Hollywood filmmakers seem to outsiders, who visit the sound stages, to be taking their time when, actually, they are making slowly their "haste" which takes time—the kind that must be taken if the finished product is to come anywhere near the perfection to which the world's film fans are entitled.

Looking back, it seems a long, long time since I did those four shows for $1.02½ each.

From what I've learned in the motion picture business, about the enormous outputs of energy and talent to satisfy the world demand for entertainment, I know now that when I got $1.02½ each for those four night club performances in Chicago, I was overpaid!

A motion picture—even only a fair one—would have given the customers a far better break for their money.

Hattie McDaniel
"WHAT HOLLYWOOD MEANS TO ME"

Hattie McDaniel, the first black performer to be honored with an Academy Award, contributed this touching and meaningful piece to the September 29, 1947, issue of The Hollywood Reporter.

An utterance of a first century Jewish scholar, "I am become all things to all men," can very aptly be applied to Hollywood—film city of the world. To the blue-nosed moralist, it is a city of gin and sin. To a producer it is an exacting place of business. To the actor or actress, it is a powerful potentate, holding in its hands honor or oblivion. To the tourist from Salt Lake, or Peoria, or Milwaukee, Hollywood is a man-made fairyland.

Sixteen years ago, I was a tourist from Milwaukee.

I had headlined on the Pantages and Orpheum circuits, but vaudeville was as dead as last month's hit song. The stock market crash of '29 had left big business paralyzed and every town had its breadline and hobo jungle. Entertainers were a dime a dozen and even at that cut-rate price there were no takers.

Milwaukee was really my springboard to Hollywood. I landed there broke. Somebody told me of a place as a maid in the ladies' room at Sam Pick's Suburban Inn. I rushed out there and took the job. One night, after midnight, when all the entertainers had left, the manager called for volunteer talent from among the help. I asked the boys in the orchestra to strike up "St. Louis Blues." I started to sing—"I hate to see that evening sun go down." . . . I never had to go back to my maid's job. For two years I starred in the floor show.

I was little more than a kid, but I was old in show business. I won a medal in dramatic art when I was 15. One year later, my oldest brother Otis, who wrote his own show and songs, persuaded my mother to let me go on the road with his company. I loved every minute of it, the tent shows, the kerosene lights, the contagious enthusiasm of the small-town crowds.

Sam Pick's patrons were nice to me, but they kept asking me one question that disturbed me—"Why don't you go to Hollywood and get in the movies?"

Some friends were driving to Los Angeles. They persuaded me to come with them. I had a shiny new pocketbook but very little cash in it.

People are always telling me about the "lucky break" I got in pictures. I don't take the trouble to tell them of all the years I sang in choruses, worked in mob scenes, thankful for the smallest thing. A call from Charlie Butler at Central Casting was like a letter from home, a bit part with a line of dialogue was like manna from heaven.

Old Father Time has a way of shuffling along and as the years went by I found myself working with such great stars as Joan Crawford, Jean Harlow, Clark Gable, Irene Dunne, Barbara Stanwyck, Will Rogers, Margaret Sullavan, Bette Davis and Jimmy Stewart. Many extras complain about getting tired of sitting around on the sets. I never tired. A soundstage was as exciting as a William Spears mystery. I learned so much, just sitting and watching.

From incidental comedy roles, David O. Selznick cast me as Mammy in *Gone With the Wind*. I was now a recognized featured player and although I had had other large roles at most of the major studios, this was my first chance at a straight dramatic role. For it, Hollywood bestowed upon me its greatest seal of approval, the Academy Award for the best supporting actress for 1939. I shall never forget that night at the Ambassador when Fay Bainter so graciously presented me with the coveted award. It was one of those always-to-be-remembered nights. Everybody was shaking hands and congratulating me. It was like Old Home Week in Kansas.

My own people were especially happy. They felt that in honoring me, Hollywood had honored the entire race. That was the way I wanted it. This was too big a moment for my personal back-slapping. I wanted this occasion to prove an inspiration to Negro youth for many years to come.

Recently, Hollywood had been criticized for its portrayal of the Negro on the screen. I have been censured by some of my race for not joining in the denouncement. Many of those loudest in their condemnation are newcomers who do not remember the days when no Negro player was given a dressingroom, when there were no hairdressers on the sets for Negro actresses, when no studio hired a Negro wardrobe girl. I have seen many changes in the film city and the trend has been one of increasing gain. We have been welcomed into the unions where the rate of pay is standardized. Members of our group have served on the board of directors of the Screen Actors Guild. Louise Beavers now serves in that capacity.

Critics have said that Hollywood insists on casting all Negroes as menials or clowns. Our memories are short-lived. In one of MGM's Dr. Gillespie series, Lionel Barrymore watched a Negro doctor (Jack Carr) perform an operation in a New York tenement house. Clarence Brooks played a Negro doctor in *Arrowsmith*. Stymie Beard, formerly of Our Gang comedies, Ida James and another Negro girl were classmates of Shirley Temple in the graduation scene of *Since You Went Away*. Leigh Whipper stood out against lynch law in *Ox-Bow Incident*, and again in *Mission to Moscow* he portrayed the Ethiopian Emperor Haile Selassie, who walked out of the Peace Conference after his prophetic voice painted the dismal picture of Fascist growth and terrorism. Caleb Peterson was a dignified veteran in *Till the End of Time*. During the war years, Rex Ingram, Kenneth Spencer and the late Ben Carter were soldiers.

I have never apologized for the roles I play. Several times I have persuaded the directors to omit dialect from modern pictures. They readily agreed to the suggestion. I have been told that I have kept alive the stereotype of the Negro servant in the minds of theatregoers. I believe my critics think the public more naive than it actually is. As I pointed out to Fredi Washington, "Arthur Treacher is indelibly stamped as a Hollywood butler, but I am sure no one would go to his home and expect him to meet them at the door with a napkin across his arm."

George S. Schuyler, brilliant Negro columnist of the *Pittsburgh Courier*, had this to say about my role in *Three's a Family*: "There is no more reason for assuming this maid to be typical of the Negro race than there is for assuming that the old, almost-blind physician in the picture is characteristic of the medical profession when he tries to deliver the wrong woman of a baby. It seems to me to be good, rousing slapstick, at which Hollywood has traditionally excelled. No farce is factual and no intelligent person expects it to be."

If I speak from a personal angle it is not because I am not aware of what Hollywood has done for others. In one picture, *Imitation of Life*, Louise Beavers became famous. Hollywood made practically unknown Lena Horne into an international singing star, it sent Eddie (Rochester) Anderson's stock sky-rocketing.

I have never gotten over my crush on Hollywood. At heart, I suppose I am still a tourist from Milwaukee!

June Allyson
"MOVIES WERE MY TEACHER"

In October of 1948, June Allyson wrote this very personal vignette for The Hollywood Reporter.

There's a great deal in that old saying, "If you want a thing enough—you'll get it." Oh, I hold no brief for these terribly determined people who will get to the top regardless of whom they hurt to do it. But I also have no patience with so many people today who sigh deeply, roll their eyes and say, "It must be wonderful to dance and act. If only I had enough money to take lessons I just know I'd succeed."

Well, money and lessons help. Let's face it. But on the other hand, if the determination is there, if that urge to dance or act or to do anything is really there, it will take more than a lack of money to smother it.

Whenever I bump into kids today who think they need careers handed to them on silver platters, my mind goes back a few years. It goes back to the year 1940, to be exact, when I ran around with a lot of youngsters in New York show business. Most of us were hoofers. Sure, we had ambitions, plenty of them. We all wanted to be actors and actresses. But lessons were definitely out. We had scarcely enough money to buy our glass of orange juice and a hot dog for dinner.

At the time, I was understudying Betty Hutton in *Panama Hattie. Pal Joey* was playing at the theatre next door. A friend of mine, Miriam Franklin, had a number of friends in the next theatre, and one in particular she thought I should meet. She invited us to her apartment one evening. Her friend turned out to be Van Johnson.

Van, just like me, and the other kids, had dreams of someday becoming an actor. But dramatic lessons were out. Our salaries, as understudies, were mighty small. But we settled for the aforementioned hot dog and orange juice at Nedick's, the open-air stand on Broadway and 45th Street, and took the money left over to buy movie tickets.

The movies proved our dramatic school. Van idolized Spencer Tracy. He still does. I thought Margaret Sullavan the greatest actress on the screen. And still do. So we automatically had dates when either of the two appeared in a film. We'd go to the movies and sit, not through a single showing, but three or four times.

Later, in the living room, or Central Park, we would act out the scenes we saw. We'd criticize each other's performances. Tear each other to pieces. Then try it again.

One night Van admitted that he, too, would like to try Hollywood. He said all the sunshine would be swell, but he was doubtful if he could make the grade as a movie actor.

I can hear him now as he said, "It would take a mighty good camera to photograph my mug." I reminded him that not all actors looked like Robert Taylor and I didn't see why he couldn't try it. We kidded and talked about what we would do when we were motion picture celebrities—how perhaps we'd even play in a picture together.

As you know, it all happened as we dreamed it would. But it didn't happen by sitting and wishing we had money to take lessons. It happened by taking the only course open—cutting down on food for the price of a theatre ticket. Watching good artists act. Going to movies to learn, not to be entertained.

It's really surprising the valuable training one can get from motion pictures if he goes with a real desire to learn. I didn't realize this myself for many years. And then one day I happened to go to one of those early pictures that Fred Astaire made with Ginger Rogers. When I saw them dance together I made up my mind. I would learn to dance.

How?

There wasn't enough in the family budget to allow for dancing lessons and so I decided to learn from the films. Fred Astaire films, that is.

I went to every Astaire picture that came to my home town, Mount Vernon, New York. And not once, but at least six or seven times.

After watching an Astaire performance I would go home and try to do the steps from memory. The incessant tapping of my feet wore the varnish off the living room floor. My attempts to duplicate the Astaire leaps proved disastrous to a valuable lamp which mother prized highly. Our attic was ransacked for a top hat and an old cane resembling those used by Astaire in some of his numbers.

But I learned to dance.

And the only teacher I ever had was Fred Astaire.

I remember *The Gay Divorcee* particularly, having seen it eighteen times to learn the routines.

Then one day I overestimated my talents in the presence of friends. I claimed to be able to dance, and well. They dared me to prove it by trying out for a Broadway show.

The sinking feeling in the pit of my stomach is still there when I remember that day. Dozens of girls were lined up for the trials. More than once I was tempted to bolt the place. But the thoughts of facing my friends kept me glued to the spot.

At last it was my turn. A piano somewhere started to pound out a rhythmic tune. I gritted my teeth, got onto the stage and did a poor imitation of an Astaire routine.

But the job was mine. It was in the chorus of *Sing Out the News* on Broadway. And it was dancing that eventually resulted in a break before the Hollywood cameras.

It was several years later that I had an opportunity to thank my unsuspecting teacher for his instruction. I had been in Hollywood six months when the meeting unexpectedly occurred.

One day I was driving my very old automobile on the lot. It stalled near a soundstage and I couldn't get it started. I got out and worked over it.

Then it occurred to me that maybe it was almost out of gas. I headed for the Metro-Goldwyn-Mayer gas station and as I rounded a corner two men suddenly loomed in front of me. They scurried out of the way but scored a near miss. Then I saw that one of them was Arthur Freed, the producer. He turned to introduce me to his companion. It was Fred Astaire.

For years I had dreamed of meeting Astaire. I had pictured myself wearing one of those lovely, flimsy gowns that Ginger Rogers always wore.

Well, it didn't turn out as glamorous as that. As a matter of fact I never mentioned the part he played in launching me on a career in the entertainment field until months later. I just blushed, mumbled something stupid, and flew down the street.

Now, this may sound detached and unimportant. But the point I'm trying to prove is the importance of motion pictures to people who feel that their future lies on the stage or before the cameras. Do without other things, if you must, but keep on going to the movies. Learn to watch with a critical eye. Decide the type of acting you want to do, then never miss a picture featuring the player you feel has the qualities you seek.

Certainly, schools and instruction are important and necessary—provided there is money enough to afford them.

But don't say "quit" if the budget won't allow it. The finest teachers in the world are at your disposal for the price of a movie admission.

Lucille Ball
"IT'S ALWAYS LUCY"

In October of 1948, Lucille Ball reminisced in The Hollywood Reporter *in this piece about her triumphant return to RKO Studios. She had left there less than famous—and had returned as a star.*

All in all, it was an overwhelming reception. I didn't really expect the brass band, the parade of clowns and animals and the huge pennants reading, "Welcome Home, Lucille Ball." I didn't expect any of that and it was lucky—because I didn't get it. But there was more excitement and self-satisfaction in the friendly smiles and warm handshakes on the RKO-Radio lot than in any of the other Ball-for-President ceremonies. After six long years away from the studio where I received my first breaks I was returning—a star, with all the trappings and privileges thereof.

When I signed for my role in *Interference* I could only daydream along Small-Town-Girl-Returns-to-the-Fatted-Calf lines. The last time I had seen RKO was on a bright summer's day in 1942, upon completion of an epic known as *Seven Days' Leave* with a "beautiful hunk of man" called Victor Mature. He was to be in *Interference* too, only now he was hailed as a sensitive, intelligent, interpretive actor. That was the first change!

I looked for others, and found them. Like being allowed to park my Buick on the lot. When I had been here before, the cops would

An early portrait of Lucille Ball.

measure my bicycle and then try to bend it double to save space!

My dressing room came as a pleasant surprise: living room, bathroom, bedroom, hot and cold running water, hot plate, refrigerator, etc. The only thing I recognized was the closet—which used to be my former dressing room! Compared to the "flat-tops" I had previously occupied, this was the Taj Mahal—with Venetian blinds, yet.

I realized as I stood there, swinging a cat without hitting any walls, that I must be prepared to act the star. After all, was I not Lucille Ball, who had toured successfully for one year in *Dream Girl?* Was I not Lucille Ball, who had starred in a succession of big pictures since leaving the lot? A sidelong glance in the mirror convinced me I was. These people had known me in my hamburger days but look at me now; I was on the RKO menu under Chef's Suggestions: "Lucille Ball Special—Ground Steak with Onions—$1.00." I had really arrived—the Leo McCarey sandwich was only 70 cents!

Arranging myself in the most soignée pose I could strike, I prepared to receive the hordes of makeup men, hairdressers, wardrobe women, publicity guys, assistant directors and dress designers who would want to consult me about my taste and desires for the role. I had barely set the stage when the first visitor arrived.

It was a grip who had worked on several of my previous films. He poked his head in the door. "Hi, Lucy," he yelled, "welcome home." Dropping my lace handkerchief, I raced over to shake his hand. What the heck—this was an old friend. That started it—I never did have another chance to play the Duse role I had assigned myself. Sure, people came around to consult me. But instead of sitting at my feet, awaiting pearls, they clapped me on the shoulder, tousled my hair, called me "Lucy," told me gags, and—and, I confess, I loved it.

These workers had known me when, through disputed talent but boundless energy, I worked myself from a $150 a week showgirl all the way down to a $50 a week actress. Now that I had achieved a degree of success, they were delighted and I realized that their tributes were sincere and true. That I had not changed to a point where they approached me, hat in hand, gave me a feeling of pride.

Everyone seemed to go out of their way to be nice to my beautiful mother and my wonderful maid and aide-de-camp, Harriet, on the set. Mother (one of those exotic women whose real name—no kidding—is Desiree) just couldn't get over how wonderful people were.

Vic Mature took her to lunch one day at Lucey's, for example, and she ordered him out of house and home—well, almost. She didn't eat breakfast that day—just anticipating that free feed with The Man. "Now I know you've arrived, kid," said Mom. "The head waiter called me *Mademoiselle* and I heard somebody say, 'There's Lucille Ball's old lady'." Mother's wonderful!

And before, when a telephone call came in for me on the set, the operators generally just threw up their hands and said, "Who's she?" Now, when Desi phones me at the studio they practically stop production to get us together over the wires. Romance—even on Gower Street—can be beautiful.

I recall that my biggest thrill came one A.M. when the publicity director, Perry Lieber (who knew me when!), forgot himself and greeted me with a cheery, "Good morning, *Miss* Ball." That, my friends, was living!

But the nicest things about returning to RKO were the memories—reminders of pictures like *Stage Door* and *The Big Street*. Somehow I always seemed to make my best friendships on this particular lot—characters like Eve Arden, Charlie Lang, Helen Parrish and (wouldn't you have known?) a fellow named Desi Arnaz, a hot-blooded gentleman I met one fine day in the commissary.

Well, I thought, there must be other compensations to star billing on a home lot. There were. I was informed that I would be allowed to eat in the executive dining room, instead of at the counter. I tried it one day: the prices were 50 cents higher and the atmosphere 30 degrees cooler. To get a steak you merely had to wave an annuity policy. Outside, it was cheaper, noisier and filled with tourists. I decided I would rather be asked for my autograph than for my opinion. Besides, I'm an incurable romantic. In the fourth booth from the door I had met Desi, and beneath this gown by Edward Stevenson lies a heart—not of gold, which is such a common metal in Hollywood—but just a heart. I like lunches well-seasoned with memories.

But there were changes. Assistant directors would phone me in my ivory tower and say, "We'll need you in an hour. Can you be ready?" instead of the well-remembered, "Where have *you* been? We've wasted three minutes looking for you." I also learned I had traveled all the way from leg shots to portraits as far as the still man was concerned. And there were special fittings in wardrobe in place of a leftover Ginger Rogers dancing dress.

One incident really clinched it. One day on the set, when everything had gone wrong, I displayed a little (how do you Americans say?) temperament. In what I considered my most ladylike manner I protested, entreated, pleaded, stormed and quivered. The net result: hilarity.

As the makeup man came over to dab the sweat from my fevered brow he murmured, "Anything for a laugh, eh, Lucy? You haven't changed a bit."

Oh, well, "star-shmar" as we used to say back home in Jamestown, New York. Just call me Lucy.

Gregory Peck
"CRITICISM IS HEALTHFUL"

Gregory Peck credits a reviewer's critical slam for helping him on the road to Hollywood success. On October 11, 1948, the following piece appeared in The Hollywood Reporter.

If it hadn't been for a critic in Philadelphia, I might not be in Hollywood now. Maybe I might not even be an actor.

Seven years ago, after I had played in several road show companies, Guthrie McClintic offered me a role in *Morning Star,* which would try out in Philadelphia before opening on Broadway. It was my first real chance and I was tense and eager.

The morning after our first performance, I riffled nervously through the newspaper, searching for the review. My eyes ran right past Gladys Cooper, Wendy Barrie, Jill Esmond and Rhys Williams and stopped when they landed on my name.

As nearly as I remember, the reviewer extolled me in these words: "Mr. Peck looks more like a wax dummy in a tailor shop than an actor headed for success on Broadway."

Well, I wasn't exactly in a state of exuberance. Never before and never since have I felt so low. I could have slithered right under that proverbial snake's belly. I wasn't even conscious of eating breakfast.

I wasn't mad nor did I feel like writing the review off as the personal dislike of one person for another individual's performance. I suspected strongly that maybe I had been too tense and too eager. Although I had played in summer theatres and had been on the road in *The Doctor's Dilemma* with Katharine Cornell and in *Punch and Julia* with Jane Cowl, I simply hadn't had the experience or the background for the excellent company I was acting with in *Morning Star.* I needed a few more years on the stage.

My wife, Greta, and I talked matters over and we decided that if we took the review to

heart and worked industriously, maybe I might look better to the New York critics by the time we arrived there. That would be a mere week hence. She sweated it out with me, helping me until far into the night, and somehow or other, that one week's prodigious effort did show up because the Broadway critics thought well of my performance.

I don't remember the name of the Philadelphia reviewer or of the newspaper because in my anxiety at the time I was only concerned with his critique, but he may easily have saved my career for me. If it hadn't been for him, I might have never known what was specifically wrong with my performance or, for that matter, that anything was wrong with it. Unlike in the movies, in a play the actor cannot sit in the audience and look himself over with a critical eye.

Since the Philadelphia episode, I have liked reviewers, those who are honest and sincere. And most of them are. Only occasionally do you find one who uses a play or a film as a peg on which to hang a witty piece of his own, often satirical, and he, of course, is not a critic but a humorist in his own right. But the drama editors who attempt to pen an impartial and unprejudiced opinion of a performance contribute vastly more to the theatre and motion pictures than some of us at times may realize.

They are not infallible, of course, and sometimes may err in their judgment, but they serve to keep us struggling to improve as actors. They save us from the great sin of contentment, and nothing perhaps is more fatal to an actor than that. In his *Study of History,* Arnold Toynbee points out that those countries and peoples achieved the most who were forced to meet and solve certain challenges, such as the challenge of environment, of external pressures, etc. In the case of the actor, the critic acts as the challenge of external pressure, which must be met and solved as only an actor may—by never-ending study and effort.

The reviewer offers more than merely a pressure, however. Sometimes he provides a blueprint, other times only clues, about how a play or scenario could have been strengthened, or the performance of a player tightened up and heightened. These may be the only clues a player ever receives. His director, at the time the play or movie was being whipped into shape, may have told him in all good conscience that he was doing an excellent job, and others may have congratulated him. They may have been extremely honest but erred because they were too close to the product for proper perspective. No one turns out a bad play or film deliberately, although the court jesters like to infer that such is often the case. Everyone in any creative field, whether it is painting, writing or acting, attempts his best. But it's only the critic, remote as he is from the creation, who brings an objective point of view.

For several years now, I've kept a scrapbook and in one part of it, I paste the bad notices. And I've had plenty of them. Some of the most unflattering remarks—those points that I think I might overcome—I have underlined in red ink. Before I begin a picture or a play, I get that scrapbook out, partly to remind one Gregory Peck that he may improve with more work and partly to study the pieces and make certain I will not repeat the same mistakes.

The day I began *Yellow Sky,* in which I play an outlaw of the post-Civil War era, I brought that scrapbook to my dressing room on the stage and between shots I would sneak it out, when no one was looking, to check over my past mistakes. As I keep telling my dog, Perry, it's only human—and dog-like—to make a mistake, but only a mutt will commit the same error twice over.

It's healthful, I'm convinced, to get whanged over the ears occasionally. It draws us all up sharp to take inventory. It makes us realize that we do not know fully the secret of acting.

The good reviews provide helium for the soul, of course, and they make a day about perfect, but I'm inclined to take the attitude of an oldtimer. Someone had praised him lavishly to the skies. He turned and said with a glint in his eyes, "Well, mother, pin a rose on me!"

Mario Lanza
"ALGER HAD NOTHING ON ME"

In 1949, Mario Lanza, whose glorious voice was compared to that of the Great Caruso, wrote a biographical article for The Hollywood Reporter. *In reading Mario's words, that old cliché about "fate" seemed more true than ever.*

I've been catching up on some back reading.

After noting in press and magazine articles that I'm a Horatio Alger character—I decided to find out whether that was bad or good.

Now I know. And while there was little time for reading books in my youth I can safely say that had I read these stories I would never have believed them. At the time, that is.

To tell the truth, I'm still not 100 percent certain that these past few years haven't been a trumped up dream anyway. Looking back at those early days on Mercy Street in Philadelphia I wonder how, of all the kids there, one Alfred Arnold Cocozza happened to be so lucky.

I wasn't born in Philadelphia but in New York City. My family moved to Mercy Street when I was only a few months old and my earliest recollection is of dodging gangster bullets that whined over my head with startling regularity.

There was no room for shy or artistic temperaments in our neighborhood. Arguments were loud and intense, and the inevitable resulting fights—bloody.

Dad and I shared a great understanding and a love for opera in general, and Caruso in particular. Any extra pennies we could scrape together, over and above the family needs, went for recordings. We listened together, my father and I, even before I could talk. It was a great bond. "Vesti la giubba," was a great

Mario Lanza and Kathryn Grayson in MGM's *That Midnight Kiss*, 1949.

favorite. At seven I knew it by heart. Five other operas, plots and main arias were added to that favorite list by my tenth birthday.

I was twenty years old before I finally sang. To this day I don't know why, or how. Sitting in my father's room listening to Caruso sing "Ch'ella mi creda" from Puccini's *Girl of the Golden West,* I suddenly opened my mouth and began to sing with him.

The record finished and I looked up and straight into the face of my father. He was standing in the doorway, tears in his eyes.

During the week that followed, time each day was spent singing with Caruso records. Then my father came to me.

"You must study," he said.

"No," I answered. "What I am doing is only noise."

But father insisted and so it was that I enrolled with a vocal coach who started work on a number of standard arias.

All of this went on without the consent of my grandfather who believed young men should work, and not waste time listening to silly music played on a music box. He put up with what he termed as "nonsense" for three months before he exploded. That explosion was louder than any of the gang wars I heard during my youth.

The inevitable result was a job with grandfather's trucking concern. From this point on the resemblance between me and the Horatio Alger boys is amazing.

My first job was to deliver a piano to the Philadelphia Academy of Music Auditorium. There, in the overalls of a moving van employee, I bumped into William K. Huff, impresario for the Philadelphia Forum concerts. Only a week before, at the insistence of my vocal coach, I had auditioned before him. He remembered me.

Huff had an idea. There was an empty dressing room adjoining that of the great conductor, Koussevitsky, who was rehearsing for a concert at that particular time. What Huff proposed was that I go into that empty dressing room and sing.

It worked. I was singing "Vesti la giubba" when Koussevitsky burst in. After bestowing a kiss on each of my grimy cheeks, the maestro insisted that I begin preparing immediately for the Berkshire Music Festival to be held that summer. I agreed, without knowing what the Berkshire Music Festival was all about.

That was one of the greatest experiences of my life. When it was over it seemed like a dream. But when offers for concerts and recordings began to arrive the reality of the experience finally dawned. Which offer to accept posed a problem, but not for long. About this time another contract arrived in the mail. It was from the United States government and began—Greetings.

The first stop in the fulfillment of this contract with the Army Air Force was Miami, Florida. After this came a period of training at the Marfa Air Base in Texas. Then, quite by accident, I met a staff sergeant, Peter Lind Hayes, who was forming an Air Force Show and in Marfa looking for talent.

The next week my transfer to Phoenix, Arizona, was effected. The show was a hit, and through it Moss Hart had Hayes, dance star Ray McDonald and me transferred to his Air Force stage show, *Winged Victory*.

Those years following my release from the Air Force were rough. I was fully aware of my great need for proper training. I also had to live. Then, at the crucial moment came a turn of events that even Horatio Alger would have found it difficult to imagine. By chance I met Sam Weiler, a business man whose hobby happened to be music. Weiler became my patron making it possible for me to study, for the first time in my life, without the worry of trying to live in addition. The first step was to find the finest teacher available. He was Enrico Rosati, an exponent of the old school.

After fifteen months of study both Rosati and

Weiler decided that the next step should be practical experience. There were numerous engagements but the motion picture chapter of this story started at a Hollywood Bowl concert. The morning following this appearance, Mr. Louis B. Mayer, head of Metro-Goldwyn-Mayer, made an offer. This was followed by a command performance at which the program of the night before was repeated for some sixty top executives gathered together on one of the studio sound stages. This, again, was the cue for dream music. I couldn't believe it—even when I walked away with a contract in my pocket.

My life in Hollywood is all that I could ask. The Metro-Goldwyn-Mayer contract is a more than generous one—permitting me to spend six months of each year making motion pictures and the remaining six months for concerts, or study, or whatever I prefer. The first picture, *That Midnight Kiss,* in which I appeared with Kathryn Grayson, Ethel Barrymore, José Iturbi and all the rest, was one of the happiest experiences of my life. Director Norman Taurog, as well as the cast, was the essence of patience and helpfulness.

Naturally, my ultimate goal is a high one—someday, somehow, to sing at the Metropolitan Opera House. But as much as I want it, as much as I dream about it—this will have to wait until I feel that I'm ready. How long this will take is a question to which there is no answer—at the present, anyway.

In the meantime I want to learn, to study, to work. It is little enough to pay for the wonderful things that have happened to me. I have had my full share of luck. The rest is up to me.

Victor Mature
"IT COULD ONLY HAPPEN IN HOLLYWOOD"

Victor Mature, one of Hollywood's all-time favorite he-men, was extremely articulate. In this vignette which he wrote for The Hollywood Reporter *he scored a lot of points with his innate wisdom. It appeared on October 31, 1949.*

It's an international pastime to knock Hollywood. Even Canasta won't replace it.

Invariably, every yarn about Hollywood's ineptness, stupidity, lack of judgment, winds up with:

"It could only happen in Hollywood!"

Hollywood and its workers are no more infallible than the people of any other vicinity or industry. Its mistakes are merely more highly publicized, more widely commented upon, because more people are interested in Hollywood's movie making and makers than in any other single occupation or art. (Praise be, or I might still be simonizing cars!)

There's always the tale of the illiterate producer. I'll tell you one myself. An author brought me a play to read. I thought it was great. I rushed it to a producer I'd met, enthused about it, begged him to produce it. He read it, commented with typical Hollywood brevity: "It stinks." Someone else produced it later (minus me) and it was acclaimed the finest play of the year.

"It could only happen in Hollywood?" It happened on Broadway!

You've heard and read repeated tales about Hollywood not recognizing talent under its nose; how pretty little geniuses have to work as waitresses to eat because they can't get inside a studio casting office, then head for Broadway and fame before Hollywood will sign them. Sure it's happened, but not only in Hollywood.

Plenty of Hollywood stars couldn't get a break on Broadway. Betsy Drake, for instance. She couldn't get a walk-on, and worked as her agent's secretary's secretary for fifteen dollars a week. She got her first real stage break in London, in *Deep Are the Roots.* Cary Grant of Hollywood saw her in that and was responsible for bringing her to Hollywood. She clicked in her first picture, and she'll be an even bigger hit in her second, *Dancing in the Dark*.

You've also heard about experienced movie players who couldn't get anywhere in Hollywood until they made a hit on Broadway. Sure, it happens. It happened to Betty Grable, who didn't get out of the rah-rah college gal pictures until she scored in *Du Barry Was a Lady* on Broadway. But, for every lovely like the *Wabash Avenue* star (Phil Harris and I are in that opus, too), there are a dozen players who never got a Broadway break until they became

Hollywood stars. Spencer Tracy, for one.

Mind you, both Broadway and Hollywood have been mighty good to me, but you don't hear the universally nasty cracks about Gotham, where a competent player can also plug along the Great White Way without attracting much attention, or achieving star billing, or getting away from "type casting." An example? Richard Widmark, who was merely a pleasantly competent Broadway leading man the world never heard of until movie director Henry Hathaway gave Dick that menace role in *Kiss of Death*. It took the movies to de-type stage actor Widmark!

A favorite cliché about Hollywood is that producers' wives are the real talent scouts for the head man. That, definitely, could only happen in Hollywood, they say. What about *Turned Up Toes* star, Paul Douglas, who knew Who's Who on Broadway and couldn't get a break on the stage. When Garson Kanin wanted "a Paul Douglas type—only an actor"—for *Born Yesterday,* it was Kanin's wife, Ruth Gordon, who suggested it might be a stroke of genius to try Paul Douglas to read for the Paul Douglas-type role. That happened on Broadway.

Then there are the tall tales and true ones about Hollywood stars who get too big for their britches, become difficult and uncooperative. Believe me, it happened on Broadway long before Hollywood had a name and became the world's target for the name-calling.

And the cracks about Hollywood stars who insist on choosing their own stories, and turn down pictures which win Academy Awards for the players who supplant them. It could only happen in Hollywood? Judy Holliday became a Broadway star in *Born Yesterday* after two big-name actresses turned down the same role.

How many times have you read high-brow dissertations on the "sterile handling of Hollywood's talented writers." Yet a recent Broadway musical, combining the talents of the nation's greatest popular composer, a noted lyricist and a famous playwright, proved a flop. No Hollywood producer was involved. Everyone makes mistakes once in a while—not just movie moguls.

As to Hollywood directors who supposedly turn down competent actors for "no good reason," despite the fact the actor read the role well. That happens, too. Maybe the actor is too young, or too old, too bald, or fat, or thin for the visual conception the producer, director, or casting director has of the character. More often than not—and I saw Cecil B. DeMille

do it often on the *Samson and Delilah* set—the director will give the actor another spot in the picture.

But if you want a weird reason for an actor losing a job, how about this one, which didn't happen in Hollywood: A New York producer once sent for Arthur Treacher to read for a role in a Galsworthy play. The producer, the author, the director all were sold on his reading of the role. But an aide spoke up, said: "I'm afraid we'll have to give the role to the other chap—Treacher's too tall for the second act scenery—the African huts, you know." Mr. Treacher suggested that they get the Singer Midgets, headed for Hollywood and film fame, which brought him better Broadway roles and salaries only a movie actor commands on Broadway.

Hollywood press agents get their share of blasting, too. Oh, those inevitable clichés, like the gateman-who-doesn't-recognize-the-star oldie! John Barrymore and a lot of famous stars before him had it happen on Broadway, and had it publicized, too. More recently, José Ferrer told me on the *Whirlpool* set that when he shaved the two-year growth of beard he wore as *Iago* in *Othello,* the stage doorman and some of his best friends failed to recognize him.

The press pokes fun at Hollywood pin-up titles; the public, they say, is weary of hearing them—The Body, The Look, The Gams, etc. But Hollywood press agents weren't the first to invent the tags. They didn't, for instance, name me "the hunk of man." It was a line Gertrude Lawrence used about me in *Lady in the Dark,* and the dignified Broadway drama critics picked it up and made it famous. To go further back, it was the French press who tagged Sarah Bernhardt "The Divine Sarah."

Speaking of Bernhardt reminds me of the wearied darts about film stars who announce their retirement, and keep on making their "last picture" year after year. It's a toss-up whether the Divine Sarah or Sir Harry Lauder, both international stage stars, made the greatest number of "farewell tours."

Other p.a. tales that irk the public are too numerous to mention. But I recall appearing with a lady playing a young and virginal creature. She was superstitious about removing her wedding ring, so wore it covered with flesh-colored adhesive tape in the play. That happened on Broadway.

But it's a favorite in-and-outdoor sport to take a poke at Hollywood's foibles, and even the Broadway-ites who have deservedly achieved both artistic and financial success in Hollywood aren't immune to the game. Moss Hart, for instance, was a house guest of *Whirlpool* producer Otto Preminger, in Hollywood, and greatly enjoyed his daily swim in Otto's pool. Hart went back to New York and let forth an amusing blast to the press agent anent Hollywood's swimming pool brigade! I recall Otto mentioning being a guest at Hart's Pennsylvania farm, which boasts a swimming pool, too. The only difference is, Hollywood pools are usually inhabited by beauteous babes. Mr. P. dived into Moss' pool and found himself swimming alongside a snake—and I don't mean the human variety.

Of course, everyone takes a crack at Hol-

lywood films—even Hollywoodians. People constantly ask why Hollywood can't produce as fine pictures as the Europeans do. Who says all European films are wonderful—certainly not Europeans. I've talked to plenty of them who admit we see only their finest films here. They wish their own run-of-the-mill productions equalled even the Hollywood B's.

There are, obviously, good and bad people and pictures in Hollywood, just as there are good, bad and indifferent people, and plays and pictures on Broadway, or anywhere else in the world.

Don't get me wrong. I love Broadway. But why keep saying: It can only happen in Hollywood!?

HOLLYWOOD ON THE HALF-SHELL
1948

In January, young actress PATRICIA NEAL was signed to co-star with RONALD REAGAN in *John Loves Mary*. Pat had the distinction of being the tallest actress on screen. She stood 5′8½″. Her nearest "rival" was Alexis Smith, a mere 5′8″. Hollywood was happy to welcome KAY and ADOLPH SPRECKELS back to town. They had sold their Beverly Hills home and lived for a while in San Francisco. But they returned and bought a huge Bel Air mansion. Gay Kay had been very much missed among the elite set.

In February, RED SKELTON and RONALD REAGAN did their good deed when they staged the first annual "Basketball Carnival of Laughs" at the Shrine Auditorium. Skelton's team was composed of GLENN FORD, BURT LANCASTER, ART LINKLETTER, DON McGUIRE, disc jockey PETER POTTER, JACKIE "Rookie of the Year" ROBINSON, MICKEY ROONEY, ANDY RUSSELL, DAVID STREET, FORREST TUCKER and KEENAN WYNN.

Reagan's group included BEN BLUE, EDDIE BRACKEN, JACKIE COOGAN, DENNIS DAY, BILL GOODWIN, JERRY LESTER, ROBERT MITCHUM, DENNIS MORGAN, WAYNE MORRIS, GENE NORMAN, MAXIE ROSENBLOOM, BARRY SULLIVAN, football great KENNY WASHINGTON and JOHN WAYNE. JACK CARSON, disc jockey AL JARVIS and BOB WATERFIELD were the referees. JACK CARSON emceed the "Giant After the Game" show, which was headed by Skelton, PEGGY LEE, BEN BLUE and DAVID STREET with the MELLO-LARKS. DORIS DAY, ANITA ELLIS and ADELE JERGENS acted as cheerleaders. The affair was sponsored by the Beverly Hills Kiwanis Club

for the benefit of the Pacific Lodge Boys Home.

There were rumors that pioneer director D. W. Griffith was not feeling well. All attempts to speak with him were frustrated until March when he gave an interview to Ezra Goodman, which appeared in *The Hollywood Reporter*.

> I am seventy-three years of age. I can say anything I want about Hollywood . . . What's the difference? I don't give a hoot what anyone says about me . . .
>
> . . . I love the change of seasons. I would love to be in New York again. The most brainless people in all the world live in Southern California . . . But, for certain financial reasons, I am exiled from the East.
>
> I was spoiled in my youth. I had my first poem, and my first play and story published at the same time—I thought I was a genius. That was a lot of baloney. Today nobody is interested in D. W. Griffith. I don't kid myself. They don't know who I am—some old s— of a b—.
>
> . . . I go out sometimes to see movies. I love the damn things because . . . my brain is negligible now . . . The best pictures I did were not popular. The lousy ones, like *Birth of a Nation,* only a cheap melodrama, were popular.

Four months later, D.W. died. Six hundred of Hollywood's most important citizens attended memorial rites. More than a thousand stood outside of the Hollywood Masonic Temple. For a few hours, Griffith was back on the

1 Attorney Greg Bautzer, one of Joan Crawford's longest-lasting flames, and Joan.   2 Mr. and Mrs. David O. Selznick (Jennifer Jones).   3 John and Shirley Agar and their baby daughter, Linda Susan, in January 1948.   4 Lana Turner on her wedding day to sportsman Bob Topping, 1948. To Lana's right is the best man, *Hollywood Reporter* publisher Billy Wilkerson, at whose home she was married. To Turner's left, Hollywood columnist Sara Hamilton. This, however, was not a lasting union.   5 Mr. and Mrs. Clark Gable on their wedding day, December 21, 1949.

boulevard he once loved. At the hour of his services, work in every major studio ceased—for three minutes.

CAROLE LANDIS and her wealthy husband, HORACE SCHMIDLAPP, split . . . CHARLIE CHAPLIN and OONA and their tiny children left for England. Rumors were that the Chaplins would make their permanent home abroad.

In April of 1948, JOAN CRAWFORD topped all of her other great parties when she gave an affair in honor of NOEL COWARD. She took over the whole Papillon Restaurant, and had her close friend, BILLY HAINES, former actor-turned-decorator, make the place into a small garden of Versailles. It was gorgeous, complete to the showers of pink gardenias which hung from every conceivable spot.

Joan's date and co-host was GREG BAUTZER. They made a divine couple. He, so handsome in his dinner clothes. She, so exquisite in an all-white gown, with the gleaming "Crawford diamonds" around her neck, on her wrists and hanging from her ears. Seated on Joan's left, Noel, her British guest of honor, beamed at the amazing turn-out of celebrities who had come to welcome him to Hollywood.

The guest list was a "Who's Who" of Tinseltown. It included such luminaries as: IRENE DUNNE and DR. FRANK GRIFFIN; GINGER ROGERS and JACK BRIGGS; DOROTHY LAMOUR, who used to date BAUTZER, with her spouse, WILLIAM HOWARD; CELESTE HOLM and her husband, SCHUYLER DUNNING; BARBARA STANWYCK and ROBERT TAYLOR; LORETTA YOUNG and TOM LEWIS; MARLENE DIETRICH; JANE WYMAN; GENE TIERNEY; the RAY MILLANDS; the ZACHARY SCOTTS; CLIFTON WEBB and his mother, MAYBELLE; DAVID NIVEN and his bride; CLAUDETTE COLBERT and DR. JOEL PRESSMAN; ANNE BAXTER and JOHN HODIAK; DICK POWELL and JUNE ALLYSON. Even two of Joan's ex-husbands, DOUG FAIRBANKS, JR., and FRANCHOT TONE were there—with *other* wives—of course. However, Crawford's most recent "ex," PHIL TERRY, was not present.

The dinner was sumptuous. The music was sweet and romantic. The entertainment was fantastic. DINAH SHORE and TONY MARTIN sang. JACK BENNY clowned and played his fiddle. Then Benny and CELESTE HOLM did a comedy patter routine. Finally, the brilliant, witty, oh-so-talented Mr. Coward sang for his supper.

In May, the biggest gag line around Hollywood: "Now that HOWARD HUGHES has bought RKO, what do I give him next Christmas?" By June, GLORIA GRAHAME had become MRS. NICHOLAS RAY . . . In July, STEWART GRANGER married JEAN SIMMONS, while JENNIFER JONES' ex, ROBERT WALKER, married director JOHN FORD's daughter BARBARA . . . CAROLE LANDIS was found in her home—a suicide. One of the most dedicated performers, she had traveled many thousands of miles during wartime to entertain the troops.

To illustrate ELSA MAXWELL's "connections," three of the guests who came to her party on the Riviera in August of 1948 were the DUKE OF WINDSOR (former KING EDWARD VIII), TYRONE POWER and CLARK GABLE. One of the discoveries of the evening was how much royalty had in common with members of the acting profession. During dinner, the Duke leaned over and asked Tyrone Power, "What's your best profile?"

Tyrone, nonplussed, replied that he hadn't given it any thought. "But I'm told I photograph pretty well from every angle," he added.

Clark Gable volunteered that *his* left profile was better than his right.

"That's more like it," replied the Duke. "Well, when I was King (*that* was an attention-getting way of starting a story), the stamp and coin people came to take my picture for a new issue. They started to arrange the pose and asked me to face right. You see, my father's picture was a left-sided profile and the tradition was that each new King's profile faced in the opposite direction.

"Well, we ran into some difficulty. I explained to the stamp and coin people that my right side was *not* my good side. They insisted that it was impossible to upset tradition but, after all, what was the point of being King if I couldn't exercise the one small prerogative of deciding from what side I wanted my face photographed!"

Profile-conscious Gable nodded understandingly. "I won the argument," said the Duke, "but it wasn't much of a victory. I posed with my good side in profile and they took the pictures—but only a few stamps were issued and the coins were never minted. Of course," added the man who gave up the throne of England for WALLY SIMPSON, "they really didn't have much time."

Also in August, West Coast television had its first Hollywood premiere on the 18th. The occasion was Don Lee's dedication of its new TV studios, on Vine Street, combined with a celebration for its promotional affiliation with Hearst's *Los Angeles Examiner* newspaper. After twenty years of rehearsal as the first station in the country, KTLA went "pro." The show they offered was strictly an "A" production.

All over Los Angeles, people rushed to see the big event. There were crowds huddled in front of store windows, as well as guests seated in those lucky livingrooms that had TV. What they saw amazed them. There were heretofore unimaginable video performances by such show business greats as Edgar Bergen, Mickey Rooney, Eddie Bracken, Johnnie Johnston and Garry Moore, who emceed. The Meglin "kiddies" performed, and Harry Zimmerman's orchestra provided the music.

The next day, the word went out: TELEVISION IS HERE!

The favorite Tinseltown quotes of the fall season came from VICTOR MATURE, who had relinquished his title as "America's Number One Sweater Boy": "I can't help it if I've got a good set of muscles. I want to prove I've got something more. I'm tired of being nothing but a male strip-teaser" . . . MICKEY ROONEY: "I think Hollywood people are as nice and normal as any neighbors you'd find anywhere. They're just a bunch of people who enjoy giving their talents and time and energy to the public. They do a lot of good and bring happiness into this world. They're completely normal, and after all, it's normal to be normal" . . . ORSON WELLES: "When I don't roll my eyes, quote Shakespeare and glow in the dark, people are disappointed" . . . And finally, from JOAN CRAWFORD: "I would play Wallace Beery's grandmother, if it was a good acting part!"

The comedy team of DEAN MARTIN and JERRY LEWIS had become the rage of Hollywood. They appeared at Slapsy Maxie's Club, were signed by HAL WALLIS and Paramount, and became the fastest-rising duo in the history of show business.

In October, ORSON WELLES confessed that he had accepted a role in *Prince of Foxes* only to raise enough money to produce and finance two Italian films starring his newest girlfriend, LEA PADOVANI . . . And INGRID BERGMAN journeyed to London to discuss making a picture in Sicily with well-known director ROBERTO ROSSELLINI. It was a meeting that would have historic repercussions . . . The BING CROSBYS celebrated eighteen years of marriage . . . And beautiful young ELIZABETH TAYLOR dated pal ARTHUR LOEW, JR., while her real boyfriend, football great GLENN DAVIS, was out of town.

In November, at a formal dinner party given by EDIE and WILLIAM GOETZ, in honor of DANNY KAYE, JANE WYMAN removed all possibilities of a reconciliation with RONNIE REAGAN when she said: "LEW AYRES is the great love of my life!" But by the following month, the AYRES-WYMAN romance had cooled off considerably . . . ZSA ZSA GABOR received a pre-engagement gift from GEORGE SANDERS—a custom-made Bentley automobile—the only other one in town like it was owned by CLARK GABLE . . . INGRID BERGMAN had definitely signed to do a film in Italy early in 1949. ROBERTO ROSSELLINI will direct it . . . And, as 1948 came to a close, owners of local bars were complaining that television had begun to cut their liquor business, while even their juke box coins were down fifty percent.

1949

January began on a sad note when famous director VICTOR FLEMING ("GWTW") died of a heart attack while on a vacation in Arizona . . . JIMMY STEWART began seriously dating socialite GLORIA MCLEAN . . . WANDA HENDRIX and the most decorated hero of World War II, AUDIE MURPHY, were married on the 8th. LAUREN BACALL brought her baby son, STEPHEN, home from the hospital . . . KEENAN WYNN married BETTY BUTLER, who used to handle fan mail at Paramount . . . And the biggest wedding news of the month: TYRONE POWER took LINDA CHRISTIAN for his wife in a regal ceremony in Rome.

In February, INGRID BERGMAN tried to convince DR. LINDSTROM to take off three months and travel to Italy with her while she filmed the ROSSELLINI picture. The good doctor was too busy—which signaled the beginning of the end of *their* marriage. NORA EDDINGTON FLYNN left ERROL and began dating singer DICK HAYMES . . . And ROSSELLINI arrived in New York on his way to Hollywood. He left his girlfriend, ANNA MAGNANI, in Rome. But their phone bills were astronomical.

In March, neighborhood movie theatres began their giveaway gimmicks again. This time it was automobiles instead of dishes . . . Rumors were that ALY KHAN's divorce would cost him millions in alimony. But obviously he felt RITA HAYWORTH was worth it . . . Poor ERROL FLYNN, he always seemed to be surrounded by troubles of a "romantic" nature. His daughter DEIRDRE's pony was stolen. It was recovered five days later—pregnant . . . And BING CROSBY, one of the owners of the Pittsburgh Pirates, took the whole baseball team to dinner at Chasen's.

In April, RONALD REAGAN's first date when he arrived in New York was with stunning singer MONICA LEWIS. They saw each other constantly while he remained in the big city . . . Both JUDY GARLAND and VINCENTE MINNELLI moved out of their home. Each comes at separate times to visit daughter LIZA . . . By the last week in the month, the ROSSELLINI-BERGMAN "situation" was about to break into headlines. R.R., quite the continental Romeo, once dated MARLENE DIETRICH. At that time, Marlene had told friends that he was the most fascinating man she had ever met. Which covered a lot of territory . . . DR. LINDSTROM left for Italy to visit INGRID. Their daughter PIA was sent to a farm in Minnesota for the summer.

By early May, l'affaire BERGMAN-ROSSELLINI had exploded. When DR. LINDSTROM physically yanked Ingrid out of a restaurant for spending too much time with her director, the incident became the number one scandal in the film business; much tougher for Hollywood to handle than the HAYWORTH—ALY KHAN travels across Europe had been. Reports from Rome that HOWARD HUGHES was ready to stop production on *After the Storm*, being filmed on the island of Stromboli, were denied by RKO. The film was shut down for only three days while Ingrid and Roberto met with Dr. Lindstrom. Meanwhile, United Artists planned to release *Stromboli*, starring ANNA MAGNANI . . .

Hollywood-type parties went on in New York, too. In mid-May, ELSA MAXWELL played hostess at what she called her "Americana" night— the occasion being the ceremony which officially changed the name of the Park Central Hotel to the Park Sheraton. No one else but the fabulous Elsa could have masterminded such a soirée, even convincing CLARK GABLE to get up on a public floor and square dance. No sooner had he recuperated from that, then she had him up again—this time competing with WILLIAM RANDOLPH HEARST, JR., and NATHAN MILSTEIN as they draped a statuesque model in chiffon.

Gable was with his favorite date of the moment, DOLLY O'BRIEN—who looked very young for a grandmother—but simultaneously possessed a will of iron. The wealthy Dolly stubbornly refused to join Clark in the square dance, so SYLVIA FAIRBANKS STANLEY and ADELE ASTAIRE DOUGLASS alternately found themselves in Clark's arms. Sylvia looked divine in a strapless white

sheer, and Adele, despite the gray streaks in her hair, still had the same ageless dancing feet as her brother, FRED.

The whole event was a fascinating sneak preview of things to come. Seven and a half months later, with her will of iron still intact, Dolly O'Brien was *out* of Clark's life. It was Sylvia Fairbanks Stanley who said the "I do's"— which turned *her* into Mrs. Clark Gable number four.

In June, MARTHA VICKERS and MICKEY ROONEY purchased a new honeymoon home right next door to Gable's Encino ranch . . . In early July, OLIVIA DE HAVILLAND, Mrs. MARCUS GOODRICH, said she was expecting a baby . . . In midmonth, DAVID O. SELZNICK and JENNIFER JONES said their wedding vows twice—once in Genoa, on land, and once on board ship . . . And ERROL FLYNN's ex, NORA EDDINGTON, said her "I do's" with DICK HAYMES.

By August, every studio was trying to sign MARLON BRANDO to a contract . . . Princess ALY KHAN, the newlywed, was pregnant . . . Longtime bachelor JIMMY STEWART married Washington socialite GLORIA MCLEAN on August 9th . . . LANA's ex, restaurateur STEVE CRANE, went off with MARTINE CAROLE, French actress, to a wedding on the Riviera . . . And a series of "what-if" gags flew around town: What if: DURANTE had been born with a small nose; SINATRA had been built like VIC MATURE; INGRID hadn't visited Stromboli and RITA hadn't fallen on her KHAN.

In mid-September, SONJA HENIE, who loved parties as much as any six-year-old, threw her biggest and best one on the occasion of her wedding reception for five hundred "intimate friends" in the Terrace Room of the Hotel Plaza. Sonja, in an effort to be sure that every detail was perfect, had CARRIE MUNN create two wedding ensembles before making her final decision. Then her caterer made a *blue* wedding cake to match her lace and tulle ballerina-length gown.

The guest list, culled from the social register and Celebrity Service, ran the gamut from Mrs. JOHN JACOB ASTOR to TOOTS SHOR. Hollywood was sparsely represented by ROBERT STACK, JEANNE CRAIN and PAUL BRINKMAN. But even minus the Tinseltown touch, the evening was as glamorous as any one of Sonja's star-studded parties in Bel Air. Next to Sonja and her handsome socialite groom, WINTHROP (WINNIE) GARDNER, the happiest face on the crowded dance floor belonged to Sonja's mother, SELMA. She *knew* that in this marriage Sonja had found

1 A few young MGM players help to celebrate Van Johnson's birthday. Left to right: Nancy Walker, Peter Lawford, June Allyson, Gloria deHaven, and Tom Drake.   2 Famous party-giver Elsa Maxwell lunches with starlet Georgia Carroll (at Maxwell's right).

Girl on Maxwell's left, unidentified.
3 Fred Astaire and Ginger Rogers in *The Barkleys of Broadway*, 1949.   4 Louis B. Mayer gets some help in celebrating MGM's Silver Anniversary from June Allyson and Jimmy Stewart, 1949.

the happiness for which she had been searching ever since her divorce from DAN TOPPING nine years before.

The new bride told guests she would not give up her estate in Holmby Hills, California, although she expected to spend more and more time in the east. Her Winnie's playboy days were over. He had taken an important job with the drug firm of Johnson & Johnson. Sonja, who made her temporary home at the Plaza Hotel during her frequent visits to New York, now made it her permanent residence. She and Winnie leased a suite there by the year.

By late September, CRAWFORD and GREG BAUTZER had split. He began dating GINGER ROGERS . . . CLARK GABLE and SYLVIA FAIRBANKS STANLEY had become a steady twosome . . . DIETRICH, in London, was dated by MICHAEL WILDING . . . And there were rumors that when JANE WYMAN returned from Europe, RONNIE REAGAN would be on the dock to meet her.

In October, ELIZABETH TAYLOR had broken her engagement to young socialite ED PAULEY. But chums said she did *not* return his $16,000 engagement ring . . . Although INGRID BERGMAN had planned to return home as soon as her film with ROSSELLINI was finished, by November the situation had changed according to reports out of Rome; Ingrid was ready to quit films. "I love Roberto," she told the correspondent. "When I am free, we will marry. He is a great artist. It is exciting to watch him work. I shall be happy to work as one of his crew, help cut his pictures, anything!"

Meanwhile, back in the States, LIZ TAYLOR was dating VIC DAMONE . . . And Boston socialite PATRICIA KENNEDY came to Hollywood to get a foot in the industry her father, JOSEPH P. KENNEDY, had been involved with several decades before.

As the Forties came to a close, WALTER WINCHELL predicted that as soon as RITA HAYWORTH KHAN had her baby, ALY would leave her. "The Prince loves the hunt and the chase too much to settle down," said Winchell . . . And CLARK GABLE and SYLVIA FAIRBANKS STANLEY were married. On their license, Clark listed his age as forty-eight. Sylvia gave hers as thirty-nine. The new Mrs. Gable apparently had had a lapse of memory. Thirteen years earlier, when she became Mrs. Douglas Fairbanks, Sr., Sylvia had stated she was thirty-two.

Clark's best man was HOWARD STRICKLING, head of publicity at MGM. REVEREND AAGE MOLLER, pastor of the Danish Lutheran Church, officiated at the single-ring ceremony. Sylvia's sister and brother-in-law, MR. and MRS. BASIL BLECK, of Cheviot Hills, California, were also in attendance. Basil gave away the bride. Another witness was GENE GARCEAU, who had served as Clark's secretary and business manager for many years.

On her wedding day, Sylvia, looking very lovely, had chosen a conservative navy blue woolen dress with matching blue shoes and white collar and cuffs. She wore a giant orchid pinned to her waist. Clark, color-coordinated in a blue business suit, looked very handsome. Sylvia was so nervous that after the ceremony, when they toasted each other with champagne, she spilled bubbly on her flower. Gallantly, Gable helped her wipe it off.

In London, news of his stepmother's elopement thrilled DOUGLAS FAIRBANKS, JR. "My wife and I read about it in the morning papers," Doug said. "It came as a complete surprise. Of course, we were both absolutely thrilled and delighted. MARY and I love her, and Clark is one of our best friends. My father always adored Sylvia. She is very vivacious, very attractive and very feminine. I'm sure she and Clark will be extremely happy . . ."

On New Year's Eve, the Gables boarded the S.S. *Lurline* in San Francisco and headed for a two-week honeymoon in Hawaii. The trip over took four-and-a-half days. When the Gables landed, they received more than the usual "aloha." Ten thousand admirers were on the dock to greet them. Then they traveled by police escort to a private home in the swank Kahala section of Honolulu. Fourteen days later, they arrived back on the mainland and began their life together on Gable's Encino Ranch—which Sylvia proceeded to redecorate—until it began to look more like the West Coast branch of a stately English mansion!

Frankly, Gable's closest friends were a bit surprised at Clark's "sudden" choice of a bride. Sylvia Fairbanks Ashley Stanley was pretty, rich and very social. Still, she was the antithesis of CAROLE LOMBARD. "Down-to-earth" was *not* one of the phrases people used in describing Sylvia. She hadn't been "one of the gang" for thirty years.

But, as the Forties ended, everyone was happy that at least Clark was no longer alone . . . Even CARY GRANT sympathized. He marched to the altar with BETSY DRAKE.

In more of a "shotgun" romance, one of the best-attended functions was the banquet honoring the first annual awards from the Television Academy of Arts and Sciences. TV's glittering "Emmy" became engaged to motion picture's gleaming "Oscar" as the trophies were given out before one thousand guests.

"Hollywood is the logical television center of the world," said the TV Academy's president.

"Not if we can help it," cried the motion picture magnates—to themselves.

After all, there was no doubt that the programs emanating from "that little box" were keeping millions of their potential customers at home. Nobody yet had quite figured out how the two media could get into bed with one another and mutually co-exist. As the Forties ended, television remained the "worst enemy" Hollywood had ever encountered.

THE FIFTIES

HOLLYWOOD TRAUMA, BIG SCREEN VS. SMALL SCREEN

A sign of the times by the mid-Fifties: Eddie Fisher and guest Mitzi Gaynor relax before Fisher's "Coke Time" television show, 1954.

HOLLYWOOD IN TRAUMA

Slowly, subtly, the face and form of Hollywood was ever-changing. Just as shaved eyebrows and exaggerated lips characterized the Thirties . . . and short hairdos and utilitarian makeup represented the wartime Forties . . . the Fifties were expected to feature yet another new look. The trouble was no one had as yet quite figured it out exactly.

It had been more than two years since television reared its ugly head—mostly in shades of black, white and fuzzy off-green. Strange faces and forms cavorted inside tiny boxes that sat on livingroom tables, or stood, unattractive hulks, intruding on the rest of the room's furnishings. Every day more and more Americans were glued to their sets. They watched old cowboy movies, cartoons and vaudeville-type acts: jugglers, ventriloquists, trained animals, dancing duos, stand-up comics, baggy-pants clowns and clumsy wrestlers.

Most of what they saw was sheer garbage. But, once the set had been purchased, it was *free*. Mom, Dad, the kids and close neighbors could sit around in jeans, or pajamas, swilling drinks and chomping food, all the while being entertained.

At the start of the decade, there were only three million sets in homes across America. That number was expected to triple, at the least, within twelve months. And, for every set, there were multiple viewers. Yet boxoffice receipts were still pretty high, and Hollywood was turning out better movies than ever. But how long would even the best movies be enough to keep people going *outside* their homes for entertainment? And there was still another problem. While the biggest of Hollywood stars had returned from the war, many of them were growing a bit long in the tooth. A whole new crop of idols was needed—and fast.

Television moguls, aware of the scarcity of celebrities available to them, created their own new idols, or resurrected semidiscarded "names." They were bringing back favorite stage comics, like Milton Berle and Ed Wynn, who rapidly developed a huge coterie of devoted fans. In the fall, NBC planned to inaugurate daytime television, converting popular radio soap operas and quiz shows into their visual medium. What would *that* do to the matinee movie trade? The thought was too horrible for filmmakers to comprehend.

In the beginning, the main television activity centered in New York and even Chicago. But networks were beginning to move west, invading Hollywood's sacred territory. CBS had even gone so far as to purchase a huge athletic field, Gilmore Stadium, and planned to spend twenty-one million dollars turning it into a fantastic "Television City."

By November of 1950, regularly scheduled *color* television was inaugurated in four big eastern cities: Philadelphia, Boston, Baltimore and Washington. The trend was obvious. Soon color would be nationwide. The movie moguls were in semishock. Their first reaction, as with radio, was to insert provisions in star contracts forbidding them from appearing on shows. It was made known, in no uncertain terms, that television was now the enemy. It was to be shunned and scorned and downplayed at every opportunity. They did everything but require their most important performers to wear signs across their chests reading: MOVIES ARE BETTER THAN EVER—HONESTLY!

Studio heads reasoned that the most immediate solution was to start turning out movies that could not be duplicated on TV. Big special epics. More adult films. Controversial themes. Films loaded with multistar names. Eventually, when that ploy failed, they would hitch their wagons to new screen processes and technologies. They would make movies that were wider, larger, taller, bigger. Films that had 3-D depth and featured innovative stereophonic sound. But all of that was at least two years away. In the meantime they had to hold down the fort. So they gathered their collective wagons in a circle and isolated Hollywood into a tight little island.

By the end of 1950, industry heads were convinced that TV was the most troublesome adversary they had ever encountered. Compared to television, night baseball, dog races, gin rummy, charades, miniature golf, and even radio were mere playthings—all like two-dollar whores—not to be taken seriously. Television, on the other hand, at least to its potential viewers, was a gorgeous, elegant, high-priced mistress. Her allure was so irresistible that hardly anyone could withstand the temptation to say so long to the old spouse, movie theatres, and climb into a permanent berth with the new gal in town, TV.

Of course, it never occurred to the film studios to opt for an immediate marriage of the two media. The thought, when a few

1

2

3

1 Wedding portrait of Nicky Hilton and Elizabeth Taylor, 1950.   2 Errol Flynn and wife number three, Patrice Wymore.
3 Charles Chaplin and wife Oona with his

daughters Josephine, 3, and future movie star Geraldine, 8, on the deck of the *Queen Elizabeth*, arriving in Southampton, September 1952. (UPI) courageous souls dared mention it, was considered nothing short of high treason. Movie studios stood firm. Top executives for 20th Century–Fox were the most vocal. Insiders felt they spoke for the entire motion picture industry.

In no uncertain terms 20th declared: "We have no intention of releasing even our old films for television. We believe that the public interest will best be served when TV can be harnessed to motion picture theatre entertainment . . ." The statement had been prompted by rumors and several items in New York gossip columns which said that 20th–Fox "planned to release for television all films made prior to 1945."

After having labeled the gossip as "completely baseless and without foundation in fact," a spokesman for 20th pointed out that they had filed an application with the FCC for experimental channels to conduct tests wherein theatres might use television as an adjunct to their programs "for the greater entertainment of the motion picture public."

The handwriting was on the wall—as well as in the offices of the Hollywood moguls. Somehow, they had to find a way to harness television, and to show it inside the auditoriums of their big movie palaces. They could not compete with that medium if people stayed at home and watched it.

A year passed. Nobody had come up with a workable solution. Universal-International, with obvious foresight and a bit of subterfuge, decided to merge with Decca Records. The recording company had fifty-five distribution centers which would handle the release of all television films to be produced by the studio. It was one way—they hoped—that they could prevent theatre exhibitors from screaming too loudly when Universal began releasing TV pictures. The first crack in the door had come!

Meanwhile, Hollywood had another big problem. Television studios were raiding their ranks—not the stars (yet!)—but the behind-the-scenes experts. The rapidly growing TV industry, while training newcomers, needed experienced technicians immediately—and the studio talent drain began.

In ivory towers all over Tinseltown, discussions were becoming more frantic. While they went about their own business of making motion pictures, careful analytical studies were made on the potential of television *within* the industry.

In late 1951, there were still no profits being made in television. Income from advertising revenue, when compared with a TV station's overhead, didn't balance out. The business was showing lots of red ink. Even if studios were to become involved eventually—God forbid—they could not accept such potential losses. The whole situation was a mess . . . The face of Hollywood was, indeed, changing. Now it had deep frown lines!

By February of 1952, yet another studio began waltzing around the outskirts of TV. Barney Balaban, president of Paramount, announced that his company might consider producing short films for advertisers. He said his company was studying the feasibility of using either their newsreel organization or cartoon studios for the purpose.

This statement brought close examination by the Federal Communications Commission. The upshot of the quiz was the revelation that Paramount might eventually apply for theatre TV channels . . . and, perhaps, sometime in the future, establish its own television network.

In conclusion, Balaban stated that various financial considerations would govern which films or special events were sold to movie theatres, to pay-as-you-see TV, to theatre TV, or to free TV. The determining factor in each case would depend on the popularity of the picture, its vintage, and so forth. It was obvious at that stage in the game that both Paramount and the FCC were on a "fishing expedition"—with neither one sure of whether or not there were even any fish to catch.

As for television programming, by 1952 it had become a mixed bag of wonderfully original variety, comedy and dramatic programs, run side by side with shows that, even for free, were pretty awful.

On Sunday nights, Ed Sullivan's "Toast of the Town" was a winner, as were the "Red Skelton Show," the "Colgate Comedy Hour," "What's My Line," and the alternating "Philco" and "Goodyear TV Playhouses."

Mondays belonged to Lucy and Desi, the "Lux Video Theatre," "Arthur Godfrey's Talent Scouts," "Robert Montgomery Presents" and "Studio One."

On Tuesday evening, the "Texaco Star Theatre," the "Fireside Theatre" and the "Armstrong Circle Theatre" all presented shows that held audience interest, some more than others, but all gallant efforts. Counterprogrammed were "Suspense," "Danger" and the "Red Buttons Show."

At midweek, the "Adventures of Ellery Queen," "Arthur Godfrey and His Friends," the "Kraft Television Theatre," "I Married Joan" and "Perry Como."

Thursday evening brought, among other shows, the "Lone Ranger," "Dinah Shore," "Burns and Allen," "Amos 'n' Andy," "Four Star Playhouse," "Dragnet," "Gangbusters," "Bit Town," "Racket Squad" and "I've Got a Secret."

Fridays were reserved for "My Friend Irma," the "Schlitz Playhouse of Stars," "Our Miss Brooks," "Mr. and Mrs. North," "The Adventures of Ozzie and Harriet" and other such "family" shows.

On Saturday night, the "Jackie Gleason Show," "You Bet Your Life," "My Little Margie" and the blockbuster Sid Caesar–Imogene Coca and company of comic characters on "Your Show of Shows."

All of that, plus ancient cowboy movies, old cartoons, popular bandleaders, Arthur and Kathryn Murray teaching America how to dance, plus sports and local programming, was certainly sufficient fare to eat into Hollywood's movie business. In fact, it was downright scary.

Still, most of the Hollywood moviemakers were garrisoned in their covered wagons, trying to figure out whether to fight the Indians—or join them. There was still a glimmer of hope left for "overcoming" television—but it was growing dimmer with each passing day.

Mary Pickford
"THE BIG BAD WOLF HAS BEEN MUZZLED"

At the close of 1934, when Billy Wilkerson asked Mary Pickford if she would write an analysis of the motion picture industry's situation in relation to the medium of television, even he could not know how prophetic she would turn out to be. Obviously, Mary was more than equal to the task. She was not only Hollywood's first really important star, but also a producer and co-founder of United Artists, as well as a very shrewd behind-the-scenes business lady. In this very candid Reporter piece, what Mary said about movies and radio, and her predictions about television, all proved quite valid. At the time it was written, however, it did not reflect the majority opinion in the industry because of Hollywood's innate fear of competition.

Producers in general and exhibitors in particular regarded the radio until recently as the Big Bad Wolf of the entertainment world. They all uttered raucous cries to the effect that it was hurting business.

Behold now a great change. The motion picture producer uses the radio to exploit his wares, even lending his stars for exploitation and sometimes for profit. One of our largest film companies, in fact, is financially involved in a bigamous marriage to a radio-chain—a scandalous situation evidently overlooked by our astute keyhole-peepers.

Fear has gone out of the producer's heart, common sense has come back to the exhibitor and calm is being restored to the ether waves that were in so tumultuous a high tide of competition.

Opposition to progress is forever futile. And he who maketh use of his enemy is indeed wise.

In my opinion, the box-office value of every star who appears to advantage on the air is greatly enhanced, and, potentially speaking, so is the stock of the company to which he or she is under contract.

So far as competition to pictures is concerned, that I view as a boon. Competition always has been, always will be, the great incentive to better effort. And I consider radio, television or any other competitive agent a benefit, not a menace. It stimulates enterprise, prevents stagnation. Of course, if we are merely going to sit with folded hands and do nothing, we will be—and should be—eliminated, all in accordance with the law of survival of the fittest.

But motion pictures have not done that. Films, on the whole, have kept pace with progress. We have been constantly setting our goal ahead, pushing up the hill in the face of competition, reaching the top of one ridge only to continue on to the summit of the next, never quite achieving our aims for the simple reason that these aims have had about them enough of the will o' the wisp quality to make them our salvation.

In other words, we have never realized our dreams and then suffered the devastating reaction of complete collapse which inevitably follows. We still find them alluring, intriguing, irresistibly brilliant, and their ephemeral, elusive quality is an incentive which gives us courage and strength to travel tricky detours and climb over obstacles which are placed in the road, not so much to discourage us as to prove our mettle, to develop our stamina and stride.

Successful though the radio has become, it is doubtful in my opinion if it can ever monopolize the entertainment field to the same extent that motion pictures do. Naturally, none can deny that it is the most economical form of amusement, especially since the price range of instruments has adjusted itself to all pocketbooks.

The great disadvantage of the radio, however, is that it does not gratify the individual's gregarious urge. No one likes to sit constantly at home, reading, talking, sewing, playing bridge or listening to the radio. The essence of entertainment is variety. And what variety is there for the housewife who has been at home all day in sitting down amid the same surroundings to listen even to the most divine symphony or the most romantic love story ever told? She wants to hear that story, of course, but not in surroundings whose charm has been dulled through constant association.

It should always be borne in mind, too, that the radio is a form of casual entertainment. One of its greatest advantages lies in the fact that it can be enjoyed to the fullest while other obligations are being discharged. The woman who is doing her dusting, for instance, can enjoy ecstatically the finest opera ever broadcast and, at the same time, continue her household task—which, by the way, is a great advantage to the cinema, for obvious reasons.

When television arrives, the same, too, will be true of that medium of entertainment. For the artist, it will be a boon, of course, for the simple reason that it will broaden his field of endeavor. But in my opinion even the novelty of television will not greatly curtail theatre business, providing the standard of film entertainment does not slip into a rut. Time will be required to eliminate the imperfections of television after it becomes a fact, no matter how skillfully it may be launched, and this in itself is very apt to minimize its novelty.

So far as motion pictures go, there is only one answer to the question of maintaining their supremacy. It is not a new answer: it is one oftimes expressed, although not always achieved.

If the supremacy of the screen is to be maintained, it must be done through quality alone. Continued improvement will assure unchallenged leadership. This and no other panacea will suffice.

Every picture of merit made since the depression engulfed us has met with financial success in spite of trying economic conditions and drastic criticism aimed at the industry from many quarters.

Much of this criticism of course was warranted. In fact constructive criticism is a marvelous tonic. It is medicine, often bitter, and usually a pill that we hate to swallow. Still, had it not been for the church drive for decency, it is difficult to predict how drastic our disaster might have been. We had become so addicted to questionable wisecracks, so proud of insidious lines with double meanings, so lop-sided with sophistication, and so befuddled by the vulgar viewpoint of that miasmic minority known as the "intelligentsia" that we completely lost sight of the fact that the majority audience of America is decent-minded. Dirt and filth under the guise of humor will never be tolerated by a nation as young as ours. We are too naive nationally, still too wholesome in our point of view, to be swayed by that Continental cynicism which the sophisticate points to as the ne plus ultra of humor.

This does not mean, however, that every play produced should be dripping sweet or saccharine enough to be innocuous as an amusement vehicle. Films properly premised can still deal with the facts of life. Virility and vitality will always be essential, but vulgarity, if or when required, can never be candy-coated and excused. Simpering or mawkish sentimentality can likewise be a cardinal offense.

The affliction of self-sufficiency is bound to pay the penalty of fallen arches at the box-office. None of us is really so important. Primarily we are part of the scheme of things, and when inflation of the ego becomes epidemic, when self-estimate reaches ability, we soon discover that the barometer of popularity recedes.

Perhaps the greatest thing about motion pictures is that no one can ever have a monopoly on ideas. Masterpieces cannot be made to order. Artistic supremacy hovers for a season over one studio, then producers bang away with their inspirational guns and chase it to another, where it perches precariously, a harried quarry soon to wing its way elsewhere, ceaselessly pursued by these diligent huntsmen.

Quite evidently we are still a Cinderella-minded nation. We love the triumph of virtue, the supremacy of success, especially when achieved at the end of an obstacle race. We are still childlike enough and healthy enough to enjoy laughter. The stonemasons of our industry are the producers, the directors, the writers, the stars. The keystone of the arch upon which they toil, however, is the story. And no arch will ever be stronger than the keystone which supports it. A faulty story will cause the collapse of any arch, the downfall of the most adroit mason.

Perhaps we are fortunate this year in that we have been given explicit directions as to how to quarry our stone. The outstanding popularity of Will Rogers, Janet Gaynor and little Shirley Temple indicates that the world wants simple, human screen fare, fundamental in emotion and wholesome in motivation. But the world does not want—and will not accept—a standard pattern.

HOLLYWOOD KALEIDOSCOPE
1950

The first year of the new decade started out with a sense of good fellowship and a modicum of euphoria. There were the usual datings, matings, startings, partings—and, par for the course, some startling quotes . . . MICKEY ROONEY and MARTHA VICKERS called off their divorce. They declared: "We thought it would be a shame to spoil our baby's first Christmas and New Year's" . . . GAIL RUSSELL and GUY MADISON separated . . . PAULETTE GODDARD and BURGESS MEREDITH split. Paulette said she would never remarry even though "marriage is the best state for a woman." Her reason? "Because I'm lazy."

RONALD REAGAN and RUTH ROMAN danced up a storm at BILLY WILKERSON's LaRue one night and on the next he was with FRANCES MURRAY at Ciro's . . . ELIZABETH TAYLOR dated NICKY HILTON at the "Key to the City" press preview. The following day there were rumors of an engagement . . . Meanwhile, TYRONE POWER slipped away from his film location at Lone Pine to celebrate his first anniversary with LINDA CHRISTIAN. He gifted her with a diamond cross.

In February, INGRID BERGMAN had a son. Nobody said whose baby it was. The legal presumption was that Ingrid's husband, DR. LINDSTROM, was the father. The American colony in Rome was nuts about her. They thought ROBERTO ROSSELLINI was "crazy," but admitted he had charm . . . There were rumors that SINATRA was dating AVA GARDNER. He denied them. Meanwhile, NANCY SINATRA's lawyer hired press agent ART JACOBS to handle the public relations concerning her separation from Frank.

By March, Liz Taylor confirmed she would become the bride of hotel heir Nicky Hilton . . . Peter Lawford went to London to ask permission from Ambassador Lewis Douglas to marry his daughter Sharman. He didn't get it . . . Elizabeth had a bridal shower. One of her favorite gifts was a petticoat embroidered "Stolen from the Hilton Hotels."

In April, friends said Dr. Peter Lindstrom would point out in court that he had provided Roberto Rossellini with a generous weekly cash allowance while the Italian producer-director was his and Ingrid's houseguest . . . Even LaRue's honored Stromboli, the island where Bergman and Rossellini were filming their epic. They put a new dish on their menu: Sea Food Pie à la Stromboli.

Over in France, Rita Hayworth paid $125,000 for a home in Paris. She borrowed the money from MCA's Jules Stein and apparently was in no hurry to return to the United States . . . Lana Turner and Bob Topping had a few friends in to celebrate their second anniversary . . . While in New York, columnist Dorothy Kilgallen reported the latest gimmick was a thing called "the Diners Club." Subscribers had one single charge account for a whole flock of cafes, nightclubs and restaurants. All they did was sign a tab, and then, at the end of the month, they received only one statement. She predicted a new trend in credit . . . Jean Arthur opened on Broadway in *Peter Pan* and was very happy with her reviews. Back in Hollywood, Janet Leigh was fuming. She and scion Arthur Loew, Jr., had been dating, but he hadn't given her an engagement ring. The fanciest thing he gifted her with was a bathmat made up of dozens of foam rubber breasts.

In May, Darryl Zanuck signed Marilyn Monroe to a long-term 20th Century–Fox contract. She was the gal who everyone said looked and acted like Jean Harlow in *The Asphalt Jungle.* 20th had her once, but dropped her . . . The press was boiling mad at Liz Taylor because of the way they were restrained at her wedding to Nicky. Only one photographer, who hid behind a church pillar, shot them kneeling at the altar.

Marilyn Monroe was dating William Morris Talent Agency bigshot Johnny Hyde . . . After a 12-year absence, Vivien Leigh arrived in Hollywood to begin work on *A Streetcar Named Desire.* Laurence Olivier, in between films, came along for the ride . . . Nearly every star in town now had a film contract which forbade their appearing on television. But Bob Hope and Bing Crosby were allowed to appear on TV—as long as it was live . . . Joan Blondell went to Las Vegas to divorce Mike Todd and checked into a motel to sit out her residence requirement.

The month of June found Errol Flynn dating lovely Princess Irene Ghika. He planned a big party in her honor. Meanwhile, the princess was getting acquainted with Errol's folks, Professor and Mrs. Flynn . . . In New York, Vic Damone, a sensational new singer, made his debut at the Waldorf-Astoria's Starlight Roof . . . Lucille Ball and Desi Arnaz appeared together on stage at the Roxy Theatre. They were a smash, and wisely packaged their act under the banner of Desilu Productions . . . Don Taylor, who appeared as the groom opposite Liz Taylor in *Father of the Bride,* received a postcard from Mrs. Hilton in Europe. It read: "Movies are better than ever—but honeymoon is better than movie!" . . . And Lucy and Desi got great news—they were "expecting a bundle of joy" in January 1951.

When July came, Rita Hayworth and Prince Aly Khan used Errol Flynn's yacht, anchored near Nice, pending his arrival in France in August . . . George Bernard Shaw turned ninety-four. When queried about television rights to some of his properties, he replied by postcard: "My works are not available for television. Television kills a living work commercially. Mine are all alive and growing. There are thousands of first-rate plays and books commercially dead. They are your natural prey."

Producer Norman Krasna dated Nancy Davis on the last day in July. By the first week in August, he had switched to Joan Crawford.

Over on the MGM lot, studio moguls said it had the hottest new prospect since Lana Turner and Judy Garland. Her name: Debbie Reynolds. She had made a big hit in *Two Weeks With Love.* . . . Ronald Reagan checked into Universal-International to prepare for his starring role in *Bedtime for Bonzo* . . . Before Patrice Wymore met Errol Flynn on location, she had been set to marry dance director Al White, who had already gone house-hunting for a honeymoon nest. Poor White had no idea he was being dumped until he read all about Pat's wedding plans with Errol in a local Hollywood column. And just prior to Flynn's third wedding, he'd told a judge he couldn't afford to pay alimony to first wife Lili Damita! . . .

The "No-TV" ban was so strict that Paramount refused to allow Bing Crosby's voice to be used in the narration of a religious film being made by the Maryknoll Fathers in the Philippines.

At the beginning of September, the INGRID BERGMAN—PETER LINDSTROM home went on the market. A potential buyer who walked through the place said Ingrid's clothes were still hanging in the bedroom closets . . . DIXIE LEE CROSBY told friends she was definitely going through with the divorce—no matter what. But by the first week in October, the Crosbys were celebrating an anniversary together. BING gifted Dixie with a gorgeous piece of jewelry. Engraved on the back: "This is the $24 question. Want to try for $25?" Two weeks later, following the death of Bing's father, his mother made one request of her son: "Do *everything* you can to make your marriage to Dixie last." He did—and it did. In early November, all was so peaceful that at Dixie Lee's birthday bash for herself and one hundred guests, Bing's brother EVERETT appeared. He and Dixie hadn't talked in ten years. But Bing, the "happy husband," did not show up.

The DANNY KAYES' "nearly Thanksgiving Day" bash for the LAURENCE OLIVIERS at the Beverly Hills Hotel was a Hollywood highlight. There hadn't been such a party since the pre-World War II soirée CARY GRANT tossed for his then bride-to-be, BARBARA HUTTON. For Sylvia and Danny, the affair was a great headache. Not for those they invited, but because of those they didn't: invitations for the special evening were pared down to a total of 158. LOUIS B. MAYER put on the most amazing performance. He danced every dance from 9 P.M. until 2:30 A.M. and looked more fit than when he'd arrived . . . Aside from L.B., the best combinations on the dance floor were GINGER ROGERS and DANNY KAYE, GREG BAUTZER and LANA TURNER, ROZ RUSSELL and VAN JOHNSON and LAURENCE OLIVIER with LYNNE BAGGETT. The biggest laugh came when Danny played MARY MARTIN to EZIO PINZA's rendition of songs from *South Pacific*—at four o'clock in the morning.

The Korean War started . . . There were rumors in Paris that RITA HAYWORTH would have to go back to work to pay off PRINCE ALY's debts . . . ELIZABETH TAYLOR's marriage to NICKY HILTON came apart at the seams. She filed for divorce.

In December, SHELLEY WINTERS was named "Miss Hollywood of 1950" by all of the studio gatemen . . . ROBERT TAYLOR returned from filming *Quo Vadis* in Rome. He and BARBARA STANWYCK dropped a bombshell, surprising even their closest friends. After eleven years, their marriage had ended. Barbara wasn't talking, and the press couldn't get any further comments from Bob. He escaped to Palm Springs in his private plane and went into seclusion in the desert . . . MARLON BRANDO said of Hollywood: "Out here everything is highly overrated. It isn't any different from anywhere else, except that it has the power of propaganda behind it. Even banalities are blown up into something big . . ."

Nineteen fifty was the year that fifty-one-year-old GLORIA SWANSON came back to "Sunset Boulevard" and proved that she was still the most glorious of all the glamour gals . . . Twenty-four-year-old beauty SHIRLEY TEMPLE announced her second marriage and her retirement simultaneously . . . And twenty-nine-year-old DEANNA DURBIN marched to the altar for the third time.

It was the year of CBS color, a sci/fi movie called *The Thing,* The DUKE OF WINDSOR's memoirs, *Guys and Dolls,* JACK BENNY, BOB HOPE, EDDIE CANTOR, BOBBY CLARK, EDGAR BERGEN and FRED ALLEN's entry into television, TALLULAH BANKHEAD's resuscitation of radio, and *King Solomon's Mines,* which unearthed the newest male heartthrob, STEWART GRANGER, while JUDY HOLLIDAY crashed through as the most exciting new actress.

AL JOLSON gave the song in his heart and his heart with it to the G.I.s in Korea and the world lost its greatest entertainer . . . JOHNNY HYDE, MARILYN MONROE's mentor, died, and FRANCES (MRS. HENRY) FONDA and EUGENE O'NEILL committed suicide.

In 1950, TYRONE POWER traveled the opposite way, to London, for his West End debut in *Mister Roberts* . . . PAULETTE GODDARD and CY HOWARD were the most amazing new couple . . . HOWARD HUGHES finally unveiled FAITH DOMERGUE . . . And CHARLIE CHAPLIN's revival of *City Lights* opened.

1951

JUDY GARLAND, who had been away from MGM for nearly a year, announced she was feeling fine and had signed a contract for a four-week

engagement at the London Palladium at $20,000 per . . . ZSA ZSA upheld the dignity of marriage by walking out on a radio show—

and her husband, GEORGE SANDERS . . . LIZ TAYLOR, who lost NICKY HILTON, found MIKE WILDING, who had lost MARLENE DIETRICH . . . Popular bachelors HOWARD DUFF, BOB STERLING, TONY CURTIS, AUDIE MURPHY and LEX BARKER went out of circulation, leaving GREG BAUTZER more pursued than ever.

When February arrived, SHIRLEY TEMPLE's husband, CHARLES BLACK, re-entered the Navy and she agreed to make a few more films . . . A local firm took an ad in *The Hollywood Reporter:* "You can survive atomic warfare—Don't be panicky, be prepared . . . With a lifestyle atomic bomb shelter . . . Visit our new model" . . . LINDA DARNELL exploded her own bomb by winning a divorce from PEV MARLEY . . . It was revealed for the first time that the Universal Studios lot had been used briefly during the war as a site for top secret experiments for the production of synthetic rubber and a new type of gasoline—made from garbage . . . ROBERT YOUNG made a pilot for a proposed television series, "Father Knows Best."

In March, MGM helped PIER ANGELI, their newest find, buy a house for her and her mother . . . ROBERT TAYLOR, still out of his former home, was said to be carrying a torch for BARBARA STANWYCK . . . RONALD REAGAN, president of the Screen Actors Guild, criticized the press during an ABC radio interview. Although he himself had never experienced a bad press, Reagan indicted the print medium for "their addition to yellow journalism, and seeking to boost circulation by going in for the flamboyant, exaggerated side of things" . . . MILTON BERLE, whose television show was number one, signed an exclusive thirty-year contract with NBC—the longest agreement ever signed in the history of show business.

There were unconfirmed rumors in April that the CLARK GABLE–SYLVIA ASHLEY FAIRBANKS merger was about to fall apart . . . RITA HAYWORTH— without ALY KHAN—visited New York's "21" Club and acted very uppity until a friend reminded her she was still a kid from Brooklyn . . . ELIZABETH TAYLOR had a brief fling with director STANLEY DONEN and gifted him with a gorgeous watch for his birthday.

By May, CLARK GABLE publicly admitted he would definitely live alone—and duck all future marriages . . . LIZ TAYLOR switched from STANLEY DONEN to dating scion LINDSAY HOWARD, JR., . . . There were rumors that RONALD REAGAN was about to elope with NANCY DAVIS . . . Hollywood welcomed a royal visitor when RAINIER, the Prince of Monaco, arrived to tour the studios—and to look for glamour girls to date.

In June, LOUIS B. MAYER said farewell to MGM, which he had co-founded twenty-six years before . . . JACK BENNY and ERROL FLYNN left for Korea to entertain the troops, the first USO show to go overseas since the end of World War II . . . When July arrived, RITA HAYWORTH decided to delay the divorce from ALY KHAN until after her current film was released. She had twenty-five percent of the profits and did not want any divorce publicity to affect the box-office grosses.

By summer's end, despite heavy financial losses, Hollywood television remained optimistically on the rise . . . JANE WYMAN was dating JOHN PAYNE . . . In early September, rumor had it that JUDY GARLAND would marry SID LUFT . . . Starlet NANCY VALENTINE announced she would become the bride of the MAHARAJAH OF COOCH BEHAR, and started instruction in the Hindu faith.

October was an off-month for living up to those wedding vows: "Until death us do part" . . . CLARK GABLE was in residence in Reno, Nevada, prepared to file for divorce from SYLVIA . . . RITA HAYWORTH said she expected to collect a three-million-dollar settlement from ALY KHAN—but word was that the prince was broke . . . LANA TURNER and BOB TOPPING's marriage had come to an end . . . GARY COOPER and his wife, VERONICA "ROCKY" BALFE, were estranged . . . Hayworth, while awaiting her settlement, said she would spend Christmas in Korea entertaining the troops . . . GABLE became so mad at SYLVIA he said he was willing to change his entire life in order to win his fight against her "unreasonable, outrageous alimony demands" . . . Romance looked brighter in November. MARION DAVIES, who fixed her sister Rose up with HORACE BROWN, decided *she* wanted him. After their marriage, they built a new Beverly Hills home . . . ELIZABETH TAYLOR, who had gone from STAN DONEN to LIN HOWARD, announced she was going to marry MICHAEL WILDING.

By December the MARILYN MONROE nude calendar went on sale—MM retained both her composure and the town's sympathy when she admitted she had posed that way because "she needed the money for food" . . . CLARK GABLE stored his furniture on the MGM lot. Every auctioneer in town fought for the account. Gable didn't care who got rid of his things. He just wanted to forget his marriage—and everything that went with it—including the marital bed ... GARY COOPER and PATRICIA NEAL's idyll was put on hold while he "made up his mind what to do about his marriage to ROCKY." Pat was "hopeful," but Hollywood insiders said Gary and Rocky would never divorce. For Miss Neal, it was "a very blue Christmas" ... The bells tolled for young and beautiful MARIA MONTEZ, FANNY BRICE, EDDY DUCHIN, novelist SINCLAIR LEWIS, composer SIGMUND ROMBERG, character actors J. EDWARD BROMBERG and LEON ERROL, BOGIE's ex, MAYO METHOT, and WILLIAM RANDOLPH HEARST.

1952

During the first month of the New Year, JUDY GARLAND and SID LUFT announced that they would become man and wife in April ... Warner Brothers' publicity department cleaned out its drawers and discovered an old photo file with layouts on MR. & MRS. MYRON FUTTERMAN: JANE WYMAN and her first husband ... ELIZABETH TAYLOR told MGM that come June, when her old contract was up, she wanted $5,000 a week and a forty-seven-week guarantee. Leo the Lion roared—but Liz got her way. What she *didn't* know: LANA TURNER had negotiated *her* new contract, and bargained for a *fifty-two*-week-a-year guarantee, but only had to show up for work *thirty-eight* weeks of the year ... When MIKE WILDING and LIZ TAYLOR "pitched woo" in New York a few months back, Mike was definitely in the doghouse with his ex-flame, MARLENE DIETRICH. But late in January, when he returned to London alone, any misunderstanding had been forgotten. Marlene shared his bon voyage luncheon at "21," then put him on the plane for home. Where this left Elizabeth was a hot topic for gossip.

MGM's woes were not over. In February, NANCY DAVIS asked Metro to cancel her contract. She said: "I'm tired of playing pregnant housewives!" ... The only other big news of the month was MARILYN MONROE's admission that she and JOE DIMAGGIO were dating—and she hoped to see a baseball game soon so she would understand why Joe was so famous.

March came in like a lion: NANCY DAVIS became MRS. RONALD REAGAN ... ELIZABETH TAYLOR honeymooned with MICHAEL WILDING ... And went out like a lamb: insiders said Mrs. Wilding was expecting.

By the beginning of April, two thousand color television sets had been sold in the city of New York alone ... In midmonth, Hollywood was all agog over the industry luncheon for QUEEN JULIANA and PRINCE BERNHARD of the Netherlands at MGM. DORE SCHARY introduced the royal party to DANA ANDREWS, ETHEL BARRYMORE, JOAN CRAWFORD, IRENE DUNNE, ZSA ZSA GABOR, SUSAN HAYWARD, DOROTHY LAMOUR, DICK POWELL, JUNE ALLYSON, VAN JOHNSON, JANE POWELL, WALTER PIDGEON, PIER ANGELI, LEO GENN, ANN MILLER, DEBBIE REYNOLDS, LOUIS CALHERN, MEL FERRER, LESLIE CARON, BARRY SULLIVAN, VERA-ELLEN, JOAN FONTAINE, BOBBY VAN, HOWARD KEEL, KIRK DOUGLAS, GENE TIERNEY, GEORGE MURPHY and JEAN-PIERRE AUMONT. CECIL B. DEMILLE, who had received numerous Dutch decorations, was a special honored guest and made a speech.

Also in April, Hollywood was saddened by the turn of events which saw distinguished producer WALTER WANGER sentenced to four months in jail for shooting agent JENNINGS LANG over a dispute involving JOAN BENNETT ... DIXIE LEE CROSBY was very ill at St. John's Hospital. SUE LADD, who had seen Dixie just prior to her hospital stay, told another close friend, with tears in her eyes, of her last visit with Dixie Lee. "She looked at me and said, 'Suzy, I know how much you like those little white gloves I always wear. Reach in my top drawer and take as many pairs as you want—I won't be needing them anymore.' " ... The only happy event of the month was SHELLEY WINTERS' marriage to Italian star VITTORIO GASSMAN.

By May, PAULETTE GODDARD had begun dating world-famous novelist ERICH MARIA REMARQUE ... VERONICA LAKE divorced ANDRÉ DE TOTH ... JOHN WAYNE and his wife, "CHATA," separated ... JOHN GARFIELD died of heart failure at age thirty-nine ... The long, hot summer saw LANA TURNER traveling to Nevada to divorce BOB TOPPING. Back home, FERNANDO LAMAS was "waiting in the wings" ... A grown-up IRVING THALBERG, JR., was expected to come into his inheritance—one million dollars in cash and stocks ... BING CROSBY made his television debut on a telethon to raise funds for the 1956 Olympic Games ... LIZ TAYLOR, filming *The Girl Who Had Everything*, expected her baby any second ... ARLENE DAHL married LEX BARKER ... The JOHN WAYNES' Encino home went up for sale, and Duke asked famed attorney JERRY GIESLER to "file for divorce and get it over with as soon as possible" ... As summer came to an end, RONNIE REAGAN reported to Universal-International to begin work on *Law and Order* ... And SHELLEY WINTERS told everybody she was expecting a little GASSMAN.

When September came, RITA HAYWORTH told

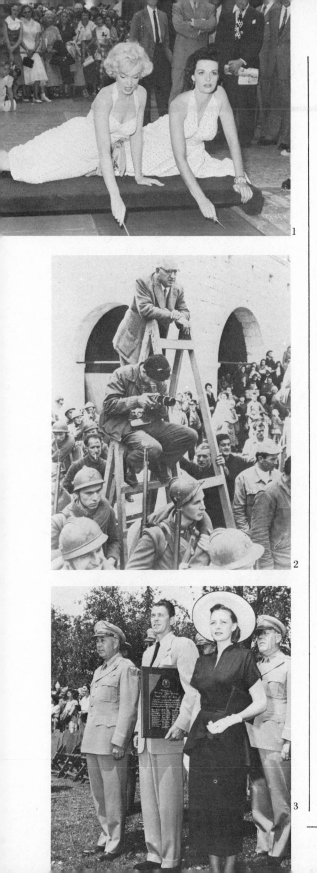

ALY KHAN their marriage was definitely, positively, absolutely over with. The Prince cried . . . GERTRUDE LAWRENCE died of liver cancer during the run of her play, *The King and I* . . . LORETTA YOUNG signed for a television series, "Your Life Story," the dramatization of true-life adventures and manners . . . ROSEMARY CLOONEY announced her forthcoming marriage to JOSÉ FERRER . . . And HOWARD HUGHES sold a big chunk of his stock in RKO—but retained the rights to JANE RUSSELL's contract.

In October, AVA GARDNER signed a new contract with MGM, and agreed to make twelve films for them at the rate of two a year . . . RALPH EDWARDS' innovative television series, "This Is Your Life," debuted and was an instant smash hit . . . Handsome "underworld figure" JOHNNY STAMPANATO severed his ties with MICKEY COHEN, went into the lovebird breeding business and started steady-dating former 20th starlet HELENE STANLEY . . . Ava, who was living apart from FRANK SINATRA, attributed their troubles to their fequent separations. "Frank had to work too hard," Ava said. "And I'm an expensive girl to keep."

On October 27, the Royal Command Film Show was different from the previous six: it was the first in the reign of the new QUEEN ELIZABETH. Among the Hollywood group presented to the Royal Family were: KIRK DOUGLAS, YVONNE DE CARLO, ROCK HUDSON, GENE KELLY, EVELYN KEYES, PATRICE MUNSEL, ALAN and SUE LADD, and practically every British star and starlet in or out of captivity.

Unfortunately, the British press did *not* appreciate the evening's onscreen entertainment. MGM's *Because You're Mine,* starring MARIO LANZA, was severely criticized. As one paper said: "The Royal Command Film Show is the occasion when the Queen is supposed to see the best film available. If this Hollywood musical is superior to all the others considered for the honor, then the state of the film

1 Marilyn Monroe and Jane Russell put their handprints at Grauman's Chinese.
2 David O. Selznick overseeing production on his film *A Farewell to Arms*. (Courtesy Selznick Properties, Ltd.)   3 SAG President Ronald Reagan accepts an award of gratitude from the United States Air Force to "American Show Business," for contributions to the World War II effort. With him, SAG member June Lockhart. (Courtesy SAG)

industry must be even more grave than we have been told" . . . The Americans were upset, and some felt like dumping tea into the Thames River!

At the end of October, SUSAN PETERS, age thirty-one, died. She had been paralyzed and in a wheel chair for eight years . . . Due to DIXIE CROSBY's critical illness, JUDY GARLAND substituted for BING on his CBS radio show. Subsequently, Dixie passed away of cancer at the age of forty-one. . . . CLARK GABLE rented a villa on Lake Como and planned to spend two months there as soon as *Mogambo* finished filming in Africa. Clark and DOROTHY DI FRASSO spent time together in Rome. The "Countess" and Gable had known each other since the Thirties when she and GARY COOPER were "an item" . . . MARIO LANZA was having personal troubles . . . JANE WYMAN started dating FRED KARGER . . . NORA and DICK HAYMES separated . . . As a "makeup" gift, SINATRA gave AVA an eleven-karat diamond ring with 174 smaller diamonds on the band . . . Ava's former hubby, MICKEY ROONEY, eloped with ELAINE MAHNKIN . . . MARILYN MONROE told a reporter she hadn't seen JOE DIMAGGIO for a long time—"almost a whole week" . . . At the end of the month, there was a star-studded premiere of ARCH OBOLER's *Bwana Devil,* the first Natural Vision 3-Dimension picture. Among those at the opening were ANN BLYTH, JEFF CHANDLER, TONY CURTIS, FERNANDO LAMAS, RAY MILLAND, ROBERT MITCHUM and RONALD REAGAN.

JOAN FONTAINE long-distanced her ex-husband BILL DOZIER in December. OLIVIA DE HAVILLAND invited her to tea for a reunion with their father, from whom both sisters had been estranged for years. Olivia's sweet gesture sent hesitant Joan back to Bill for advice. Dozier's answer: he referred Joan to her latest love, COLLIER YOUNG.

Nineteen fifty-two was the year of "I Like Ike" and "I Love Lucy" . . . The DIONNE QUINTS celebrated their 18th birthday and SHIRLEY TEMPLE had a son . . . INGRID BERGMAN experienced great happiness in the birth of her twin daughters, but heartbreak in the statement of her firstborn, PIA LINDSTROM: "I don't love my mother, I like her" . . . JUDY GARLAND brought back the two-a-day to the Palace, married SID LUFT and gave birth to a baby daughter, LORNA . . . Also joining the parent brigade were the TONY BARTLEYS (DEBORAH KERR), HOWARD DUFFS (IDA LUPINO) the LEOPOLD STOKOWSKIS (GLORIA VANDERBILT) and the RONALD REAGANS (NANCY DAVIS).

The Reagans, by the way, were still *both* actively involved in the Screen Actors Guild. In fact, contrary to subsequent widely reported accounts of their original meeting—which was supposed to have occurred in 1951—Nancy and Ronnie had become acquainted two years earlier. They had begun dating in 1949, although not steadily. However, by the late summer of 1950, they were close enough so that Davis, who adored Ronnie from the start, wanted to become involved in all of his favorite activities. Thus, in August of 1950, Nancy Davis was *appointed* to the SAG Board to serve out the term of a member who had resigned. That November, she ran for the board, but *lost.* The day after the results were known, she was again *appointed* to serve on the board. SAG President Reagan had some influence in that selection.

Nancy, never thought of as an activist in industry-related functions, ran again and won a three-year term in 1951. Shortly thereafter, on March 4, 1952, the president of SAG and his prettiest board member were married.

Nancy would run for two more three-year terms, winning elections in 1954 and 1957.

Meanwhile, in November of 1952, Reagan left office. He would return in 1955, as SAG's third vice president, replacing William Holden. In November of 1955, he was again elected to the Guild presidency. On June 6, 1960, Reagan resigned due to a conflict of business interests. But Nancy stayed on the SAG Board for another month. By July of 1960, neither was involved with the administration of SAG. Their attendance every other week at board meetings had ended. Their lives were taking them in other directions.

Without question, Reagan's long and distinguished tenure as president of SAG was an enormous boost when he ran for the governorship of California, an office he held from 1967 to 1974. Those who watched Nancy during this period, as she dutifully gazed at her husband with adoration every time he spoke publicly, feel that her devoted support helped him a great deal. Still, for some reason, this phase of the Reagan's extremely close relationship was never emphasized.

John Wayne
"READY, WILLING AND ABLE"

In 1950, John Wayne reminisced about the beginning of his career when he wrote this vignette for The Hollywood Reporter.

Recently there was an item in a Hollywood news column that stated, amongst other things, that "John Wayne is Hollywood's workingest actor." It went on to say that I have commitments with four different producing companies—Republic, Warner Bros., RKO and John Ford—that I'd just finished *Rio Grande* for Republic, was hurrying to Mexico City to supervise the final production details on a picture which I produced for Republic, *Torero,* and as soon as that was finished I had to return to Warners for my first picture there.

Yes, it sure looks like I'm a busy man— but don't get me wrong—I'm not complaining about it. I can remember the days too well when I wasn't busy. In fact, for a long while it seemed that Hollywood could make thousands of pictures without ever using John Wayne in one of them.

I had been in the acting business for approximately two years when *The Hollywood Reporter* opened shop in 1930. Our only difference was that when the *Reporter* opened its doors, they remained open. Mine were practically closed—you might even say hermetically sealed—for almost ten years.

There was a sort of freakish business about the way I landed in pictures in the first place. Basically, I became an actor because I needed the money, which is not a particularly unusual reason.

I had been attending a local university— University of Southern California if we're going to name names—but whenever I walked across the campus, I couldn't hear the jingle-jangle in my pockets. It's hard for empty pockets to jingle. I'd sit in my classrooms and my stomach would be growling so loud I couldn't hear the prof's questions.

After my second year, I managed to get a job on the labor gang during the summer months at the old Fox Studio. My first actual duty was to play shepherd to a flock of geese being used in a picture. I had to see that the geese got where they were supposed to get on time and in place. To this day I've had a peculiar aversion to geese—even the roasted variety.

Before the summer was through, I'd been given the job of prop man. The pay was regular and good. The work wasn't too rough. I tossed

An early portrait of John Wayne and horse.

a coin but waited until it landed before I called the turn. It came up heads and I decided not to return to the classrooms.

That was in 1928, two years before *The Hollywood Reporter* was born. Then the break that everyone in Hollywood hopes for came my way. I was discovered. At that time I was propping a John Ford picture, *Mother Machree,* and doing stunts for him whenever he asked me to. His friend, director Raoul Walsh, was looking for a leading man for a picture he was about to do called *The Big Trail.* Mr. Ford suggested me to him and Walsh took the suggestion. I was in pictures.

Pretty easy, you say. I thought so too. All that publicity breaking about the great new star discovery. Interviews. Cameras. Lights. Money—the folding kind that didn't jingle, just jangled. Everything was going my way. And then the picture was released.

Came the dawn and that rising new star was fast descending. A couple of minor pictures followed at Fox and that was it. Then the real struggle began. I had been an actor just long enough to really have the bug. I was determined to continue on in the acting business, but it seemed that just about every producer and director in town was just as determined that I wouldn't. The jobs were few and far between. No jingle and the growls returned.

At the time when *The Hollywood Reporter* was becoming a great force in the picture industry, John Wayne was becoming less and less a one. In fact, I could pick up *The Reporter* at any given time of any given day and not find my name mentioned in any of the pictures that were being talked about therein. The absence of that name from the cast of any picture became practically a natural thing to expect.

Finally, I went back to work in a western—the eight-day variety. This led to other westerns and other pictures. Not a lot of them, mind you, but I was eating more or less regularly again. Incidentally, in case I ever should forget those lean, hard days, I've a constant reminder today. All of those pictures are on television. But that's another story.

Universal signed me to a contract. Not long after that, I was between contracts—and meals—again. Then Republic signed me in 1938. This stuck and I'm still working for Republic.

In 1939, John Ford, who has been my good friend through all the years since *Mother Machree,* had a picture property he had wanted to make for several years. He insisted, however, that I go along with the story. That's why he'd been wanting to make it for several years and hadn't. Finally Walter Wanger agreed to take Wayne too.

The picture was *Stagecoach*. What *Public Enemy* meant to Jimmy Cagney, what *Night Nurse* meant to Clark Gable, *Stagecoach* meant to me. It was the difference between being mentioned frequently in the columns of *The Hollywood Reporter* and not being mentioned at all.

Other pictures followed, other contracts were signed. And then last year everything seemed to break at once, for no apparent reason. I'm the same person I was in *The Big Trail* and during the following years, but believe me, it's different today. I was lucky to have a series of good pictures all released at approximately the same time: *Fort Apache, Wake of the Red Witch, She Wore a Yellow Ribbon*, and *Sands of Iwo Jima.*

Consequently I'm a busy man today. But as I said earlier in this story, you'll never catch me objecting to this state of affairs. I'm ready, willing, and with luck, able to go on working like this as long as the public will have me.

Linda Darnell
"THEY DIDN'T TELL ME"

In October of 1950, glamorous star Linda Darnell wrote this vignette for The Hollywood Reporter. *Her experiences on-camera were quite a revelation!*

A few months ago I went to a party in a stunning strapless evening dress. I hadn't been there long before my friend Ann Miller came up.

"What happened to you?" she asked. "You look as though you'd gotten caught in a Mixmaster."

She was looking at some black-and-blue splotches on my shoulders so big you would have thought I'd tangled with the Notre Dame backfield.

"Oh, that," I said, trying to be gay about it. "Dick Widmark did that to me this afternoon. Hugging me."

Ann arched a pretty eyebrow and pursed her lips in the cute little way she has. It was as much as to say, "My heavens, did I hear you right or didn't I?"

"He never fakes anything," I said. "Even in rehearsal he grabs me and gets violent—very, very violent."

I mention this only to warn those girls who are studying Stanislavsky that that's not all there is to acting. Yes, I took all of the drama courses. Learned to modulate my voice, walk like a lady, maintain feather control over my eyebrows, and cry great tear drops. But I should have taken some prize fight lessons along with Stanislavsky. I should have learned something about a hammerlock and a toe hold. Because, believe you me, love scenes in the movies are hazardous. Unless a girl knows her holds, she may end up with a cracked collar bone or an esophagus out of place.

The damage I speak of was done to me for *No Way Out,* the taut drama that Darryl F. Zanuck produced for 20th Century–Fox. I played Edie, a girl drawn true to life who was hard and soft at the same time, a girl who had a remarkable intestinal fortitude to stand up against life. Edie wasn't all that she should have been but neither Edie nor I deserved the fate that so foully befell us.

The scenario, which Joseph Mankiewicz wrote and directed, called for Dick Widmark to slap me in the face, punch me in the stomach, chain whip me and pull me out of a chair by my hair, among other things. And to punish me even more cruelly, my lipstick and make-up were taken away from me and I was to appear as nature had made me, which is a horrible thing to do to any woman. Without her face on, a girl feels like she was on public view in the stockades.

As for the physical ordeal, I knew what to expect from having Dick Widmark crush me in *Slattery's Hurricane*. He's a sweet guy and I can't bring myself to say after one of these scenes, "Look at what you did." He would be hurt—because he's a gentle, kind and thoughtful individual when he's not acting. I say so and his wife says so. But he becomes so intense during a scene—he really lives the role—that he doesn't realize I'm not Gorgeous George, the wrestler.

I've had other experts get me in their clutches from time to time—Tyrone Power, Dana Andrews, Paul Douglas and George Sanders, to mention a few, and they all have the kind of technique that would have brought the Cro-Magnon man to his feet cheering, but they were preliminary boys compared to this Widmark in *No Way Out*. . . . Stanislavsky may have known his drama per se but he certainly never foresaw how the course of true love would run in the town called Hollywood, or he would have included a few chapters in the art of defense for a lady.

I wouldn't mind actually, except that after that one party and the way Ann Miller looked at me, I had to forego wearing any evening dresses except the kind that come up around my neck. Otherwise, everyone would think someone had been beating me and I couldn't very well tell them that it was only what happened when Dick Widmark embraces a gal.

The time was—and how nice it must have been—when an actress was Lady Winder-mere, something to love beneath a big yellow moon and to cherish when the roses were blooming . . . Now, all of that has changed. About ten years ago, the Neanderthal school of script writers took over in Hollywood. They wanted to shock the movie customers right out of their seats. So they knocked the pedestal out from under Woman, turned off the yellow moons, tore up the rose bushes and locked up the sylvan gardens. Those Stone Age writers work on the theory that a girl likes to be roughed up—that she knows the hero really, truly loves her if he flattens her occasionally with a haymaker to the chin.

I can remember the time when I would report for work with nothing more to worry about than my dialogue, but now I feel good if I get home nights without a broken leg. In the bath, after a hard day, I carefully examine myself to make certain I'm not missing any vertebrae, still have two ears and my nose hasn't come undone. I used to doctor the bruises but now I take them for granted. The bigger they are, the more successful I know the love scene was.

The decline of the lady began, I believe, when Jimmy Cagney pushed a grapefruit into Mae Clarke's face for *Public Enemy*. That was woman's first downfall. That was when King Arthur and his knights beat a hasty retreat and Guinevere was left to fend for herself. And for a girl who's been brought up on Sir Walter Scott's novels, and had thrilled at all of the jousts as the knights battled for their lady loves, it was a rude jolt.

Other men slapped women in the movies that followed and Carole Lombard suffered the indignity of a kick to her posterior in *Nothing Sacred*. By then, gallantry was something to talk about historically. It had taken its place with the "Battle of Bull Run." But it remained for Mr. Widmark to add a few refinements. He has brought the art to its highest form. When he sent that old lady toppling down the stairs in *Kiss of Death,* he achieved what no other man has ever dared to think about.

I'm not complaining. I'm paid well to slug it out. Only I do think Stanislavsky tricked me. He should have warned this naive girl from Texas that there was more to acting than breath control and walking like a lady.

BOXOFFICE FAVORITES

On January 6, 1950, Lauren Bacall and Humphrey Bogart's baby son, Stephen Humphrey, celebrated his first birthday. They had confounded all of the skeptics who gave their marriage three weeks, at the outset. The Bogarts were a close family unit. They either worked together or "Betty" traveled along with Bogie.

Although the location jaunt for *The African Queen*, directed by pal John Huston, was particularly rugged and arduous, they had a ball. Bogart and his co-star, Katharine Hepburn, eventually formed a mutual admiration society. But Bogie, when he talked to a reporter, could also be quite candid about Kate.

She won't let anybody get a word in sideways. She keeps emphasizing what a superior person she is. At first, I felt as though I was expected to kiss the hem of her skirt, or to lie down on my face in the dirt before her. She's really something! One day, early in the morning, Huston and I were a little red-eyed from a hard night over a large bottle. We asked Kate if she had anything that would open our eyes. She was marvelously sweet and naive. She fixed us coffee!

All the time we were working in the jungle, I always griped, about the food, the places they found to put us up, the humidity, all those crawling insects. But Kate was in heaven. She couldn't pass a tree, or a bush, without wanting to know its precise origin. She even insisted on getting the Latin names of every creature she saw swimming, flying or crawling . . .

Bogie was anxious to cut short their ten-week location. But Kate loved every second of the ordeal—and Lauren, an interested spectator, adored watching her macho husband, and the marvelous Hepburn, going through their paces. He, muttering all the way; Kate, the perennial New Englander,

surviving every experience with equanimity. And, as each week passed, she noted her husband's growing fondness and respect for the great Lady Katharine.

"After all of my years in this business," Bogie said, "I'd become used to dames who liked their close-ups big, soft-lighted and frequent. But once, Katie even suggested that Huston shoot only the back of her neck in a scene . . . And, when we finally left Africa, she made the rest of us feel like tired old men. She rented a bicycle at Shannon Airport, during our six-hour layover, and peddled all over the Irish countryside. Kate's quite a gal!"

When Bogart was finishing up work on another film, *In a Lonely Place*, he sat with *The Hollywood Reporter*'s Billy Wilkerson and, after a brew or two, started spouting off.

No one in Hollywood knows how to have fun anymore except me and Errol Flynn. So we get stiff once in a while. So we have a little fun. What's wrong with that? This is a free country, isn't it? If I want to buy a drink, that's my business. No one knows how to play anymore. In the old days, stars did plenty of brawling. But *they* captured the public's fancy with their antics. It was all good careless fun. Now, you are expected to treat this industry like a religion! Really, Flynn and I are the only ones left who do any good old-fashioned hell-raising. Oh, there are a few girls who have a little spark in them—Shelley Winters, Paulette Goddard, Lana Turner. But the old hypocrites land on us every time we cut loose . . .

People are forever reminding me of my responsibilities to my public. Well, I don't owe my public anything except a good performance. That's what they paid for and, if they get it, we're even-steven. Instead I'm expected to go around bowing and scraping to my public. Hell, if I bowed everytime they told me to, I'd be spending all my time on my knees!

While Bogie was being quotable, Bacall was being "productive." On August 23, 1952, she gave birth to their second child, a daughter they named Leslie, after Bogie's great pal and early career booster, the late Leslie Howard.

Humphrey Bogart was a paradox. A complex, well-educated, "tough softie," who loved to work, play and *talk*. In 1953, he discussed marriage, in general, his four wives, in particular—and the broad category of actresses.

I believe in marriage. And, if the three I had before Betty folded, it wasn't that I walked out on any of them. It was really the reverse. Maybe I'm just a difficult person to live with. Each of my wives has been an actress. Betty's a good one, as well as a good-looking one. It would have been plain hell to marry a bad actress. I never could have stood that. When an actor marries an actress, their differences usually develop into something more intense than they started out to be . . . Like playing a big dramatic scene. Some of the arguments I've had in my married life went on long after either of us remembered what the hell the quarrel was all about. I guess we were each thoroughly enjoying a leading role!

I like to startle people with my theory that everyone in the world is always three drinks below normal, and that if each of them took a couple of drinks, before lunch, everyday, we'd all get along much better . . . As for stardom, hell, it ruins so many people— particularly actresses. Ninety percent of them are the dullest broads in town.

Boyer and Bogie play chess while Lauren kibitzes.

They have no appeal for me whatsoever, and that goes for Marilyn Monroe, Jane Russell and Gina Lollobrigida. In fact, the only actress in town with any true allure is Lauren Bacall . . .

I don't go for those top-heavy dames at all. That isn't sexy to me, but then, I'm not a bosom man. Now, Bacall has everything: charm, wit, looks and talent. Most of those other actresses look alike to me. I can't tell the difference between most of them anyway!

In the fall of 1953, Bogart and Warners mutually agreed to cancel his contract, which still had eight more years to go. Bogart left immediately for New York to co-star with Audrey Hepburn and Bill Holden in *Sabrina Fair*, for Paramount.

The next few years were happy ones for the Bogart clan. But in March of 1956, Bogart underwent major throat surgery at Good Samaritan Hospital to remove a malignant growth in his esophagus. The operation was considered successful. Bogie said that as soon as he regained the thirty pounds he'd lost, he would be back in films. Instead, he returned to the hospital in November of 1956. At that time, his condition was described as only "a nervous disorder."

In reality, Humphrey Bogart, one of Hollywood's biggest stars for nearly two decades, was wasting away from the effects of throat cancer. Bacall tried to keep his spirits up. A few old cronies, who could bear to see their pal looking like a mere shadow of his former self, still came to visit. The end was painful, not only for Bogie, but for all of those who loved him.

He died on January 14, 1957. Three days later, hundreds of his friends paid a final tribute to him at services conducted by Reverend Kermit Castellanos in All Saints Episcopal Church. John Huston delivered a simple, touching eulogy. He talked about Bogart's indominable courage in those last days before his death, and Huston recalled one night when he and Bogart were talking about their lives. Huston had asked Bogie if there was any particular part he would like to live over again. Bogart had answered: "Yes . . . The years I've spent with Betty."

Humphrey Bogart's ashes were inurned at the Garden of Memory atop Forest Lawn Memorial Park. Along with them was a tiny gold whistle inscribed with a line of dialogue Bacall had delivered in *To Have and Have Not*, their first picture together:

"If you need anything, just whistle."

Just as a Bogart film had a ready-made audience, so, too, Betty Grable's name on theatre marquees brought people to the box-office four times between 1950 and 1951. As the star of *My Blue Heaven, Wabash Avenue, Call Me Mister* and *Meet Me After the Show*, she was able to handsomely fill the coffers of 20th Century–Fox, as befitted the reigning screen-queen of their lot. But, as 1951 ended, the mutual admiration society formed between "Miss G. and Mr. Z." was breaking down.

Zanuck had purchased a property for Grable, but Betty told Darryl she was tired and wanted a rest. The result: "the Queen" was put on suspension and received no salary for eleven months. The bone of contention revolved around a picture called *Blaze of Glory*, in which Betty was to have co-starred with Richard Widmark.

In her own candid way, Betty complained: "I have lasted in this business by doing films that were good for me . . . Pictures that my fans wanted to see me in. In *Blaze of Glory*, they wanted me to play a B-girl who picked men up in bars. I didn't think that that was right for me."

So Betty, Harry and the girls spent a lot of extra time together—and the rest and relaxation with her family helped to compensate for the enormous salary loss. By the end of 1952, Betty was back at 20th, starring in *The Farmer Takes a Wife*, opposite Dale Robertson. On the surface, things seemed peaceful again. In reality, Grable's "royal throne" was a little wobbly. In her next film, *How to Marry a Millionaire*, she *shared* star billing with *two* other actresses, Lauren Bacall and Marilyn Monroe. The picture was a 1953 blockbuster—but Betty wanted out!

All sorts of rumors flew back and forth. From the studio it was whispered that trouble had started when the film business turned sour, executives cut salaries, theatres closed and the movie industry entered a state of emergency; the front office felt Betty should have been more cooperative.

Meanwhile, certain gossip columns printed rumors that Betty wanted to retire, ". . . primarily because she was jealous of the way 20th was now tilting things in favor of a younger blonde, Marilyn Monroe."

But Betty fought back. "Nonsense," she told a reporter. "I love working in pictures. I have no plans to retire. A lot of people think I'm jealous of Marilyn. That's not true. However, I *was* told that *Gentlemen Prefer Blondes* was bought for me. Naturally, I wanted to do it. Who wouldn't? But they gave it to Marilyn—and that was her good fortune . . .

"When Judy Garland bowed out of *Annie*

Mr. and Mrs. Harry James and their private orchestra, "The Jivin' Jills," Jessica and Vicki.

Get Your Gun, I was dying to do that part. Twentieth wouldn't let me. In all the years I've been with Fox, I have never worked off the lot."

Suddenly, the arguments grew more public—and the situation more untenable. For Grable, thirteen turned out to be an unlucky number. In July of 1953, after thirteen years as a 20th star, Grable's contract was canceled "by mutual agreement"—to take effect immediately. She had starred in twenty-five Technicolor films, had been among the top ten boxoffice stars for years, and received more fan mail than anyone else at 20th. But now it was all over. The contract, still calling for Grable to star in five more pictures, with a salary of ten thousand dollars per week, on a fifty-two-week-a-year guarantee, was terminated.

In 1954, Mr. and Mrs. Harry James purchased a one-story Hawaiian mansion in Beverly Hills, for $92,500. It had three-quarters of an acre of manicured grounds, and the home featured three family bedrooms, three baths, two large dressing rooms, a formal dining room, a huge den and a barbecue in an enclosed patio. A forty-five-foot pool was being added to the property. Obviously, even sans contract, Betty did not face a reduction in her standard of living. Of course, Harry James and his orchestra, with their live appearances and record sales, were not exactly on poverty row, either.

In 1955, Betty Grable starred for Columbia pictures in *Three for the Show.* Before that year ended, she had been invited back to 20th, where she starred in *How to Be Very Very Popular.* It was the last movie she ever made.

Grable could not have ended her film career with a more significant title as her epitaph. She was, indeed, one of the very most popular stars that Hollywood had ever nurtured.

Her name had been a household word ever since she'd slipped into a white bathing suit and looked provocatively over her shoulder—displaying a gorgeous smile, a trim behind, lovely shoulders and a tiny waistline—all of which rested on two of the most beautiful legs in celluloid history.

As the Fifties ended, Betty Grable, and her gorgeous gams, were still being seen every hour on the hour—on television screens throughout America.

In 1951, Clark Gable and Sylvia seemed to get along fine. He called her "Darling"; she referred to him as "Dear"; and, out on the town, they certainly made a striking-looking couple. Gable found it enchanting that his wife had not seen him on film since *It Happened One Night.* He took delight in running all his other movies for her. The twosome spent many evenings alone at the Gable ranch while his film projector whirred off a series of Gable starrers—and they munched popcorn like a couple of kids.

But Sylvia yearned for the bright lights, and Clark, when not working, wanted to hunt and fish and go for rides on his motorcycle. Sylvia did *not* hunt, hated fishing, and couldn't quite get up the nerve to hang onto the back of Gable's speeding bike. She *did* sit a horse rather well, though, still preferring her English saddle to the western ones.

So, more and more, Clark found diversions alone—or with male cronies. Sylvia, meanwhile, helped redecorate the Gable ranch. She ordered a guest house built on the property. She bought, and/or brought from her Fairbanks beach home possessions, elegant silver, china and crystal. Suddenly, fancy linen and lace napkins and tablecloths began appearing in Clark's dining room. Even dinners for two became full-dress spectaculars.

It was obvious, even to Clark's business associates, that something was troubling him. His close cronies knew for sure that things had begun to fall apart. Then, early in 1952, Sylvia limped into the Santa Monica Courthouse. She had a broken leg, the result of an auto accident, and her attorney, Jerry Giesler, helped to support her. She was there for the purpose of testifying in a divorce action.

Sylvia told the judge that the breakup had come suddenly, unexpectedly. She stressed the fact that she had made repeated attempts to keep the marriage together.

"But when I asked him what was wrong, he couldn't specifically tell me," she remarked tearfully. "All he said was, 'There isn't anything that you have done wrong . . . You have been quite wonderful . . . I'm just not happy being a married man.' "

Sylvia went on to admit they had separated on May 26, 1951. Their marriage had lasted a total of one year, five months and six days.

"The first indication I had that anything was even wrong occurred quite suddenly," Sylvia testified. "One afternoon, my husband came to me, and said, 'I don't wish to be married to you—or anybody else—and I want you to divorce me.'

a and b. Carole and Sylvia. There couldn't have been more of a difference between the two Gable women. (a) Carole at home on the Encino ranch, 1940, with one of her favorite horses. (b) Sylvia does her best to please Clark during the filming of MGM's *Across the Wide Missouri*.

"At first, I couldn't believe he was serious. I stayed on at the house for several weeks, during which time he scarcely spoke to me. When he did, he was very sullen. I tried everything I knew how to get him to change his mind, to hold our marriage together . . . Ultimately, I had to give in."

Clark's butler, Rufus B. Martin, who had been with Gable fourteen years, confirmed Sylvia's testimony. Mr. Martin said that he, too, had noticed Mr. Gable's coldness toward his wife. "After dinner, at night, he would go directly upstairs to his room," the butler testified. "Mrs. Gable would sit alone by the television. He wouldn't talk to her. He was moody."

After Sylvia appeared in court and demanded close to a million dollars in alimony, Gable, furious, went to Nevada, seeking to divorce her. But the courts ruled he was subject to California's jurisdiction. So, on April 21st, an eleven-page document was signed by both parties. It awarded Sylvia $6,002.47 in community property, ten percent of his income from movies, radio and television for the next year, and seven percent for the following four years. Since Gable earned $500,000 a year, Lady Sylvia would get approximately $50,000 the first year, $35,000 on each of the next four years—roughly $190,000—not too bad for less than two years of marriage. Besides that, of course, she had her large inheritance from Doug, Sr., which continued to bring her huge amounts of money just in interest alone.

At one point in the proceedings, Clark became so angry he was prepared to publicly air "all of their fancy dirty linen . . . sling all of the mud possible," just to get rid of her. Gable felt he had "been taken." He was bitter over what he considered her excessive monetary demands. In the end, wiser heads prevailed. He had never been a target for unpleasant gossip. There was no reason to change his image at this stage in life. He calmed down—signed the property settlement—and Lady Sylvia went on her way.

After Clark's unpleasant separation, his first serious relationship was with Mrs. Betty Chisholm, an Arizona heiress with vast oil interests and very social connections. She had a beautiful home in Phoenix, and Clark spent time there. As "chaperones" he always took along his close friends, Mr. and Mrs. Howard Strickling. Betty, in her forties, was very active. Played golf, liked to hunt and ride. She even returned Clark's visit, and house-guested with him in Encino. But he decided she was not for him.

On his way to Europe, Gable stopped in New York. There he met a gorgeous young French model, Suzanne Dadolle, who worked for the famous dress designer, Schiaparelli. She was twenty-eight, fair-haired, stood five foot-eight inches, and had a model's tiny twenty-three-inch waist.

Clark and Suzanne dated for a while until he left on location for a film. While her measurements may have been diminutive, her mouth was somewhat larger. She revealed to a reporter that Gable had asked her to travel with him all over the world, and to be with him for the rest of his life. She added, however, "our formal engagement announcement must come from Mr. Gable himself."

In Holland, Gable's press representative said he had no plans for an engagement, a marriage, or anything else! But in Paris, the lady was still talking. She told another member of the press that she and Clark had the same tastes. They both liked quiet evenings . . . and simple foods. Their favorite dish was pepper steak and beans. She also confessed that she adored Clark because he was a strong man. "I could never love anyone weaker than I am" . . . She displayed a large topaz ring which Clark had given her, "because it was her lucky stone . . . It was not exactly meant to be an engagement ring . . . but we'll see!"

Gable hated ladies who dated and talked.

He promptly dropped lovely Suzanne flat on her derriere.

After finishing *Mogambo*, in Africa, he had a brief relationship with Grace Kelly. Clark thought her a great kid, "pretty as a picture . . . but much too young to have been allowed to go to Africa without a chaperone!"

Meanwhile, on October 26, 1954, Sylvia Gable announced her forthcoming fifth marriage to her "third title," Prince Dimitri Djordjadze, a man she had known for many years. He was fifty, owned racing cars, thoroughbred horses, and was then working as the assistant to the head of the Sherry-Netherland and Ambassador hotels in New York City. Sylvia had known the Prince even before she married Douglas Fairbanks, Sr.

In November 1954, rumors had it that Gable was romancing Marilyn Monroe. They had met for the first time at a party celebrating the completion of her latest picture, *River of No Return*. Marilyn had just divorced Joe DiMaggio on October 27th. They had a few dances together. That was all. But the rumors persisted, and the studio did release a photo of the twosome dancing cheek to cheek. Then, as Clark left for Hong Kong to film *Soldier of Fortune*, Marilyn went into the hospital for minor surgery. In a gesture of "cooperation," 20th Century–Fox was kind enough to reveal that Clark sent Marilyn three dozen roses for each day she was confined in bed—and that eventually they would do a movie together.

But when Gable returned from location, in December 1954, it was *not* Marilyn, but an "old friend," Kay Williams Spreckels, who met him at the plane. Within a few weeks, Clark was denying that he and Kay planned to be married—and that he would be retiring from pictures as soon as he completed *Soldier of Fortune*.

"Mrs. Spreckels and I have no wedding plans," he said. "And I am not retiring. I'm under contract to 20th Century–Fox."

It was almost as difficult being "The King" as it was running a large movie studio. There were so many petty annoyances. So much rumor and innuendo. But then, like a production company, Gable's "product," himself, just naturally attracted questions, reporters, wild conjecture. However, at least Clark only had his women to worry about. The moguls, well, they had much larger headaches.

Barbara Stanwyck
"RAMBLING REPORTER"

In April of 1954, Barbara Stanwyck, filling in for a vacationing Hollywood Reporter columnist, contributed this short piece which expressed her unabashed admiration for certain film and stage performers—past and present.

When I was a kid in Brooklyn there wasn't much money for anything. But, once in a great while, with a reckless disregard for the financial consequences, my sister Millie would take me to a stuffy little movie theatre to see Pearl White in her perils. It was not money wasted. Pearl White was my goddess and her courage, her grace and her triumphs lifted me out of this world. Her memory still inspires me. In my humble opinion, this explains the *why* of motion pictures.

I'm grateful to a lot of stars for performances that thrilled me as a viewer, and, in due time, as a fellow-worker. All have made me proud to have been admitted to the acting profession. I'd carry a spear and hug the backdrop just to be in one scene with that one-in-a-million actor, Walter Huston. The memory of working with him in *The Furies* is a precious one. I thank God for the privilege of pitting all the skill I could beg, borrow or steal against Walter's greater skill in scenes we played together. I never won. But it was an honor to lose every scene to a guy like that. An actor like that.

I am a devotee at the shrine of Ingrid Bergman's greatness. Her gentle beauty, the glow of her inner fire, the sure, sure timing of her work has held me spellbound, not only when that was the title of her picture but in *Dr. Jekyll and Mr. Hyde,* in *Gaslight*—even in *Arch of Triumph.* I wonder what it's like to have that talent.

There's a gal named Shirley Booth who sends me away from any performance with my head in the clouds and my throat tight. I was told to see the play *Come Back, Little Sheba,* because Hal Wallis had bought it. Would I like to play it, they wanted to know! I saw it. I wanted to play it as I have never wanted to play any other role. But all that I had learned of professional honesty from Willard Mack, who taught me to be an actress, forbade it. "Sheba" was Shirley and Shirley was "Sheba." She *had* to play the picture. I wired Hal Wallis just that. And I couldn't be more smug about anything than I am about the last line of that wire. It was: "She'll only win an Oscar with it."

The performances I can't forget are like a haunting, loved melody. Spencer Tracy in *Captains Courageous;* Jeanne Eagels in any play—*Rain* and *Cardboard Lover*—in anything at all; Henry Fonda in *The Ox-Bow Incident* on the screen, in *Mister Roberts* on the stage and screen and Hepburn and Robert Walker in *Song of Love.* Judith Anderson in *The Old Maid* and *The Furies*; and, to round out a trio of "Furies" performances, Gilbert Roland, who made his not-too-great role so great it served as a ladder to the mature career he has now.

I love to remember the poetic beauty of Robert Taylor and Vivien Leigh in *Waterloo Bridge,* and the extraordinary perfection of Anne Baxter's drunk scene in *The Razor's Edge.* I think Richard Widmark's performance in *The Kiss of Death* is the most chilling—shocking—*evil* I have ever seen, and I love every minute of it. I wrote a fan letter to Olivia De Havilland for *Snake Pit,* to Bette Davis for *Jezebel* and *Dark Victory.*

I'll never forget Victor Mature's scene at the foot of the cross in *The Robe;* nor the breath-taking, heartbreaking farewell scenes of Jack Gilbert and Renée Adorée in *The Big Parade.* There's one performance I can't forget—though I wish I could—Jack Benny's in *The Horn Blows at Midnight.* This is the man I love—with or without a good script—and not only in my opinion is he just The Greatest. I *don't* want to forget Orson Welles in *The Third Man,* which, so far, I've seen only six times! I saw Victor McLaglen in *The Informer* ten times—what an actor and wonderful guy! I cherish the memory of Jackie Cooper as *Skippy*—just writing it brings a lump to my throat and a sting to my eyes. I'll buy Claire Trevor period. And what about Ida Lupino? Ah, this *is* an artist—one of the true ones.

Robert Donat in *Mr. Chips* is wonderful remembering; Susan Hayward in *Smash-Up* and Walter Brennan, another in-anything-at-all performer. Queen of *that* category, in my book, is a little bundle of show-business, cute as a kitten and wise as an owl . . . Thelma Ritter. She's got everything—including humility.

I like to remember Joan Crawford's Oscar performance as *Mildred Pierce,* and that little guy with a big talent who got himself an Oscar, *not* because of his singing. Inseparable part of that memory is the joyous excitement of his daughter and son, at the Pantages with him when Mercedes McCambridge read: "Frank Sinatra!"

The sweetest memory in my book started with a first performance—fifteen years ago. The picture was *Golden Boy.* I was being starred in it and a kid from Pasadena was getting his break in the title role. I thought the kid had what it takes, and told him much of what Willard Mack had taught me. That time my intuition was for real. William Holden graces our profession—and has well earned his first Academy Award. I don't think it will be his last.

Memories make me wonder about the future, and I see some mighty promising talent readying for memorable performances—Marilyn Monroe, Jane Powell, Ann Blyth, Jean Peters, Rock Hudson, Robert Wagner, Steve Forrest, Robert Stack and an eighteen-year-old, brand-newcomer—Robert Dix.

Time's up—and I've only started! I lack the words to express the last but not the least of my memories—no words are worthy of the unforgettable, the incomparable—Hell! I need only one word anyway. Here it is—*Garbo!*

BRING ON THE BRAINS

Outside of the atomic scientists collected at Alamogordo, New Mexico, during World War II, and perhaps some government "eggheads" in the various technical-military branches, there were no finer scientific or engineering minds than those in Hollywood and the other film communities around the world.

The time had come to invent new processes which would defeat "the enemy television." The industry urgently needed gimmicks, innovative techniques that would bring people back to their local theatres. Hollywood prepared for its own D-Day. The moguls issued a command: "Bring on the brains. If we don't have all we need, import them. If the foreign scientists won't come here, then we'll go to them."

While the "brain safari" was in progress, experiments were conducted with a process called Phonevision. In July of 1950, Chicago was selected as the "test site." The Zenith Corporation equipped three hundred homes with a mechanism enabling occupants to order specific programs, by telephone, for which they would be billed monthly. The programs selected—Hollywood films.

In essence, Phonevision was a *home TV receiver* for feature motion pictures. The theatre exhibitors weren't all that thrilled. But it did mean potentially big money for Hollywood's studio coffers. However, the tests were called off—in October. At the last moment, Hollywood backed out. Major motion picture producers refused to supply films for the test, thus depriving th company of the type and variety of features they needed to make the experiment truly representative. The plight of movie house owners nationwide had been taken into consideration—and the threat judged too great.

In February of 1951, Phonevision was tried again anyway. They found some films to show, but the idea made no impact. The timing for this particular new process was off. It would be two more decades before anything like it was attempted again on a large scale. The experiment had failed for various reasons—the main one being Hollywood's refusal to cooperate. But it was this comparatively crude attempt which hastened the movie industry's call to arms for new theatre processes. They did *not* want to bother with ideas that might make staying at home even more inviting!

With the end of 1951 came the war of the third dimension. Producer Sol Lesser started it all when he gave the press a demonstration of the British-developed Tri-Opticon, a process requiring the audience to wear polarized glasses, as did Milton Gunzburg's Natural Vision 3-Dimension. When asked about the possibility of his obtaining the Polaroid glasses, Lesser said that if Polaroid, and its sole theatrical representative, Gunzburg, did not supply him, he would sue under antitrust. Gunzburg said he didn't know what Lesser was talking about, but if he ordered the glasses and paid for them they would be delivered.

Lesser, who had not yet signed a theatre for the American premiere of Tri-Opticon, said he would produce two full-length three-dimensional features in 1953 and roadshow a group of six 20-minute shorts to be made in color. The press audience viewed five shorts photographed in Tri-Opticon, which were shown with two standard projectors mechanically synchronized by a special rigging. The basis of Tri-Opticon was a revolutionary camera mount and mechanical calculator, the latter correlating the many factors involved in stereo photography.

While the push was on for perfecting 3-D, talent hunts for other new scientific breakthroughs were conducted around the world. One of them, Cinerama, harked back to a Thirties experiment. Technically speaking, wide screens for motion pictures were not an innovation. Toward the end of the Thirties, one of those "brainy types," Fred Waller, had demonstrated a process he called Vitarama. According to Arthur Knight, of *The Hollywood Reporter*, Waller's invention had consisted of ". . . eleven projectors linked together to throw onto as many conjoining screens an image that would encompass as much as the eye could see. Originally scheduled to debut at the 1939 New York World's Fair, it was quietly dropped as too cumbersome and expensive."

Waller scaled down his system, from eleven to three screens, and continued to show it to potential investors. While the industry moguls showed little interest, commentator-travelogue expert Lowell Thomas and producer Mike Todd did. They made a film, *This Is Cinerama*, released in 1952, captivating audiences with its enormous size, scope, and the feel of audience participation. Depending on where one sat in the theatre, there was the feeling of total involvement, whether riding a gigantic rollercoaster or flying through the Grand Canyon. By his use of peripheral vision as a substitute for mechanical 3-D, Waller had inadvertently provided the clue leading to such later processes as CinemaScope and Vista-Vision—which were 3-D *sans glasses*.

The Cinerama process, while innovative, was not perfect enough for use in feature films of a dramatic or musical nature. There were problems with screen distortion still to be worked out. But that didn't matter now. There was shouting and joy throughout Hollywoodland. The gimmick they needed had been found—and had exceeded everybody's wildest dreams.

A screening was held on Thursday, January 29, 1953, to show tests of the new wide-vision patents acquired in Paris by Spyrous Skouras some months before. Audiences would see and hear a different picture, with better sound, on a screen several times the size of those in current use. The picture, in color, with a full simulation of a 3-dimensional effect, would be more exciting than the industry had heretofore produced. The remarkable part about this process, which 20th–Fox called Cinema-Scope, was that it could be shot on 35mm raw stock, and use the *same* cameras and projectors. The biggest mechanical change would be the necessity for new screens, two or three times the size of those in existence, plus perhaps an additional set of sound horns behind them. The installation and necessary additions were minimal. It would cost the largest theatres about $25,000 and the smaller houses around $5,000.

From the audience, the full effect of each film could be had from any seat in a theatre. There would be neither the eyestrain nor any of the discomfort experienced by those who sat in the first few rows. CinemaScope was a simple, inexpensive color film device simulating 3-D. Its stereophonic sound imparted a more lifelike quality because it moved across the screen with the action. CinemaScope needed only one camera for filming and one machine for projection. It did not require audiences to wear glasses in order to appreciate the illusion of real life. It was considered as revolutionary to motion pictures as the introduction of talkies!

Screens, specially developed for extra brilliance, could be any length a theatre desired. The screen used in the first Hollywood test was 64 feet wide and 25 feet high. A big theatre, for example New York's Roxy, would use one 80 feet long, with proportionate ratio of height to width. The screen, curving to a depth of 5 feet, afforded a feeling of engulfment without reflecting any annoying light.

Due to the immensity of the screen, few entire scenes could be taken in at a glance—the moviegoer could view each one as in life or as one would watch a play. *The Robe* was 20th's first CinemaScope film to go into production. Eleven other features, both in color and CinemaScope, were scheduled to follow in rapid order.

By March of 1953, Hollywood was galvanized into action. A battle of the big screens shaped up between 20th and Paramount—Fox having the edge as they were already in production. Still, Paramount's technicians worked round the clock in an attempt to put together an immediate showing of *their* new process—VistaVision. But it would be another full year before Paramount's wide-screen features were ready to go on a big scale. The Mitchell Camera Company, the first major manufacturer to start production on the VistaVision system, would not be ready until April of 1954.

Meanwhile, in mid-March of 1953, Billy Wilkerson saw a demonstration at 20th and sounded the clarion call to the entire industry in *The Hollywood Reporter:*

We've seen CinemaScope.
We've heard the new Stereophonic sound.
We've viewed the new crystal-clear Eastman color stock.
The combination of the three, as shown at the test press showing of CinemaScope, is the answer to every exhibitor's prayer . . .
So, boys and girls, move over . . . you won't have to wear glasses to stay in the business. This process that 20th is showing has much more than 3-D, even if third-dimension is ever perfected. This is no flash-in-the-pan or quick buck device. Some of the other studios who are working on big screens may come up with something as good or better than 20th has, but until they do, we'll settle for CinemaScope.

Wilkerson was proven correct. One week after his editorial, a thousand exhibitors arrived in Hollywood to see what all the shouting was about. Never in the history of the industry had there been so much unbridled enthusiasm. When sound had been introduced, many theatre owners refused to accept it. They figured it was only a passing fancy. But the men who saw CinemaScope were convinced they were on the threshold of a new business, one that might well push motion pictures to their highest boxoffice rewards ever.

Columbia and RKO announced, however, that they still opted for the Natural Vision 3-dimensional process. Warners, which had perfected their own new color process, WarnerColor, followed suit. Jack Warner said his company was going one hundred percent into 3-D as far as their next twenty films were concerned, combining it with their new color process, plus Warner-Phonic sound. He had been spurred to this decision by his company's worldwide success with *House of Wax*, Warner's first 3-D film. Whatever size screen, or its dimension, Hollywood had begun to fight back. As Jolson had said twenty-five years earlier, "You ain't seen nothin' yet!"

In rapid order, MGM announced the development of a new lens that could take a flat picture and project it, giving the wide-screen effect and depth of both Cinema-Scope and the new 3-D. Their process was "still under wraps," Metro said. "But it looked very promising."

But, by October 1953, there was trouble in paradise. Insiders said that "the bloom was off of the rose" in regard to 3-D. Warners had a half dozen of those films still unreleased. Columbia had five, and Paramount "might be stuck with four." Both Universal-International and MGM had a trio of unreleased 3-Ds. Meanwhile, the process had not been fully accepted by the public. Once again, Hollywood, in its race to outdistance "the enemy," had gone off in all directions, competing with itself—and making some costly mistakes.

Then along came pioneer mogul Joseph M. Schenck, recently resigned from 20th. He announced the formation of another company, the Magna Theatre Corporation, organized for the manufacture, production and release of a new wide-angle medium for motion pictures. It was to be a subsidiary of United Artists, which Schenck also headed. His new process, Schenck stated, "combined scientific knowledge and the resources of the country's oldest optical organization, the American Optical Company, along with a formidable group of Broadway and Hollywood showmen. This alliance has resulted in the development of the Todd-AO process. It will be a new medium of expression, adaptable for motion picture theatres around the world," he said proudly. The industry sat up and took notice. If someone as wily and innovative as Schenck was behind *this* new process, it must have something.

In the summer of 1954, the Todd-AO process, used to film *Oklahoma!*, was unveiled—and it looked very good. Developments were coming fast and furious. By the following year, Mike Todd, in great part responsible for Todd-AO, announced he was pulling away from Schenck and the Magna Company. Rumor had it that Mike had something even better up his expensive silk sleeve.

In October of 1956, when *Around the World in 80 Days* was screened, the news was out. Todd had far surpassed both Cinerama and the original Todd-AO with refinements revealing a richer, lusher process for screen entertainment: *80 Days* presented actors in-the-round for the first time onscreen—a complete illusion of depth and audience participation. Todd also added a refined six-channel sound system, and the total effect was startling.

By this time, 20th's *The King and I*, and *The Greatest Story Ever Told*, in *their* newest 55mm CinemaScope, had been shown and the reaction was fantastic. Three-dimensional films had all but gone by the boards. The studios had learned a costly lesson.

The latter half of the Fifties became a saner, less competitive period. There was, of course, another reason: television had been perfecting *its* techniques and had come up with some sensational improvements. Color, sharper sound and enormous strides in the production of good series and cartoon animation made that medium more popular than ever. Television had grown, stride for stride, with the new motion picture. Besides, by the time the Fifties were about to end, the movie and TV industries were firmly entwined. Beating "the enemy" meant breaking one's right arm while protecting one's left!

With a faint touch of irony, the last innovation to make any impact on motion pictures during this period was a film process backed by Michael Todd, Jr. Following in his late father's dynamic footsteps, he was always on the lookout for "something great—something fantastic." The Stanley Warner Corporation had invested $100,000 in a process called "Scentvision," but then had abandoned the whole thing. It was this new gimmick which young Todd got wind of—literally.

An international chemical company claimed it had perfected a way of adding aromas which enhanced the enjoyment of motion pictures. Wisenheimers labeled it "Smell-O-Vision." But, by whatever name, it didn't turn on audiences. Todd and his stepmother, Elizabeth Taylor, went as far as screening a short film for the press. The results were less than thrilling.

David Niven
"TURNING THE TABLES ON TODD"

*With equal eloquence and wit, David Niven wrote this piece for the November 18,
1957, issue of* The Hollywood Reporter.

The time will come, I dare say, when a grandchild or three will cluster about my knobby knees with the time-honored request, "Tell us a story."

"About what?" I will ask.

"About Mike Todd and *Around the World in 80 Days,* they'll say. You see, Mike will still be around and *Around the World* will still be playing to packed houses.

I'll undoubtedly begin at the beginning, which took place one Sunday afternoon. The phone rang and a voice said, "This is Mike Todd. Can you come over right away?"

"Shall I bring my agent?" I asked. Todd said it wasn't necessary. I arrived at Mike's place to find him dressed in a Stetson, a pair of picturesque swimming trunks and a cigar.

He immediately came to the point. "Did you ever hear of Jules Verne?" he asked.

My affirmative answer elicited question number two. "Did you ever read *Around the World in 80 Days?*"

"I was weaned on it," I answered.

"Would you be interested in playing Phileas Fogg in the picture?" he asked.

"I'd do it for nothing," I shouted, my tongue working faster than my brain.

"You've got a deal," he snapped.

"Phil!" I screamed in despair to my absent agent. I got him on the phone and he rushed over. Mike didn't hold me to the gratis offer, and a deal was quickly made. This marked the beginning of the happiest and most worthwhile assignment which will ever come my way.

It was replete with laughs, locations and unforgettable experiences. I'll always remember Durango, Colorado, where we shot the train sequence on the only narrow gauge railway left in the U.S.A.

The script called for hundreds of Indians to shoot at the train and at Cantinflas and me in particular with rubber pointed arrows.

After a time, the Indians must have been affected by their own whooping and hollering, and probably started to remember what indignities their ancestors had suffered at the hands of the white man.

One arrow whizzed by me and penetrated the wood exterior of the coach not two feet away from my head. I yanked out the still quivering shaft and lo—it had a metal point as real as could be.

"Those bloody Indians are shooting at us with real arrows," I yelled at Cantinflas. He shrugged nonchalantly. I guess he didn't feel they were as sharp as the horns of the bulls he had faced.

I wasn't hit, but how could I ever forget Durango, Colorado?

Then came the time for the balloon sequence when the big gas bag was to take Cantinflas and me across the Alps.

We were to have doubles, but they just didn't look legitimate. Todd asked us to do the sequence in place of the doubles. What bothered me was acrophobia, which means I'm allergic to heights. I almost pass out when I'm standing on a chair to fix something at home, not to mention cavorting in a wicker basket at the top of a crane 180 feet above the Universal-International back lot.

But Todd is a genius. He suspended operations while we discussed the ascent, using imported champagne to neutralize the heat and dust of the location. Before long, I wasn't afraid of acrophobia or anything else and escorted Cantinflas to the balloon. The bottle and a reserve supply accompanied us. I must say that even with the influence of the bubbly stuff, the ground looked very far away, but I was able to get through with it.

It was just another case of Todd being there with the goods.

I rather got even with Mike for giving me a scare on my first offer to work for free on the occasion of going to London for the *Around the World* sequences in London.

I was about to leave New York for the plane trip to England, when Todd wired me from the British capital asking me to bring three packages for him with me and outlining the contents. The packages were delivered, and I had them placed on the plane.

Midway during the transatlantic flight, I dispatched the following telegram to Mike, who was to meet me on arrival: "Have suits, cigars and radios. Can't for the life of me find your heroin."

When I landed in London, the airport was

swarming with Scotland Yard operatives, customs and narcotics agents. Mike was completely collared as I stepped off the plane.

It took a number of hours of earnest talking to clear up the matter of the non-existent narcotic. But I swear the gag was worth all the trouble it entailed.

There are many other happy experiences I could—and probably will—tell my presently non-existent grandchildren when the proper time comes.

And when I do, I'll undoubtedly wind up with the story of the telegram I sent Todd the morning after the picture opened in New York.

It read: "Better luck next time."

THOSE VERY SPECIAL LADIES

In some ways they had a lot in common. In others, they were as different as day is from night.

Ava Gardner had literally floated into Hollywood—with absolutely no effort—and certainly no desire to become an actress, much less a star. Crawford, on the other hand, had wanted fame and fortune so desperately that she danced her legs bone-weary and smiled at so many hopefully important connections that when stardom came she felt entitled—double-in-spades.

Both wanted desperately to love and be loved. They fell hard, and fast—making heartbreaking mistakes. But neither allowed the men in their lives to become an encumbrance for too long.

Instinctively, they knew when it was time to say so long and move on.

By the spring of 1951, Ava Gardner's career was in high gear—so were her romantic entanglements. She was in Spain making *Pandora and the Flying Dutchman,* with James Mason. Of course, she already knew Frank Sinatra. Insiders said they were very close. But then, there was the bullfighter—Mario Cabre—who had a small part in Ava's film. Miss Gardner, according to the papers in Barcelona, had "fallen under Mario's spell." While the romance was partially inspired by an overactive studio publicist, Sinatra "heard whispers," and flew across the ocean, bearing gifts.

Mario, who looked like the all-American college type, was not only agile with bulls, he also wrote poetry—and talked to reporters. He told everyone who would listen that he loved Ava with all his heart and soul, and she felt the same way about him. When asked if he considered Frank a rival—and what about that piece of jewelry Sinatra had given Gardner—Cabre had a macho reply. "That diamond necklace? Well, symbolically, that would be like giving her a noose . . . trying to hang love . . . trying to rope her in!"

Sinatra, who had arrived in Spain with songwriter Jimmy Van Heusen, was short on words but quick to react. He rented a car in Barcelona and headed for a beach resort some fifteen miles south of where Ava was on location. There, in a romantic waterfront cafe, the famous twosome staged a reunion. Ava remarked to a reporter that when she fell in love for the third time, "it would be eternal"—but she would not admit whether love number three was Sinatra or her bullfighter!

Earlier in the year, Ava had been viciously attacked by Sinatra fans. They'd grown up with Frankie and were devoted to his marriage to Nancy. The letters Ava received were malicious and ugly. Pressure lessened when the fans learned that Sinatra had given Nancy a mink coat on March 26, her birthday.

When reviewers saw *Pandora and the Flying Dutchman*, they came to a single conclusion. The much publicized Sinatra, Gardner, Cabre triangle certainly helped Ava turn in the greatest screen performance of her career—particularly the love scenes.

On August 2nd, Ava was in Mexico with Frank. But their attempt to rendezvous secretly had failed. Privacy was obviously out of the question. The twosome already had been stopped by reporters at the airport in Los Angeles, then again as they changed planes in El Paso. Understandably, Sinatra had been upset and argumentative. "Why can't you guys leave us alone?" he'd shouted. "This is silly . . . What we do is our own damn business . . . It's really a fine thing when we can't even go on vacation without being chased."

Frank had refused to pose with Ava for photographers before changing planes in El Paso. He had attempted to get Ava a sandwich—she hadn't eaten aboard the flight from Los Angeles because of stomach troubles. Frank had been very solicitous of Ava because of her illness. They had acted very lovey-dovey, a stewardess reported. She also said Sinatra kept calling Ava "Angel."

By then, reports were circulating that Sinatra had decided to divorce Nancy, from whom he was already separated. But Frank dismissed any talk of an early divorce, or any divorce at all from Nancy. By August 8th, he and Ava were back in Hollywood after having spent six extremely frustrating days South of the Border trying to be alone together.

On November 2, 1951, in Philadelphia, Frank Sinatra and Ava Gardner filled out a marriage license in the privacy of Judge Charles Klein's chambers. The magistrate said Sinatra appeared highly nervous, but Ava seemed quite calm. While the judge talked to reporters, the couple slipped out a side door. The previous day, after twelve years of marriage, Sinatra had been granted a divorce from Nancy in Las Vegas. The ink was hardly dry.

According to a friend, the two planned to be married in Pennsylvania after the required seventy-two-hour waiting period. On the legal document they signed, Frank listed his age as thirty-four; his occupation as entertainer. Ava said she was twenty-eight, and an actress. Both provided blood test certificates plus official copies of their respective divorces—Sinatra's from Nancy— Ava's from both Mickey Rooney and Artie Shaw.

On Wednesday evening, November 7, 1951, in Germantown, a fashionable suburb of Philadelphia, Frank and Ava became man and wife at the home of dress manufacturer Lester Sachs. The ceremony was performed by Judge Joseph E. Sloane. When it was over, the newlyweds kissed; Frank shook the judge's hand, while Ava wrapped her arms around Sinatra's mother. Dolly burst into tears and affectionately patted her new daughter-in-law on the shoulder. Gardner looked particularly lovely in an eggshell tinted wedding gown, cut low in front, with a starched white collar, accenting prim box pleats on the bodice. Once the ceremony was over, a guest played the "Wedding March." Everyone formed a circle around the bridal couple and toasted them with champagne. Then Ava cut the seven-tiered wedding cake, topped with a green and white replica of a church bell.

Both of Sinatra's parents were present, as was Ava's sister, Bea. Although the Sachs' home was guarded by six private police detectives, fans managed to peek in through the venetian blinds. When they had arrived from New York by limousine, Frank had taken one look at the horde of reporters that was waiting for them in the rain, and he commented loudly: "How did these creeps know where we were?"

Later, Sinatra came out on the porch and

forbade photographers to take any pictures. He explained that a private photog had been hired who would do all of the shooting and provide the press with prints. When one camerman protested, Sinatra shook his fist, and yelled, "You take one picture here tonight and I'll knock you down."

In May of 1952, Ava was rushed to Cedars of Lebanon Hospital for a kidney stone operation. Frank, appearing at the Ambassador Hotel's Cocoanut Grove, was with her when she went into surgery. Ava had been ailing for weeks, but attended Frank's opening because she had wanted to be supportive. During this period she had been under suspension by MGM for refusing to travel to Mexico to make a picture. She gave them the straight reason— she did not want to leave Frank. In short order, the studio relented and Ava went back to work in Culver City.

All seemed well for the next five months. But by October the Sinatras were desperately trying to save their marriage. They had a series of terrible arguments. In a fit of pique, Ava returned her wedding ring to Frank. He, equally as pigheaded, decided not to accompany her to Africa and Europe as they'd planned, even though she would be gone for at least eighteen months. The tension between them was devastating— still, each hoped that the break could be mended. Frank left to appear at the Hotel Chase in St. Louis. Ava named the main reason for their marital troubles—her husband was always taking off to sing in another club.

To complicate matters, Ava's ring, the one she'd returned—which cost $50,000— had been lost! Frank was having a duplicate made. Wistfully, he told reporters, "I'm nuts about her . . . I don't think our love is dead . . . but it certainly is up in the air."

Although no separation or divorce had been announced, both parties were represented by New York attorney Henry Jaffe.

Meanwhile, career-wise, Sinatra never sounded better. His love songs and torch ballads carried an extra special meaning. He was doing big club business, turning the people away. In fact, critics wrote that he was once again "the old Sinatra . . . standing people in the aisles with his spectacular vocalizing."

Ava was in the limelight as well. On October 21, 1952, she made a big splash when she put her foot- and handprints in the forecourt of Grauman's Chinese Theatre. But she kept her mouth shut when reporters asked what happened the previous weekend. There had been reports of a "spirited debate" between Ava and Frank, with Lana Turner as referee. The clash had climaxed—according to rumors—when Sinatra told Gardner to get out of their house and never come back.

Still, seven days later, the twosome reconciled so publicly that it now looked as though Frank would go to Africa after all. But first they were scheduled to go to North Carolina to visit with her family, then on to New York for a couple of days—unless there was another fight between them.

On November 7, 1952, Ava celebrated one year as Mrs. Frank Sinatra. It had been a battling, wildly romantic marriage. She had been working almost constantly since that spring month in Spain when Frank first chased her halfway around the world while she was filming *Pandora*. Then she'd done *Scaramouche*. Next, RKO borrowed her for *My Forbidden Past*, where she co-starred with Robert Mitchum. They also loaned her out for "One Touch of Venus."

Then Ava left for location in Africa. She was co-starring in MGM's *Mogambo*, with Clark Gable and Grace Kelly. Frank went too. He would remain until he had to return to the States to test for the part of Maggio in *From Here to Eternity*. As she boarded the plane, all eyes were focused on her. Ava was a flawless beauty. She weighed 115 pounds, stood 5'5" tall; with a perfect complexion, brown hair, green eyes, and a very sensuous look—it was the type of special loveliness that drove men wild—none more so than Frank Sinatra.

The rest of that year, and into the next, Ava kept busy with work—and the relationship between the Sinatras seesawed between good, bad and indifferent. In September of 1953, Ava flew into New York to finish *Mogambo*. Frank was not at Idlewild Airport to meet her. He was preparing to open at Bill Miller's Riviera in New Jersey. She had no comment on the current state of their relationship, and did not attend Frankie's Riviera premiere. She deliberately flaunted her lack of interest by appearing at a rival club.

Frank, with Ava apparently out of his life, was staying at the Waldorf Towers and even answering his own phone. Chums labeled him the "new" Sinatra. He appeared to have acquired an inner security that came with his gratifying success in *From Here to Eternity*. He had never been in better voice or handled himself with more modesty.

On the eve of their second anniversary, in November 1953, Ava, back in Hollywood, confessed to a reporter that she wished she were expecting a baby, even though chances of a reconciliation with Sinatra looked slim. She was staying with her sister again, and had not been dating. She announced she would leave soon to do *The Barefoot Contessa*, in Italy.

Frank, having appeared calm and collected just the week before, wound up in Mount Sinai for a checkup. He suddenly appeared to be under a great emotional strain. Then, in yet another turn of events, Frank wound up joining Ava in Madrid for Christmas. They spent the holiday together before Ava flew off to the *Contessa* location and Frank remained behind to recuperate. From one moment to the next, neither of them knew what would happen.

In January of 1954, they were back to-

1 Co-star Clark Gable with Ava Gardner on location in Africa during the filming of MGM's *Mogambo*.   2 Frank Sinatra in a scene from Columbia's *From Here to Eternity*.

gether in Rome. But he was headed for America, while she remained in Italy to work. Ava did not see him off at the airport, "because she had the flu," Frank said. "I have to rush back to Hollywood to report to 20th Century–Fox on a project," he continued. When asked what the status of their marriage was, he smiled and said, "Fine."

By the end of May 1954, "fine" had turned into "finished." Ava Gardner had obviously dismissed thoughts of Sinatra, at least in a romantic way. She kissed handsome bullfighter Luis Miguel Dominguin goodbye at the Madrid airport before flying to London en route to New York. Once there, she announced, during a four-hour stopover, that she planned to immediately finalize divorce proceedings against Sinatra. "I was never more certain of anything," she said.

By the second week in June, Ava arrived in Reno to establish a Nevada residence for her divorce from Sinatra. She drove there from Los Angeles and rented a plush cottage in Lake Tahoe for the required six weeks' stay. When asked by a reporter what grounds she would use, she said: "The usual." In Nevada, that meant extreme cruelty. She answered no questions about her bullfighter, Dominguin. Meanwhile, at Nevada's other gambling resort, Las Vegas, Sinatra opened at the Sands Hotel, while Ava spouses number one and two, Mickey Rooney and Artie Shaw, were appearing elsewhere on the Strip. It was a veritable "Ava Gardner–Ex-Husbands–Entertainment–Festival!"

While Ava's star was continuing to rise, Joan had been at the top for more than twenty years. And she was restless. It was late 1953. Joan had been divorced from Phillip Terry for eight years. Of course, there had been men in her life since then. Glamorous attorney Greg Bautzer. A few producers. A young actor or two. Still, she was dissatisfied—she felt so insecure. There were the kids—and her work. But her life

lacked that anchor she had always yearned for.

Life still seemed a hard struggle for Crawford. She was rich. Famous. Beautiful. But it was not enough. She was still looking, constantly searching—first of all for perfection in herself and her children—a manifestation of past unhappiness.

The home she lived in, on Bristol Avenue in Brentwood, was a tangible example of her insecurity and discontent. When she first bought it, in 1929, it was a very special symbol of her earliest taste of success. A Spanish house with a tile roof, the home she shared with Douglas Fairbanks, Jr. From the moment he moved out, and Joan started on her marital merry-go-round, the house had been the target of her restlessness. She had it redone almost every year. There were fake ceilings. New floors. False walls built to hide the original stained glass windows.

Over the years, like Cinderella, the house kept changing "outfits." With Joan as fairy godmother, it went from Early Spanish to Middle Modern, to Early American, then back to Modern. By 1953, it had miraculously turned into Crawford's English Regency Castle—the only thing missing was a permanent Prince Charming.

Still, Joan kept adding rooms, subtracting rooms, redesigning her backyard. There was a pool. A formal rose garden. Neat brick patios. A special area where her beloved dogs could roam and "do their business" away from the main house. Everything could have been so perfect—yet she seemed in constant turmoil. Her servants kept changing. Most of them left because they found it impossible to keep up with her demands.

On the social side, Joan had a tight coterie of dear friends who really cared for her. From them, she needed constant reassurance that she was "really somebody" in the Hollywood sphere. If she was out of work for a week, Crawford was convinced she would never do another movie. She needed people to tell her how special she was. How important and essential Crawford films were to the industry.

Joan sometimes wrote as many as a thousand letters a month. She promptly answered every note she received. If someone sent her a "thank you" for a kind gesture, she wrote back and thanked *them* for their "thank you." All of this was a product of her inability to be content with herself—or secure in the knowledge that she truly *was* one of Hollywood's all-time great stars.

By 1954, there *was* one potential catch on the horizon—Alfred Steele, a dynamic business tycoon whom she had met in New York through her dear friends, the Sonny Werblins. He had been an advertising salesman for the *Chicago Tribune* and an executive of the Standard Oil Company of Indiana. Then he became manager for CBS in Detroit, and left there to go with Coca-Cola as a vice president. By the time Joan met him, he was a corporate officer with Coke's chief rival, Pepsi-Cola.

She visited him in New York; he came West to see her. Because he wasn't physically the matinee-idol type, Hollywood gossip columnists discounted him as a serious Crawford prospect. She had always fallen for the "gorgeous guys." Mature, gray-haired, bespectacled Alfred didn't fit the picture. But, on an evening in May of 1955, after dining at a restaurant in Beverly Hills, Joan and Alfred eloped to Las Vegas.

They were married at 2 A.M., on May 10, in a penthouse of the Flamingo Hotel. In attendance were Bert Knighton, a Pepsi executive, Mr. and Mrs. Andrew Fuller, friends of Joan's from Fort Worth, Texas, and Mr. and Mrs. Ben Goffstein and Abe Schiller of the Flamingo. Joan wore a black and gold gown with an orchid pinned to her shoulder. She had come to Nevada without any luggage. They arrived in Steele's private plane, itself an accomplishment—Joan had never flown before except on a brief hop from Catalina, twenty-six miles back to Los Angeles.

On their wedding day, they left Las Vegas at 10 A.M. and flew directly back to Hollywood. Joan had to report to Columbia Studios to finish *Queen Bee*. Steele, meanwhile, left for New York. Crawford was scheduled to join him there to begin their European honeymoon.

The moment she arrived on set, Joan's "regulars" gathered around to get all the details—as they had before when she had eloped with Phil Terry.

"It was so romantic," Crawford grinned. "We boarded Alfred's plane and took off. We went up to eleven thousand feet . . . and Alfred held me in his arms. You might say we flew on moonlit wings . . . and I haven't come down to earth yet. This is the happiest moment of my life. I'm going to make him the best wife in the world. It happened so suddenly, Alfred had to borrow a ring to put on my finger, and I had to borrow a nightie and a toothbrush."

Steele, divorced from his second wife, had a five-and-a-half-year-old boy, nicknamed Sonny, from that marriage, and a daughter, Sally, who was twenty-two.

On May 18, Joan and her fourth husband sailed from New York for the Isle of Capri. They were greeted by the villagers, who serenaded them and danced the tarantella. Then they were whisked off to begin their idyll at a villa called "Il Capricorno." At last, all was stable in Joan Crawford's world. Her Prince Charming had arrived. Her anchor had emerged. In 1956, Joan had finally found perfection or at least as much of it as any "divine creature" could hope to achieve.

Dean Martin and Jerry Lewis
"THAT'S MY BOY"

At the height of their popularity as America's leading comedy-song team, Dean Martin and Jerry Lewis wrote these short vignettes about each other for the October 29, 1951, issue of The Hollywood Reporter. *Dean had the first word.*

It takes a guy with an iron constitution, nerves of steel and the patience of a dozen Jobs to keep him from annihilating Idiot's Delight. I refer, of course, to that popular young comedian (and I use the word advisedly—I have to, it's in my contract!) Jerry Lewis. Every visual gag Jerry uses on an audience is guinea-pigged on me first. I didn't know that was to be part of Operations Lunatic. I had to learn the hard way.

A couple of months ago, for instance, during one of our television shows, Jerry brought down the house when he began cutting up my dinner jacket with a pair of big shears. The audience really went crazy. So did I—that tuxedo had just set me back a couple of hundred bucks! But, "Anything for a laugh!"—that's Jerry's motto. That's my boy!

Another time I was singing one of my best numbers on the stage of a theatre during a personal appearance. I was in great voice that night. The audience was eating it up. I had 'em right in the palm of my hand—then suddenly a few people began tittering, and pretty soon the whole audience was rocking with laughter. I really couldn't blame them. I guess I looked like a fool, singing a torchy ballad and at the same time doing what must have looked like a comic dance routine. What the audience couldn't see was "mah li'l ole pahdner" standing off in the wings throwing lighted firecrackers at me! It's little things like this that endear him to me.

There was the night, too, when I was supposed to do a very quick change for one of our routines. So what happened? So Perpetual Motion had sewed my trouser legs together!

But, underneath his moronic exterior, Jerry is true blue. He is sentimental and thoughtful. There is nothing he wouldn't do for a pal. He proved this at my wedding. He'd been clowning around and getting in my hair generally, so I told him to go jump in the pool with clothes on. Brave, fearless, intrepid Lewis—he took the dare, all right—in the new suit I'd planned to wear on my honeymoon!

But I can't complain. I had my chance to even the score for all time, but I blew it. It was in Chicago. Jerry fell asleep in the barber chair, and I bribed the guy to cut all his hair off. That backfired, but good. His new "Butch" proved a big sensation, and I was out a five-buck bribe! If I'd had any foresight at all, I'd have put the fin back in my pocket, borrowed the guy's razor, and removed Lewis' second head!

But don't get me wrong—with all his faults, I love the kid. *That's* for real!"

Then it was Jerry's turn to mouth off:

It was considerably less than a decade ago (circa 1946) that Mr. Dean Martin had the extreme good fortune to make my acquaintance. At that time, in a burst of fraternal sentiment, we made a contractual agreement to unite in presenting public entertainment fare in a light vein.

Mr. Martin was convinced that his singing voice, although far from Metropolitan caliber, was sufficiently pleasant to amuse the pleasure-seekers of that North American Riviera, Atlantic City. I was equally certain of titillating their theatrical taste buds with various antics and ludicrous capers.

Together we approached the impresario of a certain cafe and placed before him our well-thought-out plans on the subject. It was entirely natural that his interest was immediately aroused.

Dashed not a whit by the initial setback to our plans (the premiere audience had rudely forgotten to give kudos or plaudits), we followed a new pattern the next evening (one to which we have strictly adhered ever since). Its intent was to amuse and confuse. That we succeeded is now a matter of record.

Mr. Martin sang in his rather light and untutored manner while I, emulating the waiters of the establishment, gathered on to a long tray all manner of goblets, porcelain and silver from the various tables which gave onto the dance floor.

In order to divert attention from one of Mr. Martin's less true notes (which he sprinkles liberally throughout his vocal exhibitions) I allowed the heavily-laden tray to descend suddenly to the floor. The ensuing cacaphony, as the crystal and chinaware shattered into fragments, delighted the audience and they indulged in loud and great merriment. To borrow a coarse term from the argot of the theatre, "We were a wow!"

Since that initial venture *en duo,* Mr. Martin and I have traveled the length and breadth of the land, impartially distributing our individual humor to prince and pauper alike.

We have but recently, as you are undoubtedly aware, broadened our scope to include other entertainment media: wireless, television and the cinema, such as, to get in a plug, *That's My Boy.* In this latter phase, we both feel a rapport and great fulfillment of our artistic abilities.

The entire venture has been a most intriguing and educational experience. It has not only enriched the annals of theatrical lore, but has served (I must say, with a flush of quiet pride) to enrich Mr. Martin and myself as well.

Doris Day
"YOUR TOES KNOW"

When Doris Day wrote this piece for the October 30, 1950, issue of
The Hollywood Reporter, *she revealed that her original ambition*
was to become a dancer.

Sing and be dance happy!
That's your girl. That's me. That's my platform for 1950 and, I hope, for all my motion picture years to come. The Dancing Day is here.

Warner Bros.' *Tea for Two* started me kicking up my heels in front of the camera, in company with the fleet and facile Gene Nelson, and the kid's carrying on the idea in *The West Point Story,* again with Gene, and with the addition of Jimmy Cagney as a partner. From this point on in my career, given the opportunity in the script, I hope to be tapping out fast and hot rhythms with my feet. All this and singing, too. And acting! Watch out, audiences, I'm going to load you! I hope you'll like it.

While it's new for me to be dancing on screen, it's not new for Doris Day to be a dancer. Actually, that was my original ambition. I never thought of anything else. Back home in Cincinnati, I was sent to dancing school by my mother who earned the tuition money by sewing. Vera-Ellen, incidentally, was one of my classmates.

I started working long before high school age. The future looked promising for me as a dancer. I was ecstatically happy. Then came the crash. A train crash, I mean. I was on tour in the Middle-West with a Franchon and Marco show. We were en route from one city to the next, which was to be Hamilton, Ohio, to be exact. A train hit the car and carried it down the tracks. Fortunately, nobody was killed. But I broke my right leg in two places. I was in the hospital fourteen months. Almost the first day I was out jumping around with the aid of a cane, I slipped and fell and had to go back to bed and a cast for an additional four months.

It was my darkest hour when I realized my career as a dancer had come to a close. During my recuperation, when I was so depressed that all I wanted to do was cry, I turned to singing. I used to go to my singing lessons on crutches.

To be honest, I had never thought of my voice before. Not seriously. It was merely fun to sing and my friends didn't run away screaming from the spot when I obliged with a tune. But I never thought in this world that singing would be my forte.

But look what happened! I found happiness in what seemed tragedy. Singing has brought me everything, not only careerwise but personally, for I have managed to provide a wonderful home for my mother and small son.

How come I'm dancing again?

That's easy to answer. I always promised myself that one day I would try again. Then that day came along in the life of Day.

It wasn't hard for me to pick up what I knew. What I needed most was encouragement. At first, I was shy. But Gene Nelson, with that wonderful enthusiasm of his, kept my spirits soaring. We made a frolic of it, laughed and screamed and kidded. We also worked. For four hours each day, we literally sweated it out on one of the studio sound stages.

I owe Gene a great debt of gratitude. He used to call me "The Dancing Vitamin Tablet."

Another witness to our rehearsals was Smudge Pot, my French poodle. Smudgie tried to get in on the act. I thought it was a swell idea and suggested it to Gene. I said let's work a routine with the dog. Gene looked at me gravely and suggested we take a half hour's rest period. Then he talked to me. He told me the story of a dancer who always looked for his great break in a New York show. Finally, he got it. The dancer wanted to wow the public with a novelty. He thought he had found it by dreaming up a routine with a dog. What happened? Well, the show opened and "the dancing dog" got all the notices. Nobody noticed the poor guy. When Gene finished his story, I replied that I had grasped the idea. Smudge Pot did not end up in the act. In fact, he stayed home.

Dancing is the best form of exercise I know. That's how I keep fit and I've never felt better. I can eat like a horse and then work it off. I recommend a half hour at the exercise bar "limbering up." I don't need a gymnasium or a swimming pool or a running track. Women of America, get on a dancing kick like I have.

Dancing also helps your disposition. Being light on your feet seems to help discipline your thoughts to happy ones exclusively. Have you noticed that dancers, when you meet and mingle with them, are always gay and carefree?

Now that I'm dancing again for the first time since I was sixteen and hospitalized, I realize what I've missed—although singing has brought me hundreds of golden hours of happiness and success.

I even recommend dancing for older people. You're never too old to learn, and remember the idea is not to be a great one necessarily but to have the laughter and good times and the blessed fatigue that goes with dancing. It keeps you young in heart and spirit.

No, dancing will never supplant singing as "a first" in my life. But it's an endearing second.

So, pardon me now while I go into my dance. "Music, Maestro!"

HOLLYWOOD KALEIDOSCOPE
1953

Liz and Michael Wilding began the New Year with a baby son, Mike Wilding, Jr. . . . Lucy gave birth to Desi Arnaz, Jr., and big Desi snuck into the hospital and took the first photo of his "greatest production" . . . Gene Tierney, who divorced Oleg Cassini, said that as soon as she had her final papers, and Rita and Aly were legally divorced, she and the prince would be married . . .

In February, Ginger Rogers met Jacques Bergerac at the George V Hotel in Paris, and fell in love almost instantly . . . Greta Garbo, Gayelord Hauser and his friend Frey Brown sailed for Jamaica to soak up the sun in the British West Indies and dine on fresh pineapple, papaya and coconuts . . . Mr. and Mrs. Gary Cooper, firmly together, bought a four-acre estate in Brentwood . . . Lana Turner's new beau— Lex Barker . . . The Duke and Duchess of Windsor were living in the swank Waldorf-Astoria Towers—rent free . . . Janet Leigh and Tony Curtis were fighting . . . Bing Crosby's first date since Dixie's death was with pretty blonde Mona

Freeman . . . Shelley Winters' baby daughter, Victoria, had to spend the first three weeks of her life in Cedars of Lebanon Hospital.

By the time March arrived, Roz Russell had herself a smash Broadway play, *Wonderful Town* . . . Bette Davis "mergered" with Gary Merrill . . . Ginger Rogers married her handsome Parisian-turned-movie-actor . . . But Pier Angeli's mother would *not* approve of her daughter accepting Kirk Douglas' proposal . . . Vivien Leigh became ill and flew back to London with Larry Olivier and a nurse. This tragic turn of events canceled the Oliviers' theatrical plans for the Coronation season. They were to have co-starred in a new Terence Rattigan play.

In April, Prince Aly Khan's father, the Aga Khan, bought a gorgeous horse and named it "Rita" because "it had seductive calves, but a very difficult character" . . . Two of Hollywood's top glamour photographers, Wally Seawell and Paul Hesse, were invited by dictator Juan Peron to fly to Argentina and take pictures of his dead wife, EVITA, as she lay in her glass casket. The photos, to be shot in 3-D and sold to Argentinians, were the first step in Peron's move to have his late wife declared a Roman Catholic saint . . . RITA HAYWORTH said she was flattered that her former father-in-law named a horse for her; and speaking of horses, she began dating MANUEL ROJAS, a handsome Chilean polo player who came to Hollywood to ride his polo pony—and decided to stick around . . . GRETA GARBO, whose fad used to be the GAYELORD HAUSER diet, was preoccupied in the springtime with a new interest—French furniture. She had been influenced by her favorite escort ERIC ROTHSCHILD, whose impeccable taste she enlisted to redecorate her Hampshire House Hotel Suite.

Las Vegas witnessed two atomic-bomb tests over a weekend in mid-April—one of them had a tuxedo and could travel. VAN JOHNSON'S cafe appearance at the Sands Hotel proved him to be a wonderful performer in the musical comedy vein. His act: a skillful blend of songs and soft-shoe numbers—a concession to his having been discovered as a chorus boy on Broadway in *Pal Joey.*

In May, PRINCE ALY KHAN reserved a $9,500 hotel suite for himself and GENE TIERNEY so they could have a birds-eye view of QUEEN ELIZABETH's coronation route . . . VIC DAMONE and PIER ANGELI began dating . . . And the following month, JOHN WAYNE hosted a festive "I'm Almost Free at Last" divorce party for himself and his drinking buddies that went on until the wee hours of the morning . . . The LAURENCE OLIVIERS now had the same understanding as the DUKE and DUCHESS OF WINDSOR. Theirs was to be "a marriage in name—and face—only" . . . AVA and FRANK's marriage was shakier than ever . . . But there *was* one glowing Hollywood bride—ANN BLYTH married DR. JAMES McNULTY.

July was a month for partings. BETTY GRABLE left 20th Century-Fox . . . JOHN DEREK walked out on Columbia Pictures, after five years, with two more still to go on his contract . . . GAIL RUSSELL and GUY MADISON split . . . Sadly, JANET LEIGH lost her baby . . . GARY COOPER turned fifty-three . . . PRINCE ALY KHAN said he was in love with GENE TIERNEY, while his papa, the AGA, said he still favored RITA—the lady, not the horse . . . Speaking of Rita, she was holed up at the Ambassador East Hotel—with her latest love, singer DICK HAYMES . . . GRACE KELLY arrived back in Hollywood to begin filming *Dial M for Murder.* She had just closed a stage

engagement at Philadelphia's Playhouse in the Park, starring in *The Moon Is Blue* . . . KIRK DOUGLAS was so much in love with PIER ANGELI, he flew from Rome to London to help her celebrate her twenty-first birthday . . . RITA HAYWORTH so enamored of DICK HAYMES that she helped him arrange a financial settlement with NORA EDDINGTON FLYNN HAYMES so they could be married. Meanwhile, NORA said she would name Rita as the co-respondent in her divorce suit . . . The "I Love Lucy" show, rated number one for the twelfth consecutive month, claimed a TV viewership of more than fifty million a week.

Early in July TY POWER stopped in Rome before he and LINDA CHRISTIAN took off for Brussels, Amsterdam and then home to Los Angeles. Both Ty and Linda were heartsick at having to leave their favorite city. But 20th Century–Fox threatened to sue their erstwhile fair-haired boy if he didn't report back for his one-picture commitment. Obediently, but reluctantly, they took off, but planned to return to Rome for a prolonged stay come next spring.

As August arrived, GRETA GARBO's yacht, *Glen Tor,* was anchored off Santa Margherita on the Italian Riviera. The "great one" delighted onlookers when she appeared on deck in a bathing suit and then proceeded to take a dip in the Mediterranean. A Genoese newspaperman, equipped with high-powered binoculars, reported that Garbo was "still beautiful in a bathing suit," and that "her slender body was as youthful-looking as a young girl's." One evening she came ashore and visited REX HARRISON and LILLI PALMER at their villa at Portofino. Greta's next destination was the Isle of Elba—perhaps she was going to look for souvenirs from Napoleon's stay there.

With *Roman Holiday* soon to be released, the hottest new personality on the screen—AUDREY HEPBURN. Her ex-fiancé, JIM HANSON, played host for her at numerous summertime parties, still hoping to lead Audrey to the altar. Considered far more likely—gossip linking her romantically with *Roman Holiday* co-star GREG PECK. Greg, with his usual reticence, would not discuss Hepburn, except to say how much he admired Audrey as an artist. Nor would he reveal his current marital difficulties with GRETA.

In August, DARRYL ZANUCK signed a contract with a beautiful new foreign actress by the name of BEJA WERGER CAVALADE. Zanuck shortened her name to BELLA DARVI (the DAR was for Darryl; the VI for Zanuck's wife, VIRGINIA) . . . DICK HAYMES was arrested by the U.S.

Immigration Department (he had an Argentine passport). RITA decided she might start dating MANUEL ROJAS again. Where did that leave NORA HAYMES? . . . GARY COOPER found out that PATRICIA NEAL had married writer ROALD DAHL, and said, quietly, "I only hope he's a good guy" . . . ZSA ZSA dated handsome playboy-diplomat PORFIRIO RUBIROSA . . . MARIE MACDONALD and HARRY KARL split . . . VIVIEN LEIGH was back in circulation after a miraculous recovery. There was no trace of the breakdown that had tragically overtaken her five months before in Hollywood. But there *were* rumors that she and LARRY OLIVIER were on the verge of a split, despite the fact they were due to start rehearsals momentarily for *The Sleeping Prince.*

In September, AVA and FRANKIE were back together and made plans to co-star in a film for MGM, *St. Louis Woman* . . . EVIE and VAN JOHNSON's marriage was in trouble . . . SUSAN HAYWARD sued JESS BARKER for divorce . . . On September 13, LINDA CHRISTIAN POWER gave birth to a second daughter. TYRONE said Linda's astrologer had predicted they would have a son on September 16th. Except for the date and the sex, the astrologer was right on . . . AVA and FRANK had another fight, but made up over an Italian dinner, home-cooked by FRANKIE's Mama, DOLLY . . . RITA HAYWORTH not only went back to DICK HAYMES, she married him . . . And, over in Paris, GREGORY PECK lost his heart to a beautiful French reporter, VERONIQUE PASSANI . . . JEAN SIMMONS and STEWART GRANGER were having marital troubles . . . JOAN (MRS. HARRY) COHN, commenting on RITA's marriage to DICK HAYMES, said, "I've never known such a completely 'out to lunch' girl in my life!" . . . Meanwhile, everybody in Hollywood who could read purchased a copy of *The Kinsey Report* and compared notes on their sexual hangups.

In October, DEBORAH KERR opened on Broadway in *Tea and Sympathy* . . . ROBERT WAGNER signed a new long-term contract at 20th . . . AVA and FRANK had a truce, but it didn't work. Frank was singing in Las Vegas, but Ava didn't even bother going over to catch his show . . . MARILYN MONROE earned only $750 a week at Fox, while her drama coach, NATASHA

LYTESS, was paid one thousand dollars every seven days to sit on the sidelines—and prompt.

By November, forty-nine percent of all American families had at least one television set . . . Warner Brothers adopted 20th's CinemaScope process . . . The RAY MILLANDS, who had separated, reconciled on the same day GRACE KELLY came back to Hollywood. Insiders saw some connection.

In December, the movie moguls finally had something to smile about. For the first time since the advent of television, business in the movie theatres had picked up and was the best it had been in years . . . RITA HAYWORTH told a reporter she had always wanted to have a son, "but I never married a man virile enough to give me one!" . . . RICHARD LONG and SUZAN BALL, young contract players, planned to marry . . . MERCEDES MCCAMBRIDGE feuded with JOAN CRAWFORD on the set of *Johnny Guitar*. Mercedes said, "Joan Crawford is a movie queen. I never met one before. I know now what I *don't* want to be! . . . And ZSA ZSA GABOR celebrated the Christmas holidays with a lump on her forehead the size of the Hope Diamond. She said she fell. Insiders claim RUBIROSA socked her after she turned him down. Ruby said, "I'm fed up with Zsa Zsa. I'm going to marry BARBARA HUTTON!" Everyone agreed the Five and Dime heiress was certainly a terrific consolation prize.

Although 1953 was the year of Cinerama, CinemaScope, Natural Vision, three of the biggest hit pictures of the year—*From Here to Eternity, Julius Caesar* and *Roman Holiday*—were all shown on ordinary screens and in black and white . . . Hollywood watched in awe as ARLENE DAHL divorced LEX BARKER, who married LANA TURNER, who lost FERNANDO LAMAS, who found ARLENE DAHL—proving once again that what goes around, comes around! . . . There were nursery additions at the homes of the HUMPHREY BOGARTS, DEAN MARTINS, CHARLIE CHAPLINS, BEN GAGES (ESTHER WILLIAMS), VITTORIO GASSMANS, ERROL FLYNNS and KARL MALDENS . . . 1953 was also the year AUDREY HEPBURN was officially acclaimed the best actress . . . MARILYN MONROE *didn't* marry JOE DIMAGGIO, while JUNE HAVER gave back her convent veil.

1954

January was a month for mating, relating and debating in Hollywood's lovebird set. SHELLEY WINTERS left her Italian, VITTORIO GASSMAN, flat-

ter than a thin-crusted pizza . . . Heiress BARBARA HUTTON made "an honest man" of PORFIRIO RUBIROSA, and ZSA ZSA "wished them well" . . .

MARILYN MONROE and JOE DIMAGGIO decided to establish their own home base . . . JANE WYMAN hired GREG BAUTZER to handle her divorce from FRED KARGER . . . PILAR PALETTE made a movie called *Sabotage in the Forest* and began to plan her wedding to JOHN WAYNE . . . PRINCE ALY KHAN, obviously not soured on Glamour Queens, arrived in Hollywood to continue his pursuit of GENE TIERNEY.

There weren't many people in show business who could have followed the "fabulous grandma," MARLENE DIETRICH's record-breaking Las Vegas engagement. But the Sahara Hotel found the perfect formula. The DONALD O'CONNOR Show, opening right after the New Year, was labeled by first-nighters as the best bill to ever hit town.

20th's *The Robe,* in CinemaScope, set a New York boxoffice record, taking close to $3,500,000 in twelve days . . . The "New Faces of 1952" Revue introduced EARTHA KITT, ALICE GHOSTLEY, RONNY GRAHAM and PAUL LYNDE, along with a new young writer-performer, MELVIN BROOKS . . . JOAN CRAWFORD desperately wanted the female lead in *The Country Girl;* she would have done it for nothing. But the part went to relative newcomer GRACE KELLY . . . ANGIE DICKINSON, who won a beauty contest on a local Hollywood television station, KECA-TV, made her movie debut in *Lucky Me* . . . JUNE HAVER and FRED MACMURRAY began dating . . . And one of the screen's most menacing character actors, SYDNEY GREENSTREET, died at age seventy-four.

Valentine's Day brought the announcement that PETER LAWFORD would marry PATRICIA KENNEDY in April. Her father was financier and former Hollywood studio bigwig JOSEPH P. KENNEDY, and her brother was JOHN, a United States Senator . . . ERROL FLYNN and PATRICE WYMORE called their baby girl ARNELLA. Errol picked the name from a character in a book he was reading . . . HOWARD HUGHES was all set to write out a large check for the purchase of RKO Studios.

RONALD REAGAN celebrated his forty-third birthday with a new challenge. A few eyebrows were raised when he decided to do a nightclub act, but he proved himself a capable trouper. Reagan, never noted for being a comic, a dancer, or a singer, charmed a jam-packed audience at Las Vegas' Last Frontier Hotel with a lot of special material, coupled smoothly with other acts in the ninety-minute, talent-loaded revue he headlined.

Ronnie opened the show with mixed emotions. He was finally getting paid for what he had given away for years playing benefits. He humorously detailed his leap from briefcase-carrying roles in movies to the nightclub stage, then he introduced the HONEY BROTHERS. They acted as catalysts for the pandemonium which followed. Reagan reappeared and got involved in acrobatic routines—to the delight of the audience. The BLACKBURN TWINS and EVELYN WARD scored solidly with song and dance routines. Reagan then introduced the CONTINENTALS, who brought the house down with their slick harmony routines, after which Ronnie delivered a smash rendition of "Casey at the Bat." Judging by the opening-night appraisal, Reagan would have no problems should he wish to continue his career in nightclubs.

March came in like the proverbial lion with GENE TIERNEY and OLEG CASSINI battling over custody of their daughter, TINA. Oleg said Gene was an "unfit mother" because of her romance with ALY KHAN. Gene fought the "character assassination," and won . . . JANET LEIGH and TONY CURTIS celebrated their third wedding anniversary . . . BARBARA HUTTON and RUBIROSA split after only a few months of marriage. ZSA ZSA GABOR sent condolences . . . On the 20th, INGRID BERGMAN celebrated five years of living in Rome with ROSSELLINI . . . GRACE KELLY and BING CROSBY were together at a party for BEATRICE LILLIE . . . CLARK GABLE announced he would leave MGM after twenty years plus at the end of his final contract . . . ROBERT WAGNER played the lead in *Prince Valiant* and became a full-fledged star . . . Before March ended, WILL HAYS, Hollywood's first official Censor Czar, died in Sullivan, Indiana, at age seventy-four . . . SAM GOLDWYN bought *Guys and Dolls* for a cool million . . . And, fulfilling his February commitment, HOWARD HUGHES wrote a check for $23,489,478 and became the sole owner of RKO Studios.

April was a month of deals. First, FRANK SINATRA had "the last laugh." He'd been paid only $8,000 to perform in *From Here to Eternity*. To add insult to injury, Frank had been in Africa, on the *Mogambo* location with AVA, when the opportunity for the part of Maggio came up—and he'd paid his own way back to Hollywood to screen test before HARRY COHN hired him. After he'd won the Best Supporting Oscar, Columbia wanted him to star in *Pal Joey*. Frank asked Harry Cohn for $100,000—and got it! . . . Producer ALEX GOTTLIEB signed PETER LAWFORD to star in a television series,

1 The glamour trio—Ava Garner, Lana Turner, and Fernando Lamas at a Hollywood party.   2 Frank Sinatra with Billy and Tichi Wilkerson, dining in a nightclub in Monaco.   3 Frank with Nancy and Frank, Jr., at the Academy Awards. Frank won as Best Supporting Actor in *Eternity*.
4 Ronald Reagan in his nightclub debut as host-performer in a variety show at the Hotel Last Frontier in Las Vegas. Here he clowns before a billboard with his name. (Courtesy Las Vegas News Bureau)   5 Rita Hayworth and fourth husband, singer Dick Haymes.

"Dear Phoebe." After Pete filmed the first episode, he went East and claimed his bride, PATRICIA KENNEDY.

MCA packaged a deal whereby RONALD REAGAN signed a contract to host a combination live-and-film dramatic television series with top Hollywood stars for General Electric. The show, scheduled to begin in September and run for fifty-two weeks over 120 CBS-TV stations, had a substantial budget of over $1,500,000 . . . "Once in Love With AMY" was the best reason SUSAN and HANK FONDA could think of for adopting the three-month-old baby girl. Motherhood was a new experience for SUSAN (BLANCHARD), daughter of DOROTHY (Mrs. OSCAR) HAMMERSTEIN, and former contract player at 20th—Fox, but fatherhood came to Hank via his marriage to the late FRANCES BROKAW. JANE, Hank's sixteen-year-old sub-deb, and PETER, his thirteen-year-old son, will join their new stepsister on summer holidays in Honolulu. Hank will transport his whole family to Hawaii while he films *Mister Roberts*.

MARILYN MONROE signed a new seven-year contract with 20th Century-Fox. She returned to work on *There's No Business Like Show Business* the second week in April after having been on suspension since January . . . Pretty, young British actress, DAWN ADDAMS, became engaged to forty-two-year-old PRINCE VITTORIO MASSIMO . . . While Dawn was ecstatic with *her* prince, GENE TIERNEY'S mother, BELLE, was dead set against her daughter marrying ALY KHAN.

MAE WEST did *not* attend funeral services for her former manager, JIM TIMONY. Several years before his death, Mae had wanted to bring her mother, who still lived in Brooklyn, out to California. Jim convinced her it would not be the smart thing to do. Mae took his advice, and her mother passed away. West was angry and unforgiving . . . And 20th held a press conference for MARILYN MONROE. The blond beauty was *very* late arriving. Fox publicists were furious. The press was upset. But Marilyn smiled, apologized and told the columnists, "I know what a home run is now." All was forgiven.

DAWN ADDAMS' wedding to PRINCE MASSIMO, the first week in May, was the biggest social event in Rome since the 1949 TY POWER—LINDA CHRISTIAN nuptials. Even the CHARLES CHAPLINS showed up at the church . . . And FRANK SINATRA, out with MONA FREEMAN, told her, "I'm legally separated, and I don't care if Ava never comes back!" . . . Ten days later, AVA GARDNER

confided she planned to establish residence at Lake Tahoe for the purpose of getting a divorce . . . Before the month ended, the wives of Hollywood's top celebrities and movie moguls banded together to help fight mental retardation through their new organization, SHARE, INC. They planned to give a yearly fundraising party. The first Boom Town event was scheduled for Ciro's.

JUNE HAVER became MRS. FRED MACMURRAY on June 27th. The couple honeymooned on his yacht, *Blue Horizons* . . . ARLENE DAHL quietly changed the last name on her bank account to "LAMAS." Hollywoodites assumed she and FERNANDO were about to take the leap . . . JEAN PETERS, 20th Century—Fox actress, married STUART CRAMER, III . . . Rumors were hot and heavy that the GRETA—GREGORY PECK marriage was headed for the divorce courts . . . MGM paid DORIS DAY $200,000 to replace AVA GARDNER as the star of *Love Me or Leave Me* . . . And the new MRS. JOHN WAYNE, PILAR PALETTE, ordered everything in the Wayne home to be replaced—even the bathroom fixtures. Neither she nor Duke wanted any reminders of CHATA, the last Mrs. Wayne.

At the beginning of August, WALT DISNEY signed an unknown, FESS PARKER, to play the lead in the "Davy Crockett" TV series . . . FRANK SINATRA still wore his wedding ring. AVA, with the third finger on her left hand bare, had a fling with HOWARD HUGHES. Presumably DOMINGUIN, her Spanish matador, was still fighting the bulls—and awaiting her arrival in Madrid . . . MCA agent HARRY FRIEDMAN fixed ROBERT TAYLOR up on a blind date with URSULA THIESS. Shortly thereafter, Bob and Ursula became man and wife—and Taylor changed agents, going over to MCA's only rival, the William Morris office. Friedman swore off playing matchmaker . . . Rumors of a DEBBIE REYNOLDS—EDDIE FISHER marriage were all over Hollywood . . . And comedian JOHNNY CARSON was set to emcee the first live color TV show on CBS from Hollywood on August 20.

They said it wouldn't last but, in September, LANA TURNER and LEX BARKER celebrated their first wedding anniversary . . . GRACE KELLY and OLEG CASSINI are *more* than just friends, despite her family's objections . . . JANE POWELL announced she would marry PAT NEIRNEY in November . . . RICHARD BURTON, the quotable Welshman, said that, to him, "Hollywood was Heaven with Jaguars" . . . JEAN PETERS' brief marriage to STUART CRAMER was about to fall apart . . .

EDDIE CANTOR tossed a fabulous engagement party for DEBBIE and EDDIE. FISHER gave REYNOLDS a diamond watch. Their wedding rings were being custom-designed . . . A local Hollywood disc jockey introduced a record with: "This is AVA GARDNER's newest release—FRANK SINATRA!" . . . PIER ANGELI loved September, and VIC DAMONE, who gave her a three-and-a-half-karat diamond engagement ring . . . Young Broadway dancer-actress SHIRLEY MACLAINE debuted in ALFRED HITCHCOCK's *The Trouble With Harry*. MacLaine, GWEN VERDON's understudy, was spotted by talent scouts on the first night she replaced Gwen, who was out sick . . .

In late October, QUEEN ELIZABETH paid a backstage visit to *Pajama Game*. She met the cast and had champagne in JANIS PAIGE's dressing-room. Janis had been instructed to make a graceful curtsy and address the Queen as "Ma'am." In her excitement, Janis responded with typical American naturalness. She forgot the curtsy and the "Ma'am" and just shook hands.

By the first week in November, the "perfect marriage," LINDA CHRISTIAN and TY POWER, was finished. Linda, in New York, leased a place just a few blocks away from Tyrone. To show his good faith, Ty gave Linda custody of the children, a settlement handsome enough to keep her in the style to which he had accustomed her, and also gifted her with their beautiful Bel Air home lock, stock and barrel—including her own nude statuette in the garden.

On November 18, Hollywood paid final tribute to the late great LIONEL BARRYMORE, who died at the age of seventy-six . . . MARLON BRANDO, who had been dating a young French girl, JOSIE BERENGER, became engaged. His fiancée was in London, where STELLA ADLER had accepted her as a pupil.

As the Christmas holidays approached, BING CROSBY dated KATHRYN GRANT. They seemed "very cozy," dancing every dance at the El Mirador Hotel in Palm Springs . . . There were rumors that the MARILYN MONROE—JOE DIMAGGIO marriage was over . . . LUCY and DESI moved into their new home on Roxbury Drive in Beverly Hills, and became next-door neighbors of JACK and MARY BENNY . . . OLIVIA DE HAVILLAND announced that she would marry French editor PIERRE GALANTE in February of 1955 . . . ROCK HUDSON, who won't turn thirty for another year, may marry PHYLLIS GATES even sooner. He just bought a big home on Doheny Drive . . . CLARK GABLE and KAY WILLIAMS SPRECKELS were very much in love,

1 Bing Crosby, Grace Kelly, William Holden in a scene from Paramounts' *The Country Girl*, for which Grace won an Academy Award as Best Actress, 1954.   2 Tony Curtis and Janet Leigh with co-author Marcia Borie and young studio players Kathy Case and Steve Rowland. (Marcia Borie personal collection)

and looked serious . . . Sexy Laurence Harvey lived up to his reputation when he was named co-respondent in the divorce action filed by Margaret Leighton's husband . . . And producer Joe Pasternak gifted the expectant Pier Angeli with a baby carriage—Vic Damone promised to dutifully push it.

Jimmy Dean spent his Hollywood evenings with "character-around-town" Vampira. Their usual haunt was Googie's Restaurant on the Sunset Strip . . . Kirk Douglas took his bride, Ann, home to meet his mother and six sisters . . . Joanne Woodward, New York stage and TV actress, was signed by 20th to a long-term contract . . . And, for Christmas, Eddie Fisher gave Debbie Reynolds a red Thunderbird, a matching red coat, and a gorgeous white mink stole. "Little" Debbie, unaccustomed to such luxuries, was on cloud nine.

Nineteen fifty-four was the year Ernest Hemingway won the Nobel Prize and Mel Ferrer won Audrey Hepburn . . . And the latest proud parents were the Errol Flynns, Audie Murphys, Gordon MacRaes, MacDonald Careys, John Barrymores, Mario Lanzas, Ken Murrays, Bob Sterlings, Harry Belafontes, Brooks Wests (Eve Arden) and the David O. Selznicks.

Sylvia Gable annexed her fifth husband, and Greg Bautzer remained a bachelor . . . There was sadness at the passing of Dorothy di Frasso, Phyllis ("Mrs. Fred") Astaire, movie moguls Charlie Skouras and Leonard Goldstein, character actor Eugene Pallette, director Irving Pichel, L. B. Mayer's right arm, his assistant, Ida Koverman, Gladys George and author James Hilton.

It was a frantic year for celebrity marriages: splits included: the Johnnie Rays, George Hormels (Leslie Caron), George Sanders, Vittorio Gassmans, Freddie Kargers (Jane Wyman), Ed Purdoms, Mike Wallaces and Greg Pecks. But 1954 was a *wonderful* year for two Kellys— Grace and Nancy—and Lucy and Desi, Jackie Gleason, Deborah Kerr and Van Johnson.

It was a year in which television introduced only one exciting new dramatic show, "Medic," one fresh personality, George Gobel, and one new comedienne, Audrey Meadows. Bette Davis did *not* make a picture in 1954, but Gloria Vanderbilt Stokowski decided to become an actress . . . Rita Hayworth and Dick Haymes had more problems, and Clark Gable announced his retirement, but neglected to say with whom.

Eligible bachelors who went to the altar included Bob Taylor, Kirk Douglas, Dick Long, Peter Lawford, Vincente Minnelli, Groucho Marx, Fernando Lamas, Aldo Ray, John Wayne, Keenan Wynn, Steve Allen, Eddie Fisher, Pat Nerney and Wally Cox. Meanwhile, the stag line wept over the loss of Hedy Lamarr, Dawn Addams, Geraldine Page, Nina Foch, Jean Peters, Mary and Jack's daughter, Joan Benny, Marilyn Maxwell, Vera-Ellen, Mitzi Gaynor and Gloria Grahame.

1955

Marlon Brando started the year off with a bang. He announced that come June he and Josanne Berenger would "do it." Get married, he meant . . . James Dean "courted" Susan Strasberg in jeans, a dirty leather jacket and cowboy boots. Susan was as happy as if he had dressed in a tuxedo . . . Meanwhile, Linda Darnell was having trouble with her husband, tycoon Phil Liebmann. He wore nice clothes, but that didn't seem to matter.

Shirley Temple Black went into the interior decorating business in Atherton, California, and showed a great talent for the profession . . . But Vampira, Jimmy Dean's on-and-off sweetie, needed an interior and *exterior* decorator . . . And Walt Disney announced that he was going to build an amusement park, called Disneyland, for an estimated ten million dollars.

Marilyn Monroe and 20th were feuding. And, speaking of Marilyn, if John Huston weren't so popular with the press, he might have had the spotlight stolen from him, in New York, at the welcome-home party hosted by Allied Artists. In the middle of the festivities, Marilyn showed up. Monroe, who ordinarily shunned such events, came because John had given her the break in *Asphalt Jungle*, which skyrocketed her to 20th–Fox success. She was escorted by photographer Milton Greene, who left his camera at home. Among the other guests were Esther Williams and Ben Gage, Donna Reed and Tony Owen, Mike Todd, Carol Saroyan, Walter Wanger, Mary Astor and Sam Spiegel.

Sixty-four-year-old Bob Burns, one of radio and film's top comedians, passed away the first week in February . . . Marlon's Josie arrived in Hollywood . . . Elizabeth Taylor expected a baby on her twenty-third birthday, February 27th . . . ANNABELLA sold the beautiful Saltair Drive estate TYRONE POWER gave her as part of their marriage settlement. Then she stopped off in New York to see Ty's new play before she headed back to Biarritz, France, and the large farm she bought with the profits of her former Hollywood mansion . . . LINDA CHRISTIAN, TY's most recent ex, was given jewelry worth $132,000 by man-about-town BOB SCHLESINGER. After they quarreled, Bob wanted his gems back. Linda refused. Bob sued. The judge said, "A gift is a gift . . ."

MARILYN MONROE moved to New York and enrolled at the Actors Studio. She tried to put some order into her life, but wound up making enemies. In March, Marilyn reneged on her promise to sing *Diamonds Are a Girl's Best Friend* at the *East of Eden* post-premiere supper party on the Sheraton-Astor Roof, for the benefit of the Actors Studio. Despite her absence, the event was a huge success. Among the guests: the ALFRED VANDERBILTS, OSCAR HAMMERSTEINS, MILTON BERLES, TRUMAN CAPOTE, CAROL CHANNING, BETTY COMDEN, ADOLPH GREEN, CAROL SAROYAN and TENNESSEE WILLIAMS.

Eden's director, ELIA KAZAN, and his wife, MOLLY, entertained a table for ten which included JACK WARNER and his lovely daughter, BARBARA, DOROTHY and RAY (co-star of *Eden*) MASSEY, ELAINE and JOHN STEINBECK and KARL MALDEN. Steinbeck disagreed violently with one of the bad reviews of the film. "The picture is *not* like the book," he said. "But, in a larger sense, the picture *is* the book. I am more than glad that my work has contributed, among all the other contributions, to what is probably the best motion picture I have ever seen. Isn't it odd to be able to say this in humility!"

LEE and PAULA STRASBERG hosted the youngest actress at the party, an enchanting sixteen-year-old with a brilliant future, daughter SUSAN. Spotted dancing around the crowded floor were several other Strasberg prize pupils, JO VAN FLEET (superb in *Eden*), MAUREEN STAPLETON and EVA MARIE SAINT. Everyone thought Eva would give birth to her own "production" any moment. Also whirling about, GLORIA VANDERBILT, who looked like a flapper in her long-waisted, bustless, short-skirted Dior. She towered above her escort, even in her flat shoes. Her date, not the glamour-boy type, was unidentifiable except to those in the television industry. They recognized him as one of their finest young directors—SIDNEY LUMET—married to beauty Rita Gam, from whom he was separated.

CAROL CHANNING, who created *Diamonds Are a Girl's Best Friend,* was a good sport and substituted for MONROE, accompanied by composer JULE STYNE. Another sock entertainer, SAMMY DAVIS, JR. A lot of credit was due JACK WARNER. He expressed his gratitude to young talent like JAMES DEAN, JULIE HARRIS and JO VAN FLEET when he supplied *East of Eden* for the Actors Studio benefit. Strasberg's school had given all three of them training, with no fee, which helped bring them Hollywood success.

At the end of March, PAT and PETER LAWFORD had a son, CHRISTOPHER . . . JUDY GARLAND and SID LUFT named their new baby boy JOEY . . . DONALD O'CONNOR gave GLORIA NOBLE a diamond necklace, watch and ring. They were obviously very much in love . . . But love no longer existed between ZSA ZSA and "her RUBIROSA." They split for good.

At the beginning of April, MARIO LANZA'S $100,000, two-week engagement at the New Frontier Hotel, in Las Vegas, was canceled by the management when Mario said he didn't know if he would be able to go on. He had missed his opening night performance. The Hotel was already out close to $65,000. The press junket cost them $35,000, and they lost $20,000 on returned opening night reservations. In addition, the bosses had advanced Mario $10,000—which they demanded he return. Lanza refused to make himself available to the press, or anyone else, except for his immediate family and a few close advisors. But one local doctor said that Mario could have performed if he wanted to. Lanza was obviously in serious trouble. Both the Hotel and MGM, Mario's home studio, were very concerned.

In May, JEAN PETERS went to court to divorce STUART CRAMER . . . DEBBIE REYNOLDS' chums kept asking when EDDIE FISHER was going to marry her. She shrugged her shoulders. FISHER just grinned and told reporters, "I believe in long engagements!" . . . JOAN CRAWFORD eloped to Las Vegas with Pepsi-Cola business executive ALFRED STEELE . . . LILLI PALMER and REX HARRISON separated . . . ROCK HUDSON gifted PHYLLIS GATES with a diamond necklace and bracelet . . . EDMUND PURDOM (*The Egyptian*) proposed to LINDA CHRISTIAN, but she had something more urgent on her mind. She had asked for a one-million-dollar settlement from TYRONE POWER. He gave it to her. The "reasons" behind his generosity were sizzling. Linda had "an ace in the hole."

At the end of the month, DEBBIE returned from entertaining the troops in Korea, but there was still no bridal shower in her immediate future. EDDIE FISHER's managers were concerned because his phenomenal record sales had dropped off since he and Debbie had become a steady couple. They felt he was more valuable to them—and more desirable to his fans—as a single, eligible bachelor . . . And the "marriage" between blockbuster films and television looked brighter. NBC paid $500,000 for the privilege of televising one showing of LAURENCE OLIVIER's *Richard III* . . . MARILYN MONROE kissed and made up with 20th. She promised to return as soon as her Actors Studio classes were finished . . . Speaking of being finished, CLARK GABLE, contractually free of MGM, was really soaring. His salary for *The Tall Man* was fifteen times larger than the loot he had collected for *Gone With the Wind*. He was particularly angry that MGM planned to reissue a wide-screen version of "GWTW" and had not offered him even a token bonus for all of the extra millions they collected—and would earn over the years because of his efforts. If Gable had not signed on as Rhett Butler, DAVID O. SELZNICK would never have made the deal for Metro to release the picture in the first place.

By early July, the marriage of KATHRYN GRANT to BING CROSBY seemed imminent. But there were problems. After reporters found out that Kathy had ordered a wedding gown and printed the item, Bing hit the ceiling. He hated publicity of that type. Kathy dissolved in tears at his anger. On July 14th, however, wedding banns were posted in Bing's Beverly Hills parish, at the Church of the Good Shepherd, where Kathy was taking instructions in the Catholic faith. The last word was that they *would not* be married at that highly visible church. Bing wanted to avoid any more publicity.

While Bing was having pre-wedding tantrums, AVA and FRANK quietly agreed to a financial settlement . . . While over at St. John's Hospital, ROBERT TAYLOR was shouting for joy. His wife, URSULA THIESS, had given birth to a son, TERENCE . . . On July 11, KAY WILLIAMS SPRECKELS became MRS. CLARK GABLE. Ten days later, they graciously held a press conference at their Encino Ranch and fielded questions from a houseful of reporters.

The first week in August, lovely young actress SUZAN BALL re-entered the City of Hope Hospital after a recurrence of cancer. Her condition was very serious . . . COBINA WRIGHT gave a posh cocktail party at the Beverly Hills Hotel in honor of MADAME WELLINGTON KOO. GREG

BAUTZER came stag—took one look at DANA WYNTER—and sparks flew. Dana was with someone else, but Bautzer chums noted that he did not leave the affair before getting her phone number . . . GRACE KELLY took good friend CARY GRANT home with her to Philadelphia, where they co-hosted a celebrity benefit for their film *To Catch a Thief*. Then Grace flew right back to Hollywood to start *The Swan*.

The sixteen-million-dollar Beverly Hilton Hotel opened officially on August 12. Now ZSA ZSA had another place where she could stay, half-price. For old-time's sake, her ex-husband, CONRAD HILTON, allowed ZZ "a rate" in all of his hostelries . . . DEBBIE REYNOLDS tossed EDDIE FISHER a surprise twenty-seventh birthday party. She invited everybody in town but her old Burbank Girl Scout Troop . . . JEAN-PIERRE AUMONT began wooing GRACE KELLY . . . RITA HAYWORTH was all aglow as she listened to DICK HAYMES entertain at the Cocoanut Grove. He dedicated "Come Rain or Come Shine" to her.

ANN LESUEUR, JOAN CRAWFORD's mother, earned extra "pin money" with her homemade pickles and cheese straws. She sold them to Joan's friends and neighbors. Crawford wasn't *too* thrilled about the whole idea . . . JANE WITHERS married one of the Four Freshmen, KENNETH ERRAIR . . . VIC DAMONE was told by the owners of the Ambassador Hotel to stand by in case they needed a fast substitute for DICK HAYMES— who suddenly was having "troubles" again.

The first week in September, KATHY GRANT left Texas and met BING at Hayden Lake, Idaho, not far from his Elko, Nevada, ranch. Nobody knew for sure what *that* meant . . . RITA HAYWORTH and DICK HAYMES split . . . Someone gifted GRACE KELLY with a lovely cherub pin. When asked if there was any significance to the bauble, Kelly replied, "Oh, you know, Tuesday's child is full of grace . . . and I was born on a Tuesday." Having revealed that juicy fact, she left for the location site of *The Swan*, in Asheville, North Carolina.

On September 26, it finally happened. DEBBIE REYNOLDS became MRS. EDDIE FISHER. They were married at Grossinger's resort in New York's Catskill mountains . . . Rumors ran rampant that EDMUND PURDOM had run out of money, and LINDA CHRISTIAN had run out on him . . . Tragedy struck swiftly on September 30, stunning Hollywood and the nation. JAMES DEAN was killed in an auto accident. There was a Quaker funeral service, and Jimmy was buried back home in Fairmont, Indiana. The thought that his talent was stilled forever cast a shadow of gloom on the film community . . . The town was also in mourning for SUZAN BALL, who had succumbed to cancer . . . HENRY FONDA and his Susan ended their marriage . . . KAY and CLARK GABLE expected a baby come April, and happily told the world. Unfortunately, their joy was short-lived. She had a miscarriage . . . And MARILYN MONROE and JOE DIMAGGIO split.

DEBBIE and EDDIE had been married for nineteen days when his best friend, MIKE TODD, tossed them a welcome-to-the-newlyweds party, in October, on JOE SCHENCK's tented lawn. Schenck was in Palm Springs, so LOUELLA PARSONS and JIMMY MCHUGH co-hosted. Eddie exhorted his young pals, performers KATHY CASE and STEVE ROWLAND, to get married because it's a wonderful "instiTWOtion." He even spelled it out for them. Although their wedding seemed to have gone off without a hitch, Eddie admitted they had packed and unpacked three times before they decided to say their "I Do's." SHIRLEY MACLAINE came to the party in a neck brace. She and her spouse, STEVE PARKER, had tangled with another car out on the Malibu highway.

FRANCES and SAM GOLDWYN invited 450 friends to join them for a buffet dinner dance at New York's Ambassador Hotel after the charity premiere of Guys and Dolls. Frances, one of Hollywood's most charming and gracious hostesses, left the Capitol Theatre before the picture ended in order to greet her first guests, PAT NEAL and her writer-spouse, ROALD DAHL. Next to arrive were stags, MAURICE CHEVALIER and REGGIE GARDINER. A crush of photographers followed AUDREY HEPBURN and MEL FERRER. She never danced with anyone else, and he never left her side for a moment. After a year of marriage, his "Svengali" influence was as strong as ever. Obviously, Audrey thrived on it. She never looked better.

MARLON BRANDO did not bring a date. He came with agent JAY KANTOR and his lovely wife, JUDY, daughter of Paramount's BARNEY BALABAN. He did not wear a tux. His Guys and Dolls co-star, JEAN SIMMONS, looked beautiful in a cream satin sheath as she spun around the ballroom with JOE MANKIEWICZ . . . MARY MARTIN, in a black lace MAINBOCHER gown, looked radiant. She and her devoted manager-husband, RICHARD HALLIDAY, rarely attended big parties. Among the Hollywood celebrities in New York for the Goldwyn's soirée were CLIFTON WEBB, ESTHER WILLIAMS and BEN GAGE, and LAUREN BACALL and HUMPHREY BOGART. Bacall was ecstatic when she spotted two of her favorite "eggheads," EDWARD R. MURROW and presidential speechwriter BOB SHERWOOD. Whereupon BOGIE cracked, "Now, if only ADLAI STEVENSON, LOUIS BROMFIELD and JOHN HUSTON were here, we could all leave!"

ALFRED HITCHCOCK and his wife were being presented to QUEEN ELIZABETH and PRINCE PHILIP at the 10th Royal Film Performance, at the Odeon Theatre, Leicester Square, at almost the precise moment that PRINCESS MARGARET announced from Clarence House that she had decided not to marry PETER TOWNSEND. The sad news raced through the theatre like a forest fire. By the time the curtain went up on To Catch a Thief, everybody knew that Margaret had irrevocably "put duty before love."

Even the lineup of stars quizzed each other about the "big news" as they waited for the Queen to arrive. Among the celebrity guests presented were: AVA GARDNER, KATY JURADO, GINA LOLLOBRIGIDA, DIANA DORS, ROSSANO BRAZZI, STEVE COCHRAN and RICHARD ATTENBOROUGH . . . PRINCESS MARGARET, who customarily came to this annual event, spent the evening at home, alone.

By mid-November, MARILYN MONROE, back in New York, and playwright ARTHUR MILLER had discovered each other. Marilyn, all dressed in mink, and Arthur, in his usual dark blue shirt, arrived together at the opening of MAXFIELD's new ice cream parlor. Although Marilyn wasn't talking for publicity, there were rumors that Arthur would be her next husband . . . Friends close to JIMMY DEAN said that during his eighteen months in Hollywood he had accumulated an estate of $250,000—mainly in insurance policies.

As the last days of December wound down, ARLENE DAHL and FERNANDO LAMAS fought—in public . . . RITA HAYWORTH told everyone who would listen that DICK HAYMES was a "Svengali." HAYMES didn't even bother to reply. He was off planning his next wedding . . . ROCK HUDSON and PHYLLIS GATES were married . . . GLORIA VANDERBILT admitted that she and SIDNEY LUMET were "seriously in love" . . . ELIZABETH MONTGOMERY and GIG YOUNG were a "very steady couple" . . . And GRACE KELLY's much-publicized fling with JEAN-PIERRE AUMONT turned out to be "just one of those things."

Helen Hayes
"YOU BET I'M NERVOUS"

Academy award winner Helen Hayes, who holds the distinguished title "the first lady of the Broadway stage," wrote this candid piece for The Hollywood Reporter *about her experience working in a film with Ingrid Bergman in 1956.*

I'd be lying if I said I wasn't a little nervous—very nervous, in fact—about returning to films after five years away.

As a matter of fact, when 20th Century–Fox first offered me the role of the Dowager Empress in *Anastasia,* I turned them down flat.

It was before my husband [Charles MacArthur] died, and he wasn't feeling well; so part of my reason for saying no to the part was that I felt I should stay with him and not go running off to Europe.

But also I was just plain worried about working in films again. After all, the stage is my real home. I feel comfortable and competent there. The cold eye of a motion picture camera glaring at me has always unnerved me.

But after Charlie died and the offer from Fox came again, my friends—particularly Anita Loos—urged me to accept. They felt it would be good therapy for me. I'm the kind who would prefer to stay among the familiar things of home and let the solace they provide help me to mend.

Then I learned that Ingrid Bergman was playing the part of Anastasia, and that decided me.

I've known and loved Ingrid since she first came to New York, in 1939, to play the lead in Vinton Freedley's revival of *Lincoln.* That was before she had gone to Hollywood at all.

She took the old Burgess Meredith house in Rockland County, Upstate New York, and was very close to our place in Nyack. She used to visit us often and we visited her, and before she left, we had become very close friends.

In fact, when all the fuss was made over the Stromboli affair and we read about it in the New York papers, Charlie immediately sent her a telegram offering our sympathy and support. Ingrid replied with a beautiful and touching letter of gratitude.

More recently I've seen and admired Ingrid in *Joan at the Stake* in New York; so it was really the opportunity of working with her that decided me to accept the role in *Anastasia.*

When they tested me for the part, however, I almost changed my mind again. I'd never worked in a color or CinemaScope film before, and I just couldn't believe all the light that was needed to film the test. I felt like someone undergoing a third degree.

Then, too, it was scheduled to be just a make-up test, but when Tola [director Anatole Litvak] got me in there, he said, quite casually, "Why don't you read a few lines, Helen?"

I could have cheerfully killed him at the time, but I remembered most of my big "recognition" scene with Ingrid, and I went into it from the beginning.

Afterward I was grateful to Tola for doing it that way. It was like jumping right into the cold lake. I got it over with in a hurry—the first few lines in front of the camera, I mean—and now, after working for a few days with such wonderful people as Ingrid, and Yul Brynner, and Akim Tamiroff, and under Tola's sure and sensitive direction, I feel very secure.

I've decided in recent years that the most important thing to me now is working with actors I love. That's why I did *Skin of Our Teeth* last year—to work with Mary Martin. I guess at heart I'm just noncommercial; if someone offers me a fat part at a big salary, I'm frightened; but all they have to do is ask me to take a role for practically nothing, playing next to an actor I like, and I grab for it.

In the last few years, I've played two seasons at the City Centre Theatre in New York, at $80 a week, and just love it.

Although I'm now happy to be getting my feet wet in motion picture work again, I still have a fear of overacting. It's the old story of the stage actor playing to the balcony, even when he's in a closeup shot on the screen.

I remember when we were making *Farewell to Arms*—I had never gone to see the rushes, but Frank Borzage [the director] and Gary Cooper finally talked me into it, and it seemed horrible to me. I thought I was overacting all over the place, especially in the close-ups. "Old Rubberface," I called myself.

Next day, on the set, I was scared stiff to show any emotion at all. I was all tied up and wooden, and we wasted that day completely. Frank Borzage didn't suggest again that I see the rushes, and everything worked out well after all, I guess.

Now I'm a little worried again about this CinemaScope process. It's so large that it exaggerates every little twitch of the eyebrow, it would seem to me. But Tola says that, because of the added width and the greater room for movement, it's really closer to stage direction.

And then, I don't suppose I can go too far wrong working opposite Ingrid—as I do in all of my big scenes. She seems to bring out the best in any actor.

One day, for example, we were rehearsing a scene together, and I didn't know my lines too well; so I suggested that I just recite them without acting until I had learned them a little better. But as soon as we had started, I found myself acting every detail of the scene with her. Ingrid's such a persuasive and responsive person that you can't help it.

At any rate, I guess what I'm trying to say is that it's good to be in a film again—especially one like *Anastasia* and more especially with an actress like Ingrid.

She's a wonderful actress and a wonderful person, and I'm hoping that, if she comes to New York after we've finished shooting here, she will stay with me in Nyack.

A NEW KIND OF "HERO"

They no longer had names like Rudolph or Ramon. Spencer or Clark. Leslie or Humphrey. They did not radiate Gable's raw kind of animal sexuality or walk tall and shoot straight like Gary Cooper or John Wayne. They failed to radiate the native-born, Lower East Side toughness of Garfield or those same mannerisms well-brought-up Humphrey Bogart could simulate. They lacked the dimpled yet smoldering passions Tyrone Power could evoke. And they did not exhibit the daring agility of Errol Flynn. They were a different kind of heroic breed: Clift. Dean. Brando.

The magnificent fragility of Montgomery Clift was unique. The pathetically brilliant vulnerability of Jimmy Dean unparalleled. The potent power of Brando unexcelled. They were eccentrics, each in a slightly different way. Two never married. The third married a few times, and fathered several children. They were nonconformists of the first degree. Fey. Sensitive. Unfathomable.

They evoked enormous loyalties in a chosen few, and provoked equally passionate enmity and envy in most of the others. They could be crude—and often were—mainly for effect. Each had had an unusual childhood, which for one reason or another left them scarred, wary, antisocial.

All three appeared onstage before tackling films. Monty, the most. Jimmy, the least. But each had tasted the thrill of a first-night opening on Broadway. More important, they all had enormous and instantaneous impact onscreen. Montgomery Clift against John Wayne in *Red River*. Brando versus the war, and his own handicaps in *The Men*. Jimmy Dean versus Raymond Massey in *East of Eden*, and Dean against his peers and parental authority in *Rebel Without a Cause*. They were tremendously dynamic on celluloid. Their individuality leaped offscreen and made audiences laugh, or cry.

In many ways they made a tragic trio. Dean was dead right after the Fifties reached midway. Montgomery Clift, who would die of a heart attack in 1966, was among "the living dead" for quite a few years before that. Brando, the lone survivor of the group, would go from juvenile, to leading man, to character actor before our very eyes. And Jimmy and Clift remain vivid in the minds of the fans throughout the world. Cults have formed around them. In fact, Jimmy's death only enhanced his popularity. While Brando's reputation as the most brilliant actor of his generation exists to this day.

There is a premise that most performers are in part cases of arrested development. Children—never completely freed of their infantile insecurities and fears—finding safety in "emerging" only when cloaked in costumes and characters not really their own.

If that analysis is valid, Edward Montgomery Clift, born along with a twin sister on October 17, 1920, in Omaha, Nebraska, fitted the description to a remarkable degree. Monty, who felt unloved as a child and considered his parents' life-style to be nomadic—and therefore harmful to his development—simply never grew up.

His father, William Brooks Clift, Sr., was a bank executive whose position necessitated frequent travel. Monty and his sister, along with older brother William, Jr., and a tutor, were packed off from place to place while the well-to-do Clifts wandered from town to town. When the Depression hit, the senior Clifts lost nearly everything. This new condition required even more moving about. Monty, the most sensitive of the three Clift offspring, apparently never adjusted.

His first taste of the joy of becoming somebody else came in his early teens, when he had an opportunity to appear onstage, in Sarasota, Florida, the latest of the Clift residences. There, he became involved in an amateur production, *As Husbands Go*. In rapid order, Clift turned professional.

By the time he was fifteen, he was appearing onstage in New York in Thomas Mitchell's *Fly Away Home*. It ran on Broad-

1 Montgomery Clift, after the filming of *Raintree County*.   2 James Dean.
3 Marlon Brando in Paramount's *One-Eyed Jacks*.

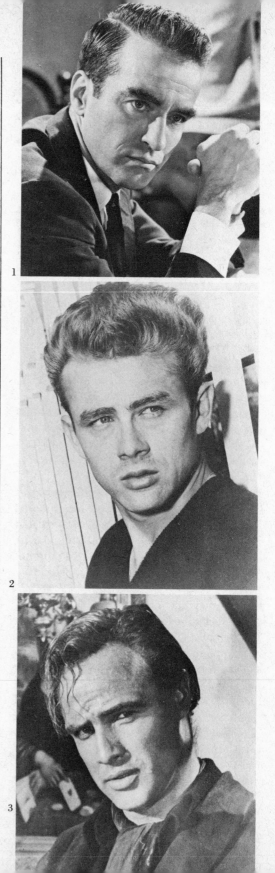

way for seven months. A succession of other plays, co-starring opposite the theatre's finest performers, kept Clift working constantly. For the next nine years his life was lived in dressing rooms and rehearsal halls. It was filled with costume fittings, learning lines, applying makeup—and then, once prepared—performing another life.

In 1946, he accepted the call to come to Hollywood. There, he made "Red River," with two of the industry's top pros, director Howard Hawks and star John Wayne. Clift's initial performance in heavy company was magnificent. Before that film was released, he traveled abroad to do *The Search*, the first picture in which he was seen by the American public. Prophetically, that also could have been the title of his autobiography. Clift's whole life would be "the Search"—but unfortunately he never seemed to find what he was looking for.

A brilliant, intense, incredibly handsome man, with blue-green eyes that mirrored every known emotion, Clift's impact on the public (particularly the female half) was swift and lasting. Wiry, sensitive, yet always manly, his succession of performances in pictures like *A Place in the Sun*, opposite Elizabeth Taylor and Shelley Winters, *The Heiress*, with Olivia de Havilland, and *Indiscretion of an American Wife*, where he co-starred with Jennifer Jones, won him an enormous following. *From Here to Eternity* and *Raintree County* solidified his position as one of America's great actors.

In his personal life, Monty had two classes of close friends—couples or "safe" women. In the first category, people like Kevin McCarthy and his wife, Augusta, to whom Monty clung tightly. The "safe" ladies, his two best female friends—both wonderful, earthy women—Elizabeth Taylor and Libby Holman. They opened their homes and their hearts to Monty.

Meanwhile, within him, the need for perfection was constantly countermanded by a gnawing, almost unconscious desire for self-destruction. Contrary to his grace onscreen, Clift was unbelievably awkward offcamera. He was always bumping into furniture or tripping over things. He chalked that up to his intense concentration. That *was* a factor. But there was also an unsettled quality in his personality that kept him continually knocking into Life—and bruising himself in the process.

Clift could be a wonderfully charming person. But he was also withdrawn. Sullen. Silent. Impenetrable. He offered such an abundance of pleasure to so many, but, unhappily, never seemed to find either sustained enjoyment or pleasure for himself. Another part of that opening premise, about childlike actors, should have included the fact that in order for some creative people to give fully of themselves they are required to sacrifice their own most personal needs.

Whatever tormented Montgomery Clift—and there is no question that he was a tortured soul—the series of brilliant performances that he gave were a testament to his consummate talent. At work, he was completely dedicated and self-disciplined. At rest, he liked to travel, to sail the seas, to soak up the sun, to keep moving. At home, usually a small, unpretentious apartment, he frequently hibernated, opening his door to only a chosen few.

Tragically, it seemed as if he could be kind and generous to everyone but himself.

When he died, September 30, 1955, in the twisted wreckage of his silver Porsche, on a lonely stretch of highway near Paso Robles, California, James Dean was twenty-four years, seven months and twenty-two days old. And had already achieved immortality. After only two major film roles, in *East of Eden* and *Rebel Without a Cause*, Dean had become an idol to millions of teenagers. His third motion picture, *Giant*, released after Jimmy was buried back home in Fairmont, Indiana, only enhanced his already impressive stature.

In his brief Hollywood career, Dean had secured two successive Academy nominations as Best Actor. Along with accolades from his peers, Dean had also garnered a reputation as a rude nonconformist and a weirdo. He was considered an ill-mannered social bore who flouted convention with the careless flick of a cigarette butt and the blink of a half-closed eye. Apparently he wanted no part of the Hollywood scene. That was the popular opinion of Dean, as viewed from the boardrooms of some studio chairmen and from the desks of numerous reporters, all of whom tried to categorize him—and came up empty.

Few people in or out of Hollywood knew the other side of Jimmy. For instance, who was aware of the fact that he died with at least two unfulfilled career ambitions? One was to re-create the character of Billy the Kid onscreen. The other was to play *Hamlet*, onstage or in films, wherever "they" would let him do it.

Throughout his later life— "later" being in Jimmy's case a pathetically relative term— he had a close friend or two. For example, he allowed actor Nick Adams to share his hopes, dreams and practical philosophy of life. Outwardly, he seemed immature, so erratically indecisive and uncaring. In truth, like some "old soul" who had lived before—and knew the score—James Byron Dean possessed some marvelously *normal* likes, dislikes and passionate opinions.

"If a person has talent and confidence in himself, he stands a pretty good chance of making the grade," Jimmy told Nick, "provided he learns to be patient."

On another occasion he confided, "One of the deepest drives of human nature is the desire to be appreciated, the longing to be liked, to be held in esteem, to be a sought-after person . . . There are six needs in life: love, security, self-esteem, recognition, new experiences, and last, but not least, the need for creative expression."

None of the above was either "weird or nonconformist." But then, Dean never said those things for publication. They were the sentiments of the *private* Jimmy. The other Jimmy was afraid to be publicly vulnerable. He believed he had been too hurt by life. Maybe they were mostly imagined hurts, but after a brief time in Hollywood, Dean refused to put his inner self "on display." He tried a few times to be part of the "in" crowd. On at least one of those occasions, "his personal idol," Marlon Brando, had put him down. Well, then, Dean decided, *he* didn't need idols. Never again would he subject himself to *that* scene. He would permit a few of those who *idolized him* to attach themselves to *his* milieu. But he would be *nobody's* satellite. For the rest of his life, Dean did not permit himself to appear affected by either knocks or raves. Praise or condemnation.

Dean once showed an intimate friend a picture of a giant California sequoia tree. "This is the largest and oldest living thing on earth," he explained. "The secret of its size and longevity, despite thousands and thousands of years of storms and bad weather, is its thick bark. It's fire-resistant and insect-proof," he added. "And it is the same thing with the human body . . . It can also have a thick bark with which to protect itself."

That was the side Jimmy presented to most of Tinseltown. And sometimes his bite was even tougher than his bark. So, in eighteen months, he managed to antagonize almost all of Hollywood's "important people." Privately they admitted that Dean was a "genius of a performer," even though they could not tolerate his public persona. Perhaps they would have viewed him in a somewhat different light if they could have seen the sentimental scrapbook he kept. It was not a record of his reviews or press clippings, but a repository for anything that touched him, really meant something to him: "The Order for the Solemnization of Marriage," the lyrics to songs like "Drink to

Me Only With Thine Eyes," "Love's Old Sweet Song" and "Puppy Love." The words to Edgar Allan Poe's "Annabel Lee." A faded newspaper cutting titled: WAYS FOR A BOY TO GET A DOG.

After Jimmy was killed, Nick Adams was asked to redub parts of the last big speech Jimmy, as Jett Rink, made in *Giant*, when he addressed all of the Texas crowd who had spurned him. It was a drunken soliloquy, and Dean, in his attempt at accurate excellence, had slurred some meaningful words so badly they had to be re-recorded. Nick, a noted Hollywood mimic, could imitate anybody from Cary Grant in *Gunga Din* to Robert Wagner in *Prince Valiant*. He was able to redo parts of Jimmy's last speech so perfectly, it was years before anyone knew all those words had not come directly from Dean's own lips. It had been a sad and secret task Adams performed for director George Stevens. And the scene, as seen onscreen, was marvelously touching. Dean was nominated posthumously for his second Oscar.

If only James Dean had remembered his own admonition to be patient, he might not have driven nearly twice the speed limit and met his death on a lonely stretch of California highway. But then, in twenty-four years, seven months and twenty-two days, he had already accomplished more on earth than most of his generation would in a normal lifespan.

There is very little that can be said about Marlon Brando that has not already been rehashed a thousand times. The place of his birth. The background of his parents. The names of his two sisters. His poor record in grade school and hatred of the military academy to which his father sent him. His unheralded arrival in New York to study acting. These are all part of the known Brando legend.

What is rarely taken into consideration is the *consistency* with which Brando has lived his "erratic" life. Since his first day in Hollywood, Marlon Brando's attitude has always been the same. By reading about the place, conversing with other New York actors who had been there and also by his own instinctive inner voice, he had the city sized up in his head before he stepped one foot on Hollywood Boulevard's pavements.

"I won't conform to anyone's dictates," he said. "This is just a small town. If you don't bow down to the powers, they hate you. So be it. If you don't buy a big house, with a large pool, you're considered a bum . . .

"When they don't see you at their special cafes and nightclubs, you're called a nonconformist. Fine. Let them label me anything they want. I have only two goals here: to act, and to live my own life. No matter how hard they try, they'll never push me into the Hollywood mold. I just don't fit!"

One of his close associates, in summing him up, said: "Marlon is like a kid. He reacts to situations in a childlike way. When he's hurt, he hits back. He's a completely free soul. He does things other people his age would do, if they weren't inhibited, or afraid of condemnation. Marlon has no inhibitions, and he doesn't give a damn what people say about his personal life. All he expects is that his work be judged fairly."

Obviously that aspiration was satisfied. Marlon was nominated four years in a row by his peers as Best Actor. In 1951, for *Streetcar*. In 1952, for *Viva Zapata!* In 1953, for *Julius Caesar*. In each of those years, he did not win. He was beaten by Bogart, Gary Cooper and William Holden. But his work had been recognized, applauded and singled out for its superior quality.

His fourth nomination, for *On the Waterfront*, brought him the golden prize. That year, he won out over Bogart, Bing Crosby, James Mason and Dan O'Herlihy. He continued to go from triumph to triumph and earned millions in the process.

He invested his money wisely, but consistently retained the same attitude he had when he first appeared on the Tinseltown scene. He did make one concession, however. He found it necessary to buy that big house, with the large pool and the high brick fence, to keep fans from intruding on his privacy. But for Marlon this was merely a convenience rather than an all-consuming passion.

Since 1954, when he showed up at the Academy Awards, wore the appropriate clothes, accepted his Oscar for *On the Waterfront*, and shared the spotlight with Grace Kelly, who also won that year, Brando has shunned industry events. After another Best Actor nomination, in 1957, for *Sayonara*, which he did not win, Marlon's peers failed to nominate him again until early in the Seventies. He did not even favor the industry with his personal appearance.

The real Marlon Brando, half spoiled child, half dedicated humanitarian, but one hundred percent genius, is among the few actors ever to beat the system. He has never been out of work, never lost a role he wanted to play, and yet he continues to thumb his nose at Hollywood's hierarchy. But, as Brando said from the beginning, "I won't be pushed into any Hollywood mold." He certainly hasn't been. Yet, behind the scenes, Marlon in his own unusual way *has* contributed more, actively *done* more, and *succeeded* more in humanitarian causes than many other more publicized Hollywood activists.

It is a fitting testament to Brando's enormous and unique ability, that he, like John Barrymore, to whom he was compared early on in his career, has sufficient genius to make him immune to the Commandments by which most people live. Brando has etched his own "Thou Shalts" on a personal tablet which only he can read.

It is enough to say: Marlon Brando is the greatest actor of his generation. He lives his life exactly the way he wants to. He is a marvelous father, devoted to his children, and a man who has given of himself for what he believes.

As an all-around human being—well, that's another story. But then, since when have the gods been judged by mortal standards?

"OKAY, WE GIVE IN!"

The unthinkable happened. On the 13th of April, 1953, 20th Century—Fox became the first major company to begin publicly figuring on the potential profits to be made from the exhibition, on television, of its older motion pictures. "The enemy" had proven that it could function *without* Hollywood films. So the movie industry, recognizing the inevitable, gave in. Twentieth, with a backlog of nine hundred movies made since the advent of sound, was only the first of many to make their new policy public. In a report to its stockholders, the company president, Spyros P. Skouras, intimated that they were getting ready to release "the gold in their vaults."

Stating that the theatregoing public eagerly went out to see CinemaScope and the other new film processes, Skouras laid his cards on the table.

In the past, we have consistently refrained from placing any valuation on our library of older motion pictures . . .

With the potential market of these subjects for television, however, such a library is becoming increasingly important. As stations increase in number, there is a potential interest in the revenue possibilities of these pictures for television . . .

Up to this time, for our own sound business reasons, we have refrained from disposing of these pictures to television stations. Among the reasons have been that we are engaged primarily in the making and distribution of pictures for theatre purposes, and the reissue, from time to time, of the older pictures for theatre exhibition.

However, with the advent of CinemaScope . . . the demand for older pictures will greatly decrease for theatres. Therefore, it is likely that these older films will be made available for television . . . We hope that these pictures will derive for your corporation very large income, running into millions of dollars.

The die was cast. The magic words had been used: "income, running into millions of dollars." The inevitable had happened: 20th was off and running.

In August of 1953, a "broad cooperative alliance" between MGM and NBC-TV was announced. This "message," however, came in a slightly different form. Metro had agreed "to make available its entire roster of talent for special appearances on NBC Television shows." Plans were being laid to allow MGM's biggest names to be seen on such top-rated programs as "Your Show of Shows" and the "Colgate Comedy Hour." There was even mention made of allowing film clips to be utilized.

Once MGM had agreed to lend stars and film clips, could the selling of feature-length movies be far behind? The answer was obvious.

By January of 1954, there were approximately 27,500,000 TV sets in American homes. The sales of new black-and-white sets was expected to raise that total to 33,000,000 by 1955. The prospect for color television was still a year or two away. But when bright-hued sets were available, it was certain sales would soar.

That same month, ABC-TV executives announced that their proposal for a film industry television program looked very good. The idea was that top movie talent would be made available for a half-hour show spotlighting scenes from three soon-to-be released movies. Advertising films on television was now also a reality.

In May of 1954, Walt Disney became the first major studio head to announce plans to make programs *directly* for television. As Walt wisely envisioned it, his weekly show would be nothing but one big advertisement for Disney products that could be seen only in theatres, as well as for his Disneyland Park, set to begin construction within two months.

By March of 1955, Warner Brothers and ABC-TV were deep in talks expected to result in one of the most significant movie-TV tieups to date. Warners had reasoned that "television was here to stay" . . . that there was room enough for everybody to make money . . . that motion picture studios and exhibitors had more to gain by "getting with it" than by trying to fight the new medium.

First, Warners was about to sell its stockpile of older films to television. Second, there was serious discussion about that studio making its own series—directly for TV. The light had finally dawned. There was money to be made from several *different* areas. Warners was ready, willing and able to cash in.

By the summer of 1955, MGM had announced it was going to make its debut in the TV field via a weekly half-program of edited shorts called "The MGM Parade." It would air on Wednesday evenings. In addition to the shorts, there would be three minutes of behind-the-scenes footage from forthcoming Metro movies "to be played exclusively in theatres."

In November of that same year, 20th Century–Fox was definitely pleased with a theatrical film which had been *remade* for TV: *The Ox-Bow Incident*. It started them out on a whole new trend. Before too long, Fox, like Warners, would be filming its own television series.

In December of 1955, David O. Selznick sold the television rights to nine of his motion pictures for one million dollars. Originally, he had offered a package of thirteen pictures, for three million, but found no takers. So Selznick held out *Rebecca, Tom Sawyer, Intermezzo* and *Spellbound*, but let the rest go to TV.

By February of 1956, Barney Balaban, president of Paramount Pictures, announced that his studio was "stepping up its activities in the television and electronic field." In June, Balaban said, Paramount would have a fabulous studio completely equipped for television production. The stages, technical equipment, office space, cutting and dubbing rooms would all be available for rental to TV—at a very nice fee.

Two weeks later, General David Sarnoff, board chairman of RCA, announced that within five years television—on an international scale—would be a reality. The market for product was growing by leaps and bounds.

Come June, and Loew's Incorporated—MGM's parent company—declared that they were "jumping into television with both feet." They planned to buy TV stations, to distribute their older movies directly to television and at the same time to begin shooting films specifically for TV. They were not only in with "both feet," they were up to their waistlines in the new medium.

The face of Hollywood was indeed changing—now it wore Max Factor's Special Television Pancake just as frequently as it donned the exotic shades and tones of the preparations required for motion pictures. In essence, the two media employed the same techniques—all geared toward removing scars, wrinkles, crow's-feet, bags and telltale signs of the previous night's hangover.

Leo the Lion was really on the prowl. By the end of the summer of 1956, Metro had sold 725 pre-1949 films, in only eleven television markets, for approximately sixteen million dollars. An earlier deal with a local Los Angeles channel involving the same films had added another four million to their coffers. But *Gone With the Wind* was *not* included in the deal, while the *Wizard of Oz* could be shown for only part of the seven-year arrangement—made mainly with CBS and its affiliates. Five months later, while still luxuriating in all of their lovely profits from old movies, MGM casually announced that at least *fifteen hundred* of their previous films had stories that could potentially be turned directly into TV series.

By the summer of 1957, Hollywood had turned into one gigantic gushing "oil field." Money from film sales to TV had all the earmarks of turning the moguls into wildcatters who had struck black gold on every square foot of land.

In February of 1958, Paramount announced its latest bonanza. The studio had sold the rights to 750 pre-1948 films to MCA for a guaranteed thirty-five million, plus fifteen additional million in the future. Simultaneously, an executive from Universal-International left that studio to join MCA-TV, while the Music Corporation of America was on a global march, opening television offices around the world, with the emphasis on the European market as well as that of the Orient.

Hooray for Hollywood—almost! But, wait a minute—the *New York Times*' movie critic, Bosley Crowther, in a page-one report, simultaneously conducted a "funeral ceremony" for the motion picture industry. It was, he said, ". . . about to go down the drain. People are spending more time watching old movies on television than they are new ones in theatres. Business in the nation's screen theatres during the last half of 1957 was some ten percent down from a corresponding period in 1956. All is lost. Television has won the fight."

For the next few years, the battle between those who had said the last rites over the movie industry, those who were making immediate millions and didn't care, and the majority, who stood firm and argued that good *new* pictures would still bring people out of their homes to the boxoffices, raged on without letup.

By the end of the decade, most of the major studios had integrated their production of theatrical and television films in order to put their studios on the soundest economic basis. Meanwhile, all of the TV networks had moved—or *were* moving—their major television production centers to Hollywood.

On December 31, 1959, there were exactly ninety-nine weekly TV series being filmed in Hollywood. In addition to network-originated shows, plus programs being produced by independents, the major studios were involved in more than one-third of all television production, with abundant new material on their drawing boards for the next season.

Walt Disney had one show. Revue-MCA (shooting on the Universal lot) had twelve. Columbia, through its subsidiary, Screen Gems, was shooting nine shows; 20th Century–Fox and United Artists–TV each had three in the works; while Warners' television division was busy with production on ten series.

As the Fifties ended, such old favorite film personalities as Walter Brennan, Raymond Burr, Rory Calhoun, Robert Stack, Ann Sothern, Barbara Stanwyck, Groucho Marx, June Allyson, Dick Powell, Robert Taylor, Ronald Reagan, Jackie Cooper, Betty Hutton, Gale Storm, ZaSu Pitts, Edmond O'Brien, Joel McCrea, James Craig, Loretta Young, Donna Reed, Robert Young, Ozzie and Harriet, Lee Bowman, Dennis O'Keefe, Keenan Wynn and Lassie had their own series.

Newcomers who would win the public's favor and become either gigantic TV stars or movie superstars were simultaneously getting their start. Among them: John Forsythe, Clint Eastwood, Richard Boone, James Arness, Dennis Weaver, Amanda Blake, Chuck Connors, Steve McQueen, David Janssen, Nick Adams, Danny Thomas, Michael Landon, Lorne Greene, Dan Blocker, Pernell Roberts, Dale Robertson, Lee Marvin, Burt Reynolds, Mike Connors, Craig Stevens, Gardner McKay, Tuesday Weld, James Garner, Connie Stevens, Robert Conrad, Roger Moore, Dorothy Provine, Will Hutchins, Clint Walker, Richard Long, Efrem Zimbalist, Jr., Roger Smith, Edd "Kookie" Byrnes, Gene Barry, George Nader, Keith Andes and Troy Donahue.

In the decade to come, more large independent television producers would join the majors in making product for "the tiny box." Yet even *that* had growing pains. Television sets now came with larger screens, and fancier cabinets became commonplace.

Even more commonplace, though not yet evident, was the role television would play as the savior of the motion picture industry. In future years, when blockbuster films failed to return profits, many picture companies would be rescued by the blessed revenues that their TV subsidiaries provided.

It was a crazy, convoluted situation. Movies and television, which in a way, would always be "enemies," had become so firmly interlocked that their "marriage"—never formally solemnized—seemed downright incestuous.

Ronald Reagan
"TV HELPS ME IN THE MOVIES"

By November of 1955, Ronald Reagan had become host of television's General Electric Theatre. The new position and the opportunities it afforded him—both in travel time and increased salary—were extremely rewarding. It was then that he wrote this piece for The Hollywood Reporter, *debunking the possibility that he would ever seriously consider running for political office.*

I have for the past months been doubling—in brass—combining television and motion picture chores. This manifold job has taught me one thing for sure: never again will I allow myself to get into a position where I must make a choice between a seat in Congress and a comfortable position in the arms of my leading lady.

Actors are citizens and should exert those rights by speaking their minds, but the actor's first duty is to his profession. Hence, you can rest assured that I will never again run for mayor or anything but head man in my own household.

You may remember a few seasons back when I was Honorary Mayor of Thousand Oaks [a San Fernando Valley community] and also a candidate for Mayor of Hollywood. It was then that someone seriously approached me with the suggestion that I run for Congress.

That proved to be the last straw!

I realized then that I was becoming a Dr. Jekyll and Mr. Hyde, and the two characters were competing to control me. I selected the Jekyll character—an actor without self-competition. This presented a chance to appear in RKO's *Cattle Queen of Montana* opposite Barbara Stanwyck. All this plus my regular weekly stint on the *General Electric Theatre* for television. In addition to my roles of host and program supervisor, I have had a number of acting assignments in offbeat roles for this series that would gladden the heart of any actor.

Now I am getting the biggest chance of my career. My *General Electric Theatre* bosses have permitted me to produce *Seeds of Hate* for their series. It's an exciting challenge and I'll have a chance to blame only myself if it doesn't pan out. At least I won't be able to do what many producers are prone to do—blame the cast if the picture fails to pan out. I started right out by signing a top name to star in this attraction.

I am a firm believer in the star system, but I also think that Hollywood should never let the stream run dry by failing to create constantly new stables of stars. The movie industry always has banked on personalities to make money. We must keep replenishing these star rosters with new talent all the time. I think the success of TV is due in a large measure to the stars already created by that medium.

Frankly, only television is doing its part right now to keep the star tradition alive.

There is no real competition between TV and movies, as some people believe. Actually, since I launched my television career, I have done more feature film work than at any time in my entire career; and, if you will pardon my pride, my pay has been boosted.

Another thing I enjoy about TV is the opportunity it affords me to get away from Hollywood, travel around the country and meet the people. Much as the movies used to send their stars out on tour, I now make coast-to-coast [trips] for my TV sponsor. In this manner I can keep in constant touch with the public and in that way better understand their moods, their likes and dislikes.

ENTER A PRINCESS . . . EXIT "THE KING"

Not even the most prescient psychic could have predicted that the third of four children born to Mr. and Mrs. John Kelly, Sr., in Philadelphia, on November 12, 1929, would one day grow up to be a movie star, an Academy Award winner—and the most titled lady in Europe. A beauty, her royal "handles" would include such honors as Princess of Monaco, Duchess of Valentinois, Marquise de Baux and Baroness de St.-Lô. Her older sister, Margaret (called Peggy), was known to be her father's favorite. Her older brother, John, Jr., was the handsome, popular, athletic kid in the family, while her younger sibling, Lizanne, was everyone's "cuddly child." Grace—well, she was known as "the shy, ethereal one."

As a youngster, she went to school at the Ravenhill Academy Convent. Then, after graduating, she attended the American Academy of Dramatic Arts. When she felt that she had completed her studies, Grace became a photographer's model, as her mother, Margaret Majer Kelly, had been before her. In the summer of 1949, she made her professional acting debut at the Bucks County Playhouse in New Hope, Pennsylvania. She appeared in a revival of a play written by her Uncle George, *The Torch Bearers*.

On November 16, 1949, four days after her twentieth birthday, Grace made her Broadway debut. She opened at the Cort Theatre in a Strindberg play, *The Father*, opposite Raymond Massey. After she had appeared in dramatic roles on "Studio One," "Robert Montgomery Presents," and several other of the better television shows, she made her first movie, a very *forgettable* picture, *Fourteen Hours*. The year was 1951.

Grace, who loved the stage, joined the Elitches Garden Theater, in Denver, and appeared in a number of plays there. Then she went back to Hollywood, and *High Noon*. In the summer of 1952, she signed a contract with MGM and was immediately cast in *Mogambo*. From that point on she never looked back. It was all uphill—to glory.

Fame and great accomplishments were not exactly new to the Kellys. Her paternal grandfather married a girl named Mary Costello. They had ten children, several of whom became very prominent. There was Walter, a vaudeville headliner for three decades, known as the "Virginia Judge." George, a Pulitzer Prize-winning playwright, and Grace's father, John, a bricklayer, who became a wealthy building contractor. But more important in terms of fame, John Kelly was the greatest sculler in American history. He participated in the 1920 and 1924 Olympic Games. In 1920, he won both the singles and doubles championships, the first and only time it had ever been accomplished. Subsequently, he was not allowed to row in the famous British Diamond Sculls Regatta at Henley. Not because, as legend had it, that he wasn't a gentleman, but because, as a laborer, his hands were extraordinarily toughened. The contest judges felt that a man who did hard physical labor would have the advantage over those contestants who did not. So he was disqualified.

Grace's mother, Margaret, a graduate of Temple University, was the first woman to teach physical education at the University of Pennsylvania. Grace's sisters both married well. Her brother eventually won the Henley race that had been denied their father. So, even without Grace's sensational rise to stardom, the Kellys of Philadelphia were a pretty fabulous family.

Meanwhile, in Hollywood, the care and handling that Kelly received was out of the ordinary. Almost from the outset, she had the most handsome and talented leading men as well as the best directors to guide her. Fortune had indeed smiled down upon her golden head.

Socially, things were a bit less exceptional. In fact, the gossip columnists had a field day with Miss Kelly. They first paired her off with the star of *High Noon*, Gary Cooper, and then played up a romance with Clark Gable, her *Mogambo* co-star. Clark, between wives when they met, was undoubtedly taken by her. Eventually he became protective and paternalistic—although

Gable and Grace *did* enjoy a photo safari or two way out in the bush, with only native bearers and wild animals as chaperones.

Next, the columns had Grace in love with Ray Milland, her *Dial M for Murder* co-star. Ray and his wife were separated at the time. But once Mal Milland got wind of the news, she effected a reconciliation with Ray rather rapidly.

There were also rumors that Grace and Bing Crosby had "had a thing." They did make two films together (*The Country Girl* and *High Society*) and, apparently, when any male star played a love scene with Grace, he was loath to stop holding her close—once the cameras had stopped rolling!

Actually, Kelly had only two "serious" affairs of the heart in Hollywood. The first was with handsome French actor Jean-Pierre Aumont. They were together for months—and made a lovely looking couple. Unfortunately, Jean-Pierre introduced Grace to his friend, designer Oleg Cassini. Before he knew what had hit him, he was sitting at home dialing Grace's number—but she was out on the town with Oleg.

The truth is that Cassini *was* a charmer. He had wooed and won the gorgeous Gene Tierney, his second wife. But that was over, and he was already divorced when he and Grace met. Oleg was short, not particularly handsome, and certainly no earth-shattering catch for a devout Catholic girl. In fact, the depth of Kelly's affection for him could be measured by the fact that for a time she continued dating Oleg over the strong objections of her family.

In the spring of 1955, Grace went to France to attend the Cannes Film Festival. Jean-Pierre was there, and they briefly came together again. But during her trip, some MGM publicity people, working in conjunction with the Parisian magazines, took Grace to pose for photographs with Rainier III of Monaco on his palace grounds. They spent less than two hours together, but obviously both were impressed. However, when

the photo session ended, they politely bid each other adieu.

What happened next was a remarkable sequence of events that Grace Kelly's closest chums would learn of in due time. Several months had passed. In the summer of 1955, Grace was home on a family visit. Friends of the Kellys', Mr. and Mrs. Russell Austin, of New Jersey, were at the house for dinner. The Austins, on their way to Europe, asked Grace for advice about various things, such as places to see—and also specifically about the Riviera. In passing, Grace mentioned Monaco. She told the Austins how lovely it was, and that she had met Prince Rainier III.

In one of those unbelievably strange quirks of fate, shortly thereafter the Austins were in Monte Carlo. As the story goes, they had difficulty getting a table at the casino. So Mr. Austin rang up the palace. He said that he and his wife were in town, and that they were close friends of Grace Kelly's. When Father Francis Tucker, Prince Rainier's personal chaplain and spiritual advisor, found out they were friends of Grace's, he immediately brought "their situation" to the attention of the Prince. They not only got a good table at the casino, but were invited to the palace.

When they met the Prince, he talked about nothing but Grace, and they all got along famously. As a parting aside, they told Rainier that when he came to America they would love to have him visit them in New Jersey. The Prince replied that he had planned a trip for the coming fall or winter, and he certainly would keep in touch.

In the meantime, Grace had finished filming *The Swan* and was home for the holidays. And the Austins had been contacted by Prince Rainier, who planned to spend Christmas Day with them in New Jersey. On December 25, 1955, the Austins arrived at the Kellys' door, with the Prince, Father Tucker and several other people in tow. Grace, of course, was delighted to see Rainier. He stayed for Christmas dinner and enjoyed meeting the whole Kelly clan. The Prince was invited to spend the night at the Kellys'. Father Tucker left with the Austins.

Fade-in . . . Fade-out . . . Within two weeks, Grace and Rainier had fallen in love. He proposed. She accepted.

By the end of January 1956, Grace was back in Hollywood, hard at work on *High Society* with Bing Crosby and Frank Sinatra. She still had four more years left on her contract. MGM was ecstatic at the prospect of having the "Princess" come back and forth for her other film commitments.

Prince Rainier arrived in town to be near his fiancée, and rented a $1,500-a-month mansion in Beverly Hills. But the Hollywood clan, anxious to meet "Gracie's catch," did not get the opportunity. Off the set, he kept to himself, as did she. They dined alone, mainly at his home. They did not mix socially with any of the movie crowd. The Prince preferred it that way.

The press had a difficult job getting a peg on Rainier. In all the time he spent in town, he spoke only briefly with one or two reporters. He told them both the same thing. He was definitely set against a wife who worked—particularly away from home. And, if Grace were to continue her career, she would have to come back to Hollywood. He, of course, was duty-bound to remain in Monaco—or at least close by. He was also not keen on his future wife making films, even in Europe. His words sounded ominous for MGM.

The Prince, who had won Grace Kelly's heart, appeared to be exceptionally conservative and very much in control. What the press and the public would soon discover was that Rainier could also be a charmer, and he had many interests and considerable talent, intelligence and wit.

On his own home grounds Rainier was "Prince Versatility." He was a skier, a yachtsman, a sports car driver and an animal lover. He studied marine biology and had a keen interest in the arts. He was highly skilled in many areas, and very well educated.

Although devout Catholics, Rainier's parents were separated. As of 1956—prior to his marriage to Grace—Rainier's sister Antoinette had acted as hostess at palace affairs. His mother, Princess Charlotte, had a large estate in France where he frequently went to hunt. He also fancied big-game hunting, but was more interested in the *care* of animals. The Prince had a large menagerie, a veritable zoo, on his palace grounds. Many of the animals roamed freely.

In addition to the palace, Rainier had a villa outside of Monaco, a place where he could be informal and relax. He also had a metal working shop, was very good at welding and achieved pleasure from working with his hands—one of his specialties was making crucifixes.

Rainier's daily routine at home—while subject to special events—rarely varied. He drove to the palace, usually every afternoon, where he stayed until nine or ten o'clock in the evening. He met with state officials from about four in the afternoon until eight o'clock.

He was a very keen seaman. He had a one hundred-fifty-foot motor yacht, *Deo Juvante II*, which had crossed the Atlantic. *Deo Juvante* was the motto of the Grimaldi family, which had ruled Monaco for more than six hundred years. A rough translation: "With the help of God."

Rainier had become quite publicity-shy because he felt he was too frequently misquoted. For instance, after he told a reporter in America the name of his yacht, it came out in the paper as "God help us"!

The Prince often sailed off for weekends. In midsummer he usually cruised the Mediterranean or West Africa. He frequently had guests on board, but he always helped to man the yacht. He was a good skin-diver and enjoyed swimming in the waters around Corsica, off the African coast, or near Sardinia.

Rainier had a chalet in the French Alps, which he preferred during the winter months. That was where he most liked to ski. As a sports car driver, he had quite a few exotic automobiles. In 1956, his special favorite was a powerful Lancia. A wealthy man, his government paid him $150,000 a year for being Prince. He also received a lavish expense account for running state business. In addition, he had his own private family property and income.

Grace Kelly's future groom had been schooled in England, Switzerland and France, and was graduated from the Paris Institute of Political Science. Those who knew him said he could converse brilliantly on a variety of subjects.

During the third week in March 1956, right after the 28th Academy Awards show, Grace Kelly left Hollywood for New York— and her trip across the seas. The marriage was a fairy tale conclusion to what had already been a charmed life. Those who heard Rainier's sentiments about the prospect of his Princess ever working again realized that Grace Kelly had left Hollywood's motion picture screens forever.

On the 19th of April, 1956, in Monaco's Cathedral of St. Nicholas, Grace formally wed the monarch of Monaco. The following year, she presented Rainier with a baby daughter, Princess Caroline. Prince Albert was born in 1958. Princess Stephanie would be born in the mid-Sixties.

By the time the Fifties came to a close, Hollywood's most royal princess had become a beloved figure among the people of Monaco. She had insured their independence from France by providing Rainier with an heir, and business in the tiny principality soared. Monaco's first family was a tourist attraction, and all threats to their

Her Serene Highness, Princess Grace of Monaco, and her bridegroom Prince Rainier III of Monaco, on their wedding day, April 19, 1956.

cherished way of life were gone. Hollywood's contribution to Monaco's royal house turned out to be a spectacular success.

Two months after Grace Kelly met her Prince, one of her favorite co-stars found the happiness he had been seeking. On July 11, 1955, Clark Gable, 54, married Kay Williams Spreckels, 37, in an informal four-minute ceremony in Minden, Nevada, forty-five miles south of Reno. As Justice of the Peace Walter Fisher officiated, close friends, Mr. and Mrs. Albert Menasco, of Los Angeles, and Kay's sister, Mrs. Elizabeth Williams Nesser, of Beverly Hills, gathered around the bridal couple. Afterward Kay and Clark left to honeymoon at the Manascos' secluded home in St. Helena, in the Napa Valley.

At last, Gable had picked himself another winner. Gorgeous, blond, warm-hearted, unpretentious Kay was the perfect wife for Clark. In fact, Gable had almost married her back in 1945, three years after Carole Lombard's tragic death. At that time, they had steadily dated—and Kay had fallen desperately in love with him. But close friends said that "Kay literally scared Clark off." She had worn her heart on her sleeve, and professed to anyone who would listen (but *not* to reporters), how much Clark meant to her. For some reason, this excess zeal frightened Gable. During this period, Clark had gone off on location to film *The Homecoming*. Kay had driven him to the plane and kissed him good-bye, assuming their relationship was still hot and heavy. She never heard from him again.

Hurt and humiliated, Kay became the wife of sugar heir Adolph Spreckels, II, on the rebound. The couple had two children and eventually she sued for divorce, alleging cruelty. By chance she was free of Adolph the same time Clark and Sylvia were divorced.

Going back even further, Kay Williams and Clark Gable first met in 1941. They were introduced by MGM executive Benny Thau. At age twenty-three, Kay was already a divorcée. She came from Erie, Pennsylvania, and had been married briefly to a young Georgia Tech student, Parker Capps. Her career as a model began in New York, where she took the town by storm. She was so beautiful that she had become the most sought-after cover girl in Manhattan. Kay used this as an entrée to Hollywood, worked briefly in pictures, but never became a star.

In 1942, Kay married Argentine cattle millionaire Martín de Alzaga Unzue, nicknamed "Macoco," a playboy well known in Hollywood circles. The unfortunate merger lasted less than two weeks.

After Carole's death, Lombard's closest friend, "Fieldsie," hoped that eventually a grieving Gable and lovely Kay might get together. She knew Kay had many of Carole's qualities. She was fun. She liked to go fishing. She played golf. She could make a good home for him just as Carole had. At that time, it just hadn't been in the cards. But Fate had indeed intended them to wind up together and in 1955 the "marriage that was destined-to-be" finally came about.

From the moment the newlyweds and her children settled down at Gable's ranch, it was sheer bliss. Clark adored his young stepchildren, Adolph Spreckels, III, called "Bunker," age six, and Joan, who was four. He added separate bedrooms to the ranch house for them, and felt part of a real family for the first time in years. There was only one other earthly thing that "the King" now desired—a child of his own—the baby Carole Lombard had been unable to give him.

On November 4, 1955, there was sad news. Kay Williams Gable lost the baby she had expected in May of 1956. She was taken by ambulance to Hollywood Presbyterian Hospital, where she miscarried. Gable was devastated. Kay's physician, Dr. Richard Clark, said she had been bedridden for three weeks with a severe case of the flu and a high fever.

Clark had been so proud of Kay when she told him she was expecting. They planned to keep it a secret, but then spontaneously announced it at a party at Mervyn LeRoy's. Still, Kay was very healthy, and she and Clark planned to try again.

Life for the Gables was marvelous. Kay and Clark and her children were regular visitors to Encino Park, and neighbors said how wonderful it was to see Gable so happy again. He and Kay really became involved in community life. When government officials threatened to close the local park, it was Gable who spearheaded the drive to keep the place open for the area children.

On Halloween he dressed up in costume; one year as a tramp; the next, as a clown. Proudly he brought "his kids" to the festive park party. Gable, slightly overweight and drinking a bit more than he should, was still the handsomest fifty-eight-year-old man in Hollywood. And, since his successful marriage to Kay, he was also the happiest.

As the Fifties came to a close, he, Kay and the children enjoyed a location jaunt to Italy, where Clark filmed *It Happened in Naples* with Sophia Loren. In his future: *The Misfits* with Marilyn Monroe and Montgomery Clift.

Nineteen fifty-nine was one of the greatest Clark Gable had ever known. Still "the King," he was earning more money than ever before . . . He had a wife he adored . . . His two stepchildren were just like his own flesh and blood . . . And maybe, just maybe, Kay would soon present him with his very own baby.

Clark Gable did not live out another full year. He died of a heart attack shortly after completing *The Misfits*, on November 16, 1960.

Four months later, on March 20, 1961, Kay gave birth to a baby boy. She named him John Clark Gable. In his whole life, there were very few things that "the King" had not seen, done, or accomplished. How

The young Gable as we will remember him . . .

sad that he could not see his greatest personal production—a child of his own to carry on the Gable name.

Jean Negulesco
"IMPRESSIONS OF SOPHIA"

Internationally known director Jean Negulesco gave the industry a personal close-up view of one of the screen's brightest stars when he wrote this vignette for The Hollywood Reporter in 1956.

Before I met her I heard all kinds of rumors—that she is huge, that she is fat, that she is built like a prizefighter, that she doesn't speak a word of English, and that, when directed, everything has to be repeated four times before it penetrates.

Well, first about her height. In her stocking feet she is five feet eight. And she is not that tall if she didn't have a fetish of keeping herself erect and always using a high, piled-up hairdo. But I have never seen anybody who

always sat so straight at any time. She enjoys being tall. As a matter of fact, when we went to dinner, I asked her to relax a bit so that we didn't have to look up to her.

With a smile, she said to me, "I enjoy being tall." Thank God I have to play her bare-footed through most of the picture we are making— *Boy on a Dolphin* for 20th-Fox—and with her hair wet from the water, that will bring her down to our level. As for her English, when I was presented to her, her first line was, "Why

Sophia Loren on location in Greece for *Boy on a Dolphin*, directed by Jean Negulesco.

Negu, you crazy mixed-up kid, how are you?" I couldn't believe my ears. I asked her where she had learned this language and she told me that Frank Sinatra had taught her in Spain.

She speaks excellent English with a very colorful accent and she has a talent for learning new words every day that is a continual source of wonder to all of us. Expressions like "Father grabber," "Mother user," and other peculiar phrases that she must have picked up from the boys for she is avid to learn as much as possible of jive talk. Of course, the only thing I can teach her is a Roumanian accent.

She is without a doubt the most extraordinary talent I have ever met. She can be a clown, a lady. She can listen seriously and talk with great wisdom.

Dancing with Sophia Loren is an experience. She is a born dancer with rhythm in her body. But dancing with her, as I said, is an experience, as she dances completely independently of you and you are just a pivot around which she dances. Of course, if by chance you try to be the "driver" and try to take hold of her and make her do what you want, after a few seconds you give up because you cannot keep up with her. And when I came back to the table after a tango and mambo with her, I was still shaking as though I'd been dancing with a vibrator.

HOLLYWOOD KALEIDOSCOPE
1956

January was a gorgeous month for NATALIE WOOD and ROBERT WAGNER. They began dating and fell madly in love . . . PATTI DEREK, reconciled to their split, though still in love with JOHN, desperately needed more money for child support. John, meanwhile, had gone off with European beauty URSULA ANDRESS . . . Another unique personality showed up on the Hollywood scene: PAUL NEWMAN. Immediately, he was compared with BRANDO and DEAN. Although he came from the "same school," and had similar training as an actor, and had also tasted success on Broadway before making his celluloid debut, both his early and later life-styles varied a great deal from theirs. Paul would not achieve enormous motion picture prominence until the Fifties were almost over. Even then, superstardom, with which he would eventually be cloaked, did not securely enfold him until the mid-Sixties. But then, his blue-eyed brilliance would explode—and place him among Hollywood's greats.

ELIZABETH TAYLOR and MIKE WILDING hit a snag. But friends said they were trying to work things out . . . FERNANDO LAMAS was in Europe, while his wife, ARLENE DAHL, was at home ill . . . EVA GABOR and TY POWER had a fling . . . DEAN MARTIN and his JEANNIE were about to "tell it to the judge" . . . And the MARLON-JOSIE "engagement" was canceled. He began dating RITA MORENO, and JOSIE went back to her French village—and anonymity.

In mid-January LIZ TAYLOR and NICKY HILTON created a sensation at the Santa Anita Race Track. MIKE WILDING was in England, and R.J. WAGNER, a chum of both, asked Liz if she would like to go to the track. Liz said yes. There, she and her ex ran into each other inside the Turf Club dining room. They spent the afternoon together—with Wagner as "chaperone."

Nicky gave Liz a winner, Free Stride, in the sixth race. Then, in the seventh, he bought her a $100 ticket, plus two ten-dollar tickets for her kids, splurging more than a $1000 on his pal, jockey EDDIE ARCARO. But Arcaro ran out of the money, whereupon Liz threw her arms around Hilton, kissed him tenderly on the cheek and said, "Nicky, you're insane—and that was why I loved you and couldn't stay married to you!"

JOHN WAYNE, in Berlin for the charity premiere of RKO's *The Conqueror,* to benefit the Motion Picture Home for German film actors, precipitated the greatest public demonstration since the anti-Red riots of June 17, 1952. Duke toured Free Berlin, and made a cautious inspection of the Russian zone without much trouble. But publicity about his appearance at the city's largest theatre resulted in a near riot that completely halted traffic and business on the Kurfürstendamm. RKO's manager for Germany anticipated only a normal turnout, but the movie house was so jammed that the screening did not begin until close to midnight. No one counted on the appeal of an American movie star to Berlin fans from *both* zones. They stormed past East German and Russian border police, surging down the main thoroughfare and screaming for a sight of Wayne. Some even offered their precious ration cards for an autograph.

LILI DAMITA took "custody" of ERROL FLYNN'S Mulholland Drive mansion, but had to pay $50,000 in liens against the house . . . A New York paper threw a damper on the GRACE KELLY–PRINCE RAINIER merger. Under the headline MONACO MARRIAGES ALWAYS FAIL, the article related that since 1869 there had never been a successful royal marriage in Monaco's Palace . . . Londoners were horrified by two story headlines: GRACE KELLY'S MOTHER TELLS ALL, plus MY GRACE IN LOVE by JOHN KELLY, SR. The Kellys were unperturbed and turned over their writing fees to charity . . . MARILYN MONROE'S newfound Democratic associates tried to press her into service for them during the next national convention.

PRINCE RAINIER came to Hollywood in February for a visit. He rented one of HOWARD HUGHES' homes in Bel Air and arranged to have all of Grace's pictures screened. It turned into a veritable Kelly Film Festival. Grace, still residing in the Pacific Palisades, kept chauffeurs busy driving her back and forth to see Rainier after work on *High Society.*

As a seventeenth birthday gift, PIA LINDSTROM will spend her summer in a reunion with INGRID BERGMAN in Paris . . . There was a new Continental romance flourishing in Tinseltown. JEAN-PIERRE AUMONT and MARISA PAVAN, PIER ANGELI'S twin sister, discovered each other . . . The DEAN MARTINS reconciled in February . . . Friends said GREG BAUTZER would finally shed his bachelor status and take the plunge with DANA WYNTER . . . And MGM referred all press requests for GRACE KELLY wedding invites to the Consulate General of Monaco . . . Designer HELEN ROSE gave Kelly her bridal shower, while the cast of *High Society* presented "Gracie" with a lovely wedding gift—a beautiful sketch of Grace and BING CROSBY, in a swimming pool sequence from the film—done by the company's art director, HAL PETERS.

In March, MARILYN MONROE stayed at the Sahara Motel, in Phoenix, and averaged at least a hundred calls a day—mostly from fraternity boys who wanted a date. While there, she celebrated a special anniversary. It had been eleven years since 20th Century–Fox dropped her original contract because they felt her chin and nose were too long—and because they said she sagged in the spots where she should have bulged . . . HUMPHREY BOGART was reported to be feeling "as good as could be expected" after nearly four hours of surgery for a throat ailment . . . RONALD REAGAN, a staunch Democrat, switched "to Ike." Ronnie said GENERAL EISENHOWER was his kind of leader—which threw his lifelong political friends into a tizzy . . . JOHN WAYNE welcomed a baby daughter, AISSA.

April brought showers and flowers and more news of Hollywood's comings and goings. The *Raintree County* company started shooting at MGM . . . ROCK HUDSON and his bride were at the "loud quarrel" stage . . . And GRACE KELLY admitted that her favorite indoor gambling sport was the high-stakes card game chemin-de-fer. MIKE TODD had taught her how to play at Deauville, France. But once the Princess of Monaco, Grace would be forbidden by law to enter her own principality's gambling casinos.

By midmonth, BING CROSBY and KATHY GRANT were still *not* married—and she was getting a bit edgy . . . All of the national advertising for *The Swan* carried the double-entendre slogan: "The Love Story of a Princess," illustrated with the sketch of a graceful swan wearing a royal crown! . . . And, as a joke, the fifteen hundred members of the international press corps, accredited to cover "the wedding" informally decided to organize and march on Monaco—which only had a sixty-two-man army . . . HELEN HAYES' beloved husband, playwright-author CHARLES MACARTHUR, passed away, and DARRYL ZANUCK tried to get her to go back to work with INGRID BERGMAN in *Anastasia* . . . ARTHUR MILLER'S family was said to be *very* upset over the news that their "wonderful son" was going to marry MARILYN MONROE . . . And brewery tycoon PHIL LIEBMANN, LINDA DARNELL'S ex, consoled all of the lovely girls competing for the coveted title of "Miss Rheingold." He informed them that GRACE KELLY had tried to win the title three times—and had come up a loser.

May was an especially hectic month. GRACE KELLY of Philadelphia became Princess Grace of Monaco, and the whole world saw television clips, plus a thirty-minute filmed documentary of all the pageantry . . . While JOHN WAYNE sang lullabys to his newest baby girl, one of his "bigger" daughters, TONI, married DON LA CAVA, son of director GREGORY LA CAVA. CARDINAL MCINTYRE performed the Catholic high mass wedding . . . With the pomp and ceremony of the Rainier nuptials still fresh in everyone's mind, Grace's mother, MRS. JOHN KELLY and her sister, PEGGY, flew back to Philadelphia—tourist class. Meanwhile, MGM planned to launch the gala premiere of *The Swan* on the Riviera, but not as part of the regular Cannes Film Festival.

JOAN CRAWFORD and ALFRED STEELE celebrated their first wedding anniversary in the Hunt Room of New York's "21" with a black-tie dinner party for a small gathering of their close personal friends, including Pepsi-Cola president HERBERT BARNETT and his wife, and LEAH RAY WERBLIN, whose husband, SONNY, was tied up with MCA business in St. Louis. It was the Werblins who had originally introduced Joan and Alfred, and Leah accepted a special thank you toast for herself and her husband. The only other "recognizable" guest was former Hollywood actor-turned-interior-decorator BILLY HAINES. The rest were corporate executive types, indicative of Joan's new circle of friends.

At the end of May, DANA WYNTER and GREG BAUTZER, who had maintained a dignified silence about their matrimonial future, announced they would be married. Determined to have a quiet and private wedding, they slipped away minus any press or guest entourage and were united in a simple ceremony. Even their honeymoon site was a well-guarded secret. Upon their return, they moved into a bungalow at the Beverly Hills Hotel for a few months until their new hilltop home in Bel Air was ready for occupancy. Greg had been Hollywood's most eligible bachelor until Dana, his fair lady from South Africa, came along. What with their merger, and the fact that half-French, half-Russian VERONIQUE PASSANI had romped off with GREG PECK, it was no wonder that the grass was greener for Dream Princes on the other side of the Atlantic . . . EVA GABOR became the bride of DR. JOHN WILLIAMS. Insiders said she started dating the doctor only to make TYRONE POWER jealous. Obviously, the whole affair was carried to its ultimate conclusion. If Ty was carrying a torch, he wasn't talking about it.

MONTGOMERY CLIFT'S favorite "protectress," wealthy LIBBY HOLMAN, sent Monty a big bouquet of flowers at Cedars of Lebanon Hospital, where he had been taken. It was a miracle that he had survived a near-fatal car-wreck on his way home from an ELIZABETH TAYLOR dinner party. It was a double miracle that Liz and the other guests, hearing the sounds of the crash, were able to rush to Monty's side in time. Liz literally crowded into the wreckage and cradled Clift's bloodied head in her lap until the ambulance arrived. Monty suffered facial damage and numerous internal injuries. Although he recovered rapidly enough to go back to work on *Raintree County,* the fabulous Clift smile was never quite the same. But he certainly had all the tender love and care possible. Mrs. Holman even leased a penthouse at the Chateau Marmont, on Sunset Boulevard, for $1,000 a month, where Clift recuperated.

And, on May 28, MARILYN MONROE had lunch with "the peasants" in the main dining room of the 20th commissary. It was the first time she had chosen not to hide away in her dressingroom since filming on *Bus Stop* began. A couple of days later, she took off for New York, where she and ARTHUR MILLER celebrated her thirtieth birthday on June 2nd . . . Two days later, Hollywood's beloved JEAN HERSHOLT was buried. He had passed away at his home at the age of sixty-nine.

As summer got under way, JOHN WAYNE had a lot to celebrate. He signed a contract with 20th Century-Fox to make four films, in four years, for two million dollars—highest star salary ever paid in the history of Hollywood to that date . . . MARLON BRANDO began steadydating Indian beauty ANNA KASHFI . . . Meanwhile, the marriage of GLENN FORD and ELEANOR POWELL was in trouble. She liked to work, but Glenn wanted his wife to spend more time "tending to the home fires" . . . And JEANNE MARTIN threw a gala party for DEAN at the L'Escoffier Room of the Beverly Hilton. For the moment, they were firmly back together, and apparently happy.

By mid-June, Mr. and Mrs. GREG BAUTZER (DANA WYNTER) were enjoying their honeymoon in Honolulu, while hometown friends of Greg's were bidding for his little black book with all of those lovely phone numbers . . . The HOLLYWOOD CHAMBER OF COMMERCE came up with a new gimmick to attract tourists. By Thanksgiving of 1956, they planned to install the first pink-pigmented sidewalks on Hollywood Boulevard, containing bronze stars with the names of celebrities and film pioneers . . . At the end of the month, LINDA CHRISTIAN and EDMUND PURDOM garnered plenty of space in the British press. Linda uttered the quote of the year when she was asked why she had not returned the $150,000 in gems from BOBBY SCHLESINGER—whose bank account did not exactly cover the gift. "It's all terribly unfair. If I had been given candy, instead of jewels, I'd have eaten it! Then what? I accepted those presents in good faith. I shouldn't have to suffer because of some sordid money transaction." Happily, she did *not* consider it a "sordid money transaction" when she collected a million dollars in alimony from TYRONE POWER.

By midmonth, PRINCESS GRACE was having the palace redecorated, but meanwhile refused to live in the Juan-les-Pins villa which RAINIER had occasionally shared with French actress GISÈLE PASCAL . . . While in Rome, BERGMAN and ROBERTO ROSSELLINI were feuding. If her 20th deal for *Anastasia* worked out, rumors were that she might return to Hollywood sans her Italian stallion . . . FRANK SINATRA was very upset that JUDY GARLAND opened at the New Frontier Hotel in Las Vegas instead of playing the Sands, where Sinatra, as an investor, shared in the profits. Pals said he was so mad that he might drum her out of membership in the Beverly Hills "Rat Pack" . . . SHELLEY WINTERS started dating TONY FRANCIOSA. She had "a thing" for handsome, talented Italian-type actors . . .

On June 21, KATHRYN GRANT was baptized in the Catholic faith . . . The DUKE and DUCHESS OF WINDSOR agreed to be the guests of honor on the first ED MURROW "Person to Person" television show of the coming fall season. They were slated to share the intimate half-hour with FRANK SINATRA . . . The TV ratings war heated up in July. STEVE ALLEN's show clobbered ED SULLIVAN's program in the Nielsens when Allen presented a special guest star: ELVIS PRESLEY.

Whether SINATRA liked it or not, JUDY GARLAND's very first saloon stand was a "Class A" act. Everyone in the Venus Room—and the hundreds who couldn't get in—seemed on edge. There was only one show, at ten P.M., and most of the stars playing other Vegas spots were able to catch her act. Judy swished out, calm, collected, cool and killed them. Every song brought an ovation.

Her proud husband, SID LUFT, said he had never seen her so happy, singing like a lark, "and with no problems at all." MCA's JULES STEIN, who remembered all of the great singers starting way back, said, "None of them could hold a candle to JUDY GARLAND." And JIMMY DURANTE said, "I'm sittin' here rememberin' when she was a little kid and we wuz both at Metro, and alluva suddin she's singin' 'Over the Rainbow' and I'm cryin' like a big joik." And SOPHIE TUCKER, who sat with DURANTE, cried too, along with MARTHA RAYE, ANNE SHIRLEY and CHARLIE LEDERER, LEX BARKER, PETE LAWFORD, BETTY FURNESS, JOHN CARROLL and dozens of more celebrities. During the evening, Judy dedicated "Happiness Is a Thing Called Joe" to her son, JOEY LUFT, and "Liza," to her daughter, young MISS MINNELLI.

KATHRYN GRANT sneaked into Mexico City in August to go sightseeing and shopping. And no, she did *not* discuss when, where and if she was going to become Mrs. Crosby . . . By September, it was reported that the ELVIS PRESLEY rock-'n'-roll craze had its subsidiary profits. Many of the nation's doctors were hailing the torso-twisting gyrations of modern crooner-dancers. Chiropractors, in particular, treated thousands of teenage patients with pelvic, sacroiliac and other misalignments formerly encountered only in their grandparents.

In October, Hollywood was all agog. The biggest event in many a moon was the fundraiser for President DWIGHT D. EISENHOWER's re-election campaign, held at the Hollywood Bowl, 26,000 in attendance. All of the Republican celebrities who could squeeze themselves in appeared en masse. Down in the Bowl dressingrooms, waiting to go on, CLINT WALKER wondered why JANE RUSSELL looked so sad. "Sad?" she replied. "I thought I was looking sexy" . . . HUGH O'BRIAN told MIKE O'SHEA how he met VIRGINIA MAYO on "Blind Date" during the war, and how she tried to talk him out of going into show business. Virginia's husband listened stoically, then asked, "What else happened on that date?"

It was ANN BLYTH's first political pitch, and

1 Honeymoon photo of Mr. and Mrs. Rock
Hudson (Phyllis Gates) taken in Jamaica.
(Photo by Kenneth A. Chinn—Marcia Borie
personal collection)   2 That spectacular
couple Mr. and Mrs. Mike Todd (Elizabeth
Taylor).   3 Marilyn Monroe and husband
number three, playwright Arthur Miller.
4 Eddie Fisher smiles as his wife, Debbie
Reynolds, grooms her puppy, Rocky, in her
dressingroom at Universal-International during the filming of *Tammy and the Bachelor.*

she had such deep convictions about Ike that she said she couldn't have slept well if she hadn't appeared . . . The Parade of Stars which preceded the President's telecast included Lou Costello, who said, "I like Ike. I like Mrs. Ike. I like the whole Republican Party." June Allyson echoed Lou's thoughts, then Dick Powell cracked: "I don't dare disagree with her . . . so do I!" They were followed in rapid succession by Art Linkletter, Louella Parsons and Anita Louise. Jeanette MacDonald remarked, "I wore this gown at Ike's last Inauguration Ball and I'll wear it at his next." Then Ginger Rogers said, "My secret ballot is Ike and Dick [Nixon]" . . . John Wayne was forceful: "We drafted him from wartime to peacetime and we'll draft him again!" Bob Hope injected a little levity: "It's amazing how fast I got here through all those crowds. I left my house at 8 and arrived here in the Bowl at 8:10—the fastest 12 hours and 10 minutes I've ever done on the Freeway."

Elizabeth Taylor's marriage to Michael Wilding was over; a divorce was in the works. At the end of November, at Mike Todd's lavish supper party, following his fabulous *Around the World in 80 Days* opening at New York's Rivoli, Liz looked like a bright poppy in a flaming red satin, strapless sheath, as she announced through a loudspeaker to Noel Coward, Marlene Dietrich, Bea Lillie, Rex Harrison, Kay Kendall, Ed Murrow, Cantinflas, Edward G. Robinson, Hermione Gingold, Milton Berle, Shirley MacLaine, Georgie Jessel, Eddie Fisher, the David Nivens, and several hundred other guests: "I've been 'Around the World' seven times, and each time I think it is the greatest entertainment I've ever seen!"

Her "world" now revolved around Todd, a consummate showman. The world premiere of *80 Days* was the most beautifully handled of any gala opening in New York, Hollywood, or abroad. After the three-hour-and-eighteen-minute screening, half of the audience moved on to the Capitol Hotel for an invitational midnight buffet. Todd hired a ballroom large enough to seat 500 guests comfortably, with a big stage for dancing.

Todd went *Around the World* for that, too, with dishes from India, China, Japan, Spain, England and America. Mike, a gambler, told his biographer, Art Cohn; "When you start thinking with your wallet you're always wondering what you *can't* do instead of what you can do" . . . Todd's reckless extravagance and courage in his pioneer solo film effort cost him multi-millions, but it eventually kept him in the caviar-and-champagne-style of living to which he had accustomed himself.

December brought one of the merriest Christmas Holidays on record to the entertainment industry. The amalgamation of Hollywood and New York, of new motion pictures on the big screen, and old movies on the small screen, filled everybody's coffers to the brim.

Nineteen fifty-six was a turning point for many celebrities . . . Gardner *didn't* pick up her divorce from Frank Sinatra, but did find romance under an Italian moon with Walter Chiari . . . Marilyn Monroe co-starred with a "prince," met a Queen and married a Miller's son . . . New babies arrived in the homes of the Stewart Grangers, Gregory Pecks, Eddie Fishers, John Waynes, Jackie Coopers, Pat Nerneys (Jane Powell), and the Dean Martins. While Fred Allen, Alexander Korda, Jean Hersholt, Columbia's Jack Cohn, Victor Young, Edward Arnold and Tommy Dorsey passed on.

Jack Benny played his violin in Carnegie Hall, and *Porgy and Bess* took Gershwin's music behind the Iron Curtain . . . Rita Hayworth came back to Columbia and Harry Cohn . . . America celebrated new young faces like Tony Perkins, Susan Strasberg, Paul Newman, Shirley MacLaine, Don Murray, Tony Franciosa, Cliff Robertson, James MacArthur, Gena Rowlands, Susan Kohner and Carroll Baker . . . And Elvis Presley and his "Blue Suede Shoes," and Pat Boone, wearing clean white bucks, both won the public's fancy.

1957

On the last day of 1955, Marilyn Monroe stayed at the Lee Strasbergs' New Year's Eve Party for five minutes. She entered, kissed the hosts, then explained, "I have to go. Someone is waiting downstairs for me in a taxi." On December 31, 1956, she came to the Strasbergs' again to welcome in 1957, and arrived *with* Arthur Miller. But this time they got only as far as the foyer. They fled after glimpsing the hundreds of guests overflowing every room of Paula and Lee's spacious apartment at the Belnord. With or without Monroe, the party was a fantastic assemblage of Actors Studio types, plus all of the other famous faces who happened to be in New York for the holidays. Among those glimpsed: SHELLEY WINTERS, arriving without a date. PATRICIA NEAL, enchantingly pregnant, along with husband ROALD DAHL. The equally expectant TAMMY GRIMES, and her handsome spouse, CHRISTOPHER PLUMMER. CLAIRE BLOOM came with GORE VIDAL, and co-hostess SUSAN STRASBERG looked very grown-up in flaming red satin.

The 1956 income tax paid by BOB HOPE, BING CROSBY and MARTIN and LEWIS was enough to cover the salaries of the entire United States Congress. And 1957 looked even brighter for DEAN and JERRY, who had each gone his own way. Martin signed a two-million-dollar television deal with NBC, while Jerry was a smash doing a Las Vegas nightclub act . . . WILLIAM EYTHE died at the age of thirty-eight . . . And, at the end of January, LAURENCE OLIVIER arrived in New York to attend a private screening of a rough cut of *The Prince and the Showgirl*. He co-starred as well as directed. Olivier was extremely pleased with the results, as was MARILYN MONROE, who attended a later showing with ARTHUR MILLER and the STRASBERGS. Lee thought it was Marilyn's finest performance to date, while Olivier himself said Marilyn was "enchanting." At the same time, he denied that Marilyn was so difficult to work with that several scenes required a few dozen retakes. According to Larry, "Those rumors were greatly exaggerated."

During the first week in February, there was an announcement which shook the studios, the recording industry and millions of teenagers—ELVIS PRESLEY was scheduled to be drafted in December. The eleven-month warning was apparently deemed sufficient to allow shock to set in, and, for those who had commitments with ELVIS, to get as much Presley product finished as possible . . . ERROL FLYNN, after an eight-year exile abroad, returned to New York, all set to resume his American film and stage career in partnership with wealthy HUNTINGTON HARTFORD . . . JULIE ANDREWS and stage designer TONY WALTON were all set to march down the aisle . . . LILLI PALMER won an uncontested divorce from REX HARRISON. His next bride, lovely British actress KAY KENDALL. Meanwhile, Lilli found happiness with her South American boyfriend, handsome actor CARLOS THOMPSON.

In March there were numerous "cheating" scandals involving several of TV's top-rated quiz shows . . . And Columbia Studios started a huge talent search to fill a role in *Pal Joey*, with FRANK SINATRA, KIM NOVAK and RITA HAYWORTH. They needed a dog who could eat bagels, cream cheese and smoked salmon—and look like he (she) really enjoyed it . . . JOAN CRAWFORD'S 17-year old, CHRISTINA, a drama student at Carnegie Tech, spent her midterm holidays in New York, and was treated to a shopping spree by Joan and stepfather AL STEELE . . . MERLE OBERON was all set to marry another millionaire, industrialist BRUNO PAGLIAI . . . MARILYN MONROE, dressed in a white beret, dark glasses and mink, and ARTHUR MILLER made one of their rare public appearances and enjoyed a midnight after-theatre supper at Sardi's . . . Word came out of Monaco that PRINCE RAINIER had completely financed the entire lavish pre- and post-wedding nuptials, ceremonies and fireworks through the extraordinary sale of Monagasque postage stamps, featuring the handsome profiles of Rainier and his lovely bride, GRACE.

EDDIE FISHER, who signed a contract for one million dollars to appear in Las Vegas for forty weeks over the next five years, had a sensational opening in April at the inauguration of the brand-new Tropicana Hotel. Eddie was introduced by MILTON BERLE, who was appearing at the El Rancho Vegas, a rival hotel. Fisher dedicated one tune, "Wait Till You See Her," to his and DEBBIE'S baby girl, CARRIE.

MIKE TODD bought "his and Liz" Rolls-Royces. His was black, ELIZABETH'S was green . . . Former Hollywood star FRANCES FARMER was spotted on her new job, clerking at the Palace Hotel in San Francisco. Frances, who had had her share of personal troubles, appeared to be accepting "her reduced state" in good spirits. However, two months later, she left her clerk's position to go back onstage at the Bucks County Playhouse in Pennsylvania . . . Sixteen-year-old RICKY NELSON, OZZIE and HARRIET'S younger son, made a smash recording hit out of a tune called "I'm Walkin," and "the new Elvis" was signed to play a series of county fairs across America . . . Meanwhile, DEAN MARTIN needed help from both BING CROSBY and FRANK SINATRA in order to make his first TV spectacular a smash hit . . . At the end of the month, producer HAL WALLIS drew such raves with his first two sneak previews of ELVIS PRESLEY'S *Loving You*, co-starring LIZ SCOTT, WENDELL COREY and DOLORES HART, he planned to release the film to the public four months ahead of time. And he had Elvis signed for another film to be completed before Presley left to start his contract with Uncle Sam.

In June, BETTE DAVIS sued WILLIAM GRANT SHERRY for divorce . . . JUDY GARLAND was a fantastic hit at the Greek Theatre in Los Angeles. After the opening, she and SID LUFT tossed a sensational party. LIZA MINNELLI and little JOEY LUFT tried to crash, but Sid sent them to bed after he said, "I never attend your marshmallow roasts" . . . JOAN COLLINS came with ARTHUR LOEW, JR. JACK WARNER did a fancy dance accompanied by a couple of fiddlers. SAMMY DAVIS, LOUELLA PARSONS, COLE PORTER and JUNE ALLYSON were among the guests seen enjoying themselves. As the evening turned into early morning, Judy sang "Accustomed to His Face" with ROGER EDENS at the piano, while LUCY and DESI, DORIS DAY and MARTY MELCHER, SCOTT BRADY, the ART LINKLETTERS, BOB MITCHUMS, SAMMY CAHNS, RAY STARKS, LAUREN BACALL and dozens of others sat and wept at the beauty of Judy's vocalizing.

MIKE TODD hit London the second week in July, and the "staid British set" was knocked for a loop by the furor he created. His visit, to launch *Around the World in 80 Days,* left an impact as explosive as an atom bomb. Whatever the eventual cost—including his Dorchester bill for the Harlequinade and Terrace suites (the most expensive in the hotel), the tickets to the charity premiere, the ruby-red Dior gown, with the ruby necklace and earrings to match for ELIZABETH (cracked Todd, after getting a close-up of the DUCHESS OF KENT'S magnificent diamond earrings and necklace: "Liz will most likely throw hers away tomorrow!")—and the fabulous party at Battersea Gardens afterward, it was worth every American dollar for the publicity he received.

Who else but Todd could have conjured up such a variety menu as champagne, hamburgers, cotton candy, fish and chips, frankfurters, toffee apples and Indian curry, or such a fabulous juxtaposition of personalities as the DUKE and DUCHESS OF MARLBOROUGH, EDDIE FISHER and DEBBIE REYNOLDS, EDMUND PURDOM, MIRIAM and DORE SCHARY, VIVIEN LEIGH and LARRY OLIVIER, MARY LEE, DOUG and DAPHNE FAIRBANKS, ROBERT MORLEY, KATE ROOSEVELT, SIR CAROL and LADY REED, DEBORAH KERR and TONY BARTLEY, ALY KHAN and BETTINA, MARY and JOHN MILLS, and Elizabeth's ex, MICHAEL WILDING, sitting at the next table to Liz, under the blue and white tent reserved for the VIPs? The only imperfection in this miracle of Todd that Mike could not control was the weather. "Will someone please turn

1 Walter Matthau and Jayne Mansfield clown backstage opening night, *Will Success Spoil Rock Hunter?* (Marcia Borie personal collection)   2 Nick Adams, James Dean's closest friend, Natalie Wood, and Elvis out on the town. (Marcia Borie personal collection)

the rain off," he kept pleading.

MARILYN MONROE, who had been elated by her pregnancy, lost the baby she and ARTHUR MILLER were expecting. The miscarriage sent Marilyn into a tailspin. Monroe's jealous detractors—they were legion—had no idea of the depth of suffering she experienced . . . GRACE KELLY'S father donated one hundred thousand dollars to the Israel Bond Drive in the honor of his newest grandchild, PRINCESS CAROLINE of MONACO . . . OLIVER "BABE" HARDY died on August 7, ending his forty-year career.

CLIFTON WEBB'S party for NOEL COWARD was the wildest of the Hollywood summer season. His mother, MAYBELLE, and writer LENNY GERSHE kicked up their heels and did a gypsy dance. Then CLAUDETTE COLBERT set the stage—a scarf and a chair—and MARLENE DIETRICH sang "Falling in Love Again." Noel, a little under the weather, but game to the bitter end, sang "I Could Have Dahnced, Dahnced, Dahnced All Night." He was followed by JUDY GARLAND, who did "Someone to Watch Over Me," while NANCY SINATRA, DOROTHY MITCHUM, SYLVIA FINE, ROCKY and GARY COOPER, SID LUFT, BARBARA STANWYCK and NANCY and RONALD REAGAN all sat, misty-eyed. CLIFTON himself reverted to his old song-and-dance-man days with "I Guess I'll Have to Change My Plans." Among the other guests having a ball: VIRGINIA ZANUCK, GEORGE CUKOR, FRANK SINATRA, COLE PORTER, TY POWER, FRED ASTAIRE, FRED BRISSON, DOLLY O'BRIEN, the JEAN-PIERRE AUMONTS, JOSEPH COTTENS and the JULES STEINS.

Before August ended, Paramount staged a twenty-four-hour round-the-clock premiere in Las Vegas of the JOE E. LEWIS biography, *The Joker Is Wild,* starring FRANK SINATRA. They flew in seventy representatives of the press, radio and TV from Hollywood, New York, Chicago and other major cities. The film also had a charity benefit in Hollywood before a star-studded audience including FRANK, LAUREN BACALL, CARY GRANT and BETSY DRAKE, PATRICIA and PETER LAWFORD, EDWARD G. ROBINSON, ANNE SHIRLEY and CHARLES LEDERER, the LELAND HAYWARDS and the SAMMY CAHNS . . . The Las Vegas festivities opened right after the Hollywood contingent arrived with a party at the Sands Hotel. The group then went on to the theatre, and continued living it up at the El Rancho Vegas Hotel after the movie. The highlight was JOE E. LEWIS, himself, who was never in better form as he roped in the press and visitors with an incredibly funny show. He and Frank, together on one stage—albeit briefly—were sensational.

In the fall, MARIO LANZA was in Rome filming *Arrivederci, Roma.* The American title was *Seven Hills of Rome.* Mario, in great shape, had slimmed down to 194 pounds.

Lanza was an idol in Italy. To the Italians, he was their "Great Caruso" come back to them. Mario, delighted at his reception, planned to make Rome his home base for two years. He leased a showplace, the white marble palace given by dictator MUSSOLINI to one of his heroic World War II generals. When Mario, his wife, BETTY, and their four children "burned their Hollywood bridges behind them," he sold his Bel Air estate. Of the vast fortune he had earned—five-and-a-quarter million dollars—during his seven years at MGM and as an RCA recording artist, the only tangible assets he had were the estate and the home he had purchased for his mother. Taxes, legal battles with business managers and agents, and his enforced suspension at MGM left little in the bank for this glorious singer, whose voice had once earned him a royalty check for $746,000 on his record sales alone.

"But I did it before and I'll do it again," said Mario. As soon as he finished this film, he planned to do four 90-minute shows for NBC-TV and record several albums for RCA Victor. He was scheduled to do his next picture in London.

In mid-October, NANCY and RONALD REAGAN made the happy announcement that they were expecting a baby by spring of 1958 . . . DICK POWELL became president of Four Star Television . . . And the police told COLONEL PARKER that ELVIS had to clean up his act during his final appearance at the Pan Pacific Auditorium before entering the Army. The local gendarmes were particularly disturbed by Presley's "Hound Dog" number, in which Elvis stretched out on the stage and rolled around with a large model of the RCA dog in his arms.

There was a gala premiere of *Raintree County* on October 16, at the Warner Brothers' Beverly Hills Theatre, followed by a terrific party at the Luau. The star of the film, LIZ TAYLOR, kicked off her shoes and danced with director PETER GLENVILLE. Everybody who was anybody showed up—including ZSA ZSA GABOR—who took one look at Taylor's diamonds and cracked, "I'm glad Liz found her Raintree!" MIKE TODD just sat beaming at his gorgeous wife . . . The following evening, three thousand miles away, Todd put on the greatest party in the history of show business at Madison Square Garden to celebrate the first anniversary of *80 Days.* In the New York arena, 18,000 guests enjoyed a delicious meal, fabulous party favors, and had front-row seats at the greatest extravaganza ever conceived. DUKE ELLINGTON'S band played for the show and dancing. The decor included a seventeen-foot-high, 1000-pound cake, iced in blue and sliced by hostess Liz Taylor. There was also a huge net strewn with garlands, which hung from the ceiling, and a twenty-foot-tall floral reproduction of the Oscar won by Todd. The following afternoon Todd took hundreds of members of the press for a champagne brunch and boatride up the Hudson. The whole party spectacle, televised over CBS, attracted a viewing audience of more than fifty million.

The third week in the month was joyous for Kathy Grant, who finally married Bing . . . But October ended sadly for all of Hollywood; dynamic Louis B. Mayer passed away at UCLA Medical Center, and the whole entertainment world mourned his loss. Funeral services were held on October 31. Jeanette MacDonald sang "Ah! Sweet Mystery of Life," and Spencer Tracy delivered the eulogy.

In November, the television-rating service, Nielsen, announced that westerns had knocked comedies out of all of the top ten spots . . . Joan Crawford and Al Steele spent a couple of weeks in Hollywood. While here, they hosted a Thanksgiving Eve dinner for Mary Martin and her husband, Dick Halliday . . . Meanwhile, Desi Arnaz, in an effort to give his Lucy the most sensational Christmas gift on record, put in a bid to buy RKO Studios . . . And Darryl and Virginia Zanuck's son, Dick, became engaged to beautiful 20th actress Lili Gentle.

With December came the news that Ingrid Bergman's "final payment" to Roberto Rossellini was her entire salary from *Indiscreet* . . . Marlon Brando walked out on Anna Kashfi and took off for New York to spend the holidays with his agent, Jay Kantor, and Jay's wife, Judy . . . Elvis Presley's entrance into the Army cost him $450,000 in movie deals at MGM and 20th.

•

The year 1957 brought Ingrid Bergman an Oscar for *Anastasia*, a triumphant return to America, a legal separation from her husband, Roberto Rossellini, which was climaxed by the Christmas dinner she shared with him and their three children in Rome . . . Jean Peters walked off with the elusive Howard Hughes . . . And Anna Kashfi married Marlon—only he left her flat.

In 1957, Lauren Bacall dated Sinatra, while Ava Gardner constantly quarreled with her Italian actor "pal," Walter Chiari . . . Marie McDonald divorced Harry Karl, dated Michael Wilding, was mysteriously kidnapped and then remarried Harry Karl . . . Bette Davis and Gary Merrill split, Joan Collins did *not* marry Arthur Loew, Jr., and "Mama" Gabor beat both Zsa Zsa and Eva to the altar by marrying a handsome Hungarian count, Edmund De Szigethy . . . Calling the whole thing off were: the Gene Kellys, the Jack Webbs, Esther Williams and Ben Gage, and Ginger Rogers and Jacques Bergerac.

By the time the year ended babies were delivered to the nurseries of Rosemary Clooney and José Ferrer, Liz and Mike Todd, the Robert Stacks, Marisa and Jean-Pierre Aumont and Ursula and Robert Taylor . . . Rita Hayworth found romance with producer James Hill, Kim Novak dated Aly Khan, and Tyrone Power found happiness in the arms of Debbie Minardos . . . Irene Dunne became a delegate to the United Nations . . . Vivien Leigh became the only lady ever to speak in the House of Lords . . . Ed Wynn, in his seventies, made a marvelous comeback . . . And the industry also bid a sad farewell to Humphrey Bogart, Erich Von Stroheim, Ezio Pinza, Jimmy Dorsey, silent star Norma Talmadge and fashion designer Christian Dior.

CENSORSHIP

It was not until 1956 that Hollywood would function under a completely revised Censorship Code. However, five years earlier, in 1951, there was a new problem on the horizon. Did the existing Code also cover motion pictures that were to be televised directly into living rooms all across America?

The question was argued in various states. Then, the rather straitlaced censors of Pennsylvania brought a suit which would have given them permission to re-censor

Hollywood pictures made for theatres that were now to be seen at home. The case went all the way up to the United States Supreme Court. But those venerable judges refused to hear Pennsylvania's argument. In essence, they ruled that state censors did not have the right to handle this area, since it was under the control of the Federal Communications Commission.

In February of 1953, yet another problem arose involving motion pictures that would be seen on home screens. This time the question revolved around the new 3-D films. With the sudden wide use of the extra dimension, which automatically increased the "realism" of movies, was more censorship necessary? It was one thing to sit in a movie house and have spears tossed so that they appeared to be headed straight for the audience—but was that permissible in living rooms with young children watching? No one knew the answer. A meeting was set up with Joseph Breen, a member of the Hollywood Censorship Board, to re-examine the potential problems.

In 1955, in the first major speech by Pius XII about films, the Pontiff declared that the motion picture industry was one "of almost magical power." Because of "this inner power of the moving picture, and because of its wide influence on the masses of men and even on moral practices," the Pope urged the "banning of corrupt movies wherever they were shown . . ." The Vatican had spoken, and had openly urged that *legal* and moral weapons be utilized to correct the situation. The industry had been put on notice.

One month later, a report came out of the Washington Senate Juvenile Delinquency Subcommittee, headed by Senator Estes Kefauver. One phrase leaped off of the printed page: ". . . the predominance of brutality in both movies and TV is making our nation's youth insensitive to human suffering."

There were other sentences that were even more bluntly directed at the motion picture industry. The government body found that ". . . the film code seems to have been administered far too laxly in the last few years. The predominance of crime, horror, violence and sex portrayed in films . . . and film advertisements . . . not only transgresses upon good taste, but also constitutes a genuinely harmful influence on young people."

Both the film and television industries were admonished to "police themselves" with respect to improper films "and not force the federal government to intervene." There was no mistake about the tenor of this report. If Hollywood did not do something—and fast—Washington would step in.

There was one further word of caution: "We are also especially interested in having those who produce films for TV come under some sort of industry regulation . . . At present, they are subject to no restrictions at all."

Eighteen months later, Hollywood acted. After a full year of re-examination a new Code was put into immediate operation. It had been precipitated not only by the growing public clamor for more restrictions, but by several "borderline" films, and what appeared to be a growing tendency to make more and more "adult" motion pictures.

REVISED MOTION PICTURE PRODUCTION CODE

On Wednesday, December 12, 1956, at high noon, a sweepingly modernized and streamlined Production Code went into effect. It represented the first major revision of the Code since its original adoption in March 1930. The old Hays Office, now headed by Eric Johnston, issued the new censorship guidelines, which had been under revision for a full year. In addition to Johnston, the Code committee for the Motion Picture Association of America (MPAA) consisted of Paramount Pictures' head man, Barney Balaban, and Columbia Studios' top executive, Abe Schneider. Martin Quigley, who drew up the original Code document in 1930, acted as consultant. The entire wording went as follows:

Motion picture producers recognize the high trust and confidence which have been placed in them by the people of the world and which have made motion pictures a universal form of entertainment. They recognize their responsibility to the public because of this trust and because entertainment and art are important influences in the life of a nation. Hence, though regarding motion pictures primarily as entertainment without any explicit purpose of teaching or propaganda, they know that the motion picture within its own field of entertainment may be directly responsible for spiritual or moral progress, for higher types of social life, and for much correct thinking.

On their part, they ask from the public and from public leaders a sympathetic understanding of the problems inherent in motion picture production and a spirit of cooperation that will allow the opportunity necessary to bring the motion picture to a still higher level of wholesome entertainment for all concerned.

GENERAL PRINCIPLES:

1. No picture shall be produced which will lower the moral standards of those who see it. Hence the sympathy of the audience shall never be thrown to the side of crime, wrong-doing, evil or sin.
2. Correct standards of life, subject only to the requirements of drama and entertainment, shall be presented.
3. Law—divine, natural or human—shall not be ridiculed, nor shall sympathy be created for its violation.

PARTICULAR APPLICATIONS:

I. CRIME:
1. Crime shall never be presented in such a way as to throw sympathy with the crime as against law and justice, or to inspire others with a desire for imitation.
2. Methods of crime shall not be explicitly presented or detailed in a manner calculated to glamorize crime or inspire imitation.
3. Action showing the taking of human life is to be held to the minimum. Its frequent presentation tends to lessen regard for the sacredness of life.
4. Suicide, as a solution of problems occurring in the development of screen drama, is to be discouraged unless absolutely necessary for the development of the plot, and shall never be justified, or glorified, or used specifically to defeat the ends of justice.
5. Excessive flaunting of weapons by criminals shall not be permitted.
6. There shall be no scenes of law-enforcing officers dying at the hands of criminals, unless such scenes are absolutely necessary to the plot.
7. Pictures dealing with criminal activities in which minors participate, or to which minors are related, shall not be approved if they tend to incur demoralizing imitation on the part of youth.

8. Murder:
   (a) The technique of murder must not be presented in a way that will inspire imitation.
   (b) Brutal killings are not to be presented in detail.
   (c) Revenge in modern times shall not be justified.
   (d) Mercy killing shall never be made to seem right or permissible.
9. Drug addiction or the illicit traffic in addiction-producing drugs shall not be shown if the portrayal:
   (a) Tends in any manner to encourage, stimulate or justify the use of such drugs; or
   (b) Stresses, visually or by dialogue, their temporarily attractive effects; or
   (c) Suggests that the drug habit may be quickly or easily broken; or
   (d) Shows details of drug procurement or of the taking of drugs in any manner; or
   (e) Emphasizes the profits of the drug traffic; or
   (f) Involves children who are shown knowingly to use or traffic in drugs.
10. Stories on the kidnapping or illegal abduction of children are acceptable under the code only (1) when the subject is handled with restraint and discretion and avoids details, gruesomeness and undue horror, and (2) the child is returned unharmed.

II. BRUTALITY:
Excessive and inhumane acts of cruelty and brutality shall not be presented. This includes all detailed and protracted presentation of physical violence, torture and abuse.

III. SEX:
The sanctity of the institution of marriage and the home shall be upheld. No film shall infer that casual or promiscuous sex relationships are the accepted or common thing.
1. Adultery and illicit sex, sometimes necessary plot material, shall not be explicitly treated, nor shall they be justified or made to seem right or permissible.
2. Scenes of Passion:
   (a) These should not be introduced except where they are definitely essential to the plot.
   (b) Lustful and open-mouth kissing, lustful embraces, suggestive posture and gestures are not to be shown.
   (c) In general, passion should be treated in such manner as not to stimulate the baser emotions.
3. Seduction or Rape:
   (a) These should never be more than suggested, and then only when essential to the plot. They should never be shown explicitly.
   (b) They are never acceptable subject matter for comedy.
   (c) They should never be made to seem right and permissible.
4. The subject of abortion shall be discouraged, shall never be more than suggested, and when referred to shall be condemned. It must never be treated lightly or made the subject of comedy. Abortion shall never be shown explicitly or by inference, and a story must not indicate that an abortion has been performed. The word "abortion" shall not be used.

5. The methods and techniques of prostitution and white slavery shall never be presented in detail, nor shall the subjects be presented unless shown in contrast to right standards of behavior. Brothels in any clear identification as such may not be shown.
6. Sex perversion or any inference of it is forbidden.
7. Sex hygiene and venereal disease are not acceptable subject matter for theatrical motion pictures.
8. Children's sex organs are never to be exposed. This provision shall not apply to infants.

IV. VULGARITY:

Vulgar expressions and double meanings having the same effect are forbidden. This shall include but not be limited to such words and expressions as chippie, fairy, goose, nuts, pansy, s.o.b., son-of-a. The treatment of low, disgusting, unpleasant, though not necessarily evil, subjects should be guided always by the dictates of good taste and a proper regard for the sensibilities of the audience.

V. OBSCENITY:

1. Dances suggesting or representing sexual actions or emphasizing indecent movements are to be regarded as obscene.
2. Obscenity in words, gesture, reference, song, joke or by suggestion, even when likely to be understood by only part of the audience, is forbidden.

VI. BLASPHEMY AND PROFANITY:

1. Blasphemy is forbidden. References to the Deity, God, Lord, Jesus, Christ, shall not be irreverent.
2. Profanity is forbidden. The words "hell" and "damn,"

while sometimes dramatically valid, will if used without moderation be considered offensive by many members of the audience. Their use shall be governed by the discretion and prudent advice of the Code Administration.

VII. COSTUMES:

1. Complete nudity, in fact or in silhouette, is never permitted, nor shall there be any licentious notice by characters in the film of suggested nudity.
2. Indecent or undue exposure is forbidden.
(a) The foregoing shall not be interpreted to exclude actual scenes photographed in a foreign land of the natives of that land, showing native life, provided: (1) Such scenes are included in a documentary film or travelogue depicting exclusively such land, its customs and civilization: and (2) Such scenes are not in themselves intrinsically objectionable.

VIII. RELIGION:

1. No film or episode shall throw ridicule on any religious faith.
2. Ministers of religion, or persons posing as such, shall not be portrayed as comic characters or as villains so as to cast disrespect on religion.
3. Ceremonies of any definite religion shall be carefully and respectfully handled.

IX. SPECIAL SUBJECTS:

The following subjects must be treated with discretion, restraint and within the careful limits of good taste.
1. Bedroom scenes.
2. Hangings and electrocutions.
3. Liquor and drinking.
4. Surgical operations and childbirth.

5. Third-degree methods.

X. NATIONAL FEELINGS:

1. The use of the flag shall be consistently respectful.
2. The history, institutions, prominent people and citizenry of all nations shall be represented fairly.
3. No picture shall be produced that tends to incite bigotry or hatred among peoples of differing races, religions or national origins. The use of such offensive words as chink, dago, frog, greaser, hunkie, kike, nigger, spig, wop, yid, should be avoided.

XI. TITLES:

The following titles shall not be used:

1. Titles which are salacious, indecent, obscene, profane or vulgar.
2. Titles which violate any other clause of this Code.

XII. CRUELTY TO ANIMALS:

In the production of motion pictures involving animals the producer shall consult with the authorized representative of the American Humane Association, and invite him to be present during the staging of such animal action. There shall be no use of any contrivance or apparatus for tripping or otherwise treating animals in an unacceptably harsh manner.

By the time the Fifties came to an end, Code violations had become rampant. But it was not until 1968 that the Production Code was scrapped completely and replaced by the Rating System. For all intents and purposes, motion picture censorship had ceased to exist—but it had taken thirty-eight years to bring the industry to its present level of maturity.

Dorothy Lamour
"SARONG, I'M RIGHT"

In this piece written for the November 19, 1956, edition of The Hollywood Reporter, *Dorothy Lamour discussed the article of clothing that first brought her fame.*

There was a time in the motion picture industry when the moon sank in the West you'd be either viewing a Fitzpatrick Traveltalk or one of my many South Sea Island pictures. The lure of the islands almost lured me into a barefoot life of sarongs, coconuts, friendly chimpanzees and hulas. The day that stands out most vividly in my mind is when I caught myself saying "aloha" instead of "good morning" to my children. It was then I decided to give my sarong a well-deserved rest.

There were many reasons for this move. I have enjoyed fame and fortune and great monetary remuneration as well, prancing in my lava-lava. I guess I first started to doubt the future for myself in this garment the day that my husband began courting me. Instead of bringing the customary flowers, he gifted me with a bunch of bananas and a coconut. My occupation is that of an actress. Webster defines this word as "one who represents fictitious or historical characters in a play, motion picture, broadcasts, etc."

I found myself either in a jungle clearing or setting up a joke for Hope or Crosby. This doesn't mean that I want to play Camille or the life of Sarah Bernhardt. I just would like to have a part where I wear shoes. One where the leading man doesn't say, "You speak English?"

Don't get me wrong. I'm not knocking my sarong, the small article of clothing which catapulted me to fame. It's just that it served its purpose. For a while I was thinking of packing it away in my cedar chest along with other memories. But after seeing the current crop of glamour cuties prancing around in those skimpy bikinis, the thought strikes me that they might be getting cold. So if any of the gals would like an article of clothing that might be warmer, its theirs.

I myself would like nothing better than cheering the heiress apparent to the throne of cinema's "Sarong Wearer." I'm looking forward to this day, and when it happens, I'll be sitting ringside in a chic Christian Dior gown and maybe a mink coat to keep my shoulders warm.

Dorothy Lamour on location on Catalina Island for *Typhoon*.

Gary Cooper
"A THREE-WORD MAN"

The articulate, urbane Gary Cooper helped to perpetuate his own "public shy-guy" legend in this vignette which he wrote for The Hollywood Reporter *in 1956.*

I think it's time we blew down the Cooper myth that I'm a two-word man. It's kind of embarrassing to go through life meeting people who expect you to say only "Yup" or "Nope."

Golly, I've seen people fall back in amazement just because I greeted them with "How do you do?"

Guess they expected me to raise my hand like an Indian chief and say "How?"

I was talking about this with William Wyler, the producer and director on my last picture for Allied Artists, *Friendly Persuasion*.

As I told Willie, a vocabulary limited to two words would be fatal to an actor. My mind reels at the thought of what would happen to an actor who could only say "Yup" to Sam Goldwyn.

As a matter of fact, I've learned that on some occasions a man can say "yup" just once and he's talking too much.

Especially if he's talking to his wife.

By the same reasoning, a man may have to say "nope" a dozen times before it takes effect. Actually, I'm more a "nope man" than a "yup man."

I know another pretty safe word, too. "Mebbe."

Gary Cooper on location.

310

I'm rather proud of "mebbe." In the first place it has two syllables, and in the second place its a dinger of a word for keeping a fellow out of trouble. The judicious use of "mebbe" can keep a problem suspended for as long as six months.

Then the problem usually disappears and you can say "nope."

Fellow has a reputation like mine and he hears all kinds of stories about himself.

For instance, they talk about the day during production of *Friendly Persuasion* when an assistant director walked up and asked if I had received some script changes Willie had sent to my house.

As the story goes, I sat silent for about a minute, then the assistant asked, "Did you hear me, Coop?"

And I'm supposed to have said, "Yup, just trying to figure which way to shake my head."

Now, of course, that's a silly story. But it goes the rounds.

Actually, all this "yup" and "nope" business started years ago when I was a guest on Edgar Bergen's radio show. I was playing a scene with Charlie McCarthy, sort of a take-off on the strong silent man of the West. It must have been pretty funny because people have never forgotten it and the tag has remained with me ever since.

Seriously, you can't just be a "yup" man in this business. Whether you like it or not, you have to learn to say "nope" and keep on saying it.

For instance, I have only found a half-dozen scripts that I could say "yup" to in the past few years. It was so tough to find stories that I didn't do a thing between *Vera Cruz* and *The Court Martial of Billy Mitchell*, and that meant I was out of action for a year.

But I must have read 70 or 80 scripts in that time, and none of them was good for me. They might have been good for somebody else, but not for me so I had to keep saying "nope."

The word is out around the country that carrying on a conversation with me is like talking to yourself. I would hate to think that's true, because I can carry on like mad if it's an interesting subject and the people are intelligent.

I talk a lot if there's anything to say. Sometimes I'm a regular chatterbox. Don't ever get me started on automobiles, guns, or hunting. There's no end to it.

Heck, I not only talk a lot but I even sing in *Friendly Persuasion*. Get into a regular barbershop rendition with Robert Middleton and Walter Catlett.

It honestly isn't the greatest singing you ever heard. To tell the truth, I think it sounds a little like hog callin'.

Dimitri Tiomkin, the music director, calls it a pleasing baritone.

Well, I won't say "yup" and I won't say "nope."

But . . . mebbe.

ELVIS AND ROCK

Singlehandedly, one young man, who began with a natural voice, homegrown sideburns, gaudy clothes and a cheap guitar, changed the face of the music industry, not only for his generation, but permanently. By November of 1955, Elvis Aron Presley, born January 8, 1935, in a shack in Tupelo, Mississippi, had risen from amateur shows and one-night stands to an RCA Victor recording contract. The story of how, and through whose guid-ance, Presley achieved so much is as well known as any show business legend. By the end of the next decade, the recorded voice of Elvis had been heard by more people in the world than that of any other performing artist.

Elvis was the Pied Piper of the Fifties, as Sinatra had been ten years before. His ability to "turn on" millions and to keep them involved and coming back for more singled him out. In January of 1956, Pres-

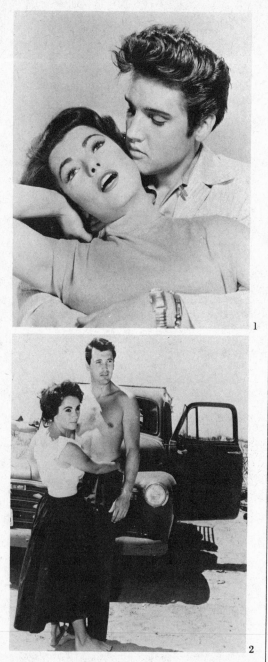

1 Elvis and Judy Tyler in MGM's *Jailhouse Rock*.   2 Elizabeth Taylor and Rock Hudson in Warner Brothers' *Giant*.

ley's first recording for RCA, "Heartbreak Hotel," started to shake up the music industry—and it remained "all shook up" for years to come. Every Elvis record went "gold." Girls wept at the sight of him. His Memphis home became a shrine. He had become the King of rock 'n' roll just as surely as Gable had been crowned on the big screen. But Presley's fiefdom was even larger than Clark's. It extended to nightclubs, outdoor arenas, feature films and TV.

His first four movies, *Love Me Tender, Loving You, Jailhouse Rock* and *King Creole*, set boxoffice records. Then, early in 1958, Presley was drafted. His advisers were worried. How could they sustain interest in him for possibly two years while he was off "protecting his country"—in peacetime? There was no cause for alarm. Through the cautious handling of Colonel Tom Parker, and Presley's own ability to become the "complete G.I.," the hunger for the sight of him, the sound of him, not only remained but increased.

There has never been a phenomenon like Presley. If he had not existed, no one could have invented him. His shy Southern ways, his weird taste in food, unusual clothes, extraordinary good looks, love for his parents, and ability to withstand the awful brickbats tossed his way by nearly all of the press—as well as the PTA—set him head and shoulders above the crowd. In fact, that was Elvis' chief quality—he had a charismatic ability to seem seven feet tall— to stick out in a group, to always seem somehow apart from—and just above—his peers.

What money, fame, power and all of the attachments eventually did to him is also part of the Presley legend. But, for most of the Fifties, and all of the Sixties, he was the biggest star of his own generation. "I believe it was God's will," he said. "I know my Mamma and Daddy sacrificed for me . . . and I just had to make it, for them. All the flash, and the cars, and jewelry and stuff—that's nice—but what really means the most to me is what I could give my folks . . . and the kids who believe in me."

When he said those words, in 1956, Elvis meant them. What he contributed to the world of show business stands as a monument. After Elvis, the floodgates were open. The Beatles. The Stones. All of the groups and single artists who came after him owe a debt to a former truck driver from Tupelo who made it so big that even the wisest prognosticators were stunned.

In the Fifties there was rock 'n' roll, but there was also *another* Rock—Hudson. Born in Winnetka, Illinois, on November 17, 1925, he grew up to his full height of 6' 4", possessed of broad shoulders, chiseled face, and a physique that made him the envy of Hollywood's males. At the beginning, he was a joke. A big, awkward, devilishly handsome young man with a funny name handed to him by agent par excellence Henry Willson. He was "created, manufactured, pushed and pummeled into a mold." Nobody thought much about his acting ability. He was there just to be shoved into bright Technicolor features—and to look good.

At first, even Rock didn't take Rock seriously. But once Universal had enough faith to give him the stellar role in *Magnificent Obsession*, Hudson came to life. "If you want to get ahead, you have to work at it constantly," he told a reporter. "At the beginning, I spent too much time in nightclubs, too many hours trying to perpetuate the image that had been created for me. I didn't work at improving myself. But the movie industry has become my life, and I have never stopped being a fan of other performers. It's my attitude that has changed from boyish hero worship to a professional admiration. I've learned to adore the challenge of doing well up there on screen. For the first few years, I really couldn't look at myself. But now, I believe in my ability.

The best advice I ever got was from director Raoul Walsh. He told me to remember that whatever I do on set will be magnified twenty times on screen. He advised me to minimize what I did . . . To be still . . . I don't think I quite understood him at first, but I know now."

By 1957, popular Rock Hudson was voted the number one boxoffice star in America. But he would reach even greater goals in the Sixties. He would play comedy, drama and swashbuckler roles with equal ease.

The Fifties spawned young heroes with names like Tab, and Troy, and Edd "Kookie" Byrnes. The leading ladies were young girls called Sandy and Connie and Annette. It was a whole new ball game. America was on a youth-cult kick, and Hollywood came up with a whole gaggle of young players who caught the public's fancy. There were no more great Crawfords or Harlows and very few good young dramatic actresses. Every once in a while one would come along to remind audiences of the old days. But primarily the Fifties were devoted to young people, young music, youthful tastes, almost sophomoric idols who fitted their times and reflected the country's attitude between wars and chaos. For every Sal Mineo, who could emote, there were twenty who didn't know one end of the camera from another.

Many of the Fifties players, however, became instant stars. They had television series which made them known nationwide virtually overnight. And they all got the star treatment. The set chairs with their names engraved in leather, the big dressingrooms, all of the perks. For every Jane Fonda and Natalie Wood, there were dozens of teenage-type dazzlers who shook their tiny behinds and smiled their toothpaste grins.

People get the kind of heroes they deserve—and require. The Fifties' kids proved that. In the next generation, the Peter Fondas, Dennis Hoppers and serious war protesters would bring yet another type to the forefront. But, in the relatively carefree Fifties, only an occasional Warren Beatty type would come along. For the most part, actors and actresses were physically all alike, interchangeable heroes and heroines— beautiful images on both the big and small screen, most of whom would pass into oblivion and be left with their scrapbooks and faded clippings.

"CINDERELLAS"

For twenty-seven years, Howard Hughes was a bachelor. His first divorce, from Ella Rice, had become final in 1930. During his "singlehood," he dated glamorous actresses, stunning socialites, winsome debutantes and willing models. If their names had been listed in alphabetical order, set in Bible-print-sized-type and laid end to end, they would have stretched longer than the wingspan of his enormous *Spruce Goose*.

When he finally bit the bullet and married again, on March 13, 1957, it was to a brown-haired, green-eyed, 5-foot, 5½-inch-tall, slim beauty, whose nickname was Pete. And when the news hit Hollywood—after the fact, of course—it took a lot of people by surprise. There was even a story, perhaps apocryphal, that some of his former flames had gathered together in a cafe and hoisted a few—in tribute to the man who got away. One was supposedly heard to mumble, "What has she got that I haven't already given him?"

To anyone who really knew Elizabeth Jean Peters, the answer was obvious—*patience*. She had waited ten years, with only one brief lapse, and had done it with dignity, independence, class and most of all, silence.

Jean was born on a farm, in East Canton, Ohio, on October 15, 1926. She grew up doing her share of chores, wearing home-sewn dresses, and aspiring to nothing more than getting good grades so she could someday become a teacher.

When she was ten, her father died. In order to survive, Jean and her mother ran a tourist camp and simultaneously kept a careful watch on the family's younger child, Shirley, age two. Over the years, through hard work and thriftiness, Jean saved enough to go away to college at Ohio State.

As an education major, she managed to make the honor roll, whip up her own clothes, and become one of the most popular coeds on campus, despite the fact that she did not pledge a sorority, because she disapproved of them. In her sophomore year, a friend, Arlen Stewart, entered Jean's name in the "Miss Ohio State" contest, which was sponsored by two Columbus newspapers. Elizabeth Jean won out over four hundred other girls. Her prize: two hundred dollars and a trip to Hollywood, with the usual routine screen test thrown in for good measure.

During the first week of her stay, Jean was tested at 20th Century–Fox. If anyone was particularly thrilled about her debut, Peters presumably knew nothing about it. At least, there were two versions about *that* part of her life. One was that 20th had offered her a contract *before* she left to head back to school. The second claimed that she had boarded a train for home in the belief that she had failed her one big chance. According to the latter anecdote, it was only *after* she was on board that a 20th executive decided to sign her—and had to track her down. Whichever version was true, Elizabeth Jean Peters *did* sign a contract for

$150 a week with options. She finished out the semester at college and then headed West.

Her first six months in town were mainly spent taking studio-sponsored drama lessons. To her fellow acting aspirants in class, Jean was considered "very un-Hollywoodish." Translation—"dull." Then, much to everyone's surprise, 20th handed her a plum assignment, the role of Tyrone Power's sweetheart in *Captain From Castille*.

She immediately went on a fifteen-week location jaunt to Morelia, Mexico, after packing her bags, sewing machine, pieces of yard goods and a stack of books. Morelia was a quaint, sleepy town—until a big bombshell exploded. The villagers had just gotten over the excitement of the film company being there, when Lana Turner arrived to visit Ty Power. Then, "quiet" Jean had another visitor, who landed in his own plane. His name was Howard Hughes.

Leave it to HH to have spotted Jean Peters *before* most of Hollywood even knew of her existence—beyond a three-line notice in *The Hollywood Reporter* when 20th signed her to a contract.

From that moment on, she was marked. Labeled. Categorized as "the mystery woman" because she had not told anyone she even knew Hughes—and refused to discuss him. When a reporter got close enough to ask if she was going to marry Howard, her only answer had been mystical: "I'm not one to kick fate in the teeth. I have elected to be an actress. I don't think I could be married and do a good job on the screen. I couldn't do both and do them well."

Over and out.

By the time she went on a 1948 location trip, to an island off the coast of Maine, for her second film, *Deep Waters*, Jean was big news. Reporters followed—or tried to—but the lid of secrecy had been partially shut. Miss Peters happily discussed her career, her new film, her dressmaking ability, but,

20th Century–Fox star Jean Peters, the woman who caught Howard Hughes.

after that, her private life was off limits.

The only tangible facts known about her nonscreen life were that she shared an unpretentious bungalow with her Aunt, Melba Doss, was a passionate baseball fan and had the reputation for being "the most frugal girl in the film colony."

Added to those startling statistics, Jean was an inveterate reader, always knew her lines, didn't like gossip, played tennis and golf, loved to eat three big meals a day and munch in between, could lay tile and bricks, plaster a room, repair furniture, fix plumbing, cook very well and make exquisite tapestries.

For the next six years, Jean Peters may or may not have been in love with Howard Hughes. She may or may not have constantly dated him. What they did, where they did it, or *if* they did it at all, remained a mystery. But the rumors were that Howard had fallen hard for Jean, and she was in love with him too.

By 1950, Jean was earning $1,500 a week, had made four films and was booked to do a whole slew of 20th movies with definite regularity. Two years later, she had changed residences, was sharing a home with her great-aunt, Cis Francomb, and had been cast to play opposite Marlon Brando in *Viva Zapata*. If she was still seeing Howard Hughes, he was the most "invisible suitor" in town. In fact, gossip columnists called Jean "Hollywood's most confirmed bachelor girl."

But 1953 brought big changes. First, it was her most exciting career year. While Jean had several pictures playing across the country, including *Niagara*, with Marilyn Monroe, Joseph Cotten and Casey Adams, she was being fitted for a glamorous wardrobe and flown off to Rome to film *Three Coins in the Fountain*, with Dorothy McGuire, Louis Jourdan, Maggie McNamara, Rossano Brazzi and Clifton Webb.

Then, somewhere between an outdoor cafe on the Via Veneto and the Fountain of Trevi, Jean Peters met handsome Stuart Cramer, III, of Charlotte, North Carolina. They immediately began a vigorous courtship and, on her return to the States, he presented her to his socially prominent parents. Although Jean told friends that she had fallen in love with Cramer after their first casual meeting, the romance was one of Hollywood's best-kept secrets.

On May 29, 1954, Elizabeth Jean Peters became Mrs. Stuart Cramer. They were married in Washington's Lincoln Church, two blocks from the White House; the historic Presbyterian church on New York Avenue where President Lincoln had worshiped. There were only three witnesses, her mother and his parents. Jean walked to the altar on the same golden carpet which Queen Elizabeth II had used on her Coronation Day. The Reverend Doctor George M. Docherty said Jean was the first bride to step on the carpet, which he had obtained from London's Westminster Abbey.

After the ceremony, when they posed for photographers, Jean, who wore a pale-blue suit with a lily-of-the-valley corsage, refused when asked to kiss Cramer. "He's not an actor yet," she said.

The handsome bridegroom, who owned part of the Mineral Wells Texas Petroleum Company, insisted he should not be described as a Texas millionaire. "Please don't call me that, because I'm not one. I'm just beginning in the business."

Back in Hollywood, Peters' wedding made front page news. If Howard Hughes was unhappy about the development, no one heard any comments. The illusive tycoon was *still* a bachelor, and his best girl—*perhaps*—had married another millionaire.

Jean and Stuart Cramer were man and wife for thirty-three days. They separated on July 1, 1954, and she returned to Hollywood. Jean made one final film, *A Man Called Peter*, and then announced her retirement from the screen.

On December 9, 1955, Jean, 29, filed suit for divorce. The Superior Court complaint charged that during the brief period she had lived with her husband, Cramer had inflicted "such mental cruelty on Miss Peters that it had become impossible for her to stay with him." She asked for no community property and made no financial demands. The only thing she walked away with was her maiden name.

Only those few insiders who claimed to know how Howard Hughes' mind worked understood the unusual situation which followed. Jean Peters had waited quietly, silently, patiently for him to marry her. Then, after seven years, she had asserted that marvelous independent streak he adored in her. She became another man's bride.

The wedding jolted him. Undoubtedly it made him regret that he had lost the most precious person in his adult life. Yet she had proven to him that she was, indeed, his kind of woman. She had just gone. There were no big scenes. No hysterical demands or ultimatums. She had simply grown tired of waiting.

At first, no one believed that Howard, down deep, wished Jean anything but the best of luck. After her divorce, everyone was convinced that although he felt a sense of relief when her marriage had not worked out, there was no future for them anymore. People just didn't walk away from Howard Hughes—not without incurring his wrath.

But, instead of being angry with her, Hughes had obviously applauded her courageous behavior. She had tried to make another life for herself. It just hadn't worked. And he was not about to let her slip through his fingers again. As soon as Jean's divorce was final and he had a few free hours, they flew off in his plane to Nevada and became man and wife. He was fifty-one, she thirty, on that March day in 1957 when the man with two hundred million dollars made the "Cinderella" girl from East Canton, Ohio, his bride.

Another Hollywood "Cinderella," was a beautiful creature with brown hair, a turned-up nose and the good fortune to be standing on the right sidewalk at the exact moment that a famous Hollywood director looked her way.

Eight years later, her unbelievable romance had its start. Natalie Wood, child star, fell in love with Robert Wagner just before she turned twelve. She was working at 20th Century–Fox, where R.J., as his friends frequently called him—short for Robert John—was the reigning young matinee idol for whom Fox had great plans. She had seen him in the flesh, gotten goosebumps and had obtained an 8 x 10 glossy fan photo of Wagner from the publicity department. She took it home and hung it in her bedroom. It was the last thing Natalie looked at before she went to sleep.

Six years later, when she was officially grown-up, he asked her out. By then, his star had risen higher, while Natalie, who had come through puberty without a blemish or a care, was a gorgeous young lady. She had publicly shown off her newfound maturity co-starring with James Dean in *Rebel Without a Cause*. For her work in that film she received an Academy Award nomination in 1954 as Best Supporting Actress.

"I never expected Bob to call and ask me out," Natalie admitted. "But when he invited me to go to a preview, I accepted. It was the night of my eighteenth birthday, July 20, 1956. I was glad to be able to celebrate in such a lovely way."

They had a few more dates after that evening. But it was not until December 6, 1956, that they officially began going steady. Then, early in 1957, Bob left on a nine weeks' location jaunt to Japan. Although they talked almost daily by transpacific phone, both were lonely. Because she was in "the business," and had to be seen at various industry functions, Natalie dated other men, most frequently Nicky Hilton. But she was simply marking time. From the moment R.J. came home, they resumed their steady dating.

Their dates consisted mostly of going to movies, out to dinner, or to small parties with friends. During their free weekends they headed for the high seas, on Bob's new boat, always properly chaperoned, of course—usually by good friends Mr. and Mrs. Richard Sale or Nick Adams and Barbara Gould. Invariably they headed for Catalina Island, twenty-six miles off the California coast. These nautical jaunts provided them an ideal escape from the public fishbowl. One of their main problems—as with all Hollywood stars—was a lack of privacy. The cruises gave them a chance to leave glamour behind and just relax.

Natasha Gurdin, a native of Northern California, had been discovered at the age of four. She and her mother were watching a film being shot on location in Santa Rosa, California. The director, Irving Pichel,

Robert Wagner and Natalie Wood (Mr. and Mrs.) during the filming of MGM's *All the Fine Young Cannibals*. The picture was released in 1960.

spotted Natalie and gave her a bit part in *Happy Land*. Two years later, remembering the enchanting child with the velvet-brown eyes, Pichel cast her in a key role in *Tomorrow Is Forever*, with Orson Welles and Claudette Colbert. Little Natasha—renamed Natalie Wood—was on her way. By the time she dated R. J. Wagner for the first time, at age eighteen, she was a veteran of twenty films and was considered one of Warner Brothers' most important young stars.

Natalie's parents, Maria and Nicholas Gurdin, were protective and quite strict with her. The oldest daughter in the family, Olga, was married. The little one, Lana, was still in knee sox and penny loafers. But Natalie, the middle child, on the verge of womanhood, really needed the love and security of a family who cared.

Robert Wagner, from a prominent Detroit family, had been raised very properly. When the time came for him and Natalie to think about getting married, R.J. did

things the only way he knew how. He called the Gurdin family, made an appointment and formally asked for Natalie's hand in marriage.

On the evening of December 6, 1957, the first anniversary of their going steady, R.J. took Natalie to the Mocambo for dinner. By prearrangement with the wine steward, Natalie was served a very *special* glass of champagne. Inside the crystal-stemmed goblet, reflecting in the sparkling pale amber liquid, was her engagement ring, a circlet of pearls and diamonds. They were married twenty-two days later.

At 12:57 P.M., on the afternoon of Saturday, December 28, 1957, the doors of the Scottsdale Methodist Church were locked and barred. Robert Wagner had personally seen to that. He and Natalie had chosen to leave Hollywood in order to make sure that their wedding was a private affair. The five-hundred-seat church contained fewer than a dozen people, all clustered together in the front row.

Nervously, R.J. waited for the signal to present himself at the altar. Nineteen-year-old Natalie, dressed in a gown of white lace and seed pearls, arranged the lace mantilla she wore on her head in place of a veil. She had been in and out of so many different costumes over her years as an actress. Yet, happily, the reflection in the mirror told her that this was the most beautiful dress she had ever worn.

The music started. She walked down the aisle on her father's arm—each holding firmly on to the other. As she passed her mother and Mrs. Wagner, and heard them weeping with joy, tears welled up in her eyes. With Lana Wood, Richard and Mary Anita Loos Sale, Nick Adams and Barbara Gould as their attendants, R.J. and Natalie became man and wife.

After a small reception, at Scottsdale's Valley Ho Hotel, the newlyweds literally raced to catch their honeymoon train. They had been misinformed about the departure time and had arrived at the station five minutes too late. The couple drove twenty miles, plus, before they were able to get the conductor to pull the emergency cord and allow them to board.

Hollywood's most "ideal young couple" would remain together until 1962. Then they divorced. Each remarried. But, in 1972—both free again—they were reunited. For their second marriage, still desiring to be alone, they were united at sea aboard a chartered yacht. Once again they repeated their vows and pledged that they would remain together "till death do us part." They did.

MORE ABOUT THOSE VERY SPECIAL LADIES

By 1956, the Alfred Steeles were ensconced in a Manhattan townhouse at 2 East 70th Street, decorated by Joan Crawford's old Hollywood chum, Billy Haines. The original eighteen rooms were transformed into eight and furnished with all the modern comforts. There was a huge closet just for Joan's three hundred pairs of shoes, another for her cosmetics and pills. There was also a special shampoo and hairdressing basin, with spray faucets for her and a massage table and whirlpool tub for him. There was a diamond-shaped table in the formal dining room. The bedroom had a wood-burning fireplace and was done in geranium pink. Visitors were asked to remove their shoes so as not to soil the carpets. The whole place was a monument to Joan's glamour, and her husband was overjoyed to give it to her.

Even Crawford's wealthy friends were awed, and dubbed the place the Taj Joan. Rumors were that Steele had borrowed huge sums of money to finance the renovation—one figure tossed about was a $387,011.65 loan made from Pepsi. Others said the amount spent was nearly twice that much. When queried, Steele admitted borrowing the money—but said it had all been repaid. Whatever the exact amount spent, the fact was that Joan now lived like the wife of a millionaire.

The first week in August 1956, the Steeles traveled to London and took up temporary residence in the posh Oliver Messel suite of the Dorchester Hotel. To her British fans, Joan represented the epitome of glamour—and she lived up to her reputation with a capital G. She arrived in London with trunkloads of elaborate clothes, fabulous jewels and furs, her own personal tycoon, and an English secretary and personal maid brought from Hollywood.

The Steeles were due to move shortly into a country retreat they had leased at Great Fosters, in suburban Egham, while Joan's film, *The Story of Esther Costello*, was in production. Everywhere, she was royally welcomed. The London Film Critics honored her at a luncheon, and the BBC-TV saluted her on the telly.

Producers John and James Woolf tossed a fabulous party in her honor at the swank Les Ambassadeurs. Aware of the vagaries of the English climate, they had the "outdoors" enclosed in a gaily decorated tent. Joan wore a creation of her own design for the occasion—an aquamarine silk organza, embroidered with green and blue sequins, short in front and long in back as a concession to the guests who were wearing *both* ballerina and full-length gowns. Around her throat glistened a glorious diamond necklace, and on her arm was an exquisite diamond bracelet, Steele's wedding gift to her.

Joan and Alfred stood on line to receive each arrival, including such old friends as Vivien Leigh and Larry Olivier, Anna Neagle and Herbert Wilcox, Binnie Barnes and Mike J. Frankovich, Helen Hayes, Hollywood hair stylist Sidney Guilaroff, Rita Hayworth, Joan Collins, "Mama" Gabor and Bessie Love. It had been almost thirty years since Joan last saw Bessie, when they both started on the MGM lot together, yet it was typical of her loyalty to old friends that she especially asked Jimmy Woolf to invite her. It had been nine years since Joan last saw Vivien Leigh, when they were both filming at Warners, Vivien, on *A Streetcar Named Desire*, and Joan, on *This Woman Is Dangerous*. Crawford's friendship with Larry dated back to the days when she was married to Doug, Jr., and Olivier was starting his Hollywood career as an unsung hero at RKO.

The Oliviers sat at Joan's table, along with Alec Guinness, Helen Hayes, Martita Hunt, Kay Hammond, John Clements and Geraldine Page. Guests at the smashing party later reported that Rita Hayworth had arrived in a black taffeta dinner frock, without any jewelry, and sans makeup except for lipstick. They said she looked thin, drawn and unglamorous, and had no escort but came in a party with the Maharajah and Maharanee of Baroda. Later, however, Rita danced practically every number with TV producer Gordon White, who had come with Joan Collins. If Joan was at all concerned at Rita's dancing away with her date, she didn't show it. She gaily whirled around the floor in the arms of Sidney Guilaroff.

Joan had even invited her first ex, but Doug, Jr., and his Mary were on holiday in Majorca and did not attend. Also among the missing were Marilyn Monroe and Arthur Miller. They had been on the guest list, but at the last minute Marilyn took to her bed with a cold. She expressed her regrets in a charming wire sent to Joan. Nevertheless, it was a star-studded and glittering affair. Joan was in seventh heaven, and Alfred proudly beamed as he and his wife whirled around the floor to the strains of "I Could Have Danced All Night."

When *Esther Costello* was finished, Joan Crawford Steele confounded her critics and surprised her chums by retiring from motion pictures. She had said from the beginning that she intended to become "the best wife in the world," and she lived up to her word. She became "Mrs. Pepsi-Cola" and traveled to all of Steele's sales meetings. Whether it was a trip to an exotic European city or a business gathering in Kansas, Joan, dressed to the teeth, stayed at her husband's side—and Pepsi sales zoomed. In the corporate world of charts and graphs, Crawford represented the ultimate in glamour, the apex of hype. And, everywhere she went, if a building, or an office, or a cafe failed to have a Pepsi dispenser, Joan took note—and the situation was remedied— pronto. At last she had found her niche. She had a husband who really needed her. A plain, "civilian" man to whom she was not competition but a complete helpmate. Speaking to a reporter, she happily explained: "We are a real husband and wife team. I love every minute of it. The reality of my life is even more unbelievable than some of the movie roles I have portrayed."

For the first time, in her "role" as a wife, Joan Crawford was totally fulfilled.

Unfortunately, fulfillment did not seem to be in the cards for the gorgeous lady from North Carolina. Ava wandered back and forth, torn between her desire to be free of marriage to Sinatra, yet, surprisingly, so deeply attached to him that it was difficult to understand her movements and motivations.

By the late fall of 1956, there were rumors that Ava Gardner had fallen in love with Italian actor Walter Chiari and was going to marry him. On the last day in December, when Frank Sinatra showed up in Milan, reporters talked to him about "the situation." Sinatra, surprisingly, did not blow his stack at being asked such a personal question. Instead, he said politely, "I loved Ava so much, I do not see why I should harass her or in any way defeat her happiness."

The whole thing was an enigma. There was no reason why, after having established her six weeks' of residence in Reno a couple of years previously, Ava should not have picked up the final papers. Yet, in all this time, she had not done so. Insiders felt that she had always hoped for a reconciliation with Frank. Meanwhile, being a man's woman, there had been others: Luis Miguel Dominguin, Chiari, and whoever else came along that attracted her fancy.

It took reporters nearly two months to catch up with Gardner and get her version of the "Chiari wedding rumors."

"For me, Walter is a very good friend . . . but there is no question of our getting married. I am not yet divorced from Frank Sinatra."

This reply came from the French Riviera, where she had just arrived, after a seventeen-hour trip from Barcelona, driving an "inconspicuous" white convertible. Chiari, meanwhile, had flown in from Genoa. They had dinner together, then he headed back to Rome.

Three months later, Ava was in Mexico City, where she wound up her location stint on *The Sun Also Rises*. In one of her handsome imported leather suitcases she carried her marriage certificate. On the 14th of June it was presented to the Department of Foreign Relations. The following day, after she and Frank had been separated for two and a half years, the divorce was filed.

Ava took off for Hollywood. Notification was sent to Sinatra. If he agreed, as he was expected to do, the divorce would be granted within a matter of days. In her complaint Ava alleged that Frank had "abandoned their home for more than six months without legally justified cause." Under Mexican law, this was sufficient grounds for divorce. The decree was signed by a civil court judge in July 1957. Sinatra did not contest the divorce.

At this point in time, Ava was living nearly the year round in Spain. Still, she clung to her American citizenship. And, when queried about her new residence, Ava responded, "Contrary to what you may have read, my decision to leave Hollywood was not made on the spur of the moment. I just don't like that town. I fell in love with Spain when I made *Pandora and the Flying Dutchman* there. I have learned to speak Spanish with practically no accent. I am able to find peace and quiet in Spain, which was almost impossible for me in Hollywood. Now that I have peace, people have started rumors and lies. I have no time to constantly defend myself. Let people believe what they like. I can't sue, or complain every day!"

In October of 1957, there were unconfirmed rumors that Ava had made a sudden trip from Madrid to London. That she arrived at the airport with her face hidden by a scarf . . . had gone to a hotel . . . had not visited any London night spots . . . had been seen by a doctor, but had refused surgery—for what, exactly, no one ever knew for sure. Then, in December, when the "mystery wound" had not healed, she had flown to New York to see a prominent American plastic surgeon.

It took nearly three months for the facts to be sorted out. Ava's gorgeous face had been damaged when she fell from a horse during a visit to the private bullring of Angel Peralta, a leading Spanish bullfighter. When finally confronted with the rumors, Ava admitted that she had suffered facial bruises in a bullring accident. But she indignantly denied she needed plastic surgery.

By this time, the story of her alleged disfigurement had gained wide circulation in London. The British press said that "she was terrified of surgery, had put off the operation, and that her face was still numb and bruised." After that report, a Madrid correspondent claimed that he had visited Ava and inspected her face. He said there was "a slight mark on her cheek." Ava said she had a blood clot which would disappear within a couple of months. The accident had occurred, she said, "while she was on horseback, testing the courage of a young bull, and had fallen off."

There were also stories that upon her arrival in New York to consult a physician, Sinatra had rushed to her side, had urged her to have the surgery—that she had agreed, then backed out.

By August of 1958, however, everything was back to normal for Ava. Sort of. There was one slight complication. Shelley Winters and her husband, Anthony Franciosa, were busy issuing denials of newspaper reports that *their* marriage was in trouble because of Ava Gardner! Franciosa, a handsome, sensitive and extremely volatile person with a potentially explosive temper that was every bit as vocal as Sinatra's could be, was furious.

"It's vicious nonsense," said Franciosa, who was playing opposite Ava in *The Naked Maja*, the story of the Spanish painter Goya and the Duchess of Alba, being filmed in Italy. In fact, Tony and Shelley had consulted Roman attorneys and wanted to sue the paper for libel. Some of the stories said that Shelley, who had arrived in Italy only a week before to visit Tony, had heard gossip about her husband and Gardner and had stalked Ava to a Rome nightclub, where she struck her.

Shelley said, "The whole thing is ridiculous!"

Ava said, "It was an accident . . . I slipped."

There was a follow-up story that *Ava hit Shelley*. Ava denied it. "I never hit her. She's a friend of mine . . . a nice girl. It's not true."

"I'm very much in love with Tony," said Shelley, who always liked to have the last word. Eventually, it turned out that Shelley and Tony were having problems which really had nothing to do with Ava. At least, with some of the celebrity set, there was never a dull moment.

In February 1959, Walter Chiari stated publicly that his romance with Ava Gardner was over. "It was a beautiful friendship," he said, from Melbourne, Australia, where he had flown many thousands of miles to see Gardner.

"Why did I fly all this way to see Ava? Because we are good friends, that's why . . . and because I also wanted to see Australia!"

Ava, who was making *On the Beach* there, had been seen in the company of handsome American tennis star Tony Trabert, who was "down under" to play in a few tournaments. Trabert, when queried, said that he and Ava and his wife, who was back in the States, were all good friends.

Ava Gardner lived out the last two years of the Fifties as though she were a gypsy moth. She was restless . . . suffered from insomnia . . . And, some said, had never really been able to come to grips with stardom: neither with all of the exotic trappings it had brought her nor with the high price she had apparently paid for her fame.

Gardner, truly one of the world's great beauties, was a paradox. She craved privacy, yet sought the inevitable spotlight by frequenting the world's most popular "in" night spots and watering holes.

In 1957, she purchased a three-bedroom brick house five miles outside of Madrid.

The place was surrounded by two acres of trees and flowers. Sister Bea, two dogs, a maid and a houseboy shared it with her. Ava furnished the place with antiques from a Spanish flea market. She loved puttering around. When Bea and the servants were away, she did her own cooking.

"Madrid is very social," Ava had said then. "I love the Spanish fiestas, the music and dancing. It's wonderful. Everybody drinks wine until dawn. Besides, Madrid is a good jumping-off point. I can fly to all the other interesting places in Europe in a couple of hours or less."

Over those restless years, the three men she had married and divorced still cared for her, and she for them. With Sinatra in particular, she maintained a continuing friendship. If ever she was in need, Frank was by her side or on the telephone, comforting her, arranging for anything she needed to make her happy.

Ava Gardner had come a long way from the start of her life as the daughter of a dirt-poor tenant farmer from North Carolina. It was her extraordinary natural beauty that had carried her most of the distance. But it was her talent that had solidified her superstar status.

Unfortunately, while she could look in the mirror and *see* her beauty, she could never quite bring herself to believe in her acting ability. More's the pity—because, when her youthful beauty turned into mature loveliness, her talent could have carried her—whenever she allowed it to.

George Burns
"WHAT'S FUNNY ABOUT A CIGAR?"

Vaudeville-radio star film personality George Burns contributed this piece about his famous trademark prop for The Hollywood Reporter *in 1957.*

I am often asked, "What's funny about a cigar?" by people who don't smoke them.

Well, this has no simple answer. Let me put it like this. If the jokes are funny, then I've got a very funny cigar. I've had a few cigars that were flops, though.

I've played straight to Gracie and to others all my life, and in this situation I'm *their* cigar—and when I have a chance to be the comic, in my monologues, the cigar has to be *my* straight man.

I have been using a cigar so long as a comedy prop that it has almost become part of my personality.

I use it to time my jokes, principally, although I confess I also enjoy smoking it, even during the show.

It's a very handy timing device. If I get a laugh with a joke, I just look at the cigar or twiddle it a little while I'm waiting for the laugh to die down. If I don't get a laugh, it's nice to have something to hang on to.

When a joke calls for a delayed laugh, I exhale my smoke slowly. If the laugh never comes at all, I swallow.

I am frequently called on to be the master of ceremonies at functions of the Friars Club, which is noted for its stag dinners honoring its members.

At those stags, even the smoke is on the blue side. For those occasions I use a darker cigar.

I receive large numbers of cigars from fans, but I always stick to my old brand.

Groucho Marx and Ken Murray also are identified with cigars, and they're pretty funny. So I get my cigars at the same place they do. If he can find a funny cigar maker, a comedian has got it made.

But there's one thing I should point out. Groucho and I light our cigars—Ken Murray just chews his. Groucho and I don't talk to Murray.

I once tried smoking cigarettes, but gave it up. I wasn't a very neat cigarette smoker, and besides the timing was off. A cigarette doesn't last long enough for one of my monologues.

I am known as one of the neatest cigar smokers in the country, which I attribute to camera angles. The camera usually just shows me from the waist up during a monologue. If it showed the condition I leave the floor in, I'd lose that reputation.

Recently, I was chosen "Cigar Smoker of the Year" by the Cigar Institute of America, and was invited to receive an award.

I had to decline the honor. They wanted me to come to Atlantic City to have 20 men blow smoke in my face, but I couldn't get away. So they flew here—all 20 of them—and blew smoke in my face here.

I started smoking cigars at the age of eight, because I wanted to look successful.

That's important when you're eight years old.

Bing Crosby
"YOU MEET SO MANY INTERESTING PEOPLE"

On November 14, 1955, Harry L. Crosby, singer-turned-journalist, wrote this biographical article for The Hollywood Reporter. *Among other facts he revealed how he received his nickname, Bing.*

I don't mean to pontificate on the subject, but my own start in the newspaper business antedates the advent of *The Hollywood Reporter* by enough seasons to qualify me as a sort of elder statesman or journalist, as you might say, in the field of publishing.

My paper, as you may know, was *The Spokesman-Review* . . . in my hometown of Spokane. I was intimately connected with this esteemed organ of public information and opinion as far back as 1917, in a capacity which one might describe as basic in conveying the news to the citizenry. (This had no bearing on the fact that the paper included a Sunday comic section called "The Bingville Bugle," and that from my weekly determination to be first in the household to read it, when a mere lad of seven, derives the monicker I bear today.)

My day with *The Spokesman-Review* started earlier than most newspapermen of today would care to contemplate. I got up each morning at four and went to the intersection of Nora and Addison Avenues, an area dotted with old wooden cars discarded by the local transit company.

We stripped this outmoded rolling stock for firewood, built a big bonfire and awaited the first car of the morning. When it came with its cargo of papers hot off the press, we folded the papers into throwable shapes by the comfortable warmth of the blaze.

My favorite style of folding was the boomerang. It had a tight twist in the middle which made it hug a porch when it hit. If it hit, that is. My best shots were sometimes on the roof, under the porch and in the bushes.

Of course, my less able colleagues ran to the three-cornered or the dog-ear fold. With me it was the boomerang fold, or nothing. Served the public interest.

I guess it's a little like that with *The Reporter*, although I have no way of knowing if its carriers are perfectionists and use the boomerang fold, or just do it the easy way with three-corner or dog-ear. The postman brings me my copy and doesn't fold it at all.

You can hardly call me a charter subscriber, though I'm old enough. I was busy at a lot of things along about 1930, when *The Reporter* made its maiden trip to the post office, but my name wasn't exactly on the list just yet. Borrowed my copies for a while; a practice you'd hardly condone as conducive to net paid circulation and all that that implies.

It is just possible you may have heard that Carl Laemmle, Sr., then head of Universal Pictures, decided to film a mammoth musical built around Paul Whiteman and his band, an organization with which I had been affiliated at the time for some three years or so.

The idea was that since "Pops" Whiteman was by far the most important and best known figure in popular music, Universal would steal a march on all the other studios. So in 1930 a deal was set for us all to come to California—the band, the singers, Whiteman, his valet, his business manager—and make *The King of Jazz*. And since we were broadcasting for Old Gold, Old Gold supplied a special train for us as an advertising stunt. Banners draped over the train plugged the cigarettes.

We didn't know it at the time, but we were to make two such trips. When we arrived we were given a big bungalow on the Universal lot as a recreation room. We all bought autos—or at least we made the downpayments with money which Pops advanced to us, then deducted from our salaries.

We loafed for a month while the big brains worked up a story which proved unsuitable to Whiteman. They'd made the mistake of trying to build him as a romantic lead. He was impressive looking, but what with his thinning thatch and his ample poundage, it was finally decided he didn't fit the script, so we bundled back to New York for a couple of months.

When we returned West, we worked on *The King of Jazz* for an age. Picture techniques weren't developed then the way they are now, and musical numbers took as much as a week to shoot. Pops had promised me a song, "Song of the Dawn," in the picture—a verse and two choruses. I rehearsed and rehearsed, then took time out to see the SC-UCLA game.

There was quite a shindig after the game in our studio bungalow, involving some tippling but not to excess. A car bumped mine after the party, and I was flung into durance vile [jail]. While things were being straightened out, came the day when the song was to be sung and I wasn't available. So it was given to another singer, John Boles, and on the strength of it he got a lot of pictures after that. I must say he had a bigger voice and a better delivery for that kind of a song than I had, and I've often wondered what might have happened to me if I had sung it. I might have flopped with the song. I might have been cut out of the picture. I might never have been given another crack at a song in any picture.

As it was, I did have a consolation number in *The King of Jazz*, something called "A Bench in the Park," rendered in company with Harry Barris and Al Rinker, my fellow members of The Rhythm Boys, and with the Three Brox Sisters.

It was very shortly afterward that I was privileged to make my in-person debut at the Montmartre [a club in Hollywood], in a Rhythm Boys engagement arranged by the same Bill Perlberg who now is a leading producer and for whom I worked most recently in *The Country Girl*.

The Montmartre was a favorite hangout then of the film colony, and Barris, Rinker and I were fairly big there. For one thing, after Whiteman had let us go, we learned a new song or two and our material improved. As sometimes happens when fresh instrumentalists or vocalists come to town, we became an overnight fad. It happened later to a lad named Vallee and to a good-looking youngster named Russ Columbo. Much later it happened to Frank Sinatra. I'm glad it happened to me then because it brought Dixie Lee to the Montmartre.

Soon after, an agent named Leonard Goldstein was booking us—the same Leonard Goldstein who went onward and upward with the motion picture arts, and who was a leading producer at the time of his passing. Under his aegis, we moved to the Cocoanut Grove. Gus Arnheim had decided to form a band and go back into the Grove, where he'd once been Abe Lyman's pianist. He signed Barris, Rinker and me, a girl singer named Loyce Whiteman, a tenor named Donald Novis, and got together a band which could do comedy group singing. When we'd rehearsed for a while, we were a pretty useful unit. The Grove had a radio outlet two hours each night. We thought this a fine thing, but we had no conception of how wonderful it actually was. Through this new medium, we built popularity all over California and as far north as Seattle, Portland and Tacoma. I found out later that even some of the people in the Midwest used to sit up until 3 A.M. to catch us.

About this time, Mack Sennett suggested I make a series of movie shorts for him. I had made one for him already, and working in pictures looked like easy money to me. The way we made these Sennett shorts reads like a quaint piece of Americana. For two days, we'd have a story conference. I was in on it. In fact, everybody was in on it—actors, cameramen, gag men and Sennett.

We sat upstairs in Sennett's office, a large room equipped with plenty of cuspidors because Sennett was a muncher of the weed. For our title we used the name of the basic song in the picture, like "I Surrender, Dear," "At Your Command," or "Just One More Chance." For our plot, we'd start with a very social mother and daughter. I'd be a band crooner with a bad reputation, and mother didn't think me quite right for her daughter. Instead she wanted her apple dumpling to marry some respectable pup, some fuddy-duddy, some very disagreeable character, a young businessman or a rising young lawyer.

Once we had this nugget of gold, Sennett would start "writing." I use writing for want of a better word. He put nothing down on paper. His story was really a series of gags. We always would end up with somebody falling in a fish pond or some other device with "punch" possibilities. Sennett would tell me, "This is the scene where you call on the girl, and you know her mother doesn't like you, and you're talking to the girl and her mother comes in and discovers you and tells you to leave the house, you louse, she doesn't want to ever see you again. So you go out, and on the way out you step into this laundry basket and you get up with the laundry hanging all over you, and you make an ignominious exit."

My next tussle with the movies was even more abortive than my original caper with the medium when I was one of the Rhythm Boys. Paramount brought me West to sing a song in a picture called *Confessions of a Co-ed*. But when the picture was edited, I wasn't even on the screen—just an off-stage voice.

But some of the studio's brains must have heard me on the radio—I'd been working for Columbia Broadcasting System by then—for when Paramount conceived the notion of a picture featuring radio performers who'd attained prominence, they signed Burns and Allen, the Mills Brothers, Kate Smith, a treacle-voiced performer known as The Street Singer—and me. Someone fluffed up a story called "The Big Broadcast," which would permit the use of our various talents.

It must have worked out well. I'm still here. And I don't think I'll ever go back to newspapering.

HOLLYWOOD KALEIDOSCOPE
1958

It was an unhappy New Year for ROCK HUDSON. He walked out on his marriage to PHYLLIS GATES and spent the holidays in New York as the houseguest of actor pal KURT KASZNER and Kurt's wife, LEORA DANA. They welcomed in 1958 at TY POWER'S Park Avenue apartment. Rock, just named Hollywood's number one boxoffice star, relaxed with NOEL COWARD, MARGARET LEIGHTON and her beloved LAURENCE HARVEY, and confided that after his Universal-International contract was up in four years he hoped to appear on Broadway, perhaps in a musical comedy. DEBBIE MINARDOS, TY's new love, co-hosted the soirée and personally supervised the delicious buffet supper. During the evening, Debbie showed her guests the beautiful mink jacket with which Tyrone had gifted her, and she just smiled when everyone asked Ty how soon they would be married.

SYLVIA HAWKES ASHLEY FAIRBANKS GABLE DJORDZADZE divorced her "prince," sold her Hollywood home and moved back to London ... There were rumors that KIM NOVAK was romancing SAMMY DAVIS, JR. . . . All of Hollywood was shocked and saddened at the sudden death of film pioneer JESSE L. LASKY ... HOWARD HUGHES purchased 400,000 shares of 20th Century–Fox, and became that studio's largest stockholder ... CLARK GABLE was paid a half a million dollars to co-star with BURT LANCASTER in *Run Silent, Run Deep* ... And RONALD REAGAN was such an effective spokesman for the movie industry when he testified before a congressional committee in Washington, D.C., that Representative JOHN BYRNES, a Republican from Wisconsin, suggested Reagan should run for Congress.

GRACIE ALLEN retired from show business in February after thirty-four years of being one-half of the leading husband-and-wife comedy team. GEORGE BURNS and his cigar remained to continue as a "single" ... And, in rapid succession, the world of entertainment lost more top industry leaders, including Columbia's HARRY COHN, and MANNY SACKS, vice-president of NBC and RCA.

In March, Hollywood received another enormous blow. MIKE TODD was killed in a plane crash one week before the Academy Awards. ELIZABETH TAYLOR was in shock as her Hollywood and New York friends rallied to her side. The industry had never seen such a dynamo as Todd. The energy he gave off, as he rushed through life, resembled a thunderbolt whose current of electricity touched everyone. Elizabeth, clutching his tiny baby, LIZA, was distraught. Just a few weeks before Todd's death, Elizabeth and he had celebrated her twenty-sixth birthday, at the stroke of midnight, while they attended the Golden Globes Awards dinner. Mike waited until the clock struck twelve before he gifted his beautiful bride with a diamond bracelet so dazzling it had the whole room aglow with its sparkle. Two weeks later, the Todds, in Palm Springs, gave a fancy dinner party at the Racquet Club, attended by every famous face who was visiting the desert spa. The thought that Mike's hustle and bustle were forever stilled cast a gloomy shadow over everybody with whom he had ever come in contact.

By April, JUDY GARLAND had ended her marriage to SID LUFT . . . SYBIL and RICHARD BURTON gave a great Hawaiian party at New York's Hotel Lexington. Everyone in town raved about this fabulous midnight-to-dawn shindig. It was the kind of party you would have expected MIKE TODD to have tossed in Hollywood, or London—not a Welsh couple in New York. Burton never went to bed at all. He just stayed up until his ten o'clock first-rehearsal call for *Wuthering Heights*. Since there was a swimming pool in the middle of the room, it was inevitable that someone would be pushed in— fully dressed. The "pushee" was TENNESSEE WILLIAMS, the "pusher" was MAUREEN STAPLETON . . . JEAN SEBERG became engaged to FRANÇOIS MOREUIL. They met in the romantic resort town of St. Tropez, on the French Riviera, while she was filming *Bonjour Tristesse* . . . And Four Star sold its TV pilot film, *Wanted: Dead or Alive*. It starred newcomer STEVE MCQUEEN as a bounty hunter in the West.

In May, there were two parties, at opposite ends of the country, rating an "A" for effort. In Hollywood, the town's top-rated charity affair, the annual SHARE Boom Town blast, was sensational. Not only was the audience star-studded, but the entertainment was worth a million dollars. DEBBIE REYNOLDS did a sensational dance to "Tequila." JO STAFFORD sang "It's Magic" as it had never been sung before. GYPSY ROSE LEE stripped down as far as she could go, and DEAN MARTIN, GOWER CHAMPION, EDDIE FISHER and GORDON MACRAE were the fabulous quartet who crooned "You Gotta Have Heart"—with a special set of lyrics penned for the occasion by SAMMY CAHN. All of that, plus SAMMY DAVIS, JR., BOB MITCHUM, GENE KELLY, MILTON BERLE and HARRY BELAFONTE made this evening one of Hollywood's most memorable. DEAN MARTIN brought down the house as he closed the show before the SHARE "girls" danced, with a parody on "All the Way," and sang: "Life is so contrary, it could lead right back to Jerry, oi and vay, all the way!"

Meanwhile, on the East Coast, LAURENCE OLIVIER invited 160 guests to a bon voyage party aboard the S.S. *Knickerbocker VII*. The cast from *Look Back in Anger* decorated the ship's decks and tables with brightly colored lanterns and tablecloths. The waiters were all dressed as English "pearlies," and the buffet featured fish 'n' chips. GREER GARSON, who had laryngitis, was all bundled up in silver mink, but most of the other guests came in sailing attire. RICHARD BURTON wore a fireman-red shirt with "HMS Olivier" embroidered (by his wife, SYBIL) across the front. LENA HORNE was decked out in a white turtleneck sweater, and DOUG FAIRBANKS dug out his Navy uniform. Host Olivier was garbed as a captain, minus the braid. Among the guests: LYNN FONTANNE and ALFRED LUNT (making one of their rare after-theatre appearances as a gesture of affection for "Captain Olivier"), the PETER USTINOVS, JEFF HAYDENS (EVA MARIE SAINT), JACK GARFEINS (CARROLL BAKER), SUSAN and PAULA STRASBERG, HENRY FONDA, JUDY HOLLIDAY, TRUMAN CAPOTE, JOAN PLOWRIGHT, EILEEN HECKART and MARY LEE FAIRBANKS.

In between soirées, on a weekend in May, TYRONE POWER married DEBBIE MINARDOS in a little chapel in her hometown of Tunica, Mississippi. By coincidence, the reverend who married them was DR. TYRONE WILLIAM . . . On May 19, RONALD COLMAN, sixty-seven, died at St. Francis Hospital, in Santa Barbara, California, from a chronic lung ailment. Colman, one of the industry's most distinguished performers, won the Best Actor Oscar in 1948 for Universal-International's *A Double Life*. He and his wife, BENITA HUME, starred in both the radio and television series "Halls of Ivy" . . . And, as the month ended, there were unconfirmed rumors that LAURENCE OLIVIER had asked VIVIEN LEIGH for a divorce so he could marry young actress JOAN PLOWRIGHT. Vivien, in London, was appearing onstage in *Duel of Angels*. While Larry, in New York, was said to be hoping to cast Plowright in the English stage version of *Two for the Seesaw*.

In June, PHYLLIS GATES, the about-to-be-ex Mrs. ROCK HUDSON, rejected Rock's offer of $200-a-week alimony and hired herself a new lawyer . . . TY and DEBBIE POWER announced that they were expecting . . . Meanwhile, in one of those "unusual" double-triangle stories, DEBORAH KERR and her husband, TONY BARTLEY, called it a day. Rumors were her next spouse would be brilliant writer PETER VIERTEL. But *he* was still legally married to the first Mrs. BUDD SCHULBERG, although *they* had separated several years previously in Paris. At that time, he had romanced BETTINA (before *she* met ALY KHAN), as well as JOAN FONTAINE. The Viertels had a four-year-old daughter, while Deborah and Tony had two little girls . . . And July found JOAN CRAWFORD, AL STEELE, her twins, and his young "SONNY," at the Brussels World Fair, along with Crawford's flotilla of luggage . . . There were rumors that the Army planned to ship ELVIS PRESLEY to Germany. Every eligible fräulein in that country immediately began primping . . . AVA GARDNER wound up seventeen years under contract to MGM. In order to re-sign her, Metro had to promise to pay her $400,000 a film, and to cast her only in movies to be made in Europe.

JENNIFER JONES and DAVID O. SELZNICK tossed a fabulous party in August that became the talk of the town because KATE HEPBURN, who never went to such big affairs, showed up. She spent most of the evening engaged in conversation with her biggest fan, LOUIS JOURDAN. It was the first time they had met, and both seemed delighted to have made a new friend. Since *Gigi*, incidentally, Jourdan was one of the hottest leading men in town. Everyone wanted to cast him in a film . . . And CYNTHIA and CLIFF ROBERTSON, who were expecting a baby, tried to prepare her young son, CHRIS (his dad was JACK LEMMON). When told he would soon have a new brother, or sister, the boy was ecstatic. Then asked politely, "May I have a monkey, too?"

VAN and EVE JOHNSON debated about putting their Beverly Hills home up for sale and seeking headquarters in Connecticut—halfway between Hollywood and Europe. Van had been spending so much time making pictures abroad, it seemed the wise thing to do. He had just returned from Holland and at the end of September was leaving again—for London. Even their ten-year-old, SCHUYLER, was getting confused . . . Speaking of confused, DICK HAYMES, RITA's ex, was getting married again. This time the bride was singer FRAN JEFFRIES . . . Meanwhile, that "ideal" couple, CARY GRANT and BETSY DRAKE, came to a friendly parting of the ways and the inevitable divorce was expected to follow.

November was another cruel month for the entertainment world. TYRONE POWER died of a heart attack shortly after being stricken on the set of *Solomon and Sheba*, while working on a dueling scene with co-star GEORGE SANDERS. TY never lived to see his baby son, who was delivered a few months after his death. While funeral arrangements were being made, YUL BRYNNER flew to Madrid to replace Power as GINA LOLLOBRIGIDA's co-star. TY, only forty-five, also left two lovely daughters by his previous marriage to LINDA CHRISTIAN . . . Ty's career had lasted twenty-three years, during which he became one of the public's all-time favorite leading men. Ironically, Power's last film footage was an appeal for the American Heart Association, which he had done just before

he left on location. In addition to his other assets, Power's estate included nearly two million dollars in deferred salaries.

With the arrival of December came the news that PHYLLIS GATES HUDSON had been awarded five percent of ROCK's next two films . . . And, in a much more meaningful financial transaction, Universal-International sold its studio property to MCA for $11,200,000, in cash, then immediately leased it back. At that time, the Music Corporation of America had no intention of using any of the studio's space for its own purposes. Under their subsidiary, Revue Productions, all of their television series were being filmed at Republic Studios . . . Speaking of MCA, JEAN, the daughter of JULES STEIN, had a lovely wedding in New York. Among the guests who flew in for the occasion was PRINCESS GRACE OF MONACO. She delighted her celebrity friends when she informed them that she kept up with all the show business news because she received daily copies of *The Hollywood Reporter* at the palace in Monaco.

Nineteen fifty-eight was the year BRIGITTE BARDOT's measurements became as well known in America as they were in France . . . LANA TURNER's defense of her daughter, CHERYL, in the JOHNNY STOMPANATO killing, was the greatest courtroom drama since *Madame X* . . . GENE TIERNEY regained her health, while MARILYN MONROE resumed her screen career after the loss of her baby . . . ROBERTO ROSSELLINI's self-righteous demands for custody of his three INGRID BERGMAN children on "moral grounds" was the ultimate in unmitigated gall . . . BING CROSBY became a father and a grandfather within the space of a few months.

JUDY GARLAND filed suit for divorce from SID LUFT on the grounds of cruelty and, after she changed her mind, later testified that Sid was a kind man who deserved custody of his son by LYNN BARI . . . MARIE MACDONALD divorced HARRY KARL again, which left him free to marry HARRY COHN's widow . . . ESTHER WILLIAMS did a double flip for JEFF CHANDLER . . . DEBRA PAGET divorced DAVID STREET before the ink was dry on their marriage license . . . SAMMY DAVIS, JR., followed his "I do" to LORAY WHITE with a solo of "I'll Walk Alone" . . . PAUL NEWMAN made JOANNE WOODWARD his bride . . . JAYNE MANSFIELD married MICKEY HARGITAY . . . And FERNANDO LAMAS, PAT BOONE, GREG PECK, MARLON BRANDO, PETER LAWFORD, TONY CURTIS, ROBERT STACK and STEVE ALLEN all became proud fathers.

January began with a few laughs. TALLULAH BANKHEAD told a friend that her doctor had advised her to eat an apple every time she had the urge to drink. She arched an eyebrow and added, "But really, dahlings, sixty apples a day!" . . . CHARLES BOYER confessed that voluptuous women scared him—quite an admission from a great screen lover . . . And television ratings for the last half of 1958, and beginning of 1959, found the top ten shows to be: "Gunsmoke," "Wagon Train," "Have Gun Will Travel," "The Rifleman," "The Danny Thomas Show," "Maverick," "Tales of Wells Fargo," "The Real McCoys," "I've Got a Secret" and "Wyatt Earp." Hollywood film moguls examined the astonishing list with keen interest. Seven of the top ten were shoot-'em-up westerns, two were comedies, and the other, a quiz program. It gave filmmakers an insight into their competition. They began a push for gigantic western stories that could not be done as effectively on the small screen.

MARLON BRANDO, both the star and the director of *One-Eyed Jacks*, debated long and hard as to whether his character should live or die. He finally allowed the actor side in him to triumph. In the latest revise, everyone but Brando got it . . . The co-stars of *Spartacus* were having *their* problems, too. KIRK DOUGLAS and LAURENCE OLIVIER had words over certain costumes Olivier was scheduled to wear, but Kirk, also the producer, would not approve. Olivier stated his case quite plainly: "Either the costumes stay in or I go out."

In the third week in February, DEBBIE REYNOLDS went to court to get her divorce from EDDIE FISHER. After having been hounded for statements by numerous columnists, Debbie declared, "The minute I leave the courtroom, the three of us will *not* be bound together in any way and will no longer be news." Her parents babysat with CARRIE and TODD FISHER while Debbie took off for the grand tour of Europe and put a lot of distance between herself, Eddie, and his new love, ELIZABETH TAYLOR . . . On March 3rd, LOU COSTELLO, one-half of Universal's biggest moneymaking comedy team, died of a heart attack a few days before his fifty-first birthday. In 1940, after Lou and BUD ABBOTT had starred in *Buck Privates*, they made millions for the studio—and for themselves. The two had split up in the mid-Fifties,

and each continued working alone. Shortly before his death, Lou had even gone dramatic on several television shows.

At the New York premiere of *Some Like It Hot*, MARILYN MONROE kept the other stars, as well as the fans, waiting an extra hour for her arrival. But the moment she showed up, it was a study in mass chaos. The police stormed the theatre and ejected hordes of photographers who followed Marilyn all the way down the aisle. One interesting side note, Monroe stood to earn over one million dollars from the film because she had made a percentage deal with the studio. As one Hollywood insider cracked, "Marilyn can really afford to keep other people waiting now that she's calling all of her own shots."

In mid-April, LANA TURNER made her live television debut with DINAH SHORE and came off brilliantly. Her phone rang off the hook with more offers—but Lana played it cool. In 1957, she had appeared with BOB HOPE, but that TV show had been pre-filmed and edited. In the most candid quote of the month, Lana commented, "I don't care what reason some of the other big stars, like GABLE, BRANDO and DIETRICH, give for refusing to go on television. The main reason we've all backed away from it is because we're frightened to death of TV . . . Yet, even though I was scared silly before I did Dinah's show live, I had to actually experience it before I realized what a wonderful challenge it was. When someone like me does a live guest appearance, not in an acting role, but just being herself, it turns out to be worth fifty personal appearances because you are seen by so many millions" . . . And the latest nationwide survey stated that there were now fifty-one million television sets in American households.

In May, FRED ASTAIRE stunned the TV audience watching the Emmy Award Show when he walked off with nine of the statuettes for "An Evening With Fred Astaire." Several days later, a delighted but embarrassed Fred tried to give his Best Actor Emmy back to the Academy. Some columnists had loudly protested the award. They claimed Astaire did *not* act—but had only performed as a singer-dancer. However, the Academy refused Fred's generous offer—and allowed the vote to stand . . . By early June, juke box operators in key

Eastern cities had inaugurated a new idea in many taverns. Billed as "Sinatrama," the jukes were filled with only FRANK SINATRA records—all of his old favorites as well as his newest releases. They drew huge crowds of Sinatra fans and the idea paid off. The same gimmick worked with PERRY COMO, ELVIS PRESLEY and BING CROSBY . . . International theatrical agent PAUL KOHNER—whose very first client was JOHN HUSTON—and who also handles dozens of famous film luminaries on numerous continents, returned from his annual trek to the Cannes Film Festival raving about the glamorous crowds, the high prices, the usual parade of undressed starlets prowling the beaches and the frantically successful merchandising Hollywood producers and studio heads did. Kohner, whose wife, LUPITA TOVAR starred in Mexico's first "talkie," was also accepting raves for his daughter SUSAN KOHNER'S latest film efforts. As the saying goes, "The Cannes Festival does not begin until Kohner arrives on the Croisette!"

The last member of the Royal Family of the stage and screen, ETHEL BARRYMORE, 79, died June 18 of a chronic heart condition in her Hollywood home. She had been bedridden for a year.

July was not only humid in New York, but also hot enough to have produced several tension-filled evenings. DEBBIE MINARDOS POWER, TYRONE'S widow, who had been dating ARTHUR LOEW, JR., attended the opening of *A Palm Tree in a Rose Garden*, marking Arthur's directorial debut. At the midnight supper party, Debbie met Arthur's mother, MICKEY, and apparently won Mrs. Loew's approval as a prospective daughter-in-law . . . Pretty, young JANE FONDA was also *very* nervous at the cocktail party JACK WARNER hosted in her honor so that she could meet the press prior to the start of her film *The Tall Story*, where she was slated to co-star with TONY PERKINS. At one point, her

1 Errol Flynn nightclubbing with his *final* girlfriend, teenager Beverly Aadland, October 14, 1959.   2 Marilyn Monroe, Milton Berle and Yves Montand at a party during the filming of 20th's *Let's Make Love*.
3 Group shot of the Screen Actors Guild Board of Directors, taken when Ronald Reagan began his sixth term as president, 1959. Seated directly in front of him, Nancy Davis Reagan, also a member of the Board. (Courtesy of the Screen Actors Guild)

knees were shaking so badly that her stepmother, AFDERA, slipped her a Miltown to calm her down.

Over in London, ELIZABETH TAYLOR and EDDIE FISHER showed up in August at the River Club with her ex-husband MICHAEL WILDING, and his current wife, SUSAN. It was the first time the foursome had been seen together publicly ... PRINCESS MARGARET made her first public appearance "since her illness." She attended a premiere and dinner party hosted by Columbia Studios to launch *The Boy and the Bridge* ... While in France, ALY KHAN was reported to be chasing an American heiress, ALICE TOPPING ... And BRIGITTE BARDOT'S ex-husband, director ROGER VADIM, was seen having drinks with her ex-fiancé, singer SACHA DISTEL. No doubt they were comparing notes—exchanging cozy anecdotes.

In September, the industry mourned the loss of four comparatively young and talented people. On the 7th, KAY KENDALL, 32, died in London of leukemia, unaware that she had been afflicted with the fatal disease for several years. The week before her death, she became gravely ill in Italy while on vacation with her husband, REX HARRISON. Rex hurriedly flew her back to London for treatment, but it was no help. Kay had appeared in a number of pictures in Hollywood and Europe; her last was Columbia's *Once More, With Feeling*. Her most outstanding Hollywood film was MGM's *Les Girls*. Kay and Rex were married in 1957, while he was appearing in the Broadway production of *My Fair Lady*.

PAUL DOUGLAS, 52, died on September 11 of a heart attack. His career had spanned thirty years, and encompassed radio, stage, screen and TV. At the time of his death, he had just signed to co-star with JACK LEMMON and SHIRLEY MacLAINE in BILLY WILDER'S *The Apartment*. He was married to actress JAN STERLING, by whom he had a three-year-old son. He also left a teenage daughter from his previous marriage to performer VIRGINIA FIELD.

JANET GAYNOR'S husband, GILBERT ADRIAN, 56, the famous Hollywood fashion designer, died on September 13 of a stroke ... The following day, former Warner Brothers star WAYNE MORRIS, 45, had a heart attack. He died while visiting his former United States Navy flying squadron leader aboard the aircraft carrier *Bonhomme Richard*, which was docked in Oakland, California. Morris had been a naval flying ace during World War II.

There was a lot of excitement in Hollywood on September 19, occasioned by the arrival of Soviet Premier NIKITA KHRUSHCHEV. Everybody invited to the luncheon in his honor, at 20th Century–Fox, busily prepared for the big do. There were, however, two Hollywoodites who did *not* attend—for different reasons. RONALD REAGAN was asked, but *refused* to come, while teenager SANDRA DEE, of Russian heritage—who spoke the language—was sorely disappointed because no one had invited her. She was in tears at the thought of missing the big event. The luncheon was a star-studded affair. SHIRLEY MacLAINE entertained the premier when she, JULIET PROWSE and a troupe of girls did a dance from *Can Can*, raised their skirts and exposed their panties at the end of the number. Nikita and his wife—Hollywood later learned—were very offended. The Soviet leader really was mad because the State Department refused to allow him and his traveling entourage to visit Disneyland because of the security risk it entailed. It was just as well, DONALD DUCK and MICKEY MOUSE might have proved equally as shocking.

In New York, at BARBARA RUSH'S cocktail party, JOANNE WOODWARD revealed she was taking a Hebrew lesson every day in preparation for her "exodus" to Israel with PAUL NEWMAN in January of 1960. She and Paul and their baby planned to remain abroad after Newman finished the OTTO PREMINGER assignment. They were scheduled to do some extensive traveling— most specifically to London, where they planned to catch pal CHRISTOPHER PLUMMER'S debut in the TV production of "Hamlet."

At the end of the month, handsome and virile YVES MONTAND, the best entertainer to come out of France since MAURICE CHEVALIER, opened at New York's HENRY MILLER Theatre. He sang sad songs, fun songs and love songs with variety and style, and danced with the grace of FRED ASTAIRE, whom he imitated in one number. Montand's long-awaited American debut was greeted by one of the most glamorous first-night audiences of the season. MARILYN MONROE, who wore a sensational "Some Like It Hot" gown, stopped traffic in the aisle where she sat with MONTGOMERY CLIFT, whom some mistook for ARTHUR MILLER, and others didn't recognize at all. INGRID BERGMAN, with LARS SCHMIDT, garnered plenty of attention, as did LAUREN BACALL and SYDNEY CHAPLIN, and MARLENE DIETRICH with GODDARD LIEBERSON, head of Columbia Records for whom Montand recorded. SIMONE SIGNORET, YVES' perfect, self-effacing wife, wouldn't give any *Room at the*

Top interviews until after her husband's premiere. Still, Montand's opening-night audience gave her an ovation as she walked down the aisle to her seat. Yves, who heard this sudden burst of applause, peered from behind the curtain. He expected to see GARBO, at least, and was bowled over with pride at this tribute to his brilliantly talented wife.

In mid-October, 20th abandoned plans to star ELVIS PRESLEY in an untitled screenplay with a Mississippi riverboat background and went shopping around for another vehicle for the actor-singer. In the meantime, PRESLEY was set to do three features back-to-back after his Army discharge in March of 1960. The first would be *G.I. Blues*, for HAL WALLIS and Paramount. Backgrounds for that film were currently being shot in Germany, where Elvis was stationed.

On October 7, MARIO LANZA died in Rome at the age of thirty-eight. The official cause listed was a heart attack. He had been hospitalized for a week prior to his death with what had been described as a minor illness. Rumors were that Mario had been on a severe weight-loss regimen and this had weakened his already overtaxed heart . . . Exactly one week later, ERROL FLYNN, age fifty, died of a heart attack in Vancouver, British Columbia. Twenty-seven days before his death, Flynn told *The Hollywood Reporter*, "I don't care what you columnists say about me. I'm gonna have fun because I'll be dead in five years anyway." Errol beat his own deadline.

He had been in Vancouver with his fiancée, BEVERLY AADLAND, to sell his yacht, *Zaca*. He shocked newsmen upon his arrival when he gave an unprintable answer to a female reporter who asked why he dated young girls. Then he stopped and bought a case of vodka. Four days prior to his heart attack, he came down with a high fever. The Canadian doctor who examined him told him, "Quit drinking or you'll be dead in a year." At which point Beverly butted in with, "But, doctor, I drink every bit as much as Errol does."

The medic looked at her sternly and replied, "The difference, my dear, is that you also take out time to eat!"

When November arrived, newlyweds DEBBIE POWER and ARTHUR LOEW, JR., were in New York at the Savoy-Hilton for a three-week whirl. The senior Loews were thrilled at having a "ready-made" grandson, TYRONE POWER, IV.

MARLENE DIETRICH made the Christmas holidays brighter for Las Vegas visitors. She played the Sahara Hotel and looked as glamorous as ever, still trim and exotic in her flesh-colored gown and feathered stole. Marlene, a living monument to aging gracefully, gave audiences what they wanted to hear—and see. She won standing ovations throughout her entire engagement.

The year 1959 seemed to have a much more chaotic mixture of happiness and sadness than the years of the decade which preceded it. The deaths were shocking and sudden . . . The breakups equally sudden and upsetting . . . The new brides: ELIZABETH TAYLOR, BRIGITTE BARDOT, JULIE ANDREWS, EVA GABOR, CLAIRE BLOOM and DEBBIE POWER LOEW were all destined to eventually hit the divorce courts—and move on to other men.

STARS AS THEIR OWN PRODUCERS

Two of Hollywood's top leading men, John Wayne and Robert Mitchum, gave their colleagues a special insight into the ramifications of both starring in as well as producing their own films. In November of 1957, Billy Wilkerson's readers got a bird's-eye view of what their respective location jaunts were like—Wayne's to Africa—Mitchum's to Asheville, North Carolina. But whether it was problems with camels or moonshiners, both of these screen idols were up to their hip pockets in the details that are attendant to any major film—especially films that are shot away from the comparative sanity and security of a studio lot.

John Wayne
"SHOOTING IN THE SAHARA"

John Wayne was one of the most prolific celebrity contributors to The Hollywood
Reporter. *He wrote this fascinating piece for the twenty-seventh anniversary issue,
which ran on November 18, 1957.*

After more than 25 years as an actor in
motion pictures I believe I can answer
a question which has been asked of me
many times—"What was your toughest screen
assignment?" I would now reply with just four
words, *Legend of the Lost.*

I have never before had the feelings about
a movie that I have about *Legend of the Lost.*
I have always, during my career as an actor
and as head of Batjac Productions, Inc., left
it up to those fellows I believe the trade refers
to as "tub-thumpers," or publicity men, to shout
the praises of a product or personality with
which I have been connected. I have never
personally concerned myself with any of these
functions. I made the pictures—and I would
rather someone else disposed of them.

However, this is not the case with *Legend
of the Lost.* This film has had a particularly
exhilarating effect on me. Perhaps it was because we traveled halfway around the globe
to live in a tent city on the desolate North
Africa desert. Perhaps it was because our first
day's shooting took place on a barren sand
dune hundreds of miles in the Libyan desert
cut off from civilization. Perhaps it was because I realized we were living a great experience.

The story behind the making of the film is
as interesting as its actual production. It all
started when I bumped into an old friend, a
director, Henry Hathaway, at lunch one day,
and he told me a story he'd like me to read.
To be truthful, Henry, whose screen credits
are outstanding, had carried the story around
in his head for many years, saving it for the
right time and the right actors. He had engaged the famous novelist Ben Hecht and another fine writer by the name of Robert Presnell,
Jr., to write the screenplay—and after many
more months of chatting and typing they had
it down on paper. Henry said it was right for
me. I took the script home.

Needless to say, I did approve. *Legend* was
a great romantic-adventure story between the
yellow covers of a script. I felt it would be
just as exciting and interesting as a motion
picture. It was at lunch the next day that Henry
and I shook hands. We had a deal.

Henry would produce and direct for Batjac,
and we talked with United Artists, probably
the biggest distributors of films in the world,
who were as eager and enthusiastic as we
after reading the script. UA would release
Legend of the Lost, and it would be a three-
million-dollar project.

Our first meeting on the film was historic.
"There's a spot of sand," I said, "out near
Mojave, California, that would be a great desert if we scooped up some dunes with bulldozers and . . ." Henry interrupted. "The script,"
he said slowly, "says the Sahara Desert."

"Yes, I know," I retorted. "But that's way
the hell and gone on the other side of the
world. Have you ever seen those Texas deserts? They have more sand in Texas than . . ."
Henry interrupted again. "The sand in the Sahara," he continued, "is golden, yellow gold,
and God made the dunes without bulldozers.
The people will be able to tell the difference."

Obviously Henry didn't believe the old adage
"A tree is a tree; shoot it in Griffith Park." To
be honest, neither did I. Henry was right. The
people would know. They would want something they can't find at home on television. If
we took them to the Sahara, it was an adventure, even if it meant taking 200 people with
us, building a camp city and airfield, a food
supply depot, a hospital, film vaults and all
the rest. I signed the contract and committed
myself to obligations that were soon to pyramid. I never regretted it.

Those of us in the industry know that the
making of a movie requires many gifted hands.
After we made our deal with UA for the financing and release of the film, we had to
gather together all of the people needed to
make a movie. We got a crew—and it was a
good one. They had to be, inasmuch as we
were going to a distant land which couldn't
supply us with props or equipment. What a
gigantic task it was. Items ranged from 2000
blankets, to tons of canned food, reflectors,
miles of cable and wiring, generators, arcs,
and so on and so on. We had conferences far
into each night, prior to our departure, where
Henry, our production manager, Nate Edwards, and other staff members and myself

tore apart the script for costs and requirements.

Before the film began shooting, Henry, Nate and our art director, Al Ybarra, planed to the Middle East. We wanted the Sahara, but we also needed a native village we could transform into historic Timbuctoo, and a ruin of a Roman city. It had to be authentic. They started looking in Egypt. It exploded in their faces. Bombs fell, riots flared, tanks raced through the streets—and Henry and his men got out damn quick. Dauntless, they travelled again—thousands of miles by plane, bus and jeep. And they didn't return until they had found the location sites they wanted. I was at home, in Encino, that night when I got their cable—"We found it!" We would film our picture in Libya.

Within a week, they were back home. Our conferences started anew. First we would go to Rome to set up production offices and a base of operations. Then we would go to Libya, most primitive of the nations of North Africa, yet possessor of the scenic qualities that we needed. We would get our cast together immediately and start moving our men and equipment there.

Our cast? We needed a woman and a man. Both had to have fire, be good performers, and have names that would sell tickets at the box-office. We began looking at film. Before long, we had two names written down on a slip of paper—Sophia Loren and Rossano Brazzi.

Scripts had to be sent abroad. Time went by, and we sat with our fingers crossed. Then came the cables. "Okay for Brazzi, send contracts." And then the other, "Loren loves script; draw up agreement." It was a big day. We had a fine script, an excellent director, a fascinating background, and now Sophia Loren and Rossano Brazzi would join me in a picture which seemed destined to be big.

Things happened fast and furious for the next few weeks. Sets were sketched, words were translated into dollars, props and costumes were gathered, contracts written, and our transportation people began making the vital and extensive arrangements to ship us, bag and baggage, around to the other side of the earth. Before long we were on our way.

We got to Rome a couple of weeks before Christmas, moved into three different hotels, and set up our offices. We had many setbacks. It took our equipment, sailing from San Pedro, 55 days to arrive in Genoa. No less of a job was the shipping of supplies from Genoa to Tripoli, on the North Africa coast. Vessels were away to rescue Italian refugees from troubled Egypt, or there was not a ship big enough in the Mediterranean trade to carry all our materials at once. After much bargaining, we arranged to have the supplies shipped.

On Christmas Day [1956], the lot of us sat around a big table, decorated in the center with holly, atop of which flew the American, Italian and British flags (the latter in honor of our excellent cameraman, Jack Cardiff). It was great fun, but we were all pretty homesick that night.

The next day a group of us boarded a plane for Tripoli. The weather was stimulating and the Arab world interesting to observe upon our arrival. North Africa was strange, I'll admit, but exciting.

Our next stop was Ghadames. This was an oasis of 3000 population, about 2000 years old, which would be our base of operations while in the Libyan desert. Incidentally, we arrived in Ghadames, on a chilly morning, in a chartered DC-3 that was rigged to carry cargo and passengers in the same compartment. Our stay in the village was not long, for we were soon soaring, in our plane again, across the reddish-brown sandy waste that changed to a golden yellow when the sun grew high in the sky.

Ghadames. Erg. We moved like chessmen on a strange chessboard. At Erg, we landed on an airstrip that had been built by the French during World War II. The entire village turned out to meet us. We were ushered to the local hotel.

Did I say hotel? Better say a small mud building of fourteen rooms built twenty some-odd years before by the great Italian aviator [Italo] Balbo as a desert retreat. Naturally, we had to convert it, beginning with fumigation. As this was going on, planeloads of material began flowing in every few hours, and a tent city was erected capable of taking care of the comforts of 150 men and a handful of women. It was a tent city complete with everything from showers to an elaborate kitchen.

Anyway, here we were, I thought, 500 miles in the desolate Libyan desert, ready to start a motion picture. Let's go to work.

The first day of shooting was unlike any beginning of a picture I have ever seen. Forty trucks, carrying people and equipment, lumbered out into the rocky, then sandy section of the desert, into the Great Eastern Erg, while the sun peeked over the horizon. It was a spectacular and breathtaking sight.

Ironically, that first morning every large piece of equipment was stuck in the sand. One by one, we hauled our expensive but hapless vehicles to firm ground. At 8 o'clock in the morning it seemed we were off to a gloomy start. Much thanks go to our crew and the French Army for what they did to help us that day and on many other mornings.

The Sahara Desert had always been to me a place of forbidding and intense heat. I soon learned that there were other things to fear. The sand, for example, was sometimes moist and hard, the next hour dry and powdery like talcum. And then, there was the cold, a biting cold, that chills to the bone. And there was the sun, bright and relentless. Last but far from least, there was the Gibli, the dread sandstorm of the desert which beleagured us with its ferocity and penetrating sand. It was like this for the ten weeks we spent in its heart.

We encountered other problems. For the cameraman, the desert light was tricky. In order to take advantage of the light, we often had to start for our location long before sun-up and drive many mornings 60 miles into the desert to shoot the day's scenes. Our property man had equal difficulties. In Hollywood, he would pick up a phone and order what he needed. In the desert it's not that easy. If you need 150 camels, like we did for one sequence, you send scouts into the desert assigned to return with the animals. Also, negotiations for the Arab people to work in the picture had to be handled tactfully and with diplomacy. We read up on our Arab etiquette. They worked for us but I secretly suspect that they thought us a pack of lunatics invading their domain for some sort of mechanical horseplay.

It didn't take long for any of us to come to the conclusion that the Arab burnoose was the most practical garment ever constructed by man. We would sit on the ground and pull the hood of this great overcoat over our heads and around our ears to keep from freezing in the cold night or roasting in the burning sun. By day's end, exhaustion was common to all of us, and we sat silently and chewed our food, and then staggered blind-eyed off to bed.

Our water was flown from Tripoli, and the liquid we were drinking cost almost as much per bottle as the finest champagne. Fresh fruit and vegetables were other luxury items. Another necessary expense was having our own doctor with a completely equipped infirmary and drugstore.

We spent better than $1,500,000 in the heart of the Sahara.

When we completed exterior shooting on *Legend of the Lost*, we abandoned most of our equipment because the cost of bringing it out was prohibitive. We said our goodbyes. But when we left, we all looked back with strong feelings upon the sight of an experience that would remain with us.

We finished our picture at Cinecittà Studios in Rome. I look back at it all as an adventure, but I am also stirred by a feeling of accomplishment and a knowledge that my associates and I have been honest in creating what we are trying to sell. We have made a picture as it might have happened in actual life.

Robert Mitchum
"PROBLEMS OF PRODUCING"

On November 18, 1957, Robert Mitchum shared his new experiences as a film producer with the readers of The Hollywood Reporter.

You got problems? Well, climb on the pad and tell old Dad. I don't have any.

Or, I didn't have until producing a picture messed me up. I flipped for the whole enchilada. Now my troubles come in color, wide-screen and third-dimension.

Our setup is monickered DRM (for Dorothy and Robert Mitchum) Productions, and the first film, for United Artists release, rolled this past fall at location sites around Asheville, North Carolina. By now it should be known as either *Thunder Road* or *The Whippoorwill*.

We danced around on that little obstacle for a few weeks, too. But, I'm getting ahead of myself.

As the man said, "It all started with a cloud in the sky no bigger than a man's fist." Home crouched on the couch one night, it occurred to me that we might get a motion picture out of moonshiners and government tax men trying to outwit each other in the southeastern area of the United States. I had a smattering of knowledge about that part of Uncle Sam's domain; I was raised there.

A good story line beat through and writers James Atlee Phillips and Walter Wise went to work on it. At times, I soothe my ego by shouting about actors' problems, and I have a loud voice. Sure, actors have problems, but I've found production problems come lower than a hungover snake.

We got our script licked. Those two writers scratched, wrote and polished for months. Phillips spent five weeks at the Library of Congress in Washington, just studying folk music. Research takes time, but we wanted it right. Now it's right and tight. We've used the Treasury Department's Alcohol and Tobacco Tax Division files; we have case histories that'd curl Yul Brynner's hair. (I'm hoping to cozen one of the Internal men and maybe get some income taxes wholesale).

Research brought out some interesting facts: the mountains are crawling with descendants of English, Welsh, Irish and Scottish families who landed there before that tea caper in Boston Harbor sometime back. They can trace their ancestry back to Elizabethan times. For 250 years, these backwoods socialites have been brewing moonshine in those mountains. They are proud of it and their product. No stigma comes from doing time for trying to slip an unstamped jug past your Uncle Sammy's tax men. While most leading families of the area wouldn't buy any unstamped liquor today, a short walk into the hills will put you on the spot where the family fortunes were founded. Illegally.

As we sat in Hollywood, breathing smog, our representative, John E. Burch, combed the area to find some sixteen-year-old Mercury cars. These are hopped up by moonshiner transporters and used to outrun the pursuing government agents. In our story, the car is an integral, generic accessory to our storytelling. So could we find one or two? No. Here was old Dan with a pocket full of Hollywood green; everytime we found what we needed, we also found one of the local mountain boys had just bought it or outbid us!

Meantime, back at the DRM Productions ranch, a few details pressed in: signing co-star Gene Barry, persuading my son Jim to debut in pictures as my younger brother, finding director Arthur Ripley, finding a crew, casting some of the roles we didn't pick up in the area, overseeing the script, listening to proposed music, choosing wardrobe for both men and women, dispatching technical equipment across the continent and wondering what the best attack might be for me in *The Whippoorwill*, or is it *Thunder Road*, as an actor. Another little detail—we had to film a drunken pig; revenue men are sometimes led to illegal stills by following pigs who've gotten into the mash, gotten stoned and are rooting around the mountain. Where do you advertise for an alcoholic pig, Dad? We finally found one, treated it like a piece of Ming dynasty china until we'd gotten it photographed, then couldn't get anyone to claim it. The revenooers, remember?

I've probably forgotten something, and if I have, it cost me money. MONEY?

Lord, Lord, think of that.

"Reva [Mitchum's secretary at that time, Reva Fredericks]! Get me the bank on the blower. Can't you hear me calling, Carolina?"

Mickey Rooney
"BRING MY SON UP AN ACTOR? . . . OF COURSE"

Mickey Rooney, one of Hollywood's most brilliant stars, began working in show business as a child. On November 24, 1958, he wrote this article for The Hollywood Reporter. It had an interesting message about his profession that he wanted to share.

How do I like it now that one of my offspring, eight-year-old Teddy, has decided on show business as a career? I'm delighted. Let me explain.

I've been infuriated many times to hear fellow actors say, "Bring up my kid to be an actor? Never in a million years"—or words to that effect. Believe me, this attitude is both prevalent and unjustified.

Why is it that a large number of entertainment personalities feel the need to apologize for being members of a wonderful profession? It has me completely mystified. Particularly since most of those who belittle show business owe to it a great debt in terms of fame and fortune.

While I never, by any means, used undue influence on Teddy to push him into a career he wouldn't want, I've tried to make him as proud as I am of this great business. Fortunately, Teddy is taking it beautifully. The happiest days of my life were when we worked together in *Andy Hardy Comes Home*, in which Teddy was typecast as my son. And to prove that his career isn't a matter of nepotism, he left for Connecticut the day after his last scene in our picture to work with Jack Lemmon and Doris Day in Columbia's *Miss Casey Jones.*

As I look back on my 36 years in show business, I am convinced there's absolutely no other way in which I would have wanted to earn my living. I love the business and it's been good to me. I can only hope that the marriage of Teddy Rooney to the entertainment industry will be as happy.

This isn't to say that I haven't had my downs as well as my ups. There were plenty of times when I was convinced my career was at a dead end, or even finished. But even the pain and discouragement that come to us all in this business is all for the best.

The problems teach us fortitude and, when the pendulum swings upwards again, the joy and elation are all the keener. Teddy won't have it easy in his apparently chosen career, unless he's the exception which proves the rule, but he'll be all the better for it.

Why am I so delighted that my kid is joining his pop in show business? Well, there are many reasons. And when I think of those reasons, I feel all the more bitter that people who have derived so much from this profession feel the need to keep their children away from it.

Through the years, I've been surrounded by a host of generous, interesting, hard-working people who have become wonderful friends. I've made a lot of money—not that I've kept it all. I've had the opportunity to travel widely, and to meet all walks of people, from the President of the United States, to the guy named Joe.

Also, being an actor has given me the chance to be creative, something which is denied people in many other lines of business. And this, as most of us know, provides both stimulation and a wonderful kind of emotional satisfaction.

Show business has come a long way from the days when respectable citizens thought of the theatre in terms of scorn. Today, owing to the fact that our profession has prestige and influence, it is a great force for good throughout the world.

As the years pass, this influence for good will continue to grow. I couldn't be happier that the present direction of Teddy's life indicates he'll be a part of it.

HOLLYWOOD IN TRANSITION—AGAIN

In the final months of 1959, Hollywood was once more a town full of secondhand roses and two-time tulips. This time it wasn't the lack of funds, but the expediency of time saved. Blossoms used on sets of feature motion pictures were hastily rushed to the next soundstage to be used as props for a weekly television series produced by the same studio.

Once more, Hollywood was a town in transition. A community in crisis. The problems were different. The economics had changed. But paranoia and fear were causing the same headaches and chills to sweep across the sun-baked hills of Hollywood. At the start of the decade, all of the moguls were firmly in control. By the end of it, all of them—except Jack Warner—were gone.

And even J. L. was losing ground to the newest phenomenon, the independents.

Undoubtedly the most telling shift in the balance of power had been Darryl F. Zanuck's resignation, in 1956, as the head of production of 20th Century–Fox. DF had anticipated the new trend earlier than those moguls who still survived. He had left his sumptuous office, all the perks and the power of running a major studio, to form his own autonomous, independent production unit. Instead of supervising thirty to fifty films a year, he had opted for personally producing two to three pictures annually. Exit Zanuck and his "Greek Chorus"—the old guard was no more!

The breakup of the studio system was in full swing. Contract players were the exception rather than the rule. Studios, reasoning that it was more economical to hire stars on a per picture basis rather than carry them fifty weeks of the year, had made a tragic mistake. Now, those same stars cost twice as much—and also expected—no, *demanded*—a piece of the profits. The same held true of the top directors, producers, writers and other creative behind-the-scenes talent. All of them were suddenly in a position to make very impressive deals.

By government decree, studios had divested themselves, or were in the process of selling, their theatre chains. And, to add to Hollywood's other woes, the foreign film market had realized an enormous surge in business because of a lady named Bardot, who was turning out films of an "adult" nature that seemed to be the only fare taking people away from their TV sets. *And God Created Woman* was such a sensation that studio heads wondered why God had forsaken *them*—and pondered how to best compete.

The face of Hollywood wore yet another expression—pained. It wasn't the same game anymore. The players were different . . . The rules had changed . . . The main cen-

ters of power had given way to a whole new crop of producers. The era of the conglomerates had not yet arrived—but the big corporate powers were waiting in the wings to splurge and merge.

Television and motion pictures, now more firmly married than ever before, wobbled along together, just like any typical couple—happy with each other one day, on the outs the next. Even the glamour had faded. The gorgeous gowns and trailing furs had been replaced by torn T-shirts and faded blue jeans. The rock 'n' roll era was in full swing. Many people spent their money on records rather than at the boxoffice.

But what was valid on the day Billy Wilkerson opened the doors of *The Hollywood Reporter*, September 3, 1930, was still the operative code for success: give the public good pictures and they'll come! But good pictures cost lots of money, and as usual there were economic problems to be overcome.

Even the girl who had begun the Thirties as the consummate flapper with Doug Fairbanks, Jr., in her bed and the world at her feet was about to undergo a final change as a middle-aged matron.

On April 19, 1959, at 9 A.M., Joan Crawford found her fifty-seven-year-old husband dead. They had just returned from a six weeks' business trip and had spent the previous evening playing a few hands of gin rummy and discussing a ten-day vacation they planned to take to Jamaica. At midnight, Alfred said he felt unusually tired. Since they were scheduled to leave on their holiday the next afternoon, Steele kissed his wife and went off to sleep. He apparently suffered a heart attack during the night and never woke up.

Several days later, Joan, still under a doctor's care, attended her husband's funeral services at St. Thomas Protestant Episcopal Church.

Right after Steele's burial, there were

conflicting reports on the status of Joan's finances. Some friends reported that Joan told them she did not have a penny to her name; that, although Steele thought he was leaving her a lot, his entire estate would go for income taxes and debts. At that point, they said, Joan considered selling her Brentwood home because it was too big and, besides, she could not afford to keep it. There were rumors that the only money she would have was the $60,000-a-year salary she would receive from Pepsi-Cola to continue on as their spokesperson.

When Steele's will was probated, ten days after his death, Joan was left everything but $5,000 dollars, which was bequeathed to Mrs. Sally Steele Comer, of San Juan, Puerto Rico, his daughter by a previous marriage. There was another problem attendant to Steele's death. His first wife, Lillian, was supposed to collect alimony from the Steele estate which ended only if she remarried. But there was no money to pay that alimony since Steele had sunk his fortune into the apartment in which he and Joan lived.

On May 28, 1959, five weeks after Steele's death, Crawford returned to Hollywood to star in her first film since 1956. She had a very prominent cameo role in 20th's *The Best of Everything*, for Jerry Wald. Joan was required to work only four weeks and was expected to receive somewhere between $75,000 and $100,000 for her performance. She was, once more, the family breadwinner.

For the rest of the year she commuted between Hollywood and New York and also went out on trips for Pepsi. Her spirits seemed to alternately rise and fall—and her friends were concerned about her being alone again.

But by December there were whispers of a new Crawford love interest. On December 30th, she ended a holiday visit with a wealthy Carolinian, Robert Huffines, by meeting his relatives. Both denied rumors of any romance. He was the former president of Burlington Mills of New York, and of Textron. In 1959, he was on the board of directors of Paramount Studios and of American Broadcasting Company. His wife had died the previous May.

Huffines was attending a board meeting in California when he and Joan met. They had shared plans for Christmas and had decided to spend it together. He told her he was taking his children to South Carolina, to his farm, and invited Joan and her twin daughters to join them. And that's exactly what Crawford did.

Joan and Cindy and Cathy had arrived at the Huffines' Cherokee Plantation near Walterboro, South Carolina, where the girls had a wonderful visit. It was the first time they had gone to a formal dance, and the two families mixed very nicely. There were plans for Joan and Robert to meet again— perhaps. Huffines then lived in Greenwich, Connecticut. A tycoon and industrialist, he was said to have a large real estate investment in Connecticut.

But, as the Fifties came to an end, Joan Crawford was still a widow. After so many years of the good fight, the fast pursuit, even she had slowed down. She would remain unmarried for the rest of her life— and die, alone, in her New York apartment on May 18, 1977—still one of the greatest glamour queens Hollywood had ever known.

Crawford was, in a way, symbolic of the industry. She was capable of cruelty and compassion. But she had grown. Matured. Changed. Switched her goals and her focus. The old excitement was gone, replaced by the world of business and corporate finance; the trailing foxes and the gleaming diamonds no longer as important as the substance which lay underneath.

Hollywood, too, had grown. Matured. Become more flexible. Less rooted in past ways. By the end of the next decade, even the archaic Purity Seal would have gone the way of all flesh—having bowed down to the foreign films with their "exotic exposure" and steamy love scenes. Jack Valenti, a far cry from Hollywood's original censor, Will Hays (although he, too, had come to Tinseltown after a post in a presidential administration), as the new head of the MPAA, had ruled that *any* picture could be made so long as producers accepted his organization's classification system. Films would now be released in various categories from G (general audience) all the way up to X (no one under seventeen admitted).

Hollywood's floodgates would be opened. Everything formerly taboo would be permitted—under the proper circumstances. The industry in the Sixties would enrich tens of millions with unique subject matter and a more mature quality never seen on its screens before.

Hollywood was and always will be the greatest center of moviemaking in the world. There will always be many frustrating problems . . . "enemies" . . . economic worries . . . new technological advances . . . competition from the most unexpected sources. Industryites will always be looking over their shoulders in fear and panic. But, just as Crawford somehow survived to a ripe old age and lives on through her cinematic accomplishments, so, too, Hollywood—with a few more wrinkles in its pantyhose—will not only survive, but thrive!

One look back at this fabulous star. Joan Crawford plants her handprint in Grauman's Chinese Theatre forecourt, September 14, 1929. (Courtesy Bruce Torrence Historical Collection)

There will continue to be a constant crop of creative talents. There will always be new vision. Great courage. And, most of all, there will be an unending stream of dynamic people to dream new dreams. Occasionally, there may still be a secondhand rose. A two-time tulip. But, more often, there will be the scent and mystery of fresh gardenias and violets—the stuff of which romance and dreams will perpetually be made.

Index